1 ... k Loan

# Analysis and Design for Systems Ninth Edition

# Analysis and Design for Systems Ninth Edition

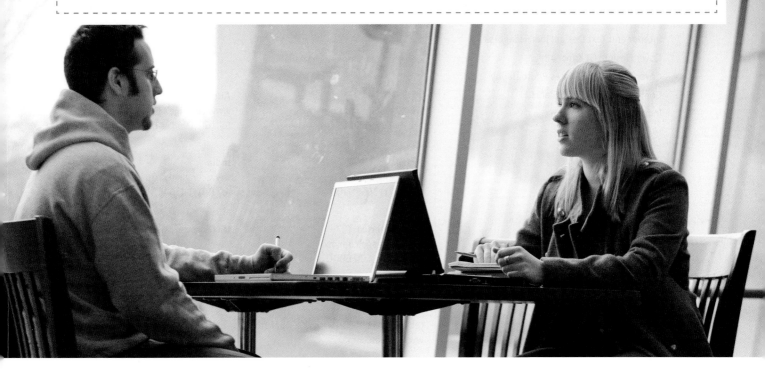

**Gary B. Shelly**
**Harry J. Rosenblatt**

**Shelly Cashman Series®**
*An imprint of Course Technology, Cengage Learning*

COURSE TECHNOLOGY
CENGAGE Learning™

Australia • Brazil • Japan • Korea • Mexico • Singapore • Spain • United Kingdom • United States

## COURSE TECHNOLOGY
### CENGAGE Learning™

**Analysis and Design for Systems, Ninth Edition**
Gary B. Shelly
Harry J. Rosenblatt

Vice President, Publisher: Nicole Pinard

Executive Editor: Kathleen McMahon

Associate Acquisitions Editor: Reed Curry

Associate Product Manager: Aimee Poirier

Editorial Assistant: Angela Giannopoulos

Director of Marketing: Elisa Roberts

Marketing Manager: Tristen Kendall

Marketing Coordinator: Adrienne Fung

Print Buyer: Julio Esperas

Director of Production: Patty Stephan

Content Project Manager: Matthew Hutchinson

Development Editor: Deb Kaufmann

Proofreader: Kim Kosmatka

Art Director: Marissa Falco

Interior and Text Design: Joel Sadagursky

Cover Design: GEX Inc

Cover Photos: Tom Kates Photography

Compositor: PreMediaGlobal

Indexer: Liz Cunningham

Library of Congress Control Number: 2010943248

International Edition:

ISBN-13: 978-0-538-48162-5

ISBN-10: 0-538-48162-5

Cengage Learning International Offices

**Asia**
www.cengageasia.com
tel: (65) 6410 1200

**Australia/New Zealand**
www.cengage.com.au
tel: (61) 3 9685 4111

**Brazil**
www.cengage.com.br
tel: (55) 11 3665 9900

**India**
www.cengage.co.in
tel: (91) 11 4364 1111

**Latin America**
www.cengage.com.mx
tel: (52) 55 1500 6000

**UK/Europe/Middle East/Africa**
www.cengage.co.uk
tel: (44) 0 1264 332 424

**Represented in Canada by Nelson Education, Ltd.**
tel: (416) 752 9100/(800) 668 0671
www.nelson.com

Cengage Learning is a leading provider of customized learning solutions with office locations around the globe, including Singapore, the United Kingdom, Australia, Mexico, Brazil, and Japan. Locate your local office at: **www.cengage.com/global**

For product information: **www.cengage.com/international**
Visit your local office: **www.cengage.com/global**
Visit our corporate website: **www.cengage.com**

Printed in China by China Translation & Printing Services Limited
1 2 3 4 5 6 7 16 15 14 13 12 11

# BRIEF CONTENTS

# TABLE OF CONTENTS

# Chapter 3
## Project Management

# PHASE 2: SYSTEMS ANALYSIS

# Chapter 4
## Determining Requirements

# Chapter 5

## Data and Process Analysis

# Chapter 6

## Object Analysis

# Chapter 7

## Options for Development

## PHASE 3: SYSTEMS DESIGN

# Chapter 8

## Designing the Interface

# Chapter 9

## Designing the Data

# Appendix B

## Software Engineering

# Appendix C

## Cost-Benefit Analysis

# Appendix D

## Internet Resources

# PREFACE

The Shelly Cashman Series® offers the finest textbooks in computer education. We are proud that our previous editions of *Analysis and Design for Systems* have been so well received by instructors and students. *Analysis and Design for Systems, Ninth Edition* continues with the innovation, quality, and reliability you have come to expect from the Shelly Cashman Series.

## Overview

*Analysis and Design for Systems, Ninth Edition* includes exciting Video Learning Sessions, developed to maximize the learning experience. The Video Learning Sessions combined with the text offer an interactive, multimedia approach to information systems development. Many two- and four-year colleges and schools use this book in information systems, computer science, and e-commerce curriculums. The textbook emphasizes the role of the systems analyst in a dynamic, business-related environment.

Facing a challenging global marketplace, companies need strong IT resources to survive and compete effectively. Many of today's students will become the systems analysts, managers, and IT professionals of tomorrow. This textbook will help prepare them for those roles.

Using this book, students learn how to translate business requirements into information systems that support a company's short- and long-term objectives. Case studies and assignments teach analytical and problem-solving skills. Students learn about traditional structured analysis, object-oriented concepts, and agile methods. Extensive end-of-chapter exercises emphasize critical-thinking skills.

The *Ninth Edition* introduces several major new features, including four new Video Learning Sessions and a new end-of-chapter assignment called *Ready for a Challenge*, which stresses critical thinking skills. This edition also includes significant updates on topics such as agile development, IT security, and Web 2.0 trends.

## Objectives of This Textbook

*Analysis and Design for Systems, Ninth Edition* is intended for a three credit-hour introductory systems analysis and design course. This textbook is designed to:

- Enhance critical thinking skills with the new Ready for a Challenge feature at the end of each chapter. The scenario-based tasks and sample answers help students develop perception, organization, analysis, problem-solving, and decision-making skills that they can take to the workplace.

- Explain systems analysis and design using an appealing full-color format, numerous screen shots and illustrations, and an easy-to-read style that invites students to learn.

- Introduce project management concepts early in the systems development process, with a new chapter that explains project management tools and techniques.

- Challenge students with a Question of Ethics mini-case in each chapter that asks them to respond to real-life ethical issues in an IT environment.

- Provide multi-method coverage, including a comparison of structured, object-oriented, and agile systems development methods.

- Emphasize the importance of planning, implementing, and managing an effective IT security program.

- Explain how IT supports business requirements in today's intensely competitive environment, and describe major IT developments and trends.

- Describe a systems analyst's job in a typical business organization, and show students how to use various tools and techniques to improve their skills and manage their careers.

- Provide students with a comprehensive Systems Analyst's Appendix that highlights four major cross-functional tools, including: Communicating, Software Engineering, Cost-Benefit Analysis, and Internet Resources.

## Video Learning Sessions

Eighteen multimedia Video Learning Sessions describe key systems analysis skills and concepts and provide students with a self-paced, interactive learning tool that reinforces the text. The sessions provide step-by-step explanations that are easy to follow and understand.

Each session includes practice tasks, sample answers, and challenge tasks to keep students interested and engaged as they learn.

- Topics include DFDs, object-oriented analysis, functional decomposition diagrams, structure charts, data normalization, entity-relationship diagrams, decision tables, financial tools, and project management.

- A **Your Turn** feature in every Video Learning Session challenges students to apply their skills and check their work against sample answers. This hands-on practice can help students better handle actual assignments and tasks.

- The Video Learning Sessions offer a self-paced multimedia format that students can review at their convenience.

- Instructors may use the Video Learning Sessions as classroom presentations, distance-education support, student review tools, and exam preparation.

## Other New and Updated Features in This Text

*Analysis and Design for Systems, Ninth Edition* offers these exciting new and expanded features:

- New Ready for a Challenge end-of-chapter assignment allows students to practice critical thinking skills, first by trying *Practice Tasks* and viewing sample answers, and then by completing the *Challenge Tasks*. These tasks can help students develop perception, organization, analysis, problem-solving, and decision-making skills that they can take to the workplace.

- Increased emphasis on project management skills and techniques, with one or more Gantt charts in each chapter, work breakdown structures, and realistic project examples. A link to Open Workbench connects students to open-source project management software that they can download and install.

- Question of Ethics mini-case in each chapter challenges students with real-life ethical issues in an IT environment.

- Multi-method coverage provides comparison of structured, object-oriented, and agile development methods, starting in Chapter 1. New material on agile methods includes examples of extreme programming, scrum, spiral models, and related topics.

- New coverage of risk management, both in a project management context and as a key element of IT security planning.

- Extensive update of networking coverage, including new material on switches, routers, and multistation access units. New coverage of wireless networks, including wireless standards, topologies, and trends.

- Expansion of IT security material, including risk management, fault management, backup and recovery, wireless security issues, and a six-level security framework.

- Expanded coverage of IT trends, including cloud computing, Web 2.0, social networking, RFID, wireless networks, mobile computing, offshore outsourcing, e-business, ERP, Web hosting, client/server architecture, network concepts, Webinars, podcasts, RSS feeds, Web-based applications, and others.

- Updated Systems Analyst's Appendix teaches students IT support skills in four cross-functional areas, including Communicating, Software Engineering, Cost-Benefit Analysis, and Internet Resources.

- New Management Information Systems CourseMate Web site for *Analysis and Design for Systems, Ninth Edition* available for a fully digital course solution. CourseMate provides one location for all interactive activities, Video Learning Sessions, and an interactive e-book. EngagementTracker provides the ability to assess student understanding of concepts through the interactive activities.

## Organization of This Textbook

*Analysis and Design for Systems, Ninth Edition,* contains 16 learning units in twelve chapters and a four-part Systems Analyst's Appendix that teaches valuable cross-functional skills.

**Chapter 1 – Systems Analysis Fundamentals** Chapter 1 provides an up-to-date overview of IT issues, major trends, and various systems development approaches, including structured, object-oriented, and agile methods. The chapter emphasizes the important role of systems analysis and design in supporting business objectives.

**Chapter 2 – Business Justification** Chapter 2 offers a business-related starting point for successful systems analysis. Topics include strategic planning, review of systems requests, how to conduct a feasibility study, and the steps in a preliminary investigation.

**Chapter 3 – Project Management** Chapter 3 explains project management, cost estimating, and change control for information systems. This chapter includes hands-on skills that systems analysts can use to create Gantt charts and PERT charts.

**Chapter 4 – Determining Requirements** Chapter 4 describes fact-finding techniques and team-based modeling methods, including JAD and RAD, that systems analysts use to model and document a new system.

**Chapter 5 – Data and Process Analysis** Chapter 5 explains how systems analysts create a logical model for the new system by using data flow diagrams and process description tools, including structured English, decision tables, and decision trees.

**Chapter 6 – Object Analysis** Chapter 6 explains object-oriented tools and techniques, including use case diagrams, class diagrams, sequence diagrams, state-transition diagrams, activity diagrams, and the Unified Modeling Language.

**Chapter 7 – Options for Development** Chapter 7 focuses on software acquisition options, including outsourcing and offshore outsourcing options, application service providers, and other trends that view software as a service rather than a product.

**Chapter 8 – Designing the Interface** Chapter 8 highlights output and report design, the interaction between humans and computers, including usability issues, graphical screen design, input issues, and data entry guidelines.

**Chapter 9 – Designing the Data** Chapter 9 describes data design terms, concepts, and skills including entity-relationship diagrams, cardinality, data normalization rules, data warehousing, data mining, a comparison of logical and physical records, and data control measures.

**Chapter 10 – System Construction Planning** Chapter 10 explains the elements of system architecture, with emphasis on RFID, ERP, supply chain management, client/server architecture, and network topology, including wireless networking standards and trends.

**Chapter 11 – Making the System Operational** Chapter 11 includes coverage of application development and implementation topics, including structure charts, documentation techniques, system testing, user training, data conversion, changeover methods, and post-implementation evaluation.

**Chapter 12 – Securing and Supporting the System** Chapter 12 describes user support, maintenance techniques, and factors that indicate the end of a system's useful life. This chapter explains IT security concepts, techniques, and tools, and specifically addresses six security levels: physical, network, application, file, user, and procedural security. Chapter 12 also describes risk management, data backup and disaster recovery, and explains future challenges and opportunities that IT professionals will face in a dynamic workplace.

**Appendix A – Communicating** Appendix A describes oral and written communication tools that can make a systems analyst more effective. Topics include guidelines for successful communications, tips for better readability, how to organize and plan a presentation, effective speaking techniques, and managing communication skills.

**Appendix B – Software Engineering** Appendix B focuses on computer-aided software engineering (CASE) tools that systems analysts use to document, model, and develop information systems. Examples of several popular CASE tools are provided, along with sample screens that show CASE tool features.

**Appendix C – Cost-Benefit Analysis** Appendix C explains various tools that systems analysts use to determine feasibility and evaluate the costs and benefits of an information system. Specific tools include payback analysis, return on investment (ROI), and net present value (NPV).

**Appendix D – Internet Resources** Appendix D explains Internet-based information gathering strategies. Topics include search engines, subject directories, the invisible Web, advanced search techniques, Boolean logic and Venn diagrams. This Appendix also discusses social networking, newsgroups, newsletters, blogs, podcasts, RSS feeds, Webinars, mailing lists, Web-based discussion groups, chat rooms, instant messaging, and online learning opportunities.

## FOR THE STUDENT

The Shelly Cashman Series wants you to have a valuable learning experience that will provide the knowledge and skills you need to be successful. With that goal in mind, we have included many activities, games, and learning tools, that we hope you will find interesting, challenging, and enjoyable. For example, because a picture is worth a thousand words, each systems development phase begins with an eye-catching Dilbert© cartoon and a multi-color Gantt chart that provides a "*You are Here*" roadmap.

## Chapter Opening Features

Each chapter contains the following features to help you get started:

- **Chapter Introduction** Read the Chapter Introduction for a brief overview of the chapter.

- **Chapter Objectives** The Chapter Objectives lists the main skills and knowledge you will have when you finish the chapter.

- **Chapter Introduction Case: Mountain View College Bookstore** The Mountain View College Bookstore case is a continuing case study that provides a real-world overview of the topics that will be covered in each chapter. As you work through the textbook, you will see how the Mountain View IT team discusses the issues, identifies the key points, and creates specific task lists.

## Learning Tools within the Chapter

As you work through each chapter, you will find these helpful tools and features:

- **Video Learning Sessions** An online library of 18 self-paced multimedia sessions is available to you and the text includes reminders about them. Depending on your personal learning style, you might use the videos in various ways. For example, one approach might be to review the chapter, watch the VLS, try the Your Turn tasks, and then check your answers.

- **A Question of Ethics** A mini-case in each chapter will challenge you with real-life ethical issues in an IT environment.

- **Case in Point** This exciting feature provides four embedded mini-case opportunities for you to analyze and apply the skills and concepts you are learning in the chapter.

- **Margin Notes** The Systems Analyst's Appendix explains skills that you can apply at any point in the textbook. Marginal notes remind you about the Appendix, where to find it, and how it might help you address the issues or material in the chapter.

- **On the Web** Learn more about a topic by visiting the suggested Web sites and exploring the links we have provided.

## End-of-Chapter Exercises

The following exercises are in every text chapter:

- **Learn It Online** Each chapter features a Learn It Online page that includes six exercises. These exercises utilize the Web to offer chapter-related reinforcement activities that will help you gain confidence in systems analysis and design. These exercises include True/False, Multiple Choice, Short Answer, Flash Cards, Practice Test, and several learning games.

- **CASE SIM: SCR Associates** This is an interactive Web-based case study, with a work session at the end of each chapter. Visit SCR's Web site and log on to the company's intranet to read e-mail messages addressed to you, listen to voice mail messages, and perform assigned tasks in a realistic corporate setting. In this simulation you report to Jesse Baker, but you e-mail your completed assignments to your instructor. Detailed instructions on how to use this case are available in the Management Information Systems CourseMate Web site for *Analysis and Design for Systems, Ninth Edition* at www.cengagebrain.com. To log on to the SCR intranet, you must use the password *sad9*. When you log on to the SCR intranet, you also will be asked to enter your first and last name so your e-mail can be addressed to you correctly.

- **Chapter Exercises** In this section, you will find 10 Review Questions and four Discussion Topics. These exercises allow you to apply your understanding of the material and will help to prepare you for tests and assessments.

- **Apply Your Knowledge** This section includes four mini-cases per chapter. Each mini-case requires you to use the knowledge and skills you learned in the chapter.

- **Case Studies** Case studies provide practical experience and allow you to practice specific skills learned in the chapter. Each chapter contains several case studies, two of which (New Century Health Clinic and Personal Trainer, Inc.) continue throughout the textbook. You can complete your assignments using Microsoft Word and Excel forms, available in the Management Information Systems CourseMate Web site for *Analysis and Design for Systems, Ninth Edition* at www.cengagebrain.com.

- **Chapter Capstone Case: SoftWear, Limited** SoftWear, Limited (SWL) is a continuing case study where students act as members of the SWL systems development team and perform various assignments in each chapter, including a set of project management tasks and a sample Gantt chart.

- **Ready for a Challenge** This new end-of-chapter assignment stresses critical thinking skills, which many educators and employers believe are very important in the workplace. Perform the Practice Tasks first, view the sample answers, and apply your knowledge and skill to the Challenge Tasks. *Ready for a Challenge* can help you develop perception, organization, analysis, problem-solving, and decision-making skills that you can take to the workplace.

## Additional Support Tools

These additional tools can enhance your learning experience:

**GLOSSARY/INDEX** This edition of the textbook includes a glossary/index feature to assist your understanding of key terms and phrases, or to use as a quick reference tool.

**STUDENT STUDY TOOL** This interactive study tool, accessible via the Management Information Systems CourseMate Web site for *Analysis and Design for Systems, Ninth Edition* provides:

- Detailed outlines of every chapter that highlight key topics covered and can be used as a guide when reviewing for an exam
- Chapter glossaries that allow you to look up all key terms in one place, and provide page references where key terms can be found if you need more information
- Figures and Test Yourself questions that provide additional reinforcement of chapter concepts
- User guide for Open Workbench (a free, open-source project management program), and links to download and install a trial version of Microsoft Project and a full version of Open Workbench

**MANAGEMENT INFORMATION SYSTEMS COURSEMATE** Broaden your learning experience and enhance your understanding of the material in each chapter with the Management Information Systems CourseMate Web site. Visit www.cengagebrain.com for access to:

- Full, interactive digital e-book
- Video Learning Sessions and Your Turn exercises
- Ready for a Challenge Practice Tasks and Challenge Tasks
- On the Web links
- Learn It Online exercises, including True/False, Multiple Choice, Short Answer, Flash Cards, Practice Test, and several learning games
- SCR Associates Internet and intranet sites
- Forms Library
- Project Management Resources

## FOR THE INSTRUCTOR

The Shelly Cashman Series is dedicated to providing you all of the tools you need to make your class a success.

## Instructor Resources

The Instructor Resources companion website, www.cengage.com/international, for this textbook includes both teaching and testing aids. The contents of this site are listed below:

- **Instructor's Manual** Includes lecture notes summarizing the chapter sections, figures and boxed elements found in every chapter, teacher tips, classroom activities, lab activities, and quick quizzes in Microsoft Word files.

- **Syllabus** Easily customizable sample syllabus that covers policies, assignments, exams, and other course information. Also included is a Microsoft Project file used to create the five Phase Opener Gantt charts. An instructor can use this project file to create a visual syllabus that could include additional tasks, quizzes, and projects. The project file also can be used to track class progress through the course. Instructors are welcome to distribute this file to students, and show them how to manage tasks, resources, and deadlines for team projects that might be assigned.

- **PowerPoint Presentations** A multimedia lecture presentation system provides slides for each chapter, based on chapter objectives.

- **Figure Files** Illustrations for every figure in the textbook in electronic form.

- **Solutions to Exercises** Includes solutions for end-of-chapter exercises, including Ready for a Challenge Practice and Challenge Task solutions, chapter reinforcement exercises, and extra case studies.

- **Test Bank & Test Engine** Test Banks include 112 questions for every chapter, and feature objective-based and critical thinking question types, page number references, and figure references when appropriate. The ExamView test engine is the ultimate tool for your testing needs.

- **Additional Activities for Students** The forms that students can use to complete the Case Studies are included. Two additional case studies are also provided for every chapter, to be assigned as homework, extra credit, or assessment tools. Chapter Reinforcement Exercises, which are true/false, multiple-choice, and short answer questions that help students gain confidence in the material learned are included, as are the Your Turn Practice Tasks and sample solutions.

- **Additional Faculty Files** A copy of the powerful CASE tool, Visible Analyst — Student Edition, is provided for your evaluation. Several sample solutions to case study tasks also are included. To install this program, you follow a simple registration process that entitles you to use the software and obtain support. Detailed instructions are provided on the Instructor Resources disc. Also included are Word document versions of the e-mail and voice mail messages posted for students on the SCR Web site and the Interview Summaries for the New Century Case Study.

**SOFTWARE BUNDLING OPPORTUNITIES** *Analysis and Design for Systems, Ninth Edition* can be bundled with several popular software programs:

- **Visible Analyst Student Edition** Whether you are designing e-business applications, developing a data warehouse, or integrating legacy systems with new enterprise applications, Visible Analyst is a valuable software based learning tool that helps students become more marketable with its advanced, affordable, and easy to use modeling capabilities. Visible Analyst was recently awarded the "Best Systems Analysis & Design Modeling Tool" by the Indian Education Ministry. Key users include: Business Analysts who analyze the organization and design of businesses or government departments and assess business models and their integration with technology; other professions that use systems analysis and design methods and techniques include Systems Analysts, Database Engineers, Computer Scientists, and Software Engineers. Visible Analyst is a separate software tool available individually as a Student Edition or as a University Edition with concurrent floating licenses for college or university computer labs. For more information about Visible Analyst, please visit: www.visible.com/Modeler/index.htm or contact sales@visible.com.

- **Microsoft Visio**  The advanced diagramming tools of Visio 2010 help you simplify complexity with dynamic, data-driven visuals and new ways to share on the Web in real time. Start by building your diagram with professional-looking templates and modern, pre-drawn shapes. Then, easily link your diagram to popular data sources (such as Excel). You'll see data automatically refresh right within your diagram, reflected in vibrant visuals such as icons, symbols, colors, and bar graphs. Finally, with just a few clicks, publish your data-linked diagram to SharePoint, and provide access to others on the Web, even if they don't have Visio. Together, simplicity, data-driven shapes, and Web sharing make Visio 2010 one of the most powerful ways to see and understand important information.

- **Microsoft Project**  Microsoft® Project 2010 delivers powerful, visually enhanced ways to effectively manage a wide range of projects and programs. From meeting crucial deadlines to selecting the right resources and empowering your teams, Project 2010 offers easier and more intuitive experiences to help you simply be more productive and realize amazing results.

## ACKNOWLEDGMENTS

First, special thanks to Deb Kaufmann, our development editor, who made an enormous contribution to this edition. Her insight and suggestions were extremely valuable. Thanks to Larry Brock, Andrew Page, and Ron Savilla. As former students at Central Piedmont Community College, their ideas were especially valuable, and helped shape the new edition. Thanks also to David Rosenblatt, who contributed to an earlier edition of *Analysis and Design for Systems,* and returned to help with the Ninth Edition.

Finally, thanks to our students for their feedback and comments. They suggested that we add additional *Video Learning Sessions* and interactive content such as *Ready for a Challenge* and *Your Turn.* We hope they continue to offer suggestions, and we will certainly continue to listen to them.

## ABOUT OUR COVERS

The Shelly Cashman Series is continually updating our approach and content to reflect the way today's students learn and experience new technology. This focus on student success is reflected on our covers, which feature real students from Bryant University using the Shelly Cashman Series in their courses, and reflect the varied ages and backgrounds of the students learning with our books. When you use the Shelly Cashman Series, you can be assured that you are learning computer skills using the most effective courseware available.

# PHASE

## SYSTEMS PLANNING

As the Dilbert cartoon suggests, it is always a good idea to know whether a project fits the company's overall strategy. You will learn more about the relationship between systems projects and corporate strategies in the systems planning phase.

Systems planning is the first of five phases in the systems development life cycle. After an introduction to systems analysis and design, you will learn how systems projects get started, how to evaluate a project proposal to determine its feasibility, and how to use project management tools and techniques. The deliverable for this phase is the preliminary investigation report.

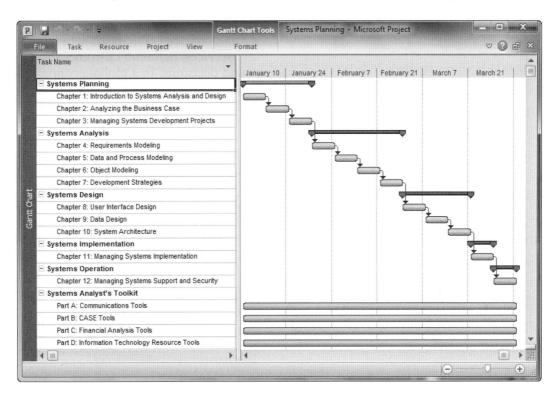

# CHAPTER | Systems Analysis Fundamentals

**Chapter 1** is the first of three chapters in the systems planning phase. This chapter describes the role of information technology in today's dynamic business environment. In this chapter, you will learn about the development of information systems, systems analysis and design concepts, and various systems development methods. This chapter also describes the role of the information technology department and its people.

## INTRODUCTION

## OBJECTIVES

*When you finish this chapter, you will be able to:*

• Describe the impact of information technology on business strategy and success

• Define an information system and describe its components

• Explain how profiles and models can represent business functions and operations

• Explain how the Internet has affected business strategies and relationships

• Identify various types of information systems and explain who uses them

• Distinguish between structured analysis, object-oriented analysis, and agile methods

• Compare the traditional waterfall model with agile methods and models

• Apply five basic guidelines for systems development

• Discuss the role of the information technology department and the systems analysts who work there

The headlines in Figure 1-1 offer dramatic examples of how information technology affects our society. Companies use information as a weapon in the battle to increase productivity, deliver quality products and services, maintain customer loyalty, and make sound decisions. In a global economy with intense competition, information technology can mean the difference between success and failure.

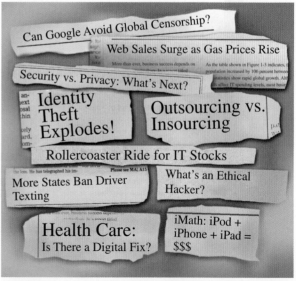

**FIGURE 1-1** These headlines show the enormous impact of information technology in the twenty-first century.

## CHAPTER INTRODUCTION CASE:   Mountain View College Bookstore

**Background:** Mountain View College is located in New England. The school has grown rapidly and now has 8,000 students at three campuses, each with a branch bookstore. Wendy Lee, manager of college services, is responsible for all bookstore operations. Wendy wants a new information system that will increase efficiency and improve customer service.

As the case begins, Tina Allen, a systems analyst in the college's Information Technology department, is talking with David Conroe. David is majoring in information systems at Mountain View College and is earning credit toward his degree by working part-time as a student intern.

**Participants:**     Tina and David
**Location:**     Tina's office, 10 a.m. Monday morning, August 22, 2011
**Project status:**     Initial discussion
**Discussion topics:**     Basic systems development concepts

| | |
|---|---|
| **Tina:** | Welcome aboard, David. |
| **David:** | *I'm glad to be here. What's on the agenda?* |
| **Tina:** | Well, there's been some talk about a new bookstore information system. Wendy says nothing is definite yet, but she suggested that we should get ready. |
| **David:** | *So we start by learning about the bookstore business?* |
| **Tina:** | Yes, the best system in the world isn't worth much unless it supports business and information needs. But let's not get ahead of ourselves. First, we need to talk about business information systems in general. Then we'll build a business model so we can understand the specific operations and processes at the bookstore. We'll also discuss systems analysis and design tools and techniques. Let's start with an overview of information systems and their characteristics. |
| **David:** | *That makes sense. What about the basic systems analysis techniques you mentioned? Can you tell me a bit more?* |
| **Tina:** | On this project, we'll use what's called a structured method, which is based on the concept of a systems development life cycle, or SDLC for short. I'll also explain object-oriented and agile methods, and you'll learn about modeling tools and techniques. We'll follow a set of basic system development guidelines as we go along. |
| **David:** | *How does the SDLC work?* |
| **Tina:** | The SDLC is like constructing a building. First, you would list specific objectives for the project. Then, you might hire an architect to create drawings that show the finished building. Later, you'd need detailed blueprints for the construction workers. When the building is done, you would check everything, turn it over to the new owners, and make sure they're happy with the results. |
| **David:** | *And that's how we'll develop new information systems?* |
| **Tina:** | It sure is. We'll use a program called Microsoft Project to create a list of tasks we can work on. |

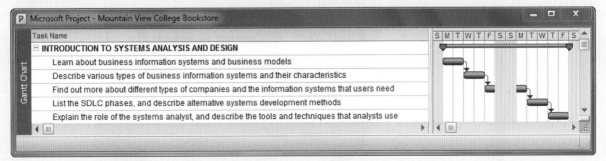

**FIGURE 1-2**   Typical introductory tasks for systems projects

## THE IMPACT OF INFORMATION TECHNOLOGY

**Information technology** (IT) refers to the combination of hardware, software, and services that people use to manage, communicate, and share information. Although fictitious, the bold headlines in Figure 1-1 show the huge impact of IT on our society.

More than ever, business success depends on information technology. IT is driving a new digital economy, where advances in hardware, software, and connectivity can provide enormous benefits to businesses and individuals. Although economic trends affect IT spending levels, most firms give IT budgets a high priority, in good times or bad. The reason is simple — during periods of growth, companies cannot afford to lag behind the IT curve. Conversely, when the economy slows down, firms often use IT to reduce operating costs and improve efficiency.

### The Future

To learn more about the future of IT, visit the Management Information Systems CourseMate Web site at **www. cengagebrain. com**, navigate to **On the Web Links** for this chapter, and locate The Future of IT link.

If you ask a group of IT professionals to name a company that has been successful for over 100 years, the answer probably would be IBM. As its name suggests, International Business Machines was a major supplier of typewriters and data processing equipment long before the computer era. As a longtime IT leader, IBM's predictions deserve close attention.

The company that became IBM was founded in 1896 by Herman Hollerith, who invented the punched card system shown in Figure 1-3. Hollerith wanted to analyze the 1890 census data, and his idea was brilliant. First, letters and numbers were coded by being punched into specific locations on a card. His machines then used a simple

**FIGURE 1-3** Several years before the Wright brothers made their first flight, Herman Hollerith devised a machine that could manage data stored on punched cards.

electrical circuit to detect the position of the holes and recognize the characters. This concept transformed a set of punched cards into what we would call a database, which could be sorted, queried, and printed. Punched card technology revolutionized data storage, and was the main form of information management well into the 1960s and beyond. The concept still is used with some types of voting forms and other documents.

Today, IBM is a global giant with a half-million employees, numerous patents, and more Nobel Prize winners than any other IT firm. In its 2009 Annual Report, IBM chairman Samuel J. Palmisano noted three issues that will shape the future of IT and guide the company's strategy. As shown in Figure 1-4, these include changes in the world, changes in technology, and changes in client demand. IT professionals should study these trends and prepare for the future. The table in Figure 1-5 on the next page summarizes IBM's vision and how it might affect the IT industry and the people who work in it.

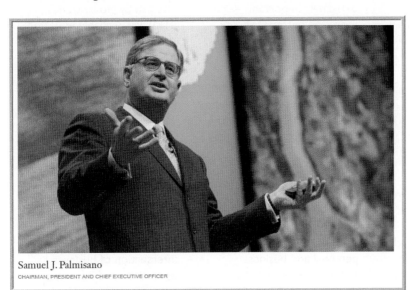

Samuel J. Palmisano
CHAIRMAN, PRESIDENT AND CHIEF EXECUTIVE OFFICER

**1. Changes in the World:** The lowering of trade barriers, the rise of the developing world and the emergence of the World Wide Web were unleashing the flow of work on a global scale. We believed these changes were powerful and irreversible, and that they would lead to new business models and a new form of the corporation itself—what we came to call the globally integrated enterprise.

**2. Changes in Technology:** At the same time, a new model of computing was replacing the PC-based, client/server approach. Computational capability was being put into things no one would recognize as computers: phones, cameras, cars, appliances, roadways, power lines, clothes—and even natural systems, such as agriculture and rivers. All of this was being connected through the Internet. And we now had the computing power, advanced analytics and new models (now known as "clouds") to turn mountains of data into insight. As a result, the economic, societal and physical systems of the world were becoming instrumented, interconnected and intelligent. Our planet was becoming smarter.

**3. Changes in Client Demand:** Compelled by the new opportunities and competitive demands of these first two shifts, enterprises and institutions were no longer content with cost savings from off-the-shelf technologies and solutions. They now sought to innovate—not just in their products and services, but also their business processes, management systems, policies and core business models. To accomplish that, they needed to integrate advanced technology far deeper into their operations.

**FIGURE I-4**   The 2009 IBM Annual Report points out three key issues that affect the company's strategy and operational plans.

## Systems Development

Business information systems are developed by people who are technically qualified, business-oriented, and highly motivated. Successful developers also must be good communicators with strong analytical and critical thinking skills.

| TOPIC | IBM'S VISION | HOW WILL THIS AFFECT IT JOBS GENERALLY? | WHAT WILL BE THE IMPACT ON FUTURE SYSTEMS ANALYSTS? |
|---|---|---|---|
| **Changes in the World** | IBM foresees a new kind of corporation: a globally integrated enterprise, driven by the Internet and free of traditional trade barriers. | Language skills will be extremely important — the more the better. Diversity will open new opportunities, and developing countries will be able to compete more effectively. Where the physical work is done will be less important than how the virtual company deploys its assets. | Systems analysts will be affected by global trends. They will probably work for more firms in their careers, be exposed to more information, and see greater change than at any time in history. |
| **Changes in Technology** | Powered by an enormous increase in computing power, new IT models will include networks with smart, interconnected devices such as communication systems, automobiles, entertainment, highway infrastructure, and power grids. | Technical skills will be in demand, but so will the ability to "think outside the box." New technology will drive major changes in how personal and business services are provided. Firms will compete in a global marketplace that will reward innovation, creativity, and positive societal outcomes. | The systems analyst will need to have both business savvy and technical skills. He or she will have a unique opportunity to work at the intersection of business operations and information technology. The synergy between technology growth and globalization will create jobs and opportunities for people with the right skills. |
| **Changes in Client Demand** | In the face of worldwide competition and enormous technology change, firms will stress innovation, vision, and the ability to adapt rapidly. Every aspect of their business plans, processes, and operations will be affected. | Successful IT workers must be able to innovate, analyze, and communicate effectively. The winners will be those who can adapt to change and embrace new technology and new ways of doing business. | Students preparing for the workplace of tomorrow will need a strong skill set. Systems analysts will be expected to bring communications, modeling, problem-solving, decision-making, and critical thinking skills to the workplace — and to be aware of ethical issues that might affect them. |

**FIGURE 1-5** If IBM's vision is accurate, what will it mean to IT professionals?

## Systems Analysis and Design

**Systems analysis and design** is a
step-by-step process for developing
high-quality information systems.
An **information system** combines
information technology, people, and
data to support business requirements. For example, information
systems handle daily business transactions, improve company productivity, and help managers make
sound decisions. The IT department
team includes **systems analysts** who
plan, develop, and maintain information systems.

With increasing demand for talented people, employment experts
predict a shortage of qualified applicants to fill IT positions. Many companies list employment opportunities
on their Web sites, as shown in Figure 1-6.

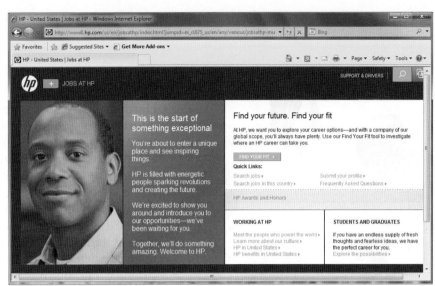

**FIGURE 1-6**   HP invites potential candidates to search for jobs on its Web site.

## Who Develops Information Systems?

Traditionally, a company either developed its own information systems, called **in-house
applications,** or purchased systems called **software packages** from outside vendors.
Today, the choice is much more complex. Options include Internet-based application
services, outsourcing, custom solutions from IT consultants, and enterprise-wide software strategies.

Regardless of the development method, launching a new information system involves
risks as well as benefits. The greatest risk occurs when a company tries to decide *how* the
system will be constructed before determining *what* the system needs to do. Instead of
putting the cart before the horse, a company must begin by outlining its business needs
and identifying possible IT solutions. Typically, this important work is performed by
systems analysts and other IT professionals. A firm should not consider implementation options until it has a clear set of objectives. Later on, as the system is developed,
a systems analyst's role will vary depending on the implementation option selected.

## INFORMATION SYSTEM COMPONENTS

A **system** is a set of related components that produces specific
results. For example, specialized systems route Internet traffic,
manufacture microchips, and control complex entities like the
Mars Rover shown in Figure 1-7. A **mission-critical system** is one
that is vital to a company's operations. An order processing system, for example, is mission-critical because the company cannot do business without it.

Every system requires input data. For example, your computer
receives data when you press a key or click a menu command. In
an information system, **data** consists of basic facts that are the
system's raw material. **Information** is data that has been transformed into output that is valuable to users.

**FIGURE 1-7**   Imagine the complexity of the
systems used to launch and operate the Mars Rover.

An information system has five key components, as shown in Figure 1-8: hardware, software, data, processes, and people.

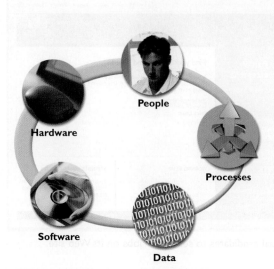

**FIGURE 1-8** The five main components of an information system.

## Hardware

**Hardware** consists of everything in the physical layer of the information system. For example, hardware can include servers, workstations, networks, telecommunications equipment, fiber-optic cables, mobile devices, scanners, digital capture devices, and other technology-based infrastructure. As new technologies emerge, manufacturers race to market the innovations and reap the rewards.

Hardware purchasers today face a wide array of technology choices and decisions. In 1965, Gordon Moore, a cofounder of Intel, predicted that the number of transistors on an integrated circuit would double about every 24 months. His concept, called **Moore's Law**, has remained valid for more than 50 years. Fortunately, as hardware became more powerful, it also became much less expensive. Large businesses with thousands or millions of sales transactions require company-wide information systems and powerful servers, such as those shown in Figure 1-9.

**FIGURE 1-9** Multiple servers provide the power and speed that modern IT systems require.

## Software

**Software** refers to the programs that control the hardware and produce the desired information or results. Software consists of system software and application software.

**System software** manages the hardware components, which can include a single workstation or a global network with many thousands of clients. Either the hardware manufacturer supplies the system software or a company purchases it from a vendor. Examples of system software include the operating system, security software that protects the computer from intrusion, device drivers that communicate with hardware such as printers, and utility programs that handle specific tasks such as data backup and disk management. System software also controls the flow of data, provides data security, and manages network operations. In today's interconnected business world, network software is vitally important.

**Application software** consists of programs that support day-to-day business functions and provide users with the information they require. Application software can serve one user or thousands of people throughout an organization. Examples of company-wide applications, called **enterprise applications**, include order processing systems, payroll systems, and company communications networks. On a smaller scale, individual users increase their productivity with tools such as spreadsheets, word processors, and database management systems.

Application software includes horizontal and vertical systems. A **horizontal system** is a system, such as an inventory or payroll application, that can be adapted for use in many different types of companies. A **vertical system** is designed to meet the unique requirements of a specific business or industry, such as a Web-based retailer, a medical practice, or a video chain.

**ON THE WEB**

To learn more about Moore's Law, visit the Management Information Systems CourseMate Web site at **www.cengagebrain.com**, navigate to **On the Web Links** for this chapter, and locate the Moore's Law link.

Most companies use a combination of software that is acquired at various times. When planning an information system, a company must consider how a new system will interface with older systems, which are called **legacy systems**. For example, a new human resources system might need to exchange data with an older payroll application.

## Data

Data is the raw material that an information system transforms into useful information. An information system can store data in various locations, called tables. By linking the tables, the system can extract specific information. Figure 1-10 shows a payroll system that stores data in four separate tables. Notice that the linked tables work together to supply 19 different data items to the screen form. Users, who would not know or care where the data is stored, see an integrated form, which is their window into the payroll system.

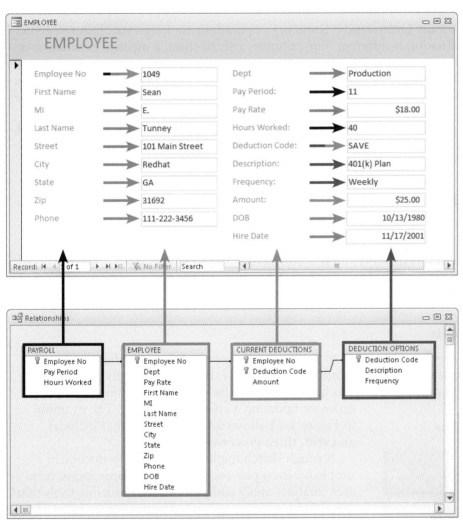

**FIGURE 1-10**   In a typical payroll system, data is stored in separate tables, which are joined together to form a database that contains all the information.

## Processes

**Processes** describe the tasks and business functions that users, managers, and IT staff members perform to achieve specific results. Processes are the building blocks of an information system because they represent actual day-to-day business operations. To build a successful information system, analysts must understand business processes and document them carefully.

## People

People who have an interest in an information system are called **stakeholders**. Stakeholders include the management group responsible for the system, the **users** (sometimes called **end users**) inside and outside the company who will interact with the system, and IT staff members, such as systems analysts, programmers, and network administrators who develop and support the system.

Each stakeholder group has a vital interest in the information system, but most experienced IT professionals agree that the success or failure of a system usually depends on whether it meets the needs of its users. For that reason, it is essential to understand user requirements and expectations throughout the development process.

## UNDERSTAND THE BUSINESS

Business process modeling tools, which are described in Appendix B, can help you document and describe business operations. To learn more about these tools, turn to Appendix B.

IT professionals must understand a company's operations to design successful systems. Each business situation is different. For example, a retail store, a medical practice, and a hotel chain all have unique information systems requirements. Systems analysts use a process called **business process modeling** to represent company operations and information needs. Business process modeling requires a business profile and a series of models that document business processes.

As the business world changes, systems analysts can expect to work in new kinds of companies that require innovative IT solutions, including Web-based systems that serve customers and carry out online transactions with other businesses.

### Business Profile

A **business profile** is an overview of a company's mission, functions, organization, products, services, customers, suppliers, competitors, constraints, and future direction. Although much of this information is readily available, a systems analyst usually needs to do additional research and fact-finding. A business profile is the starting point for the modeling process.

### Business Process

A **business process** is a specific set of transactions, events, and results that can be described and documented. A **business process model (BPM)** graphically displays one or more business processes, such as handling an airline reservation, filling a product order, or updating a customer account. The example in Figure 1-11 shows a simple model that includes an event, three processes, and a result.

A rough sketch might be sufficient to document a simple business process. For complex operations, however, analysts apply computer-based modeling tools that use a standard language called **business process modeling notation (BPMN)**. BPMN includes various shapes and symbols to represent events, processes, and workflows, as shown in the example in Figure 1-12. Modeling tools include multi-purpose graphical applications, such as Microsoft Visio, and computer-aided software engineering programs such as Visible Analyst. Business process modeling is described in more detail in Appendix B.

BUSINESS MODEL: HANDLE SALES ORDER

Event: **Receive Sales Order**

Process: **Check Customer Status**

Process: **Verify Customer Credit**

Result: **Completed Sales Order**

Process: **Enter Customer Order Data**

**FIGURE 1-11**  A simple business model might consist of an event, three processes, and a result.

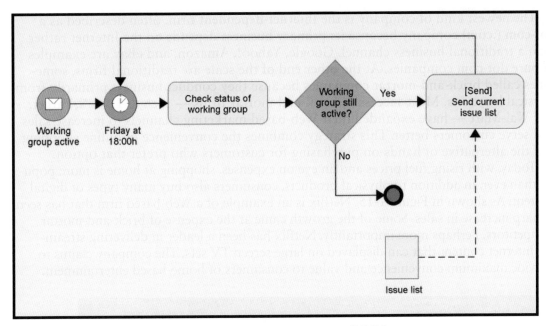

**FIGURE 1-12** This sample uses business process modeling notation (BPMN) to represent events, processes, and workflow.

## New Kinds of Companies

Traditionally, IT companies were identified as product-oriented or service-oriented. **Product-oriented** firms manufactured computers, routers, or the microchips shown in Figure 1-13, whereas **service-oriented** companies included vendors, software developers, and service providers.

Today, those distinctions are gone. Most successful IT companies offer a mix of products, services, and support. Value-added services such as consulting, financing, and technical support can be more profitable than hardware. In a striking example of this trend, IBM stated in its 2009 annual report that software, services, and financing produced 93 percent of pre-tax income, while hardware accounted for only 7 percent. Even more interesting is the contrast shown in Figure 1-14. Over a nine-year period, hardware profits declined by two-thirds, while software, services and financing income grew rapidly.

**FIGURE 1-13** Intel is an example of a product-oriented company that manufactures technology products, such as the microchip shown here.

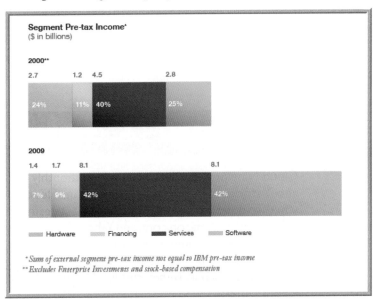

**FIGURE 1-14** IBM's 2009 report shows a sharp increase in profitable business segments such as software and services, and a decline in profit from hardware sales.
*Source:* IBM Annual Report, 2009.

The newest kind of company is the **Internet-dependent** firm, often described as a **dot-com (.com)** company because its primary business depends on the Internet rather than a traditional business channel. Google, Yahoo!, Amazon, and eBay are examples of pure dot-com companies. At the other end of the scale are traditional firms, sometimes called **brick-and-mortar** companies because they conduct business primarily from physical locations. Most successful brick-and-mortar firms — such as Lowe's, Target, and Wal-Mart — have expanded their Web-based marketing channels to increase sales and serve customers better. This strategy combines the convenience of online shopping *and* the alternative of hands-on purchasing for customers who prefer that option.

Today, with rising fuel prices and an eye on expenses, shopping at home is more popular than ever. In addition to physical products, consumers also buy many types of digital content. As shown in Figure 1-15, Netflix is an example of a Web-based firm that has seen a sharp increase in sales. Some of the growth came at the expense of brick-and-mortar competitors. Perhaps more importantly, Netflix has been a leader in delivering streaming Internet content that can displayed on large screen TV sets. The company claims to provide maximum convenience and value to consumers of home-based entertainment.

**FIGURE 1-15**  Netflix offers an Internet portal for digital content that can be viewed on large screen TVs.

## CASE IN POINT 1.1: CLOUD NINE FINANCIAL ADVISORS

Cloud Nine provides its clients with a monthly newsletter that offers recommendations about stocks to buy or sell. Doug Layton, Cloud Nine's president, has asked your opinion on whether dot-com stocks might be good investments for the future. He specifically mentioned Google, eBay, Amazon.com, and Yahoo!, but he said you could suggest other companies. Doug wants you to do some Internet research to learn more about these Web-based companies and their future prospects. You can use a search engine, or start by visiting the Web sites of publications such as *Forbes*, *Fortune Magazine*, *Business Week*, or *The Wall Street Journal*, among others.

## IMPACT OF THE INTERNET

Internet-based commerce is called **e-commerce (electronic commerce)** or **I-commerce (Internet commerce)**.

Internet-based systems involve various hardware and software designs, but a typical model is a series of Web pages that provides a user interface, which communicates with database management software and a Web-based data server. As Internet-based commerce continues to grow, career opportunities will expand significantly for IT professionals such as Web designers, database developers, and systems analysts. The surge in demand will come from dot-com companies large and small, and from mainstream retailers.

E-commerce includes two main sectors: **B2C (business-to-consumer)** and **B2B (business-to-business)**.

### B2C (Business-to-Consumer)

Using the Internet, consumers can go online to purchase an enormous variety of products and services. This new shopping environment allows customers to do research, compare prices and features, check availability, arrange delivery, and choose payment methods in a single convenient session. Many companies, such as airlines, offer incentives for online transactions because Web-based processing costs are lower than traditional methods. By making flight information available online to last-minute travelers, some airlines also offer special discounts on seats that might otherwise go unfilled.

B2C commerce is changing traditional business models and creating new ones. For example, a common business model is a retail store that sells a product to a customer. To carry out that same transaction on the Internet, the company must develop an online store and deal with a totally different set of marketing, advertising, and profit-ability issues. Some companies have found new ways to use established business models. For example, eBay.com has transformed a traditional auction concept into a popular and successful method of selling goods and services.

In the e-commerce battles, the real winners will be online consumers, who will have access to more information, better choices, and an enhanced shopping experience. For example, in addition to the traditional offerings, the Lowe's Web site shown in Figure 1-16 includes a gift advisor, buying guides, how-to clinics, and interactive design tools.

**ON THE WEB**

To learn more about electronic commerce, visit the Management Information Systems CourseMate Web site at **www.cengagebrain.com**, navigate to **On the Web Links** for this chapter, and locate the Electronic Commerce link.

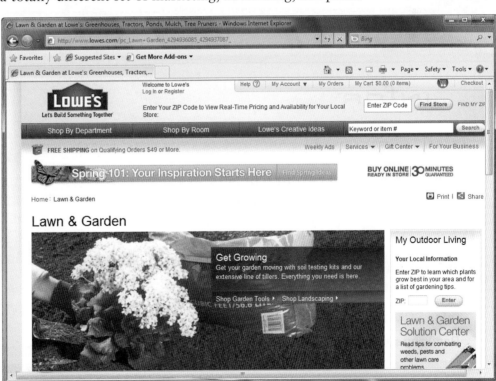

**FIGURE 1-16**  Lowe's is an example of a mainstream retailer that effectively combines traditional and online marketing strategies.

### B2B (Business-to-Business)

Although the business-to-consumer (B2C) sector is more familiar to retail customers, the volume of business-to-business (B2B) transactions is many times greater. Industry observers predict that B2B sales will increase sharply as more firms seek to improve efficiency and reduce costs.

Initially, electronic commerce between two companies used a data sharing arrangement called **electronic data interchange (EDI)**. EDI enabled computer-to-computer data transfer, usually over private telecommunications lines. Firms used EDI to plan production, adjust inventory levels, or stock up on raw materials using data from another company's information system. As B2B volume soared, the development of **extensible markup language (XML)** enabled company-to-company traffic to migrate to the Internet, which offered standard protocols, universal availability, and low communication costs. XML is a flexible data description language that allows Web-based communication between different hardware and software environments.

Because it allows companies to reach the global marketplace, B2B is especially important to smaller suppliers and customers who need instant information about market prices and availability. On an industry-wide scale, many B2B sites exist where buyers, sellers, distributors, and manufacturers can offer products, submit specifications, and transact business. This popular form of online B2B interaction is called **supply chain management (SCM)**, or **supplier relationship management (SRM)**. Figure 1-17 shows a software vendor that offers SCM solutions designed to reduce supply chain costs.

**ON THE WEB**

To learn more about XML, visit the Management Information Systems CourseMate Web site at **www. cengagebrain. com**, navigate to **On the Web Links** for this chapter, and locate the Extensible Markup Language link.

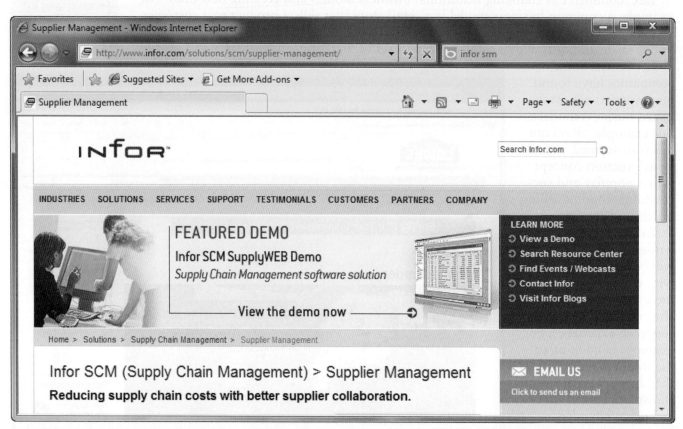

**FIGURE I-17**  Infor is a software vendor that offers SCM solutions based on real-time supplier collaboration.

# BUSINESS INFORMATION SYSTEMS

In the past, IT managers divided systems into categories based on the user group the system served. Categories and users included office systems (administrative staff), operational systems (operational personnel), decision support systems (middle-managers and knowledge workers), and executive information systems (top managers).

Today, traditional labels no longer apply. For example, all employees, including top managers, use office productivity systems. Similarly, operational users often require decision support systems. As business changes, information use also changes in most companies. Today, it makes more sense to identify a system by its functions and features, rather than by its users. A new set of system definitions includes enterprise computing systems, transaction processing systems, business support systems, knowledge management systems, and user productivity systems.

## Enterprise Computing

**Enterprise computing** refers to information systems that support company-wide operations and data management requirements. Wal-Mart's inventory control system, Boeing's production control system, and Hilton Hotels' reservation system are examples of enterprise computing systems. The main objective of enterprise computing is to integrate a company's primary functions (such as production, sales, services, inventory control, and accounting) to improve efficiency, reduce costs, and help managers make key decisions. Enterprise computing also improves data security and reliability by imposing a company-wide framework for data access and storage.

In many large companies, applications called **enterprise resource planning (ERP)** systems provide cost-effective support for users and managers throughout the company. For example, a car rental company can use ERP to forecast customer demand for rental cars at hundreds of locations.

By providing a company-wide computing environment, many firms have been able to achieve dramatic cost reductions. Other companies have been disappointed in the time, money, and commitment necessary to implement ERP successfully. A potential disadvantage of ERP is that ERP systems generally impose an overall structure that might or might not

**ON THE WEB**

To learn more about enterprise resource planning, visit the Management Information Systems CourseMate Web site at **www. cengagebrain. com**, navigate to **On the Web Links** for this chapter, and locate the Enterprise Resource Planning link.

match the way a company operates. ERP is described in more detail in Chapter 7, which discusses system development strategies.

Because of its growth and potential, many hardware and software vendors target the enterprise computing market and offer a wide array of products and services. Figure 1-18 shows a Web site that is dedicated to marketing enterprise computing software and solutions.

## Transaction Processing

**Transaction processing (TP) systems** process data generated by day-to-day business operations. Examples of TP systems include customer order processing, accounts receivable, and warranty claim processing.

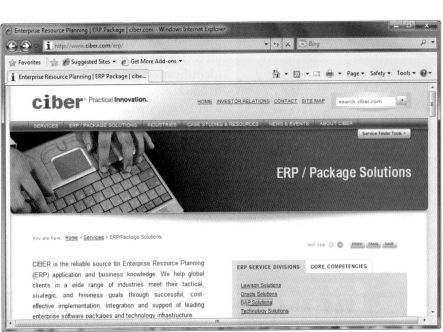

**FIGURE 1-18**   Ciber offers ERP applications and consulting, using software from leading software providers.

**FIGURE 1-19** A single sales transaction consists of six separate tasks, which the TP system processes as a group.

**FIGURE 1-20** Retailers use RFID tags for security and inventory control.

TP systems perform a series of tasks whenever a specific transaction occurs. In the example shown in Figure 1-19, a TP system verifies customer data, checks the customer's credit status, posts the invoice to the accounts receivable system, checks to ensure that the item is in stock, adjusts inventory data to reflect a sale, and updates the sales activity file. TP systems typically involve large amounts of data and are mission-critical systems because the enterprise cannot function without them.

TP systems are efficient because they process a set of transaction-related commands as a group rather than individually. To protect data integrity, however, TP systems ensure that if any single element of a transaction fails, the system does not process the rest of the transaction.

## Business Support

**Business support systems** provide job-related information support to users at all levels of a company. These systems can analyze transactional data, generate information needed to manage and control business processes, and provide information that leads to better decision-making.

The earliest business computer systems replaced manual tasks, such as payroll processing. Companies soon realized that computers also could produce valuable information. The new systems were called **management information systems (MIS)** because managers were the primary users. Today, employees at *all* levels need information to perform their jobs, and they rely on information systems for that support.

A business support system can work hand in hand with a TP system. For example, when a company sells merchandise to a customer, a TP system records the sale, updates the customer's balance, and makes a deduction from inventory. A related business support system highlights slow- or fast-moving items, customers with past due balances, and inventory levels that need adjustment.

To compete effectively, firms must collect production, sales, and shipping data and update the company-wide business support system immediately. The newest development in data acquisition is called **radio frequency identification (RFID)** technology, which uses high-frequency radio waves to track physical objects, such as the item shown in Figure 1-20. RFID's dramatic growth has been fueled by companies like Wal-Mart, which requires its suppliers to add RFID tags to all items.

An important feature of a business support system is decision support capability. Decision support helps users make decisions by creating a computer model and applying a set of variables. For example, a truck fleet dispatcher might run a series of **what-if** scenarios to determine the impact of increased shipments or bad weather. Alternatively, a retailer might use what-if analysis to determine the price it must charge to increase profits by a specific amount while volume and costs remain unchanged.

## Knowledge Management

**Knowledge management systems** are called **expert systems** because they simulate human reasoning by combining a knowledge base and inference rules that determine how the knowledge is applied.

A **knowledge base** consists of a large database that allows users to find information by entering keywords or questions in normal English phrases. A knowledge management system uses **inference rules**, which are logical rules that identify data patterns and relationships.

Figure 1-21 shows a knowledge management system that Toshiba maintains for its customers and users. After a user enters a symptom, problem, or question, Toshiba's Knowledge Base searches for a solution and displays the results.

**FIGURE 1-21**  The interactive Toshiba Knowledge Base allows users to search for solutions.

Knowledge management systems do not use strict logical rules. Instead, many knowledge management systems use a technique called **fuzzy logic** that allows inferences to be drawn from imprecise relationships. Using fuzzy logic, values need not be black and white, like binary logic, but can be many shades of gray. The results of a fuzzy logic search will display in priority order, with the most relevant results at the top of the list.

**ON THE WEB**

To learn more about knowledge management systems, visit the Management Information Systems CourseMate Web site at **www.cengagebrain.com**, navigate to **On the Web Links** for this chapter, and locate the Knowledge Management Systems link.

## User Productivity

Companies provide employees at all levels with technology that improves productivity. Examples of **user productivity systems** include e-mail, voice mail, fax, video and Web conferencing, word processing, automated calendars, database management, spreadsheets, desktop publishing, presentation graphics, company intranets, and high-speed Internet access. User productivity systems also include groupware. **Groupware** programs run on a company intranet and enable users to share data, collaborate on projects, and work in teams. GroupWise, offered by Novell, is a popular example of groupware.

When companies first installed word processing systems, managers expected to reduce the number of employees as office efficiency increased. That did not happen, primarily because the basic nature of clerical work changed. With computers performing most of the repetitive work, managers realized that office personnel could handle tasks that required more judgment, decision-making, and access to information.

Computer-based office work expanded rapidly as companies assigned more responsibility to employees at lower organizational levels. Relatively inexpensive hardware, powerful networks, corporate downsizing, and a move toward employee empowerment also contributed to this trend. Today, administrative assistants and company presidents alike are networked, use computer workstations, and need to share corporate data to perform their jobs.

## Information Systems Integration

Most large companies require systems that combine transaction processing, business support, knowledge management, and user productivity features. For example, suppose an international customer has a problem with a product and makes a warranty claim. A customer service representative enters the claim into a TP system. The transaction updates two other systems: a knowledge management system that tracks product problems and warranty activity, and a quality control system with decision support capabilities. A quality control engineer uses what-if analysis to determine if it would be advantageous to make product design changes to reduce warranty claims. In this example, a TP system is integrated with a knowledge management system and a business support system with decision support features.

## WHAT INFORMATION DO USERS NEED?

Corporate organizational structure has changed considerably in recent years. As part of downsizing and business process reengineering, many companies reduced the number of management levels and delegated responsibility to operational personnel. Although modern organization charts tend to be flatter, an organizational hierarchy still exists in most companies.

A typical organizational model identifies business functions and organizational levels, as shown in Figure 1-22. Within the functional areas, operational personnel report to supervisors and team leaders. The next level includes middle managers and knowledge workers, who, in turn, report to top managers. In a corporate structure, the top managers report to a board of directors elected by the company's shareholders.

A systems analyst must understand the company's organizational model to recognize who is responsible for specific processes and decisions and to be aware of what information is required by whom.

**FIGURE 1-22**  A typical organizational model identifies business functions and organizational levels.

### Top Managers

Top managers develop long-range plans, called **strategic plans**, which define the company's overall mission and goals. To plot a future course, top managers ask questions such as "How much should the company invest in information technology?" or "How much will Internet sales grow in the next five years?" or "Should the company build new factories or contract out the production functions?"

Strategic planning affects the company's future survival and growth, including long-term IT plans. Top managers focus on the overall business enterprise and use IT to set the company's course and direction. To develop a strategic plan, top managers also need information from outside the company, such as economic forecasts, technology trends, competitive threats, and governmental issues.

### Middle Managers and Knowledge Workers

Just below the top management level, most companies have a layer of middle managers and knowledge workers. Middle managers provide direction, necessary resources, and performance feedback to supervisors and team leaders. Because they focus on a somewhat shorter time frame, middle managers need more detailed information than top managers, but somewhat less than supervisors who oversee day-to-day operations. For example, a middle manager might review a weekly sales summary for a three-state area, whereas a local sales team leader would need a daily report on customer sales at a single location.

In addition to middle managers, every company has people called knowledge workers. **Knowledge workers** include professional staff members such as systems analysts, programmers, accountants, researchers, trainers, and human resource specialists. Knowledge workers also use business support systems, knowledge management systems, and user productivity systems. Knowledge workers provide support for the organization's basic functions. Just as a military unit requires logistical support, a successful company needs knowledge workers to carry out its mission.

## Supervisors and Team Leaders

Supervisors, often called team leaders, oversee operational employees and carry out day-to-day functions. They coordinate operational tasks and people, make necessary decisions, and ensure that the right tools, materials, and training are available. Like other managers, supervisors and team leaders need decision support information, knowledge management systems, and user productivity systems to carry out their responsibilities.

## Operational Employees

Operational employees include users who rely on TP systems to enter and receive data they need to perform their jobs. In many companies, operational users also need information to handle tasks and make decisions that were assigned previously to supervisors. This trend, called **empowerment**, gives employees more responsibility and accountability. Many companies find that empowerment improves employee motivation and increases customer satisfaction.

## SYSTEMS DEVELOPMENT TOOLS

In addition to understanding business operations, systems analysts must know how to use a variety of techniques, such as modeling, prototyping, and computer-aided systems engineering tools to plan, design, and implement information systems. Systems analysts work with these tools in a team environment, where input from users, managers, and IT staff contributes to the system design.

## Modeling

**Modeling** produces a graphical representation of a concept or process that systems developers can analyze, test, and modify. A systems analyst can describe and simplify an information system by using a set of business, data, object, network, and process models.

A **business model**, or **requirements model**, describes the information that a system must provide. A **data model** describes data structures and design. An **object model** describes objects, which combine data and processes. A **network model** describes the design and protocols of telecommunications links. A **process model** describes the logic that programmers use to write code modules. Although the models might appear to overlap, they actually work together to describe the same environment from different points of view.

System developers often use multipurpose charting tools such as Microsoft Visio to display business-related models. Visio is a popular tool that systems analysts can use to create business process diagrams, flowcharts, organization charts, network diagrams, floor plans, project timelines, and work flow diagrams, among others.

The CASE tools in Appendix B can help you develop and maintain complex information systems. To learn more about these tools, turn to Appendix B.

**FIGURE 1-23** Microsoft Visio 2010 allows you to drag and drop various symbols and connect them to show a business process.

**ON THE WEB**

To learn more about CASE Tools, visit the Management Information Systems CourseMate Web site at **www. cengagebrain. com**, navigate to **On the Web Links** for this chapter, and locate the CASE Tools link.

Figure 1-23 shows how you can drag and drop various symbols from the left pane into the drawing on the right, and connect them to show a business process.

You will learn about many types of models in this textbook, including data flow diagrams, object diagrams, and entity-relationship diagrams. Business process modeling is explained in more detail in Appendix B.

## Prototyping

Prototyping tests system concepts and provides an opportunity to examine input, output, and user interfaces before final decisions are made. A **prototype** is an early working version of an information system. Just as an aircraft manufacturer tests a new design in a wind tunnel, systems analysts construct and study information system prototypes. A prototype can serve as an initial model that is used as a benchmark to evaluate the finished system, or the prototype itself can develop into the final version of the system. Either way, prototyping speeds up the development process significantly.

A possible disadvantage of prototyping is that important decisions might be made too early, before business or IT issues are understood thoroughly. A prototype based on careful fact-finding and modeling techniques, however, can be an extremely valuable tool.

## Computer-Aided Systems Engineering (CASE) Tools

Computer-aided systems engineering (CASE), also called **computer-aided software engineering**, is a technique that uses powerful software, called **CASE tools**, to help systems analysts develop and maintain information systems. CASE tools provide an overall framework for systems development and support a wide variety of design methodologies, including structured analysis and object-oriented analysis.

Because CASE tools make it easier to build an information system, they boost IT productivity and improve the quality of the finished product. Appendix B explains how analysts use CASE tools to create business profiles, build business models, and document complex processes. After developing a model, many CASE tools can generate program code, which speeds the implementation process. Figure 1-24 shows the Web site for Visible Systems Corporation, a leading vendor of CASE tools.

**FIGURE 1-24** Visible Systems Corporation offers a wide array of software engineering tools, including Visible Analyst, a popular CASE tool.

## SYSTEMS DEVELOPMENT METHODS

Many options exist for developing information systems, but the most popular alternatives are **structured analysis**, which is a traditional method that still is widely used, **object-oriented (O-O) analysis**, which is a more recent approach that many analysts prefer, and **agile methods**, also called **adaptive methods**, which include the latest trends in software development. Figure 1-25 provides an overview of the three methods, which are discussed in the following sections.

|  | STRUCTURED ANALYSIS | OBJECT-ORIENTED ANALYSIS | AGILE/ADAPTIVE METHODS |
|---|---|---|---|
| **Description** | Represents the system in terms of data and the processes that act upon that data. System development is organized into phases, with deliverables and milestones to measure progress. The SDLC waterfall model typically consists of five phases. Iteration is possible among the phases, as shown in Figure 1-27. | Views the system in terms of objects that combine data and processes. The objects represent actual people, things, transactions, and events, as shown in Figure 1-28. Compared to structured analysis, O-O phases tend to be more interactive. Can use the waterfall model or the model that stresses greater iteration, as shown in Figure 1-29. | Stresses intense team-based effort, as shown in Figures 1-30 and 1-31. Breaks development process down into cycles, or iterations that add functionality. Each iteration is designed, built, and tested in an ongoing process. Attempts to reduce major risks by incremental steps in short time intervals. Typically uses a spiral model, as shown in Figure 1-32. |
| **Modeling tools** | Data flow diagrams (DFDs) and process descriptions, which are described in Chapter 5. Also, business process modeling, which is explained in Appendix B. | Various object-oriented diagrams depict system actors, methods, and messages, which are described in Chapter 6. Also, business process modeling, which is explained in Appendix B. | Tools that enhance communication, such as collaborative software, brainstorming, and whiteboards. Business process modeling, which is explained in Appendix B, works well with agile methods. |
| **Pros** | Traditional method, which has been very popular over time. Relies heavily on written documentation. Frequent phase iteration can provide flexibility comparable with other methods. Well-suited to project management tools and techniques. | Integrates easily with object-oriented programming languages. Code is modular and reusable, which can reduce cost and development time. Easy to maintain and expand as new objects can be cloned using inherited properties. | Very flexible and efficient in dealing with change. Stresses team interaction and reflects a set of community-based values. Frequent deliverables constantly validate the project and reduce risk. |
| **Cons** | Changes can be costly, especially in later phases. Requirements are defined early, and can change during development. Users might not be able to describe their needs until they can see examples of features and functions. | Somewhat newer method might be less familiar to development team members. Interaction of objects and classes can be complex in larger systems. | Team members need a high level of technical and communications skills. Lack of structure and documentation can introduce risk factors. Overall project might be subject to scope change as user requirements change. |

**FIGURE 1-25** Comparison of structured, object-oriented, and agile/adaptive development methods.

Although most projects utilize one of these approaches, it is not unusual for system developers to mix and match methods to gain a better perspective. In addition to these three main development methods, some organizations choose to develop their own in-house approaches or use techniques offered by software suppliers, CASE tool vendors, or consultants. Many alternatives exist, and most IT experts agree that no one system development method is best in all cases. An approach that works well for one project might have major disadvantages or risks in another situation. The important thing is for a systems analyst to understand the various methods and the strengths and weaknesses of each approach.

Regardless of the development strategy, people, tasks, timetables, and costs must be managed effectively. Complex projects can involve dozens of people, hundreds of tasks, and many thousands of dollars. **Project management** is the process of planning, scheduling, monitoring, controlling, and reporting upon the development of an information system. Chapter 3 describes project management tools and techniques in detail.

## Structured Analysis

Structured analysis is a traditional systems development technique that is time-tested and easy to understand. Structured analysis uses a series of phases, called the **systems development life cycle (SDLC)**, to plan, analyze, design, implement, and support an information system. Although structured analysis evolved many years ago, it remains a popular systems development method. Structured analysis is based on an overall plan, similar to a blueprint for constructing a building, so it is called a **predictive** approach.

Structured analysis uses a set of process models to describe a system graphically. Because it focuses on processes that transform data into useful information, structured analysis is called a **process-centered** technique. In addition to modeling the processes, structured analysis also addresses data organization and structure, relational database design, and user interface issues.

A process model shows the data that flows in and out of system processes. Inside each process, input data is transformed by **business rules** that generate the output. Figure 1-26 shows a process model that was created with Visible Analyst, a popular software development tool. The model, which represents a school registration system, is a called a **data flow diagram (DFD)** because it uses various symbols and shapes to represent data flow, processing, and storage. You will learn more about DFDs in Chapter 5, and you can view a Video Learning Session that explains DFDs and how they are used as modeling tools.

Structured analysis uses the SDLC to plan and manage the systems development process. The SDLC describes activities and functions that all systems developers perform, regardless of which approach they use. In the **waterfall model**, the result of each phase is called a **deliverable**, or **end product**, which flows into the next phase.

Some analysts see a disadvantage in the built-in structure of the SDLC, because the waterfall model does not emphasize interactivity among the phases. This criticism can be valid if the SDLC phases are followed too rigidly. However, adjacent phases usually interact, as shown

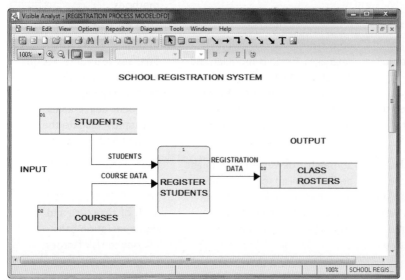

**FIGURE 1-26**  This Visible Analyst screen shows a process model for a school registration system. The REGISTER STUDENTS process accepts input data from two sources and transforms it into output data.

by the dotted lines in Figure 1-27 and interaction among several phases is not uncommon. Other analysts regard the waterfall model as a two-way *water flow* model, with emphasis on iteration and user input. Used in this manner, the traditional model is not as different from agile methods as it might appear to be.

The SDLC model usually includes five steps, which are described in the following sections: systems planning, systems analysis, systems design, systems implementation, and systems support and security.

**SYSTEMS PLANNING** The **systems planning phase** usually begins with a formal request to the IT department, called a **systems request**, which describes problems or desired changes in an information system or a business process. In many companies, IT systems planning is an integral part of overall business planning. When managers and users develop their business plans, they usually include IT requirements that generate systems requests. A systems request can come from a top manager, a planning team, a department head, or the IT department itself. The request can be very significant or relatively minor. A major request might involve a new information system or the upgrading of an existing system. In contrast, a minor request might ask for a new feature or a change to the user interface.

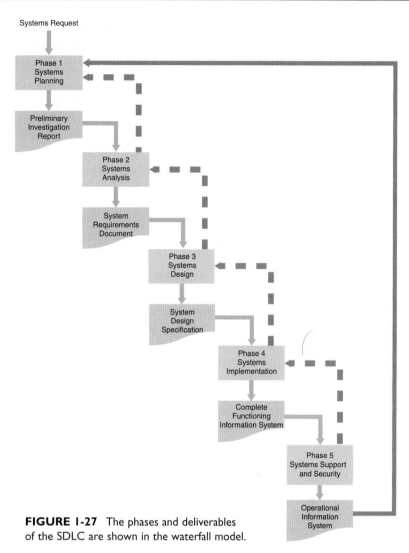

**FIGURE 1-27** The phases and deliverables of the SDLC are shown in the waterfall model.

The purpose of this phase is to perform a **preliminary investigation** to evaluate an IT-related business opportunity or problem. The preliminary investigation is a critical step because the outcome will affect the entire development process. A key part of the preliminary investigation is a **feasibility study** that reviews anticipated costs and benefits and recommends a course of action based on operational, technical, economic, and time factors.

Suppose you are a systems analyst and you receive a request for a system change or improvement. Your first step is to determine whether it makes sense to launch a preliminary investigation at all. Often you will need to learn more about business operations before you can reach a conclusion. After an investigation, you might find that the information system functions properly, but users need more training. In some situations, you might recommend a business process review, rather than an IT solution. In other cases, you might conclude that a full-scale systems review is necessary. If the development process continues, the next step is the systems analysis phase.

**SYSTEMS ANALYSIS** The purpose of the **systems analysis phase** is to build a logical model of the new system. The first step is **requirements modeling**, where you investigate business processes and document what the new system must do to satisfy users. Requirements modeling continues the investigation that began during the systems planning phase. To understand the system, you perform fact-finding using techniques such as interviews, surveys, document review, observation, and sampling. You use the fact-finding results to build business models, data and process models, and object models.

The deliverable for the systems analysis phase is the **system requirements document**. The system requirements document describes management and user requirements, costs and benefits, and outlines alternative development strategies.

**SYSTEMS DESIGN** The purpose of the **systems design phase** is to create a physical model that will satisfy all documented requirements for the system. At this stage, you design the user interface and identify necessary outputs, inputs, and processes. In addition, you design internal and external controls, including computer-based and manual features to guarantee that the system will be reliable, accurate, maintainable, and secure. During the systems design phase, you also determine the application architecture, which programmers will use to transform the logical design into program modules and code.

The deliverable for this phase is the **system design specification**, which is presented to management and users for review and approval. Management and user involvement is critical to avoid any misunderstanding about what the new system will do, how it will do it, and what it will cost.

**SYSTEMS IMPLEMENTATION** During the **systems implementation phase,** the new system is constructed. Whether the developers use structured analysis or O-O methods, the procedure is the same — programs are written, tested, and documented, and the system is installed. If the system was purchased as a package, systems analysts configure the software and perform any necessary modifications. The objective of the systems implementation phase is to deliver a completely functioning and documented information system. At the conclusion of this phase, the system is ready for use. Final preparations include converting data to the new system's files, training users, and performing the actual transition to the new system.

The systems implementation phase also includes an assessment, called a **systems evaluation**, to determine whether the system operates properly and if costs and benefits are within expectations.

**SYSTEMS SUPPORT AND SECURITY** During the **systems support and security phase,** the IT staff maintains, enhances, and protects the system. Maintenance changes correct errors and adapt to changes in the environment, such as new tax rates. Enhancements provide new features and benefits. The objective during this phase is to maximize return on the IT investment. Security controls safeguard the system from both external and internal threats. A well-designed system must be secure, reliable, maintainable, and scalable. A **scalable** design can expand to meet new business requirements and volumes. Information systems development is always a work in progress. Business processes change rapidly, and most information systems need to be updated significantly or replaced after several years of operation.

**VIDEO LEARNING SESSIONS**

To learn more about object modeling, visit the Management Information Systems CourseMate Web site at **www. cengagebrain. com** and navigate to the **Video Learning Sessions** for this book. These sessions can help you understand key concepts, practice your skills, and check your work.

## Object-Oriented Analysis

Whereas structured analysis treats processes and data as separate components, object-oriented analysis combines data and the processes that act on the data into things called **objects**. Systems analysts use O-O to model real-world business processes and operations. The result is a set of software objects that represent actual people, things, transactions, and events. Using an O-O programming language, a programmer then writes the code that creates the objects.

An object is a member of a **class**, which is a collection of similar objects. Objects possess characteristics called **properties**, which the object inherits from its class or possesses on its own. As shown in Figure 1-28, the class called PERSON includes INSTRUCTOR and STUDENT. Because the PERSON class has a property called Address, a STUDENT inherits the Address property. A STUDENT also has a property called Major that is not shared by other members of the PERSON class.

In O-O design, built-in processes called **methods** can change an object's properties. For example, in a Web-based catalog store, an ORDER object might have a property called STATUS that changes when a CUSTOMER object clicks to place, confirm, or cancel the order.

One object can send information to another object by using a message. A **message** requests specific behavior or information from another object. For example, an ORDER object might send a message to a CUSTOMER object that requests a shipping address. When it receives the message, the CUSTOMER object supplies the information. The ORDER object has the capability to send the message, and the CUSTOMER object knows what actions to perform when it receives the message. O-O analysis uses object models to represent data and behavior, and to show how objects affect other objects. By describing the objects and methods needed to support a business operation, a system developer can design reusable components that speed up system implementation and reduce development cost.

**FIGURE 1-28** The PERSON class includes INSTRUCTOR and STUDENT objects, which have their own properties and inherited properties.

Object-oriented methods usually follow a series of analysis and design phases that are similar to the SDLC, although there is less agreement on the number of phases and their names. In an O-O model, the phases tend to be more interactive. Figure 1-29 shows a system development model where planning, analysis, and design tasks interact continuously to produce prototypes that can be tested and implemented. The result is an **interactive model** that can accurately depict real-world business processes.

O-O methodology is popular because it provides an easy transition to O-O programming languages such as Java, Smalltalk, C++, Python, and Perl. Chapter 6 covers O-O analysis and design, with a detailed description of O-O terms, concepts, tools, and techniques.

**FIGURE 1-29** An interactive model often is used with O-O development methods. In this model, planning, analysis, and design tasks interact continuously.

## Agile Methods

Development techniques change over time. For example, structured analysis is a traditional approach, and agile methods are the newest development. Structured analysis builds an overall plan for the information system, just as a contractor might use a blueprint for constructing a building. Agile methods, in contrast, attempt to develop a system incrementally, by building a series of prototypes and constantly adjusting them to user requirements. As the agile process continues, developers revise, extend, and merge earlier versions into the final product. An agile approach emphasizes continuous feedback, and each incremental step is affected by what was learned in the prior steps.

Although relatively new to software development, the notion of **iterative** development can be traced back to Japanese auto firms that were able to boost productivity by using a flexible manufacturing system, where team-based effort and short-term milestones helped keep quality up and costs down. Agile methods have attracted a wide following and an entire community of users, as shown in Figure 1-30 on the next page.

 **ON THE WEB**

To learn more about agile systems development methods, visit the Management Information Systems CourseMate Web site at **www.cengagebrain.com**, navigate to **On the Web Links** for this chapter, and locate the Agile Methods link.

**FIGURE 1-30** Agile methods have attracted a wide following and an entire community of users.

Agile methods typically use a **spiral model**, which represents a series of iterations, or revisions, based on user feedback. As the process continues, the final product gradually evolves. An agile approach requires intense interactivity between developers and individual users, and does not begin with an overall objective. Instead, the agile process determines the end result. Proponents of the spiral model believe that this approach reduces risks and speeds up software development.

Spiral models initially were suggested in the 1990s by Barry Boehm, a noted software engineering professor. He stated that each iteration, or phase, of the model must have a specific goal that is accepted, rejected, or changed by the user, or client. Thus, each iteration produces feedback and enhancements, which enable the team to reach the overall project goal. Typically, each iteration in a spiral model includes planning, risk analysis, engineering, and evaluation, as shown in the table in Figure 1-31. The repeated iterations produce a series of prototypes, which evolve into the finished system. Notice that these phases resemble SDLC tasks, which also can be iterative.

| PHASE | TASKS |
| --- | --- |
| Planning | Define objectives, constraints, and deliverables |
| Risk analysis | Identify risks and develop acceptable resolutions |
| Engineering | Develop a prototype that includes all deliverables |
| Evaluation | Perform assessment and testing to develop objectives for next iteration |

**FIGURE 1-31** Typical phases and tasks in a spiral model.

Numerous other adaptive variations and related methods exist, and most IT developers expect this trend to continue in the future. Two examples are Scrum and Extreme Programming (XP), which are discussed in detail in Chapter 4, Determining Requirements, and in Chapter 11, Making the System Operational.

Although agile methods are becoming popular, analysts should recognize that these approaches have advantages and disadvantages. By their nature, agile methods can allow developers to be much more flexible and responsive, but can be riskier than more traditional methods. For example, without a detailed set of system requirements, certain features requested by some users might not be consistent with the company's larger game plan.

Other potential disadvantages of agile methods can include weak documentation, blurred lines of accountability, and too little emphasis on the larger business picture. Also, unless properly implemented, a long series of iterations might actually add to project cost and development time. The bottom line is that systems analysts should understand the pros and cons of any approach before selecting a development method for a specific project.

## Other Development Methods

IT professionals know that the key to success is user input — before, during, and after a system is developed. Over time, many companies discovered that systems development teams composed of IT staff, users, and managers could complete their work more rapidly and produce better results. Two methodologies became popular: **joint application development (JAD)** and **rapid application development (RAD)**.

Both JAD and RAD use teams composed of users, managers, and IT staff. The difference is that JAD focuses on team-based fact-finding, which is only one phase of the development process, whereas RAD is more like a compressed version of the entire process. JAD, RAD, and agile methods are described in more detail in Chapter 4.

In addition to the methods described in this chapter, you might encounter other systems development techniques. If a systems analyst wants additional choices, he or she can choose from an entire industry of IT software companies and consulting firms. For example, a popular approach offered by the Rational group at IBM is called the **Rational Unified Process (RUP®)**. According to IBM, RUP® offers a flexible, iterative process for managing software development projects that can minimize risk, ensure predictable results, and deliver high-quality software on time.

Another option is what Microsoft calls **Microsoft Solutions Framework (MSF)**, which documents the experience of its own software development teams. Although the Microsoft process differs from the SDLC phase-oriented approach, MSF developers perform the same kind of planning, ask the same kinds of fact-finding questions, deal with the same kinds of design and implementation issues, and resolve the same kinds of problems. Using this approach, MSF examines a broader business and organizational context that surrounds the development of an information system.

Companies often choose to follow their own methodology. Using CASE tools, an IT team can apply a variety of techniques rather than being bound to a single, rigid methodology. As shown in Appendix B, many CASE tools offer a complete set of analysis and modeling tools that support various methods and strategies. Regardless of the development model, it will be necessary to manage people, tasks, timetables, and expenses by using various project management tools and techniques.

**ON THE WEB**

To learn more about Microsoft Solutions Framework, visit the Management Information Systems CourseMate Web site at **www. cengagebrain. com**, navigate to **On the Web Links** for this chapter, and locate the Microsoft Solutions Framework link.

## SYSTEMS DEVELOPMENT GUIDELINES

The basic principles in Figure 1-32 apply to any IT project, large or small. Although you will develop your own methods and techniques, these guidelines will help you achieve success as a systems analyst.

| FIVE BASIC SYSTEMS DEVELOPMENT GUIDELINES | |
|---|---|
| **Develop a Plan** | Prepare an overall project plan and stick to it. Complete the tasks in a logical sequence. Develop a clear set of ground rules and be sure that everyone on the team understands them clearly. |
| **Involve Users and Listen Carefully to Them** | Ensure that users are involved in the development process, especially when identifying and modeling system requirements. When you interact with users, listen closely to what they are saying. Chapter 4 describes fact-finding and how to get the most out of face-to-face communication. |
| **Use Project Management Tools and Techniques** | Try to keep the project on track and avoid surprises. Create a reasonable number of checkpoints — too many can be burdensome, but too few will not provide adequate control. In Chapter 3, you will learn how to use Microsoft Project to help you manage tasks, allocate resources, and monitor progress. |
| **Develop Accurate Cost and Benefit Information** | Managers need to know the cost of developing and operating a system, and the value of the benefits it will provide. You must provide accurate, realistic cost and benefit estimates, and update them as necessary. |
| **Remain Flexible** | Be flexible within the framework of your plan. Systems development is a dynamic process, and overlap often exists among tasks. The ability to react quickly is especially important when you are working on a system that must be developed rapidly. |

**FIGURE 1-32**  These basic guidelines apply throughout the systems development process.

## THE INFORMATION TECHNOLOGY DEPARTMENT

The IT department develops and maintains information systems. The structure of the IT department varies among companies, as does its name and placement within the organization. In a small firm, one person might handle all computer support activities and services, whereas a large corporation might require many people with specialized skills to provide information systems support. Figure 1-33 shows a typical IT organization in a company that has networked PCs, enterprise-wide databases, centralized processing, and Web-based operations.

The IT group provides **technical support**, which includes six main functions: application development, systems support and security, user support, database administration, network administration, and Web support. These functions overlap considerably and often have different names in different companies.

**FIGURE 1-33** Depending on its size, an IT department might have separate organizational units for these functions, or they might be combined into a smaller number of teams.

### Application Development

The IT **application development** group typically provides leadership and overall guidance, but the systems themselves are developed by teams consisting of users, managers, and IT staff members. A popular model for information systems development is a project-oriented team using RAD or JAD, with IT professionals providing overall coordination, guidance, and technical support.

## CASE IN POINT 1.2:   GLOBAL HOTELS AND MOMMA'S MOTELS

Suppose you work in the IT department of Global Hotels, a multinational hotel chain. Global Hotels runs several specialized business support systems, including a guest reservations system that was developed in-house to meet the requirements of a large company with worldwide operations. Guests can make one-stop online reservations by visiting Global's Web site, which has links to all major travel industry sites.

Global Hotels just acquired Momma's, a regional chain of 20 motels in western Canada. Momma's uses a vertical reservations package suitable for small- to medium-sized businesses, and a generic accounting and finance package. Should Momma's use Global Hotels' information systems or continue with its own? In your answer, consider issues such as business profiles, business processes, system interactivity, EDI, XML, e-commerce, and the characteristics of both information systems. What additional information would be helpful to you in making a recommendation?

## Systems Support and Security

**Systems support and security** provides vital protection and maintenance services for system hardware and software, including enterprise computing systems, networks, transaction processing systems, and corporate IT infrastructure. The systems support and security group implements and monitors physical and electronic security hardware, software, and procedures. This group also installs and supports operating systems, telecommunications software, and centralized database management systems. In addition, systems support and security technicians provide technical assistance to other groups in the IT department. If a site has a large number of remote clients, the systems support group often includes a **deployment team** that installs and configures the workstations.

## User Support

**User support** provides users with technical information, training, and productivity support. The user support function usually is called a **help desk** or **information center** (IC). A help desk's staff trains users and managers on application software such as e-mail, word processing spreadsheets, and graphics packages. User support specialists answer questions, troubleshoot problems, and serve as a clearinghouse for user problems and solutions.

## Database Administration

**Database administration** involves data design, management, security, backup, and access. In small- and medium-sized companies, an IT support person performs those roles in addition to other duties. Regardless of company size, mission-critical database applications require continuous attention and technical support.

## Network Administration

Business operations depend on networks that enable company-wide information systems. **Network administration** includes hardware and software maintenance, support, and security. In addition to controlling user access, network administrators install, configure, manage, monitor, and maintain network applications. Network administration is discussed in more detail in Chapter 10.

## Web Support

**Web support** is a vital technical support function. Web support specialists design and construct Web pages, monitor traffic, manage hardware and software, and link Web-based applications to the company's information systems. Reliable, high-quality Web support is especially critical for companies engaged in e-commerce.

## Quality Assurance (QA)

Many large IT departments also use a **quality assurance (QA)** team that reviews and tests all applications and systems changes to verify specifications and software quality standards. The QA team usually is a separate unit that reports directly to IT management.

## CASE IN POINT 1.3: WHAT SHOULD LISA DO?

Lisa Jameson has two job offers. One is from Pembroke Boats, a boat manufacturer that employs 200 people in a small Ohio town. Pembroke does not have an IT department and wants her to create one. The job position is called information coordinator, but she would be the only IT person.

The other offer, which pays about $7,500 more annually, is from Albemarle Express, a nationwide trucking firm located in Detroit. At Albemarle Express, Lisa would be a programmer-analyst, with the promise that if she does well in her position, she eventually will move into a systems analyst position and work on new systems development. Lisa has heard a rumor that another company might acquire Albemarle Express, but that rumor has occurred before and nothing has ever happened. What should Lisa do, and why?

## THE SYSTEMS ANALYST

A systems analyst investigates, analyzes, designs, develops, installs, evaluates, and maintains a company's information systems. To perform those tasks, a systems analyst constantly interacts with users and managers within and outside the company. On large projects, the analyst works as a member of an IT department team; on smaller assignments, he or she might work alone.

Most companies assign systems analysts to the IT department, but analysts also can report to a specific user area such as marketing, sales, or accounting. As a member of a functional team, an analyst is better able to understand the needs of that group and how information systems support the department's mission. Smaller companies often use consultants to perform systems analysis work on an as-needed basis.

### Responsibilities

The communications tools in Appendix A can help you develop better reports and presentations. To learn more about these tools, turn to Appendix A.

The systems analyst's job overlaps business and technical issues. Analysts help translate business requirements into IT projects. When assigned to a systems development team, an analyst might help document business profiles, review business processes, select hardware and software packages, design information systems, train users, and plan e-commerce Web sites.

A systems analyst plans projects, develops schedules, and estimates costs. To keep managers and users informed, the analyst conducts meetings, delivers presentations, and writes memos, reports, and documentation. The Systems Analyst's Appendix that follows Chapter 12 includes various tools to help you with each of those important skills.

### Knowledge, Skills, and Education

A successful systems analyst needs technical knowledge, oral and written communication skills, an understanding of business operations, and critical thinking skills. Educational requirements vary widely depending on the company and the position. In a rapidly changing IT marketplace, a systems analyst must manage his or her own career and have a plan for professional development.

**TECHNICAL KNOWLEDGE** State-of-the-art knowledge is extremely important in a rapidly changing business and technical environment. The Internet offers numerous opportunities to update technical knowledge and skills. Many sites, such as the one shown in Figure 1-34 offer a convenient way for IT professionals to learn about technical developments, exchange experiences, and get answers to questions. Analysts also maintain their skills by attending training courses, both on-site and online. Networking with colleagues is another way to keep up with new developments, and membership in professional associations also is important.

**COMMUNICATION SKILLS** A systems analyst needs strong oral and written communication skills, and the ability to interact with people at all levels, from operational staff to senior executives. Often, the analyst must work with people outside the company, such as software and hardware vendors, customers, and government officials. Analysts often coordinate IT project teams, where they use communication skills to guide and motivate team members.

**BUSINESS SKILLS** A systems analyst works closely with managers, supervisors, and operational employees. To be effective, he or she must understand business operations and processes, communicate clearly, and translate business needs into requirements that can be understood by programmers and systems developers. A successful analyst is business-oriented, curious, comfortable with financial tools, and able to see the big picture. Chapter 2, Business Justification describes some basic concepts, including strategic planning, SWOT analysis, and feasibility tests. In addition, the Systems Analyst's Appendix, which follows Chapter 12, explains communication and financial tools that can help analysts handle business-related tasks.

**CRITICAL THINKING SKILLS** Although no standard definition exists, most educators agree that **critical thinking skills** include the ability to compare, classify, evaluate, recognize patterns, analyze cause-and-effect, and apply logic. Critical thinkers often use a *what-if* approach, and they have the ability to evaluate their own thinking and reasoning.

Critical thinking skills are valuable in the IT industry, where employers seek job candidates who can demonstrate these skills and bring them to the workplace. Figure 1-35 shows the Foundation for Critical Thinking site, which offers many resources to support the critical thinking community.

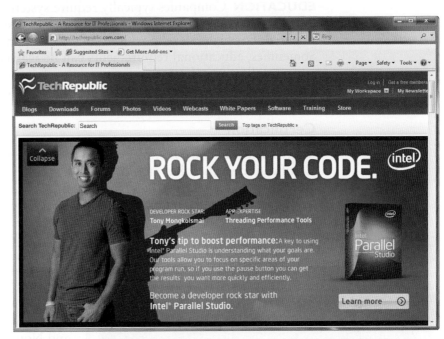

**FIGURE 1-34** The TechRepublic Web site offers support for IT professionals. Features include newsletters, forums, product information, and a searchable knowledge base.

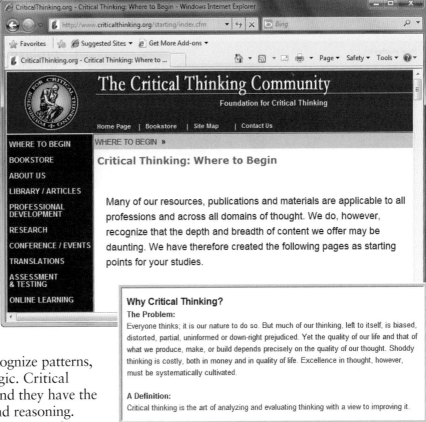

**FIGURE 1-35** The Critical Thinking Community is a nonprofit organization that provides encouragement and resources for critical thinkers.

**EDUCATION** Companies typically require systems analysts to have a college degree in information systems, computer science, or business, and some IT experience usually is required. For higher-level positions, many companies require an advanced degree. Sometimes, educational requirements can be waived if a candidate has significant experience, skills, or professional certifications. Appendix D describes many valuable IT resources for personal and professional development.

## Certification

Many hardware and software companies offer certification for IT professionals. **Certification** verifies that an individual demonstrated a certain level of knowledge and skill on a standardized test. Certification is an excellent way for IT professionals to learn new skills and gain recognition for their efforts. Although certification does not guarantee competence or ability, many companies regard certification as an important credential for hiring or promotion. You can learn more about certification in Chapter 12, Securing and Supporting the System, and by visiting the Web sites of individual companies such as Microsoft, Cisco Systems, Sun Microsystems, and Novell.

In addition to traditional hardware and software certifications, some firms are exploring ways to assess critical thinking skills, as shown in Figure 1-3. These skills include perception, organization, analysis, problem-solving, and decision-making. Whether or not formal certification is involved, these skills are extremely valuable to IT professionals and the employers who hire them.

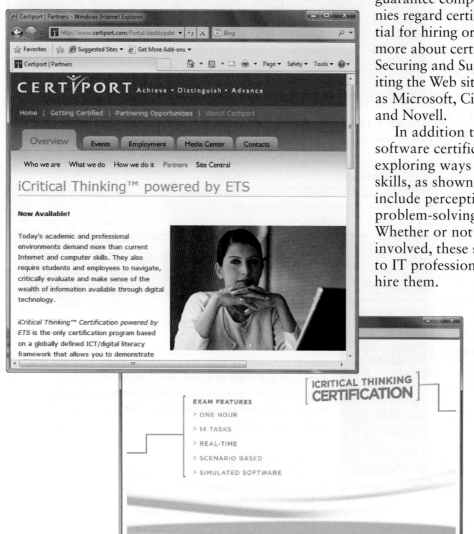

**FIGURE 1-36** Employers want to hire people who think logically and effectively. Some firms are working on certification exams designed to measure these skills.

## Career Opportunities

The demand for systems analysts is expected to remain strong. Companies will need systems analysts to apply new information technology, and the explosion in e-commerce will fuel IT job growth. The systems analyst position is a challenging and rewarding one that can lead to a top management position. With an understanding of technical and business issues, a systems analyst has an unlimited horizon. Many companies have presidents and senior managers who started in IT departments as systems analysts.

The responsibilities of a systems analyst at a small firm are different from those at a large corporation. Would you be better off at a small or large company? Where will you find the best opportunity for experience and professional growth? Each person looks for different rewards in a job. What will be important to you?

**JOB TITLES** First, do not rely on job titles alone. Some positions are called systems analysts, but involve only programming or technical support. In other cases, systems analyst responsibilities are found in positions titled computer specialist, programmer, programmer/analyst, systems designer, software engineer, and various others. Be sure the responsibilities of the job are stated clearly when you consider a position.

**COMPANY ORGANIZATION** Find out all you can about the company and where the IT department fits in the organization chart. Where are IT functions performed, and by whom? A firm might have a central IT group, but decentralize the systems development function. This situation sometimes occurs in large conglomerates, where the parent company consolidates information that actually is developed and managed at the subsidiary level. Where would you rather work?

**COMPANY SIZE** If you like more variety, a smaller firm might suit you best. If you want to specialize, however, then consider a larger company with state-of-the-art systems. Although you might have more responsibility in a smaller company, the promotional opportunities and financial rewards often are greater in larger companies. You also might want to consider working as an independent consultant, either on your own or with others. Many consulting firms have been successful in offering their services to smaller business enterprises that do not have the expertise to handle systems development on their own.

> The information technology resource tools in Appendix D can help you obtain technical data, advance your career, and network with other IT professionals. To learn more about these tools, turn to Appendix D.

**CORPORATE CULTURE** In addition to having goals, methods, and information systems requirements, every firm has an underlying **corporate culture**. A corporate culture is the set of beliefs, rules, traditions, values, and attitudes that define a company and influence its way of doing business. To be successful, a systems analyst must understand the corporate culture and how it affects the way information is managed. Companies sometimes include statements about corporate culture in their mission statements, which are explained in Chapter 2.

**SALARY, LOCATION, AND FUTURE GROWTH** Finally, consider salary, location, and the company's prospects for future growth and success. Think about your impressions of the company and the people you met during your interviews. Most important, review your short- and long-term goals very carefully before deciding which position is best for you.

## CASE IN POINT 1.4: JUST-IN-TIME AIRFREIGHT, INC.

Suppose you are the IT director at Just-in-Time Airfreight, and you have received authorization to hire another systems analyst. This will be an entry-level position, and the person will assist senior systems analysts on various projects involving the reservations and the human resources systems. Using the information in this chapter, draft an ad that would appear in *The Wall Street Journal*, local newspapers, and online. You can get some ideas by visiting monster.com, or a similar site. In your ad, be sure to list desired skills, experience, and educational requirements.

## A QUESTION OF ETHICS

You are enjoying your job as a summer intern in the IT department of a local company. At lunch yesterday, several people were discussing ethical issues. You learned that some of them belong to IT organizations that have ethical codes to guide members and set professional standards. For example, Ann, your supervisor, belongs to the Association for Computing Machinery (ACM), which has over 97,000 members and a Web site at **acm.org.** Ann said that the ACM code of ethics is important to her, and would definitely influence her views. On the other hand, Jack, a senior programmer, believes that his own personal standards would be sufficient to guide him if ethical questions were to arise.

Because you are excited about your career as an IT professional, you decide to examine the ACM code of ethics and make up your own mind. After you do so, would you tend to agree more with Ann or with Jack?

## CHAPTER SUMMARY

In this chapter, you learned that information technology (IT) refers to the combination of hardware, software, and services that people use to manage, communicate, and share information. Technology is changing rapidly, and IT professionals must prepare for the future. IT supports business operations, improves productivity, and helps managers make decisions. Systems analysis and design is the process of developing information systems that transform data into useful information.

Traditionally, companies either developed in-house applications or purchased software packages from vendors. Today, the choice is much more complex, but it is always important for companies to plan the system carefully before considering implementation options.

The essential components of an information system are hardware, software, data, processes, and people. Hardware consists of everything in the physical layer of the information system. Software consists of system software, which manages the hardware components, and application software, which supports day-to-day business operations. Data is the raw material that an information system transforms into useful information. Processes describe the tasks and functions that users, managers, and IT staff members perform. People who interact with a system include users, from both within and outside the company.

A systems analyst starts with a business profile, which is an overview of company functions, and then he or she creates a series of business models that represent business processes, which describe specific transactions, events, tasks, and results. Analysts use business process modeling tools to document complex operations.

Most successful companies offer a mix of products, technical and financial services, consulting, and customer support. A rapidly growing business category is the Internet-dependent (dot-com) firm, which relies solely on Internet-based operations. E-commerce includes business-to-consumer (B2C) sales, and business-to-business (B2B) transactions that use Internet-based digital marketplaces or private electronic data interchange (EDI) systems.

Based on their functions and features, business information systems are identified as enterprise computing systems, transaction processing systems, business support systems, knowledge management systems, or user productivity systems. In most companies, significant overlap and integration exists among the various types of information systems.

A typical organization structure includes top managers, middle managers and knowledge workers, supervisors and team leaders, and operational employees. Top managers develop strategic plans, which define an overall mission and goals. Middle managers provide direction, resources, and feedback to supervisors and team leaders.

Knowledge workers include various professionals who function as support staff. Supervisors and team leaders oversee operational employees. Each organizational level has a different set of responsibilities and information needs.

Systems analysts use modeling, prototyping, and computer-aided systems engineering (CASE) tools. Modeling produces a graphical representation of a concept or process, whereas prototyping involves the creation of an early working model of the information or its components. A systems analyst uses CASE tools to perform various systems development tasks.

Three popular system development approaches are structured analysis, which is a traditional method that still is widely used, object-oriented analysis (O-O), which is a more recent approach that many analysts prefer, and agile methods, also called adaptive methods, which include the latest trends in software development.

Structured analysis uses a series of phases, called the systems development life cycle (SDLC) that usually is shown as a waterfall model. Structured analysis uses an overall plan, similar to a blueprint for constructing a building, so it is called a predictive approach. This method uses a set of process models to describe a system graphically, and also addresses data organization and structure, relational database design, and user interface issues.

Object-oriented analysis combines data and the processes that act on the data into things called objects that represent people, things, transactions, and events. Objects have characteristics called properties, built-in processes called methods, and can send information to other objects by using messages. Using an O-O programming language, a programmer then writes the code that creates the objects. Object-oriented methods usually follow a series of analysis and design phases similar to the SDLC, but the phases are more interactive.

Agile methods are the newest development approach, and attempt to develop a system incrementally by building a series of prototypes and constantly adjusting them to user requirements. Agile methods typically use a spiral model, which represents a series of iterations, or revisions, based on user feedback. The repeated iterations produce a series of prototypes, which evolve into the finished system.

Regardless of the development strategy, people, tasks, timetables, and costs must be managed effectively using project management tools and techniques, which are described in detail in Chapter 3.

Some firms choose to develop their own in-house methods or adopt techniques offered by software suppliers, CASE tool vendors, or consultants. Companies also use team-based strategies called joint application development (JAD) and rapid application development (RAD). JAD focuses on team-based fact-finding, whereas RAD is more like a compressed version of the entire process. JAD and RAD are described in more detail in Chapter 4.

The IT department develops, maintains, and operates a company's information systems. IT staff members provide technical support, including application development, systems support, user support, database administration, network administration, and Web support. These functions overlap considerably and often have different names in different companies.

In addition to technical knowledge, a systems analyst must understand the business, think critically, and communicate effectively. Valuable credentials such as certifications are available to systems analysts. A systems analyst's responsibilities depend on a company's organization, size, and culture. Systems analysts need to consider salary, location, and future growth potential when making a career decision.

# Key Terms and Phrases

adaptive methods *21*

agile methods *21*

application development *28*

application software *8*

B2B (business-to-business) *13*

B2C (business-to-consumer) *13*

brick-and-mortar *12*

business model *19*

business process *10*

business process model (BPM) *10*

business process modeling *10*

business process modeling notation (BPMN) *10*

business process reengineering (BPR) *18*

business profile *10*

business rules *22*

business support systems *16*

CASE tools *20*

certification *32*

class *24*

computer-aided software engineering (CASE) *20*

computer-aided systems engineering (CASE) *20*

corporate culture *33*

critical thinking skills *31*

data *7*

data flow diagram (DFD) *22*

data model *19*

database administration *29*

deliverable *22*

deployment team *29*

dot-com (.com) *12*

e-commerce (electronic commerce) *13*

electronic data interchange (EDI) *14*

empowerment *19*

end product *22*

end users *10*

enterprise applications *8*

enterprise computing *15*

enterprise resource planning (ERP) *15*

expert systems *16*

extensible markup language (XML) *14*

feasibility study *23*

fuzzy logic *17*

groupware *17*

hardware *8*

help desk *29*

horizontal system *8*

I-commerce (Internet commerce) *13*

inference rules *17*

information *7*

information center (IC) *29*

information system *7*

information technology (IT) *4*

in-house applications *7*

interactive model *25*

Internet-dependent *12*

iterative *25*

joint application development (JAD) *26*

knowledge base *17*

knowledge management systems *16*

knowledge workers *19*

legacy systems *9*

management information systems (MIS) *16*

message *25*

methods *25*

Microsoft Solutions Framework (MSF) *27*

mission-critical system *7*

modeling *19*

Moore's Law *8*

network administration *29*

network model *19*

object-oriented (O-O) analysis *21*

object model *19*

objects *24*

predictive *22*

preliminary investigation *23*

process model *19*

process-centered *22*

processes *9*

product-oriented *11*

project management *22*

properties *24*

prototype *20*

quality assurance (QA) *29*

radio frequency identification (RFID) *16*

rapid application development (RAD) *26*

Rational Unified Process (RUP®) *27*

requirements model *19*

requirements modeling *23*

scalable *24*

service-oriented *11*

software *8*

software packages *7*

spiral model *26*

stakeholders *10*

strategic plans *18*

structured analysis *21*

supplier relationship management (SRM) *14*

supply chain management (SCM) *14*

system *7*

system design specification *24*

system requirements document *24*

system software *8*

systems analysis and design *7*

systems analysis phase *23*

systems analysts *7*

systems design phase *24*

systems development life cycle (SDLC) *22*

systems evaluation *24*

systems implementation phase *24*

systems planning phase *23*

systems request *23*

systems support and security *29*

systems support and security phase *24*

technical support *28*

transaction processing (TP) systems *15*

user productivity systems *17*

user support *29*

users *10*

vertical system *8*

waterfall model *22*

Web support *29*

what-if *16*

# Learn It Online

**Instructions:**   To complete the Learn It Online exercises, visit the Management Information Systems CourseMate Web site at **www.cengagebrain.com**, navigate to the resources for this chapter, and click the link for the exercise you want to complete.

## 1 Chapter Reinforcement

### TF, MC, and SA

Click the Chapter Reinforcement link. Print the quiz by clicking Print on the File menu for each page. Answer each question.

## 2 Flash Cards

Click the Flash Cards link and read the instructions. Type 20 (or a number specified by your instructor) in the Number of playing cards text box, type your name in the Enter your Name text box, and then click the Flip Card button. When the flash card is displayed, read the question and then click the ANSWER box arrow to select an answer. Flip through the Flash Cards. If your score is 15 (75%) correct or greater, click Print on the File menu to print your results. If your score is less than 15 (75%) correct, then redo this exercise by clicking the Replay button.

## 3 Practice Test

Click the Practice Test link. Answer each question, enter your first and last name at the bottom of the page, and then click the Grade Test button. When the graded practice test is displayed on your screen, click Print on the File menu to print a hard copy. Continue to take practice tests until you score 80% or better.

## 4 Who Wants To Be a Computer Genius?

Click the Computer Genius link. Read the instructions, enter your first and last name at the bottom of the page, and then click the Play button. When your score is displayed, click the PRINT RESULTS link to print a hard copy.

## 5 Wheel of Terms

Click the Wheel of Terms link. Read the instructions, and then enter your first and last name and your school name. Click the PLAY button. When your score is displayed on the screen, right-click the score and then click Print on the shortcut menu to print a hard copy.

## 6 Crossword Puzzle Challenge

Click the Crossword Puzzle Challenge link. Read the instructions, and then enter your first and last name. Click the SUBMIT button. Work the crossword puzzle. When you are finished, click the Submit button. When the crossword puzzle is redisplayed, click the Print Puzzle button to print a hard copy.

## SCR Associates Case Simulation  Session 1: Introduction

### Overview

The SCR Associates case study is a Web-based simulation that allows you to practice your skills in a real-world environment. The case study transports you to SCR's intranet, where you complete 12 work sessions, each aligning with a chapter. As you work on the case, you will receive e-mail and voice mail messages, obtain information from SCR's online libraries, and perform various tasks.

### Background

SCR Associates is an IT consulting firm that offers solutions and training. SCR has decided to expand by opening a high-tech training center.  The company needs to develop an information system to support operations at the new training center. The new system will be called TIMS (Training Information Management System).

As a newly hired systems analyst, you report to Jesse Baker, systems group manager. She will expect you to apply the knowledge and skills you learn in each chapter. Your work should be accurate, thorough, and have a professional appearance.

### What's in the textbook?

- A preview of each work session, to set the stage for your tasks.
- A list of the session tasks for easy reference.

### What's on the Web?

- A realistic simulation that includes the SCR Web site and a link to the company intranet. The Web site contains public information about the company, including its organization, mission, values, goals, and services.
- An intranet portal that asks you to enter your name and a password.
- Links for e-mail and voice mail that explain your tasks and add realism.
- A task list, with four specific tasks per session.
- Background information you will need, including a data library, a forms library, and resources list.

### How do I use the case?

- Review the background material.
- Read the preview for this session and study the Task List. You might need to review the chapter material in order to perform the tasks.
- Visit the Management Information Systems CourseMate Web site at **www.cengagebrain. com**, navigate to the **SCR Case Simulation**, and locate the intranet link.
- Enter your name and the password **sad9e.** An opening screen will display the work sessions.
- Select a work session.
- Check your e-mail and voice mail messages carefully, and then begin working on the task list.

## Preview: Session I

This is your second day on the job as a systems analyst at SCR Associates. You spent most of yesterday filling out personnel forms and learning your way around the office. This morning, you sit at your desk and examine SCR's Internet site. You explore the entire site, which reflects SCR's history, purpose, and values. You especially are impressed with the emphasis SCR puts on its relationships with clients. When you finish examining the site, you are more convinced than ever that SCR will be a great career opportunity. You are excited about your new job, and eager to get started.

## Task List

| | |
|---|---|
| 1. | Investigate SCR's Internet site and learn about the company's history, purpose, and values. Send Jesse a brief memo with suggestions to expand or improve these sections. |
| 2. | On the SCR intranet, visit the data, forms, and resource libraries and review a sample of the information in each library. |
| 3. | Using the SCR functions and organization listed in the data library, create an organization chart using Microsoft Word, Visio, or a drawing program. |
| 4. | Jesse says that SCR has plenty of competition in the IT consulting field. Get on the Internet and find three other IT consulting firms. She wants a brief description of each firm and the services it offers. |

**FIGURE 1-37**   Task list: Session 1.

# Chapter Exercises

## Review Questions

1. What is information technology, and why is it important to a business?
2. Define business profiles, processes, and modeling.
3. Identify the main components of an information system, and describe the system's stakeholders.
4. Explain the difference between vertical and horizontal systems packages.
5. How do companies use EDI? What are some advantages of using XML?
6. Describe five types of information systems, and give an example of each.
7. Describe four organizational levels of a typical business and their information requirements.
8. Describe the phases of the systems development life cycle, and compare the SDLC waterfall model with the spiral model.
9. Explain the use of models, prototypes, and CASE tools in the systems development process. Also explain the pros and cons of agile development methods.
10. What is object-oriented analysis, and how does it differ from structured analysis?

## Discussion Topics

1. Some experts believe that the growth in e-commerce will cause states and local governments to lose a significant amount of sales tax revenue, unless Internet transactions are subject to sales tax. Do you agree? Why or why not?
2. Present an argument for and against the following proposition: Because IT managers must understand all phases of the business, a company should fill top management vacancies by promoting IT managers.
3. The head of the IT group in a company often is called the chief information officer (CIO) or chief technology officer (CTO). Should the CIO or CTO report to the company president, to the finance department, where many of the information systems are used, or to someone or somewhere else? Why would it matter?
4. Computers perform many jobs that previously were performed by people. Will computer-based transactions and expanded e-commerce eventually replace person-to-person contact? From a customer's point of view, is this better? Why or why not?

# Apply Your Knowledge

The Apply Your Knowledge section contains four mini-cases. Each case describes a situation, explains your role in the case, and asks you to respond to questions. You can answer the questions by applying knowledge you learned in the chapter.

## 1 Low-Voltage Components

**Situation:**

You are the IT manager at Low-Voltage Components, a medium-sized firm that makes specialized circuit boards. Low-Voltage's largest customer, TX Industries, recently installed a computerized purchasing system. If Low-Voltage connects to the TX system, TX will be able to submit purchase orders electronically. Although Low-Voltage has a computerized accounting system, that system is not capable of handling EDI.

1. Should Low-Voltage develop a system to connect with TX Industries' purchasing system? Why or why not?
2. What terms or concepts describe the proposed computer-to-computer relationship between Low-Voltage and TX Industries?
3. Is Low-Voltage's proposed new system a transaction processing system? Why or why not?
4. Before Low-Voltage makes a final decision, should the company consider an ERP system? Why or why not?

## 2 Systems Analyst Salaries

**Situation:**

As part of your job search, you decide to find out more about salaries and qualifications for systems analysts in the area where you would like to work. To increase your knowledge, search the Internet to perform the following research:

1. Find information about a career as a systems analyst.
2. Using the Internet, determine whether the Federal Bureau of Labor Statistics lists salary information for systems analysts. If so, summarize the information you find.
3. Find at least two online ads for systems analysts and list the employers, the qualifications, and the salaries, if mentioned.
4. Find at least one ad for an IT position that specifically mentions e-commerce.

## 3  MultiTech Interview

**Situation:**

You have an interview for an IT position with MultiTech, a large telecommunications company, and you want to learn more about the firm and its organizational structure. To prepare for the interview, you decide to review your knowledge about corporations, including the following questions:

1. What are the four organizational levels in a typical company?
2. How can you classify companies based on their mix of products and services?
3. What is empowerment?
4. What types of information systems might a large company use?

## 4  Rainbow's End Interview

**Situation:**

Your MultiTech interview seemed to go well, but you did not get the job. During the meeting, the interviewer mentioned that MultiTech uses structured analysis and relies heavily on modeling, prototyping, and CASE tools. Thinking back, you realize that you did not fully understand those terms. As you prepare for an interview with Rainbow's End, a large retail chain, you decide to review some IT terms and concepts. You want to be ready for the following questions:

1. What are the main differences between structured, O-O, and agile development methods?
2. What is a CASE tool and what does it do?
3. What is business process modeling and how is it done?
4. What is prototyping and why is it important?

# Case Studies

Case studies allow you to practice specific skills learned in the chapter. Each chapter contains several case studies that continue throughout the textbook, and a chapter capstone case.

### New Century Health Clinic

New Century Health Clinic offers preventive medicine and traditional medical care. In your role as an IT consultant, you will help New Century develop a new information system.

#### Background

Five years ago, cardiologists Timothy Jones and Dolores Garcia decided to combine their individual practices in Brea, California, to form New Century Health Clinic. They wanted to concentrate on preventive medicine by helping patients maintain health and fitness and by providing traditional medical care. Dr. Jones recently asked you to work with him as an IT consultant. He wants you to help New Century develop an information system that will support the clinic's operations and future growth. At your initial meeting, he provided you with some background information and asked for your suggestions about how to begin.

At your desk, you begin to review New Century's situation. The clinic is located near a new shopping mall in a busy section of the city. New Century's staff includes four doctors, three registered nurses, four physical therapists, and six office staff workers. The clinic currently has a patient base of 3,500 patients from 275 different employers, many of which provide insurance coverage for employee wellness and health maintenance. Currently, New Century accepts 34 different insurance policies.

Anita Davenport, who has been with New Century since its inception, is the office manager. She supervises the staff, including Fred Brown, Susan Gifford, Tom Capaletti, Lisa Sung, and Carla Herrera. Fred Brown handles office payroll, tax reporting, and profit distribution among the associates. Susan Gifford is responsible for the maintenance of patient records. Tom Capaletti handles most of the paperwork concerning insurance reporting and accounting. Lisa Sung has the primary responsibility for the appointment book, and her duties include making reminder calls to patients and preparing daily appointment lists. Carla Herrera is concerned primarily with ordering and organizing office and clinic supplies.

Each of the six office staff people has one or more primary responsibilities; however, all members of the staff help out whenever necessary with patient records, insurance processing, and appointment processing. In addition to their regular responsibilities, all six office workers are involved in the preparation of patient statements at the end of each month.

Using this information, you begin to prepare for your next meeting with Dr. Jones.

#### Assignments

1. Create an organization chart of the office staff using Microsoft Word or a similar program, or you can draw it by hand. In Word 2010 and Word 2007, click the Insert tab on the Ribbon, then Smart Art, then Hierarchy.

2. Identify at least three business processes that New Century performs, and explain who is responsible for the specific tasks.

3. Explain how New Century might use a transaction processing system, a business support system, and a user productivity system. For each type of system, provide a specific example, and explain how the system would benefit the clinic.

4. During the systems development process, should New Century consider any of the following: B2B, vertical and horizontal system packages, or Internet-based solutions? Explain your answers.

## PERSONAL TRAINER, INC.

Personal Trainer, Inc. owns and operates fitness centers in a dozen midwestern cities. The centers have done well, and the company is planning an international expansion by opening a new "supercenter" in the Toronto area.

### Background

Cassia Umi, president, heads Personal Trainer's management team. Three managers report to her at the firm's Chicago headquarters: Janet McDonald, manager, finance; Tai Tranh, manager, sales and marketing; and Reed Cotter, manager, operations. The managers who run the 12 existing centers all report to Reed.

Cassia wants the new supercenter to emphasize a wide variety of personal services and special programs for members. If the supercenter approach is successful, it will become the model for Personal Trainer's future growth. Cassia personally selected Gray Lewis, a manager with three years of fitness center experience, to run the new facility.

The new supercenter will feature a large exercise area with state-of-the-art equipment, a swimming pool, a sporting goods shop, a health food store, and a snack bar. In addition, the center will offer child care with special programs for various ages, a teen center, and a computer café. Cassia also wants members to have online access to customized training programs and progress reports.

Personal Trainer currently uses BumbleBee, a popular accounting package, to manage its receivables, payables, and general ledger. Membership lists and word processing are handled with Microsoft Office products.

Cassia believes the new supercenter will require additional data management capability, and she decided to hire Patterson and Wilder, an IT consulting firm, to help Personal Trainer develop an information system for the new operation. The firm assigned Susan Park, an experienced consultant, to work with the Personal Trainer team.

Susan's first task was to learn more about business operations at the new center, so she requested a meeting with Gray. After some small talk, the discussion went like this:

**Susan:**   Tell me about your plans for the new operation. I'm especially interested in what kind of information management you'll need.

**Gray:**   *Cassia thinks that we'll need more information support because of the size and complexity of the new operation. To tell the truth, I'm not so sure. We've had no problem with BumbleBee at the other centers, and I don't really want to reinvent the wheel.*

**Susan:**   Maybe we should start by looking at the similarities — and the differences — between the new center and the existing ones.

**Gray:**   *Okay, let's do that. First of all, we offer the same basic services everywhere. That includes the exercise equipment, a pool, and, in most centers, a snack bar. Some centers also sell sporting goods, and one offers child care — but not child-fitness programs. It is true that we've never put all this together under one roof. And, I admit, we've never offered online access. To be honest, I'm not absolutely sure what Cassia has in mind when she talks about 24/7 Web-based access. One more feature — we plan to set up two levels of membership — let's call them silver and gold for now. Silver members can use all the basic services, but will pay additional fees for some special programs, such as child fitness. Gold members will have unlimited use of all services.*

**Susan:**   So, with all this going on, wouldn't an overall system make your job easier?

**Gray:**   *Yes, but I don't know where to start.*

*(continued)*

| | |
|---|---|
| **Susan:** | Gray, that's why I'm here. I'll work with you and the rest of the team to come up with a solution that supports your business. |
| **Gray:** | *Sounds good to me. When can we start?* |
| **Susan:** | Let's get together first thing tomorrow. Bring along an organization chart and think about how you plan to run the new facility. We'll try to build a model of the new operation so we can identify the business functions. When we know what the functions are, we can figure out what kind of information is needed or generated by each function. That will be our starting point. |

### Assignments

1. Develop a business profile for Personal Trainer, based on the facts provided. List at least three of Personal Trainer's business processes.

2. Create an organization chart for Personal Trainer using Microsoft Word or a similar program, or you can draw it by hand. In Word 2010 and Word 2007, click the Insert tab on the Ribbon, then Smart Art, then Hierarchy.

3. Review the conversation between Susan and Gray. In your opinion, is Gray totally supportive of the new system? Why or why not? Do you agree with the way that Susan responds to Gray's comments? Why or why not?

4. Should Personal Trainer consider any of the following systems: enterprise computing, transaction processing, business support, knowledge management, or user productivity? Why or why not? What opportunities might Personal Trainer have for Web-based B2C transactions in the future? What about B2B?

### Original Kayak Adventures

Original Kayak Adventures (OKA) offers guided eco-tours and kayak rentals along the Hudson River.

### Background

John and Edie Caputo, who are avid kayakers and amateur naturalists, founded OKA two years ago. The Caputos spent many weekends and vacations exploring the Hudson's numerous creeks and tributaries. John was a sales representative and Edie worked for a Web design firm. Two years ago, John's division was purchased by a rival company, which announced plans to move operations to another state. Rather than relocate, the Caputos decided to launch OKA. They reasoned that Edie could leave her job and work as a freelance Web designer, which would provide some income while John tried to build OKA into a profitable business. John and Edie are convinced that the ecotourism market will expand greatly, and they look forward to sharing their experience and knowledge with others who enjoy nature and kayaking.

Original Kayak Adventures advertises in regional magazines and maintains a Web site, which Edie designed. Customers say that the site is attractive and informative, but the Caputos are not sure of its effectiveness in attracting new business. At this time, no other kayak rental firms operate within 20 miles of OKA's location.

So far, the Caputos' plan is working out well. OKA rents space at a nearby marina, where Edie runs the office and operates her Web design business. She also handles rentals when John is giving lessons or busy with a tour group. On summer weekends and holidays, Janet Jacobs, a local college student, handles telephone inquiries and reservations.

OKA's inventory includes 16 rental kayaks of various types, eight car-top carriers, and a large assortment of accessories and safety equipment. Based on customer requests, Edie is considering adding a selection of books and videos about kayaking and ecotourism.

OKA has three main business segments: rentals, instruction, and guided tours. Most customers make advance reservations for scheduled tours and instruction sessions, but sometimes space is available for last-minute customers. Rentals are split evenly between reservations and walk-in customers.

Reservations are entered in a loose-leaf binder, with separate tabs for each business activity. Edie also created a Microsoft Access database to record reservations. When she has time, she enters the reservation date, the reservation details and kayak type, and the customer information into a table, which is sorted by reservation date. Each day, she prints a reservation list. For quick reference, Edie also displays kayak availability on a wall-mounted board with color-coded magnets that show the available or reserved status of each rental kayak. In addition to the database, Edie uses an inexpensive accounting package to keep OKA's books.

Although the OKA database handles the basic information, the Caputos have noticed some drawbacks. For example, reservations for guided tours or instruction sessions sometimes conflict with John's or Edie's availability. The Caputos also would like to get more information about rental patterns, customer profiles, advertising effectiveness, and future business opportunities. John and Edie have talked about updating the system, but they have been too busy to do so.

## Assignments

1. Develop a business profile for Original Kayak Adventures. The profile should include information about OKA's business activities, organization, resources, customers, and potential opportunity to engage in e-commerce.

2. List OKA's main functions and business processes. Draw a model of an OKA business process, including possible events, processes, and results.

3. What types of information systems does OKA use? Do these systems support its current and future business objectives? Why or why not?

4. From an object-oriented viewpoint, OKA treats reservations as a class. Based on the background information provided, what are some properties of reservation objects?

## CHAPTER CAPSTONE CASE:   SoftWear, Limited

SoftWear, Limited (SWL) is a continuing case study that illustrates the knowledge and skills described in each chapter. In this case study, the student acts as a member of the SWL systems development team and performs various tasks.

### Background

SoftWear, Limited, manufactures and sells casual and recreational clothing for men and women. SWL was formed about 10 years ago when a national firm sold the division during a corporate downsizing. A group of managers obtained financing and became owners of the company. With clever marketing, competitive pricing, and efficient production, SWL has grown to more than 450 employees, including the corporate headquarters and manufacturing plants. Last year, SWL had sales of $700 million.

The company employs 90 people at its Raleigh, North Carolina, headquarters, including officers, managers, and support staff. Another 30 salaried and 340 hourly people are employed at production facilities in Haskell, California, and Florence, Texas. The company also is considering new factories in Canada and Australia.

SWL maintains a Web site with information about the company and its products. SWL's Web site features text, graphics, and audio and allows customers to send e-mail, order products from the SoftWear catalog, and request special promotional items, including beach umbrellas, hats, and T-shirts customized with the purchaser's logo. SWL also is studying other ways to use the Internet to boost product sales and expand its marketing efforts, including a special European promotion designed to increase awareness of SWL's Web site.

### Organization

SWL's headquarters includes the executive, operations, marketing, finance, and human resources departments. Figure 1-38 shows the organization chart of the management positions within SWL. Notice that the director of information technology, Ann Hon, reports to Michael Jeremy, vice president of finance. The director of the payroll department, Amy Calico, also reports to Mr. Jeremy.

**FIGURE 1-38** Organization chart of SoftWear, Limited.

## CHAPTER CAPSTONE CASE:   SoftWear, Limited (continued)          SWL

The IT department includes Ann Hon, the director; Jane Rossman, the systems support manager; Zachary Ridgefield, the user support manager; and Ella Trung, the Web support manager. Figure 1-39 shows the organization of the IT department. At SWL, the systems support group also handles new systems development, network administration, and database administration.

**FIGURE 1-39**  Organization chart of the IT department of SoftWear, Limited.

Systems analysts and programmers report to Jane Rossman, systems support manager. Systems analysts primarily analyze and design information systems. Programmers primarily develop, test, and implement code necessary for systems development, enhancements, and maintenance. In addition to the current staff, SWL is planning to hire a programmer-analyst who will divide his or her time between systems analysis and programming duties.

The technical support staff members are responsible for the system software on all SWL computers. They also provide technical advice and guidance to the other groups within the IT department.

The operations staff is responsible for centralized IT functions, including SWL's mainframe computer, and provides network and database administration.

### Current Systems

SWL uses a manufacturing and inventory control system at its factories, but the system does not exchange data with SWL's suppliers at this time. The company's sales processing system handles online and catalog transactions, and produces sales reports. The marketing staff, however, wants even more information about sales trends and marketing analysis data. A company intranet connects employees at all locations, and provides e-mail, shared calendars, and a document library. Most administrative employees have workstations with Microsoft Office applications, but SWL has not provided company-wide training or help desk support.

## CHAPTER CAPSTONE CASE: SoftWear, Limited (continued)

### SWL Team Tasks

1. Write an employment advertisement for a new systems analyst position at SWL. Perform Internet research to locate examples of advertisements for systems analysts, and consider SWL's business profile when you write the advertisement.
2. Should SWL consider any of the following systems: ERP, business support, or knowledge management? Why or why not?
3. What opportunities might SWL have for Web-based B2B transactions in the future?
4. Should SWL consider ways to increase a sense of empowerment among its employees? Why or why not? Could user productivity software play a role in that effort? How?

### Manage the SWL Project

You have been asked to manage SWL's new information system project. One of your most important activities will be to identify project tasks and determine when they will be performed. Before you begin, you should review the SWL case in this chapter. Then list and analyze the tasks, as follows:

**LIST THE TASKS** Start by listing and numbering at least 10 tasks that the SWL team needs to perform to fulfill the objectives of this chapter. Your list can include SWL Team Tasks and any other tasks that are described in this chapter. For example, Task 3 might be to Draw an SWL organization chart, and Task 6 might be to Identify the various levels of SWL management.

**ANALYZE THE TASKS** Now study the tasks to determine the order in which they should be performed. First identify all concurrent tasks, which are not dependent on other tasks. In the example shown in Figure 1-40, Tasks 1, 2, 3, 4, and 5 are concurrent tasks, and could begin at the same time if resources were available.

Other tasks are called dependent tasks, because they cannot be performed until one or more earlier tasks have been completed. For each dependent task, you must identify specific tasks that need to be completed before this task can begin. For example, you would want an organization chart to help you identify the management levels, so Task 6 cannot begin until Task 3 is completed, as Figure 1-40 shows.

**FIGURE 1-40** Tasks 1, 2, 3, 4, and 5 are concurrent tasks that could be performed at the same time. Task 6 is a dependent task that cannot be performed until Task 3 has been completed.

Chapter 3 describes project management tools, techniques, and software. To learn more, you can use the Features section on your Student Study Tool CD-ROM, or visit the Management Information Systems CourseMate Web site at **www.cengagebrain.com** and locate the project management resources library for this book. On the Web, Microsoft offers demo versions, training, and tips for using Project 2010. You also can visit the OpenWorkbench.org site to learn more about this free, open-source software.

# Ready for a Challenge?

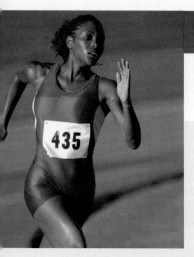

In additional to technical skills, IT professionals need critical thinking skills such as perception, organization, analysis, problem-solving, and decision-making. The Ready for a Challenge feature can help you learn, practice, and apply critical thinking skills that you can take to the workplace.

You are a summer intern in the IT department at Game Technology. You report to the IT director, Mike McGee. Mike assigned you to work with two systems analysts: Lauren Jacksina and Cathy Ross. Lauren and Cathy both report to Felesia Stukes, manager — IT development, who reports to Mike. Joe Turner, manager — IT operations also reports to Mike. Dawn Rountree, database administrator, and Greg Wade, network administrator, report to Joe.

As an intern, you are expected to keep a journal to record your day-to-day experiences and things you learn. This week, you need to list some characteristics of various systems development methods used by the IT team. Your journal should include the following topics:
- Which development method relies heavily on written documentation?
- Which development method depicts system actors using diagrams?
- Which development method uses a spiral model?

## Practice Tasks

A. Draw an organization chart showing all IT department positions, You can use Microsoft Word or a similar program, or you can draw it by hand. In Word 2010 and Word 2007, click the Insert tab on the Ribbon, then click Smart Art, then Hierarchy.
B. Write a journal entry that answers the questions about development methods.

   After you complete the Practice Tasks, to check your work and view sample answers, visit the Management Information Systems CourseMate Web site at **www.cengagebrain. com**, navigate to the resources for this chapter, and locate Ready for a Challenge?.

## The Challenge

Three weeks ago, Mike McGee left to join a larger company, and management decided to reorganize the IT department. Felesia Stukes was promoted to IT director, and to save money, her old job was eliminated.  You, Lauren, Cathy, and Joe will report to her. The rest of the team is unchanged, except that a new programmer, Annie Edenton, has been hired, reporting to Dawn Rountree. Dawn's title has been changed to data design specialist.

To update your journal, you need to add three more pieces of information:
- Which development method uses a five-phase model?
- Which development method stresses intense team-based efforts?
- Which development method uses a waterfall model?

## Challenge Tasks

A. Draw a new organization chart showing the changes, with full names and titles.
B. Write a journal entry that answers the new questions about development methods.

# CHAPTER 2 Business Justification

**Chapter 2** explains how to analyze a business case. This chapter also explains why it is important to understand business operations and requirements, how IT projects support a company's overall strategic plan, how systems projects get started, and how systems analysts conduct a preliminary investigation and feasibility study.

## INTRODUCTION

### OBJECTIVES

*When you finish this chapter, you will be able to:*

- Explain the concept of a business case and how a business case affects an IT project
- Describe the strategic planning process and why it is important to the IT team
- Conduct a SWOT analysis and describe the four factors involved
- Explain the purpose of a mission statement
- Explain how the SDLC serves as a framework for systems development
- List reasons for systems projects and factors that affect such projects
- Describe systems requests and the role of the systems review committee
- Define operational, technical, economic, and schedule feasibility
- Describe the steps and the end product of a preliminary investigation

During the systems planning phase, the IT team reviews a proposal to determine if it presents a strong business case. The term **business case** refers to the reasons, or justification, for a proposal. A strong business case suggests that the company should pursue the alternative, above other options, because it would be in the firm's best interest to do so. To analyze the business case for a specific proposal, the analyst must consider the company's overall mission, objectives, and IT needs.

This chapter begins with a discussion of strategic planning, because the IT team must understand, support, and help plan long-term strategic goals. Along with financial, marketing, and human resources, companies need information technology to achieve growth and success.

Systems development typically starts with a systems request, followed by a preliminary investigation, which includes a feasibility study. You will learn how systems requests originate, how they are evaluated, and how to conduct a preliminary investigation. You also will learn about fact-finding techniques that begin at this point and carry over into later development phases. Finally, you will examine the report to management, which concludes the systems planning phase.

## CHAPTER INTRODUCTION CASE: Mountain View College Bookstore

**Background:** Wendy Lee, manager of college services at Mountain View College, wants a new information system that will improve efficiency and service at the three college bookstores.

In this part of the case, Tina Allen (systems analyst) and David Conroe (student intern) are talking about justification for the new system and the project's feasibility.

| | |
|---|---|
| **Participants:** | Tina and David |
| **Location:** | Mountain View College cafeteria, Tuesday afternoon, September 6, 2011. |
| **Project status:** | Tina has received a systems request from Wendy Lee for a new bookstore information system. |
| **Discussion topics:** | Analysis of business justification and project feasibility |

**Tina:** Hi, David. Are you ready to get started?

**David:** *Sure. What's our next step?*

**Tina:** Well, when we analyze a specific systems request, we need to see how the proposal fits into the overall picture at the college. In other words, we have to analyze the business case for the request.

**David:** *What's a business case?*

**Tina:** A business case is the justification for a project. A strong business case means that a proposal will add substantial value to the organization and support our strategic plan.

**David:** *What's a strategic plan?*

**Tina:** A strategic plan is like a road map for the future. Without a long-range plan, it's hard to know if you're heading in the right direction. Our plan starts with a mission statement, which reflects our purpose, our vision, and our values.

**David:** *I see what you mean. I read the mission statement this morning. It says that we will strive to be an efficient, customer-friendly bookstore that uses a mix of interpersonal skills and technology to serve our students and support the overall objectives of the college. That says a lot in just one sentence.*

**Tina:** It sure does. Now, let's get to the specifics. I just received a systems request from the college business manager. She wants us to develop a new information system for the bookstore.

**David:** *Do we have a green light to get started?*

**Tina:** Yes and no. Mountain View College doesn't have a formal procedure for evaluating IT requests, and we don't have a systems review committee. Maybe that's something we should consider for the future. Meanwhile, we need to conduct a preliminary investigation to see whether this request is feasible.

**David:** *What do you mean by "feasible"?*

**Tina:** To see if a systems request is feasible, we have to look at four separate yardsticks: operational feasibility, technical feasibility, economic feasibility, and schedule feasibility. If the request passes all the tests, we continue working on the system. If not, we stop.

**David:** *How will we know if the request passes the tests?*

**Tina:** That's our next step. Here's a task list to get us started:

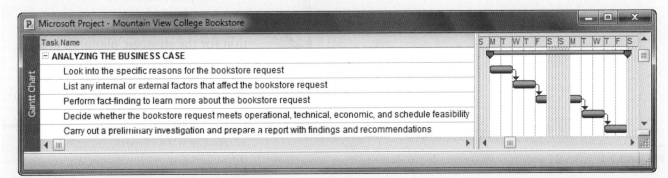

**FIGURE 2-1** Typical business case analysis task list.

# STRATEGIC PLANNING — A FRAMEWORK FOR IT SYSTEMS DEVELOPMENT

Companies develop and maintain IT systems to support their current and future business operations. Some IT needs are immediate, such as fixing a logic problem in a payroll system. Other needs might be on the horizon, such as planning IT support for a new factory, a future merger, or a corporate restructuring. In most companies, the IT team reviews each IT-related proposal, project, and systems request to determine if it presents a strong business case, or justification.

Most successful IT managers engage in long-range planning, even as they handle day-to-day maintenance and support. To carry out this task effectively, they must understand and participate in the firm's strategic planning process. **Strategic planning** is the process of identifying long-term organizational goals, strategies, and resources. Strategic planning looks beyond day-to-day activities and focuses on a horizon that is 3, 5, 10, or more years in the future.

## Strategic Planning Overview

Why does a systems analyst need to know about strategic planning? The answer might be found in an old story about two stonecutters who were hard at work when a passerby asked them what they were doing. "I am cutting stones," said the first worker. The second worker replied, "I am building a cathedral." So it is with information technology: One analyst might say, "I am using a CASE tool," whereas another might say, "I am helping the company succeed in a major new business venture." Systems analysts should focus on the larger, strategic role of IT as they carry out their day-to-day responsibilities.

Strategic planning starts with a management review called a **SWOT analysis**. The letters stand for strengths, weaknesses, opportunities, and threats. A SWOT analysis usually starts with a broad overview. The first step is for top management to respond to questions like these:

- What are our strengths, and how can we use them to achieve our business goals?

- What are our weaknesses, and how can we reduce or eliminate them?

- What are our opportunities, and how do we plan to take advantage of them?

- What are our threats, and how can we assess, manage, and respond to the possible risks?

A SWOT analysis is a solid foundation for the strategic planning process, because it examines a firm's technical, human, and financial resources. In Figure 2-2, the bulleted lists show samples of typical strengths, weaknesses, opportunities, and threats.

As the SWOT process continues, management reviews specific resources and business operations. For example,

**STRENGTHS**
- Excellent Web design staff
- Low systems analyst turnover
- Recently upgraded network

**WEAKNESSES**
- Still using several legacy systems
- Budget increase was turned down
- Documentation needs updating

**OPPORTUNITIES**
- Well-positioned for expansion
- Can be first with new software
- High potential for B2B growth

**THREATS**
- Aggressive new Web competition
- Impact of new FCC rules
- Other firms offer better benefits

**FIGURE 2-2**  A SWOT analysis might produce results similar to those shown here.

suppose that during a SWOT analysis, a firm studies an important patent that the company owns. The patent review might generate input like the examples shown in Figure 2-3.

**SWOT ANALYSIS**

| | |
|---|---|
| **Strength** | Our patent covers valuable technology that we can use in many popular products. |
| **Weakness** | Our patent, like every patent, has a limited life, and when it expires, the technology will no longer be protected. |
| **Opportunity** | We might be able to use the patented technology in more products, license it to other firms, or expand our research to develop new patents based on the original technology. |
| **Threat** | There is a chance that a competitor will develop technology that is similar to ours, but does not technically infringe upon our patent. |

**FIGURE 2-3**  Sample SWOT analysis of a specific asset, such as a patent.

There is no standard approach to strategic planning. Some managers believe that a firm's **mission statement** should contain an inspirational message to its stakeholders. Others feel that unless a firm starts with a realistic SWOT assessment, it might develop a mission statement that is unachievable. The majority of companies view the strategic planning process as a dynamic interaction, similar to the diagram in Figure 2-4, where the company's mission statement reflects a long-term horizon, but sets forth goals that are achievable and consistent with real-world conditions. Figure 2-5 on the next page shows how purpose, vision, and values are revealed in one company's Web site.

**FIGURE 2-4**  Strategic planning is a dynamic process that identifies specific goals and objectives that support the company's mission.

**FIGURE 2-5** PepsiCo's Web site presents a combination of values, mission, and vision.

**ON THE WEB**

To learn more about mission statements, visit the Management Information Systems CourseMate Web site at **www. cengagebrain. com,** navigate to **On the Web Links** for this chapter, and locate the Mission Statements link.

A mission statement is just the starting point. Next, the company identifies a set of goals that will accomplish the mission. For example, the company might establish one-year, three-year, and five-year goals for expanding market share. To achieve those goals, the company develops a list of shorter-term objectives. For example, if a goal is to increase Web-based orders by 30% next year, a company might set quarterly objectives with monthly milestones. Objectives also might include tactical plans, such as creating a new Web site and training a special customer support group to answer e-mail inquiries. Finally, the objectives translate into day-to-day business operations, supported by IT and other corporate resources. The outcome is a set of business results that affect company stakeholders.

## CASE IN POINT 2.1:  LO CARB MEALS

Lo Carb is a successful new company that has published several cookbooks, and marketed its own line of low-carbohydrate meals. Joe Turner, Lo Carb's president, has asked your opinion. He wants to know whether a mission statement really is necessary. After you review the chapter material, write a brief memo with your views. Be sure to include good (and not-so-good) examples of actual mission statements that you find on the Web.

## A CASE Tool Example

You are a systems analyst working for Sally, the IT manager for a large hotel chain. Sally is working with top management to develop a strategic plan, and she asked you to assist her. The plan will guide future company goals and objectives, including IT projects.

Sally has experience with the Visible Analyst CASE tool, but she has never used it for strategic planning, so she asked you to do some research. First, you navigate to the strategic planning section, where you can enter planning statements such as assumptions, goals, objectives, critical success factors, and others. Planning statements also can document strengths, weaknesses, opportunities, and threats, as shown in Figure 2-6. After you visit the Help section to learn more about the strategic planning features, you feel confident that you can work effectively with this powerful tool.

When you present your results to Sally, she seems pleased. Because the term is new to you, you ask her what critical success factors are, and she replies that **critical success factors** are vital objectives that must be achieved for the company to fulfill its mission.

**FIGURE 2-6**  The Visible Analyst CASE tool supports strategic planning and allows a user to enter many kinds of information. Notice the four SWOT categories in the list.

## The Role of the IT Department in Project Evaluation

Management leadership and information technology are linked closely, and remarkable changes have occurred in both areas. Ten years ago, a typical IT department handled all aspects of systems development and consulted users only when, and if, the department wanted user input. Today, systems development is much more team-oriented. New approaches to systems development, such as joint application development (JAD) and rapid application development (RAD), typically involve groups of users, managers, and IT staff working together right from the start.

Although team-oriented development is the norm, some companies see the role of the IT department as a gatekeeper, responsible for screening and evaluating systems requests. Should the IT department perform the initial evaluation, or should a cross-functional team do it? The answer depends on the company's size and organization, and whether IT is tightly integrated into business operations. In smaller companies or firms where only one person has IT skills, that person acts as a coordinator and consults closely with users and managers to evaluate systems requests. Larger firms are more likely to use an evaluation team or systems review committee.

## The Future

If you could look into the future, here is what you might see: new industries, products, and services emerging from amazing advances in information technology, customers who expect world-class IT support, a surge in Internet-based commerce, and a global business environment that is dynamic and incredibly challenging. To some firms, these changes will be threatening; other companies will see opportunities and take advantage of them by creating and following a strategic plan.

## CASE IN POINT 2.2: ATTAWAY AIRLINES, PART ONE

You are the IT director at Attaway Airlines, a small regional air carrier. You chair the company's systems review committee, and you currently are dealing with strong disagreements about two key projects. Dan Esposito, the marketing manager, says it is vital to have a new computerized reservation system that can provide better customer service and reduce operational costs. Molly Kinnon, vice president of finance, is equally adamant that a new accounting system is needed immediately, because it will be very expensive to adjust the current system to new federal reporting requirements. Molly outranks Dan, and she is your boss. The next meeting, which promises to be a real showdown, is set for 9:00 a.m. tomorrow. How will you prepare for the meeting? What questions and issues should be discussed?

## WHAT IS A BUSINESS CASE?

As mentioned earlier, the term *business case* refers to the reasons, or justification, for a proposal. A business case should be comprehensive, yet easy to understand. It should describe the project clearly, provide the justification to proceed, and estimate the project's financial impact. ProSci's BPR Online Learning Center, as shown in Figure 2-7, offers a Business Case Tutorial Series. According to ProSci, the business case should answer questions such as the following:

- Why are we doing this project?
- What is the project about?
- How does this solution address key business issues?

- How much will it cost and how long will it take?

- Will we suffer a productivity loss during the transition?

- What is the return on investment and payback period?

- What are the risks of doing the project? What are the risks of *not* doing the project?

- How will we measure success?

- What alternatives exist?

## INFORMATION SYSTEMS PROJECTS

This section discusses reasons for systems projects and the internal and external

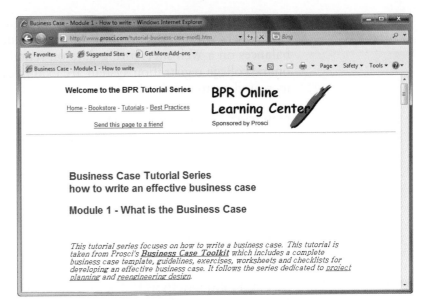

**FIGURE 2-7**   ProSci's BPR Online Learning Center offers a Business Case Tutorial Series that focuses on how to write a business case.

factors that affect systems projects. The section also includes a preview of project management, which is discussed in detail in Chapter 3.

### Main Reasons for Systems Projects

The starting point for most projects is called a **systems request**, which is a formal way of asking for IT support. A systems request might propose enhancements for an existing system, the correction of problems, the replacement of an older system, or the development of an entirely new information system that is needed to support a company's current and future business needs.

As Figure 2-8 shows, the main reasons for systems requests are improved service to customers, better performance, support for new products and services, more information, stronger controls, and reduced cost.

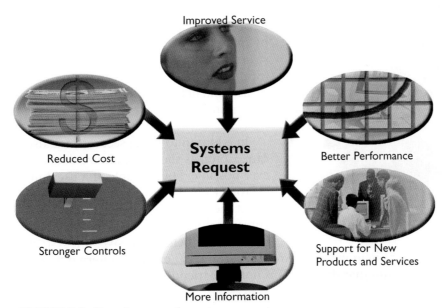

**FIGURE 2-8**   Six main reasons for systems requests.

**IMPROVED SERVICE** Systems requests often are aimed at improving service to customers or users within the company. Allowing mutual fund investors to check their account balances on a Web site, storing data on rental car customer preferences, or creating an online college registration system are examples that provide valuable services and increased customer satisfaction.

**SUPPORT FOR NEW PRODUCTS AND SERVICES** New products and services often require new types or levels of IT support. For example, a software vendor might offer an automatic upgrade service for subscribers; or a package delivery company might add a special service for RFID-tagged shipments. In situations like these, it is most likely that additional IT support will be required. At the other end of the spectrum, product obsolescence can also be an important factor in IT planning. As new products enter the marketplace, vendors often announce that they will no longer provide support for older versions. A lack of vendor support would be an important consideration in deciding whether or not to upgrade.

**ON THE WEB**

To learn more about biometric devices, visit the Management Information Systems CourseMate Web site at **www. cengagebrain. com**, navigate to **On the Web Links** for this chapter, and locate the Biometric Devices link.

**BETTER PERFORMANCE** The current system might not meet performance requirements. For example, it might respond slowly to data inquiries at certain times, or it might be unable to support company growth. Performance limitations also result when a system that was designed for a specific hardware configuration becomes obsolete when new hardware is introduced.

**MORE INFORMATION** The system might produce information that is insufficient, incomplete, or unable to support the company's changing information needs. For example, a system that tracks customer orders might not be capable of analyzing and predicting marketing trends. In the face of intense competition and rapid product development cycles, managers need the best possible information to make major decisions on planning, designing, and marketing new products and services.

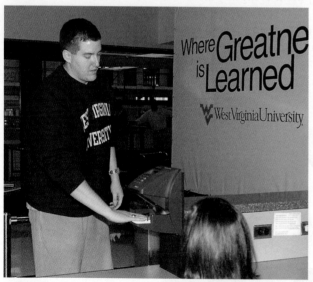

**STRONGER CONTROLS** A system must have effective controls to ensure that data is secure and accurate. Some common security controls include passwords, various levels of user access, and **encryption**, or coding of data to keep it safe from unauthorized users. Hardware-based security controls include **biometric devices** that can identify a person by a retina scan or by mapping a facial pattern. A new biometric tool scans hands, rather than faces. The technology uses infrared scanners that create images with thousands of measurements of hand and finger characteristics, as shown in Figure 2-9.

**FIGURE 2-9** Students at West Virginia University use a hand scanning device to identify themselves.

In addition to being secure, data also must be accurate. Controls should minimize data entry errors whenever possible. For example, if a user enters an invalid customer number, the order processing system should reject the entry immediately and prompt the user to enter a valid number. Data entry controls must be effective without being excessive. If a system requires users to confirm every item with an "Are you sure? Y/N" message, internal users and customers might complain that the system is not user-friendly.

**REDUCED COST** The current system could be expensive to operate or maintain as a result of technical problems, design weaknesses, or the changing demands of the business. It might be possible to adapt the system to newer technology or upgrade it. On the other hand, cost-benefit analysis might show that a new system would be more cost effective and provide better support for long-term objectives.

## CASE IN POINT 2.3: TRENT COLLEGE

Trent College is a private school in a small Maryland town. The college has outgrown its computerized registration system and is considering a new system. Althea Riddick, the college president, has asked you to list the reasons for systems projects, which are described on pages 59–61, and assign a relative weight to each reason, using a scale of 1 – 10, low to high. She said to use your best judgment, and support your conclusions in a brief memo to her. She also wants you to create a Microsoft Excel spreadsheet that will calculate the weighted values automatically for each reason.

### Factors that Affect Systems Projects

Internal and external factors affect every business decision that a company makes, and IT systems projects are no exception. Figure 2-10 shows the main internal and external factors.

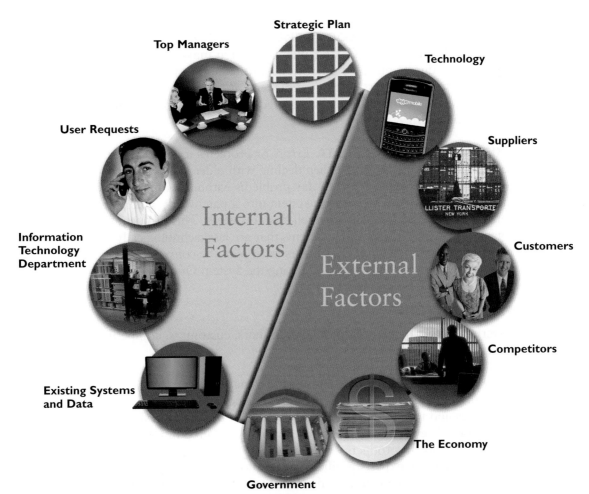

**FIGURE 2-10** Internal and external factors that affect IT systems projects.

## Internal Factors

Internal factors include the strategic plan, top managers, user requests, information technology department, and existing systems and data.

**STRATEGIC PLAN** A company's strategic plan sets the overall direction for the firm and has an important impact on IT projects. Company goals and objectives that need IT support will generate systems requests and influence IT priorities. A strategic plan that stresses technology tends to create a favorable climate for IT projects that extends throughout the organization.

**TOP MANAGERS** Directives from top managers are a prime source of large-scale systems projects. Those directives often result from strategic business decisions that require new IT systems, more information for decision making, or better support for mission-critical information systems.

**USER REQUESTS** As users rely more heavily on information systems to perform their jobs, they are likely to request even more IT services and support. For example, sales reps might request improvements to the company's Web site, a more powerful sales analysis report, a network to link all sales locations, or an online system that allows customers to obtain the status of their orders instantly. Or, users might not be satisfied with the current system because it is difficult to learn or lacks flexibility. They might want information systems support for business requirements that did not even exist when the system was developed.

**INFORMATION TECHNOLOGY DEPARTMENT** Many systems project requests come from the IT department. IT staff members often make recommendations based on their knowledge of business operations and technology trends. IT proposals might be strictly technical matters, such as replacement of certain network components, or suggestions might be more business oriented, such as proposing a new reporting or data collection system.

**EXISTING SYSTEMS AND DATA** Errors or problems in existing systems can trigger requests for systems projects. When dealing with older systems, analysts sometimes spend too much time reacting to day-to-day problems without looking at underlying causes. This approach can turn an information system into a patchwork of corrections and changes that cannot support the company's overall business needs. This problem typically occurs with legacy systems, which are older systems that are less technologically advanced. When migrating to a new system, IT planners must plan the conversion of existing data, which is described in detail in Chapter 11, Making the System Operational.

## External Factors

External factors include technology, suppliers, customers, competitors, the economy, and government.

To learn more about JIT systems, visit the Management Information Systems CourseMate Web site at **www. cengagebrain. com**, navigate to **On the Web Links** for this chapter, and locate the JIT Systems link.

**TECHNOLOGY** Changing technology is a major force affecting business and society in general. For example, the rapid growth of telecommunications has created entire new industries and technologies. Technology also dramatically reshapes existing business operations. The success of scanner technology resulted in universal bar coding that now affects virtually all products.

Some industry experts predict that bar code technology will be overshadowed in the future by **electronic product code (EPC)** technology that uses RFID tags to identify and monitor the movement of each individual product, from the factory floor to the retail checkout counter.

**SUPPLIERS** With the growth of electronic data interchange (EDI), relationships with suppliers are critically important. For example, an automobile company might require that suppliers code their parts in a certain manner to match the auto company's inventory control system. EDI also enables **just-in-time (JIT)** inventory systems, as shown in Figure 2-11, which rely on computer-to-computer data exchange to minimize unnecessary inventory. The purpose of a JIT system is to provide the right product at the right place at the right time.

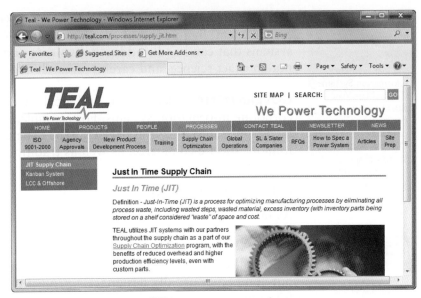

**FIGURE 2-11** Just-in-time (JIT) inventory systems rely on computer-to-computer data exchange to minimize unnecessary inventory.

**CUSTOMERS** Customers are vitally important to any business. Information systems that interact with customers usually receive top priority. Many companies implement **customer relationship management (CRM)** systems that integrate all customer-related events and transactions, including marketing, sales, and customer service activities. Vendor-oriented CRM systems often interconnect with supplier relationship management (SRM) systems, which were discussed in Chapter 1. CRM components can provide automated responses to sales inquiries, Web-based order processing, and online inventory tracking. Because an efficient warehouse is just as important as a successful Web site, suppliers use *smart* forklifts that can read RFID tags or UPC numbers and transmit data to a CRM system, as shown in Figure 2-12.

One of the newest RFID applications is called **electronic proof of delivery (EPOD)**. Using EPOD, a supplier uses RFID tags on each crate, case, or shipping unit to create a digital shipping list. The customer receives the list and scans the incoming shipment. If a discrepancy is detected, it is reported and adjusted automatically. Because they would be expensive to investigate manually, small shipping inconsistencies might not otherwise be traced. This is an example of technology-related cost control.

**COMPETITORS** Competition drives many information systems decisions. For example, if one cellular telephone provider offers a new type of digital service, other firms must match the plan in order to remain competitive. New product research and development, marketing, sales, and service all require IT support.

**FIGURE 2-12** In an efficient warehouse, *smart* forklifts can read RFID tags or UPC numbers and transmit data to a CRM system.

**ON THE WEB**

To learn more about CRM systems, visit the Management Information Systems CourseMate Web site at **www. cengagebrain. com**, navigate to **On the Web Links** for this chapter, and locate the CRM Systems link.

**VIDEO LEARNING SESSIONS**

To learn more about project management, visit the Management Information Systems CourseMate Web site at **www. cengagebrain. com** and navigate to the **Video Learning Sessions** for this book. These sessions can help you understand key concepts, practice your skills, and check your work.

**THE ECONOMY** Economic activity has a powerful influence on corporate information management. In a period of economic expansion, firms need to be ready with scalable systems that can handle additional volume and growth. Predicting the business cycle is not an exact science, and careful research and planning is critically important.

**GOVERNMENT** Federal, state, and local government regulations affect the design of corporate information systems. For example, income tax reporting requirements must be designed into a payroll package. The debate about Internet sales tax issues could profoundly affect e-commerce, as well as traditional retail businesses.

## Project Management

As mentioned earlier, business case analysis involves consideration of project reasons, costs, benefits, and risks. At the end of the preliminary investigation, if the project is approved, it can be planned, scheduled, monitored and controlled, and reported upon. Individual analysts or IT staff members often handle small projects, but companies usually designate a project manager to coordinate the overall effort for complex projects.

In Chapter 3, you will study project management concepts, skills, tools, and techniques. You also will learn about project risk management, and how to perform the following tasks:

- Develop a project risk management plan
- Identify the risks
- Analyze the risks
- Create a risk response plan
- Monitor and respond to risks

Figure 2-13 shows the latest version of Microsoft Project, a popular project management tool. Using this program, a project manager can define project tasks, list activities and participants, plan the sequence of work, estimate milestone dates, and track costs.

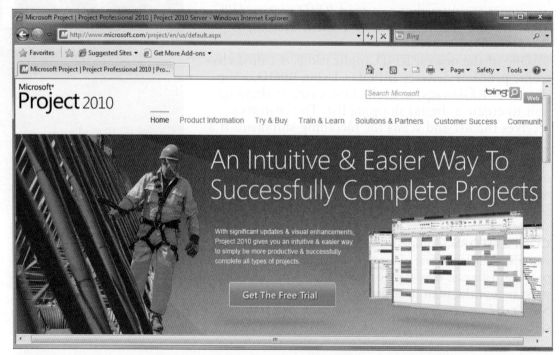

**FIGURE 2-13**  Microsoft Project is a powerful, popular software tool for project management.

## EVALUATION OF SYSTEMS REQUESTS

In most organizations, the IT department receives more systems requests than it can handle. Many organizations assign responsibility for evaluating systems requests to a group of key managers and users. Many companies call this group a **systems review committee** or a **computer resources committee**. Regardless of the name, the objective is to use the combined judgment and experience of several managers to evaluate systems projects.

### Systems Request Forms

Many organizations use a special form for systems requests, similar to the online sample shown in Figure 2-14. A properly designed form streamlines the request process and ensures consistency. The form must be easy to understand and include clear instructions. It should include enough space for all required information and should indicate what supporting documents are needed. Many companies use online systems request forms that can be filled in and submitted electronically.

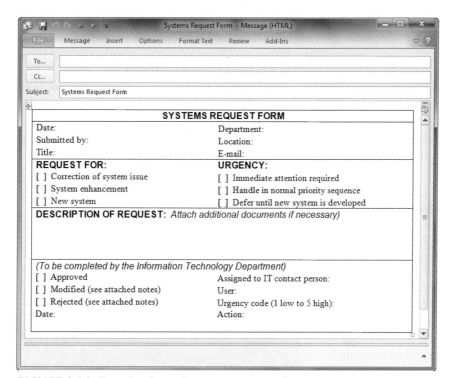

**FIGURE 2-14** Example of an online systems request form.

When a systems request form is received, a systems analyst or IT manager examines it to determine what IT resources are required for the preliminary investigation. A designated person or a committee then decides whether to proceed with a preliminary investigation. Occasionally a situation will arise that requires an immediate response. For example, if the problem involves a mission-critical system, an IT maintenance team would attempt to restore normal operations. When the system is functioning properly, the team conducts a review and prepares a systems request to cover the work that was performed.

## Systems Review Committee

Most large companies use a systems review committee to evaluate systems requests. Instead of relying on a single individual, a committee approach provides a variety of experience and knowledge. With a broader viewpoint, a committee can establish priorities more effectively than an individual, and one person's bias is less likely to affect the decisions. A typical committee consists of the IT director and several managers from other departments. The IT director usually serves as a technical consultant to ensure that committee members are aware of crucial issues, problems, and opportunities.

Although a committee offers many advantages, some disadvantages exist. For example, action on requests must wait until the committee meets. To avoid delay, committee members typically use e-mail and teleconferencing to communicate. Another potential disadvantage of a committee is that members might favor projects requested by their own departments, and internal political differences could delay important decisions.

Many smaller companies rely on one person to evaluate system requests instead of a committee. If only one person has the necessary IT skills and experience, that person must consult closely with users and managers throughout the company to ensure that business and operational needs are considered carefully.

Whether one person or a committee is responsible, the goal is to evaluate the requests and set priorities. Suppose four requests must be reviewed: the marketing group wants to analyze current customer spending habits and forecast future trends; the technical support group wants a cellular link so service representatives can download technical data instantly; the accounting department wants to redesign customer statements and allow Internet access; and the production staff wants an inventory control system that can exchange data with major suppliers. Which projects should the firm pursue? What criteria should be applied? How should priorities be determined? To answer those questions, the individual or the committee must assess the feasibility of each request.

## OVERVIEW OF FEASIBILITY

As you learned in Chapter 1, a systems request must pass several tests, called a feasibility study, to see whether it is worthwhile to proceed further. As shown in Figure 2-15, a feasibility study uses four main yardsticks to measure a proposal: operational feasibility, technical feasibility, economic feasibility, and schedule feasibility.

Sometimes a feasibility study is quite simple and can be done in a few hours. If the request involves a new system or a major change, however, extensive fact-finding and investigation is required.

How much effort needs to go into a feasibility study? That depends on the

**FIGURE 2-15**  A feasibility study includes tests for operational, technical, economic, and schedule feasibility.

Overview of Feasibility                                                                     67

request. For example, if a department wants an existing report sorted in a different order, the analyst can decide quickly whether the request is feasible. On the other hand, a proposal by the marketing department for a new market research system to predict sales trends requires more effort. In both cases, the systems analyst asks these important questions:

- Is the proposal desirable in an operational sense? Is it a practical approach that will solve a problem or take advantage of an opportunity to achieve company goals?
- Is the proposal technically feasible? Are the necessary technical resources and people available for the project?
- Is the proposal economically desirable? What are the projected savings and costs? Are other intangible factors involved, such as customer satisfaction or company image? Is the problem worth solving, and will the request result in a sound business investment?
- Can the proposal be accomplished within an acceptable time frame?

To obtain more information about a systems request, you might perform initial fact-finding by studying organization charts, performing interviews, reviewing current documentation, observing operations, and surveying users. If the systems request is approved, more intensive fact-finding will continue during the systems analysis phase.

## Operational Feasibility

**Operational feasibility** means that a proposed system will be used effectively after it has been developed. If users have difficulty with a new system, it will not produce the expected benefits. Operational feasibility depends on several vital issues. For example, consider the following questions:

- Does management support the project? Do users support the project? Is the current system well liked and effectively used? Do users see the need for change?
- Will the new system result in a workforce reduction? If so, what will happen to affected employees?
- Will the new system require training for users? If so, is the company prepared to provide the necessary resources for training current employees?
- Will users be involved in planning the new system right from the start?
- Will the new system place any new demands on users or require any operating changes? For example, will any information be less accessible or produced less frequently? Will performance decline in any way? If so, will an overall gain to the organization outweigh individual losses?
- Will customers experience adverse effects in any way, either temporarily or permanently?
- Will any risk to the company's image or goodwill result?
- Does the development schedule conflict with other company priorities?
- Do legal or ethical issues need to be considered?

## Technical Feasibility

**Technical feasibility** refers to the technical resources needed to develop, purchase, install, or operate the system. When assessing technical feasibility, an analyst must consider the following points:

- Does the company have the necessary hardware, software, and network resources? If not, can those resources be acquired without difficulty?

- Does the company have the needed technical expertise? If not, can it be acquired?

- Does the proposed platform have sufficient capacity for future needs? If not, can it be expanded?

- Will a prototype be required?

- Will the hardware and software environment be reliable? Will it integrate with other company information systems, both now and in the future? Will it interface properly with external systems operated by customers and suppliers?

- Will the combination of hardware and software supply adequate performance? Do clear expectations and performance specifications exist?

- Will the system be able to handle future transaction volume and company growth?

## Economic Feasibility

**Economic feasibility** means that the projected benefits of the proposed system outweigh the estimated costs usually considered the **total cost of ownership (TCO)**, which includes ongoing support and maintenance costs, as well as acquisition costs. To determine TCO, the analyst must estimate costs in each of the following areas:

- People, including IT staff and users

- Hardware and equipment

- Software, including in-house development as well as purchases from vendors

- Formal and informal training

- Licenses and fees

- Consulting expenses

- Facility costs

- The estimated cost of not developing the system or postponing the project

In addition to costs, you need to assess tangible and intangible benefits to the company. The systems review committee will use those figures, along with your cost estimates, to decide whether to pursue the project beyond the preliminary investigation phase.

**Tangible benefits** are benefits that can be measured in dollars. Tangible benefits result from a decrease in expenses, an increase in revenues, or both. Examples of tangible benefits include the following:

- A new scheduling system that reduces overtime

- An online package tracking system that improves service and decreases the need for clerical staff

- A sophisticated inventory control system that cuts excess inventory and eliminates production delays

**Intangible benefits** are advantages that are difficult to measure in dollars but are important to the company. Examples of intangible benefits include the following:

- A user-friendly system that improves employee job satisfaction

- A sales tracking system that supplies better information for marketing decisions

- A new Web site that enhances the company's image

You also must consider the development timetable, because some benefits might occur as soon as the system is operational, but others might not take place until later.

**ON THE WEB**

To learn more about TCO, visit the Management Information Systems CourseMate Web site at **www. cengagebrain. com**, navigate to **On the Web Links** for this chapter, and locate the TCO link.

**VIDEO LEARNING SESSIONS**

To learn more about financial tools, visit the Management Information Systems CourseMate Web site at **www. cengagebrain. com** and navigate to the **Video Learning Sessions** for this book. These sessions can help you understand key concepts, practice your skills, and check your work.

The Financial Analysis tools in Appendix C can help you analyze project costs, benefits, and economic feasibility. To learn more about these tools, turn to Appendix C.

## Schedule Feasibility

**Schedule feasibility** means that a project can be implemented in an acceptable time frame. When assessing schedule feasibility, a systems analyst must consider the interaction between time and costs. For example, speeding up a project schedule might make a project feasible, but much more expensive.

Other issues that relate to schedule feasibility include the following:

- Can the company or the IT team control the factors that affect schedule feasibility?
- Has management established a firm timetable for the project?
- What conditions must be satisfied during the development of the system?
- Will an accelerated schedule pose any risks? If so, are the risks acceptable?
- Will project management techniques be available to coordinate and control the project?
- Will a project manager be appointed?

Chapter 3 describes various project management tools and techniques.

## EVALUATING FEASIBILITY

The first step in evaluating feasibility is to identify and weed out systems requests that are not feasible. For example, a request would not be feasible if it required hardware or software that the company already had rejected.

Even if the request is feasible, it might not be necessary. For example, a request for multiple versions of a report could require considerable design and programming effort. A better alternative might be to download the server data to a personal computer-based software package and show users how to produce their own reports. In this case, training users would be a better investment than producing reports for them.

Also keep in mind that systems requests that are not currently feasible can be resubmitted as new hardware, software, or expertise becomes available. Development costs might decrease, or the value of benefits might increase enough that a systems request eventually becomes feasible. Conversely, an initially feasible project can be rejected later. As the project progresses, conditions often change. Acquisition costs might increase, and the project might become more expensive than anticipated. In addition, managers and users sometimes lose confidence in a project. For all those reasons, feasibility analysis is an ongoing task that must be performed throughout the systems development process.

## SETTING PRIORITIES

After rejecting systems requests that are not feasible, the systems review committee must establish priorities for the remaining items. The highest priority goes to projects that provide the greatest benefit, at the lowest cost, in the shortest period of time. Many factors, however, influence project evaluation.

## Factors that Affect Priority

When assessing a project's priority, a systems analyst should consider the following:

- Will the proposed system reduce costs? Where? When? How? How much?
- Will the system increase revenue for the company? Where? When? How? How much?
- Will the systems project result in more information or produce better results? How? Are the results measurable?
- Will the system serve customers better?
- Will the system serve the organization better?
- Can the project be implemented in a reasonable time period? How long will the results last?
- Are the necessary financial, human, and technical resources available?

Very few projects will score high in all areas. Some proposed systems might not reduce costs but will provide important new features. Other systems might reduce operating costs substantially but require the purchase or lease of additional hardware. Some systems might be very desirable but require several years of development before producing significant benefits.

Whenever possible, the analyst should evaluate a proposed project based on tangible costs and benefits that represent actual (or approximate) dollar values. For example, a reduction of $8,000 in network maintenance is an example of a tangible benefit.

Often, the evaluation involves intangible costs or benefits, as described in the section on economic feasibility. In contrast to tangible benefits, such as the network cost reduction example, it is more difficult to assign dollar values to intangible benefits such as enhancing the organization's image, raising employee morale, or improving customer service. Intangible costs and benefits often influence systems decisions and priorities and must be considered carefully.

## Discretionary and Nondiscretionary Projects

Is the project absolutely necessary? Projects where management has a choice in implementing them are called **discretionary projects**. Projects where no choice exists are called **nondiscretionary projects**. Creating a new report for a user is an example of a discretionary project; adding a report required by a new federal law is an example of a nondiscretionary project.

If a particular project is not discretionary, is it really necessary for the systems review committee to evaluate it? Some people believe that waiting for committee approval delays critical nondiscretionary projects unnecessarily. Others believe that by submitting all systems requests to the systems review committee, the committee is kept aware of all projects that compete for the resources of the IT department. As a result, the committee assesses the priority of discretionary projects and can schedule them more realistically. Additionally, the committee might need to prioritize nondiscretionary projects when funds or staff are limited.

Many nondiscretionary projects are predictable. Examples include annual updates to payroll, tax percentages, or quarterly changes in reporting requirements for an insurance processing system. By planning ahead for predictable projects, the IT department manages its resources better and keeps the systems review committee fully informed without needing prior approval in every case.

## CASE IN POINT 2.4:   ATTAWAY AIRLINES, PART TWO

Back at Attaway Airlines, the morning meeting ended with no agreement between Dan Esposito and Molly Kinnon. In fact, a new issue arose. Molly now says that the new accounting system is entitled to the highest priority because the federal government soon will require the reporting of certain types of company-paid health insurance premiums. Because the current system will not handle this report, she insists that the entire accounting system is a nondiscretionary project. As you might expect, Dan is upset. Can part of a project be nondiscretionary? What issues need to be discussed? The committee meets again tomorrow, and the members will look to you, as the IT director, for guidance.

## PRELIMINARY INVESTIGATION OVERVIEW

A systems analyst conducts a **preliminary investigation** to study the systems request and recommend specific action. After obtaining an authorization to proceed, the analyst interacts with managers and users, as shown in the model in Figure 2-16. The analyst gathers facts about the problem or opportunity, project scope and constraints, project benefits, and estimated development time and costs. The end product of the preliminary investigation is a report to management.

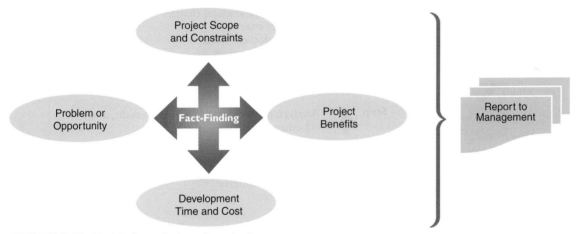

**FIGURE 2-16**  Model of a preliminary investigation.

### Interaction with Managers and Users

Before beginning a preliminary investigation, a memo or an e-mail message should let people know about the investigation and explain your role. You should meet with key managers, users, and IT staff to describe the project, explain your responsibilities, answer questions, and invite comments. This starts an important dialogue with users that will continue throughout the entire development process.

A systems project often produces significant changes in company operations. Employees may be curious, concerned, or even opposed to those changes. It is not surprising to encounter some user resistance during a preliminary investigation. Employee attitudes and reactions are important and must be considered.

When interacting with users, you should be careful in your use of the word *problem*, because generally it has a negative meaning. When you ask users about *problems*, some will stress current system limitations rather than desirable new features or enhancements. Instead of focusing on difficulties, you should question users about additional capability they would like to have. Using this approach, you highlight ways to improve the user's job, you get a better understanding of operations, and you build better, more positive relationships with users.

## Planning the Preliminary Investigation

During a preliminary investigation, a systems analyst typically follows a series of steps, as shown in Figure 2-17. The exact procedure depends on the nature of the request, the size of the project, and the degree of urgency.

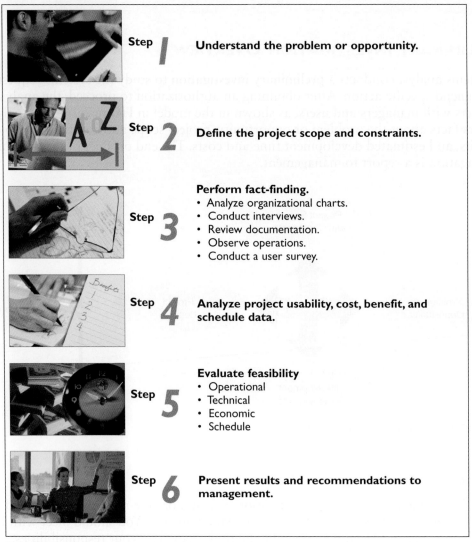

**Step 1**  Understand the problem or opportunity.

**Step 2**  Define the project scope and constraints.

**Step 3**  Perform fact-finding.
- Analyze organizational charts.
- Conduct interviews.
- Review documentation.
- Observe operations.
- Conduct a user survey.

**Step 4**  Analyze project usability, cost, benefit, and schedule data.

**Step 5**  Evaluate feasibility
- Operational
- Technical
- Economic
- Schedule

**Step 6**  Present results and recommendations to management.

**FIGURE 2-17**  Six steps in a preliminary investigation.

Figure 2-18 shows how a systems analyst might use Microsoft Project to plan and manage the preliminary investigation. Notice that the analyst has listed the tasks, estimated the duration of each task, and designated a specific order in which the tasks must be performed.

## Step 1: Understand the Problem or Opportunity

If the systems request involves a new information system or a substantial change in an existing system, systems analysts might need to develop a business profile that describes business processes and functions, as explained in Chapter 1. Even where the request involves relatively minor changes or enhancements, you need to understand how those modifications will affect business operations and other information systems. Often a change in one system has an unexpected effect on another system. When you analyze a systems request, you need to determine which departments, users, and business processes are involved.

In many cases, the systems request does not reveal the underlying problem, but only a symptom. For example, a request to investigate mainframe processing delays might reveal improper scheduling practices rather than hardware problems. Similarly, a request for analysis of customer complaints might disclose a lack of sales representative training, rather than problems with the product.

A popular technique for investigating causes and effects is called a **fishbone diagram**, or **Ishikawa diagram**, as shown in Figure 2-19. A fishbone diagram is an analysis tool that represents the possible causes of a problem

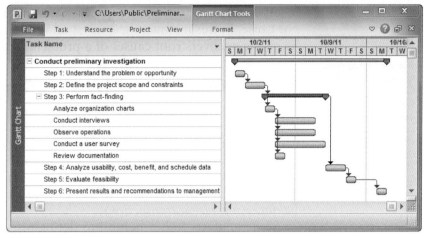

**FIGURE 2-18** An analyst could use Microsoft Project to plan and manage a preliminary investigation.

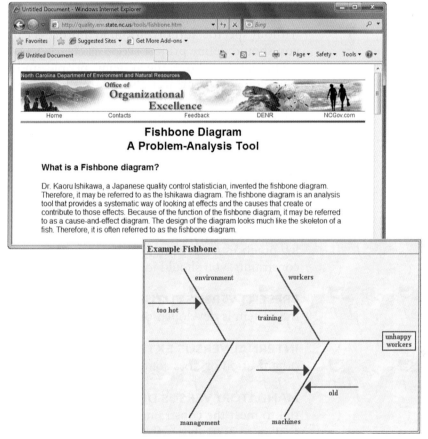

**FIGURE 2-19** A fishbone diagram displays the causes of a problem. Typically, you must dig deeper to identify actual *causes* rather than just symptoms.

as a graphical outline. When using a fishbone diagram, an analyst first states the problem and draws a main bone with sub-bones that represent possible causes of the problem. In the example shown in Figure 2-19, the problem is *unhappy workers*, and the analyst has identified four areas to investigate: *environment, workers, management,* and *machines.* In each area, the analyst identifies possible causes and draws them as horizontal sub-bones. For example, *too hot* is a possible cause in the *environment* bone. For each cause, the analyst must dig deeper and ask the question: What could be causing *this* symptom to occur? For example, *why* is it too hot? If the answer is

To learn more about fishbone diagrams, visit the Management Information Systems CourseMate Web site at **www. cengagebrain. com**, navigate to **On the Web Links** for this chapter, and locate the Fishbone Diagram link.

insufficient air conditioning capacity, the analyst indicates this as a sub-bone to the *too hot* cause. In this manner, the analyst adds additional sub-bones to the diagram, until he or she uncovers root causes of a problem, rather than just the symptoms.

## Step 2: Define the Project Scope and Constraints

Determining the **project scope** means defining the specific boundaries, or extent, of the project. For example, a statement that, *payroll is not being produced accurately* is very general, compared with the statement *overtime pay is not being calculated correctly for production workers on the second shift at the Yorktown plant.* Similarly, the statement, *the project scope is to modify the accounts receivable system*, is not as specific as the statement, *the project scope is to allow customers to inquire online about account balances and recent transactions.*

Some analysts find it helpful to define project scope by creating a list with sections called *Must Do, Should Do, Could Do,* and *Won't Do.* This list can be reviewed later, during the systems analysis phase, when the systems requirements document is developed.

Projects with very general scope definitions are at risk of expanding gradually, without specific authorization, in a process called **project creep**. To avoid this problem, you should define project scope as clearly as possible. You might want to use a graphical model that shows the systems, people, and business processes that will be affected. The scope of the project also establishes the boundaries of the preliminary investigation itself. A systems analyst should limit the focus to the problem at hand and avoid unnecessary expenditure of time and money.

Along with defining the scope of the project, you need to identify any constraints on the system. A **constraint** is a requirement or condition that the system must satisfy or an outcome that the system must achieve. A constraint can involve hardware, software, time, policy, law, or cost. System constraints also define project scope. For example, if the system must operate with existing hardware, that is a constraint that affects potential solutions. Other examples of constraints are: The order entry system must accept input from 15 remote sites; the human resources information system must produce statistics on hiring practices; and the new Web site must be operational by March 1. When examining constraints, you should identify their characteristics.

**PRESENT VERSUS FUTURE** Is the constraint something that must be met as soon as the system is developed or modified, or is the constraint necessary at some future time?

**INTERNAL VERSUS EXTERNAL** Is the constraint due to a requirement within the organization or does some external force, such as government regulation, impose it?

**MANDATORY VERSUS DESIRABLE** Is the constraint mandatory? Is it absolutely essential to meet the constraint, or is it merely desirable?

Figure 2-20 shows five examples of constraints. Notice that each constraint has three characteristics, which are indicated by its position in the figure and by the symbol that represents the constraint. The constraint in Example A is present, external, and mandatory. The constraint in Example B is future, external, and mandatory. The constraint in Example C is present, internal, and desirable. The constraint in Example D is present, internal, and mandatory. The constraint in Example E is future, internal, and desirable.

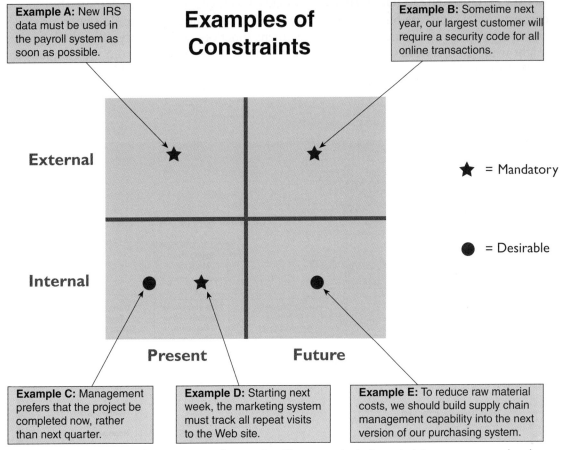

**Examples of Constraints**

**Example A:** New IRS data must be used in the payroll system as soon as possible.

**Example B:** Sometime next year, our largest customer will require a security code for all online transactions.

External

Internal

Present     Future

★ = Mandatory

● = Desirable

**Example C:** Management prefers that the project be completed now, rather than next quarter.

**Example D:** Starting next week, the marketing system must track all repeat visits to the Web site.

**Example E:** To reduce raw material costs, we should build supply chain management capability into the next version of our purchasing system.

**FIGURE 2-20** Examples of various types of constraints. The constraint in Example A is present, external, and mandatory. The constraint in Example B is future, external, and mandatory. The constraint in Example C is present, internal, and desirable. The constraint in Example D is present, internal, and mandatory. The constraint in Example E is future, internal, and desirable.

Regardless of the type, all constraints should be identified as early as possible to avoid future problems and surprises. A clear definition of project scope and constraints avoids misunderstandings that arise when managers assume that the system will have a certain feature or support for a project, but later find that the feature is not included.

## Step 3: Perform Fact-Finding

The objective of fact-finding is to gather data about project usability, costs, benefits, and schedules. Fact-finding involves various techniques, which are described below. Depending on what information is needed to investigate the systems request, fact-finding might consume several hours, days, or weeks. For example, a change in a report format or data entry screen might require a single telephone call or e-mail message to a user, whereas a new inventory system would involve a series of interviews. During fact-finding, you might analyze organization charts, conduct interviews, review current documentation, observe operations, and carry out a user survey.

**ANALYZE ORGANIZATION CHARTS**  In many instances, you will not know the organizational structure of departments involved in the study. You should obtain organization charts to understand how the department functions and identify individuals you might want to interview. Organization charts often can be obtained from the company's human resources department. If such charts are unavailable, you should obtain the necessary information directly from department personnel and then construct your own charts, as shown in Figure 2-21.

**FIGURE 2-21**    Microsoft Visio includes an organization chart drawing tool that is powerful and easy to use.

When organization charts are available, you should verify their accuracy. Keep in mind that organization charts show formal reporting relationships but not the informal alignment of a group, which also is important.

**CONDUCT INTERVIEWS**  The primary method of obtaining information during the preliminary investigation is the interview. The interviewing process involves a series of steps:

1. Determine the people to interview.
2. Establish objectives for the interview.
3. Develop interview questions.
4. Prepare for the interview.
5. Conduct the interview.
6. Document the interview.
7. Evaluate the interview.

These seven steps are discussed in detail in Chapter 4, which describes fact-finding techniques that occur during the systems analysis phase of the SDLC.

Remember that the purpose of the interview, and of the preliminary investigation itself, is to uncover facts, not to convince others that the project is justified. Your primary role in an interview is to ask effective questions and listen carefully. If you plan to talk to several people about the same topic, you should prepare a standard set of questions for all the interviews. Also be sure to include open-ended questions, such as "What else do you think I should know about the system?" or "Is there any other relevant information that we have not discussed?"

When conducting interviews during the preliminary investigation, you should interview managers and supervisors who have a broad knowledge of the system and can give you an overview of the business processes involved. Depending on the situation, you might talk to operational personnel to learn how the system functions on a day-to-day basis.

**REVIEW DOCUMENTATION** Although interviews are an extremely important method of obtaining information, you also might want to investigate the current system documentation. The documentation might not be up to date, so you should check with users to confirm that you are receiving accurate and complete information.

**OBSERVE OPERATIONS** Another fact-finding method is to observe the current system in operation, as shown in Figure 2-22. You might see how workers carry out typical tasks. You might choose to trace or follow the actual paths taken by input source documents or output reports. In addition to observing operations, you might want to sample the inputs or outputs of the system. Using sampling techniques described in Chapter 4, you can obtain valuable information about the nature and frequency of the problem.

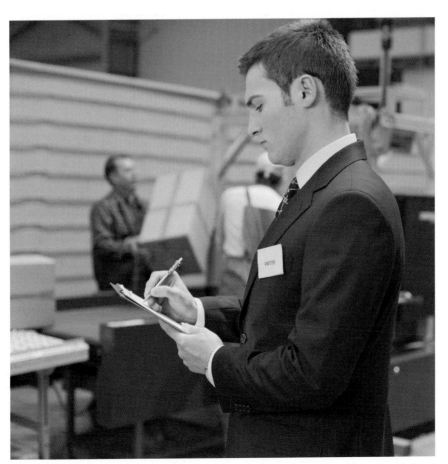

**FIGURE 2-22** Sometimes, an analyst can get a better understanding of a system by watching actual operations.

**CONDUCT A USER SURVEY** Interviews can be time consuming. Sometimes you can obtain information from a larger group by conducting a user survey. In this case, you design a form that users complete and return to you for tabulation. A survey is not as flexible as a series of interviews, but it is less expensive, generally takes less time, and can involve a broad cross-section of people.

**ANALYZE THE DATA** Systems analysts use many techniques to locate the source of a problem. For example, the **Pareto chart** is a widely used tool for visualizing issues that need attention. Named for a nineteenth century economist, a Pareto chart is drawn as a vertical bar graph, as shown in Figure 2-23. The bars, which represent various causes of a problem, are arranged in descending order, so the team can focus on the most important causes. In the example shown, a systems analyst might use a Pareto chart to learn more about the causes of inventory system problems, so that necessary improvements can be made. Creating Pareto charts with Excel is a simple process.

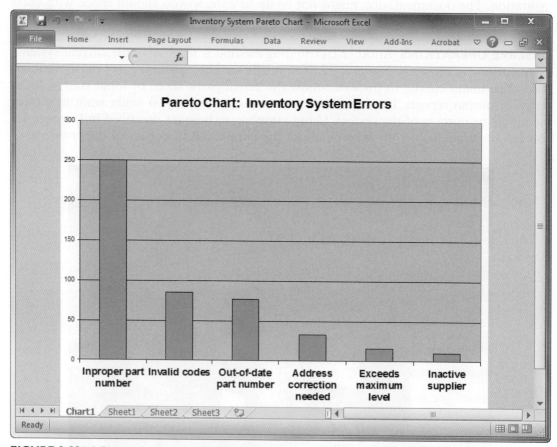

**FIGURE 2-23** A Pareto chart can display and prioritize the causes of a problem, enabling an analyst to focus on the most important issues.

The **XY chart**, sometimes called a **scatter diagram**, is another problem-solving tool. Often, an analyst looks for a correlation between two variables. For example, suppose you are getting complaints about network response time, and you want to determine the cause. You would try to identify variables, such as the number of users, to see whether there is a correlation, or pattern. Figure 2-24 shows two XY charts with data samples. The first chart sample would suggest that there is no correlation between the delays and the number of users, and you would look elsewhere for the source of the problem. However, if the data resembles the second XY sample, it indicates a strong relationship between the number of users and the longer response times. That information would be extremely valuable in the problem-solving process.

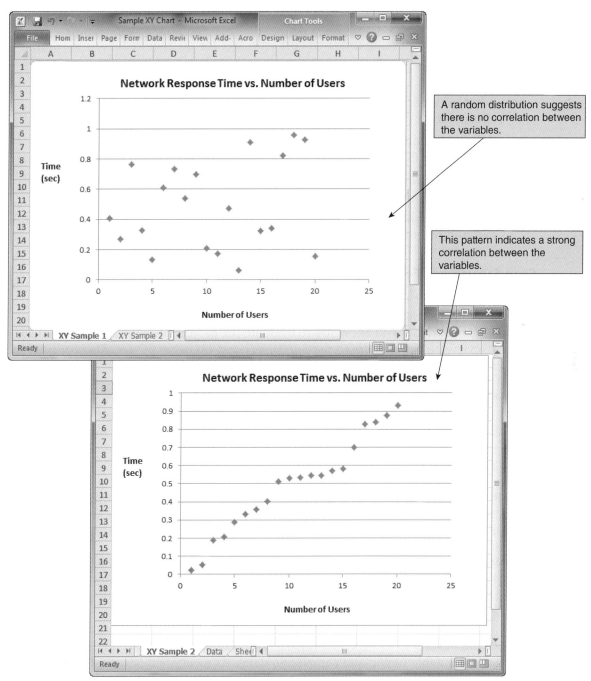

**FIGURE 2-24** An XY chart shows correlation between variables, which is very important in problem-solving. Conversely, a *lack* of correlation suggests that the variables are independent, and that you should look elsewhere for the cause.

## Step 4:  Analyze Project Usability, Cost, Benefit, and Schedule Data

During fact-finding, you gathered data about the project's predicted costs, anticipated benefits, and schedule issues that could affect implementation. Before you can evaluate feasibility, you must analyze this data carefully. If you conducted interviews or used surveys, you should tabulate the data to make it easier to understand. If you observed current operations, you should review the results and highlight key facts that will be useful in the feasibility analysis. If you gathered cost and benefit data, you should be able to prepare financial analysis and impact statements using spreadsheets and other decision support tools.

Also, you should develop time and cost estimates for the requirements modeling tasks for the next SDLC phase, systems analysis. Specifically, you should consider the following:

- What information must you obtain, and how will you gather and analyze the information?

- Will you conduct interviews? How many people will you interview, and how much time will you need to meet with the people and summarize their responses?

- Will you conduct a survey? Who will be involved? How much time will it take people to complete it? How much time will it take to tabulate the results?

- How much will it cost to analyze the information and prepare a report with findings and recommendations?

## Step 5: Evaluate Feasibility

You have analyzed the problem or opportunity, defined the project scope and constraints, and performed fact-finding to evaluate project usability, costs, benefits, and time constraints. Now you are ready to evaluate the project's feasibility. You should start by reviewing the answers to the questions listed on pages 67–69. Also consider the following guidelines:

**OPERATIONAL FEASIBILITY** Your fact-finding should have included a review of user needs, requirements, and expectations. When you analyze this data, you should look for areas that might present problems for system users and how they might be resolved. Because operational feasibility means that a system will be used effectively, this is a vital area of concern.

**TECHNICAL FEASIBILITY** The fact-finding data should identify the hardware, software, and network resources needed to develop, install, and operate the system. With this data, you can develop a checklist that will highlight technical costs and concerns, if any.

**ECONOMIC FEASIBILITY** Using the fact-finding data, you can apply the financial analysis tools described in Appendix C to assess feasibility. The cost-benefit data will be an important factor for management to consider. Also, a cost estimate for the project development team will be built into the project management plan.

**SCHEDULE FEASIBILITY** The fact-finding data should include stakeholder expectations regarding acceptable timing and completion dates. As mentioned previously, often a trade-off exists between a project's schedule and its costs. For example, compressing a project schedule might be possible, but only if the budget is increased accordingly. The schedule data will be incorporated into the project plan in the form of task durations and milestones.

## Step 6: Present Results and Recommendations to Management

At this stage, you have several alternatives. You might find that no action is necessary or that some other strategy, such as additional training, is needed. To solve a minor problem, you might implement a simple solution without performing further analysis. In other situations, you will recommend that the project proceed to the next development phase, which is systems analysis.

The final task in the preliminary investigation is to prepare a report to management, and possibly deliver a presentation, as shown in Figure 2-25. The report includes an evaluation of the systems request, an estimate of costs and benefits, and a **case for action**, which is a summary of the project request and a specific recommendation.

The format of a preliminary investigation report varies from one company to another. A typical report might consist of the following sections:

The Communication Tools in Appendix A can help you develop better reports and presentations. To learn more about these tools, turn to Appendix A.

- *Introduction* — the first section is an overview of the report. The introduction contains a brief description of the system, the name of the person or group who performed the investigation, and the name of the person or group who initiated the investigation.

- *Systems Request Summary* — the summary describes the basis of the systems request.

- *Findings* — the findings section contains the results of your preliminary investigation, including a description of the project's scope, constraints, and feasibility.

- *Case for Action* — a summary of the project request and a specific recommendation. Management will make the final decision, but the IT department's input is an important factor.

**FIGURE 2-25**  Oral presentations often are required during systems development, and systems analysts need to develop strong presentation skills.

- *Project Roles* — this section lists the people who will participate in the project, and describes each person's role.

- *Time and Cost Estimates* — this section describes the cost of acquiring and installing the system, and the total cost of ownership during the system's useful life.

- *Expected Benefits* — this section includes anticipated tangible and intangible benefits and a timetable that shows when they are to occur.

- *Appendix* — an appendix is included in the report if you need to attach supporting information. For example, you might list the interviews you conducted, the documentation you reviewed, and other sources for the information you obtained. You do not need detailed reports of the interviews or other lengthy documentation. It is critical that you retain those documents to support your findings and for future reference.

# A QUESTION OF ETHICS

As a new systems analyst at Premier Financial Services, you are getting quite an education. You report to Mary, the IT manager, who also chairs the systems review committee. Several months ago, the committee rejected a request from Jack, the finance director, for an expensive new accounts payable system, because the benefits did not appear to outweigh the costs.

Yesterday, Mary's boss called her in and asked her to reconsider Jack's request, and to persuade the other members to approve it. Mary wanted to discuss the merits of the request, but he cut her off rather abruptly. Mary happens to know that Jack and her boss are longtime friends.

Mary has confided in you. She is very uncomfortable about the meeting with her boss, and she believes that his request would undermine the integrity of the systems review process. Mary feels it would be unethical to grant preferred treatment just because a friendship is involved. She is thinking of submitting a request to step down as review committee chair, even though that might harm her career at the company.

Is this an ethical question, or just a matter of office politics? What would you say to Mary?

## CHAPTER SUMMARY

Systems planning is the first phase of the systems development life cycle. Effective information systems help an organization support its business processes, carry out its mission, and serve its stakeholders. Strategic planning allows a company to examine its purpose, vision, and values and develops a mission statement, which leads to goals, objectives, day-to-day operations, and business results that affect company stakeholders.

During the systems planning phase, an analyst reviews the business case, which is the basis, or reason, for a proposed system. A business case should describe the project clearly, provide the justification to proceed, and estimate the project's financial impact.

Systems projects are initiated to improve performance, provide more information, reduce costs, strengthen controls, or provide better service. Various internal and external factors affect systems projects, such as user requests, top management directives, existing systems, the IT department, software and hardware vendors, technology, customers, competitors, the economy, and government.

During the preliminary investigation, the analyst evaluates the systems request and determines whether the project is feasible from an operation, technical, economic, and schedule standpoint. Analysts evaluate systems requests on the basis of their expected costs and benefits, both tangible and intangible.

The steps in the preliminary investigation are to understand the problem or opportunity; define the project scope and constraints; perform fact-finding; analyze project usability, cost, benefit, and schedule data; evaluate feasibility; and present results and recommendations to management. During the preliminary investigation, analysts often use investigative tools such as fishbone or Ishikawa diagrams, Pareto charts, and XY charts. The last task in a preliminary investigation is to prepare a report to management. The report must include an estimate of time, staffing requirements, costs, benefits, and expected results for the next phase of the SDLC.

# Key Terms and Phrases

biometric devices 60

business case 52

case for action 81

computer resources committee 65

constraint 74

critical success factors 57

customer relationship management (CRM) 63

discretionary projects 70

economic feasibility 68

electronic product code (EPC) 62

electronic proof of delivery (EPOD) 63

encryption 60

fishbone diagram 73

intangible benefits 68

Ishikawa diagram 73

just-in-time (JIT) 63

mission statement 55

nondiscretionary projects 70

operational feasibility 67

Pareto chart 78

preliminary investigation 71

project creep 74

project scope 74

scatter diagram, 78

schedule feasibility 69

strategic planning 54

SWOT analysis 54

systems request 59

systems review committee 65

tangible benefits 68

technical feasibility 67

total cost of ownership (TCO) 68

XY chart 78

# Learn It Online

**Instructions:** To complete the Learn It Online exercises, visit the Management Information Systems CourseMate Web site at **www.cengagebrain.com**, navigate to the resources for this chapter, and click the link for the exercise you want to complete.

## 1 Chapter Reinforcement

### TF, MC, and SA

Click the Chapter Reinforcement link. Print the quiz by clicking Print on the File menu for each page. Answer each question.

## 2 Flash Cards

Click the Flash Cards link and read the instructions. Type 20 (or a number specified by your instructor) in the Number of playing cards text box, type your name in the Enter your Name text box, and then click the Flip Card button. When the flash card is displayed, read the question and then click the ANSWER box arrow to select an answer. Flip through the Flash Cards. If your score is 15 (75%) correct or greater, click Print on the File menu to print your results. If your score is less than 15 (75%) correct, then redo this exercise by clicking the Replay button.

## 3 Practice Test

Click the Practice Test link. Answer each question, enter your first and last name at the bottom of the page, and then click the Grade Test button. When the graded practice test is displayed on your screen, click Print on the File menu to print a hard copy. Continue to take practice tests until you score 80% or better.

## 4 Who Wants To Be a Computer Genius?

Click the Computer Genius link. Read the instructions, enter your first and last name at the bottom of the page, and then click the Play button. When your score is displayed, click the PRINT RESULTS link to print a hard copy.

## 5 Wheel of Terms

Click the Wheel of Terms link. Read the instructions, and then enter your first and last name and your school name. Click the PLAY button. When your score is displayed on the screen, right-click the score and then click Print on the shortcut menu to print a hard copy.

## 6 Crossword Puzzle Challenge

Click the Crossword Puzzle Challenge link. Read the instructions, and then enter your first and last name. Click the SUBMIT button. Work the crossword puzzle. When you are finished, click the Submit button. When the crossword puzzle is displayed, click the Print Puzzle button to print a hard copy.

## SCR Associates Case Simulation  Session 2: Analyzing the Business Case

### Overview

The SCR Associates case study is a Web-based simulation that allows you to practice your skills in a real-world environment. The case study transports you to SCR's intranet, where you complete 12 work sessions, each aligning with a chapter. As you work on the case, you will receive e-mail and voice mail messages, obtain information from SCR's online libraries, and perform various tasks.

### How do I use the case?

- Review the SCR background material in Chapter 1.
- Read the Preview for this session and study the Task List
- Visit the Management Information Systems CourseMate Web site at **www.cengagebrain.com**, navigate to the **SCR Case Simulation**, and locate the intranet link.
- Enter your name and the password **sad9e**. An opening screen will display the 12 sessions.
- Select this session. Check your e-mail and voice mail carefully, and then work on the tasks.

### Preview: Session 2

During your orientation, you found your way around the office and had a chance to explore the SCR Internet site. Now, after a week on the job, your supervisor, Jesse Baker, has explained the new TIMS system and asked you to lead the systems development effort. She suggested that you review SCR's mission statement, think about a systems review committee, draft a project scope statement, and prepare to interview people to learn more about the new system.

### Task List

| |
|---|
| 1.  We need a corporate goal for SCR that refers to our new training activity. Prepare a draft to show Jesse. |
| 2.  Jesse wants my opinion on whether or not SCR needs a system review committee. Need to prepare a recommendation and reasons. |
| 3.  Draft a project scope statement for the TIMS system and describe the constraints. She said be specific. |
| 4.  Need to identify the people I want to interview to learn more about the new training activity, and prepare a list of the questions I will ask. |

**FIGURE 2-26**  Task list: Session 2.

# Chapter Exercises

## Review Questions

1. What is a business case? How does a business case affect an IT project?
2. What is a SWOT analysis and why is it important?
3. What are five common reasons for systems projects?
4. What are some internal and external factors that affect systems projects?
5. What are some advantages and disadvantages of a systems review committee?
6. What is feasibility? List and briefly discuss four feasibility tests.
7. How do tangible benefits differ from intangible benefits?
8. What are the steps in a preliminary investigation?
9. What is project scope? What is a constraint? In what three ways are constraints classified?
10. Explain how you might use fishbone diagrams, Pareto charts, and XY charts in problem-solving. Be specific, and describe the advantages of each tool.

## Discussion Topics

1. Directives from top management often trigger IT projects. Suppose that the vice president of marketing tells you to write a program to create mailing labels for a one-time advertising promotion. As the IT manager, you know that the labels can be prepared more efficiently by simply exporting the data to a word processing program with a mail merge feature. How would you handle this situation?
2. The vice president of accounting says to you, the IT director, "This systems development life cycle stuff takes too long." She tells you that her people know what they are doing and that all systems requests coming from her department are necessary and important to the organization. She suggests that the IT department bypass the initial steps for any accounting department request and immediately get to work at the solution. What would you say to her?
3. One of your coworkers says, "Mission statements are nice, but they really don't change things down here where the work gets done." How would you reply?
4. Would you continue to work for a company if you disagreed with the firm's mission statement? Why or why not?

# Apply Your Knowledge

The section contains four mini-cases. Each case describes a situation, explains your role in the case, and asks you to respond to questions. You can answer the questions by applying knowledge you learned in the chapter.

## 1  Last Chance Securities

**Situation:**

The IT director opened the department staff meeting today by saying "I've got some good news and some bad news. The good news is that management approved the payroll system project this morning. The new system will reduce clerical time and errors, improve morale in the payroll department, and avoid possible fines and penalties for noncompliance. The bad news is that the system must be installed by the end of December in order to meet new federal reporting rules, costs must be within the budgeted amount, the new system must interact with existing systems, and the vice president of finance insists on approving the final design."

1. Name the constraints and indicate whether each is present, future, internal, external, mandatory, or desirable.
2. Explain why it is important to define the payroll project's scope. Explain how to define project scope.
3. Identify tangible and intangible benefits of the new payroll system.
4. What topics should be included in a report to management at the end of the preliminary investigation?

## 2  Way Out Bikes

**Situation:**

The owner of Way Out Bikes asked you for advice about acquiring an information system for her business. The company specializes in helping customers select exactly the right bicycle for their needs and lifestyles. Way Out cannot compete on price with mass merchandisers, but it seeks to offer value and expertise for which customers are willing to pay. You ask the owner whether she has long-range plans for the company, and she replies that she has not really thought beyond a one-year time frame.

1. Explain the concept of strategic planning to Way Out's owner.
2. Decide what else you might want to know about Way Out. Consider the internal and external factors described on pages 59 to 61, and make a list of questions to ask the  owner.
3. Draft a mission statement for Way Out.
4. Make a list of Way Out's stakeholders.

## 3 The Monday IT Department Staff Meeting

**Situation:**

Your boss, the IT manager, was ready to explode. "Why can't we get our priorities straight?" he fumed. "Here we go again, working on a low-value project, just because it's a favorite of the marketing group. I wish we could get away from departmental politics! I want you to draft a memo that proposes a systems review committee for this company. Explain the advantages, but don't step on anyone's toes!"

1. Write a draft of the proposal, as your boss requested.
2. Write a memo to your boss explaining potential disadvantages of the committee approach.
3. Draft a set of ground rules for committee meetings. Try to suggest rules that will minimize political differences and focus on the overall benefit to the company.
4. Most people serve on a committee at some point in their lives. Write a brief memo describing your committee experiences, good or bad.

## 4 The Friday IT Department Staff Meeting

**Situation:**

By the end of the week, things quieted down. The IT staff discussed how to prioritize IT project requests, taking into account technical, operational, economic, and schedule feasibility. The IT manager asked for suggestions from the group.

1. Provide three examples of why a project might lack technical feasibility.
2. Provide three examples of why a project might lack operational feasibility.
3. Provide three examples of why a project might lack economic feasibility.
4. Provide three examples of why a project might lack schedule feasibility.

# Case Studies

Case studies allow you to practice specific skills learned in the chapter. Each chapter contains several case studies that continue throughout the textbook, and a chapter capstone case.

## NEW CENTURY HEALTH CLINIC

New Century Health Clinic offers preventive medicine and traditional medical care. In your role as an IT consultant, you will help New Century develop a new information system.

### Background

New Century Health Clinic's office manager, Anita Davenport, recently asked permission to hire an additional office clerk because she feels the current staff can no longer handle the growing workload. The associates discussed Anita's request during a recent meeting. They were not surprised that the office staff was feeling overwhelmed by the constantly growing workload.

Because the clinic was busier and more profitable than ever, they all agreed that New Century could afford to hire another office worker. Dr. Jones then came up with another idea. He suggested that they investigate the possibility of computerizing New Century's office systems. Dr. Jones said that a computerized system could keep track of patients, appointments, charges, and insurance claim processing and reduce paperwork. All the associates were enthusiastic about the possibilities and voted to follow up on the suggestion. Dr. Jones agreed to direct the project.

Because no member of the staff had computer experience, Dr. Jones decided to hire a consultant to study the current office systems and recommend a course of action. Several friends recommended you as a person who has considerable experience with computerized business applications.

### Assignments

1. Dr. Jones has arranged an introductory meeting between the associates of New Century Health Clinic and you to determine if mutual interest exists in pursuing the project. What should the associates try to learn about you? What should you try to learn in this meeting?
2. Does the proposed system present a strong business case? Why or why not?
3. For each type of feasibility, prepare at least two questions that will help you reach a feasibility determination.
4. You begin the preliminary investigation. What information is needed? From whom will you obtain it? What techniques will you use in your fact-finding?

## PERSONAL TRAINER, INC.

Personal Trainer, Inc., owns and operates fitness centers in a dozen midwestern cities. The centers have done well, and the company is planning an international expansion by opening a new "supercenter" in the Toronto area. Personal Trainer's president, Cassia Umi, hired an IT consultant, Susan Park, to help develop an information system for the new facility. During the project, Susan will work closely with Gray Lewis, who will manage the new operation.

### Background

At their initial meeting, Susan and Gray discussed some initial steps in planning a new information system for the new facility. The next morning, they worked together on a business profile, drew an organization chart, discussed feasibility issues, and talked about various types of information systems that would provide the best support for the supercenter's operations. Their main objective was to carry out a preliminary investigation of the new system and report their recommendations to Personal Trainer's top managers.

After the working session with Gray, Susan returned to her office and reviewed her notes. She knew that Personal Trainer's president, Cassia Umi, wanted the supercenter to become a model for the company's future growth, but she did not remember any mention of an overall strategic plan for the company. Susan also wondered whether the firm had done a SWOT analysis or analyzed the internal and external factors that might affect an information system for the supercenter.

Because the new operation would be so important to the company, Susan believed that Personal Trainer should consider an enterprise resource planning strategy that could provide a company-wide framework for information management. After she finished compiling her notes, Susan listed several topics that might need more study and called Gray to arrange another meeting the following day.

### Assignments

1. Based on the background facts described in Chapter 1, draft a mission statement for Personal Trainer. Consider the firm's overall direction, and the services, products, and experiences the company might want to offer its customers in the future. In your statement, consider all the stakeholders affected by Personal Trainer's operations.

2. Susan and Gray probably will need more information about the proposed system. Make a list of people whom they might want to interview. Also, suggest other fact-finding techniques they should consider.

3. Consider the internal and external factors that affect information systems. Which factors, in your opinion, will have the greatest impact on the system proposed for the new supercenter? Explain your answer.

4. At the conclusion of the preliminary investigation, Susan and Gray will deliver a written summary of the results and deliver a brief presentation to Personal Trainer's management team. Prepare a list of recommendations that will help make their written and oral communications more effective. Put your list in priority order, starting with what you consider to be the most important suggestions. Before you complete this task, you should review Appendix A, which provides suggestions for oral and written presentations.

## ORIGINAL KAYAK ADVENTURES

Original Kayak Adventures (OKA) offers guided eco-tours and kayak rentals along the Hudson River.

### Background

In Chapter 1, you learned that John and Edie Caputo founded OKA two years ago. Now John and Edie are thinking about replacing their current system, which is a mix of manual and computer-based techniques, with a new information system that would meet their current and future needs. Before you answer the following questions, you should review the fact statement in Chapter 1.

### Assignments

1. Does a strong business case exist for developing an information system to support the Caputos' business? Explain your answer.

2. In a small- to medium-sized business, such as OKA, is it really important to use a structured approach for information systems development? Why or why not?

3. Based on the facts provided, draft a mission statement for OKA. In your statement, consider all the stakeholders who might be affected by OKA operations.

4. What internal and external factors might affect OKA's business success?

## TOWN OF EDEN BAY

The town of Eden Bay owns and maintains a fleet of vehicles. You are a systems analyst reporting to Dawn, the town's IT manager.

### Background

Eden Bay is a medium-sized municipality. The town has grown rapidly, and so has the demand for town services. Eden Bay currently owns 90 vehicles, which the town's equipment department maintains. The fleet includes police cars, sanitation trucks, fire trucks, and other vehicles assigned to town employees. The maintenance budget has risen sharply in recent years, and people are asking whether the town should continue to perform its own maintenance or outsource it to private firms.

This morning, Dawn called you into her office to discuss the situation. A summary of her comments follows.

**Dawn (IT manager):** When I came here two years ago, I was told that Eden Bay had a computerized information system for vehicle maintenance. What I found was a spreadsheet application designed by a part-time employee as a quick answer to a much more complex problem. It's probably better than no system at all, but I can't justify spending any time on it. The system should never have been designed as a spreadsheet in the first place.

I've discussed the situation with the equipment department people. Rather than tinker with the current system, I think we should press for a new information system project, and I've developed an initial proposal. I've code-named the new system RAVE, which stands for Repair Analysis for Vehicular Equipment. I know that commercial fleet maintenance packages exist, but they are very expensive.

I did some fact-finding, and I want you to start by reading the interview summaries I prepared.

### Before You Begin ...

Review the following interview summaries from Marie (town manager), Martin (equipment department manager), Phil (maintenance supervisor), Alice (maintenance clerk), and Joe (mechanic).

**Marie (town manager):** Maintenance costs have risen 14 to 16% annually. I'm not sure that we have any real control over these costs. Some members of the town council think we should get out of the maintenance business and contract it out to a private firm. That might mean laying off current employees, and I'm not sure whether outsourcing is the right way to go.

Both the equipment department manager and the IT manager tell me that our current record-keeping system is outdated, and I wonder if a new information system would give us a better handle on the problem. My own view is that if there's a way we can become more efficient, we should continue to perform our own maintenance.

Dawn, our IT manager, tells me that she has developed a proposal for a maintenance information system. I plan to bring it up at the next council meeting.

**Martin (equipment department manager):** I hear a lot of criticism about the maintenance budget, but I'm doing the best I can. We operate from one budget year to the next, without a long-term plan. I belong to a professional association of fleet maintenance managers, and I know that we should be developing a strategic plan instead of juggling annual budget figures.

I'd like to build this department into a first-class organization. Our people are great, but they could use more technical training. Our shop and equipment are generally adequate for what we do, but we haven't kept up with some of the newer diagnostic equipment. We have a real problem in record keeping. Instead of a short-term solution, Eden Bay should have developed a maintenance information system years ago. Prior to taking this position, I was assistant maintenance manager in a medium-sized city, and they had developed a system that handled scheduling and cost analysis, in addition to day-to-day maintenance operations.

**Phil (maintenance supervisor):** I'm in the middle — I get pressure from above to cut costs, and I get complaints from below that management doesn't know what it's doing. One thing for sure — short-term solutions are not the answer. I hope they don't ask me to cut back on preventive maintenance. The last time we did that, we extended routine oil changes and servicing, and we ended up with even more repairs than we had previously.

My mechanics are capable people, and they're doing the best they can. One problem I see is that it's hard to pull up a history for a particular vehicle. We keep the data on a computer, but different people used different codes and procedures over the years, and the system probably needs a good overhaul.

**Alice (maintenance clerk):** I'm in charge of maintenance record keeping. We use a spreadsheet system that was designed by a part-time employee who is no longer around. Because we work on a monthly budget, the spreadsheet has a separate page for each month. When the year is over, we start a new set of monthly pages. The spreadsheet is supposed to record labor and parts used, and assign the cost to a specific vehicle, but it doesn't always work out that way.

I also use a notebook to keep track of vehicle mileage and scheduled service intervals, so I can let the department heads know when a vehicle needs to come in for service. I write up work orders for scheduled service or necessary repairs, but often a mechanic finds other problems and has to write up an additional charges form.

Each time a vehicle comes into the shop, I start a new row on the spreadsheet. I enter the vehicle number, mileage, and date. Then I enter the rest of the data into the columns for parts, labor hours, job code, shop supplies, and miscellaneous charges. At the end of the month, I calculate total costs from the spreadsheet, and we compare these with actual payroll and parts vouchers for the month. If the totals are close, everyone is happy. If not, we try to figure out what work didn't get reported and entered into the spreadsheet.

The labor codes also are a problem. Specific codes are assigned for certain types of shop labor, but these were changed three years ago when the new Director arrived. Also, about half the labor can be coded, but the rest has to be entered manually — and there are no standards. Two mechanics might do the same job, and one records four specific tasks, while the other calls it a tune-up.

I know the mechanics don't like paperwork, but what can I do? I asked the IT manager if she could do anything to help, but she says that it isn't worthwhile to update the current system. She says she has heard some talk about developing a new information system specifically designed for vehicle fleet maintenance. It can't be soon enough for me.

**Joe (mechanic):** I love my job, but I hate the paperwork. We get a work order from the clerk for all scheduled maintenance, but if we find other problems, we have to handwrite an additional work ticket. Personally, I think some of these vehicles should be retired before they get too expensive to maintain.

I would hate to see the town contract out the maintenance. I've put in 17 years here, and I don't want to lose my job, but I know that some specialized repairs would be less expensive on the outside. Most of the mechanics realize this, but let management figure it out — they're the ones with the fancy computer system.

### Assignments

1. Upon investigation, you learn that the town does not have a strategic plan or a mission statement. In your view, does this affect the current situation? Why or why not?

2. Based on the fact statements provided, summarize the maintenance department's most important strengths, weaknesses, opportunities, and threats.

3. Describe the specific steps you will follow during a preliminary investigation, including any fact-finding techniques you will use. Be sure to include the tools mentioned in this chapter.

4. Of the four tests of feasibility — operational, technical, economic, and schedule — which would you perform first to measure the system project's feasibility? Why?

# CHAPTER CAPSTONE CASE:   SoftWear, Limited

SoftWear, Limited (SWL), is a continuing case study that illustrates the knowledge and skills described in each chapter. In this case study, the student acts as a member of the SWL systems development team and performs various tasks.

## Background

SWL outsources the company's payroll processing to an outside firm called Business Information Systems (BIS). SWL's payroll department submits data to BIS, which uses its own hardware and software to produce employee paychecks and generate payroll reports. BIS performs payroll processing for dozens of companies. Contractual agreements between BIS and its customers identify specific information processing services and prices.

SWL's information technology department is located at the company headquarters in Raleigh and reports to the vice president of finance. The IT staff is responsible for SWL's mainframe computer and supports the company's Web site and the inventory, marketing, customer order entry, and accounting systems.

Robert Lansing, SWL's president, believes that IT support is vital to the company's strategic long-range plans and has approved increased IT budgets and expansion of the IT staff. In addition to the mainframe, the company networked personal computers in all offices and many shop floor locations and implemented a company intranet linking all SWL locations.

Even though it could handle its own payroll processing, SWL continues to use BIS for payroll services because BIS does a good job at a reasonable cost, and it relieves SWL of this responsibility. Recently, problems with the payroll system developed, and SWL's payroll department employees had to work overtime to correct errors involving employee deductions.

SWL employees can make two types of voluntary payroll deductions. Starting in 2007, employees could contribute to the newly formed SWL credit union. To enroll or make changes, an employee must complete a deduction form. In 2009, the company gave employees an opportunity to purchase SWL company stock through payroll deductions. Employees enroll in the stock purchase plan or change their deductions by visiting the human resources department, which then sends a weekly list of transactions to SWL's payroll department.

In addition to the credit union and stock purchase deductions, SWL employees soon may have other savings and investment choices. SWL's top management, with strong support from the vice president of human resources, may consider a new Employee Savings and Investment Plan (ESIP) that allows employees to purchase mutual funds, stocks, and other investments through regular payroll deductions. Under this new 401(k) plan, an outside investment firm, Court Street Securities, manages tax-sheltered deductions and services the individual accounts. Each employee maintains direct control over his or her investments using a 24-hour toll-free number or accessing the Court Street Securities Web site. Management expects to make a final decision about the new ESIP in several months.

## Request for Information Technology Services

Rob King, vice president of human resources, learned that a number of SWL employees had complained about improper paycheck deductions, and he became concerned about employee morale. He decided to discuss the subject with Michael Jeremy, vice president of finance. After the meeting, Mr. Jeremy met with Amy Calico, director of payroll, to ask her about the problem — and a recent increase in overtime pay in her group. Amy stated that the overtime became necessary because payroll operations recently required more time and effort. She also noted that, because this workload increase came about recently, she lacked the money in her budget to hire any additional people. She did not provide any specific explanation for the payroll deduction errors.

**CHAPTER CAPSTONE CASE: SoftWear, Limited (continued)**    **SWL**

Mr. Jeremy then decided to ask the IT department to investigate the payroll system. He prepared a systems request, as shown in Figure 2-27, and sent it to the IT department for action. In the request, he mentioned problems with the payroll system and requested help but did not identify the causes of the problems or propose a solution.

Jane Rossman, manager of applications, normally receives systems requests and does an initial review. After a quick look at Mr. Jeremy's request, Jane decided to contact her boss, Ann Hon, director of information technology. After discussing the proposal, Jane and Ann decided that a preliminary investigation should start right away. Given that the system was eight years old and had never received a major update, it seemed likely that they would find some problems. Jane assigned Rick Williams, a systems analyst, to conduct the preliminary investigation.

**FIGURE 2-27** Michael Jeremy's systems request.

## Payroll Department Organization

Rick's first meeting was with Rob King, vice president of human resources. He gave Rick copies of job descriptions for all payroll department positions but did not have a current organization chart for that group.

After reviewing the descriptions, Rick visited Amy Calico, director of payroll. She explained how the payroll department was organized. She explained that two people report directly to her: Nelson White, payroll manager, and Nancy Farmer, administrative assistant. Two payroll technicians, Britton Ellis and Debra Williams, report to Nelson White.

## Interviews

Rick next decided to interview Michael Jeremy, Amy Calico, and Mike Feiner, director of human resources.

Mr. Jeremy provided an overview of the recent problems within the payroll system, including the costs of the current system. He had no specific data, but he thought that the majority of the errors involved stock purchases rather than credit union deductions.

Later that day, in his meeting with Mike Feiner, Rick found out more about the reported deduction errors. He learned that stock purchase enrollments and changes are handled differently from credit union deductions. For legal reasons, Mike explained, employees must complete a special form for stock purchase plan transactions. When enrolling or making changes, an employee visits the human resources department for a brochure and an information package called a prospectus, which also includes the form required to enroll. At the end of each week, the human resources department prepares a summary of deduction requests and sends it to the payroll department. Payroll clerks then file the changes with the employee's master record.

The next morning, Rick again met with Amy Calico. In the interview, Amy told Rick that some problems with deductions existed, but she did not feel that the payroll clerks were at fault. She suggested that he look elsewhere for the source of the problem. Amy stated that the payroll process generally works well, although it requires a substantial amount of manual effort. She said that if she could hire two additional clerks, it would resolve any remaining problems. During the course of the meeting, Rick began to feel that Amy's opinion might be somewhat biased. As payroll director, she might not want to call attention to problems in her department, and Rick guessed, that some other issues might be involved. He decided to keep this possibility in mind as the investigation continued.

## Current Documentation

After completing the three interviews, Rick reviewed his notes and decided to find out more about the actual sequence of operations in the current system. He studied the documentation and found that it provided step-by-step procedures for preparing the payroll. When he asked the payroll clerks about those procedures, he learned that some sections were outdated. The actual sequence of events is shown in Figure 2-28.

**Step 1:** A new SWL employee completes an employee master sheet and a W-4 form. The human resources department then enters the employee's status and pay rate. Copies of these forms are sent to the payroll department. The payroll department updates the employee master sheet whenever changes are received from the employee or the human resources department. Updates are made with various forms, including forms for credit union and employee stock purchase plan enrollment and changes.

**Step 2:** On the last day of a weekly pay period, the payroll department prepares and distributes time sheets to all SWL departments. The time sheets list each employee, with codes for various status items such as regular pay, overtime, sick leave, vacation, jury duty, and personal leave.

**Step 3:** Department heads complete the time sheets on the first business day after the end of a pay period. The sheets then go to the payroll department, where they are reviewed. A payroll clerk enters pay rates and deduction information and forwards the time sheets to the BIS service bureau.

**Step 4:** BIS enters and processes the time sheet data, prints SWL paychecks, and prepares a payroll register.

**Step 5:** The checks, time sheets, and payroll register are returned to SWL. The payroll department distributes checks to each department, creates reports for credit union and stock purchase plan deductions, and then transfers necessary funds.

**FIGURE 2-28**  Sequence of events in payroll processing at SoftWear, Limited.

Rick also discovered that the payroll department never sees a copy of the form that an employee fills out in the human resources department when joining the stock purchase plan or changing deductions. Rick obtained a copy of the SWL stock purchase form from the human resources department and copies of several forms from the payroll department — including employee master sheets, employee time sheets, and credit union deduction forms. Rick put them in a file for later review.

During the preliminary investigation, Rick did not show concern with the detailed information on each form. He would review that information only after management authorized the IT department to continue with the systems analysis phase.

## CHAPTER CAPSTONE CASE:   SoftWear, Limited (continued)

### Presentation to Management

After Rick finished his investigation, he analyzed his findings, prepared a preliminary investigation report, and met with Jane and Ann to plan the presentation to management. Ann sent an advance copy of the report to Mr. Jeremy with an e-mail that announced the time and location of the presentation.

Figure 2-29 shows the preliminary investigation report. Following the presentation to SWL's top managers and department heads, a question-and-answer session took place. The management group discussed the findings and recommendations and decided that the payroll system needed further analysis. The group also wanted to know if the BIS service bureau could handle the ESIP using their current arrangement. Ann replied that no clear answer could be given, and everyone agreed that the project scope should be broadened to include that question.

---

**Preliminary Investigation Report:  SWL Payroll System**          **October 10, 2011**

**Introduction**
The IT department completed a preliminary investigation of the payroll system on October 8. This investigation was the result of a systems request submitted by Michael Jeremy, vice president, finance, on September 17.

**Systems Request Summary**
Two problems were mentioned in the request: incorrect deductions from employee paychecks, and excessive payroll department overtime to perform manual processing tasks and make corrections.

**Preliminary Investigation Findings**
1.     The human resources department sends a summary of employee stock purchase deductions to the payroll department. It is likely that data errors occur during this process. Although the errors are corrected, we believe that incorrect payroll information adversely affects employee morale.

2.     The payroll processing arrangement with Business Information Systems (BIS) requires considerable manual effort. BIS does not provide summary reports that SWL needs to verify and apply credit union and stock purchase deductions. Currently, the payroll department handles these tasks manually at the end of each pay period.

3.     Payroll department overtime averages about eight hours per week, plus an additional eight hours at the end of the month, when stock purchase deductions are applied. Total annual overtime is about 512 hours. The average hourly base rate for payroll staff is $16.00, with an overtime rate of $24.00 per hour. The additional expense is about $12,288 per year.

4.     SWL developed its current payroll procedures 10 years ago, when the company had only 75 employees. At that time, the only payroll deductions were legally required tax items. Today, the payroll system handles over 450 people and many deduction options that must be verified and applied manually.

**Recommendations**
The current problems will intensify as SWL continues to grow. At this point, it is unclear whether the current system can be modified to handle tasks that are being done manually. Accordingly, the IT department recommends a full analysis of the current system and possible solutions. The project should focus on two main areas: manual processing at SWL and computer-based payroll processing at BIS.

**Time and Cost Estimates**
We can perform a study during a two-week period. In addition to the time spent by IT staff, we will conduct about 20 hours of interviews with people outside the IT department. The following is a rough estimate of costs through the systems analysis phase:

| | | |
|---|---|---|
| Systems analyst | 2.0 weeks @ $1,400 per week | $2,800 |
| Other SWL staff | 0.5 weeks @ $1,000 per week (average) | 500 |
| | Total: | $3,300 |

If the project continues beyond the systems analysis phase, total cost will depend on what development strategy is followed. If the current system can be modified, we estimate a total project effort of $20,000 to $30,000 over a four-month period. If modification is not feasible, a revised cost estimate will be submitted.

**Expected Benefits**
A sharp reduction in overtime costs and processing errors will avoid unnecessary expense and improve employee morale. During the systems analysis phase, the IT department will investigate various strategies and solutions to address current problems and strengthen SWL's ability to handle payroll-related IT issues in the future.

---

**FIGURE 2-29**  A typical preliminary investigation report includes findings, recommendations, and estimated costs and benefits.

## CHAPTER CAPSTONE CASE:    SoftWear, Limited (continued)    SWL

### SWL Team Tasks

1.  You have been assigned to write a formal mission statement for SWL. Start by reviewing SWL's background in Chapter 1, then do Internet research to find mission statements that seem clear, focused, and easy to understand. Pay special attention to Web-based and catalog retail firms to see how they approach the issue.

2.  Review the preliminary investigation report to see whether all four feasibility tests were discussed in the report. Write a brief summary of your findings.

3.  Review the payroll department organization information on page 94. Using this information, prepare an organization chart for this group. In Word 2010 and Word 2007, click the Insert tab on the Ribbon, then SmartArt, then Hierarchy.

4.  Rick asked you to investigate other firms that offer payroll processing services. Perform an Internet search using the term "payroll processing services." Try your search both with and without placing quotes around the phrase and notice what happens. Based on your search results, select an example of a payroll processing firm and write a brief report to Rick. Include the firm's name, Web address, and services offered.

### Manage the SWL Project

You have been asked to manage SWL's new information system project. One of your most important activities will be to identify project tasks and determine when they will be performed. Before you begin, you should review the SWL case in this chapter. Then list and analyze the tasks, as follows:

**LIST THE TASKS** Start by listing and numbering at least 10 tasks that the SWL team needs to perform to fulfill the objectives of this chapter. Your list can include SWL Team Tasks and any other tasks that are described in this chapter. For example, Task 3 might be to Prepare a payroll department organization chart, and Task 6 might be to Review payroll department job descriptions.

**ANALYZE THE TASKS** Now study the tasks to determine the order in which they should be performed. First identify all concurrent tasks, which are not dependent on other tasks. In the example shown in Figure 2-30, Tasks 1, 2, 3, 4, and 5 are concurrent tasks, and could begin at the same time if resources were available.

Other tasks are called dependent tasks, because they cannot be performed until one or more earlier tasks have been completed. For each dependent task, you must identify specific tasks that need to be completed before this task can begin. For example, you would want an organization chart to help you identify the payroll department positions, so Task 6 cannot begin until Task 3 is completed, as Figure 2-30 shows.

**FIGURE 2-30**  Tasks 1, 2, 3, 4, and 5 are concurrent tasks that could be performed at the same time. Task 6 is a dependent task that cannot be performed until Task 3 has been completed.

## CHAPTER CAPSTONE CASE:   SoftWear, Limited (continued)

Chapter 3 describes project management tools, techniques, and software. To learn more, you can use the Features section on your Student Study Tool CD-ROM, or visit the Management Information Systems CourseMate Web site at **www.cengagebrain.com** and locate the project management resources library for this book. On the Web, Microsoft offers demo versions, training, and tips for using Project 2010 and 2007. You also can visit the OpenWorkbench.org site to learn more about this free, open-source software.

# Ready for a Challenge?

In additional to technical skills, IT professionals need critical thinking skills such as perception, organization, analysis, problem-solving, and decision-making. The Ready for a Challenge feature can help you learn, practice, and apply critical thinking skills that you can take to the workplace.

As an IT intern at Game Technology, you often assist analysts with feasibility studies. The work can include intense fact-finding and tight deadlines. You decide to add a new section to your journal to describe the four different types of feasibility. In your journal, you want to include a definition of each feasibility type, and a sample statement that would indicate a *lack* of feasibility.

For example:
- The hardware has limited capacity for future needs.
- Our users will resist the new system because it is the third change in 18 months.
- The project will take too long to pay for itself.
- Development cannot begin until next year, which is too late.

You also want to learn more about project constraints. You know that constraints can be grouped into various categories: present vs. future, internal vs. external, and mandatory vs. desirable. You plan to use a grid chart like the one in Figure 2-20 on page 75 to show the constraints. To get started, you come up with three sample constraints:
- The new IRS tax rates must go into effect as soon as possible.
- From now on, we should try to hire technicians with A+ certifications.
- Starting next year, government regulations will require a detailed security analysis.

## Practice Tasks

A. Define each feasibility type and include an example that shows a lack of feasibility.
B. Create a grid chart that shows the sample constraints. Use Figure 2-20 as a model.

After you complete the Practice Tasks, to check your work and view sample answers, visit the Management Information Systems CourseMate Web site at **www.cengagebrain.com**, navigate to the resources for this chapter, and locate Ready for a Challenge?.

## The Challenge

It's fortunate that you studied various feasibility types. Felisia Stukes, the IT director, wants you to review the following statements and decide which type of feasibility applies:
- Based on the future cost of support and maintenance, TCO will be very high.
- The network will not be ready until next year, which might be too late.
- Expensive training will be required.
- The current system is well liked and effective, and users see no need for change.
- The hardware is unreliable and will not integrate with other company systems.
- The new system will cause a workforce reduction, and employees are very concerned.
- The platform does not have capacity for future needs, and cannot be expanded.
- The project does not meet the company policy for acceptable return on investment.
- The projected benefits do not outweigh the estimated costs.
- The software will not be available until May, and that will cause an unacceptable delay.

Felesia wants to see a grid chart that will properly show the following constraints:
- Management told all departments to include "green" goals in next year's plan.
- The inventory system would be more effective if we add RFID capability next year.
- Management just announced a change in travel policy: No more first class air travel!
- Effective immediately, our products must meet all government standards.

## Challenge Tasks

A. Reply to Felesia and indicate the type of feasibility for each statement.
B. Draw a grid chart that shows the constraints. Use Figure 2–20 as a model.

# CHAPTER 3 Project Management

**Chapter 3** is the final chapter in the systems planning phase of the SDLC. In this chapter, you will learn about project management and how to plan, schedule, monitor, and report on IT projects.

## INTRODUCTION

### OBJECTIVES

*When you finish this chapter, you will be able to:*

- Explain project planning, scheduling, monitoring, and reporting

- Describe work breakdown structures, task patterns, and critical path analysis

- Explain techniques for estimating task completion times and costs

- Describe various scheduling tools, including Gantt charts and PERT/CPM charts

- Analyze task dependencies, durations, start dates, and end dates

- Describe project management software and how it can assist you in project planning, estimating, scheduling, monitoring, and reporting

- Discuss the importance of project risk management

- Understand why projects sometimes fail

Chapter 3 explains project management for IT projects. You will learn about project planning, scheduling, monitoring, reporting, and the use of project management software. You will learn how to create a work breakdown structure, identify task patterns, and calculate a critical path. You will also learn how to use Gantt charts and PERT/CPM techniques to schedule and monitor projects. Finally, you will learn how to control and manage project changes as they occur.

In addition to the project management material in this chapter, you can visit the Features section on your Student Study Tool CD-ROM, where you can learn more about Microsoft Project and Open Workbench, an open-source project management program that you can download and install. You can also visit the MIS CourseMate Web site for this book at **www.cengagebrain.com** and explore links in the SWL project management resources library.

Chapter 3 includes three Video Learning Sessions that show you how to create a work breakdown structure (WBS), how to identify task patterns, and how to calculate a project's critical path.

## CHAPTER INTRODUCTION CASE:    Mountain View College Bookstore

**Background:** Wendy Lee, manager of college services at Mountain View College, wants a new information system that will improve efficiency and customer service at the three college bookstores.

In this part of the case, Tina Allen, systems analyst, and David Conroe, student intern, are talking about project management tools and techniques.

**Participants:** Tina and David
**Location:** Mountain View College Cafeteria, Wednesday afternoon, September 21, 2011
**Discussion topics:** Project planning, Gantt charts, PERT/CPM charts, Microsoft Project and Open Workbench software, project monitoring, and risk management techniques.

**Tina:** Hi, David. Glad I ran into you. I'd like to talk with you about project management, which we'll be using as we plan and execute the bookstore information system project.

**David:** *Sure. I've read a little about project management, but I don't know the specifics.*

**Tina:** Well, we manage business and personal projects every day, but we don't always give it much thought. To manage large-scale IT projects, you need specific tools and techniques. You also need a project manager, who is responsible for planning, leading, organizing, and controlling all the tasks.

**David:** *I guess that's you?*

**Tina:** Sure is. No matter which tools you use, the idea is to break the project down into individual tasks, determine the order in which the tasks need to be performed, and figure out how long each task will take. With this information, you can use Gantt charts or PERT/CPM charts to schedule and manage the work.

**David:** *I've seen Gantt charts — they're the ones that look like horizontal bar charts?*

**Tina:** Right. In addition to Gantt charts, we'll use PERT/CPM charts, which look like network diagrams that show all the tasks, patterns, and calculations that we'll need. We'll learn how to create PERT/CPM charts manually, and we'll also experiment with Microsoft Project and Open Workbench, which are powerful project management tools.

**David:** *Anything else we need to know?*

**Tina:** Yes. After we have a specific plan, we need to monitor it carefully, report the progress, and employ a process called risk management. If you are ready, here's a task list to get us started:

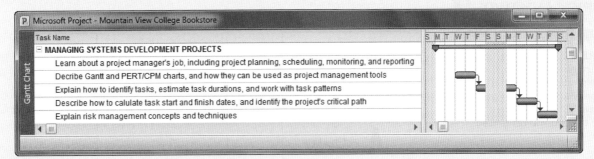

**FIGURE 3-1**   Typical project management tasks.

**FIGURE 3-2** Building construction and systems development projects both need careful management and monitoring.

# OVERVIEW OF PROJECT MANAGEMENT

Whether you are developing an information system or working on a construction project like the one in Figure 3-2, the process is the same. The only difference is the nature of the project. **Project management** for IT professionals includes planning, scheduling, monitoring and controlling, and reporting on information system development.

## What Shapes a Project?

A successful project must be completed on time, within budget, and deliver a quality product that satisfies users and meets requirements. Project management techniques can be used throughout the SDLC. System developers can initiate a formal project as early as the preliminary investigation stage, or later on, as analysis, design, and implementation activities occur.

As the sign in Figure 3-3 suggests, sometimes you have to decide what is most important. The same concept applies to systems development, where the factors include budget limits, time constraints, and quality standards. As long as everything is in balance, like the see-saw in Figure 3-4, the project will be successful. However, if one factor changes, adjustments must be made. Because the factors interact constantly, a project manager must respond quickly. For example, if an extremely time-critical project starts to slip, the project manager might have to trim some features, seek approval for a budget increase, simplify the testing plan, or a combination of all three actions.

Unfortunately, many systems projects do fail. A report by The Standish Group noted that only a third of all software development projects were successful, in the sense that they met budget, schedule, and quality targets. Standish chairman Jim Johnson said that improvement will require better project management tools, more iterative methods, and better communication between project developers and users.

**FIGURE 3-3** The sign at this imaginary garage tells an old story, which also applies to project management. Sometimes, if you can't have all three, you must choose the two you really need.

**FIGURE 3-4** If one factor changes, adjustments must be made to keep things in balance.

## What Does a Project Manager Do?

Whether a project involves a new office building or an information system, good leadership is essential. In a systems project, the **project manager**, or **project leader**, usually is a senior systems analyst or an IT department manager if the project is large. An analyst or a programmer/analyst might manage smaller projects. In addition to the project manager, most large projects have a project coordinator. A **project coordinator** handles administrative responsibilities for the team and negotiates with users who might have conflicting requirements or want changes that would require additional time or expense. Project managers typically perform four activities, or functions: planning, scheduling, monitoring, and reporting.

- **Project planning** includes identifying all project tasks and estimating the completion time and cost of each.

- **Project scheduling** involves the creation of a specific timetable, usually in the form of charts that show tasks, task dependencies, and critical tasks that might delay the project. Scheduling also involves selecting and staffing the project team and assigning specific tasks to team members. Project scheduling uses Gantt charts and PERT/CPM charts, which are explained in the following sections.

- **Project monitoring** requires guiding, supervising, and coordinating the project team's workload. The project manager must monitor the progress, evaluate the results, and take corrective action when necessary to control the project and stay on target.

- **Project reporting** includes regular progress reports to management, users, and the project team itself. Effective reporting requires strong communication skills and a sense of what others want and need to know about the project.

## CASE IN POINT 3.1:  Spring Forward Products

After three years with the company, you recently were asked to manage several IT projects. You are confident that you have the technical skills you need, but you are concerned about morale at the company. There has been some downsizing, and many employees are worried about the future.

As a longtime fan of the Dilbert cartoon strip, you know that maintaining morale can be a real challenge. Your current project involves a team of a dozen people, several of whom remind you of Dilbert and his coworkers. What are some techniques that you might use to motivate the team and inspire its members? What are some things you might *not* want to do?

## Project Activities and Planning Steps

On any given day, a project manager might perform one or more of the activities listed above. However, as Figure 3-5 suggests, each activity is part of a larger framework, which includes three key steps in project planning:

- Create a work breakdown structure.
- Identify task patterns.
- Calculate the critical path.

The matrix in Figure 3-5 on the next page shows typical activities that the project leader performs as the project develops. When the project becomes operational, he or she also manages the people, the schedule, the budget, and the progress.

| | Planning | Scheduling | Monitoring | Reporting |
|---|---|---|---|---|
| STEP1: Create a work breakdown structure | ✓ | | | |
| STEP 2: Identify task patterns | ✓ | ✓ | | |
| STEP 3: Calculate the critical path | ✓ | ✓ | | |
| Manage the operational project | | | ✓ | ✓ |

**FIGURE 3-5** The matrix is a typical sample of management activities performed while the project is being developed, and when it is launched.

The following sections describe the three project development steps. You can view a Video Learning Session before, during, or after you study each step.

## STEP 1: CREATE A WORK BREAKDOWN STRUCTURE

A **work breakdown structure (WBS)** involves breaking a project down into a series of smaller tasks. Before creating work breakdown structures, you should understand the two primary chart types: Gantt charts and PERT/CPM charts.

### What Is a Gantt Chart?

Gantt charts were developed almost 100 years ago by Henry L. Gantt, a mechanical engineer and management consultant. His goal was to design a chart that could show planned and actual progress on a project. A **Gantt chart** is a horizontal bar chart that represents a set of tasks. For example, the Gantt chart in Figure 3-6 displays five tasks in a vertical array, with time shown on the horizontal axis. The position of the bar shows the planned starting and ending time of each task, and the length of the bar indicates its duration. On the horizontal axis, time can be shown as elapsed time from a fixed starting point, or as actual calendar dates. A Gantt chart also can simplify a complex project by combining several activities into a **task group**. For example, in Figure 3-6, Task 4 might consist of five separate tasks, which are hidden in this view.

## VIDEO LEARNING SESSION: WORK BREAKDOWN STRUCTURES

Video Learning Sessions can help you understand key concepts, practice your skills, and check your work. To access the sessions, visit the Management Information Systems CourseMate Web site at **www.cengagebrain.com** and navigate to the **Video Learning Sessions** for this book. This session is about work breakdown structures. You'll learn what a work breakdown is and why it is important, how to create a work breakdown structure, and how to use Microsoft Project to display a work breakdown structure.

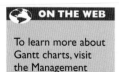

**ON THE WEB**

To learn more about Gantt charts, visit the Management Information Systems CourseMate Web site at **www. cengagebrain. com**, navigate to **On the Web Links** for this chapter, and locate the Gantt Charts link.

**FIGURE 3-6** In this Gantt chart, notice the task group represented by Task 4. Also notice the yellow bars that show the percentage of task completion.

A Gantt chart can show task status by adding a contrasting color to the horizontal bars. For example, a vertical arrow marks the current date in Figure 3-6. With a fixed reference point, it is easy to see that Task 1 is way behind schedule, Task 2 is only about 80 percent done and is running behind schedule, Task 3 should have started, but no work has been done, Task 4 actually is running ahead of schedule, and Task 5 will begin in several weeks.

Gantt charts can present an overview of the project's status, but they do not provide enough detailed information, which is necessary when managing a complex project. Most project managers find that PERT/CPM charts, which are discussed in the following section, are better tools for managing large projects.

## What Is a PERT/CPM Chart?

The **Program Evaluation Review Technique (PERT)** was developed by the U.S. Navy to manage very complex projects, such as the construction of nuclear submarines. At approximately the same time, the **Critical Path Method (CPM)** was developed by private industry to meet similar project management needs. The distinction between the two methods has disappeared over time, and today the technique is called either PERT, CPM, or **PERT/CPM**. The textbook will use the term PERT chart.

PERT is a **bottom-up technique**, because it analyzes a large, complex project as a series of individual tasks. To create a PERT chart, you first identify all the project tasks and estimate how much time each task will take to perform. Next, you must determine the logical order in which the tasks must be performed. For example, some tasks cannot start until other tasks have been completed. In other situations, several tasks can be performed at the same time.

Once you know the tasks, their durations, and the order in which they must be performed, you can calculate the time that it will take to complete the project. You also can identify the specific tasks that will be critical to the project's on-time completion. An example of a PERT chart, which Microsoft calls a **network diagram**, is shown in the lower screen in Figure 3-7.

## Which Type of Chart Is Better?

Although a Gantt chart offers a valuable snapshot view of the project, PERT charts are more useful for scheduling, monitoring, and controlling the actual work. With a PERT chart, a project manager can convert task start and finish times to actual dates by laying out the entire project on a calendar. Then, on any given day, the manager can compare what *should* be happening with what *is* taking place, and react accordingly. Also, a PERT chart displays complex task patterns and relationships. This information is valuable to a manager who is trying to address high priority issues. PERT and Gantt charts are not mutually exclusive techniques, and project managers often use both methods.

Figure 3-7 shows both chart types. The top screen is a Gantt chart with 11 tasks. The PERT chart in the bottom screen shows the same project, using a separate box for each task instead of a horizontal

**ON THE WEB**

To learn more about PERT/CPM, visit the Management Information Systems CourseMate Web site at **www. cengagebrain. com**, navigate to **On the Web Links** for this chapter, and locate the PERT/ CPM link.

**FIGURE 3-7**   The top screen is a Gantt chart with 11 tasks, and a PERT chart in the bottom screen shows the same project. Although not visible in this zoomed-out view, the PERT chart boxes provide detailed information about task duration, start dates, and finish dates.

bar. Although they both show the task patterns and flow, the PERT chart boxes can provide more detailed information, such as task duration, start date, and finish date. You will learn how to create PERT charts in following sections.

## Identifying Tasks in a Work Breakdown Structure

A work breakdown structure must clearly identify each task and include an estimated duration. A **task**, or **activity**, is any work that has a beginning and an end and requires the use of company resources such as people, time, or money. Examples of tasks include conducting interviews, designing a report, selecting software, waiting for the delivery of equipment, or training users. Tasks are basic units of work that the project manager plans, schedules, and monitors — so they should be relatively small and manageable.

Event or Milestone

Task

**FIGURE 3-8** Using a questionnaire requires a series of tasks and events to track the progress. The illustration shows the relationship between the tasks and the events, or milestones, that mark the beginning and end of each task.

In addition to tasks, every project has events, or milestones. An **event**, or **milestone**, is a recognizable reference point that you can use to monitor progress. For example, an event might be the start of user training, the conversion of system data, or the completion of interviews. A milestone such as *Complete 50 percent of program testing* would not be useful information unless you could determine exactly when that event will occur.

Figure 3-8 shows tasks and events that might be involved in the creation, distribution, and tabulation of a questionnaire. Notice that the beginning and end of each task is marked by a recognizable event. If you tried to manage a project as one large task, it would be impossible. Instead, you break the project down into smaller tasks, creating a work breakdown structure (WBS). The first step in creating a WBS is to list all the tasks.

**LISTING THE TASKS**   While this step sounds simple, it can be challenging, because the tasks might be embedded in a document, such as the one shown in the first version of Figure 3-9. One trick is to start by highlighting the individual tasks, as shown in the second version. Adding bullets makes the tasks stand out more clearly, as shown in the third version. The next step is to number the tasks and create a table, similar to the one shown in Figure 3-10, with columns for task number, description, duration, and predecessor tasks.

### First version

First, reserve the meeting room. Then order the marketing materials and brief the managers. After the briefings, send out customer e-mails and burn sample DVDs. When the e-mails are sent and the DVDs are ready, load the new software. When the marketing materials have arrived and the software is ready, do a dress rehearsal.

### Second version

First, *reserve the meeting room.* Then *order the marketing materials* and *brief the managers.* After the briefings, *send out customer e-mails* and *burn sample DVDs.* When the e-mails are sent and the DVDs are ready, *load the new software.* When the marketing materials have arrived and the software is ready, *do a dress rehearsal.*

### Third version

- First, *reserve the meeting room.*
- Then *order the marketing materials* and *brief the managers.*
- After the briefings, *send out customer e-mails* and *burn sample DVDs.*
- When the e-mails are sent and the DVDs are ready, *load the new software.*
- When the marketing materials have arrived and the software is ready, *do a dress rehearsal.*

**FIGURE 3-9**   The three versions show how to transform a task statement into a list of specific tasks for a work breakdown structure.

| Task No. | Description | Duration (Days) | Predecessor Tasks |
|---|---|---|---|
| 1 | Reserve the meeting room | | |
| 2 | Order the marketing materials | | |
| 3 | Brief the managers | | |
| 4 | Send out customer e-mails | | |
| 5 | Burn sample DVDs | | |
| 6 | Load the new software | | |
| 7 | Do a dress rehearsal | | |

**FIGURE 3-10**   In this table, columns have been added for task number, description, duration, and predecessor tasks.

## CASE IN POINT 3.2:  PARALLEL SERVICES

The project management team at Parallel Services is having a debate about how to define tasks in the work breakdown structure (WBS). Ann, the project manager, wants to break tasks down into the smallest possible units. For example, she objected to a broad task statement called *Develop a training schedule*. Instead, she suggested three subtasks: (1) *Determine availability of training room*, (2) *Determine availability of attendees*, and (3) *Select specific dates and training times*.

   Karen, another project team member, disagrees. She feels that the broader task statement is better, because it allows more flexibility and will produce the same result. Karen says that if you break tasks into pieces that are too small, you risk overmanaging the work and spending more time on monitoring than actually performing the tasks. As a member of the team, would you tend to agree more with Ann or Karen? What are the pros and cons of each approach?

**ESTIMATING TASK DURATION**   Task duration can be hours, days, or weeks — depending on the project. Because the following example uses days, the units of measurement are called person-days. A **person-day** represents the work that one person can complete in one day. This approach, however, can present some problems. For example, if it will take one person 20 days to perform a particular task, it might not be true that two people could complete the same task in 10 days or that 10 people could perform the task in two days. Some tasks can be divided evenly so it is possible to use different combinations of time and people, up to a point. For instance, if it takes two person-days to install the cables for a new local area network, one person might do the task in two days, two people in one day, or four people in half a day. In most systems analysis tasks, however, time and people are not interchangeable. If one analyst needs two hours to interview a user, two analysts also will need two hours to do the same interview.

   Project managers often use a weighted formula for estimating the duration of each task. The project manager first makes three time estimates for each task: an optimistic, or **best-case estimate** (B), a **probable-case estimate** (P), and a pessimistic, or **worst-case estimate** (W). The manager then assigns a **weight**, which is an importance value, to each estimate. The weight can vary, but a common approach is to use a ratio of B = 1, P = 4, and W = 1. The expected task duration is calculated as follows:

$$\frac{(B+4P+W)}{6}$$

   For example, a project manager might estimate that a file-conversion task could be completed in as few as 20 days or could take as many as 34 days, but most likely will require 24 days. Using the formula, the expected task duration is 25 days, calculated as follows:

$$\frac{(20+(4*24)+34)}{6} = 25$$

### Factors Affecting Duration

When developing duration estimates, project managers consider four factors:

- Project size
- Human resources
- Experience with similar projects
- Constraints

**PROJECT SIZE** You learned in Chapter 1 that information systems have various characteristics that affect their complexity and cost. In addition to considering those factors, a project manager must estimate the time required to complete each project phase. To develop accurate estimates, a project manager must identify all project tasks, from initial fact-finding to system implementation. Regardless of the systems development methodology used, the project manager must determine how much time will be needed to perform each task. In developing an estimate, the project manager must allow time for meetings, project reviews, training, and any other factors that could affect the productivity of the development team.

**HUMAN RESOURCES** Companies must invest heavily in cutting-edge technology and Web-based systems to remain competitive in a connected world. In many areas, skilled IT professionals are in great demand, and firms must work hard to attract and retain the talent they need. A project manager must assemble and guide a development team that has the skill and experience to handle the project. If necessary, additional systems analysts or programmers must be hired or trained, and this must be accomplished within a specific time frame. After a project gets under way, the project manager must deal with turnover, job vacancies, and escalating salaries in the technology sector — all of which can affect whether the project can be completed on time and within budget.

**EXPERIENCE WITH SIMILAR PROJECTS** A project manager can develop time and cost estimates based on the resources used for similar, previously developed information systems. The experience method works best for small- or medium-sized projects where the two systems are similar in size, basic content, and operating environment. In large systems with more variables, the estimates are less reliable.

In addition, you might not be able to use experience from projects that were developed in a different environment. For example, when you use a new Web-based database application, you might not have previous experience to measure in this environment. In this situation, you could design a prototype or pilot system to gain technical and cost estimating experience.

**CONSTRAINTS** You learned in Chapter 2 that constraints are defined during the preliminary investigation. A constraint is a condition, restriction, or requirement that the system must satisfy. For example, a constraint might involve maximums for one or more resources, such as time, dollars, or people. A project manager must define system requirements that can be achieved realistically within the required constraints. In the

## CASE IN POINT 3.3: SUNRISE SOFTWARE

A lively discussion is under way at Sunrise Software, where you are a project manager. The main question is whether the person-days concept has limitations. In other words, if a task will require 100 person-days, does it matter whether the work is performed by two people in 50 days, five people in 20 days, 10 people in 10 days, or some other combination that adds up to 100?

Programmers Paula and Ethan seem to think it doesn't matter. On the other hand, Hector, a systems analyst, says it is ridiculous to think that any combination would work. To support his point, he offers this extreme example: Could a task estimated at 100 person-days be accomplished by 100 people in one day?

Is Hector correct? If so, what are the limits in the people versus days equation? Taking the concept a step farther, is there an *optimum* number of people to be assigned to a task? If so, how would that number be determined? You need to offer some guidance at the next project team meeting. What will you say?

absence of constraints, the project manager simply calculates the resources needed. However, if constraints are present, the project manager must adjust other resources or change the scope of the project. This approach is similar to the what-if analysis that is described in Chapter 12.

### Displaying the Work Breakdown Structure

After you enter the task durations, the work breakdown structure will look like Figure 3-11. If you are managing a complex project with many tasks, you can use task groups, just as you would in a Gantt chart, to simplify the list. If you are using Microsoft Project, the WBS might resemble Figure 3-12.

| Task No. | Description | Duration (Days) | Predecessor Tasks |
|---|---|---|---|
| 1 | Reserve the meeting room | 1 | |
| 2 | Order the marketing materials | 9 | |
| 3 | Brief the managers | 2 | |
| 4 | Send out customer e-mails | 3 | |
| 5 | Burn sample DVDs | 3 | |
| 6 | Load the new software | 2 | |
| 7 | Do a dress rehearsal | 1 | |

**FIGURE 3-11**   Task durations have been added, and the WBS is complete except for predecessor task information. The predecessor tasks will determine task patterns and sequence of performance.

| | Task Name | Duration |
|---|---|---|
| 1 | Reserve the meeting room | 1 day |
| 2 | Order marketing materials | 9 days |
| 3 | Brief the managers | 2 days |
| 4 | Send out customer e-mails | 3 days |
| 5 | Burn sample DVDs | 3 days |
| 6 | Load the new software | 2 days |
| 7 | Do a dress rehearsal | 1 day |

Microsoft Project - VLS Project Manageme...  (Gantt Chart)

**FIGURE 3-12**   A Microsoft project screen displays the same WBS, including task number, description, during, and predecessors.

## VIDEO LEARNING SESSION:  TASK PATTERNS

Video Learning Sessions can help you understand key concepts, practice your skills, and check your work. To access the sessions, visit the Management Information Systems CourseMate Web site at **www.cengagebrain.com** and navigate to the **Video Learning Sessions** for this book. This session is about task patterns. You'll learn what task patterns are and why are they important, how to identify and use task patterns, and how to use Microsoft Project to show task patterns.

## TASK BOX FORMAT

| Task Name | |
| --- | --- |
| Start Day/Date | Task ID |
| Finish Day/Date | Task Duration |

**FIGURE 3-13** Each section of the task box contains important information about the task, including the Task Name, Task ID, Task Duration, Start Day/Date, and Finish Day/Date.

## STEP 2: IDENTIFY TASK PATTERNS

Tasks in a work breakdown structure must be arranged in a logical sequence called a **task pattern**. This section will show you how to understand and create graphical models of these patterns.

### What Are Task Patterns?

In any project, large or small, tasks depend on each other and must be performed in a sequence, not unlike the commands in a software program. Task patterns can involve dependent tasks, multiple successor tasks, and multiple predecessor tasks. In larger projects, these patterns can be very complex, and an analyst must study the logical flow carefully.

### How Do I Use Task Boxes to Create a Model?

In a PERT/CPM chart, project tasks are shown as rectangular boxes, arranged in the sequence in which they must be performed. Each rectangular box, called a **task box**, has five sections, as shown in Figure 3-13. Each section of the task box contains important information about the task, including the Task Name, Task ID, Task Duration, Start Day/Date, and Finish Day/Date.

**TASK NAME** The **task name** should be brief and descriptive, but it does not have to be unique in the project. For example, a task named *Conduct Interviews* might occur in several phases of the project.

**TASK ID** The **task ID** can be a number or code that provides unique identification.

**TASK DURATION** The **duration** is the amount of time it will take to complete a task. All tasks must use the same time units, which can be hours, days, weeks, or months, depending on the project. An actual project starts on a specific date, but can also be measured from a point in time, such as *Day 1*.

**START DAY/DATE** The **start day/date** is the time that a task is scheduled to begin. For example, suppose that a simple project has two tasks: Task 1 and Task 2. Also suppose that Task 2 cannot begin until Task 1 is finished. An analogy might be that you cannot run a program until you turn on your computer. If Task 1 begins on Day 1 and has a duration of three days, it will finish on Day 3. Because Task 2 cannot begin until Task 1 is completed, the start time for Task 2 is Day 4, which is the day *after* Task 1 is finished.

**FINISH DAY/DATE** The **finish day/date** is the time that a task is scheduled to be completed. To calculate the finish day or date, you add the duration to the start day or date. When you do this, you must be very careful not to add too many days. For example, if a task starts on Day 10 and has a duration of 5 days, then the finish would be on Day 14 — *not* Day 15.

### What Are the Main Types of Task Patterns?

A project is based on a pattern of tasks. In a large project the overall pattern would be quite complex, but it can be broken down into three basic patterns: dependent tasks, multiple successor tasks, and multiple predecessor tasks.

**DEPENDENT TASKS**   When tasks must be completed one after another, like the relay race shown in Figure 3-14, they are called **dependent tasks,** because one depends on the other. For example, Figure 3-15 shows that Task 2 depends on Task 1, because Task 2 cannot start until Task 1 is completed. In this example, the finish time of Task 1, Day 5, controls the start date of Task 2, which is Day 6.

**MULTIPLE SUCCESSOR TASKS**   When several tasks can start at the same time, each is called a **concurrent task.** Often, two or more concurrent tasks depend on a single prior task, which is called a **predecessor task.** In this situation, each concurrent task is called a **successor task.** In the example shown in Figure 3-16, successor Tasks 2 and 3 both can begin as soon as Task 1 is finished. Notice that the finish time for Task 1 determines the start time for both Tasks 2 and 3. In other words, the earliest that Task 1 can finish is day 30, so day 31 is the earliest that Tasks 2 and 3 can start.

**MULTIPLE PREDECESSOR TASKS**   Suppose that a task requires two or more prior tasks to be completed before it can start. Figure 3-17 on the next page shows that example, because Task 3 cannot begin until Tasks 1 and 2 are both completed. Since the two tasks might not finish at the same time, the longest (latest) predecessor task becomes the controlling factor. Notice that the start for Task 3 is Day 16, *not* Day 6. Why is this so? Because Task 3 depends on two predecessor tasks, Tasks 1 and 2, Task 3 cannot begin until the *later* of those tasks is complete. Therefore, the start time for a successor task must be the latest (largest) finish time for any of its preceding tasks. In the example shown, Task 1 ends on Day 15, while Task 2 ends on Day 5, so Task 1 controls the start time for Task 3.

## How Do I Identify Task Patterns?

You can identify task patterns by looking carefully at the wording of the task statement. Words like *then, when,* or *and* are action words that signal a sequence of events. Here are three simple examples:

- *Do Task 1, then do Task 2* describes dependent tasks that must be completed one after the other.

- *When Task 2 is finished, start two tasks: Task 3 and Task 4* describes multiple successor tasks that can both start as soon as Task 2 is finished.

- *When Tasks 5 and 6 are done, start Task 7* indicates that Task 7 is a multiple predecessor task because it can't start until two or more previous tasks all are completed.

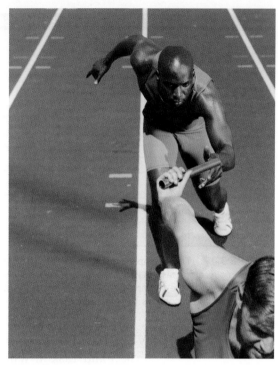

**FIGURE 3-14**   In a relay race, each runner is dependent on the preceding runner and cannot start until the earlier runner finishes.

| EXAMPLE OF A DEPENDENT TASK | | | |
|---|---|---|---|

| Prepare Outline | | Create Document | |
|---|---|---|---|
| Start: Day 1 | ID: 1 | Start: Day 6 | ID: 2 |
| Finish: Day 5 | Dur: 5 | Finish: Day 14 | Dur: 9 |

**FIGURE 3-15**   This example of a dependent task shows that the finish time of Task 1, Day 5, controls the start date of Task 2, which is Day 6.

| EXAMPLE OF MULTIPLE SUCCESSOR TASKS | |
|---|---|

| Arrange Interviews | |
|---|---|
| Start: Day 31 | ID: 2 |
| Finish: Day 60 | Dur: 30 |

| Develop Plan | |
|---|---|
| Start: Day 1 | ID: 1 |
| Finish: Day 30 | Dur: 30 |

| Design Survey | |
|---|---|
| Start: Day 31 | ID: 3 |
| Finish: Day 40 | Dur: 10 |

**FIGURE 3-16**   This example of multiple successor tasks shows that the finish time for Task 1 determines the start time for both Tasks 2 and 3.

EXAMPLE OF MULTIPLE PREDECESSOR TASKS

**FIGURE 3-17**   This example of multiple predecessor tasks shows that the start time for a successor task must be the latest (largest) finish time for any of its preceding tasks. In the example shown, Task 1 ends on Day 15, while Task 2 ends on Day 5, so Task 1 controls the start time for Task 3.

## How Do I Work With Complex Task Patterns?

When several task patterns combine, you must study the facts very carefully to understand the logic and sequence. A project schedule will not be accurate if the underlying task pattern is incorrect. For example, consider the following three fact statements and the task patterns they represent. Examples of the task patterns are shown Figures 3-18, 3-19, and 3-20.

**DEPENDENT TASKS**   Perform Task 1. When Task 1 is complete, perform Task 2.

**DEPENDENT TASKS AND MULTIPLE SUCCESSOR TASKS**   Perform Task 1. When Task 1 is complete, perform Task 2. When Task 2 is finished, start two tasks: Task 3 and Task 4. When Task 3 is complete, start two more tasks: Task 5 and Task 6.

**DEPENDENT TASKS, MULTIPLE SUCCESSOR TASKS, AND MULTIPLE PREDECESSOR TASKS**   Perform Task 1. When Task 1 is complete, perform Task 2. When Task 2 is finished, start two Tasks: Task 3 and Task 4. When Task 3 is complete, start two more tasks: Task 5 and Task 6. When Tasks 5 and 6 are done, start Task 7. Then, when Tasks 4 and 7 are finished, perform Task 8.

**FIGURE 3-18**   Dependent tasks.

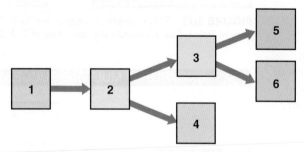

**FIGURE 3-19**   Dependent tasks and multiple successor tasks.

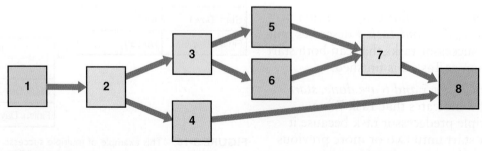

**FIGURE 3-20**   Dependent tasks, multiple successor tasks, and multiple predecessor tasks.

## VIDEO LEARNING SESSION:  CRITICAL PATH ANALYSIS

Video Learning Sessions can help you understand key concepts, practice your skills, and check your work. To access the sessions, visit the Management Information Systems CourseMate Web site at **www.cengagebrain.com** and navigate to the **Video Learning Sessions** for this book. This session is about critical path analysis. You'll learn what a critical path is and why it is important, how to calculate task dates and identify the critical path, and how to use Microsoft Project to analyze and display the critical path.

## STEP 3: CALCULATE THE CRITICAL PATH

Task patterns determine the order in which the tasks are performed. Once the task sequence has been defined, a project manager can schedule the tasks and calculate the critical path.

### What Is a Critical Path?

A **critical path** is a series of tasks which, if delayed, would affect the completion date of the overall project. If any task on the critical path falls behind schedule, the entire project will be delayed. For example, suppose that you invite Joan and Jim to your home for dinner. Joan arrives on time, but Jim arrives 30 minutes late. Jim's arrival is part of the critical path, because you do not want to start without him, so the meal will be served 30 minutes later than originally planned.

Project managers always must be aware of the critical path, so they can respond quickly to keep the project on track. Microsoft Project and other **project management software** can highlight the series of tasks that form the critical path.

### How Do I Calculate the Critical Path?

Figure 3-21 shows a training project with five tasks. Notice that the analyst has arranged the tasks and entered task names, IDs, and durations. First, you should review the task patterns. In this example, Task 1 is followed by Task 2, which is a dependent task. Task 2 has two successor tasks: Task 3 and Task 4. Tasks 3 and 4 are predecessor tasks for Task 5.

The next step is to determine start and finish dates, which will determine the critical path for the project. The following explanation will guide you through a step-by-step process. The result is shown in Figure 3-22 on the next page.

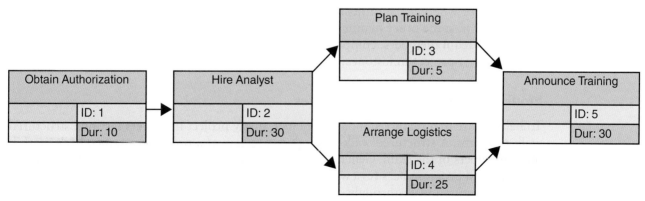

**FIGURE 3-21**   Example of a PERT/CPM chart with five tasks. Task 2 is a dependent task that has multiple successor tasks. Task 5 has multiple predecessor tasks. In this figure, the analyst has arranged the tasks and entered task names, IDs, and durations.

CRITICAL PATH:1-2-4-5

**FIGURE 3-22**   Now the analyst has entered the start and finish times, using the rules explained in this section. Notice that the overall project has a duration of 95 days.

- Task 1 starts on Day 1 and has a duration of 10 days, so the finish date is Day 10.

- Task 2, which is dependent on Task 1, can start on Day 11 — the day *after* Task 1 ends. With a duration of 30 days, Task 2 will end on Day 40.

- Tasks 3 and 4 are multiple successor tasks that can start after Task 2 is done. Task 2 ends on Day 40, so Tasks 3 and 4 *both* can start on Day 41. Task 3 has a duration of 5 days, and will end on Day 45. Task 4 has a duration of 25 days, and will not end until Day 65.

- Task 5 depends on Tasks 3 and 4, which are multiple predecessors. Because Task 5 depends on *both* tasks, it cannot start until the later of the two tasks is complete. In this example, Task 3 ends earlier, but Task 4 will not be completed until Day 65, so Task 5 cannot start until Day 66.

Recall that the critical path is a series of tasks which, if delayed, would affect the final completion date of the overall project. In this example, Tasks 1 and 2 are the first tasks on the critical path. Now look at Task 5, which cannot start until both Tasks 3 and 4 are done. In this case, Task 4 is the controlling factor, because Task 4 finishes on Day 65, which is 20 days later than Task 3, which is completed on Day 45. Therefore, the start date for Task 5 is determined by the finish date for Task 4. In contrast, Task 3 has slack time, and could be delayed up to 20 days without affecting Task 5. **Slack time** is the amount of time that the task could be late without pushing back the completion date of the entire project. Tasks 1, 2, 4, and 5 represent the critical path, which is highlighted with red arrows in Figure 3-22.

## PROJECT MONITORING AND CONTROL

Regardless of whether the project was planned and scheduled with project management software or in some other manner, the project manager must keep track of the tasks and progress of team members, compare actual progress with the project plan, verify the completion of project milestones, and set standards and ensure that they are followed.

### Monitoring and Control Techniques

To help ensure that quality standards are met, many project managers institute structured walk-throughs. A **structured walk-through** is a review of a project team member's work by other members of the team. Generally, systems analysts review the work of other systems analysts, and programmers review the work of other programmers, as a form of peer review. Structured walk-throughs take place throughout the SDLC and are called **design reviews**, **code reviews**, or **testing reviews**, depending on the phase in which they occur.

## Maintaining a Schedule

Maintaining a project schedule can be challenging, and most projects run into at least some problems or delays. By monitoring and controlling the work, the project manager tries to anticipate problems, avoid them or minimize their impact, identify potential solutions, and select the best way to solve the problem.

The better the original plan, the easier it will be to control the project. If clear, verifiable milestones exist, it will be simple to determine if and when those targets are achieved. If enough milestones and frequent checkpoints exist, problems will be detected rapidly. A project that is planned and scheduled with PERT/CPM can be tracked and controlled using these same techniques. As work continues, the project manager revises the plan to record actual times for completed tasks and revises times for tasks that are not yet finished.

Project managers spend most of their time tracking the tasks along the critical path, because delays in those tasks have the greatest potential to delay or jeopardize the project. Other tasks cannot be ignored, however. For example, suppose that a task not on the critical path takes too long and depletes the allotted slack time. At that point, the task actually becomes part of the critical path, and any further delay will push back the overall project.

## REPORTING

Members of the project team regularly report their progress to the project manager, who in turn reports to management and users. As shown in Figure 3-23, the project manager collects, verifies, organizes, and evaluates the information he or she receives from the team. Then the manager decides which information needs to be passed along, prepares a summary that can be understood easily, adds comments and explanations if needed, and submits it to management and users.

The Communication Tools in Appendix A can help you develop better reports and presentations. To learn more about these tools, turn to Appendix A.

## Project Status Meetings

Project managers, like the one shown in Figure 3-24, schedule regular meetings to update the team and discuss project status, issues, problems, and opportunities. Although meetings can be time consuming, most project managers believe they are worth the effort. The sessions give team members an opportunity to share information, discuss common problems, and explain new techniques. The meetings also give the project manager an opportunity to seek input and conduct brainstorming sessions.

## Project Status Reports

Before going further, you should read the *Question of Ethics* feature on page 125, which describes an interesting conflict at Final Four Industries.

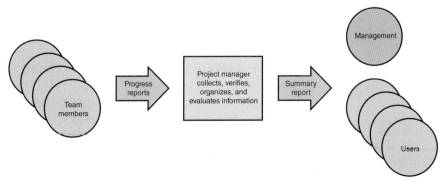

**FIGURE 3-23** Members of the project team regularly report their progress to the project manager, who in turn reports to management and users.

**FIGURE 3-24** Project managers schedule regular meetings to update the project team and discuss project status, issues, problems, and opportunities.

A project is in trouble, but the project manager is reluctant to report the problems. The case highlights important ethical issues that often arise in this situation.

A project manager must report regularly to his or her immediate supervisor, upper management, and users. Although a progress report might be given verbally to an immediate supervisor, reports to management and users usually are written. Gantt charts often are included in progress reports to show project status graphically. Deciding how to handle potential problems can be difficult. At what point should you inform management about the possibility of cost overruns, schedule delays, or technical problems? At one extreme is the overly cautious project manager who alerts management to every potential snag and slight delay. The danger here is that the manager loses credibility over a period of time, and management might ignore potentially serious situations. At the other extreme is the project manager who tries to handle all situations single-handedly and does not alert management until a problem is serious. By the time management learns of the problem, little time might remain in which to react or devise a solution.

A project manager's best course of action lies somewhere between the two extremes, but is probably closer to the first. If you are unsure of the consequences, you should be cautious and warn management about the possibility of a problem. When you report the situation, you also should explain what you are doing to handle and monitor the problem. If you believe the situation is beyond your control, you might want to suggest possible actions that management can take to resolve the situation. Most managers recognize that problems do occur on most projects; it is better to alert management sooner rather than later.

## PROJECT MANAGEMENT EXAMPLES

You can use these examples to practice the skills you learned in this chapter. You will also see how you can use project management software to help you manage and display the tasks.

### PERT/CPM Example

Figure 3-25 shows a list of 11 tasks. The example is more complex, but the same guidelines apply. Notice that each task has an ID, a description, a duration, and a reference to predecessor tasks, if any, which must be completed before the task can begin. Also notice that dependent tasks can have one predecessor task, or several. You construct a PERT/CPM chart from this task list in a two-step process:

| Task No. | Description | Duration (Days) | Predecessor Tasks |
|---|---|---|---|
| 1 | Develop Plan | 1 | - |
| 2 | Assign Tasks | 4 | 1 |
| 3 | Obtain Hardware | 17 | 1 |
| 4 | Programming | 70 | 2 |
| 5 | Install Hardware | 10 | 3 |
| 6 | Program Test | 30 | 4 |
| 7 | Write User Manual | 25 | 5 |
| 8 | Convert Files | 20 | 5 |
| 9 | System Test | 25 | 6 |
| 10 | User Training | 20 | 7, 8 |
| 11 | User Test | 25 | 9, 10 |

**FIGURE 3-25**  Example of a table listing 11 tasks, together with their descriptions, durations, and predecessor tasks.

**STEP 1: CREATE THE WORK BREAKDOWN STRUCTURE**  In the first step, as shown in Figure 3-26 on the next page, you identify the tasks, determine task dependencies, and enter the task name, ID, and duration. Notice that this example includes dependent tasks, multiple successor tasks, and multiple predecessor tasks.

**STEP 2: ENTER START AND FINISH TIMES**  In the second step, as shown in Figure 3-27, you enter the start and finish times by applying the guidelines in this section. For example, Task 1 has a one-day duration, so you enter the start and finish times for Task 1 as Day 1. Then you enter Day 2 as the start time for successor Tasks 2 and 3. Continuing from left to right, you add the task duration for each task

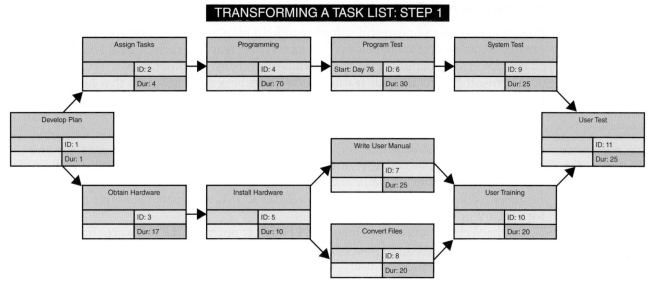

**FIGURE 3-26**   To transform a task list into a PERT/CPM chart, you first enter the task name, ID, duration, and predecessors for each task. Notice that this example includes dependent tasks, tasks with multiple successors, and tasks with multiple predecessors.

to its start time to determine its finish time. As you proceed, there are three important rules you must keep in mind:

- If a successor task has more than one predecessor task, use the *latest* finish time of the predecessor tasks to determine the start time for the successor task.

- If a predecessor task has more than one successor task, use the predecessor task's finish time to determine the start time for *all* successor tasks.

- Continuing from left to right, add the task duration for each task to its start time to determine and enter its finish time. Again, be very careful not to add too many days. For example, if a task starts on Day 10 and has a duration of 5 days, then the finish would be Day 14 — *not* Day 15.

When you enter all the start and finish times, you determine that the project will be completed on Day 155. Also, you note that Tasks 1, 2, 4, 6, 9, and 11 represent the critical path shown by the red arrows.

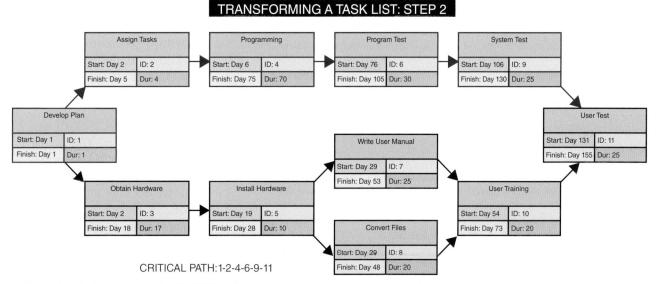

**FIGURE 3-27**   To complete the PERT/CPM chart, you apply the guidelines explained in this section. For example, Task 1 has a one-day duration, so you enter the start and finish for Task 1 as Day 1. Then you enter Day 2 as the start for successor Tasks 2 and 3.

**ON THE WEB**

To learn more about project management software, visit the Management Information Systems CourseMate Web site at **www. cengagebrain. com**, navigate to **On the Web Links** for this chapter, and locate the Project Management Software link.

## Software-Driven Example

Project managers use powerful software to help plan, schedule, monitor, and report on a project. Most project management programs offer features such as PERT/CPM, Gantt charts, resource scheduling, project calendars, and cost tracking.

**Microsoft Project** is a full-featured project management program that holds the dominant share of the market. On the Web, Microsoft offers demo versions, training, and tips. Although Microsoft is the industry leader, many other vendors offer project management software, and you can explore these options by searching on the Web. One product, **Open Workbench**, is available as free software, complete with manuals and sample projects, as shown in Figure 3-28. You can download the latest version from the Open Workbench site at *openworkbench.org*, or you can use the download link in the Features section of the Student Study Tool CD-ROM, which also contains a user manual for Open Workbench.

As the Web site explains, Open Workbench is **open-source software** that is supported by a large group of users and developers. Support options include community forums that are open to all users, various training packages, and third-party support. For many small to medium-sized projects, Open Workbench would be a cost-effective alternative that would compare favorably to Microsoft Project. Open Workbench also can exchange files with Microsoft Project by importing and exporting the data in XML file format.

When you use project management software, you follow the same step-by-step process to develop a WBS and create various types of charts. The following sections focus on some basic concepts, but most programs include many powerful features, such as automated reporting tools, and convenient data import-export tools. You can sample these features by reviewing the Open Workbench User Guide, which is included in your Student Study Tool CD-ROM.

**FIGURE 3-28** Open Workbench is a free, open-source project management program with powerful features and capabilities.

**Please study the following task summary:**
- First, we will review the systems request. That will take three days.
- Then, two tasks can begin at once: We can review the documentation, which will take three days, and review the Internet access delays, which will take two days.
- When the documentation and the Internet access delays have been analyzed, we can contact managers about the interviews, which will take two days.
- After we contact the managers, we can plan the interview schedule, which will take two days.
- Next, we can prepare the preliminary investigation report, which will take two days.
- When the report is ready, we can deliver our presentation to the committee, which will take two days.
- After the presentation, three tasks can begin at once: We plan the interview questions, which will take one day; contact the interviewees, which will take one day; and send out the questionnaire, which will be returned in five days.
- When the interview questions are ready and the interviewees have been contacted, we can conduct the interviews, which will take three days.
- Finally, when the interviews have been conducted and the questionnaire results are back, we can tabulate all results, which will take one day.

**FIGURE 3-29** A sample task summary.

**WORK BREAKDOWN STRUCTURE** You already know how to create a work breakdown structure. If you are using Microsoft Project or Open Workbench, the process is exactly the same. You must identify the tasks, durations, and task patterns. You might have to develop this information on your own, or you might work with a task summary like the one in Figure 3-29. Your manager would like you to create a Gantt chart and a PERT chart that show all tasks, dependencies, dates, and total project duration. Your first step is to create a Gantt chart showing the necessary information. You decide to use Microsoft Project to construct the chart. As you enter each task, you also enter the duration and the predecessor tasks, if any.

**GANTT CHART**   As you enter the tasks, durations, and predecessor tasks, the program automatically performs the calculations, detects the task patterns, and creates a Gantt chart similar to the one shown in Figure 3-30. The chart consists of 12 horizontal bars, connected with arrows that indicate the task dependencies. Notice that Saturdays and Sundays are shown as shaded columns, because no work will be performed on those days. The

**FIGURE 3-30**   Open Workbench can show the sample project as a Gantt chart, or as a PERT chart that includes tasks, durations, dependencies, and a highlighted critical path.

program makes these adjustments automatically. For example, Task 2, which has a duration of three days, starts on Thursday and ends on Monday.

**NETWORK DIAGRAM**   After you complete the Gantt chart, you decide to view the data in the form of a Microsoft Project network diagram, which is similar to a PERT chart. When you select the Network Diagram option on the View menu, you can see the project tasks and dependencies, as shown in Figure 3-31. You study the diagram and see that the program has calculated a start and finish date for each task. Notice that the diagram displays the same information as the Gantt chart, including task dependencies, and also includes a red line that indicates the project's critical path. According to the diagram, if the

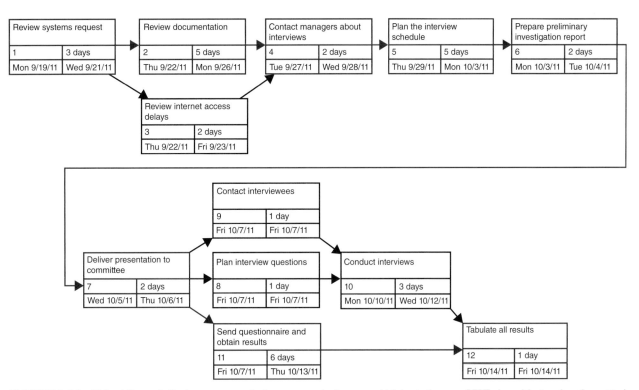

**FIGURE 3-31**   Using Microsoft Project, you can display a network diagram, which is similar to a PERT chart. Notice that the critical path appears as a red line.

project remains on schedule, the last task will be completed on Friday, October 14, 2011. Notice that the task boxes in Microsoft Project are similar to PERT/CPM task boxes. Using Microsoft Project, you can assign each task to one or more people, assign budget targets, produce progress reports, and readjust schedules and deadlines as necessary.

The latest version of Project is Microsoft Project 2010. This release is offered in a Standard version, a Professional version, and a Server version that includes support for large, enterprise-wide projects. In addition to providing a full description, demos, and training on its Web site, Microsoft also offers a free 60-day trial version that allows you to install, use, and evaluate the program.

An alternative to Microsoft Project is the Open Workbench program, which is free. Figure 3-32 shows the Open Workbench version of the same project shown in Figure 3-30 on the previous page. Using Open Workbench, you create tasks and durations, indicate dependencies, and assign resources, just as you would in Microsoft Project. Notice that the critical path is highlighted, both in the Gantt chart and the network diagram.

Regardless of which software you use, you can see from these examples that project schedules, task estimates, and personnel assignments all are interrelated. Therefore, project planning is a dynamic task and involves constant change. One significant advantage of integrated interactive project management software is that it allows the project manager to adjust schedules, estimates, and resource assignments rapidly to develop a workable plan.

**FIGURE 3-32**   Open Workbench can show the sample project as a Gantt chart, or as a PERT chart that includes tasks, durations, dependencies, and a highlighted critical path.

## CASE IN POINT 3.4:  Census 2010

In April 2008, the U.S. Commerce Department canceled a plan to acquire 500,000 handheld computers to tabulate data during the 2010 census. According to Commerce Secretary Carlos Gutierrez, costs had skyrocketed. He blamed the problem on "a lack of effective communications with one of our major suppliers."

Apparently, there was plenty of blame to go around. Secretary Gutierrez noted that the Census Bureau had submitted numerous technical changes to the vendor, Harris Corporation. This greatly increased the cost and the complexity of the devices. Gutierrez stated, "The Census Bureau was unaccustomed to working with an outside vendor on such a large contract." He also pointed out that the vendor had submitted an initial estimate of $36 million to operate a help desk to assist census-takers, but that figure had jumped to $217 million. "It was a bad estimate. I can't think of a better way to say it. Harris gave us the number. We accepted it. It was totally underestimated."

What can be learned from the failure of this project, and could it have been prevented? Suppose you were asked to head up a similar project. What would you do to prevent a similar outcome?

## RISK MANAGEMENT

Every IT project involves risks that systems analysts and project managers must address. A **risk** is an event that could affect the project negatively. **Risk management** is the process of identifying, analyzing, anticipating, and monitoring risks to minimize their impact on the project.

### Steps in Risk Management

The first step in risk management is to develop a specific plan. Although project management experts differ with regard to the number of steps or phases, a basic list would include the following tasks:

- *Develop a risk management plan.* A **risk management plan** includes a review of the project's scope, stakeholders, budget, schedule, and any other internal or external factors that might affect the project. The plan should define project roles and responsibilities, risk management methods and procedures, categories of risks, and contingency plans.

- *Identify the risks.* **Risk identification** lists each risk and assesses the likelihood that it could affect the project. The details would depend on the specific project, but most lists would include a means of identification, and a brief description of the risk, what might cause it to occur, who would be responsible for responding, and the potential impact of the risk.

- *Analyze the risks.* This typically is a two-step process: Qualitative risk analysis and quantitative risk analysis. **Qualitative risk analysis** evaluates each risk by estimating the probability that it will occur and the degree of impact. Project managers can use a formula to weigh risk and impact values, or they can display the results in a two-axis grid. For example, a Microsoft Excel XY chart can be used to display the matrix, as shown in Figure 3-33. In the chart, notice the various combinations of risk and impact ratings for the five sample values. This tool can help a project manager focus on the most critical areas, where risk probability and potential impact are high.

**FIGURE 3-33**   You can use a Microsoft Excel XY chart type to display a risk matrix that shows risk probability and potential impact.

**FIGURE 3-34**   Intaver Institute offers an add-on risk management package for Microsoft Project.

The purpose of **quantitative risk analysis** is to understand the actual impact in terms of dollars, time, project scope, or quality. Quantitative risk analysis can involve a modeling process called what-if analysis, which allows a project manager to vary one or more element(s) in a model to measure the effect on other elements. This topic is discussed in more detail in Chapter 12, Securing and Supporting the System.

- Create a risk response plan. A **risk response plan** is a proactive effort to anticipate a risk and describe an action plan to deal with it. An effective risk response plan can reduce the overall impact by triggering timely and appropriate action.

- Monitor risks. This activity is ongoing throughout the risk management process. It is important to conduct a continuous tracking process that can identify new risks, notice changes in existing risks, and update any other areas of the risk management plan.

## Risk Management Software

Most project management software includes powerful features that allow a project manager to assign specific dates as constraints, align task dependencies, note external factors that might affect a task, track progress, and display tasks that are behind schedule. In addition, some vendors offer risk management add-ons, such as the one shown in Figure 3-34.

The enterprise edition of Microsoft Project, Microsoft Project Server 2010, has a built-in risk management capability that can be used for large, corporate-wide projects. Microsoft claims that the software can link risks with specific tasks and projects, specify probability and impact, assign ownership, and track progress to manage projects more efficiently. Microsoft's risk management model includes the following factors:

- Probability, which represents the likelihood that the risk will happen, expressed as a percentage

- Impact, which indicates the degree of adverse effect should the risk occur, on a scale of 1 to 10

- Cost, which indicates the potential financial impact of the risk

- Category, which specifies the risk type

- Description, which specifies the nature of the risk

- Mitigation plan, which identifies plans to control or limit the risk

- Contingency plan, which specifies actions to be taken if the risk occurs
- Trigger, which identifies a condition that would initiate the contingency plan

Armed with this information, the IT team can make a recommendation regarding the risks associated with the project. Depending on the nature and magnitude of the risks, the final decision might be made by management.

## MANAGING FOR SUCCESS

To be successful, an information system must satisfy business requirements, stay within budget, be completed on time, and — most important of all — be managed effectively. When a project develops problems, the reasons typically involve business, budget, or schedule issues, as explained in the following sections. In addition to planning and managing the project, a project manager must be able to recognize problems and deal with them effectively.

### Business Issues

The major objective of every system is to provide a solution to a business problem or opportunity. If the system does not do this, then it is a failure — regardless of positive reaction from users, acceptable budget performance, or timely delivery. When the information system does not meet business requirements, causes might include unidentified or unclear requirements, inadequately defined scope, imprecise targets, shortcuts or sloppy work during systems analysis, poor design choices, insufficient testing or inadequate testing procedures, and lack of change control procedures. Systems also fail because of changes in the organization's culture, funding, or objectives. A system that falls short of business needs also produces problems for users and reduces employee morale and productivity.

As you learned in Chapter 2, projects without clear scope definitions are risky, because they tend to expand gradually, without specific authorization, in a process called **project creep**. However, even when a project is clearly described, it must be managed constantly.

### Budget Issues

Cost overruns typically result from one or more of the following:

- Unrealistic estimates that are too optimistic or based on incomplete information
- Failure to develop an accurate forecast that considers all costs over the life of the project
- Poor monitoring of progress and slow response to early warning signs of problems
- Schedule delays due to factors that were not foreseen
- Human resource issues, including turnover, inadequate training, and motivation

### Schedule Issues

Problems with timetables and project milestones can indicate a failure to recognize task dependencies, confusion between effort and progress, poor monitoring and control methods, personality conflicts among team members, or turnover of project personnel. The failure of an IT project also can be caused by poor project management techniques.

If the project manager fails to plan, staff, organize, supervise, communicate, motivate, evaluate, direct, and control properly, then the project is certain to fail. Even when factors outside his or her control contribute to the failure, the project manager is responsible for recognizing the early warning signs and handling them effectively.

## THE BOTTOM LINE

Project management is a challenging task. Project managers must be alert, technically competent, and highly resourceful. They also must be good communicators with strong human resource skills. A project manager can be proud when he or she handles a successful project that helps the company achieve its business objectives, such as the Apple product launch shown in Figure 3-35.

Unfortunately, projects can and do get derailed for a wide variety of reasons. When problems occur, the project manager's ability to handle the situation becomes the critical factor. When a project manager first recognizes that a project is in trouble, what options are available? Alternatives can include trimming the project requirements, adding to the project resources, delaying the project deadline, and improving management controls and procedures. Sometimes, when a project experiences delays or cost overruns, the system still can be delivered on time and within budget if several less critical requirements are trimmed. The system can be delivered to satisfy the most necessary requirements, and additional features can be added later as a part of a maintenance or enhancement project.

If a project is in trouble because of a lack of resources or organizational support, management might be willing to give the project more commitment and higher priority. For example, management might agree to add more people to a project that is behind schedule. Adding staff, however, will reduce the project's completion time only if the additional people can be integrated effectively into the development team. If team members lack experience with certain aspects of the required technology, temporary help might be obtained from IT consultants or part-time staff. Adding staff can mean training and orienting the new people, however. In some situations, adding more people to a project actually might increase the time necessary to complete the project because of a principle called **Brooks' Law**. This interesting concept was stated by Frederick Brooks, Jr., an IBM engineer, who observed that adding manpower to a late software project only makes it later. Brooks reached this conclusion when he saw that new workers on a project first had to be educated and instructed by existing employees whose own productivity was reduced accordingly.

**FIGURE 3-35** When a complex project is successful, the project manager has a right to be proud.

# A QUESTION OF ETHICS

"Better blow the whistle," says Roy, your friend and project teammate at Final Four Industries. "The project is out of control, and you know it!" "Maybe so," you respond, "But that's not my call — I'm not the project manager." What you don't say is that Stephanie, the project manager, feels like her career is on the line and she is reluctant to bring bad news to management at this time. She honestly believes that the project can catch up, and says that a bad report on a major project could result in bad publicity for the firm and frighten potential customers.

To be fair, the next management progress report is scheduled in three weeks. It is possible that the team could catch up, but you doubt it. You wonder if there is an ethical question here: Even though the report isn't due yet, should a significant problem be reported to management as soon as possible? You are concerned about the issue, and you decide to discuss it with Stephanie. What will you say to her?

## CHAPTER SUMMARY

Project management is the process of planning, scheduling, monitoring, and reporting on the development of an information system. A successful project must be completed on time, within budget, and deliver a quality product that satisfies users and meets requirements. Project management techniques can be used throughout the SDLC.

Project managers are responsible for project planning, scheduling, monitoring, and reporting. Planning includes identifying all project tasks and estimating the completion time and cost of each. Project scheduling involves the creation of a specific timetable, usually in the form of charts that show tasks, task dependencies, and critical tasks that might delay the project. Project monitoring requires guiding, supervising, and coordinating the project team's workload. The project manager must monitor the progress, evaluate the results, and take corrective action when necessary to control the project and stay on target. Project reporting includes regular progress reports to management, users, and the project team itself. Effective reporting requires strong communication skills and a sense of what others want and need to know about the project.

Planning, scheduling, monitoring and reporting all take place within a larger project development framework, which includes three key steps: creating a work breakdown structure, identifying task patterns, and calculating the critical path.

A work breakdown structure must clearly identify each task and include an estimated duration. A task, or activity, is any work that has a beginning and an end and requires the use of company resources such as people, time, or money. Time and cost estimates for tasks usually are made in person-days. A person-day represents the work that one person can accomplish in one day. Estimating the time for project activities is more difficult with larger systems. Project managers must consider the project size and scope, IT resources, prior experience with similar projects or systems, and applicable constraints. In addition to tasks, every project has events, or milestones. An event, or milestone, is a recognizable reference point that you can use to monitor progress.

Task patterns establish the sequence of work in a project. Task patterns involve dependent tasks, multiple successor tasks, and multiple predecessor tasks. In larger projects, these patterns can be very complex.

A critical path is a series of tasks which, if delayed, would affect the completion date of the overall project. If any task on the critical path falls behind schedule, the entire project will be delayed. Tasks on the critical path cannot have slack time. To identify the critical path, you calculate the start and finish date for each task, which will determine the critical path for the project.

In project scheduling, the project manager develops a specific time for each task, based on available resources and whether or not the task is dependent on other predecessor tasks. The manager can use graphical tools such as Gantt charts and PERT charts to assist in the scheduling process.

A Gantt chart is a horizontal bar chart that represents the project schedule with time on the horizontal axis and tasks arranged vertically. It shows individual tasks and task groups, which include several tasks. In a Gantt chart, the length of the bar indicates the duration of the tasks. A Gantt chart can display progress, but does not show task dependency details or resource assignment unless the chart was created with a project management program that supports dependency linking and the entry of other information.

A PERT/CPM chart shows the project as a network diagram with tasks connected by arrows. Using a prescribed calculation method, the project manager uses a PERT chart to determine the overall duration of the project and provide specific information for each task, including the task IDs, their durations, start and finish times, and the order in which they must be performed. With this information, the manager can determine the critical path, which is the sequence of tasks that have no slack time and must be performed on schedule in order to meet the overall project deadline.

Most project managers use powerful software such as Microsoft Project and Open Workbench to plan, schedule, and monitor projects. Project managers are responsible for risk management, which is the process of identifying, analyzing, anticipating, and monitoring risks to minimize their impact on the project.

In the end, every successful information system must support business requirements, stay within budget, and be completed on time. Sound project management involves the same skills as any other management. The project manager must be perceptive, analytical, well-organized, and a good communicator. If the project manager senses that the project is off-track, he or she must take immediate steps to diagnose and solve the problem. If the project manager fails to plan, staff, organize, supervise, communicate, motivate, evaluate, direct, and control properly, then the project is certain to fail. Even when factors outside his or her control contribute to the failure, the project manager is responsible for recognizing the early warning signs and handling them effectively.

# Key Terms and Phrases

activity *106*

best-case estimate *107*

bottom-up technique *105*

Brooks' Law *124*

code review *114*

concurrent tasks *111*

critical path *113*

Critical Path Method (CPM) *105*

dependent task *111*

design review *114*

duration *110*

event *106*

finish day/date *110*

Gantt chart *104*

Microsoft Project *118*

milestone *106*

network diagram *105*

Open Workbench *118*

open-source software *118*

person-day *107*

PERT/CPM *105*

predecessor task *111*

probable-case estimate *107*

Program Evaluation Review Technique (PERT) *105*

project coordinator *103*

project creep *123*

project leader *103*

project management *102*

project management software *113*

project manager *103*

project monitoring *103*

project planning *103*

project reporting *103*

project scheduling *103*

qualitative risk analysis *121*

quantitative risk analysis *122*

risk *121*

risk identification *121*

risk management *121*

risk management plan *121*

risk response plan *122*

slack time *114*

start day/date *110*

structured walk-through *114*

successor task *111*

task *105*

task box *110*

task group *104*

task ID *110*

task name *110*

task pattern *110*

testing review *114*

weight *107*

work breakdown structure (WBS) *104*

worst-case estimate *107*

# Learn It Online

**Instructions:**   To complete the Learn It Online exercises, visit the Management Information Systems CourseMate Web site at **www.cengagebrain.com**, navigate to the resources for this chapter, and click the link for the exercise you want to complete.

## 1 Chapter Reinforcement
### TF, MC, and SA

Click the Chapter Reinforcement link. Print the quiz by clicking Print on the File menu for each page. Answer each question.

## 2 Flash Cards

Click the Flash Cards link and read the instructions. Type 20 (or a number specified by your instructor) in the Number of playing cards text box, type your name in the Enter your name text box, and then click the Flip Card button. When the flash card is displayed, read the question and then click the ANSWER box arrow to select an answer. Flip through the Flash Cards. If your score is 15 (75%) correct or greater, click Print on the File menu to print your results. If your score is less than 15 (75%) correct, then redo this exercise by clicking the Replay button.

## 3 Practice Test

Click the Practice Test link. Answer each question, enter your first and last name at the bottom of the page, and then click the Grade Test button. When the graded practice test is displayed on your screen, click Print on the File menu to print a hard copy. Continue to take practice tests until you score 80% or better.

## 4 Who Wants To Be a Computer Genius?

Click the Computer Genius link. Read the instructions, enter your first and last name at the bottom of the page, and then click the Play button. When your score is displayed, click the PRINT RESULTS link to print a hard copy.

## 5 Wheel of Terms

Click the Wheel of Terms link. Read the instructions, and then enter your first and last name and your school name. Click the PLAY button. When your score is displayed on the screen, right-click the score and then click Print on the shortcut menu to print a hard copy.

## 6 Crossword Puzzle Challenge

Click the Crossword Puzzle Challenge link. Read the instructions, and then enter your first and last name. Click the SUBMIT button. Work the crossword puzzle. When you are finished, click the SUBMIT button. When the crossword puzzle is redisplayed, click the Print Puzzle button to print a hard copy.

## SCR Associates Case Simulation    Session 3: Managing Systems Projects

### Overview

The SCR Associates case study is a Web-based simulation that allows you to practice your skills in a real-world environment. The case study transports you to SCR's intranet, where you complete 12 work sessions, each aligning with a chapter. As you work on the case, you will receive e-mail and voice mail messages, obtain information from SCR's online libraries, and perform various tasks.

### How do I use the case?

* Review the SCR background material in Chapter 1.
* Read the Preview for this session and study the Task List
* Visit the Management Information Systems CourseMate Web site at **www.cengagebrain. com**, navigate to the **SCR Case Simulation**, and locate the intranet link.
* Enter your name and the password **sad9e**. An opening screen will display the 12 sessions.
* Select this session. Check your e-mail and voice mail carefully, and then work on the tasks.

### Preview: Session 3

The TIMS system was approved by top management. Jesse Baker, systems group manager, has asked you to help her manage the project. She said it will be a great opportunity to learn more about project management and practice your skills, so you'll be able to handle a future project on your own. She specifically suggested that you become familiar with work breakdown structures, task patterns, and critical path calculations. To make sure that you are prepared, you decide to study the project management chapter in your textbook before starting the tasks.

### Task List

| |
|---|
| 1. Jesse wants me to investigate Open Workbench software to determine whether it would be suitable for SCR. She asked me to prepare a summary of pros and cons, and a sample of screen shots and information. |
| 2. Jesse likes the idea of using task completion estimates with best-case, probable-case, and worst-case estimates. She said that I should use typical formulas and weight values to create a Microsoft Excel spreadsheet that would make it easier to calculate expected task durations. |
| 3. To practice my skills, Jesse asked me to create an imaginary project with 10 tasks, which include dependent, multiple predecessor, and multiple successor tasks. She wants me to create a list showing the tasks and dependencies, and then lay it out on paper to show the logical flow, and the duration, start, and finish for each task. |
| 4. I'm excited to be part of the project team, and Jesse wants me to prepare a brief handout for the other team members with some do's and don'ts regarding project management. She said to make it look like a checklist of keys to project success. |

**FIGURE 3-36**    Task list: Session 3.

# Chapter Exercises

## Review Questions

1. What is project management, and what are its main objectives?
2. What is the relationship between tasks and events, or milestones?
3. What is a work breakdown structure? How do you create one?
4. What are task patterns, and how can you recognize them?
5. Compare the advantages and disadvantages of Gantt and PERT/CPM charts.
6. Define the following terms: best-case estimate, probable-case estimate, and worst-case estimate, and describe how project managers use these concepts.
7. How does a project manager calculate start and finish times?
8. What is a critical path, and why is it important to project managers? How do you identify the critical path?
9. What are some project reporting and communication techniques?
10. What is risk management, and why is it important?

## Discussion Topics

1. In *Poor Richard's Almanac*, Benjamin Franklin penned the familiar lines: "For the want of a nail the shoe was lost, for the want of a shoe the horse was lost, for the want of a horse the rider was lost, for the want of a rider the battle was lost, for the want of a battle the kingdom was lost — and all for the want of a horseshoe nail." Looking at the outcome in hindsight, could project management concepts have avoided the loss of the kingdom? Explain your answers.
2. Microsoft Project is an example of software that is very powerful, but quite expensive. As a project manager, how would you justify the purchase of this software? Also, would you consider using Open Workbench? Why or why not?
3. Suppose you want to manage a relatively small project, but you have no access to project management software of any kind. How could you use a spreadsheet program or a database program to manage the project? Share your ideas with the class.
4. Many managers claim to have "seat of the pants" intuition when it comes to project management. In your view, does this kind of intuition actually exist? Can you think of examples to support your views?

# Apply Your Knowledge

The Apply Your Knowledge section contains four mini-cases. Each case describes a situation, explains your role in the case, and asks you to respond to questions. You can answer the questions by applying knowledge you learned in the chapter.

## 1 Countywide Construction

At Countywide Construction, you are trying to convince your boss that he should consider modern project management techniques to manage a complex project. Your boss says that he doesn't need anything fancy, and that he can guess the total time by the seat of his pants.

To prove your point, you decide to use a very simple example of a commercial construction project, with eight tasks. You create a hypothetical work breakdown structure, as follows:

- Prepare the foundation (10 days). Then assemble the building (4 days).
- When the building is assembled, start two tasks at once: Finish the interior work (4 days) and set up an appointment for the final building inspection (30 days).
- When the interior work is done, start two more tasks at once: landscaping (5 days) and driveway paving (2 days).
- When the landscaping and driveway are done, do the painting (5 days).
- Finally, when the painting is done and the final inspection has occurred, arrange the sale (3 days).

Now you ask your boss to estimate the total time and write his answer on a piece of paper. You look at the paper and see that his guess is wrong.

1. What is the correct answer?
2. What is the critical path?
3. Create a Gantt chart that shows the WBS.
4. Create a PERT/CPM chart.

## 2 Pleasantville High School Class

The computer science instructor at Pleasantville High School has asked you to visit her class and give a presentation about project management. You have just a few days to prepare, and you need to develop a presentation that briefly describes project management tools and techniques. You can be creative, and you might want to include examples of actual projects that you know about. In any case, try to describe how projects are planned, scheduled, monitored, and reported upon. Your presentation can be in the form of a Microsoft Word outline with notes, or as a set of PowerPoint slides.

1. Prepare opening comments that give the class an overview of project management.
2. Provide the class with a glossary of the most important project management terms and definitions.
3. Think of a common event like buying a new home, and show the class how a project manager might handle the matter.
4. Create a short scenario with 4 – 6 tasks, some of which depend on each other. You can use the two preceding cases as a model. Develop a sample answer that you will show the students after you give them a chance to analyze the tasks.

**3  Lightfoot Industries**

You have been asked to lead a training session for new employees at Lightfoot Industries. You must develop a specific schedule for the tasks listed below (the estimated task duration for each is shown in parentheses):

- First, you need to contact the participants and explain their roles (1 day). Then you must obtain approval from their department managers (5 days).
- After you obtain the approval, two tasks can begin at the same time: You can arrange the meeting room (4 days) and prepare an agenda for the initial session (11 days).
- When the agenda is ready, you can start two more concurrent tasks: Prepare the information packets (4 days) and create visual aids (8 days).
- When the meeting room is arranged and the information packets are ready, you can send out an e-mail to participants (1 day).
- Finally, after the e-mail is sent to participants and the visual aids are ready, you can conduct the JAD sessions (5 days).

1. Prepare a list showing all tasks and their durations.
2. Analyze the fact situation carefully to determine which tasks are concurrent and which ones are dependent on other tasks.
3. Using PERT/CPM techniques, develop a chart that shows the project. Use a format similar to Figure 3-27 on page 117. If project management software is available, use it to develop the chart.
4. What is the critical path for this project? How do you know?

**4  Riverside Financial**

At Riverside Financial, where you work as a project manager, you have been asked to conduct user training sessions during the implementation phase for a new information system. You must develop a specific schedule for the tasks (the estimated task duration for each is shown in parentheses):

- First, you need to send an e-mail message to all department managers announcing the training sessions (1 day).
- After the e-mail message goes out, two tasks can begin at the same time: You can develop the training material (4 days) and confirm arrangements for the training facility you plan to use (11 days).
- As soon as the training material is complete, you can work on two tasks at once: Arrange to have copies of handout material printed (3 days) and develop a set of PowerPoint slides (4 days).
- When the PowerPoint slides are ready, you conduct a practice training session with the instructor who will assist you (1 day).
- Finally, when the practice session is over, the handout material is ready, and the training facility is confirmed, you conduct the user training sessions (3 days).

1. Prepare a list showing all tasks and their durations.
2. Analyze the fact situation carefully to determine which tasks are concurrent and which ones are dependant on other tasks.
3. Using PERT/CPM techniques, develop a chart that shows the project. Use a format similar to Figure 3-27 on page 117. If project management software is available, use it to develop the chart.
4. What is the critical path for this project? How do you know?

# Case Studies

Case studies allow you to practice specific skills learned in the chapter. Each chapter contains several case studies that continue throughout the textbook, and a chapter capstone case.

## NEW CENTURY HEALTH CLINIC

New Century Health Clinic offers preventive medicine and traditional medical care. In your role as an IT consultant, you will help New Century develop a new information system.

### Background

To ensure the quality, cost, and timeliness of the new information system, New Century is considering a project management approach. To obtain a better understanding of project management, Dr. Jones contacted Precision Planning, a consulting firm that specializes in managing projects of this type. He invited the company to deliver a brief presentation on project management concepts and advantages, and to submit a proposal for project management consulting services.

You joined Precision Planning two years ago as a project assistant, after working two summers as a student intern. Your supervisor, Charlie West, asked you to develop the presentation for New Century and you are excited about the opportunity. Charlie said that the main objective is to provide a clear, informative presentation.

Charlie wants you to include the following topics in your presentation: an overview of project management and its history, a description of the process, and an explanation of the most important terms and concepts. Charlie also wants you to describe task identification, various types of relationships among tasks, and schedule development. He says you should show how Gantt and PERT/CPM charts are developed, and how they can be used to plan, track, and control projects. Charlie also said that your presentation should include a specific example to illustrate all the main points.

### Assignments

1. Create a Microsoft PowerPoint presentation that will meet the requirements that Charlie outlined to you.
2. Create a Microsoft Word handout that will meet the requirements that Charlie outlined to you.
3. Create a project management example with at least six tasks. Assign durations and task dependencies. At least three of the tasks should be dependent on other tasks. Use this example to display a Gantt chart.
4. Use the same data as Assignment 3 to display a PERT/CPM chart.

## PERSONAL TRAINER, INC.

Personal Trainer, Inc. owns and operates fitness centers in a dozen Midwestern cities. The centers have done well, and the company is planning an international expansion by opening a new "supercenter" in the Toronto area. Personal Trainer's president, Cassia Umi, hired an IT consultant, Susan Park, to help develop an information system for the new facility. During the project, Susan will work closely with Gray Lewis, who will manage the new operation.

### Background

You are enjoying your job as a student intern at Personal Trainer. Last week, Susan asked you to help her plan the new information system project. Susan knows that you have completed several information systems courses at the local college, and that you have studied project management tools and techniques.

Specifically, she wants you to get ready for the next set of systems development tasks, which will be requirements modeling for the new system. Yesterday, Susan called you into her office to discuss the specific tasks she wants you to perform. After meeting with Susan, you sit down and review your notes. She wants you to treat the set of tasks as a project, and to use project management skills to plan the tasks.

Here is what she suggested to you as a work breakdown structure, including the duration she estimated for each task:

- First, you need to meet with fitness center managers at other Personal Trainer locations (10 days).
- After these meetings, you can conduct a series of interviews (8 days).
- When the interviews are complete, two tasks can begin at the same time: You can review company records (2 days) and observe business operations (7 days).
- When you have reviewed the records and observed business operations, you can analyze the BumbleBee accounting software (3 days) and study a sample of sales and billing transactions (1 day).

You are excited about the opportunity to practice your skills, and you start to work on the following list.

### Assignments

1. Create a table listing all tasks separately, with their duration.
2. Identify all dependent tasks, and indicate what predecessor tasks are required.
3. Construct a PERT/CPM chart similar to the one in Figure 3-27 on page 117. If you have access to Microsoft Project or other project management software, you can use it to help you create the chart.
4. Determine the overall duration of the project, and identify the critical path.

# CHAPTER CAPSTONE CASE:   SoftWear, Limited

SoftWear, Limited (SWL) is a continuing case study that illustrates the knowledge and skills described in each chapter. In this case study, the student acts as a member of the SWL systems development team and performs various tasks.

## Background

At a recent management meeting, SWL's president, Robert Lansing, announced a major effort to control costs and improve quality. To help achieve this goal, Mr. Lansing stated that SWL would use project management tools and techniques to plan and manage all major corporate projects. He named several people who would work as an interdepartmental team to coordinate SWL's project management efforts. Team members included April Lane, director of planning; Mike Feiner, director of human resources; and Ann Hon, director of information technology.

## The Interdepartmental Team

At their first meeting, the team came up with three main goals: Establish a company-wide understanding of project management concepts, identify suitable project management software, and develop comprehensive training for all SWL managers. Since Ann Hon had the most experience with project management, she agreed to serve as team leader. She also agreed to develop a list of concepts that the team could use as a starting point.

## Project Management Concepts

The team met again a week later, and Ann distributed a list of 10 key questions:

1.   What is a project?
2.   What are project characteristics, constraints, and risks?
3.   What is a project stakeholder?
4.   What is the role of a project manager?
5.   What is project planning?
6.   What is project scheduling?
7.   What is project monitoring and controlling?
8.   What is project reporting?
9.   What is project risk management?
10.   What are the indications of project success or failure?

As the team members reviewed the list, Ann said that a set of working definitions would be a good first step in developing a company-wide approach for managing projects. She suggested that the answers were available from various sources, including a considerable body of literature and numerous online links. She also pointed out that the answers would be a key part of the proposed training program for SWL managers. The team decided to split up the research tasks and share the results at the next meeting.

## Project Management Software

Ann made arrangements for the other team members to obtain a copy of Microsoft Project, which is the leading project management program. She also suggested that each of them try the brief Project training courses that are available on the Microsoft Web site. She then walked them though a two-hour session that demonstrated the software. She showed examples of Gantt charts, PERT charts, milestones, task dependencies, and resource assignments.

*(continues)*

## CHAPTER CAPSTONE CASE:   SoftWear, Limited (continued)

Ann also pointed out that other software alternatives exist, including free, open-source programs, such as Open Workbench, which is supported by a large user group. For now, the team agreed to obtain pricing and licensing information for Microsoft Project, and to look into other alternatives to determine whether the other programs could exchange data with Microsoft Project.

### Project Management Training

Ann suggested that the team compare the pros and cons of in-house training versus vendor-supplied training options. Again, Ann suggested the Microsoft Web site as a good starting point to evaluate third-party solutions. Using information on the site, the team was able to identify three training providers. After contacting these firms, the team had some realistic time and cost estimates for outside training solutions.

Ann suggested that the team should also consider a train-the-trainer approach where she would instruct an initial group from all SWL departments, and the training team would then provide training sessions within their respective departments. Meanwhile, Mike Feiner wondered whether any current SWL employees had listed project management experience and skills in their applications or résumés.

### SWL Team Tasks

1. Using the material in this chapter and other reference material if necessary, develop a set of answers to the 10 questions that Ann presented to the team.
2. Suppose that Ann asked you to create an outline for her two-hour demo session. You can use Microsoft Project if it is available to you, or you can download a free demo version from the Microsoft Web site. In your outline, try to mention the basic information that a user would need to get started with a simple project.
3. Visit the Web site for Open Workbench and write a description of the product. Try to include as many features as possible, and list the pros and cons of the program. Determine whether the program can exchange information with Microsoft Project, and whether any special techniques are necessary to accomplish the transfer.
4. Microsoft has launched MPUG, which stands for Microsoft Project User Group. MPUG's stated mission is to deliver Microsoft Office Project content, resources, opportunities, and community networking worldwide. Explore the site at mpug.com and note the various levels of membership. Should SWL encourage IT staff members to join this group? Write up a recommendation with your reasons.

### Manage the SWL Project

You have been asked to manage SWL's new information system project. One of your most important activities will be to identify project tasks and determine when they will be performed. Before you begin, you should review the SWL case in this chapter. Then list and analyze the tasks, as follows:

**LIST THE TASKS**   Start by listing and numbering at least 10 tasks that the SWL team needs to perform to fulfill the objectives of this chapter. Your list can include SWL Team Tasks and any other tasks that are described in this chapter. For example, Task 3 might be to Identify the project tasks and Task 6 might be to Analyze task relationships.

# CHAPTER CAPSTONE CASE:    SoftWear, Limited (continued)

**ANALYZE THE TASKS**    Now study the tasks to determine the order in which they should be performed. First identify all concurrent tasks, which are not dependent on other tasks. In the example shown in Figure 3-37, Tasks 1, 2, 3, 4, and 5 are concurrent tasks, and could begin at the same time if resources are available.

Other tasks are dependent tasks, because they cannot be performed until one or more earlier tasks have been completed. For each dependent task, you must identify specific tasks that need to be completed before these tasks can begin. For example, you need to identify the project tasks before you can analyze the task relationships, so Task 6 cannot begin until Task 3 is completed, as Figure 3-37 shows.

This chapter describes project management tools, techniques, and software. To learn more, you can use the Features section on your Student Study Tool CD-ROM, or visit the Management Information Systems CourseMate Web site at **www.cengagebrain.com** and locate the project management resources library for this book. On the Web, Microsoft offers demo versions, training, and tips for using Project 2010. You also can visit the OpenWorkbench.org site to learn more about this free, open-source software.

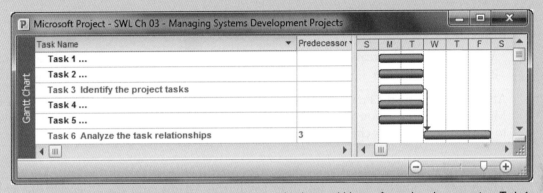

**FIGURE 3-37**    Tasks 1, 2, 3, 4, and 5 are concurrent tasks that could be performed at the same time. Task 6 is a dependent task that cannot be performed until Task 3 has been completed.

## Ready for a Challenge?

In additional to technical skills, IT professionals need critical thinking skills such as perception, organization, analysis, problem-solving, and decision-making. The Ready for a Challenge feature can help you learn, practice, and apply critical thinking skills that you can take to the workplace.

The IT group at Game Technology has received approval to add a new entry-level systems analyst position. You will help set up the hiring timetable and tasks. After speaking to several people in the department, you identified seven tasks and the order in which they should be performed.

Using your notes, you write up the following statement: First, review the applications (2 days). Then start three tasks: notify the IT team (2 days), reserve a conference room (1 day), and set up an interview schedule (5 days). When the team has been notified and the conference room reserved, prepare a set of interview questions (2 days). When the questions are ready and the interview schedule has been developed, conduct the interviews (5 days). After the interviews are done, meet with the hiring committee to select a candidate (1 day).

### Practice Tasks

A.  Prepare a work breakdown structure showing tasks, durations, and predecessor tasks.

B.  Calculate the start and finish date for each task, and determine the critical path.

After you complete the Practice Tasks, to check your work and view sample answers, visit the Management Information Systems CourseMate Web site at **www.cengagebrain.com**, navigate to the resources for this chapter, and locate Ready for a Challenge?.

### The Challenge

The hiring committee made a job offer to Sharon Adams, and she accepted. She will start her new job in three weeks. As IT department intern, you were asked to set up an orientation for her, including meetings with human resources, users, and the IT team. She also would go on a tour of the company, and confirm a security clearance. After thinking about this, you come up with a suggested orientation schedule, as follows:

First, Sharon would meet with human resources to learn about company benefits and policies (3 hours). When that meeting is over, she could handle three tasks at once: she could tour the company offices (4 hours), meet with users (3 hours), and work on the necessary paperwork (2 hours). After the tour and user meetings, she could meet with the IT managers (1 hour). Then, after meeting the IT managers and with all the paperwork completed, she would meet with the entire IT team for a brief introduction (1 hour).

### Challenge Tasks

A.  Prepare a work breakdown structure showing tasks, durations, and predecessor tasks.

B.  Calculate the start and finish date for each task, and determine the critical path.

# PHASE 2 SYSTEMS ANALYSIS

As the Dilbert cartoon suggests, a successful project manager must determine the requirements before starting the design process, not the other way around. You will learn more about fact-finding and modeling system requirements in the systems analysis phase.

Systems analysis is the second of five phases in the systems development life cycle. In the previous phase, systems planning, you conducted a preliminary investigation to determine the project's feasibility. Now you will use requirements modeling, data and process modeling, and object modeling techniques to represent the new system. You also will consider various development strategies for the new system, and plan for the transition to systems design tasks. The deliverable for this phase is the system requirements document.

# CHAPTER 4 Determining Requirements

**Chapter 4** is the first of four chapters in the systems analysis phase. This chapter describes the process of gathering facts about a systems project, preparing documentation, and creating models that will be used to design and develop the system.

## INTRODUCTION

After an overview of the systems analysis phase, this chapter describes requirements modeling techniques and team-based methods that systems analysts use to visualize and document new systems. The chapter then discusses system requirements and fact-finding techniques, which include interviewing, documentation review, observation, surveys and questionnaires, sampling, and research.

Chapter 4 includes a Video Learning Session that shows you how to use a functional decomposition diagram (FDD) to model business functions and processes.

## OBJECTIVES

*When you finish this chapter, you will be able to:*

- Describe systems analysis phase activities

- Explain joint application development (JAD), rapid application development (RAD), and agile methods

- Use a functional decomposition diagram (FDD) to model business functions and processes

- Describe the Unified Modeling Language (UML) and examples of UML diagrams

- List and describe system requirements, including outputs, inputs, processes, performance, and controls

- Explain the concept of scalability

- Use fact-finding techniques, including interviews, documentation review, observation, questionnaires, sampling, and research

- Define total cost of ownership (TCO)

- Conduct a successful interview

- Develop effective documentation methods to use during systems development

## CHAPTER INTRODUCTION CASE:   Mountain View College Bookstore

**Background:** Wendy Lee, manager of college services at Mountain View College, wants a new information system that will improve efficiency and customer service at the three college bookstores.

In this part of the case, Tina Allen (systems analyst) and David Conroe (student intern) are talking about requirements modeling tasks and concepts.

| | |
|---|---|
| **Participants:** | Tina and David |
| **Location:** | Tina's office, Monday morning, October 3, 2011 |
| **Project status:** | The project has advanced to the systems analysis phase. Now, Tina and David will work on modeling, fact-finding, and the documentation they need to build a requirements model for the proposed bookstore information system. |
| **Discussion topics:** | Modeling, team-based development strategies, fact-finding techniques, and documentation |

**Tina:** Before I tell you about the project, look at this Dilbert cartoon. You'll like it!

**David:** *It's funny, but scary too. Hope it doesn't apply to us!*

**Tina:** Me too. That's why we have to do a good job of requirements modeling.

**David:** *So, what do we do next?*

**Tina:** We need to create a model of the new system. We call this a requirements model, because it will include all the outputs, inputs, processes, and controls for the new system. The model will consist of various diagrams, charts, and documentation.

**David:** *How will we use the model when we're done?*

DILBERT: © Scott Adams/Dist. by United Feature Syndicate, Inc.

**Tina:** We'll study it carefully and review it frequently with system users.

**David:** *Who are the users?*

**Tina:** Users might include bookstore staff, students, faculty members, and the college business office. External users might include textbook publishers and suppliers of bookstore merchandise. The main thing is to work with users every step of the way. We'll perform fact-finding, and we'll document everything carefully. Here's a task list to get us started:

**FIGURE 4-1**   Typical requirements modeling task list.

## Systems Analysis Phase Tasks

**FIGURE 4-2** The systems analysis phase consists of requirements modeling, data and process modeling, object modeling, and consideration of development strategies. Notice that the systems analysis tasks are interactive, even though the waterfall model generally depicts sequential development.

# SYSTEMS ANALYSIS PHASE OVERVIEW

The overall objective of the systems analysis phase is to understand the proposed project, ensure that it will support business requirements, and build a solid foundation for system development. In this phase, you use models and other documentation tools to visualize and describe the proposed system.

## Systems Analysis Activities

The systems analysis phase includes the four main activities shown in Figure 4-2: requirements modeling, data and process modeling, object modeling, and consideration of development strategies.

Although the waterfall model shows sequential SDLC phases, it is not uncommon for several phases (or certain tasks within a phase) to interact during the development process, just as they would in an adaptive model. For example, this occurs whenever new facts are learned or system requirements change during the modeling process. Figure 4-2 shows typical interaction among the three modeling tasks: requirements modeling, data and process modeling, and object modeling.

To learn more about data flow diagrams, visit the Management Information Systems CourseMate Web site at **www.cengagebrain.com** and navigate to the **Video Learning Sessions** for this book. These sessions can help you understand key concepts, practice your skills, and check your work.

**REQUIREMENTS MODELING** This chapter describes **requirements modeling**, which involves fact-finding to describe the current system and identification of the requirements for the new system, such as outputs, inputs, processes, performance, and security. **Outputs** refer to electronic or printed information produced by the system. **Inputs** refer to necessary data that enters the system, either manually or in an automated manner. **Processes** refer to the logical rules that are applied to transform the data into meaningful information. **Performance** refers to system characteristics such as speed, volume, capacity, availability, and reliability. **Security** refers to hardware, software, and procedural controls that safeguard and protect the system and its data from internal or external threats.

**DATA AND PROCESS MODELING** In Chapter 5, Data and Process Modeling, you will continue the modeling process by learning how to represent graphically system data and processes using traditional structured analysis techniques. As you learned in Chapter 1, structured analysis identifies the data flowing into a process, the business rules that transform the data, and the resulting output data flow.

**OBJECT MODELING** Chapter 6 discusses object modeling, which is another popular modeling technique. While structured analysis treats processes and data as separate components, object-oriented analysis (O-O) combines data and the processes that act on the data into things called objects. These objects represent actual people, things, transactions, and events that affect the system. During the system development process, analysts often use both modeling methods to gain as much information as possible.

**DEVELOPMENT STRATEGIES** In Chapter 7, Development Strategies, you will consider various development options and prepare for the transition to the systems design phase of the SDLC. You will learn about software trends, acquisition and development alternatives, outsourcing, and formally documenting requirements for the new system.

The deliverable, or end product, of the systems analysis phase is a **system requirements document**, which is an overall design for the new system. In addition, each activity within the systems analysis phase has an end product and one or more milestones. As you learned in Chapter 3, project managers use various tools and techniques to coordinate people, tasks, timetables, and budgets.

## Systems Analysis Skills

You will need strong analytical and interpersonal skills to build an accurate model of the new system. **Analytical skills** enable you to identify a problem, evaluate the key elements, and develop a useful solution. **Interpersonal skills** are especially valuable to a systems analyst who must work with people at all organizational levels, balance conflicting needs of users, and communicate effectively.

Because information systems affect people throughout the company, you should consider team-oriented strategies as you begin the systems analysis phase.

## Team-Based Techniques: JAD, RAD, and Agile Methods

The IT department's goal is to deliver the best possible information system, at the lowest possible cost, in the shortest possible time. To achieve the best results, system developers view users as partners in the development process. Greater user involvement usually results in better communication, faster development times, and more satisfied users.

The traditional model for systems development was an IT department that used structured analysis and consulted users only when their input or approval was needed. Although the IT staff still has a central role, and structured analysis remains a popular method of systems development, most IT managers invite system users to participate actively in various development tasks.

As you learned in Chapter 1, team-based approaches have been around for some time. A popular example is **joint application development (JAD)**, which is a user-oriented technique for fact-finding and requirements modeling. Because it is not linked to a specific development methodology, systems developers use JAD whenever group input and interaction are desired.

Another popular user-oriented method is **rapid application development (RAD)**. RAD resembles a condensed version of the entire SDLC, with users involved every step of the way. While JAD typically focuses only on fact-finding and requirements determination, RAD provides a fast-track approach to a full spectrum of system development tasks, including planning, design, construction, and implementation.

Finally, as you learned in Chapter 1, **agile methods** represent a recent trend that stresses intense interaction between system developers and users. JAD, RAD, and agile methods are discussed in the following sections.

## JOINT APPLICATION DEVELOPMENT

Joint application development (JAD) is a popular fact-finding technique that brings users into the development process as active participants.

**VIDEO LEARNING SESSIONS**

To learn more about obect modeling, visit the Management Information Systems CourseMate Web site at **www. cengagebrain. com** and navigate to the **Video Learning Sessions** for this book. These sessions can help you understand key concepts, practice your skills, and check your work.

**ON THE WEB**

To learn more about interpersonal skills, visit the Management Information Systems CourseMate Web site at **www. cengagebrain. com**, navigate to **On the Web Links** for this chapter, and locate the Interpersonal Skills link.

## User Involvement

Users have a vital stake in an information system, and they should participate fully in the development process. Until recent years, the IT department usually had sole responsibility for systems development, and users had a relatively passive role. During the development process, the IT staff would collect information from users, define system requirements, and construct the new system. At various stages of the process, the IT staff might ask users to review the design, offer comments, and submit changes.

Today, users typically have a much more active role in systems development. IT professionals now recognize that successful systems must be user-oriented, and users need to be involved, formally or informally, at every stage of system development.

One popular strategy for user involvement is a JAD team approach, which involves a task force of users, managers, and IT professionals that works together to gather information, discuss business needs, and define the new system requirements.

## JAD Participants and Roles

A JAD team usually meets over a period of days or weeks in a special conference room or at an off-site location. Either way, JAD participants should be insulated from the distraction of day-to-day operations. The objective is to analyze the existing system, obtain user input and expectations, and document user requirements for the new system.

The JAD group usually has a project leader, who needs strong interpersonal and organizational skills, and one or more members who document and record the results and decisions. Figure 4-3 describes typical JAD participants and their roles. IT staff members often serve as JAD project leaders, but that is not always the case. Systems analysts on the JAD team participate in discussions, ask questions, take notes, and provide support to the team. If CASE tools are available, analysts can develop models and enter documentation from the JAD session directly into the CASE tool.

A typical JAD session agenda is shown in Figure 4-4. The JAD process involves intensive effort by all team members. Because of the wide range of input and constant interaction among the participants, many companies believe that a JAD group produces the best possible definition of the new system.

| JAD PARTICIPANT | ROLE |
|---|---|
| JAD project leader | Develops an agenda, acts as a facilitator, and leads the JAD session |
| Top management | Provides enterprise-level authorization and support for the project |
| Managers | Provide department-level support for the project and understanding of how the project must support business functions and requirements |
| Users | Provide operational-level input on current operations, desired changes, input and output requirements, user interface issues, and how the project will support day-to-day tasks |
| Systems analysts and other IT staff members | Provide technical assistance and resources for JAD team members on issues such as security, backup, hardware, software, and network capability |
| Recorder | Documents results of JAD sessions and works with systems analysts to build system models and develop CASE tool documentation |

**FIGURE 4-3** Typical JAD participants and roles.

| Project leader | • Introduce all JAD team members<br>• Discuss ground rules, goals, and objectives for the JAD sessions<br>• Explain methods of documentation and use of CASE tools, if any |
| --- | --- |
| Top management (sometimes called the project owner or sponsor) | • Explain the reason for the project and express top management authorization and support |
| Project leader | • Provide overview of the current system and proposed project scope and constraints<br>• Present outline of specific topics and issues to be investigated |
| Open discussion session, moderated by project leader | • Review the main business processes, tasks, user roles, input, and output<br>• Identify specific areas of agreement or disagreement<br>• Break team into smaller groups to study specific issues and assign group leaders |
| JAD team members working in smaller group sessions, supported by IT staff | • Discuss and document all system requirements<br>• Develop models and prototypes |
| Group leaders | • Report on results and assigned tasks and topics<br>• Present issues that should be addressed by the overall JAD team |
| Open discussion session, moderated by project leader | • Review reports from small group sessions<br>• Reach consensus on main issues<br>• Document all topics |
| Project leader | • Present overall recap of JAD session<br>• Prepare report that will be sent to JAD team members |

**FIGURE 4-4**   Typical agenda for a JAD session.

## JAD Advantages and Disadvantages

Compared with traditional methods, JAD is more expensive and can be cumbersome if the group is too large relative to the size of the project. Many companies find, however, that JAD allows key users to participate effectively in the requirements modeling process. When users participate in the systems development process, they are more likely to feel a sense of ownership in the results, and support for the new system. When properly used, JAD can result in a more accurate statement of system requirements, a better understanding of common goals, and a stronger commitment to the success of the new system.

## RAPID APPLICATION DEVELOPMENT

Rapid application development (RAD) is a team-based technique that speeds up information systems development and produces a functioning information system. Like JAD, RAD uses a group approach, but goes much further. While the end product of JAD is a requirements model, the end product of RAD is the new information system. RAD is a complete methodology, with a four-phase life cycle that parallels the traditional SDLC phases. Companies use RAD to reduce cost and development time, and increase the probability of success.

RAD relies heavily on prototyping and user involvement. The RAD process allows users to examine a working model as early as possible, determine if it meets their needs, and suggest necessary changes. Based on user input, the prototype is modified and the interactive process continues until the system is completely developed and users are satisfied. The project team uses CASE tools to build the prototypes and create a continuous stream of documentation.

### RAD Phases and Activities

The RAD model consists of four phases: requirements planning, user design, construction, and cutover, as shown in Figure 4-5. Notice the continuous interaction between the user design and construction phases.

**ON THE WEB**

To learn more about RAD, visit the Management Information Systems CourseMate Web site at **www. cengagebrain. com**, navigate to **On the Web Links** for this chapter, and locate the RAD link.

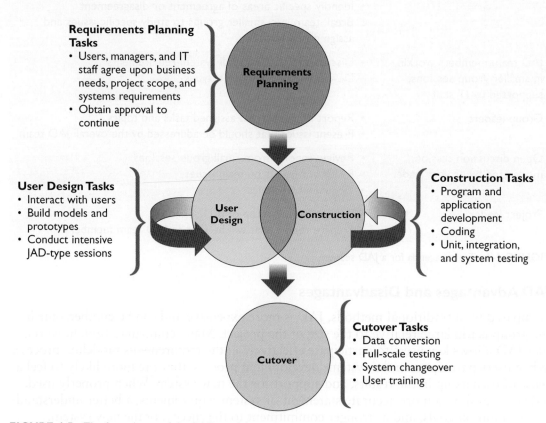

**FIGURE 4-5**  The four phases of the RAD model are requirements planning, user design, construction, and cutover. Notice the continuous interaction between the user design and construction phases.

**REQUIREMENTS PLANNING**  The **requirements planning phase** combines elements of the systems planning and systems analysis phases of the SDLC. Users, managers, and IT staff members discuss and agree on business needs, project scope, constraints, and system requirements. The requirements planning phase ends when the team agrees on the key issues and obtains management authorization to continue.

**USER DESIGN**  During the **user design phase,** users interact with systems analysts and develop models and prototypes that represent all system processes, outputs, and inputs. The RAD group or subgroups typically use a combination of JAD techniques and CASE tools to translate user needs into working models. User design is a continuous, interactive process that allows users to understand, modify, and eventually approve a working model of the system that meets their needs.

**CONSTRUCTION** The **construction phase** focuses on program and application development tasks similar to the SDLC. In RAD, however, users continue to participate and still can suggest changes or improvements as actual screens or reports are developed.

**CUTOVER** The **cutover phase** resembles the final tasks in the SDLC implementation phase, including data conversion, testing, changeover to the new system, and user training. Compared with traditional methods, the entire process is compressed. As a result, the new system is built, delivered, and placed in operation much sooner.

## RAD Objectives

The main objective of all RAD approaches is to cut development time and expense by involving users in every phase of systems development. Because it is a continuous process, RAD allows the development team to make necessary modifications quickly, as the design evolves. In times of tight corporate budgets, it is especially important to limit the cost of changes that typically occur in a long, drawn-out development schedule.

In addition to user involvement, a successful RAD team must have IT resources, skills, and management support. Because it is a dynamic, user-driven process, RAD is especially valuable when a company needs an information system to support a new business function. By obtaining user input from the beginning, RAD also helps a development team design a system that requires a highly interactive or complex user interface.

## RAD Advantages and Disadvantages

RAD has advantages and disadvantages compared with traditional structured analysis methods. The primary advantage is that systems can be developed more quickly with significant cost savings. A disadvantage is that RAD stresses the mechanics of the system itself and does not emphasize the company's strategic business needs. The risk is that a system might work well in the short term, but the corporate and long-term objectives for the system might not be met. Another potential disadvantage is that the accelerated time cycle might allow less time to develop quality, consistency, and design standards. RAD can be an attractive alternative, however, if an organization understands the possible risks.

# AGILE METHODS

In Chapter 1, you learned that agile methods attempt to develop a system incrementally, by building a series of prototypes and constantly adjusting them to user requirements. As the agile process continues, developers revise, extend, and merge earlier versions into the final product. An agile approach emphasizes continuous feedback, and each incremental step is affected by what was learned in the prior steps.

As agile methods become more popular, a large community of agile-related software and services has evolved. For example, Visual Paradigm offers Agilian, which includes a set of agile modeling tools, as shown in Figure 4-6 on the next page. The Agilian modeling toolset includes support for many modeling tools, such as the Unified Modeling Language, entity-relationship diagrams, data flow diagrams, and business process modeling, among others.

**FIGURE 4-6**   Visual Paradigm's Agilian includes many types of agile modeling tools.

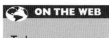

**ON THE WEB**

To learn more about agile methods, visit the Management Information Systems CourseMate Web site at **www. cengagebrain. com**, navigate to **On the Web Links** for this chapter, and locate the Agile Methods link.

Some agile developers prefer not to use CASE tools at all, and rely instead on whiteboard displays and arrangements of movable sticky notes. This approach, they believe, reinforces the agile strategy: simple, rapid, flexible, and user-oriented.

**Scrum** is another agile approach. The name is derived from the rugby term *scrum* (Figure 4-7), where team members prepare to lunge at each other to achieve their objectives. The systems development version of Scrum involves the same intense interaction, though more mental than physical. In a Scrum session, agile team members play specific roles, including colorful designations as *pigs* or *chickens*. These roles are based on the old joke about the pig and chicken who discuss a restaurant where ham and eggs would be served. However, the pig declines, because that role would require a total commitment, while for the chicken, it would only be a contribution.

In the agile world, the *pigs* include the product owner, the facilitator, and the development team; while the *chickens* include users, other stakeholders, and managers. Scrum sessions have specific guidelines that emphasize time blocks, interaction, and team-based activities that result in deliverable software.

**FIGURE 4-7**   In a rugby scrum, team members prepare to lunge at each other to achieve their objectives.

## Agile Method Advantages and Disadvantages

Agile, or adaptive, methods are very flexible and efficient in dealing with change. They are popular because they stress team interaction and reflect a set of community-based values. Also, frequent deliverables constantly validate the project and reduce risk.

However, some potential problems exist. For example, team members need a high level of technical and interpersonal skills. Also, a lack of structure and documentation can introduce risk factors. Finally, the overall project may be subject to significant change in scope as user requirements continue to evolve during the project.

## CASE IN POINT 4.1: NORTH HILLS COLLEGE

North Hills College has decided to implement a new registration system that will allow students to register online, as well as in person. As IT manager, you decide to set up a JAD session to help define the requirements for the new system. The North Hills organization is fairly typical, with administrative staff that includes a registrar, a student support and services team, a business office, an IT group, and a number of academic departments. Using this information, you start work on a plan to carry out the JAD session. Who would you invite to the session, and why? What would be your agenda for the session, and what would take place at each stage of the session?

## MODELING TOOLS AND TECHNIQUES

Models help users, managers, and IT professionals understand the design of a system. Modeling involves graphical methods and nontechnical language that represent the system at various stages of development. During requirements modeling, you can use various tools to describe business processes, requirements, and user interaction with the system.

In Chapter 1, you learned about CASE tools that offer powerful modeling features. CASE tool modeling is discussed in detail in Appendix B.

Systems analysts use modeling and fact-finding interactively — first they build fact-finding results into models, then they study the models to determine whether additional fact-finding is needed. To help them understand system requirements, analysts use functional decomposition diagrams, business process models, data flow diagrams, and Unified Modeling Language diagrams. Any of these diagrams can be created with CASE tools or standalone drawing tools if desired.

## VIDEO LEARNING SESSION: FUNCTIONAL DECOMPOSITION DIAGRAMS (FDDs)

Video Learning Sessions can help you understand key concepts, practice your skills, and check your work. To access the sessions, visit the Management Information Systems CourseMate Web site at **www.cengagebrain.com** and navigate to the **Video Learning Sessions** for this book. This session is about functional decomposition diagrams (FDDs). You'll learn about FDDs and why they are important, how to use FDDs to model business functions and processes, and how to use CASE tools to create FDDs.

### Functional Decomposition Diagrams

A **functional decomposition diagram (FDD)** is a top-down representation of a function or process. Using an FDD, an analyst can show business functions and break them down into lower-level functions and processes. Creating an FDD is similar to drawing an organization chart — you start at the top and work your way down. Figure 4-8 shows an FDD of a library system drawn with the Visible Analyst CASE tool. FDDs can be used at several stages of systems development. During requirements modeling, analysts use FDDs to model business functions and show how they are organized into

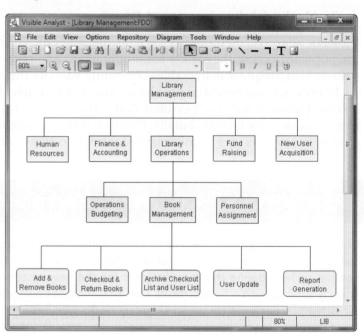

**FIGURE 4-8**   FDD showing five top-level functions. The Library Operations function includes two additional levels that show processes and subprocesses.

The CASE tools in Appendix B can help you document business functions and processes, develop graphical models, and provide an overall framework for information system development. To learn more about these tools, turn to Appendix B.

lower-level processes. Those processes translate into program modules during application development.

### Business Process Modeling

As you learned in Chapter 1, a **business process model (BPM)** describes one or more business processes, such as handling an airline reservation, filling a product order, or updating a customer account. During requirements modeling, analysts often create models that use a standard language called **business process modeling notation (BPMN)**. BPMN includes various shapes and symbols to represent events, processes, and workflows.

When you create a business process model using a CASE tool such as Visible Analyst, your diagram automatically becomes part of the overall model. In the example shown in Figure 4-9, using BPMN terminology, the overall diagram is called a **pool**, and the designated customer areas are called **swim lanes**. Integrating BPM into the CASE development process leads to faster results, fewer errors, and reduced cost. Appendix B describes business process modeling in more detail.

## Data Flow Diagrams

Working from a functional decomposition diagram, analysts can create **data flow diagrams (DFDs)** to show how the system stores, processes, and transforms data. The DFD in Figure 4-10 describes adding and removing books, which is a function shown in the Library Management diagram in Figure 4-8. Notice that the two shapes in the DFD represent processes, each with various inputs and outputs. Additional levels of information and detail are depicted in other, related DFDs. Data and process modeling is described in detail in Chapter 5.

## Unified Modeling Language

The **Unified Modeling Language (UML)** is a widely used method of visualizing and documenting software systems design. UML uses object-oriented design concepts, but it is independent of any specific programming language and can be used to describe business processes and requirements generally.

UML provides various graphical tools, such as use case diagrams and sequence diagrams. During requirements modeling, a systems analyst can utilize the UML to represent the information system from a user's viewpoint. Use case diagrams, sequence diagrams, and other UML concepts are discussed in more detail in Chapter 6, along with other object-oriented analysis concepts. A brief description of each technique follows.

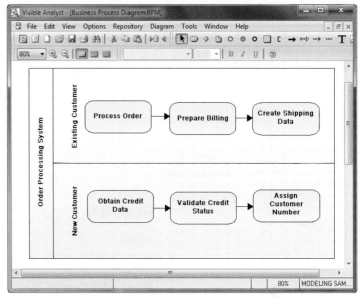

**FIGURE 4-9**  Using the Visible Analyst CASE tool, an analyst can create a business process diagram. The overall diagram is called a pool, and the two separate customer areas are called swim lanes.

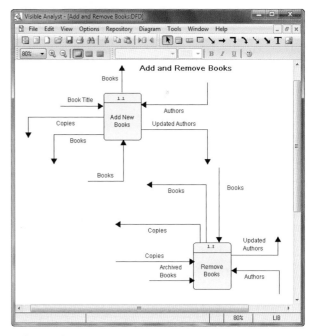

**FIGURE 4-10**  A library system DFD shows how books are added and removed.

**USE CASE DIAGRAMS**  During requirements modeling, systems analysts and users work together to document requirements and model system functions. A **use case diagram** visually represents the interaction between users and the information system. In a use case diagram, the user becomes an **actor**, with a specific role that describes how he or she interacts with the system. Systems analysts can draw use case diagrams freehand or use CASE tools that integrate the use cases into the overall system design.

Figure 4-11 shows a simple use case diagram for a sales system where the actor is a customer and the use case involves a credit card validation that is performed by the system. Because use cases depict the system through the eyes of a user, common business

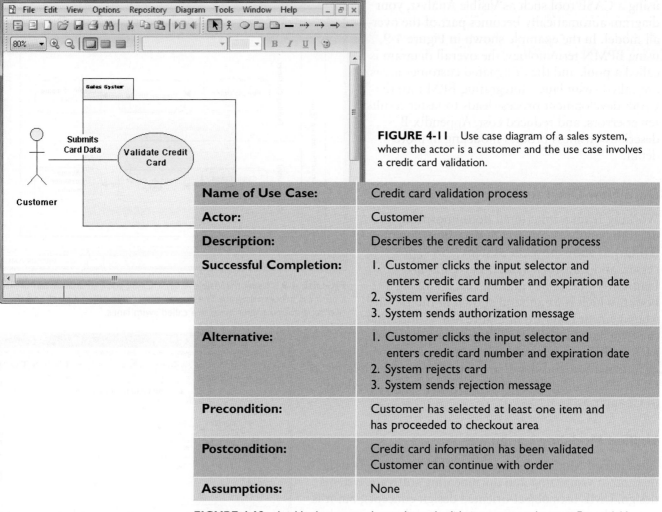

**FIGURE 4-11** Use case diagram of a sales system, where the actor is a customer and the use case involves a credit card validation.

| Name of Use Case: | Credit card validation process |
|---|---|
| Actor: | Customer |
| Description: | Describes the credit card validation process |
| Successful Completion: | 1. Customer clicks the input selector and enters credit card number and expiration date<br>2. System verifies card<br>3. System sends authorization message |
| Alternative: | 1. Customer clicks the input selector and enters credit card number and expiration date<br>2. System rejects card<br>3. System sends rejection message |
| Precondition: | Customer has selected at least one item and has proceeded to checkout area |
| Postcondition: | Credit card information has been validated Customer can continue with order |
| Assumptions: | None |

**FIGURE 4-12** A table documents the credit card validation use case shown in Figure 4-11.

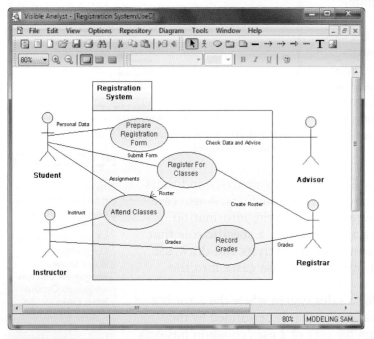

**FIGURE 4-13** Use case diagram of a student records system.

language can be used to describe the transactions. For example, Figure 4-12 shows a table that documents the credit card validation use case, and Figure 4-13 shows a student records system, with several use cases and actors.

**SEQUENCE DIAGRAMS** A sequence diagram shows the timing of interactions between objects as they occur. A systems analyst might use a sequence diagram to show all possible outcomes, or focus on a single scenario. Figure 4-14 shows a simple sequence diagram of a successful credit card validation. The interaction proceeds from top to bottom along a vertical timeline, while the horizontal arrows represent messages from one object to another.

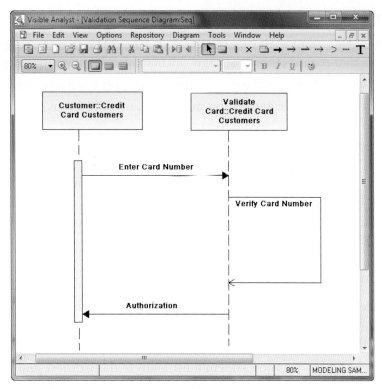

**FIGURE 4-14**  Sequence diagram showing a credit card validation process.

## SYSTEM REQUIREMENTS CHECKLIST

During requirements modeling, systems developers must identify and describe all system requirements. A **system requirement** is a characteristic or feature that must be included in an information system to satisfy business requirements and be acceptable to users. System requirements serve as benchmarks to measure the overall acceptability of the finished system.

System requirements fall into five general categories: outputs, inputs, processes, performance, and controls. Typical examples of system requirements for each category are listed below.

### Output Examples

✓ The Web site must report online volume statistics every four hours, and hourly during peak periods.

✓ The inventory system must produce a daily report showing the part number, description, quantity on hand, quantity allocated, quantity available, and unit cost of all sorted by part number.

✓ The contact management system must generate a daily reminder list for all sales reps.

✓ The purchasing system must provide suppliers with up-to-date specifications.

✓ The sales tracking system must produce a daily fast-moving-item report, listing all products that exceed the forecasted sales volume grouped by style, color, size, and reorder status.

✓ The customer analysis system must produce a quarterly report that identifies changes in ordering patterns or trends with statistical comparisons to the previous four quarters.

## Input Examples

✓ Manufacturing employees must swipe their ID cards into online data collection terminals that record labor costs and calculate production efficiency.

✓ The department head must enter overtime hours on a separate screen.

✓ Student grades must be entered on machine-scannable forms prepared by the instructor.

✓ Each input form must include date, time, product code, customer number, and quantity.

✓ Data entry screens must be uniform, except for background color, which can be changed by the user.

✓ A data entry person at the medical group must input patient services into the billing system.

## Process Examples

✓ The student records system must calculate the GPA at the end of each semester.

✓ As the final step in year-end processing, the payroll system must update employee salaries, bonuses, and benefits and produce tax data required by the IRS.

✓ The warehouse distribution system must analyze daily orders and create a routing pattern for delivery trucks that maximizes efficiency and reduces unnecessary mileage.

✓ The human resources system must interface properly with the existing payroll system.

✓ The video rental system must not execute new rental transactions for customers who have overdue videos.

✓ The prescription system must automatically generate an insurance claim form.

## Performance Examples

✓ The system must support 25 users online simultaneously.

✓ Response time must not exceed four seconds.

✓ The system must be operational seven days a week, 365 days a year.

✓ The accounts receivable system must prepare customer statements by the third business day of the following month.

✓ The student records system must produce class lists within five hours after the end of registration.

✓ The online inventory control system must flag all low-stock items within one hour after the quantity falls below a predetermined minimum.

## Control Examples

✓ The system must provide logon security at the operating system level and at the application level.

✓ An employee record must be added, changed, or deleted only by a member of the human resources department.

✓ The system must maintain separate levels of security for users and the system administrator.

✓ All transactions must have audit trails.

✓ The manager of the sales department must approve orders that exceed a customer's credit limit.

✓ The system must create an error log file that includes the error type, description, and time.

## FUTURE GROWTH, COSTS, AND BENEFITS

In addition to the system requirements, systems analysts must consider scalability, which determines how a system will handle future growth and demands, and the total cost of ownership, which includes all future operational and support costs.

### Scalability

**Scalability** refers to a system's ability to handle increased business volume and transactions in the future. Because it will have a longer useful life, a scalable system offers a better return on the initial investment.

To evaluate scalability, you need information about projected future volume for all outputs, inputs, and processes. For example, for a Web-based order processing system, you would need to know the maximum projected number of concurrent users, the periods of peak online activity, the number and types of data items required for each transaction, and the method of accessing and updating customer files.

Even to print customer statements, you need to know the number of active accounts and have a forecast for one, two, or five years, because that information affects future hardware decisions. In addition, with realistic volume projections, you can provide reliable cost estimates for related expenses, such as postage and online charges.

Similarly, to ensure that a Web-based hotel reservation system is sufficiently scalable, you would need to project activity levels for several years of operation. For example, you might forecast the frequency of online queries about room availability and estimate the time required for each query and the average response time. With that information, you could estimate server transaction volume and network requirements.

Transaction volume has a significant impact on operating costs. When volume exceeds a system's limitations, maintenance costs increase sharply. Volume can change dramatically if a company expands or enters a new line of business. For example, a new Internet-based marketing effort might require an additional server and 24-hour technical support.

Data storage also is an important scalability issue. You need to determine how much data storage is required currently and predict future needs based on system activity and growth. Those requirements affect hardware, software, and network bandwidth needed to maintain system performance. You also must consider data retention requirements and determine whether data can be deleted or archived on a specific timetable.

### Total Cost of Ownership

In addition to direct costs, systems developers must identify and document indirect expenses that contribute to the **total cost of ownership (TCO)**. TCO is especially important if the development team is assessing several alternatives. After considering the indirect costs, which are not always apparent, a system that seems inexpensive initially might actually turn out to be the most costly choice. One problem is that cost estimates tend to understate indirect costs such as user support and downtime productivity losses. Even if accurate figures are unavailable, systems analysts should try to identify indirect costs and include them in TCO estimates.

The financial analysis tools in Appendix C can help you analyze project costs, benefits, and economic feasibility. To learn more about these tools, turn to Appendix C.

To learn more about REJ, visit the Management Information Systems CourseMate Web site at **www. cengagebrain. com**, navigate to **On the Web Links** for this chapter, and locate the REJ link.

Microsoft has developed a method for measuring total costs and benefits, called **Rapid Economic Justification (REJ)**, which is described in Figure 4-15. According to Microsoft, REJ is a framework to help IT professionals analyze and optimize IT investments. Notice that the primary emphasis is on business improvement, rather than operational efficiency. As the Web site points out, the strategic role of IT investments should be included, even when the specific benefits are difficult to quantify.

**FIGURE 4-15**  Microsoft developed Rapid Economic Justification (REJ) as a framework to help IT professionals analyze and optimize IT investments.

## FACT-FINDING

Now that you understand the categories of system requirements, scalability, and TCO, the next step is to begin collecting information. Whether you are working on your own or as a member of a JAD team, during requirements modeling you will use various fact-finding techniques, including interviews, document review, observation, surveys and questionnaires, sampling, and research.

### Fact-Finding Overview

Although software can help you to gather and analyze facts, no program actually performs fact-finding for you. First, you must identify the information you need. Typically, you begin by asking a series of questions, such as these:

- What business functions are supported by the current system?
- What strategic objectives and business requirements must be supported by the new system?
- What are the benefits and TCO of the proposed system?
- What transactions will the system process?
- What information do users and managers need from the system?

- Must the new system interface with legacy systems?
- What procedures could be eliminated by business process reengineering?
- What security issues exist?
- What risks are acceptable?
- What budget and timetable constraints will affect system development?

To obtain answers to these questions, you develop a fact-finding plan, which can involve another series of questions (*who*, *what*, *where*, *when*, and *how*), or use a more structured approach such as the Zachman Framework, which is explained in a following section. Either way, you will develop a strategy, carry out fact-finding techniques, document the results, and prepare a system requirements document, which is presented to management.

## Who, What, Where, When, How, and Why?

Fact-finding involves answers to five familiar questions: *who*, *what*, *where*, *when*, and *how*. For each of those questions, you also must ask another very important question: *why*. Some examples of these questions are:

1. *Who?* Who performs each of the procedures within the system? Why? Are the correct people performing the activity? Could other people perform the tasks more effectively?

2. *What?* What is being done? What procedures are being followed? Why is that process necessary? Often, procedures are followed for many years and no one knows why. You should question why a procedure is being followed at all.

3. *Where?* Where are operations being performed? Why? Where could they be performed? Could they be performed more efficiently elsewhere?

4. *When?* When is a procedure performed? Why is it being performed at this time? Is this the best time?

5. *How?* How is a procedure performed? Why is it performed in that manner? Could it be performed better, more efficiently, or less expensively in some other manner?

There is a difference between asking what *is* being done and what *could* or *should* be done. The systems analyst first must understand the current situation. Only then can he or she tackle the question of what *should* be done. Figure 4-16 lists the basic questions and when they should be asked. Notice that the first two columns relate to the current system, but the third column focuses on the proposed system.

| CURRENT SYSTEM | | PROPOSED SYSTEM |
|---|---|---|
| Who does it? | Why does this person do it? | Who should do it? |
| What is done? | Why is it done? | What should be done? |
| Where is it done? | Why is it done there? | Where should it be done? |
| When is it done? | Why is it done then? | When should it be done? |
| How is it done? | Why is it done this way? | How should it be done? |

**FIGURE 4-16**   Sample questions during requirements modeling as the focus shifts from the current system to the proposed system.

**ON THE WEB**

To learn more about the Zachman Framework, visit the Management Information Systems CourseMate Web site at **www. cengagebrain. com**, navigate to **On the Web Links** for this chapter, and locate The Zachman Framework link.

## The Zachman Framework

In the 1980s, John Zachman observed how industries such as architecture and construction handled complex projects, and he suggested that the same ideas could be applied to information systems development. His concept, the **Zachman Framework for Enterprise Architecture,** is a model that asks the traditional fact-finding questions in a systems development context, as shown in Figure 4-17. The Zachman Framework is a popular approach, and the Visible Analyst CASE tool now includes a Zachman Framework interface that allows users to view a systems project from different perspectives and levels of detail. The Zachman Framework helps managers and users understand the model and ensures that overall business goals translate into successful IT projects.

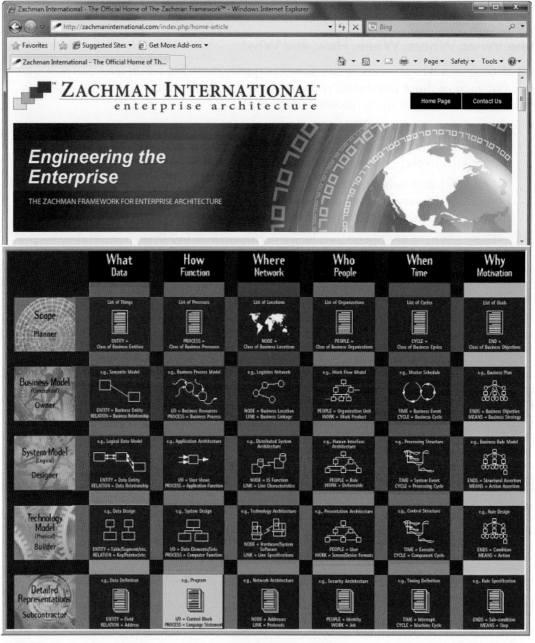

**FIGURE 4-17**  Visible Analyst uses the Zachman Framework for Enterprise Architecture. The Zachman concept presents traditional fact-finding questions in a systems development context.

## INTERVIEWS

Interviewing is an important fact-finding tool during the systems analysis phase. An **interview** is a planned meeting during which you obtain information from another person. You must have the skills needed to plan, conduct, document, and evaluate interviews successfully.

After you identify the information you need, as described earlier in the chapter, you can begin the interviewing process, which consists of seven steps for each interview:

1. Determine the people to interview.
2. Establish objectives for the interview.
3. Develop interview questions.
4. Prepare for the interview.
5. Conduct the interview.
6. Document the interview.
7. Evaluate the interview.

### Step 1: Determine the People to Interview

To get an accurate picture, you must select the right people to interview and ask them the right questions. During the preliminary investigation, you talked mainly to middle managers or department heads. Now, during the systems analysis phase, you might need to interview people from all levels of the organization.

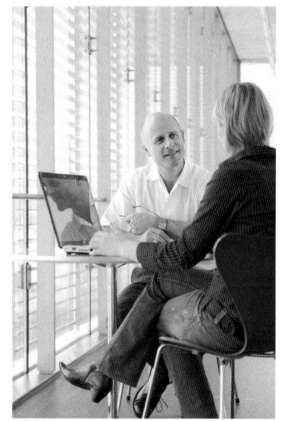

Although you can select your interview candidates from the formal organization charts that you reviewed earlier, you also must consider any informal structures that exist in the organization. Informal structures usually are based on interpersonal relationships and can develop from previous work assignments, physical proximity, unofficial procedures, or personal relationships such as the informal gathering shown in Figure 4-18. In an **informal structure**, some people have more influence or knowledge than appears on an organization chart. Your knowledge of the company's formal and informal structures helps you determine the people to interview during the systems analysis phase.

Should you interview several people at the same time? Group interviews can save time and provide an opportunity to observe interaction among the participants. Group interviews also can present problems. One person might dominate the conversation, even when questions are addressed specifically to others. Organization level also can present a problem, as the presence of senior managers in an interview might prevent lower-level employees from expressing themselves candidly.

### Step 2: Establish Objectives for the Interview

After deciding on the people to interview, you must establish objectives for the session. First, you should determine the general areas to be discussed, and then list the facts you want to gather. You also should try to solicit ideas, suggestions, and opinions during the interview.

**FIGURE 4-18**  When setting up interviews, an analyst should look outside a formal organization chart to identify people who might provide valuable information.

The objectives of an interview depend on the role of the person being interviewed. Upper-level managers can provide the big picture and help you to understand the system as a whole. Specific details about operations and business processes are best learned from people who actually work with the system on a daily basis.

In the early stages of systems analysis, interviews usually are general. As the fact-finding process continues, however, the interviews focus more on specific topics. Interview objectives also vary at different stages of the investigation. By setting specific objectives, you create a framework that helps you decide what questions to ask and how to phrase the questions.

## Step 3: Develop Interview Questions

Creating a standard list of interview questions helps to keep you on track and avoid unnecessary tangents. Also, if you interview several people who perform the same job, a standard question list allows you to compare their answers. Although you have a list of specific questions, you might decide to depart from it because an answer to one question leads to another topic that you want to pursue. That question or topic then should be included in a revised set of questions used to conduct future interviews. If the question proves to be extremely important, you may need to return to a previous interviewee to query him or her on the topic.

The interview should consist of several different kinds of questions: open-ended, closed-ended, or questions with a range of responses. When you phrase your questions, you should avoid **leading questions** that suggest or favor a particular reply. For example, rather than asking, "What advantages do you see in the proposed system?" you might ask, "Do you see any advantages in the proposed system?"

**OPEN-ENDED QUESTIONS** Open-ended **questions** encourage spontaneous and unstructured responses. Such questions are useful when you want to understand a larger process or draw out the interviewee's opinions, attitudes, or suggestions. Here are some examples of open-ended questions: What are users saying about the new system? How is this task performed? Why do you perform the task that way? How are the checks reconciled? What added features would you like to have in the new billing system? Also, you can use an open-ended question to probe further by asking: Is there anything else you can tell me about this topic?

**CLOSED-ENDED QUESTIONS** Closed-ended **questions** limit or restrict the response. You use closed-ended questions when you want information that is more specific or when you need to verify facts. Examples of closed-ended questions include the following: How many personal computers do you have in this department? Do you review the reports before they are sent out? How many hours of training does a clerk receive? Is the calculation procedure described in the manual? How many customers ordered products from the Web site last month?

**RANGE-OF-RESPONSE QUESTIONS** Range-of-response **questions** are closed-ended questions that ask the person to evaluate something by providing limited answers to specific responses or on a numeric scale. This method makes it easier to tabulate the answers and interpret the results. Range-of-response questions might include these: On a scale of 1 to 10, with 1 the lowest and 10 the highest, how effective was your training? How would you rate the severity of the problem: low, medium, or high? Is the system shutdown something that occurs never, sometimes, often, usually, or always?

## Step 4: Prepare for the Interview

After setting the objectives and developing the questions, you must prepare for the interview. Careful preparation is essential because an interview is an important meeting and not just a casual chat. When you schedule the interview, suggest a specific day and time and let the interviewee know how long you expect the meeting to last. It is also a good idea to send an e-mail or place a reminder call the day before the interview.

Remember that the interview is an interruption of the other person's routine, so you should limit the interview to no more than one hour. If business pressures force a postponement of the meeting, you should schedule another appointment as soon as it is convenient. Remember to keep department managers informed of your meetings with their staff members. Sending a message to each department manager listing your planned appointments is a good way to keep them informed. Figure 4-19 is an example of such a message.

You should send a list of topics to an interviewee several days before the meeting, especially when detailed information is needed, so the person can prepare for the interview and minimize the need for a follow-up meeting. Figure 4-20 shows a sample message that lists specific questions and confirms the date, time, location, purpose, and anticipated duration of the interview.

If you have questions about documents, ask the interviewee to have samples available at the meeting. Your advance memo should include a list of the documents you want to discuss, if you know what they are. Also, you can make a general request for documents, as the analyst did in her e-mail shown in Figure 4-20.

Two schools of thought exist about the best location for an interview. Some analysts believe that interviews should take place in the interviewee's office, whereas other analysts feel that a neutral location such as a conference room is better.

Supporters of interviews in the interviewee's office believe that is the best location because it makes the interviewee feel comfortable during the meeting. A second

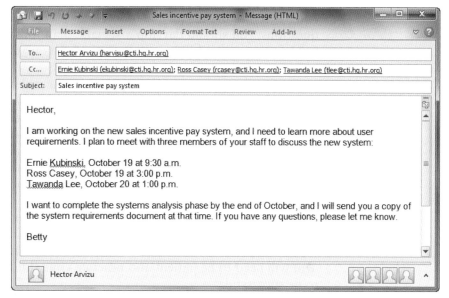

**FIGURE 4-19**   Sample message to a department head about interviews.

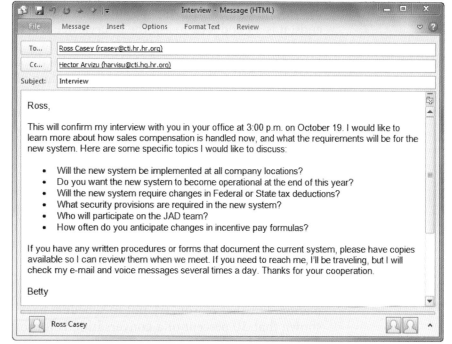

**FIGURE 4-20**   Sample message to confirm an interview.

argument in favor of the interviewee's office is that the office is where he or she has the easiest access to supporting material that might be needed during the discussion. If you provide a complete list of topics in advance, however, the interviewee can bring the necessary items to a conference room or other location.

Supporters of neutral locations stress the importance of keeping interruptions to a minimum so both people can concentrate fully. In addition, an interview that is free of interruptions takes less time. If the meeting does take place in the interviewee's office, you should suggest tactfully that all calls be held until the conclusion of the interview.

## Step 5: Conduct the Interview

After determining the people to interview, setting your objectives, and preparing the questions, you should develop a specific plan for the meeting. When conducting an interview, you should begin by introducing yourself, describing the project, and explaining your interview objectives.

During the interview, ask questions in the order in which you prepared them, and give the interviewee sufficient time to provide thoughtful answers. Establishing a good rapport with the interviewee is important, especially if this is your first meeting. If the other person feels comfortable and at ease, you probably will receive more complete and candid answers. Your primary responsibility during an interview is to listen carefully to the answers. Analysts sometimes hear only what they expect to hear. You must concentrate on what is said and notice any nonverbal communication that takes place. This process is called **engaged listening**.

After asking a question, allow the person enough time to think about the question and arrive at an answer. Studies have shown that the maximum pause during a conversation is usually three to five seconds. After that interval, one person will begin talking. You will need to be patient and practice your skills in many actual interview situations to be successful.

When you finish asking your questions, summarize the main points covered in the interview and explain the next course of action. For example, mention that you will send a follow-up memo or that the interviewee should get back to you with certain information. When you conclude the interview, thank the person and encourage him or her to contact you with any questions or additional comments. Also, when the interview ends, it is a good idea to ask the interviewee whether he or she can suggest any additional topics that should be discussed.

After an interview, you should summarize the session and seek a confirmation from the other person. By stating your understanding of the discussion, the interviewee can respond and correct you, if necessary. One approach is to rephrase the interviewee's answers. For example, you can say, "If I understand you correctly, you are saying that ..." and then reiterate the information given by the interviewee.

## Step 6: Document the Interview

Although taking notes during an interview has both advantages and disadvantages, the accepted view is that note taking should be kept to a minimum. Although you should write down a few notes to jog your memory after the interview, you should avoid writing everything that is said. Too much writing distracts the other person and makes it harder to establish a good rapport.

After conducting the interview, you must record the information quickly. You should set aside time right after the meeting to record the facts and evaluate the information. For that reason, try not to schedule back-to-back interviews. Studies have shown that 50 percent of a conversation is forgotten within 30 minutes. You, therefore, should use your notes to record the facts immediately so you will not forget them. You can summarize the facts by preparing a narrative describing what took place or by recording the answers you received next to each question on your prepared question list.

Tape recorders are effective tools for an interview; however, many people feel uncomfortable when recorders are present. Before using a recorder, you should discuss its use with the interviewee. Assure the interviewee that you will erase the tape after you transcribe your notes and that you will stop and rewind the tape anytime during the interview at his or her request. If you ask sensitive questions or the interviewee wants to answer a question without being recorded, explain that you will turn off the tape for a period of time during the interview.

Even with a tape recorder in use, you should listen carefully to the interviewee's responses so you can ask good follow-up questions. Otherwise, you might have to return for a second visit to ask the questions you missed the first time. Also, remember that each recorded interview takes twice the amount of time, because you must listen to or view the recorded meeting again after conducting the interview itself.

After the interview, send a memo to the interviewee expressing your appreciation for his or her time and cooperation. In the memo, you should note the date, time, location, purpose of the interview, and the main points you discussed so the interviewee has a written summary and can offer additions or corrections.

## Step 7: Evaluate the Interview

In addition to recording the facts obtained in an interview, try to identify any possible biases. For example, an interviewee who tries to protect his or her own area or function might give incomplete answers or refrain from volunteering information. Or, an interviewee with strong opinions about the current or future system might distort the facts. Some interviewees might answer your questions in an attempt to be helpful even though they do not have the necessary experience to provide accurate information.

## CASE IN POINT 4.2:  DEEP RIVER COLLEGE

Deep River College is a two-year school in Southern California. Twice a year, the fundraising office at Deep River mails requests for donations to the alumni. The staff uses a word processing program and a personal information database to create personalized letters. Data on past contributions and other alumni information, however, is stored manually. The dean, Alexandra Ali, recently submitted a systems request asking the college's IT department to develop a computerized alumni information system. The school does not have a formal systems review committee, and each department has an individual budget for information services.

Eddie Bateman, a systems analyst, performed a preliminary investigation and he concluded that the system met all the feasibility tests. After reading his report, Alexandra asked him to proceed with the systems analysis phase. Eddie has scheduled an interview with her, and he has asked you to help him prepare for the meeting. Specifically, he wants you to list all the topics he should cover during the interview. Eddie also wants you to prepare a list of specific questions that he should ask. Be sure to include open-ended, closed-ended, and range-of-response questions.

## Unsuccessful Interviews

No matter how well you prepare for interviews, some are not successful. One of the main reasons could be that you and the interviewee did not get along well. Such a situation can be caused by several factors. For example, a misunderstanding or personality conflict could affect the interview negatively, or the interviewee might be afraid that the new system will eliminate or change his or her job.

In other cases, the interviewee might give only short or incomplete responses to your open-ended questions. If so, you should switch to closed-ended questions or questions with a range of responses, or try rephrasing your open-ended questions into those types of questions. If that still does not help, you should find a tactful way to conclude the meeting.

Continuing an unproductive interview is difficult. The interviewee could be more cooperative later, or you might find the information you seek elsewhere. If failure to obtain specific information will jeopardize the success of the project, inform your supervisor, who can help you decide what action to take. Your supervisor might contact the interviewee's supervisor, ask another systems analyst to interview the person, or find some other way to get the needed information.

## CASE IN POINT 4.3: FastPak Overnight Package System

FastPak, the nation's fourth-largest overnight package system, is headquartered in Los Angeles, California. Jesse Evans is a systems analyst on an IT team that is studying ways to update FastPak's package tracking system. Jesse prepared well for her interview with Jason Tanya, FastPak's executive vice president. Mr. Tanya did not ask his assistant to hold his calls during the meeting, however. After several interruptions, Jesse tactfully suggested that she could come back another time, or perhaps that Mr. Tanya might ask his assistant to hold his calls. "No way," he replied. "I'm a very busy man and we'll just have to fit this in as we can, even if it takes all day." Jesse was unprepared for his response. What are her options? Is an analyst always in control of this kind of situation? Why or why not?

## OTHER FACT-FINDING TECHNIQUES

In addition to interviewing, systems analysts use other fact-finding techniques, including document review, observation, questionnaires and surveys, sampling, and research. Such techniques are used before interviewing begins to obtain a good overview and to help develop better interview questions.

### Document Review

**Document review** can help you understand how the current system is supposed to work. Remember that system documentation sometimes is out of date. Forms can change or be discontinued, and documented procedures often are modified or eliminated. You should obtain copies of actual forms and operating documents currently in use. You also should review blank copies of forms, as well as samples of actual completed forms. You usually can obtain document samples during interviews with the people who perform that procedure. If the system uses a software package, you should review the documentation for that software.

### Observation

The **observation** of current operating procedures is another fact-finding technique. Seeing the system in action gives you additional perspective and a better understanding of system procedures. Personal observation also allows you to verify statements made in interviews and determine whether procedures really operate as they are described.

Through observation, you might discover that neither the system documentation nor the interview statements are accurate.

Personal observation also can provide important advantages as the development process continues. For example, recommendations often are better accepted when they are based on personal observation of actual operations. Observation also can provide the knowledge needed to test or install future changes and can help build relationships with the users who will work with the new system.

Plan your observations in advance by preparing a checklist of specific tasks you want to observe and questions you want to ask. Consider the following issues when you prepare your list:

1. Ask sufficient questions to ensure that you have a complete understanding of the present system operation. A primary goal is to identify the methods of handling situations that are not covered by standard operating procedures. For example, what happens in a payroll system if an employee loses a time card? What is the procedure if an employee starts a shift 10 minutes late but then works 20 minutes overtime? Often, the rules for exceptions such as these are not written or formalized; therefore, you must try to document any procedures for handling exceptions.

2. Observe all the steps in a transaction and note the documents, inputs, outputs, and processes involved.

3. Examine each form, record, and report. Determine the purpose each item of information serves.

4. Consider each user who works with the system and the following questions: What information does that person receive from other people? What information does this person generate? How is the information communicated? How often do interruptions occur? How much downtime occurs? How much support does the user require, and who provides it?

5. Talk to the people who receive current reports to see whether the reports are complete, timely, accurate, and in a useful form. Ask whether information can be eliminated or improved and whether people would like to receive additional information.

As you observe people at work, as shown in Figure 4-21, consider a factor called the **Hawthorne Effect**. The name comes from a well-known study performed in the Hawthorne plant of the Western Electric Company in the 1920s. The purpose of the study was to determine how various changes in the work environment would affect employee productivity. The surprising result was that productivity improved during observation whether the conditions were made better or worse. Researchers concluded that productivity seemed to improve whenever the workers knew they were being observed.

Although some recent studies have raised questions about the original findings, you should be aware that observation can and does have an effect on normal

**FIGURE 4-21**   The Hawthorne study suggested that worker productivity improves during observation. Always consider the Hawthorne Effect when observing the operation of an existing system.

operations. With this in mind, always give advance notice to the supervisor in that area. In some situations, it might be helpful to explain the purpose of your visit to the people being observed.

## Questionnaires and Surveys

In projects where it is desirable to obtain input from a large number of people, a questionnaire can be a valuable tool. A **questionnaire**, also called a **survey**, is a document containing a number of standard questions that can be sent to many individuals.

Questionnaires can be used to obtain information about a wide range of topics, including workloads, reports received, volumes of transactions handled, job duties, difficulties, and opinions of how the job could be performed better or more efficiently. Figure 4-22 shows a sample questionnaire that includes several different question and response formats.

**PURCHASE REQUISITION QUESTIONNAIRE**

Pat Kline, Vice President, Finance, has asked us to investigate the purchase requisition process to see if it can be improved. Your input concerning this requisition process will be very valuable. We would greatly appreciate it if you could complete the following questionnaire and return it by March 10 to Dana Juarez in information technology. If you have any questions, please call Dana at x2561.

**A. YOUR OBSERVATIONS**
Please answer each question by checking one box.

1. How many purchase requisitions did you process in the past five working days? _____

2. What percentage of your time is spent processing requisitions?
[ ] under 20%    [ ] 60–79%
[ ] 21–39%       [ ] 80% or more
[ ] 40–59%

3. Do you believe too many errors exist on requisitions?
[ ] yes
[ ] no

4. Out of every 100 requisitions you process, how many contain errors?
[ ] fewer than 5    [ ] 20 to 29
[ ] 5 to 9          [ ] 30 to 39
[ ] 10 to 14        [ ] 40 to 49
[ ] 15 to 19        [ ] 50 or more

5. What errors do you see most often on requisitions? (Place a 1 next to the most common error, place a 2 next to the second, etc.)
[ ] incorrect charge number     [ ] missing authorization
[ ] missing charge information  [ ] other (please explain) _____
[ ] arithmetic errors
[ ] incorrect discount percent used

**B. YOUR SUGGESTIONS**
Please be specific, and give examples if possible.

1. If the currently used purchase requisition form were to be redesigned, what changes to the form would you recommend?

(If necessary, please attach another sheet)

2. Would you be interested in meeting with an information technology representative to discuss your ideas further? If so, please complete the following information:

Name _____    Department _____

Telephone _____    E-mail address _____

**FIGURE 4-22** Sample questionnaire. Does it follow the suggested guidelines?

A typical questionnaire starts with a heading, which includes a title, a brief statement of purpose, the name and telephone number of the contact person, the deadline date for completion, and how and where to return the form. The heading usually is followed by general instructions that provide clear guidance on how to answer the questions. Headings also are used to introduce each main section or portion of the survey and include instructions when the type of question or response changes. A long questionnaire might end with a conclusion that thanks the participants and reminds them how to return the form.

What about the issue of anonymity? Should people be asked to sign the questionnaire, or is it better to allow anonymous responses? The answer depends on two questions. First, does an analyst really need to know who the respondents are in order to match or correlate information? For example, it might be important to know what percentage of users need a certain software feature, but specific usernames might not be relevant. Second, does the questionnaire include any sensitive or controversial topics? Many people do not want to be identified when answering a question such as "How well has your supervisor explained the system to you?" In such cases, anonymous responses might provide better information.

When designing a questionnaire, the most important rule of all is to make sure that your questions collect the right data in a form that you can use to further your fact-finding. Here are some additional ideas to keep in mind when designing your questionnaire:

- Keep the questionnaire brief and user-friendly.

- Provide clear instructions that will answer all anticipated questions.

- Arrange the questions in a logical order, going from simple to more complex topics.

- Phrase questions to avoid misunderstandings; use simple terms and wording.

- Try not to lead the response or use questions that give clues to expected answers.

- Limit the use of open-ended questions that are difficult to tabulate.

- Limit the use of questions that can raise concerns about job security or other negative issues.

- Include a section at the end of the questionnaire for general comments.

- Test the questionnaire whenever possible on a small test group before finalizing it and distributing to a large group.

A questionnaire can be a traditional paper form, or you can create a **fill-in form** and collect data on the Internet or a company intranet. For example, you can use Microsoft Word, as shown in Figure 4-23, to create form fields, including text boxes, date pickers, and drop-down lists where users can click selections. Before you publish the form, you should protect it so users can fill it in but cannot change the layout or design. Forms also can be automated, so if a user answers *no* to question three, he or she goes directly to question eight, where the form-filling resumes.

## Sampling

When studying an information system, you should collect examples of actual documents using a process called **sampling**. The samples might include records, reports, operational logs,

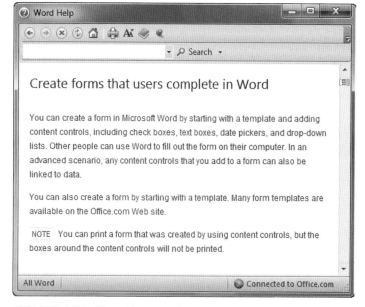

**FIGURE 4-23**  Using Microsoft Word, you can create a fill-in form with text boxes, date pickers, and drop-down lists.

data entry documents, complaint summaries, work requests, and various types of forms. Sampling techniques include systematic sampling, stratified sampling, and random sampling.

Suppose you have a list of 200 customers who complained about errors in their statements, and you want to review a representative sample of 20 customers. A **systematic sample** would select every tenth customer for review. If you want to ensure that the sample is balanced geographically, however, you could use a **stratified sample** to select five customers from each of four zip codes. Another example of stratified sampling is to select a certain percentage of transactions from each zip code, rather than a fixed number. Finally, a **random sample** selects any 20 customers.

The main objective of a sample is to ensure that it represents the overall population accurately. If you are analyzing inventory transactions, for example, you should select a sample of transactions that are typical of actual inventory operations and do not include unusual or unrelated examples. For instance, if a company performs special processing on the last business day of the month, that day is not a good time to sample *typical* daily operations. To be useful, a sample must be large enough to provide a fair representation of the overall data.

You also should consider sampling when using interviews or questionnaires. Rather than interviewing everyone or sending a questionnaire to the entire group, you can use a sample of participants. You must use sound sampling techniques to reflect the overall population and obtain an accurate picture.

**ON THE WEB**

To learn more about sampling, visit the Management Information Systems CourseMate Web site at **www.cengagebrain.com**, navigate to **On the Web Links** for this chapter, and locate the Sampling link.

## Research

**Research** is another important fact-finding technique. Your research can include the Internet, IT magazines, and books to obtain background information, technical material, and news about industry trends and developments. In addition, you can attend professional meetings, seminars, and discussions with other IT professionals, which can be very helpful in problem solving.

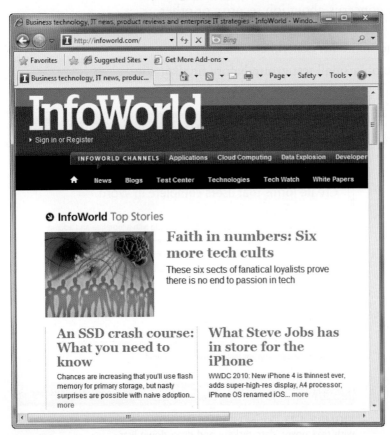

The Internet is an extremely valuable resource. Appendix D describes a variety of Internet resource tools. Using the Internet, you also can access information from federal and state governments, as well as from publishers, universities, and libraries around the world. Online forums and newsgroups are good resources for exchanging information with other professionals, seeking answers to questions, and monitoring discussions that are of interest to you.

All major hardware and software vendors maintain sites on the Web where you can obtain information about products and services offered by the company and send e-mail with specific questions to company representatives. In addition to contacting specific firms, you can access Web sites maintained by publishers and independent firms that provide links to hundreds of hardware and software vendors, as shown in Figure 4-24. Such sites are one-stop information centers where IT professionals can find information, share ideas, and keep posted on developments in technology.

**FIGURE 4-24**  InfoWorld's Web site offers many resources for IT professionals.

Research also can involve a visit to a physical location, called a **site visit**, where the objective is to observe a system in use at another location. If you are studying your firm's human resources information system, for example, you might want to see how another company's system works. Site visits also are important when considering the purchase of a software package. If the software vendor suggests possible sites to visit, be aware that such sites might constitute a biased sample. A single site visit seldom gives you true pictures, so you should try to visit more than one installation.

Before a site visit such as the one shown in Figure 4-25, prepare just as you would for an interview. Contact the appropriate manager and explain the purpose of your visit. Decide what questions you will ask and what processes you will observe. During your visit, observe how the system works and note any problems or limitations. You also will want to learn about the support provided by the vendor, the quality of the system documentation, and so on.

**FIGURE 4-25** A site visit provides an opportunity to observe a system in use.

## Interviews versus Questionnaires

When you seek input from a large group, a questionnaire is a very useful tool. On the other hand, if you require detailed information from only a few people, then you probably should interview each person individually. Is it better to interview or use a questionnaire? Each situation is different, and you must consider the type of information, time constraints, and expense factors.

The interview is more familiar and personal than a questionnaire. People who are unwilling to put critical or controversial comments in writing might talk more freely in person. Moreover, during a face-to-face interview, you can react immediately to anything the interviewee says. If surprising or confusing statements are made, you can pursue the topic with additional questions. In addition, during a personal interview, you can watch for clues to help you determine if responses are knowledgeable and unbiased. Participation in interviews also can affect user attitudes, because people who are asked for their opinions often view the project more favorably.

Interviewing, however, is a costly and time-consuming process. In addition to the meeting itself, both people must prepare, and the interviewer has to do follow-up work. When a number of interviews are planned, the total cost can be quite substantial. The personal interview usually is the most expensive fact-finding technique.

In contrast, a questionnaire gives many people the opportunity to provide input and suggestions. Questionnaire recipients can answer the questions at their convenience and do not have to set aside a block of time for an interview. If the questionnaire allows anonymous responses, people might offer more candid responses than they would in an interview.

Preparing a good questionnaire, however, like a good interview, requires skill and time. If a question is misinterpreted, you cannot clarify the meaning as you can in a face-to-face interview. Furthermore, unless questionnaires are designed well, recipients might view them as intrusive, time-consuming, and impersonal. As an analyst, you should select the technique that will work best in a particular situation.

Another popular method of obtaining input is called **brainstorming**, which refers to a small group discussion of a specific problem, opportunity, or issue. This technique encourages new ideas, allows team participation, and enables participants to build on each other's inputs and thoughts. Brainstorming can be structured or unstructured. In **structured brainstorming**, each participant speaks when it is his or her turn, or passes. In **unstructured brainstorming**, anyone can speak at any time. At some point, the results are recorded and made part of the fact-finding documentation process.

## CASE IN POINT 4.4:  CYBERSTUFF

Ann Ellis is a systems analyst at CyberStuff, a large company that sells computer hardware and software via telephone, mail order, and the Internet. CyberStuff processes several thousand transactions per week on a three-shift operation and employs 50 full-time and 125 part-time employees. Lately, the billing department has experienced an increase in the number of customer complaints about incorrect bills. During the preliminary investigation, Ann learned that some CyberStuff representatives did not follow established order entry procedures. She feels that with more information, she might find a pattern and identify a solution for the problem.

Ann is not sure how to proceed. She came to you, her supervisor, with two separate questions. First, is a questionnaire the best approach, or would interviews be better? Second, whether she uses interviews, a questionnaire, or both techniques, should she select the participants at random, include an equal number of people from each shift, or use some other approach? As Ann's supervisor, what would you suggest, and why?

## DOCUMENTATION

Keeping accurate records of interviews, facts, ideas, and observations is essential to successful systems development. The ability to manage information is the mark of a successful systems analyst and an important skill for all IT professionals.

### The Need for Recording the Facts

As you gather information, the importance of a single item can be overlooked or complex system details can be forgotten. The basic rule is to write it down. You should document your work according to the following principles:

- Record information as soon as you obtain it.
- Use the simplest recording method possible.
- Record your findings in such a way that they can be understood by someone else.
- Organize your documentation so related material is located easily.

Often, systems analysts use special forms for describing a system, recording interviews, and summarizing documents. One type of documentation is a narrative list with simple statements about what is occurring, apparent problems, and suggestions for improvement. Other forms of documentation that are described in Chapter 4 include data flow diagrams, flowcharts, sample forms, and screen captures.

### Software Tools

Many software programs are available to help you record and document information. Some examples are described here.

**CASE TOOLS**  You can use CASE tools at every stage of systems development. This chapter contains several examples of CASE tools. Appendix B describes other features and capabilities of CASE tools.

**PRODUCTIVITY SOFTWARE**  Productivity software includes word processing, spreadsheet, database management, presentation graphics, and collaboration software programs. Although Microsoft Office is the best-known set of productivity software programs, other vendors offer products in each of these categories.

Using word processing software such as Microsoft Word, Corel WordPerfect, or OpenOffice.org Writer, you can create reports, summaries, tables, and forms. In addition to standard document preparation, the program can help you organize a presentation with templates, bookmarks, annotations, revision control, and an index. You can consult the program's Help system for more information about those and other features. You also can create fill-in forms to conduct surveys and questionnaires, as described earlier in this chapter.

Spreadsheet software, such as Microsoft Excel, Corel Quattro Pro, or OpenOffice.org Calc, can help you track and manage numeric data or financial information. You also can generate graphs and charts that display the data and show possible patterns, and you can use the statistical functions in a spreadsheet to tabulate and analyze questionnaire data. A graphical format often is used in quality control analysis because it highlights problems and their possible causes, and it is effective when presenting results to management. A common tool for showing the distribution of questionnaire or sampling results is a vertical bar chart called a **histogram**. Most spreadsheet programs can create histograms and other charts that can display data you have collected. Figure 4-26 displays a typical histogram that might have resulted from the questionnaire shown in Figure 4-22 on page 166.

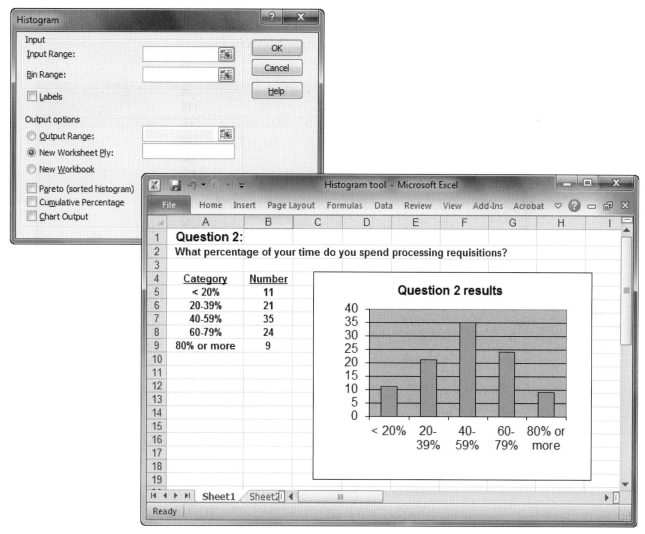

**FIGURE 4-26**   This histogram displays results from Question 2 in the questionnaire shown in Figure 4-22 on page 166.

Database management software allows you to document and organize fact-finding results such as events, observations, and data samples. You can use a database program such as Microsoft Access to manage the details of a complex project, create queries to retrieve specific information, and generate custom reports.

Presentation graphics software, such as Microsoft PowerPoint, Apple Keynote, or OpenOffice.org Impress, is a powerful tool for organizing and developing your formal presentation. Presentation graphics programs enable you to create organization charts that can be used in a preliminary investigation and later during requirements modeling. These high-quality charts also can be included in written reports and management presentations.

Collaboration software is the latest weapon in the struggle to boost productivity. More than ever, people work in teams and use Web-based software such as Google Docs and Microsoft Web Apps to access data and share files. Google and others are betting that cloud computing will create a virtual workplace, where people will be able to interact in real time, with all the benefits of a traditional face-to-face workplace, but none of the limitations.

**GRAPHIC MODELING SOFTWARE** Microsoft Visio is a popular graphic modeling tool that can produce a wide range of charts and diagrams. Visio includes a library of templates, stencils, and shapes. An analyst can use Visio to create many types of visual models, including business processes, flowcharts, network diagrams, organization charts, and Web site maps, such as the one shown in Figure 4-27.

**FIGURE 4-27** This Microsoft Visio screen shows shapes that can be used to create a Web site map.

**PERSONAL INFORMATION MANAGERS** A busy analyst needs to keep track of meetings, interviews, appointments, and deadlines. A **personal information manager** (**PIM**), such as Microsoft Outlook or IBM's Lotus Organizer, can help manage those tasks using a personal calendar and a to-do list, with priorities and the capability to check off completed items.

In addition to desktop-based organizers, handheld computers are popular. Some handheld computers, also called **personal digital assistants** (**PDAs**), accept handwritten input, while others have small keyboards. These devices can handle calendars, schedules, appointments, telephone lists, and calculations. A PDA can be standalone, Bluetooth-capable to synchronize with a desktop, or fully wireless-enabled, such as the HP iPAQ shown in Figure 4-28.

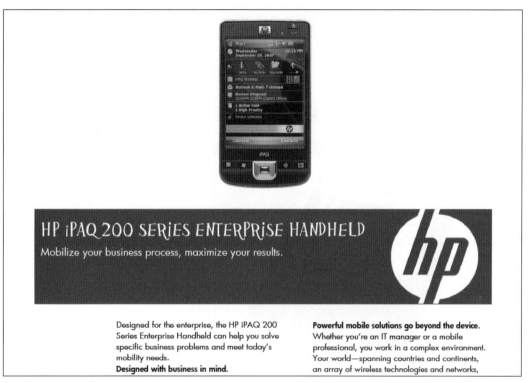

**FIGURE 4-28**   HP's iPAQ is a powerful wireless device that HP describes as a mobile handheld computer.

**WIRELESS COMMUNICATION DEVICES** Even in the dynamic world of IT, the recent explosion in wireless technology is almost unprecedented. The latest wireless standard, called **4G** (**fourth generation**), is opening new frontiers in broadband Web access, e-mail, social networking, file exchange, and streaming multimedia. Users enjoy new hardware and software, easy synchronization with office networks, and innovative services designed for a *wired* generation.

The rapid growth of wireless communication has resulted in a merger of various technologies. Many people swear by **all-in-one devices** such as Research in Motion's BlackBerry or **smart phones**, such as the Apple iPhone. Others are devoted to products that use Google's Android operating system, which is a **mobile device platform** adopted by many hardware vendors, including Motorola, Kyocera, and LG. Figure 4-29 on the next page shows some examples of these products.

Beyond hardware choices, users can select from literally thousands of portable applications for business and personal use. No one can predict the future with certainty, but it is apparent that portable wireless technology is having an enormous impact on business practices, everyday communications, and social interaction.

**FIGURE 4-29**   Three popular examples of current wireless technology.

## PREVIEW OF LOGICAL MODELING

At the conclusion of requirements modeling, systems developers should have a clear understanding of business processes and system requirements. The next step is to construct a logical model of the system.

Data and process modeling, which is described in Chapter 5, uses a structured analysis approach. Structured analysis is a popular, traditional technique that describes the system in terms of data and the processes that act on that data.

An alternative to structured analysis modeling is object modeling, which is described in Chapter 6. Object modeling is a methodology that combines data and processes into things called objects that represent actual people, things, transactions, and events. Systems analysts use object models to visualize and document real-world business processes and operations.

IT professionals have differing views about systems development methodologies, and no universally accepted approach exists. By studying both structured analysis and object-oriented methods, you gain valuable knowledge, skills, and perspective. You then can use that information to determine what method, or combination of methods, is best for the different situations you will face in your career.

# A QUESTION OF ETHICS

Your supervisor manages the corporate office where you work as a systems analyst. Several weeks ago, after hearing rumors of employee dissatisfaction, he asked you to create a survey for all IT employees. After the responses were returned and tabulated, he was disappointed to learn that many employees assigned low ratings to morale and management policies.

This morning he called you into his office and asked whether you could identify the departments that submitted the lowest ratings. No names were used on the individual survey forms. However, with a little analysis, you probably could identify the departments, because several questions were department-related.

Now you are not sure how to respond. The expectation was that the survey would be anonymous. Even though no individuals would be identified, would it be ethical to reveal which departments sent in the low ratings? Would your supervisor's motives for wanting this information matter?

## CHAPTER SUMMARY

The systems analysis phase includes three activities: requirements modeling, data and process modeling, and consideration of development strategies. The main objective is to understand the proposed project, ensure that it will support business requirements, and build a solid foundation for the systems design phase.

During requirements modeling, you identify the business-related requirements for the new information system, including outputs, inputs, processes, performance, and controls. You consider scalability to ensure that the system can support future growth and expansion. You also estimate total cost of ownership (TCO) to identify all costs, including indirect costs.

Popular team-based approaches include JAD, RAD, and agile methods. Joint application development (JAD) is a popular, team-based approach to fact-finding and requirements modeling. JAD involves an interactive group of users, managers, and IT professionals who participate in requirements modeling and develop a greater commitment to the project and to their common goals.

Rapid application development (RAD) is a team-based technique that speeds up information systems development and produces a functioning information system. RAD is a complete methodology, with a four-phase life cycle that parallels the traditional SDLC phases.

Agile methods attempt to develop a system incrementally, by building a series of prototypes and constantly adjusting them to user requirements.

Systems analysts use various tools and techniques to model system requirements. Unified Modeling Language (UML) is a widely used method of visualizing and documenting software design through the eyes of the business user. UML tools include use case diagrams and sequence diagrams to represent actors, their roles, and the sequence of transactions that occurs.

A functional decomposition diagram (FDD) is a model of business functions and processes. A CASE tool can generate a set of data flow diagrams directly from a FDD.

The fact-finding process includes interviewing, document review, observation, questionnaires, sampling, and research. Successful interviewing requires good planning and strong interpersonal and communication skills. The systems analyst must decide on the people to interview, set interview objectives, and prepare for, conduct, and analyze interviews. The analyst also might find it helpful to use one or more software tools during fact-finding.

Systems analysts should carefully record and document factual information as it is collected, and various software tools can help an analyst visualize and describe an information system. The chapter concluded with a preview of logical modeling. Data and process modeling is a structured analysis approach that views the system in terms of data and the processes that act on that data. Object modeling is an approach that views the system in terms of data and the processes that act on that data.

# Key Terms and Phrases

4G (fourth generation) *173*

actor *151*

agile methods *143*

analytical skills *143*

brainstorming *169*

business process model (BPM) *150*

business process modeling notation (BPMN) *150*

closed-ended questions *160*

construction phase *147*

cutover phase *147*

data flow diagram (DFD) *151*

document review *164*

engaged listening *162*

fill-in form *167*

functional decomposition diagram (FDD) *150*

Hawthorne Effect *165*

histogram *171*

informal structure *159*

inputs *142*

interpersonal skills *143*

interview *159*

joint application development (JAD) *143*

leading questions *160*

observation *164*

open-ended questions *160*

outputs *142*

performance *142*

personal digital assistant (PDA) *173*

personal information manager (PIM) *173*

pool *151*

processes *142*

productivity software *170*

questionnaire *166*

random sample *168*

range-of-response questions *160*

rapid application development (RAD) *143*

Rapid Economic Justification (REJ) *156*

requirements modeling *142*

requirements planning phase *146*

research *168*

sampling *167*

scalability *155*

Scrum *148*

security *142*

sequence diagram *152*

site visit *169*

smart phone *173*

stratified sample *168*

structured brainstorming *169*

survey *166*

swim lanes *151*

system requirement *153*

system requirements document *143*

systematic sample *168*

total cost of ownership (TCO) *155*

Unified Modeling Language (UML) *151*

unstructured brainstorming *169*

use case diagram *151*

user design phase *146*

Zachman Framework for Enterprise Architecture *158*

# Learn It Online

**Instructions:** To complete the Learn It Online exercises, visit the Management Information Systems CourseMate Web site at **www.cengagebrain.com**, navigate to the resources for this chapter, and click the link for the exercise you want to complete.

**1  Chapter Reinforcement**

**TF, MC, and SA**

Click one of the Chapter Reinforcement links for Multiple Choice, True/False, or Short Answer. Answer each question and submit to your instructor.

**2  Flash Cards**

Click the Flash Cards link and read the instructions. Type 20 (or a number specified by your instructor) in the Number of playing cards text box, type your name in the Enter your Name text box, and then click the Flip Card button. When the flash card is displayed, read the question and then click the ANSWER box arrow to select an answer. Flip through the Flash Cards. If your score is 15 (75%) correct or greater, click Print on the File menu to print your results. If your score is less than 15 (75%) correct, then redo this exercise by clicking the Replay button.

**3  Practice Test**

Click the Practice Test link. Answer each question, enter your first and last name at the bottom of the page, and then click the Grade Test button. When the graded practice test is displayed on your screen, click Print on the File menu to print a hard copy. Continue to take practice tests until you score 80% or better.

**4  Who Wants To Be a Computer Genius?**

Click the Computer Genius link. Read the instructions, enter your first and last name at the bottom of the page, and then click the Play button. When your score is displayed, click the PRINT RESULTS link to print a hard copy.

**5  Wheel of Terms**

Click the Wheel of Terms link. Read the instructions, and then enter your first and last name and your school name. Click the PLAY button. When your score is displayed on the screen, right-click the score and then click Print on the shortcut menu to print a hard copy.

**6  Crossword Puzzle Challenge**

Click the Crossword Puzzle Challenge link. Read the instructions, and then click the Continue button. Work the crossword puzzle. When you are finished, click the Submit button. When the crossword puzzle is redisplayed, submit it to your instructor.

## SCR Associates Case Simulation Session 4: Requirements Modeling

### Overview

The SCR Associates case study is a Web-based simulation that allows you to practice your skills in a real-world environment. The case study transports you to SCR's intranet, where you complete 12 work sessions, each aligning with a chapter. As you work on the case, you will receive e-mail and voice mail messages, obtain information from SCR's online libraries, and perform various tasks.

### How do I use the case?

- Review the SCR background material in Chapter 1.
- Read the Preview for this session and study the Task List.
- Visit the Management Information Systems CourseMate Web site at **www.cengagebrain. com**, navigate to the **SCR Case Simulation**, and locate the intranet link.
- Enter your name and the password **sad9e**. An opening screen will display the 12 sessions.
- Select this session. Check your e-mail and voice mail carefully, and then work on the tasks.

### Preview: Session 4

As you begin the requirements modeling process, you receive specific directions from your supervisor, Jesse Baker. She wants you to conduct a survey of former and prospective students, lead a JAD group session, and draft a list of system requirements based on the results of the JAD session. She also wants to see a functional decomposition diagram showing the main TIMS functions.

### Task List

1. Group managers said it was OK for their people to attend a three-day JAD session next week. Send a message to the JAD team members, with a brief explanation of JAD methods and a proposed agenda.

2. Design a questionnaire for former and potential students in SCR's training classes. Also, reply to Jesse's message about sampling. Give her a recommendation and reasons.

3. Read the JAD session summary in the Data Library and put together a list of system requirements, including outputs, inputs, processes, performance, and controls.

4. Draw an FDD of the main functions for TIMS and send it to Jesse. Be sure to show at least one or two levels of detail.

**FIGURE 4-30**   Task list: Session 4.

## Chapter Exercises

### Review Questions

1. What are the five questions typically used in fact-finding? What additional question can be asked during this process?
2. What is a systems requirement, and how are systems requirements classified?
3. What are JAD and RAD, and how do they differ from traditional fact-finding methods? What are their pros and cons?
4. What is total cost of ownership (TCO), and why is it important?
5. Provide examples of closed-ended, open-ended, and range-of-response questions.
6. What are three types of sampling, and why would you use them?
7. What is the Hawthorne Effect? Why is it significant?
8. What is a functional decomposition diagram (FDD) and why would you use one? Explain how to create an FDD.
9. What are agile methods, and what are some pros and cons of this approach?
10. To what three different audiences might you have to give a presentation? How would the presentation differ for each?

Answer question 10 after you complete the presentations section in Appendix A.

### Discussion Topics

1. A group meeting sometimes is suggested as a useful compromise between interviews and questionnaires. In such a group meeting, one systems analyst meets with and asks questions of a number of users at one time. Discuss the advantages and disadvantages of such a group meeting.
2. JAD requires strong interpersonal and communication skills on the part of the systems analyst. Are those skills different from the ones that an analyst needs when conducting one-to-one interviews? Explain your answer.
3. Research the Internet, magazines, or textbooks to find examples of each of the following types of visual aids: bar chart, pie chart, line chart, table, diagram, and bulleted list of key points. How effective do you think each aid is? Find at least one example that you feel could be improved. Discuss its shortcomings and prepare an improved version.
4. Review the presentations section in Appendix A, then attend a speech or presentation and analyze its effectiveness. Consider the speaker's delivery and how he or she organized the material, used visual aids, and handled audience questions. Describe specifically how the speech or presentation was most effective, as well as how it could have been improved.

# Apply Your Knowledge

The Apply Your Knowledge section contains four mini-cases. Each case describes a situation, explains your role in the case, and asks you to respond to questions. You can answer the questions by applying knowledge you learned in the chapter.

## 1  Elmwood College

**Situation:**

The school is considering a new system that will speed up the registration process. As a systems analyst, you are asked to develop a plan for fact-finding.

1. List all the possible techniques that you might use.
2. Describe an advantage for each technique.
3. Suppose the development budget is tight. How might that affect the fact-finding process?
4. What are five important questions to use during fact-finding?

## 2  JAD Session I

**Situation:**

You are an IT advisor to a JAD team that is studying a new inventory system. The proposed system will provide more information and faster updates, and automatically monitor fast- or slow-moving items. Some controversy exists about whether to use an on-site or off-site location for the JAD sessions.

1. How would you advise the project leader?
2. Who should be on the JAD team, and what would be their roles as team members?
3. The JAD project leader asked for advice about how to get the first session started. How would you reply?
4. You invited the senior vice president to the opening JAD session, but she says she is quite busy and might not be able to attend unless it is really important. What would you say to her?

**3** **JAD Session 2**

**Situation:**

The JAD team wants you to draw up a checklist of requirements for the new system.

1. List the five main categories of system requirements.
2. Use your imagination and provide at least one example per category of a system requirement that might be appropriate for an inventory system.
3. The project leader wants you to explain the concept of scalability to the team. How will you do that?
4. Several managers on the team have heard of TCO but are not quite sure what it is. How will you explain it to them?

**4** **Better Hardware Marketing System**

**Situation:**

Your boss, the IT director, wants you to explain the UML to a group of company managers and users who will serve on a systems development team for the new marketing system.

1. Describe the Unified Modeling Language (UML) and how it can be used during systems development.
2. Explain use case diagrams to the group, and provide a simple example.
3. Explain sequence diagrams to the group, and provide a simple example.
4. During the meeting, a manager asks you to explain why it is desirable to describe the system through the eyes of a user. How would you answer?

# Case Studies

Case studies allow you to practice specific skills learned in the chapter. Each chapter contains several case studies that continue throughout the textbook, and a chapter capstone case.

## NEW CENTURY HEALTH CLINIC

New Century Health Clinic offers preventive medicine and traditional medical care. In your role as an IT consultant, you will help New Century develop a new information system.

### Background

New Century Health Clinic has decided to computerize its office systems. The associates hired you, a local computer consultant, to perform a preliminary investigation. You had several meetings with Dr. Tim Jones to discuss the various office records and accounting systems. Anita Davenport, New Century's office manager, participated in those meetings.

In a report to the associates at the end of your investigation, you recommended conducting a detailed analysis of the patient record system, the patient and insurance billing systems, and the patient scheduling system. You believe that New Century would benefit most from implementing those three systems. Although the systems could be developed independently, you recommended analyzing all three systems together because of the significant interaction among them.

You presented your findings and recommendations at a late afternoon meeting of the associates. After answering several questions, you left the meeting so they could discuss the matter privately. Dr. Jones began the discussion by stating that he was impressed with your knowledge and professionalism, as well as your report and presentation.

Dr. Jones recommended accepting your proposal and hiring you immediately to conduct the systems analysis phase. Dr. Garcia, however, was not as enthusiastic and pointed out that such a study would certainly disrupt office procedures. The staff already had more work than they could handle, she argued, and taking time to answer your questions would only make the situation worse. Dr. Jones countered that the office workload was going to increase in any event, and that it was important to find a long-term solution to the problem. After some additional discussion, Dr. Garcia finally agreed with Dr. Jones's assessment. The next morning, Dr. Jones called you and asked you to go ahead with the systems analysis phase of the project.

### Assignments

1. Review the office organization chart you prepared in Chapter 1 for New Century.
2. List the individuals you would like to interview during the systems analysis phase.
3. Prepare a list of objectives for each of the interviews you will conduct.
4. Prepare a list of specific questions for each individual you will interview.
5. Conduct the interviews. (Consult your instructor regarding how to accomplish this. One possibility is through role-playing.)
6. Prepare a written summary of the information gained from each of the interviews. (Your instructor may want you to use a standard set of interview results.)
7. Design a questionnaire that will go to a sample of New Century patients to find out if they were satisfied with current insurance and scheduling procedures. Your questionnaire should follow the suggestions in this chapter. Also, decide what sampling method you will use and explain the reason for your choice.

## PERSONAL TRAINER, INC.

Personal Trainer, Inc., owns and operates fitness centers in a dozen Midwestern cities. The centers have done well, and the company is planning an international expansion by opening a new "supercenter" in the Toronto area. Personal Trainer's president, Cassia Umi, hired an IT consultant, Susan Park, to help develop an information system for the new facility. During the project, Susan will work closely with Gray Lewis, who will manage the new operation.

### Background

During requirements modeling for the new system, Susan Park met with fitness center managers at several Personal Trainer locations. She conducted a series of interviews, reviewed company records, observed business operations, analyzed the BumbleBee accounting software, and studied a sample of sales and billing transactions. Susan's objective was to develop a list of system requirements for the proposed system.

### Fact-Finding Summary

- A typical center has 300–500 members, with two membership levels: full and limited. Full members have access to all activities. Limited members are restricted to activities they have selected, but they can participate in other activities by paying a usage fee. All members have charge privileges. Charges for merchandise and services are recorded on a charge slip, which is signed by the member. At the end of each day, cash sales and charges are entered into the BumbleBee accounting software, which runs on a computer workstation at each location. Daily cash receipts are deposited in a local bank and credited to the corporate Personal Trainer account. The BumbleBee program produces a daily activity report with a listing of all sales transactions. At the end of the month, the local manager uses BumbleBee to transmit an accounts receivable summary to the Personal Trainer headquarters in Chicago, where member statements are prepared and mailed. Members mail their payments to the Personal Trainer headquarters, where the payment is applied to the member account.

- The BumbleBee program stores basic member information, but does not include information about member preferences, activities, and history.

- Currently, the BumbleBee program produces one local report (the daily activity report) and three reports that are prepared at the headquarters location: a monthly member sales report, an exception report for inactive members and late payers, and a quarterly profit-and-loss report that shows a breakdown of revenue and costs for each separate activity.

During the interviews, Susan received a number of "wish list" comments from local managers and staff members. For example, many managers wanted more analytical features so they could spot trends and experiment with what-if scenarios for special promotions and discounts. The most frequent complaint was that managers wanted more frequent information about the profitability of the business activities at their centers.

To enhance their business, managers wanted to offer a computerized activity and wellness log, a personal coach service, and e-mail communication with members. Managers also wanted better ways to manage information about part-time instructors and staff. Several staff members suggested a redesign for the charge slips or scannable ID cards.

### Assignments

1. List the system requirements, with examples for each category. Review the information that Susan gathered, and assume that she will add her own ideas to achieve more effective outputs, inputs, processes, performance, and controls.
2. Are there scalability issues that Susan should consider? What are they?
3. If Susan wants to conduct a survey of current or prospective members to obtain their input, what type of sampling should she use? Why?
4. Draw an FDD that shows the main operations described in the fact statement.

## BAXTER COMMUNITY COLLEGE

Baxter Community College is a two-year school in New Jersey. Twice a year, the records office at Baxter mails requests for donations to the alumni. The staff uses a word processing merge file to create personalized letters, but the data on past contributions and other alumni information is stored manually. The registrar, Mary Louise, recently submitted a systems request asking the college's IT department to develop a computerized alumni information system. The school does not have a formal systems review committee, and each department head has an individual budget for routine information services.

Todd Wagner, a systems analyst, was assigned to perform a preliminary investigation. After reading his report, Mary asked him to proceed with the systems analysis phase, saying that a formal presentation was unnecessary. Todd has scheduled an interview tomorrow with her, and he asked you to help him prepare for the meeting.

### Assignments

1. Make a list of the topics that you think Todd should cover during the interview.
2. Prepare a list of specific questions that Todd should ask. Include open-ended, closed-ended, and range-of-response questions.
3. Conduct student-to-student interviews, with half the students assuming Todd's role and the other half playing the registrar.
4. Document the information covered during the interviews.

## TOWN OF EDEN BAY

The town of Eden Bay owns and maintains a fleet of vehicles. You are a systems analyst reporting to Dawn, the town's IT manager.

### Background

In Chapter 2, you learned that the town's maintenance budget has risen sharply in recent years. Based on a preliminary investigation, the town has decided to develop a new information system to manage maintenance information and costs more effectively. The new system will be named RAVE, which stands for Repair Analysis for Vehicular Equipment.

Dawn has asked you to perform additional fact-finding to document the requirements for the new system.

### Assignments

1. Review the interview summaries in Chapter 2. For each person (Marie, Martin, Phil, Alice, and Joe), develop three additional questions: an open-ended question, a closed-ended question, and a range-of-response question.
2. Based on what you know so far, list the system requirements for the new system. You can use your imagination if the facts are insufficient. Consider outputs, inputs, processes, performance, and controls. Include at least two examples for each category.
3. You decide to analyze a sample of vehicle records. What sampling methods are available to you? Which one should you use, and why?
4. Dawn thinks it would be a good idea to conduct a JAD session to perform additional fact-finding. Draft a message to the participants, with a brief explanation of JAD methods and a proposed agenda.

# CHAPTER CAPSTONE CASE:   SoftWear, Limited

SoftWear, Limited (SWL), is a continuing case study that illustrates the knowledge and skills described in each chapter. In this case study, the student acts as a member of the SWL systems development team and performs various tasks.

## Background

In Chapter 2, you learned that SWL's vice president of finance, Michael Jeremy, requested an investigation into problems with the company's payroll system. Jane Rossman, applications manager, assigned systems analyst Rick Williams to conduct a preliminary investigation.

Rick found several problems, including input errors and a need for manual preparation of reports. The payroll department often required overtime to correct those errors and produce the reports.

The IT department recommended an in-depth analysis of the problem areas and Mr. Jeremy approved the study. Now, as the systems analysis phase begins, the next step is requirements modeling.

## Human Resources Department Interview

During the preliminary investigation phase, Rick prepared the organization chart of the human resources department shown in Figure 4-31.

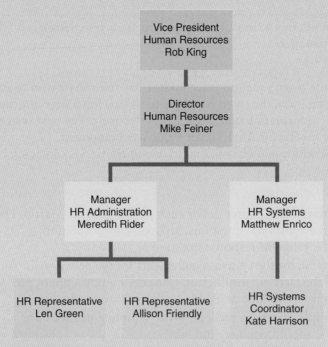

**FIGURE 4-31**   Human resources department organization chart.

Rick learned that some errors involved employee stock purchase deductions, so he decided to study that process. He knew that the human resources department initiates stock purchase deductions, so he decided to interview Meredith Rider, manager of human resources administration. Meredith is responsible for completing the paperwork for newly hired employees and sending the forms to the payroll department.

Rick called Meredith to make an appointment and sent her the confirmation message shown in Figure 4-32 that described the topics and requested copies of related forms.

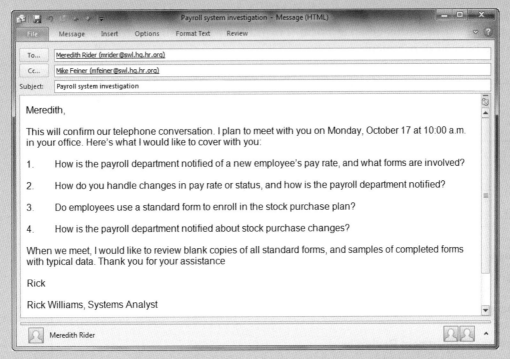

**FIGURE 4-32** Rick Williams's message to Meredith Rider regarding preparation for the interview.

In the interview, Meredith explained that new employees fill in the top portion of a Payroll Master Record Form (Form PR-1). The human resources department then adds the pay rate and other data and sends a copy of the PR-1 form to the payroll department. Meredith showed Rick a blank copy of an online PR-1 form shown in Figure 4-33. She explained that because payroll and personnel information is confidential, she could not give Rick a completed form.

**PAYROLL MASTER RECORD FORM**
(Form PR-1)

SSN _____
Name _____
last            first            middle
Address _____
street          city          state    zip
Department _____
Job title _____
Pay rate _____ per _____

Status ☐ Exempt ☐ Non-exempt ☐ Orientation ☐ Insurance
☐ W-4 OK ☐ Citizenship OK ☐ Credit Union ☐ Handbook

Checked by _____ Date _____

**FIGURE 4-33** Payroll Master Record Form (Form PR-1).

Also, when an employee's pay rate or status changes, the human resources department completes the online Payroll Status Change Form (Form PR-2) shown in Figure 4-34 and sends a copy to the payroll department.

```
                          PAYROLL STATUS CHANGE FORM
    (Form PR-2)

    SSN
                    _____
    Name
                    _____    _____  _____
                    last                         first     middle
    Department      _____  Location _____

    Status change     ☐    Old: _____    New: _____

    Pay change        ☐    Old: _____ per _____  New: _____ per _____

    Position change   ☐    Old: _____    New: _____


    Human Resources Department Review by: _____
    Date  _____
```

**FIGURE 4-34**   Payroll Status Change Form (Form PR-2).

Meredith also explained that after a 90-day probationary period, employees can participate in the SWL Credit Union. An employee submits the Payroll Deduction Change Form (Form PR-3) shown in Figure 4-35 to the human resources department, which forwards it to the payroll department.

```
                        PAYROLL DEDUCTION CHANGE FORM
    (Form PR-3)

        SSN     _____    Date _____
        Name
                _____    _____  _____
                last                   first       middle
    Department
                _____    Location _____

    W-4 exemption change     ☐    Old: _____    New: _____

    Credit Union change      ☐    Old: _____    New: _____

    Position change          ☐    Old: _____    New: _____
    _____
    (For Human Resources Department Use Only)
    Effective date of change _____
                                            By:  Human Resources Department
```

**FIGURE 4-35**   Payroll Deduction Change Form (Form PR-3).

SWL also has an Employee Stock Purchase Plan, which an employee can join after 180 days. To enroll, the employee completes an Employee Stock Purchase Plan Enrollment and Change Form (Form PR-4). The human resources department prepares a weekly report of all stock plan enrollments and changes on the Employee Stock Purchase Plan Weekly Deduction Summary Report (Form PR-5) shown in Figure 4-36 and sends a copy to the payroll department.

### EMPLOYEE STOCK PURCHASE PLAN
#### Weekly Deduction Summary Report

(Form PR-5)                                              Week ending:

| Code:<br>N= New<br>C = Change | SSN | Employee Name | Deduction Amount |
|---|---|---|---|
|  |  |  |  |
|  |  |  |  |
|  |  |  |  |
|  |  |  |  |
|  |  |  |  |
|  |  |  |  |
|  |  |  |  |
|  |  |  |  |

**FIGURE 4-36**  Employee Stock Purchase Plan Weekly Deduction Summary Report (Form PR-5).

After the interview with Meredith, Rick sent the follow-up message shown in Figure 4-37 and attached a copy of the interview documentation shown in Figure 4-37.

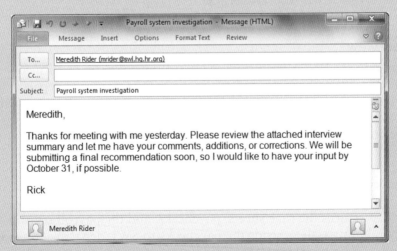

**FIGURE 4-37**  Follow-up message from Rick Williams to Meredith Rider, with a request for her comments on the interview summary.

## CHAPTER CAPSTONE CASE:  SoftWear, Limited (continued)                     SWL

Name of System:   Payroll
Date:             October 21, 2011
Prepared by:      Rick Williams
Title:            Systems Analyst
Purpose:          Interview Summary: Meredith Rider, Manager of Human Resources Administration
Location:         Raleigh

Five basic forms are used by the human resources department that relate to the payroll system:
1.  Payroll Master Record Form (Form PR-I)
2.  Payroll Status Change Form (Form PR-2)
3.  Payroll Deduction Change Form (Form PR-3)
4.  Employee Stock Purchase Plan Enrollment and Change Form (Form PR-4)
S.  Employee Stock Purchase Plan Weekly Deduction Summary Report (Form PR-S)

When an employee is hired, the following takes place:
1.  The human resources department prepares a Payroll Master Record Form (Form PR-I) with employee
    data, including Social Security number, name, address, telephone, emergency contact, and information
    about the position, title, and initial pay rate.
2.  A copy of this form is sent to the payroll department, where it is filed and maintained.
3.  Subsequent pay rate or status changes are submitted by the human resources department to the payroll
    department on a Payroll Status Change Form (Form PR-2). Payroll then files these change forms with
    the employee's PR-I form.

After 180 days of employment, the employee is eligible to enroll in the SWL Stock Purchase Plan.
1.  To enroll, an employee completes an Employee Stock Purchase Plan Enrollment and Change Form
    (Form PR-4).
2.  The human resources department prepares an Employee Stock Purchase Plan Weekly Deduction
    Summary Report Form (Form PR-S) and sends it to the payroll department with copies of the PR-4 forms,
    which then are filed with the employee's PR-I form.

I have identified several problems with the current procedures:
1.  Data errors can occur when the human resources staff prepares the weekly summary of employee stock
    purchase deductions, and no system verification takes place until incorrect deductions are reported.
2.  The system performs no verification of employment dates, and it is possible that the 90- and 180-day
    eligibility periods are applied incorrectly.
3.  The filing of the PR-2, PR-3, and PR-4 forms with the Payroll Master Record Forms in the payroll
    department could lead to problems. If any of the forms are lost or misfiled, incorrect data is entered into
    the s stem.

**FIGURE 4-38**   Documentation of the interview with Meredith Rider.

## Payroll Department Interview

Rick's next interview was with the lead payroll clerk, Nelson White. Nelson confirmed that when an employee is hired, a PR-1 form is completed in the human resources department, and a copy is sent to payroll. He also explained that each week, the payroll department sends a time sheet to every SWL department manager. The time sheet lists the employees, with space to record regular hours, vacation, sick leave, jury duty, and other codes.

After each pay period, SWL managers complete the time sheets and return them to the payroll department. Payroll then enters the pay rates and deduction information, and delivers the sheets to Business Information Systems (BIS), the service bureau that prepares SWL's payroll.

After BIS runs the payroll, it returns the time sheets, paychecks, and the payroll register to SWL. The director of payroll, Amy Calico, sends the paychecks to SWL department heads for distribution to employees.

Nelson uses the weekly payroll register to prepare a report of credit union deductions and a check to the credit union for the total amount deducted. Stock purchases, on the other hand, are processed monthly, based on the stock's closing price on the last business day of the month. Using the weekly payroll registers, Nelson manually prepares a monthly report of employee stock purchases and forwards a copy of the report and a funds transfer authorization to Carolina National Bank, which is SWL's stock transfer agent.

Rick asked Nelson why BIS did not produce a report on employee stock purchase deductions. Nelson replied that although the payroll is run weekly, the stock deductions are invested only once a month. Because the two cycles do not match, the BIS system could not handle the task.

Nelson then referred Rick to the SWL Systems and Procedures Manual page that describes how monthly Employee Stock Purchase Plan investment amounts are calculated, as shown in Figure 4-39. After blanking out the employee's name and Social Security number, Nelson also gave Rick a sample of two monthly deduction registers, as shown in Figure 4-40.

 **Procedures Manual**

**Employee Stock Purchase Plan**

To enroll in the SWL stock purchase plan, an employee submits a PR-4 form. Human resources sends a copy of the form to the payroll department. At the end of the month, accumulated deductions for that month are invested in shares of SWL stock at the current market price.

However, because weeks and months do not match up exactly, the following calculation must be used:
  a. Divide the weekly deduction by seven to get a daily deduction rate.
  b. Then multiply the number of days in the month times the daily deduction rate. The result is the total stock investment amount for that month.

Here is an example for the month of January:
  • Employee A authorizes a weekly stock plan deduction of $20.00.
  • $20.00 divided by 7 = a $2.857 daily deduction rate.
  • January has 31 calendar days, so 31 × $2.857 = $88.57, which will be the stock investment amount for January.

At the end of each month, the payroll department prepares a deduction register (PR-6) that shows weekly deductions and monthly totals.

**FIGURE 4-39**   Sample page from SWL Systems and Procedures Manual.

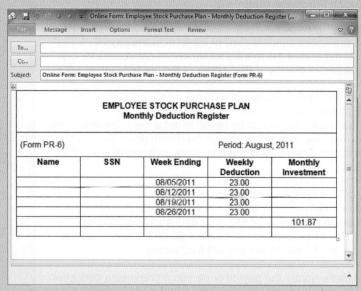

**FIGURE 4-40**   Sample of the ESIP Monthly Deduction Register for July and August, 2009.

Rick began to see why it was taking so much effort to prepare the reports. The interview with Nelson provided much more detail than the general description that Rick had received during the preliminary investigation.

## BIS Interview

Rick decided that he should talk with someone at the BIS service bureau to find out more about its operations. He learned from Nelson that Linda DeMarco was BIS's customer relations manager, so he scheduled an appointment with her.

When Rick arrived at BIS, Linda greeted him warmly. She explained that she had planned to meet with members of SWL's payroll department within the next month or two to discuss the latest developments. Because Rick now was working on SWL's payroll system, however, this meeting would save her a trip. Rick temporarily abandoned his interview plan and asked Linda what she had in mind.

"The payroll system that your company is using, which we call GAPP, for Generalized Automated Payroll Program, originally was developed here at BIS about eight years ago," Linda began. "In fact, SoftWear, Limited was one of our very first customers. We've worked together for a long time, and we are very committed to your firm. As you know, GAPP was modified and updated many times. But let's face it, even with the patches, GAPP is an antique! Anyway, I have some exciting news. We decided to develop a new, state-of-the-art payroll system. We are going to call it CHIPS, for Comprehensive High-powered Interactive Payroll System. I'm looking forward to working with SWL when you switch over to CHIPS," Linda said.

Rick took a few moments to consider this surprising development. He then asked what would happen with GAPP. Linda stated that GAPP would be available to customers for another year or two, but that BIS would make no further enhancements to the system. Using BIS resources to maintain an obsolete system would not make sense, she explained.

Before this meeting, Rick had hoped that BIS could make some minor changes to solve SWL's payroll problems. He now realized that was impossible, so he decided to learn more about CHIPS.

Rick described the problem with the mismatched deduction cycles and asked if CHIPS would handle that. Linda said that she already had looked into the matter. She pointed out that SWL was their only customer with more than one deduction application cycle. From BIS's point of view, programming CHIPS to handle multiple cycle reports did not make sense. Linda suggested that perhaps a special add-on module could be written, once CHIPS was up and running. BIS could do that kind of job on a contract basis, she added.

Rick then asked when the new system would be available and what the cost would be. Linda stated that current plans were to begin offering CHIPS sometime in the following year. She explained that the system was still in development, and she could not be more specific about timetables and costs. She was sure, however, that the monthly fee for CHIPS would not increase more than 30 percent above the current GAPP charges.

As Rick was preparing to leave, Linda urged him to keep in touch. In the next few months, she explained, plans for CHIPS would become more specific, and she would be able to answer all his questions.

### New Developments

When Rick returned from his meeting with Linda, he immediately went to his manager, Jane Rossman. After he described his visit to BIS, Jane telephoned Ann Hon, director of information technology. Within the hour, Jane and Rick held a meeting with Ann in her office. Rick repeated the details of his visit, and Ann asked for his opinion on how the developments at BIS would affect SWL's current systems analysis.

Rick explained that one of the problems — possible input errors when transferring data from the human resources summary list — might be solved easily by developing a new form or procedure. Nevertheless, he saw no obvious solutions for the stock purchase deduction problems, except to change the scope of the payroll project.

Jane, Rick, and Ann then analyzed the situation. They all agreed that because of the upcoming changes at BIS, the current payroll system project would produce very limited results and should be expanded in scope. They totaled the costs of the SWL project to that point and prepared estimates for a detailed investigation of the entire payroll system in order to meet SWL's current and future needs.

Later that week, Ann met with Michael Jeremy, vice president of finance, to discuss the situation and present her proposal to expand the project. Before she even started, however, Mr. Jeremy filled her in on the latest announcement from SWL's top management: The company had decided to move forward with the new Employee Savings and Investment Plan (ESIP) under consideration. He said that in December, Robert Lansing, SWL's president, would announce a target date of April 1, 2012, for the new ESIP plan. Mr. Jeremy explained that the new plan would be a 401(k) plan with tax advantages for employees.

Facing the new constraints on top of the existing payroll system problems, it looked like SWL would need a new payroll system after all.

## The Revised Project

Jane Rossman assigned Carla Moore, a programmer-analyst, to work with Rick Williams on the revised system project. Because they now had to determine the requirements for the complete payroll system, Rick and Carla conducted follow-up interviews with Nelson White and Meredith Rider, as well as Allison Friendly, a human resources representative, and both payroll clerks, Britton Ellis and Debra Williams. During the payroll department interviews, the payroll staff prepared samples of all the existing payroll reports. At the end of the fact-finding process, Rick and Carla decided to prepare the functional decomposition diagram shown in Figure 4-41. The diagram shows the main functions identified during the interviews.

**FIGURE 4-41**   A functional decomposition diagram (FDD) shows the main functions that were identified during the interviews.

The Payroll Register is shown in Figure 4-42. Each employee is listed on a separate line, along with his or her earnings, deductions, and net pay. BIS creates three copies of this report each week. One copy is sent to Michael Jeremy, and one copy goes to Amy Calico. The third copy is used by the payroll department for determining SWL's obligation for tax withholding and FICA payments and for applying credit union and stock purchase plan deductions.

## CHAPTER CAPSTONE CASE:   SoftWear, Limited (continued)                    SWL

**SWL**                                **PAYROLL REGISTER**

Week Ending _____                                        *Page 1*

| Employee Data | | Earnings | | | Deductions | | | | | Net Pay | |
|---|---|---|---|---|---|---|---|---|---|---|---|
| Name | SSN | Regular Pay | Overtime Pay | Total Pay | Federal Tax | State Tax | FICA | Credit Union | Stock Plan | Net Amount | Check Number |
| | | | | | | | | | | | |
| | | | | | | | | | | | |
| | | | | | | | | | | | |
| | | | | | | | | | | | |
| | | | | | | | | | | | |

**FIGURE 4-42**   Sample page of SWL Payroll Register report.

Mr. Jeremy receives a weekly overtime report from BIS that lists every employee who worked overtime that week. When Carla asked him about that report, he stated that he consulted it occasionally but admitted that he did not need the report every week. He also receives an accounting report, but he routinely forwards it to the accounting department. He mentioned that an overall financial summary was more valuable to him.

### SWL Team Tasks

1. When Rick Williams met with Meredith Rider in the human resources department, he asked for copies of actual reports and forms that contained confidential information, but Meredith declined to provide them. Rick has asked you to suggest a reasonable compromise between confidentiality requirements and the need for analysts to review actual records, instead of fictitious data. Think about this, and write a message to Rick with your views.

2. Assume that you were with Rick at the meeting with Linda DeMarco. Review the fact statement, then write an interview summary that documents the main topics that Rick and Linda discussed.

3. Rick asked you to design a questionnaire that would measure employee satisfaction with the current payroll deduction system. Review the sample questionnaire in the chapter, and prepare a draft for Rick. Rick also wants you to suggest various sampling methods so he can make a choice. Include a brief description of various methods, and be sure to include your recommendation and reasons.

4. Rick wants you to interview several employees to learn more about their levels of satisfaction with the current system. Prepare a set of interview questions, and be sure to include at least examples of open-ended, closed-ended, and range-of-response questions. If possible, conduct role-play interviews with other students.

### Manage the SWL Project

You have been asked to manage SWL's new information system project. One of your most important activities will be to identify project tasks and determine when they will be performed. Before you begin, you should review the SWL case in this chapter. Then list and analyze the tasks, as follows:

**LIST THE TASKS** Start by listing and numbering at least 10 tasks that the SWL team needs to perform to fulfill the objectives of this chapter. Your list can include SWL Team Tasks and any other tasks that are described in this chapter. For example, Task 3 might be to Identify people to interview, and Task 6 might be to Conduct interviews.

**CHAPTER CAPSTONE CASE:    SoftWear, Limited (continued)**    **SWL**

**ANALYZE THE TASKS**  Now study the tasks to determine the order in which they should be performed. First identify all concurrent tasks, which are not dependent on other tasks. In the example shown in Figure 4-43, Tasks 1, 2, 3, 4, and 5 are concurrent tasks, and could begin at the same time if resources were available.

Other tasks are called dependent tasks, because they cannot be performed until one or more earlier tasks have been completed. For each dependent task, you must identify specific tasks that need to be completed before this task can begin. For example, you would need to identify the people to interview before you conducted the interviews, so Task 6 cannot begin until Task 3 is completed, as Figure 4-43 shows.

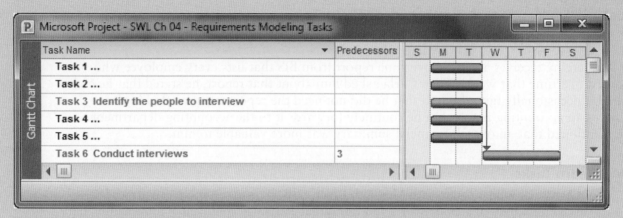

**FIGURE 4-43**    Tasks 1, 2, 3, 4, and 5 are concurrent tasks that could be performed at the same time. Task 6 is a dependent task that cannot be performed until Task 3 has been completed.

Chapter 3 describes project management tools, techniques, and software. To learn more, you can use the Features section on your Student Study Tool CD-ROM, or visit the Management Information Systems CourseMate Web site at **www.cengagebrain.com** and locate the project management resources library for this book. On the Web, Microsoft offers demo versions, training, and tips for using Project 2010. You also can visit the OpenWorkbench.org site to learn more about this free, open-source software.

# Ready for a Challenge?

In additional to technical skills, IT professionals need critical thinking skills such as perception, organization, analysis, problem-solving, and decision-making. The Ready for a Challenge feature can help you learn, practice, and apply critical thinking skills that you can take to the workplace.

As a leader in the game development field, Game Technology has many customers. The company wants to add a customer contact management feature to the sales system, and you will assist the IT team on this project. One of your first tasks is to interview users to find out what functions they want. When you have this information, you can construct a functional decomposition diagram (FDD) to list and organize the functions.

Before you talk to the users, you decide to practice your interviewing skills. Specifically, you want to use a mix of open-ended, closed-ended, and range-of-response questions.

To test yourself, you ask a team member to develop some practice questions for you to identify, as follows:

| Question | Code:   O = open-ended<br>C = closed-ended<br>R = range-of-response |
|---|---|
| Do you foresee any problems with this system?<br>On a scale of one (low) to five (high), how important is the project?<br>Do you maintain current e-mail addresses for customers?<br>Who is responsible for entering these records?<br>What would be some benefits of the new feature? | |

After you finish the interviews, you study the following results before preparing the FDD.

### Interview results

The starting point should be an overview screen that allows users to look up a customer, add a customer, edit a customer, delete a customer, or get help. The Help option should allow a user to search a knowledge base or contact the IT Help Desk. If users select the knowledge base option, they can search by keyword or by topic. If they select the IT Help Desk, they can either select e-mail or a telephone call-back option.

### Practice Tasks

  A. For each question listed, enter a code that correctly identifies the question.
  B. Draw an FDD that follows the guidelines in the textbook.

After you complete the Practice Tasks, to check your work and view sample answers, visit the Management Information Systems CourseMate Web site at **www.cengagebrain.com**, navigate to the resources for this chapter, and locate Ready for a Challenge?.

### The Challenge

The interviews were successful, but you want more details. Specifically, you want to learn more about the user interface, built-in error checking, and reports that could be generated for users. Using these topics, or others you think would be relevant, prepare two samples of each type of question.

Also, your FDD was good, but now you must add a Reports function to the overview screen. By selecting that option, users should be able to list all reports by name or by type. Users also should be able to view or print a report. If they select the Print option, they should be able to print the full report, the current page, or selected pages.

### Challenge Tasks

  A. Prepare the six questions described above (two of each type), indicating the type for each question.
  B. Draw an FDD that shows the Reports function and subfunctions.

# CHAPTER 5 Data and Process Analysis

**Chapter 5** is the second of four chapters in the systems analysis phase of the SDLC. This chapter discusses data and process modeling techniques that analysts use to show how the system transforms data into useful information. The deliverable, or end product, of data and process modeling is a logical model that will support business operations and meet user needs.

# INTRODUCTION

## OBJECTIVES

*When you finish this chapter, you will be able to:*

- Describe data and process modeling concepts and tools, including data flow diagrams, a data dictionary, and process descriptions
- Describe the symbols used in data flow diagrams and explain the rules for their use
- Draw data flow diagrams in a sequence, from general to specific
- Explain how to level and balance a set of data flow diagrams
- Describe how a data dictionary is used and what it contains
- Use process description tools, including structured English, decision tables, and decision trees
- Describe the relationship between logical and physical models

During the requirements modeling process described in Chapter 4, you used fact-finding techniques to investigate the current system and identify user requirements. Now, in Chapters 5 and 6 you will use that information to develop a logical model of the proposed system and document the system requirements. A **logical model** shows *what* the system must do, regardless of how it will be implemented physically. Later, in the systems design phase, you build a **physical model** that describes *how* the system will be constructed. Data and process modeling involves three main tools: data flow diagrams, a data dictionary, and process descriptions.

Chapter 5 includes four Video Learning Sessions that show you how to work with DFD symbols and diagrams, how to create a context diagram, how to create a diagram 0 DFD, and how to use a decision table.

# CHAPTER INTRODUCTION CASE:   Mountain View College Bookstore

**Background:** Wendy Lee, manager of college services at Mountain View College, wants a new information system that will improve efficiency and customer service at the three college bookstores.

In this part of the case, Tina Allen (systems analyst) and David Conroe (student intern) are talking about data and process modeling tasks and concepts.

| | |
|---|---|
| **Participants:** | Tina and David |
| **Location:** | Tina's office, Monday afternoon, October 17, 2011. |
| **Project status:** | Tina and David have completed fact-finding for the new system and are ready to develop a requirements model using various diagrams and a data dictionary that will describe and document the proposed system. |
| **Discussion topics:** | Data flow diagrams, data dictionaries, and process description tools |

**Tina:**    Hi, David. Any questions about the fact-finding we did?

**David:**   *Well, I found out that fact-finding is hard work.*

**Tina:**    Yes, but it was worth it. Look at what we learned — now we understand how the current system operates, and we know what users expect in the new system. This information will help us build a requirements model that we can present to Wendy and her staff.

**David:**   *What's the next step?*

**Tina:**    We need to draw a set of data flow diagrams, or DFDs for short.

**David:**   *Do we use a CASE tool to draw the DFDs?*

**Tina:**    We can draw the initial versions by hand. We'll use a CASE tool to prepare the final version of the diagrams.

**David:**   *What goes into a DFD?*

**Tina:**    DFDs use four basic symbols that represent processes, data flows, data stores, and entities. You'll learn about these as we go along. I'll also show you how we use techniques called leveling and balancing to develop accurate, consistent DFDs.

**David:**   *Apart from the diagrams, do we need to develop any other documentation?*

**Tina:**    Yes, we need to create a data dictionary and process descriptions. The data dictionary is an overall storehouse of information about the system, and serves as a central clearinghouse for all documentation. We use process descriptions to explain the logical steps that each process performs. To create these descriptions, we use three tools: structured English statements, decision tables, and decision trees.

**David:**   *Sounds like a lot to do. Where do we begin?*

**Tina:**    Here's a task list to get us started:

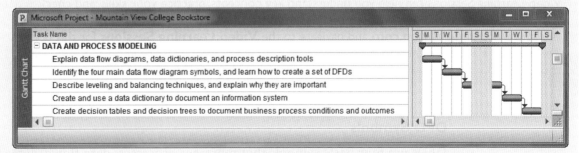

**FIGURE 5-1** Typical data and process modeling task list.

## OVERVIEW OF DATA AND PROCESS MODELING TOOLS

The CASE Tools in Appendix B can help you document business functions and processes, develop graphical models, and provide an overall framework for information system development. To learn more about these tools, turn to Appendix B.

Systems analysts use many graphical techniques to describe an information system. One popular method is to draw a set of data flow diagrams. A **data flow diagram** (**DFD**) uses various symbols to show how the system transforms input data into useful information. Other graphical tools include object models, which are explained in Chapter 6 (Object Analysis), and entity-relationship diagrams, which are described in Chapter 9 (Designing the Data).

## DATA FLOW DIAGRAMS

In Appendix A, you learn how to use visual aids to help explain a concept, as shown in Figure 5-2. Similarly, during the systems analysis phase, you learn how to create a visual model of the information system using a set of data flow diagrams.

A data flow diagram (DFD) shows how data moves through an information system but does not show program logic or processing steps. A set of DFDs provides a logical model that shows *what* the system does, not *how* it does it. That distinction is important because focusing on implementation issues at this point would restrict your search for the most effective system design.

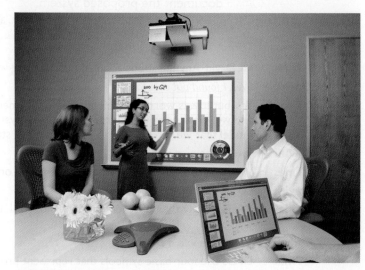

**FIGURE 5-2** Systems analysts often use visual aids during presentations.

## VIDEO LEARNING SESSION: DFD SYMBOLS AND DIAGRAMS

Video Learning Sessions can help you understand key concepts, practice your skills, and check your work. To access the sessions, visit the Management Information Systems CourseMate Web site at **www.cengagebrain.com** and navigate to the **Video Learning Sessions** for this book. This session is about DFD symbols and diagrams. You'll learn why DFDs are important modeling tools, how to use DFD symbols, and how you can use a CASE tool to create DFDs.

### DFD Symbols

DFDs use four basic symbols that represent processes, data flows, data stores, and entities. Several different versions of DFD symbols exist, but they all serve the same purpose. DFD examples in this textbook use the **Gane and Sarson** symbol set. Another popular symbol set is the **Yourdon** symbol set. Figure 5-3 shows examples of both versions. Symbols are referenced by using all capital letters for the symbol name.

**PROCESS SYMBOL** A **process** receives input data and produces output that has a different content, form, or both. For instance, the process for calculating pay uses two inputs (pay rate and hours worked) to produce one output (total pay). Processes can be very simple or quite complex. In a typical company, processes might include calculating sales trends, filing online insurance claims, ordering inventory from a supplier's system, or verifying e-mail addresses for Web customers. Processes contain the **business logic**, also called **business rules**, that transform the data and produce the required results.

The symbol for a process is a rectangle with rounded corners. The name of the process appears inside the rectangle. The process name identifies a specific function and consists of a verb (and an adjective, if necessary) followed by a singular noun. Examples of process names are APPLY RENT PAYMENT, CALCULATE COMMISSION, ASSIGN FINAL GRADE, VERIFY ORDER, and FILL ORDER.

Processing details are not shown in a DFD. For example, you might have a process named DEPOSIT PAYMENT. The process symbol does not reveal the business logic for the DEPOSIT PAYMENT process. To document the logic, you create a process description, which is explained later in this chapter.

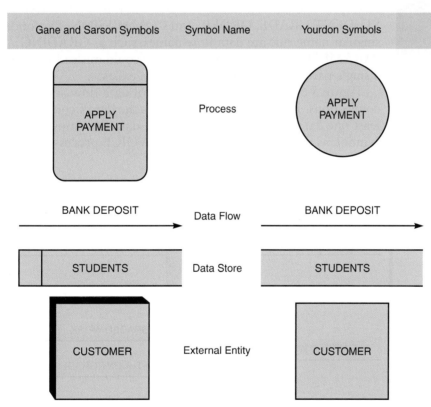

**ON THE WEB**

To learn more about Yourdon symbols, visit the Management Information Systems CourseMate Web site at **www. cengagebrain.com**, navigate to **On the Web Links** for this chapter, and locate the Yourdon Symbols link.

**FIGURE 5-3** Data flow diagram symbols, symbol names, and examples of the Gane and Sarson and Yourdon symbol sets.

In DFDs, a process symbol can be referred to as a **black box,** because the inputs, outputs, and general functions of the process are known, but the underlying details and logic of the process are hidden. By showing processes as black boxes, an analyst can create DFDs that show how the system functions, but avoid unnecessary detail and clutter. When the analyst wishes to show additional levels of detail, he or she can zoom in on a process symbol and create a more in-depth DFD that shows the process's internal workings — which might reveal even more processes, data flows, and data stores. In this manner, the information system can be modeled as a series of increasingly detailed pictures.

**FIGURE 5-4** Networks use various devices that act like *black boxes*. Cables carry data in and out, but internal operations are hidden inside the case.

The network router shown in Figure 5-4 is an example of a black box. An observer can see cables that carry data into and out of the router, but the router's internal operations are not revealed — only the results are apparent.

**DATA FLOW SYMBOL** A **data flow** is a path for data to move from one part of the information system to another. A data flow in a DFD represents one or more data items. For example, a data flow could consist of a single data item (such as a student ID number) or it could include a set of data (such as a class roster with student ID numbers, names, and registration dates for a specific class). Although the DFD does not show the detailed contents of a data flow, that information is included in the data dictionary, which is described later in this chapter.

The symbol for a data flow is a line with a single or double arrowhead. The data flow name appears above, below, or alongside the line. A data flow name consists of a singular noun and an adjective, if needed. Examples of data flow names are DEPOSIT, INVOICE PAYMENT, STUDENT GRADE, ORDER, and COMMISSION. Exceptions to the singular name rule are data flow names, such as GRADING PARAMETERS, where a singular name could mislead you into thinking a single parameter or single item of data exists.

Figure 5-5 shows correct examples of data flow and process symbol connections. Because a process changes the data's content or form, at least one data flow must enter and one data flow must exit each process symbol, as they do in the CREATE INVOICE process. A process symbol

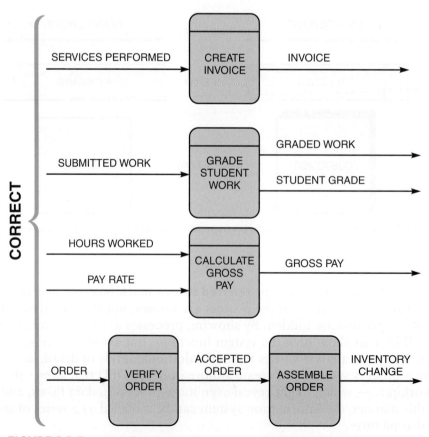

**FIGURE 5-5** Examples of correct combinations of data flow and process symbols.

can have more than one outgoing data flow, as shown in the GRADE STUDENT WORK process, or more than one incoming data flow, as shown in the CALCULATE GROSS PAY process. A process also can connect to any other symbol, including another process symbol, as shown by the connection between VERIFY ORDER and ASSEMBLE ORDER in Figure 5-5. A data flow, therefore, *must* have a process symbol on at least one end.

Figure 5-6 shows three data flow and process combinations that you must avoid:

- **Spontaneous generation.** The APPLY INSURANCE PREMIUM process, for instance, produces output, but has no input data flow. Because it has no input, the process is called a spontaneous generation process.

- **Black hole.** The CALCULATE GROSS PAY is called a black hole process, which is a process that has input, but produces no output.

- **Gray hole.** A gray hole is a process that has at least one input and one output, but the input obviously is insufficient to generate the output shown. For example, a date of birth input is not sufficient to produce a final grade output in the CALCULATE GRADE process.

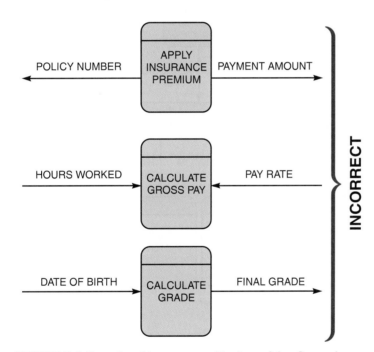

**FIGURE 5-6** Examples of incorrect combinations of data flow and process symbols. APPLY INSURANCE PREMIUM has no input and is called a spontaneous generation process. CALCULATE GROSS PAY has no outputs and is called a black hole process. CALCULATE GRADE has an input that is obviously unable to produce the output. This process is called a gray hole.

Spontaneous generation, black holes, and gray holes are impossible logically in a DFD because a process must act on input, shown by an incoming data flow, and produce output, represented by an outgoing data flow.

**DATA STORE SYMBOL** A **data store** is used in a DFD to represent data that the system stores because one or more processes need to use the data at a later time. For instance, instructors need to store student scores on tests and assignments during the semester so they can assign final grades at the end of the term. Similarly, a company stores employee salary and deduction data during the year in order to print W-2 forms with total earnings and deductions at the end of the year. A DFD does not show the detailed contents of a data store — the specific structure and data elements are defined in the data dictionary, which is discussed later in this chapter.

The physical characteristics of a data store are unimportant because you are concerned only with a logical model. Also, the length of time that the data is stored is unimportant — it can be a matter of seconds while a transaction is processed or a period of months while data is accumulated for year-end processing. What is important is that a process needs access to the data at some later time.

In a DFD, the Gane and Sarson symbol for a data store is a flat rectangle that is open on the right side and closed on the left side. The name of the data store appears between the lines and identifies the data it contains. A data store name is a plural name consisting of a noun and adjectives, if needed. Examples of data store names are STUDENTS, ACCOUNTS RECEIVABLE, PRODUCTS, DAILY PAYMENTS, PURCHASE ORDERS, OUTSTANDING CHECKS, INSURANCE POLICIES, and EMPLOYEES. Exceptions to the plural name rule are collective nouns that represent multiple occurrences of objects. For example, GRADEBOOK represents a group of students and their scores.

A data store must be connected to a process with a data flow. Figure 5-7 illustrates typical examples of data stores. In each case, the data store has at least one incoming and one outgoing data flow and is connected to a process symbol with a data flow.

Violations of the rule that a data store must have at least one incoming and one outgoing data flow are shown in Figure 5-8. In the first example, two data stores are connected incorrectly because no process is between them. Also, COURSES has no incoming data flow and STUDENTS has no outgoing data flow. In the second and third examples, the data stores lack either an outgoing or incoming data flow.

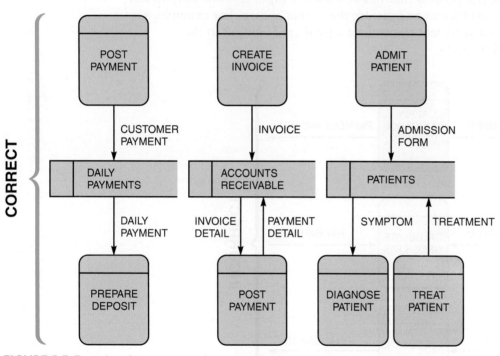

**FIGURE 5-7** Examples of correct uses of data store symbols in a data flow diagram.

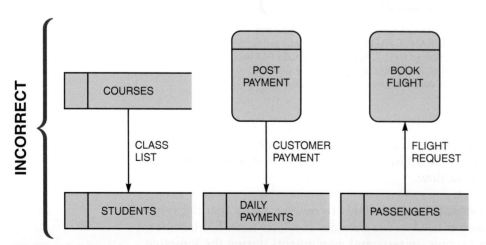

**FIGURE 5-8** Examples of incorrect uses of data store symbols: Two data stores cannot be connected by a data flow without an intervening process, and each data store should have an outgoing and incoming data flow.

There is an exception to the requirement that a data store must have at least one incoming and one outgoing data flow. In some situations, a data store has no input data flow because it contains fixed reference data that is not updated by the system. For example, consider a data store called TAX TABLE, which contains withholding tax data that a company downloads from the Internal Revenue Service. When the company runs its payroll, the CALCULATE WITHHOLDING process accesses data from this data store. On a DFD, this would be represented as a one-way outgoing data flow from the TAX TABLE data store into the CALCULATE WITHHOLDING process.

**ENTITY SYMBOL** The symbol for an **entity** is a rectangle, which may be shaded to make it look three-dimensional. The name of the entity appears inside the symbol.

A DFD shows only external entities that provide data to the system or receive output from the system. A DFD shows the boundaries of the system and how the system interfaces with the outside world. For example, a customer entity submits an order to an order processing system. Other examples of entities include a patient who supplies data to a medical records system, a homeowner who receives a bill from a city property tax system, or an accounts payable system that receives data from the company's purchasing system.

DFD entities also are called **terminators,** because they are data origins or final destinations. Systems analysts call an entity that supplies data to the system a **source,** and an entity that receives data from the system a **sink**. An entity name is the singular form of a department, outside organization, other information system, or person. An external entity can be a source or a sink or both, but each entity must be connected to a process by a data flow. Figures 5-9 and 5-10 show correct and incorrect examples of this rule.

With an understanding of the proper use of DFD symbols, you are ready to construct diagrams that use these symbols. Figure 5-11 on the next page shows a summary of the rules for using DFD symbols.

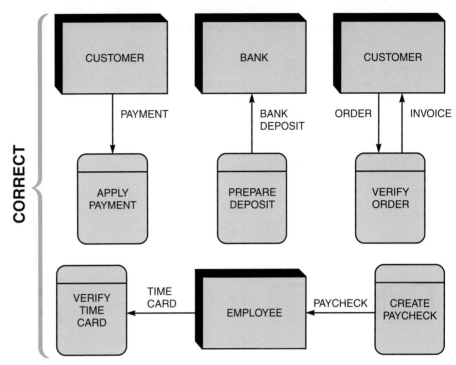

FIGURE 5-9 Examples of correct uses of external entities in a data flow diagram.

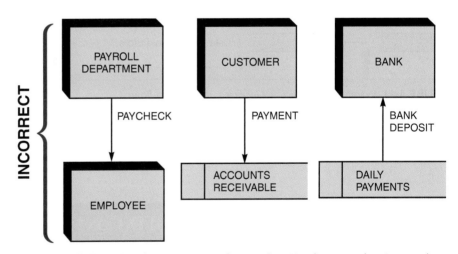

FIGURE 5-10 Examples of incorrect uses of external entities. An external entity must be connected by a data flow to a process, and not directly to a data store or to another external entity.

| Correct and Incorrect Examples of Data Flows | | |
|---|---|---|
| | Process to Process | ✓ |
| | Process to External Entity | ✓ |
| | Process to Data Store | ✓ |
| | External Entity to External Entity | ✗ |
| | External Entity to Data Store | ✗ |
| | Data Store to Data Store | ✗ |

**FIGURE 5-11** Examples of correct and incorrect uses of data flows.

## CREATING A SET OF DFDs

During requirements modeling, you used interviews, questionnaires, and other techniques to gather facts about the system, and you learned how the various people, departments, data, and processes fit together to support business operations. Now you are ready to create a graphical model of the information system based on your fact-finding results.

To learn how to construct DFDs, you will use examples of two information systems. The first example is a grading system that instructors use to assign final grades based on the scores that students receive during the term. The second example is an order system that a company uses to enter orders and apply payments against a customer's balance. First, you will review a set of guidelines for drawing DFDs. Then you will learn how to apply these guidelines and create a set of DFDs using a three-step process.

## VIDEO LEARNING SESSION: DFD CONTEXT DIAGRAMS

Video Learning Sessions can help you understand key concepts, practice your skills, and check your work. To access the sessions, visit the Management Information Systems CourseMate Web site at **www.cengagebrain.com** and navigate to the **Video Learning Sessions** for this book. This session is about DFD context diagrams, why they are important, how to construct a context diagram, and how you can use a CASE tool to create a context diagram.

### Guidelines for Drawing DFDs

When you draw a context diagram and other DFDs, you should follow several guidelines:

- Draw the context diagram so it fits on one page.
- Use the name of the information system as the process name in the context diagram. For example, the process name in Figure 5-12 is GRADING SYSTEM. Notice that the process name is the same as the system name. This is because the

context diagram shows the entire information system as if it were a single process. For processes in lower-level DFDs, you would use a verb followed by a descriptive noun, such as ESTABLISH GRADEBOOK, ASSIGN FINAL GRADE, or PRODUCE GRADE REPORT.

- Use unique names within each set of symbols. For instance, the diagram in Figure 5-12 shows only one entity named STUDENT and only one data flow named FINAL GRADE. Whenever you see the entity STUDENT on any other DFD in the grading system, you know that you are dealing with the same entity. Whenever the FINAL GRADE data flow appears, you know that you are dealing with the same data flow. The naming convention also applies to data stores.

- Do not cross lines. One way to achieve that goal is to restrict the number of symbols in any DFD. On lower-level diagrams with multiple processes, you should not have more than nine process symbols. Including more than nine symbols usually is a signal that your diagram is too complex and that you should reconsider your analysis. Another way to avoid crossing lines is to duplicate an entity or data store. When duplicating a symbol on a diagram, make sure to document the duplication to avoid possible confusion. A special notation, such as an asterisk, next to the symbol name and inside the duplicated symbols signifies that they are duplicated on the diagram.

- Provide a unique name and reference number for each process. Because it is the highest-level DFD, the context diagram contains process 0, which represents the entire information system, but does not show the internal workings. To describe the next level of detail inside process 0, you must create a DFD named diagram 0, which will reveal additional processes that must be named and numbered. As you continue to create lower-level DFDs, you assign unique names and reference numbers to all processes, until you complete the logical model.

- Obtain as much user input and feedback as possible. Your main objective is to ensure that the model is accurate, easy to understand, and meets the needs of its users.

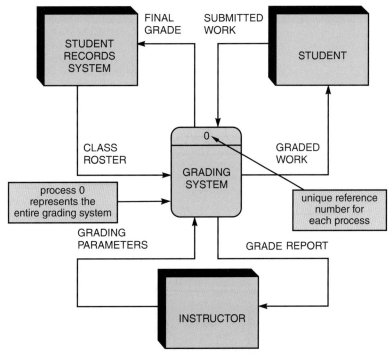

**FIGURE 5-12** Context diagram DFD for a grading system.

### Step 1: Draw a Context Diagram

The first step in constructing a set of DFDs is to draw a context diagram. A **context diagram** is a top-level view of an information system that shows the system's boundaries and scope. To draw a context diagram, you start by placing a single process symbol in the center of the page. The symbol represents the entire information system, and you identify it as **process 0** (the numeral zero, and not the letter O). Then you place the system entities around the perimeter of the page and use data flows to connect the entities to the central process. Data stores are not shown in the context diagram because they are contained within the system and remain hidden until more detailed diagrams are created.

How do you know which entities and data flows to place in the context diagram? You begin by reviewing the system requirements to identify all external data sources and destinations. During that process, you identify the entities, the name and content of the data flows, and the direction of the data flows. If you do that carefully, and you did a good job of fact-finding in the previous stage, you should have no difficulty drawing the context diagram. Now review the following context diagram examples.

**EXAMPLE:  CONTEXT DIAGRAM FOR A GRADING SYSTEM**  The context diagram for a grading system is shown in Figure 5-12 on the previous page. The GRADING SYSTEM process is at the center of the diagram. The three entities (STUDENT RECORDS SYSTEM, STUDENT, and INSTRUCTOR) are placed around the central process. Interaction among the central process and the entities involves six different data flows. The STUDENT RECORDS SYSTEM entity supplies data through the CLASS ROSTER data flow and receives data through the FINAL GRADE data flow. The STUDENT entity supplies data through the SUBMITTED WORK data flow and receives data through the GRADED WORK data flow. Finally, the INSTRUCTOR entity supplies data through the GRADING PARAMETERS data flow and receives data through the GRADE REPORT data flow.

**EXAMPLE:  CONTEXT DIAGRAM FOR AN ORDER SYSTEM**  The context diagram for an order system is shown in Figure 5-13. Notice that the ORDER SYSTEM process is at the center of the diagram and five entities surround the process. Three of the entities, SALES REP, BANK, and ACCOUNTING, have single incoming data flows for

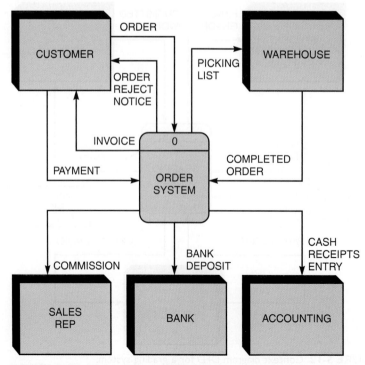

**FIGURE 5-13** Context diagram DFD for an order system.

COMMISSION, BANK DEPOSIT, and CASH RECEIPTS ENTRY, respectively. The WAREHOUSE entity has one incoming data flow — PICKING LIST — that is, a report that shows the items ordered and their quantity, location, and sequence to pick from the warehouse. The WAREHOUSE entity has one outgoing data flow, COMPLETED ORDER. Finally, the CUSTOMER entity has two outgoing data flows, ORDER and PAYMENT, and two incoming data flows, ORDER REJECT NOTICE and INVOICE.

The context diagram for the order system appears more complex than the grading system because it has two more entities and three more data flows. What makes one system more complex than another is the number of components, the number of levels, and the degree of interaction among its processes, entities, data stores, and data flows.

## VIDEO LEARNING SESSION:  DFD DIAGRAM 0

Video Learning Sessions can help you understand key concepts, practice your skills, and check your work. To access the sessions, visit the Management Information Systems CourseMate Web site at **www.cengagebrain.com** and navigate to the **Video Learning Sessions** for this book. This session is about DFD diagram 0. You'll learn what a DFD diagram 0 is, how to create a diagram 0, and how you can use a CASE tool to create a DFD diagram 0.

### Step 2: Draw a Diagram 0 DFD

In the previous step, you learned that a context diagram provides the most general view of an information system and contains a single process symbol, which is like a black box. To show the detail inside the black box, you create DFD diagram 0. **Diagram 0** (the numeral zero, and not the letter O) zooms in on the system and shows major internal processes, data flows, and data stores. Diagram 0 also repeats the entities and data flows that appear in the context diagram. When you expand the context diagram into DFD diagram 0, you must retain all the connections that flow into and out of process 0.

The real-life scene in Figure 5-14 represents a complex manufacturing system with many interactive processes and data. In a large system such as this, each process in

**FIGURE 5-14** Complex manufacturing systems require many interactive processes and data sources.

diagram 0 could represent a separate system such as inventory, production control, and scheduling. Diagram 0 provides an overview of all the components that interact to form the overall system. Now review the following diagram 0 examples.

#### EXAMPLE:  DIAGRAM 0 DFD FOR A GRADING SYSTEM

Figure 5-15 on the next page shows a context diagram at the top and diagram 0 beneath it. Notice that diagram 0 is an expansion of process 0. Also notice that the three same entities (STUDENT RECORDS SYSTEM, STUDENT, and INSTRUCTOR) and the same six data flows (FINAL GRADE, CLASS ROSTER, SUBMITTED WORK, GRADED WORK, GRADING PARAMETERS, and GRADE REPORT) appear in both diagrams. In addition, diagram 0 expands process 0 to reveal four internal processes, one data store, and five additional data flows.

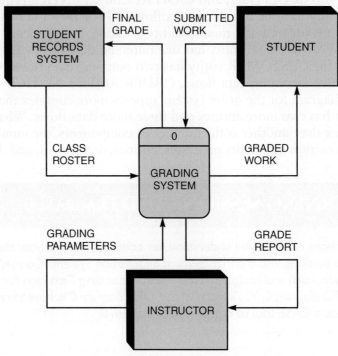

**CONTEXT DIAGRAM FOR GRADING SYSTEM**

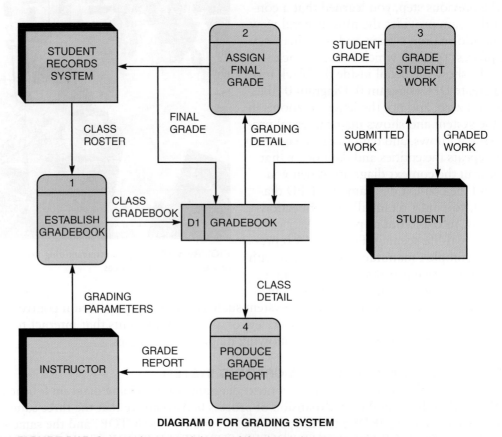

**DIAGRAM 0 FOR GRADING SYSTEM**

**FIGURE 5-15**   Context diagram and diagram 0 for the grading system.

Notice that each process in diagram 0 has a reference number: ESTABLISH GRADEBOOK is 1, ASSIGN FINAL GRADE is 2, GRADE STUDENT WORK is 3, and PRODUCE GRADE REPORT is 4. These reference numbers are important because they identify a series of DFDs. If more detail were needed for ESTABLISH GRADEBOOK, for example, you would draw a diagram 1, because ESTABLISH GRADEBOOK is process 1.

The process numbers do not suggest that the processes are accomplished in a sequential order. Each process always is considered to be available, active, and awaiting data to be processed. If processes must be performed in a specific sequence, you document the information in the process descriptions (discussed later in this chapter), not in the DFD.

The FINAL GRADE data flow output from the ASSIGN FINAL GRADE process is a diverging data flow that becomes an input to the STUDENT RECORDS SYSTEM entity and to the GRADEBOOK data store. A **diverging data flow** is a data flow in which the same data travels to two or more different locations. In that situation, a diverging data flow is the best way to show the flow rather than showing two identical data flows, which could be misleading.

If the same data flows in both directions, you can use a double-headed arrow to connect the symbols. To identify specific data flows into and out of a symbol, however, you use separate data flow symbols with single arrowheads. For example, in Figure 5-15, the separate data flows (SUBMITTED WORK and GRADED WORK) go into and out of the GRADE STUDENT WORK process.

Because diagram 0 is an exploded version of process 0, it shows considerably more detail than the context diagram. You also can refer to diagram 0 as a partitioned or decomposed view of process 0. When you explode a DFD, the higher-level diagram is called the **parent diagram**, and the lower-level diagram is referred to as the **child diagram**. The grading system is simple enough that you do not need any additional DFDs to model the system. At that point, the four processes, the one data store, and the 10 data flows can be documented in the data dictionary.

When you create a set of DFDs for a system, you break the processing logic down into smaller units, called functional primitives, that programmers will use to develop code. A **functional primitive** is a process that consists of a single function that is not exploded further. For example, each of the four processes shown in the lower portion of Figure 5-15 is a functional primitive. You document the logic for a functional primitive by writing a process description in the data dictionary. Later, when the logical design is implemented as a physical system, programmers will transform each functional primitive into program code and modules that carry out the required steps. Deciding whether to explode a process further or determine that it is a functional primitive is a matter of experience, judgment, and interaction with programmers who must translate the logical design into code.

**EXAMPLE: DIAGRAM 0 DFD FOR AN ORDER SYSTEM**    Figure 5-16 on the next page shows the diagram 0 for an order system. Process 0 on the order system's context diagram is exploded to reveal three processes (FILL ORDER, CREATE INVOICE, and APPLY PAYMENT), one data store (ACCOUNTS RECEIVABLE), two additional data flows (INVOICE DETAIL and PAYMENT DETAIL), and one diverging data flow (INVOICE).

The following walkthrough explains the DFD shown in Figure 5-16:

1. A CUSTOMER submits an ORDER. Depending on the processing logic, the FILL ORDER process either sends an ORDER REJECT NOTICE back to the customer or sends a PICKING LIST to the WAREHOUSE.

2. A COMPLETED ORDER from the WAREHOUSE is input to the CREATE INVOICE process, which outputs an INVOICE to both the CUSTOMER process and the ACCOUNTS RECEIVABLE data store.

3. A CUSTOMER makes a PAYMENT that is processed by APPLY PAYMENT. APPLY PAYMENT requires INVOICE DETAIL input from the ACCOUNTS

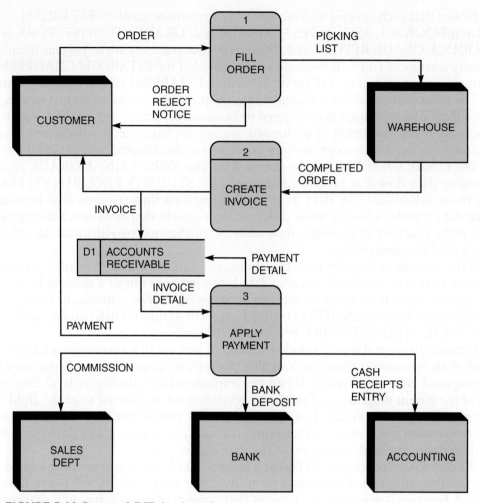

**FIGURE 5-16** Diagram 0 DFD for the order system.

RECEIVABLE data store along with the PAYMENT. APPLY PAYMENT also outputs PAYMENT DETAIL back to the ACCOUNTS RECEIVABLE data store and outputs COMMISSION to the SALES DEPT, BANK DEPOSIT to the BANK, and CASH RECEIPTS ENTRY to ACCOUNTING.

The walkthrough of diagram 0 illustrates the basic requirements of the order system. To learn more, you would examine the detailed description of each separate process.

### Step 3: Draw the Lower-Level Diagrams

This set of lower-level DFDs is based on the order system. To create lower-level diagrams, you must use leveling and balancing techniques. **Leveling** is the process of drawing a series of increasingly detailed diagrams, until all functional primitives are identified. **Balancing** maintains consistency among a set of DFDs by ensuring that input and output data flows align properly. Leveling and balancing are described in more detail in the following sections.

**LEVELING EXAMPLES** Leveling uses a series of increasingly detailed DFDs to describe an information system. For example, a system might consist of dozens, or even hundreds, of separate processes. Using leveling, an analyst starts with an overall view, which is a context diagram with a single process symbol. Next, the analyst creates diagram 0, which shows more detail. The analyst continues to create lower-level DFDs until all processes are identified as functional primitives, which represent single processing functions. More complex systems have more processes, and analysts must work through many levels to identify the functional primitives. Leveling also is called **exploding, partitioning,** or **decomposing**.

Figures 5-16 and 5-17 provide an example of leveling. Figure 5-16 shows diagram 0 for an order system, with the FILL ORDER process labeled as process 1. Now consider Figure 5-17, which provides an exploded view of the FILL ORDER process. Notice that FILL ORDER (process 1) actually consists of three processes: VERIFY ORDER (process 1.1), PREPARE REJECT NOTICE (process 1.2), and ASSEMBLE ORDER (process 1.3).

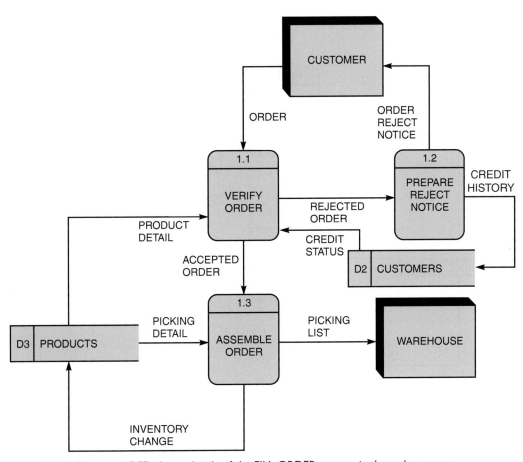

**FIGURE 5-17** Diagram I DFD shows details of the FILL ORDER process in the order system.

As Figure 5-17 shows, all processes are numbered using a decimal notation consisting of the parent's reference number, a decimal point, and a sequence number within the new diagram. In Figure 5-17, the parent process of diagram 1 is process 1, so the processes in diagram 1 have reference numbers of 1.1, 1.2, and 1.3. If process 1.3, ASSEMBLE ORDER, is decomposed further, then it would appear in diagram 1.3 and the processes in diagram 1.3 would be numbered as 1.3.1, 1.3.2, 1.3.3, and so on. This numbering technique makes it easy to integrate and identify all DFDs.

When you compare Figures 5-16 and 5-17, you will notice that Figure 5-17 (the exploded FILL ORDER process) shows two data stores (CUSTOMERS and PRODUCTS) that do not appear on Figure 5-16, which is the parent DFD. Why not? The answer is based on a simple rule: When drawing DFDs, you show a data store only when two or more processes use that data store. The CUSTOMERS and PRODUCTS data stores were internal to the FILL ORDER process, so the analyst did not show them on diagram 0, which is the parent. When you explode the FILL ORDER process into diagram 1 DFD, however, you see that three processes (1.1, 1.2, and 1.3) interact with the two data stores, which now are shown.

Now compare Figure 5-17 (on the previous page) and Figure 5-18. Notice that Figure 5-18 shows the same data flows as Figure 5-17, but does not show the CUSTOMER and WAREHOUSE entities. Analysts often use this technique to simplify a DFD and reduce unnecessary clutter. Because the missing symbols appear on the parent DFD, you can refer to that diagram to identify the source or destination of the data flows.

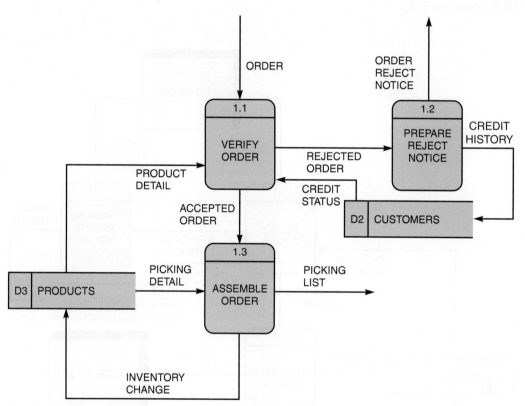

**FIGURE 5-18** This diagram does not show the symbols that connect to data flows entering or leaving FILL ORDER on the context diagram.

**BALANCING EXAMPLES** Balancing ensures that the input and output data flows of the parent DFD are maintained on the child DFD. For example, Figure 5-19 shows two DFDs: The order system diagram 0 is shown at the top of the figure, and the exploded diagram 3 DFD is shown at the bottom.

The two DFDs are balanced, because the child diagram at the bottom has the same input and output flows as the parent process 3 shown at the top. To verify the balancing, notice that the parent process 3, APPLY PAYMENT, has one incoming data flow from an external entity, and three outgoing data flows to external entities. Now examine the child DFD, which is diagram 3. Now, ignore the internal data flows and count the data flows to and from external entities. You will see that the three processes maintain the same one incoming and three outgoing data flows as the parent process.

**Order System Diagram 0 DFD**

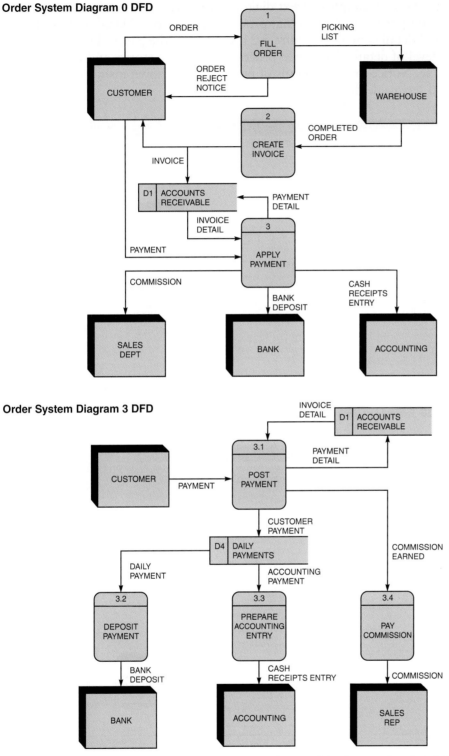

**Order System Diagram 3 DFD**

**FIGURE 5-19** The order system diagram 0 is shown at the top of the figure, and exploded diagram 3 DFD (for the APPLY PAYMENT process) is shown at the bottom. The two DFDs are balanced, because the child diagram at the bottom has the same input and output flows as the parent process 3 shown at the top.

Another example of balancing is shown in Figures 5-20 and 5-21 on the next page. The DFDs in these figures were created using Visible Analyst, a popular CASE tool.

Figure 5-20 shows a sample context diagram. The process 0 symbol has two input flows and two output flows. Notice that process 0 can be considered as a black box, with no internal detail shown. In Figure 5-21, process 0 (the parent DFD) is exploded into the next level of detail. Now three processes, two data stores, and four internal data flows are visible. Notice that the details of process 0 are shown inside a dashed line, just as if you could see inside the process.

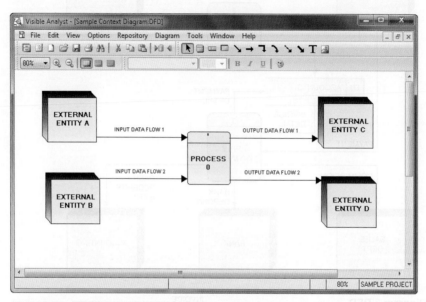

**FIGURE 5-20** Example of a parent DFD diagram, showing process 0 as a black box.

**FIGURE 5-21** In the next level of detail, the process 0 black box reveals three processes, two data stores, and four internal data flows — all of which are shown inside the dashed line.

The DFDs in Figures 5-20 and 5-21 are balanced, because the four data flows into and out of process 0 are maintained on the child DFD. The DFDs also are leveled, because each internal process is numbered to show that it is a child of the parent process.

## CASE IN POINT 5.1:  BIG TEN UNIVERSITY

You are the IT director at Big Ten University. As part of a training program, you decide to draw a DFD that includes some obvious mistakes to see whether your newly hired junior analysts can find them. You came up with the diagram 0 DFD shown in Figure 5-22. Based on the rules explained in this chapter, how many problems should the analysts find?

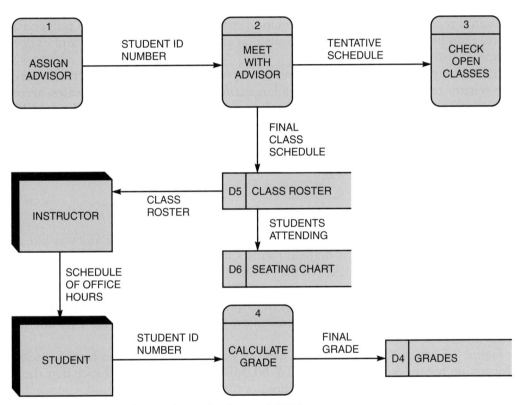

**FIGURE 5-22** What are the mistakes in this diagram 0 DFD?

## DATA DICTIONARY

A set of DFDs produces a logical model of the system, but the details within those DFDs are documented separately in a data dictionary, which is the second component of structured analysis.

A **data dictionary**, or **data repository**, is a central storehouse of information about the system's data. An analyst uses the data dictionary to collect, document, and organize specific facts about the system, including the contents of data flows, data stores, entities, and processes. The data dictionary also defines and describes all data elements and meaningful combinations of data elements. A **data element**, also called a **data item** or **field**, is the smallest piece of data that has meaning within an information system. Examples of data elements are student grade, salary, Social Security number, account balance, and company name. Data elements are combined into **records**, also called **data structures**. A record is a meaningful combination of related data elements that is included in a data flow or retained in a data store. For example, an auto parts store inventory record might include part number, description, supplier code, minimum and maximum stock levels, cost, and list price.

**ON THE WEB**

To learn more about data dictionaries, visit the Management Information Systems CourseMate Web site at **www. cengagebrain.com**, navigate to **On the Web Links** for this chapter, and locate the Data Dictionaries link.

Significant relationships exist among the items in a data dictionary. For example, data stores and data flows are based on data structures, which in turn are composed of data elements. Data flows are connected to data stores, entities, and processes. Accurately documenting these relationships is essential so the data dictionary is consistent with the DFDs. You can use CASE software to help you document the design.

## Using CASE Tools for Documentation

The CASE tools in Appendix B can help you document business functions and processes. To learn more about these tools, turn to Appendix B.

The more complex the system, the more difficult it is to maintain full and accurate documentation. Fortunately, modern CASE tools simplify the task. For example, in the Visible Analyst CASE tool, documentation automatically flows from the modeling diagrams into the central repository, along with information entered by the user. This section contains several examples of Visible Analyst screens that show the data repository and its contents.

A CASE repository ensures data consistency, which is especially important where multiple systems require the same data. In a large company, for example, the sales, accounting, and shipping systems all might use a data element called CUSTOMER NUMBER. Once the CUSTOMER NUMBER element has been defined in the repository, it can be accessed by other processes, data flows, and data stores. The result is that all systems across the enterprise can share data that is up to date and consistent. You will learn more about CASE tools in Appendix B.

## Documenting the Data Elements

You must document every data element in the data dictionary. Some analysts like to record their notes on online or manual forms. Others prefer to enter the information directly into a CASE tool. Several of the DFDs and data dictionary entries that appear in this chapter were created using a popular CASE tool called Visible Analyst. Although other CASE tools might use other terms or display the information differently, the objective is the same: to provide clear, comprehensive information about the data and processes that make up the system.

Figure 5-23 shows how the analyst used an online documentation form to record information for the SOCIAL SECURITY NUMBER data element. Notice that the figure caption identifies eight specific characteristics for this data element.

1. Online or manual documentation entries often indicate which system is involved. This is not necessary with a CASE tool because all information is stored in one file that is named for the system.
2. The data element has a standard label that provides consistency throughout the data dictionary.
3. The data element can have an alternative name, or alias.
4. This entry indicates that the data element consists of nine numeric characters.
5. Depending on the data element, strict limits might be placed on acceptable values.
6. The data comes from the employee's job application.
7. This entry indicates that only the payroll department has authority to update or change this data.
8. This entry indicates the individual or department responsible for entering and changing data.

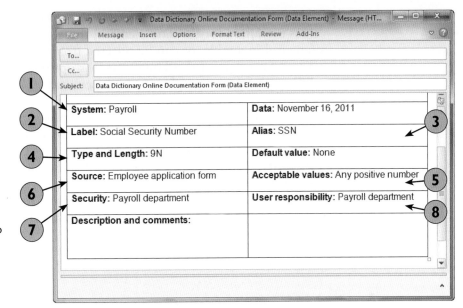

**FIGURE 5-23** Using an online documentation form, the analyst has recorded information for a data element named SOCIAL SECURITY NUMBER. Later, the analyst will create a data dictionary entry using a CASE tool.

Figure 5-24 shows a sample screen that illustrates how the SOCIAL SECURITY NUMBER data element might be recorded in the Visible Analyst data dictionary.

Regardless of the terminology or method, the following attributes usually are recorded and described in the data dictionary:

**Data element name or label.** The data element's standard name, which should be meaningful to users.

**Alias.** Any name(s) other than the standard data element name; this alternate name is called an **alias.** For example, if you have a data element named CURRENT BALANCE, various users might refer to it by alternate names such as OUTSTANDING BALANCE, CUSTOMER BALANCE, RECEIVABLE BALANCE, or AMOUNT OWED.

**Type and length. Type** refers to whether the data element contains numeric, alphabetic, or character values. **Length** is the maximum number of characters for an alphabetic or character data element or the maximum number of digits and number of decimal positions for a numeric data element. In addition to text and numeric data, sounds and images also can be stored in digital form. In some systems, these binary data objects are managed and processed just as traditional data elements are. For example, an employee record might include a digitized photo image of the person.

**Default value.** The value for the data element if a value otherwise is not entered for it. For example, all new customers might have a default value of $500 for the CREDIT LIMIT data element.

**FIGURE 5-24** A Visible Analyst screen describes the data element named SOCIAL SECURITY NUMBER. Notice that many of the items were entered from the online form shown in Figure 5-23.

**Acceptable values.** Specification of the data element's **domain,** which is the set of values permitted for the data element; these values either can be specifically listed or referenced in a table, or can be selected from a specified range of values. You also would indicate if a value for the data element is optional. Some data elements have additional **validity rules.** For example, an employee's salary must be within the range defined for the employee's job classification.

**Source.** The specification for the origination point for the data element's values. The source could be a specific form, a department or outside organization, another information system, or the result of a calculation.

**Security.** Identification for the individual or department that has access or update privileges for each data element. For example, only a credit manager has the authority to change a credit limit, while sales reps are authorized to access data in a read-only mode.

**Responsible user(s).** Identification of the user(s) responsible for entering and changing values for the data element.

**Description and comments.** This part of the documentation allows you to enter additional notes.

## Documenting the Data Flows

In addition to documenting each data element, you must document all data flows in the data dictionary. Figure 5-25 shows a definition for a data flow named COMMISSION. The information on the manual form at the top was entered into the CASE tool data dictionary at the bottom of Figure 5-25.

Although terms can vary, the typical attributes are as follows:

**Data flow name or label.** The data flow name as it appears on the DFDs.

**Description.** Describes the data flow and its purpose.

**Alternate name(s).** Aliases for the DFD data flow name(s).

**Origin.** The DFD beginning, or source, for the data flow; the origin can be a process, a data store, or an entity.

**Destination.** The DFD ending point(s) for the data flow; the destination can be a process, a data store, or an entity.

**Record.** Each data flow represents a group of related data elements called a record or data structure. In most data dictionaries, records are defined separately from the data flows and data stores. When records are defined, more than one data flow or data store can use the same record, if necessary.

**Volume and frequency.** Describes the expected number of occurrences for the data flow per unit of time. For example, if a company has 300 employees, a TIME CARD data flow would involve 300 transactions and records each week, as employees submit their work hour data.

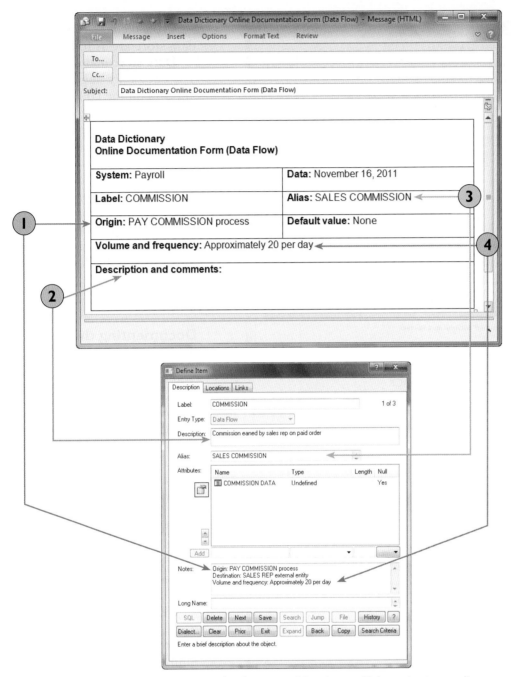

**FIGURE 5-25** In the upper screen, an analyst has entered four items of information in an online documentation form. The lower screen shows the same four items entered into a Visible Analyst data dictionary form.

## Documenting the Data Stores

You must document every DFD data store in the data dictionary. Figure 5-26 on the next page shows the definition of a data store named IN STOCK.

1. This data store has an alternative name, or alias.
2. For consistency, data flow names are standardized throughout the data dictionary.
3. It is important to document these estimates, because they will affect design decisions in subsequent SDLC phases.

**FIGURE 5-26** Visible Analyst screen that documents a data store named IN STOCK.

1. The process number identifies this process. Any subprocesses are numbered 1.1, 1.2, 1.3, and so on.
2. These data flows will be described specifically elsewhere in the data dictionary.

**FIGURE 5-27** Visible Analyst screen that describes a process named VERIFY ORDER.

Typical characteristics of a data store are as follows:

**Data store name or label.** The data store name as it appears on the DFDs.

**Description.** Describes the data store and its purpose.

**Alternate name(s).** Aliases for the DFD data store name.

**Attributes.** Standard DFD names that enter or leave the data store.

**Volume and frequency.** Describes the estimated number of records in the data store and how frequently they are updated.

## Documenting the Processes

You must document every process, as shown in Figure 5-27. Your documentation includes a description of the process's characteristics and, for functional primitives, a process description, which is a model that documents the processing steps and business logic.

The following are typical characteristics of a process:

**Process name or label.** The process name as it appears on the DFDs.

**Description.** A brief statement of the process's purpose.

**Process number.** A reference number that identifies the process and indicates relationships among various levels in the system.

**Process description.** This section includes the input and output data flows. For functional primitives, the process description also documents the processing steps and business logic. You will learn how to write process descriptions in the next section.

## Documenting the Entities

By documenting all entities, the data dictionary can describe all external entities that interact with the system. Figure 5-28 shows a definition for an external entity named WAREHOUSE.

Typical characteristics of an entity include the following:

**Entity name.** The entity name as it appears on the DFDs.

**Description.** Describe the entity and its purpose.

**Alternate name(s).** Any aliases for the entity name.

**Input data flows.** The standard DFD names for the input data flows to the entity.

**Output data flows.** The standard DFD names for the data flows leaving the entity.

1. The external entity also can have an alternative name, or alias, if properly documented.
2. For consistency, these data flow names are standardized throughout the data dictionary.

**FIGURE 5-28** Visible Analyst screen that documents an external entity named WAREHOUSE.

## Documenting the Records

A record is a data structure that contains a set of related data elements that are stored and processed together. Data flows and data stores consist of records that you must document in the data dictionary. You define characteristics of each record, as shown in Figure 5-29.

Typical characteristics of a record include the following:

**Record or data structure name.** The record name as it appears in the related data flow and data store entries in the data dictionary.

**Definition or description.** A brief definition of the record.

**Alternate name(s).** Any aliases for the record name.

**Attributes.** A list of all the data elements included in the record. The data element names must match exactly what you entered in the data dictionary.

1. This data structure is named CREDIT STATUS.

2. The CREDIT STATUS data structure consists of two data elements: CUSTOMER NUMBER and CUSTOMER STATUS CODE.

**FIGURE 5-29** Visible Analyst screen that documents a record, or data structure named CREDIT STATUS.

## Data Dictionary Reports

The data dictionary serves as a central storehouse of documentation for an information system. A data dictionary is created when the system is developed, and is updated constantly as the system is implemented, operated, and maintained. In addition to describing each data element, data flow, data store, record, entity, and process, the data dictionary documents the relationships among these components. You can obtain many valuable reports from a data dictionary, including the following:

- An alphabetized list of all data elements by name
- A report describing each data element and indicating the user or department that is responsible for data entry, updating, or deletion
- A report of all data flows and data stores that use a particular data element
- Detailed reports showing all characteristics of data elements, records, data flows, processes, or any other selected item stored in the data dictionary

## PROCESS DESCRIPTION TOOLS

A **process description** documents the details of a functional primitive, and represents a specific set of processing steps and business logic. Using a set of process description tools, you create a model that is accurate, complete, and concise. Typical process description tools include structured English, decision tables, and decision trees. When you analyze a functional primitive, you break the processing steps down into smaller units in a process called modular design.

It should be noted that this chapter deals with structured analysis, but the process description tools also can be used in object-oriented development, which is described in Chapter 6. You learned in Chapter 1 that O-O analysis combines data and the processes that act on the data into things called objects, that similar objects can be grouped together into classes, and that O-O processes are called methods. Although O-O programmers use different terminology, they create the same kind of modular coding structures, except that the processes, or methods, are stored inside the objects, rather than as separate components.

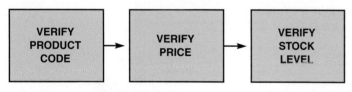

**FIGURE 5-30** Sequence structure.

## Modular Design

**Modular design** is based on combinations of three **logical structures**, sometimes called **control structures**, which serve as building blocks for the process. Each logical structure must have a single entry and exit point. The three structures are called sequence, selection, and iteration. A rectangle represents a step or process, a diamond shape represents a condition or decision, and the logic follows the lines in the direction indicated by the arrows.

1. **Sequence.** The completion of steps in sequential order, one after another, as shown in Figure 5-30. One or more of the steps might represent a subprocess that contains additional logical structures.

2. **Selection.** The completion of one of two or more process steps based on the results of a test or condition. In the example shown in Figure 5-31, the system tests the input, and if the hours are greater than 40, it performs the CALCULATE OVERTIME PAY process.

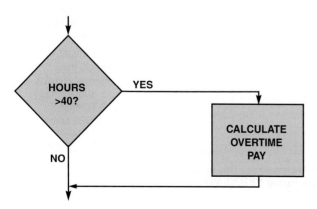

**FIGURE 5-31** Selection structure.

3. **Iteration**. The completion of a process step that is repeated until a specific condition changes, as shown in Figure 5-32. An example of iteration is a process that continues to print paychecks until it reaches the end of the payroll file. Iteration also is called **looping**.

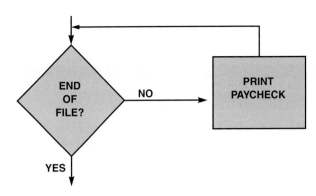

Sequence, selection, and iteration structures can be combined in various ways to describe processing logic.

**FIGURE 5-32** Iteration structure.

## Structured English

**Structured English** is a subset of standard English that describes logical processes clearly and accurately. When you use structured English, you must conform to the following rules:

- Use only the three building blocks of sequence, selection, and iteration.
- Use indentation for readability.
- Use a limited vocabulary, including standard terms used in the data dictionary and specific words that describe the processing rules.

An example of structured English appears in Figure 5-33, which shows the VERIFY ORDER process that was illustrated earlier. Notice that the structured English version documents the actual logic that will be coded into the system. Structured English can help make your process descriptions accurate and understandable to users and system developers.

Structured English might look familiar to programming students because it resembles **pseudocode**, which is used in program design. Although the techniques are similar, the primary purpose of structured English is to describe the underlying business logic, while programmers, who are concerned with coding, mainly use pseudocode as a shorthand notation for the actual code.

Figure 5-34 shows another example of structured English. After you study the sales promotion policy, notice that the structured English version describes the processing logic that the system must apply. Following structured English rules ensures that your process descriptions are

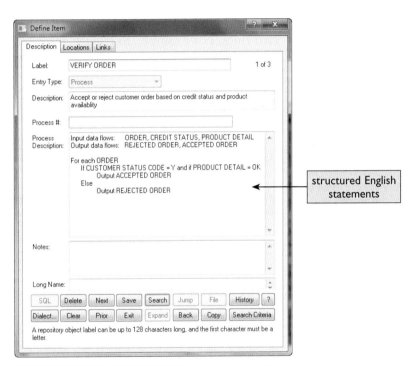

**FIGURE 5-33** The VERIFY ORDER process description includes logical rules and a structured English version of the policy. Notice the alignment and indentation of the logic statements.

understandable to users who must confirm that the process is correct, as well as to other analysts and programmers who must design the information system from your descriptions.

# VIDEO LEARNING SESSION: DECISION TABLES

Video Learning Sessions can help you understand key concepts, practice your skills, and check your work. To access the sessions, visit the Management Information Systems CourseMate Web site at **www.cengagebrain.com** and navigate to the **Video Learning Sessions** for this book. This session is about decision tables, why they are important process description tools, how to create decision tables, and how to analyze conditions and outcomes in a decision table.

## Decision Tables

A **decision table** is a logical structure that shows every combination of conditions and outcomes. Analysts often use decision tables to describe a process and ensure that they have considered all possible situations. You can create decision tables using Microsoft PowerPoint, Word, or Excel.

**TABLES WITH ONE CONDITION** If a process has a single condition, there only are two possibilities – *yes* or *no*. Either the condition is present or it is not, so there are only two rules. For example, to trigger an overtime calculation, the process condition might be: *Are the hours greater than 40?* If so, the calculation is made. Otherwise, it is not.

**TABLES WITH TWO CONDITIONS** Suppose you want to create a decision table based on the Verify Order business process shown in Figure 5-34. When documenting a process, it is important to ensure that you list every possibility. In this example, the process description contains two conditions: product stock status and customer credit status. If *both* conditions are met, the order is accepted. Otherwise the order is rejected.

1. Place the name of the process in a heading at the top left.
2. Enter the conditions under the heading, with one condition per line, to represent the customer status and availability of products.
3. Enter all potential combinations of Y/N (for yes and no) for the conditions. Each column represents a numbered possibility called a rule.
4. Place an X in the action entries area for each rule to indicate whether to accept or reject the order.

## VERIFY ORDER Business Process with Two Conditions

- An order will be accepted only if the product is in stock and the customer's credit status is OK.

- All other orders will be rejected.

**FIGURE 5-34** The Verify Order business process has two conditions. For an order to be accepted, the product must be in stock and the customer must have an acceptable credit status.

After you identify all the conditions and outcomes, you are ready to create a decision table similar to the one shown in Figure 5-35. To create the table, follow the four steps listed in the margin.

**① → VERIFY ORDER Process**

| | 1 | 2 | 3 | 4 | |
|---|---|---|---|---|---|
| **② →** Credit status is OK | Y | Y | N | N | } ③ |
| **→** Product is in stock | Y | N | Y | N | |
| Accept order | X | | | | } ④ |
| Reject order | | X | X | X | |

**FIGURE 5-35** Example of a simple decision table showing the processing logic of the VERIFY ORDER process.

Notice that each condition has two possible values, so the number of rules doubles each time you add another condition. For example, one condition creates two rules, two conditions create four rules, three conditions create eight rules, and so on. In the two-condition example in Figure 5-35, four possibilities exist, but Rule 1 is the *only* combination that will accept an order.

**TABLES WITH THREE CONDITIONS** Suppose the company now decides that the credit manager can waive the customer credit requirement, as shown in Figure 5-36. That creates a third condition, so there will be eight possible rules. The new decision table might resemble the one shown in Figure 5-37.

## VERIFY ORDER Business Process with Three Conditions

- An order will be accepted only if the product is in stock and the customer's credit status is OK.
- The credit manager can waive the credit status requirement.
- All other orders will be rejected.

**FIGURE 5-36** A third condition has been added to the Verify Order business process. For an order to be accepted, the product must be in stock and the customer must have an acceptable credit status. However, the credit manager now has the authority to waive the credit status requirement.

## VERIFY ORDER Process with Credit Waiver (initial version)

|  | 1 | 2 | 3 | 4 | 5 | 6 | 7 | 8 |
|---|---|---|---|---|---|---|---|---|
| Credit status is OK | Y | Y | Y | Y | N | N | N | N |
| Product is in stock | Y | Y | N | N | Y | Y | N | N |
| Waiver from credit manager | Y | N | Y | N | Y | N | Y | N |
| Accept order | X | X |  |  | X |  |  |  |
| Reject order |  |  | X | X |  | X | X | X |

**FIGURE 5-37** This table is based on the Verify Order conditions shown in Figure 5-36. With three conditions, there are eight possible combinations, or rules.

First, you must fill in the Y-N patterns, as shown in Figure 5-37. The best way to assure that all combinations appear is to use patterns like these. The first condition uses a pattern of Y-Y-Y-Y followed by N-N-N-N; the second condition uses a repeating Y-Y-N-N pattern; and the pattern in the third condition is a series of Y-Ns.

The next step is very important, regardless of the number of conditions. Each numbered column, or rule, represents a different set of conditions. You must analyze the logic carefully and show the outcome for each rule. Before going further, study the table in Figure 5-37 and be sure you understand the logical outcome for each of the eight rules.

When all the outcomes have been determined, you are ready to simplify the table. In a multi-condition table, some rules might be duplicates, redundant, or unrealistic. To simplify the table, follow these steps:

1. Study each combination of conditions and outcomes. When you have rules with three conditions, only one or two of them may control the outcome, and the other conditions simply do not matter.

2. If you identify conditions that do not affect the outcome, mark them with dashes (-) as shown in the first table in Figure 5-38.

3. Now combine and renumber the rules, as shown in the second table in Figure 5-38.

## VERIFY ORDER Process with Credit Waiver (with rules marked for combination)

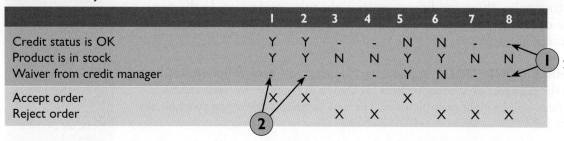

| | 1 | 2 | 3 | 4 | 5 | 6 | 7 | 8 |
|---|---|---|---|---|---|---|---|---|
| Credit status is OK | Y | Y | - | - | N | N | - | - |
| Product is in stock | Y | Y | N | N | Y | Y | N | N |
| Waiver from credit manager | - | - | - | - | Y | N | - | - |
| Accept order | X | X | | | X | | | |
| Reject order | | | X | X | | X | X | X |

1. Because the product is not in stock, the other conditions do not matter.
2. Because the other conditions are met, the waiver does not matter.

## VERIFY ORDER Process with Credit Waiver (after rule combination and simplification)

| | 1 (COMBINES PREVIOUS 1, 2) | 2 (PREVIOUS 5) | 3 (PREVIOUS 6) | 4 (COMBINES PREVIOUS 3, 4, 7, 8) |
|---|---|---|---|---|
| Credit status is OK | Y | N | N | - |
| Product is in stock | Y | Y | Y | N |
| Waiver from credit manager | - | Y | N | - |
| Accept order | X | X | | |
| Reject order | | | X | X |

**FIGURE 5-38** In the first table, dashes have been added to indicate that a condition is not relevant. In the second version, rules have been combined. Notice that in final version, only four rules remain. These rules document the logic, and will be transformed into program code when the system is developed.

If you follow these steps, you will see that Rules 1 and 2 can be combined because credit status is OK in both rules, so the waiver would not matter. Rules 3, 4, 7, and 8 also can be combined because the product is not in stock, so other conditions do not matter. The result is that instead of eight possibilities, only four logical rules control the Verify Order process.

**MULTIPLE OUTCOMES** In addition to multiple conditions, decision tables can have more than two possible outcomes. For example, the sales promotion policy shown in Figure 5-39 includes three conditions: Was the customer a preferred customer, did the customer order $1,000 or more, and did the customer use our company charge card? Based on these conditions, four possible actions can occur, as shown in the decision table in Figure 5-40.

### SALES PROMOTION POLICY – Holiday Season, 2011

- Preferred customers who order $1,000 or more are entitled to a 5% discount, and an additional 5% discount if they use our charge card.

- Preferred customers who do not order $1,000 or more will receive a $25 bonus coupon.

- All other customers will receive a $5 bonus coupon.

**FIGURE 5-39** A sales promotion policy with three conditions. Notice that the first statement contains two *separate* conditions – one for the 5% discount, and another for the additional discount.

## Sales Promotion Policy (initial version)

|  | 1 | 2 | 3 | 4 | 5 | 6 | 7 | 8 |
|---|---|---|---|---|---|---|---|---|
| Preferred customer | Y | Y | Y | Y | N | N | N | N |
| Ordered $1,000 or more | Y | Y | N | N | Y | Y | N | N |
| Used our charge card | Y | N | Y | N | Y | N | Y | N |
| 5% discount | X | X |  |  |  |  |  |  |
| Additional 5% discount | X |  |  |  |  |  |  |  |
| $25 bonus coupon |  |  | X | X |  |  |  |  |
| $5 bonus coupon |  |  |  |  | X | X | X | X |

**FIGURE 5-40** This decision table is based on the sales promotion policy in Figure 5-39. This is the initial version of the table, before simplification.

As explained in the preceding section, most tables can be simplified, and this one is no exception. When you study the conditions and outcomes, you realize that:

- In Rule 1, all three conditions are met, so *both* 5% discounts apply.

- In Rule 2, a preferred customer orders $1,000 or more, but does not use our charge card, so only *one* 5% discount applies.

- Rules 3 and 4 can be combined into a single rule. Why? If preferred customers do not order $1,000 or more, it does not matter whether they use our charge card – either way, they only earn a $25 bonus coupon. Therefore, Rules 3 and 4 really are a single rule.

- Rules 5, 6, 7, and 8 also can be combined into a single rule – because if the person is *not* a preferred customer, he or she can *only* receive a $5 bonus coupon, and the other conditions simply do not matter. So, you insert a dash if a condition is irrelevant, as shown in Figure 5-41.

If you add dashes for rules that are not relevant, your table should resemble the one shown in Figure 5-41. When you combine and simplify the results, only four rules remain: Rule 1, Rule 2, Rule 3 (a combination of initial Rules 3 and 4), and Rule 4 (a combination of initial Rules 5, 6, 7, and 8).

## Sales Promotion Policy (final version)

|  | 1 | 2 | 3 | 4 | 5 | 6 | 7 | 8 |
|---|---|---|---|---|---|---|---|---|
| Preferred customer | Y | Y | Y | Y | N | N | N | N |
| Ordered $1,000 or more | Y | Y | N | N | - | - | - | - |
| Used our charge card | Y | N | - | - | - | - | - | - |
| 5% discount | X | X |  |  |  |  |  |  |
| Additional 5% discount | X |  |  |  |  |  |  |  |
| $25 bonus coupon |  |  | X | X |  |  |  |  |
| $5 bonus coupon |  |  |  |  | X | X | X | X |

**FIGURE 5-41** In this version, dashes have been added to indicate that a condition is not relevant. At this point, it appears that several rules can be combined.

Decision tables often are the best way to describe a complex set of conditions. Many analysts use decision tables because they are easy to construct and understand, and programmers find it easy to work from a decision table when developing code.

# CASE IN POINT 5.2:   ROCK SOLID OUTFITTERS (PART 1)

Leah Jones is the IT manager at Rock Solid Outfitters, a medium-sized supplier of outdoor climbing and camping gear. Steve Allen, the marketing director, has asked Leah to develop a special Web-based promotion. As Steve described it to Leah, Rock Solid will provide free shipping for any customer who either completes an online survey form or signs up for the Rock Solid online newsletter. Additionally, if a customer completes the survey *and* signs up for the newsletter, Rock Solid will provide a $10 merchandise credit for orders of $100 or more. Leah has asked you to develop a decision table that will reflect the promotional rules that a programmer will use. She wants you to show all possibilities, then to simplify the results to eliminate any combinations that would be unrealistic or redundant.

## Decision Trees

A **decision tree** is a graphical representation of the conditions, actions, and rules found in a decision table. Decision trees show the logic structure in a horizontal form that resembles a tree with the roots at the left and the branches to the right. Like flowcharts, decision trees are useful ways to present the system to management. Decision trees and decision tables provide the same results, but in different forms. In many situations, a graphic is the most effective means of communication.

Figure 5-42 is based on the sales promotion policy shown in Figure 5-39 on page 228. A decision tree is read from left to right, with the conditions along the various branches and the actions at the far right. Because the example has two conditions with four resulting sets of actions, the example has four terminating branches at the right side of the tree.

**FIGURE 5-42** This example is based on the same Sales Promotion Policy shown in the decision tables in Figures 5-40 and 5-41 on the previous page. Like a decision table, a decision tree shows all combinations of conditions and outcomes. The main difference is the graphical format, which many viewers find easier to interpret.

Whether to use a decision table or a decision tree often is a matter of personal preference. A decision table might be a better way to handle complex combinations of conditions. On the other hand, a decision tree is an effective way to describe a relatively simple process.

# CASE IN POINT 5.3:   ROCK SOLID OUTFITTERS (PART 2)

Leah Jones, the IT manager at Rock Solid Outfitters, thinks you did a good job on the decision table task she assigned to you. Now she wants you to use the same data to develop a decision tree that will show all the possibilities for the Web-based promotion described in Part 1 of the case. She also wants you to discuss the pros and cons of decisions tables versus decision trees.

## LOGICAL VERSUS PHYSICAL MODELS

While structured analysis tools are used to develop a logical model for a new information system, such tools also can be used to develop physical models of an information system. A physical model shows how the system's requirements are implemented. During the systems design phase, you create a physical model of the new information system that follows from the logical model and involves operational tasks and techniques.

### Sequence of Models

What is the relationship between logical and physical models? Think back to the beginning of the systems analysis phase, when you were trying to understand the existing system. Rather than starting with a logical model, you first studied the physical operations of the existing system to understand how the current tasks were carried out. Many systems analysts create a physical model of the current system and then develop a logical model of the current system before tackling a logical model of the new system. Performing that extra step allows them to understand the current system better.

### Four-Model Approach

Many analysts follow a **four-model approach,** which means that they develop a physical model of the current system, a logical model of the current system, a logical model of the new system, and a physical model of the new system. The major benefit of the four-model approach is that it gives you a clear picture of current system functions before you make any modifications or improvements. That is important because mistakes made early in systems development will affect later SDLC phases and can result in unhappy users and additional costs. Taking additional steps to avoid these potentially costly mistakes can prove to be well worth the effort. Another advantage is that the requirements of a new information system often are quite similar to those of the current information system, especially where the proposal is based on new computer technology rather than a large number of new requirements. Adapting the current system logical model to the new system logical model in these cases is a straightforward process.

The only disadvantage of the four-model approach is the added time and cost needed to develop a logical and physical model of the current system. Most projects have very tight schedules that might not allow time to create the current system models. Additionally, users and managers want to see progress on the new system — they are much less concerned about documenting the current system. As a systems analyst, you must stress the importance of careful documentation and resist the pressure to hurry the development process at the risk of creating serious problems later.

## CASE IN POINT 5.4:   TIP TOP STAFFING

Tip Top Staffing supplies employees to hundreds of IT firms that require specialized skills for specific projects. Systems analysts Lisa Nuevo and Bill Goodman are working on the logical model of Tip Top's billing and records system, using DFDs, a data dictionary, and process descriptions. At some point while working on the logical model of the system, Lisa felt that some improvements should be made in the data forms that Tip Top uses to obtain information about job applicants. Was the subject of improving the forms a physical implementation issue? Is Lisa going off on a tangent by considering *how* something will be done, instead of sticking to *what* will be done?

# A QUESTION OF ETHICS

This is your first week in your new job at Safety Zone, a leading producer of IT modeling software. Your prior experience with a smaller competitor gave you an edge in landing the job, and you are excited about joining a larger company in the same field.

So far, all is going well and you are getting used to the new routine. However, you are concerned about one issue. In your initial meeting with the IT manager, she seemed very interested in the details of your prior position, and some of her questions made you a little uncomfortable. She did not actually ask you to reveal any proprietary information, but she made it clear that Safety Zone likes to know as much as possible about its competitors.

Thinking about it some more, you try to draw a line between information that is OK to discuss, and topics such as software specifics or strategy that should be considered private. This is the first time you have ever been in a situation like this. How will you handle it?

## CHAPTER SUMMARY

During data and process modeling, a systems analyst develops graphical models to show how the system transforms data into useful information. The end product of data and process modeling is a logical model that will support business operations and meet user needs. Data and process modeling involves three main tools: data flow diagrams, a data dictionary, and process descriptions.

Data flow diagrams (DFDs) graphically show the movement and transformation of data in the information system. DFDs use four symbols: The process symbol transforms data; the data flow symbol shows data movement; the data store symbol shows data at rest; and the external entity symbol represents someone or something connected to the information system. Various rules and techniques are used to name, number, arrange, and annotate the set of DFDs to make them consistent and understandable.

A set of DFDs is like a pyramid with the context diagram at the top. The context diagram represents the information system's scope and its external connections but not its internal workings. Diagram 0 displays the information system's major processes, data stores, and data flows and is the exploded version of the context diagram's process symbol, which represents the entire information system. Lower-level DFDs show additional detail of the information system through the leveling technique of numbering and partitioning. Leveling continues until you reach the functional primitive processes, which are not decomposed further and are documented with process descriptions. All diagrams must be balanced to ensure their consistency and accuracy.

The data dictionary is the central documentation tool for structured analysis. All data elements, data flows, data stores, processes, entities, and records are documented in the data dictionary. Consolidating documentation in one location allows you to verify the information system's accuracy and consistency more easily and generate a variety of useful reports.

Each functional primitive process is documented using structured English, decision tables, and decision trees. Structured English uses a subset of standard English that defines each process with combinations of the basic building blocks of sequence, selection, and iteration. You also can document the logic by using decision tables or decision trees.

Structured analysis tools can be used to develop a logical model during one systems analysis phase, and a physical model during the systems design phase. Many analysts use a four-model approach, which involves a physical model of the current system, a logical model of the current system, a logical model of the new system, and a physical model of the new system.

# Key Terms and Phrases

# Learn It Online

**Instructions:** To complete the Learn It Online exercises, visit the Management Information Systems CourseMate Web site at **www.cengagebrain.com**, navigate to the resources for this chapter, and click the link for the exercise you want to complete.

**1 Chapter Reinforcement**

**TF, MC, and SA**

Click one of the Chapter Reinforcement links for Multiple Choice, True/False, or Short Answer. Answer each question and submit to your instructor.

**2 Flash Cards**

Click the Flash Cards link and read the instructions. Type 20 (or a number specified by your instructor) in the Number of playing cards text box, type your name in the Enter your Name text box, and then click the Flip Card button. When the flash card is displayed, read the question and then click the ANSWER box arrow to select an answer. Flip through the Flash Cards. If your score is 15 (75%) correct or greater, click Print on the File menu to print your results. If your score is less than 15 (75%) correct, then redo this exercise by clicking the Replay button.

**3 Practice Test**

Click the Practice Test link. Answer each question, enter your first and last name at the bottom of the page, and then click the Grade Test button. When the graded practice test is displayed on your screen, click Print on the File menu to print a hard copy. Continue to take practice tests until you score 80% or better.

**4 Who Wants To Be a Computer Genius?**

Click the Computer Genius link. Read the instructions, enter your first and last name at the bottom of the page, and then click the Play button. When your score is displayed, click the PRINT RESULTS link to print a hard copy.

**5 Wheel of Terms**

Click the Wheel of Terms link. Read the instructions, and then enter your first and last name and your school name. Click the PLAY button. When your score is displayed on the screen, right-click the score and then click Print on the shortcut menu to print a hard copy.

**6 Crossword Puzzle Challenge**

Click the Crossword Puzzle Challenge link. Read the instructions, and then click the Continue button. Work the crossword puzzle. When you are finished, click the Submit button. When the crossword puzzle is redisplayed, submit it to your instructor.

## SCR Associates Case Simulation **Session 5: Data and Process Modeling**

### Overview

The SCR Associates case study is a Web-based simulation that allows you to practice your skills in a real-world environment. The case study transports you to SCR's intranet, where you complete 12 work sessions, each aligning with a chapter. As you work on the case, you will receive e-mail and voice mail messages, obtain information from SCR's online libraries, and perform various tasks.

### How do I use the case?

- Review the SCR background material in Chapter 1.
- Read the Preview for this session and study the Task List.
- Visit the Management Information Systems CourseMate Web site at **www.cengagebrain. com**, navigate to the **SCR Case Simulation**, and locate the intranet link.
- Enter your name and the password **sad9e**. An opening screen will display the 12 sessions.
- Select this session. Check your e-mail and voice mail carefully, and then work on the tasks.

### Preview: Session 5

You recently completed requirements modeling tasks for the new Training Information Management System (TIMS). Now you are ready to begin data and process modeling, which will produce a logical model of the new system. You will create DFDs, develop a data dictionary, and use decision tables and trees.

### Task List

| |
|---|
| 1.  Jesse wants to see a context diagram and a diagram 0 DFD for TIMS. |
| 2.  Need to review the JAD session summary again! Try to identify four main TIMS functions and draw a lower-level DFD for each process. |
| 3.  Prepare a reply to Jesse's message about CASE tools. Search the Internet to find two more alternatives. |
| 4.  Prepare a decision table and a decision tree that show the logical rules described in Jesse's message about fees and discounts. |

**FIGURE 5-43** Task list: Session 5.

# Chapter Exercises

## Review Questions

1. Describe data and process modeling, and name the main data and process modeling techniques.
2. Describe the Gane and Sarson symbols used for processes, data flows, data stores, and entities. Give four examples of typical names for processes, data flows, data stores, and entities.
3. What is the relationship between a context diagram and diagram 0, and which symbol is not used in a context diagram?
4. What is meant by an exploded DFD?
5. Describe a data dictionary and give examples of how and when it is used.
6. Explain the DFD leveling technique.
7. What is a balanced DFD?
8. Describe the steps in creating a decision table.
9. Discuss the pros and cons of decision tables versus decision trees.
10. What is structured English?

## Discussion Topics

1. Suppose you were assigned to develop a logical model of the registration system at a school or college. Would you be better off using a top-down approach, or would a bottom-up strategy be better? What would influence your decision?
2. Some systems analysts find it better to start with a decision table, then construct a decision tree. Others believe it is easier to do it in the reverse order. Which do you prefer? Why?
3. A systems analyst attended a weeklong workshop on structured analysis. When she returned to her job, she told her boss that structured analysis was not worth the time to learn and use on the job. Her view was that it was too academic and had too much new terminology to be useful in a practical setting. Do you agree or disagree? Defend your position.
4. This chapter describes a black box concept that allows more detail to be shown as a process is exploded. Can the concept be applied in business management generally, or is it limited to information systems design? Provide reasons and examples with your answer.

# Apply Your Knowledge

The Apply Your Knowledge section contains four mini-cases. Each case describes a situation, explains your role in the case, and asks you to respond to questions. You can answer the questions by applying knowledge you learned in the chapter.

## 1 Digital Consulting

### Situation:

You are a senior systems analyst at Digital Consulting, a growing IT consulting firm. You are leading the development team for a major client. You need to explain structured analysis to your two newly hired junior analysts (Sara and Mike) before meeting with the client tomorrow afternoon.

1. Describe the rules for creating a context diagram.
2. Make a basic list of dos and don'ts when developing DFDs.
3. Explain the importance of leveling and balancing.
4. Ask Sara and Mike to review the order system context diagram on page 208, and compare it with the order system diagram 0 DFD on page 212. Then ask them to answer the following questions: (a) How many external entities are shown in each diagram? (b) In each diagram, how many data flows connect to the external entities? (c) How many subprocesses are identified in the diagram 0 DFD? (d) Could the data store have been shown in the context diagram? Why or why not?

## 2 Precision Tools

### Situation:

Precision Tools sells a line of high-quality woodworking tools. When customers place orders on the company's Web site, the system checks to see if the items are in stock, issues a status message to the customer, and generates a shipping order to the warehouse, which fills the order. When the order is shipped, the customer is billed. The system also produces various reports.

1. Draw a context diagram for the order system.
2. Draw a diagram 0 DFD for the order system.
3. Name four attributes that you can use to define a process in the order system.
4. Name four attributes that you can use to define an entity in the order system.

## 3   Claremont School

**Situation:**

The Claremont School course catalog reads as follows: "To enroll in CIS 288, which is an advanced course, a student must complete two prerequisites: CIS 110 and CIS 286. A student who completes either one of these prerequisites and obtains the instructor's permission, however, will be allowed to take CIS 288."

1. Create a decision table that describes the Claremont School course catalog regarding eligibility for CIS 288. Show all possible rules.
2. Simplify the table you just created. Describe the results.
3. Draw a simplified decision tree to represent the Claremont School catalog. Describe the results.
4. Why might you use a decision tree rather than a decision table?

## 4   City Bus Lines

**Situation:**

City Bus Lines is developing an information system that will monitor passenger traffic, peak travel hours, and equipment requirements. The IT manager wants you to document a process called BALANCE that determines whether extra buses currently are needed on a particular route. The BALANCE process automatically assigns additional buses to that route, but *only* if all other routes are operating on schedule. In any case, a supervisor can override the automatic BALANCE process if he or she so desires.

1. Create a decision table that describes the bus transfer process.
2. Draw a decision tree that describes the bus transfer process.
3. Name four attributes that you can use to define a data flow in the bus information system.
4. Name four attributes that you can use to define a data store in the bus information system.

# Case Studies

Case studies allow you to practice specific skills learned in the chapter. Each chapter contains several case studies that continue throughout the textbook, and a chapter capstone case.

## New Century Health Clinic

New Century Health Clinic offers preventive medicine and traditional medical care. In your role as an IT consultant, you will help New Century develop a new information system.

### Background

You began the systems analysis phase at New Century Health Clinic by completing a series of interviews, reviewing existing reports, and observing office operations. (Your instructor may provide you with a sample set of interview summaries.)

As you learned, the doctors, nurses, and physical therapists provide services and perform various medical procedures. All procedures are coded according to Current Procedure Terminology, which is published by the American Medical Association. The procedure codes consist of five numeric digits and a two-digit suffix, and are used for all billing and insurance claims.

From your fact-finding, you determined that seven reports are required at the clinic. The first report is the daily appointment list for each provider. The list shows all scheduled appointment times, patient names, and services to be performed, including the procedure code and description. A second daily report is the call list, which shows the patients who are to be reminded of their next day's appointments. The call list includes the patient name, telephone number, appointment time, and provider name. The third report is the weekly provider report that lists each of the providers and the weekly charges generated, plus a month-to-date (MTD) and a year-to-date (YTD) summary.

The fourth report is the statement — a preprinted form that is produced monthly and mailed in a window envelope. Statement header information includes the statement date, head of household name and address, the previous month's balance, the total household charges MTD, the total payments MTD, and the current balance. The bottom section of the statement lists all activity for the month in date order. For each service performed, a line shows the patient's name, the service date, the procedure code and description, and the charge. The statement also shows the date and amount of all payments and insurance claims. When an insurance payment is received, the source and amount are noted on the form. If the claim is denied or only partially paid, a code is used to explain the reason. A running balance appears at the far right of each activity line.

The associates also require two insurance reports: the weekly Insurance Company Report and the monthly Claim Status Summary. In addition to these six reports, the office staff would like to have mailing labels and computer-generated postcards for sending reminders to patients when it is time to schedule their next appointment. Reminders usually are mailed twice monthly. Now you are ready to organize the facts you gathered and prepare a system requirements document that represents a logical model of the proposed system. Your tools will include DFDs, a data dictionary, and process descriptions.

### Assignments

1. Prepare a context diagram for New Century's information system.
2. Prepare a diagram 0 DFD for New Century. Be sure to show numbered processes for handling appointment processing, payment and insurance processing, report processing, and records maintenance. Also, prepare lower-level DFDs for each numbered process.

3. Prepare a list of data stores and data flows needed for the system. Under each data store, list the data elements required.

4. Prepare a data dictionary entry and process description for one of the system's functional primitives.

## PERSONAL TRAINER, INC.

Personal Trainer, Inc., owns and operates fitness centers in a dozen Midwestern cities. The centers have done well, and the company is planning an international expansion by opening a new "supercenter" in the Toronto area. Personal Trainer's president, Cassia Umi, hired an IT consultant, Susan Park, to help develop an information system for the new facility. During the project, Susan will work closely with Gray Lewis, who will manage the new operation.

### Background

Susan Park has completed a preliminary investigation and performed the fact-finding tasks that were described in Chapters 2 and 4. Now, she will use the results to develop a logical model of the proposed information system.

### Assignments

Before you perform the following tasks, you should review the information provided in Chapters 2 and 4 of the case.

1. Prepare a context diagram for the new system.
2. Prepare a diagram 0 DFD for the new system.
3. Write a brief memo that explains the importance of leveling a set of DFDs.
4. Write a brief memo that explains the importance of balancing a set of DFDs.

## CHAPTER CAPSTONE CASE: SoftWear, Limited

SoftWear, Limited (SWL), is a continuing case study that illustrates the knowledge and skills described in each chapter. In this case study, the student acts as a member of the SWL systems development team and performs various tasks.

### Background

Rick Williams, a systems analyst, and Carla Moore, a programmer/analyst, continued their work on the SWL payroll system project. After completing detailed interviews and other fact-finding activities, Rick and Carla now understand how the current system operates and the new requirements desired by users. They are ready to organize and document their findings by preparing a logical model of the payroll system.

### Data Flow Diagrams

After they completed the preliminary investigation, Rick and Carla felt that they knew more about the system entities and how they interacted.

The two analysts knew that the payroll department issues paychecks based on timesheet data submitted by department heads, and that each employee receives a W-2 form at the end of the year. They also knew that the human resources department prepares employee status changes, and the payroll department enters the pay data. The diagram also noted the output of state and federal government reports and internal reports to SWL's finance and payroll departments. The credit union and the SWL stock transfer department reports and fund transfers also were included.

Using this information, Rick and Carla prepared a sketch of a context diagram and scheduled a meeting for the next day with Amy Calico, director of the payroll department, to discuss the diagram. At the meeting, Amy made several comments:

- The human resources department would be setting up additional ESIP deduction choices for employees under a new 401(k) plan. Human resources also would receive ESIP reports from the payroll system.

- The payroll department enters timesheet data received from department heads, who do not interact directly with the system. Rather than showing the department head entity symbol on the context diagram, the input data flow from the payroll department should be expanded and called PAY DETAIL.

- State and federal reporting requirements differ, so they should be treated as two separate entities. Also, periodic changes in government tax rates should be shown as inputs to the payroll system.

- All accounting reports, except for an overall financial summary, should be distributed to the accounting department instead of to the finance department. The accounting department also should receive a copy of the payroll report.

- The bank returns cleared payroll checks to the payroll department once a month. Amy reminded the analysts that the payroll system handles the reconciliation of payroll checks.

After discussing Amy's comments, Rick and Carla prepared the final version of the payroll system context diagram shown in Figure 5-44.

**FIGURE 5-44**  Final context diagram for SoftWear, Limited's payroll system.

## CHAPTER CAPSTONE CASE:  SoftWear, Limited (continued)

While their conversation with Amy Calico still was fresh in her mind, Carla proposed that they construct the diagram 0 DFD. After going through several draft versions, they completed the diagram 0 shown in Figure 5-45. They identified four processes: the check reconciliation subsystem, the pay employee subsystem, the payroll accounting subsystem, and a subsystem that would handle all voluntary deductions, which they called the ESIP deduction subsystem.

FIGURE 5-45  Diagram 0 DFD for SoftWear, Limited's payroll system.

## CHAPTER CAPSTONE CASE:   SoftWear, Limited (continued)

SWL

Over the next few days, Rick concentrated on partitioning the pay employee subsystem and the ESIP subsystem, while Carla developed the lower-level diagrams for the other two subsystems.

At that point, Rick considered the problem of applying certain deductions on a monthly cycle, even though the deductions were made weekly. To provide flexibility, he decided to use two separate processes, as shown in Figure 5-46. When he finished, his diagram 4 DFD contained the two processes EXTRACT DEDUCTION and APPLY DEDUCTION, as well as a local data store, UNAPPLIED DEDUCTIONS. Several local data flows also were included. The first process, EXTRACT DEDUCTION, would deduct the proper amount in each pay period. The deductions would be held in the temporary data store

**FIGURE 5-46** Diagram 4 DFD for SoftWear, Limited's payroll system shows the detail of process 4, the ESIP DEDUCTION SUBSYSTEM.

and then applied in the APPLY DEDUCTION process on a weekly or monthly basis, depending on the type of deduction. Rick decided that those processes were functional primitives and he did not need to partition them further. That task completed the logical model of the new SWL payroll system.

Rick and Carla also considered the physical design of the ESIP deduction subsystem that would be completed later. They knew that it would be necessary to add some new forms and to redesign others. They saw that the human resources department would need a new form for enrollments or deduction changes for the credit union, SWL stock purchase plan, or any new ESIP choices that might be offered in the future. The payroll department then could use the form as its official notification. To provide for future expansion and add flexibility, the human resources department also would need a form to notify payroll of any new type of deduction, with a deduction code, the name of the deduction, and the payroll cycle involved. Rick anticipated that the new system would eliminate problems with improper deductions, while adding flexibility and reducing maintenance costs.

## Data Dictionary and Process Descriptions

As they constructed the DFDs for the payroll system, Rick and Carla also developed the data dictionary entries with supporting process descriptions. After completing the documentation of the ESIP deduction subsystem, Carla and Rick met with Amy to review the logical model for the subsystem. After a thorough discussion of all proposed changes and processing, Amy approved the model.

Rick and Carla continued their analysis and documentation of the payroll system over the next several days. As they completed a model of a portion of the information system, they would meet with the appropriate users at SWL to review the model, obtain user input, make necessary adjustments to the model, and obtain the users' approval. After Rick and Carla finished the complete payroll information system logical model, they turned their attention to completing the rest of the system requirements document.

## SWL Team Tasks

Suppose that you are working with Rick and Carla when a new systems request comes in. SWL's vice president of marketing, Amy Neal, wants to change the catalog mailing program and provide a reward for customers who use the Internet.

Amy's plan specifies that customers will remain on SWL's mailing list if they either requested a catalog, ordered from SWL in the last two years, or signed the guest register on SWL's new Web site. To encourage Internet visitors, customers who register on the Web site also will receive a special discount certificate.

To document the requirements, Rick wants you to design a decision table. Initially, it appears to have eight rules, but you notice that some of those rules are duplicates, or might not be realistic combinations.

1. Design the decision table with all possibilities.
2. Simplify the table by combining rules where appropriate.
3. Draw a decision tree that reflects Amy Neal's policy.
4. Create a set of structured English statements that accurately describes the policy.

# Chapter Capstone Case:   SoftWear, Limited (continued)         SWL

## Manage the SWL Project

You have been asked to manage SWL's new information system project. One of your most important activities will be to identify project tasks and determine when they will be performed. Before you begin, you should review the SWL case in this chapter. Then list and analyze the tasks, as follows:

**LIST THE TASKS** Start by listing and numbering at least 10 tasks that the SWL team needs to perform to fulfill the objectives of this chapter. Your list can include SWL Team Tasks and any other tasks that are described in this chapter. For example, Task 3 might be to Identify the system entities, and Task 6 might be to Draw a context diagram.

**ANALYZE THE TASKS** Now study the tasks to determine the order in which they should be performed. First identify all concurrent tasks, which are not dependent on other tasks. In the example shown in Figure 5-47, Tasks 1, 2, 3, 4, and 5 are concurrent tasks, and could begin at the same time if resources were available.

Other tasks are called dependent tasks, because they cannot be performed until one or more earlier tasks have been completed. For each dependent task, you must identify specific tasks that need to be completed before this task can begin. For example, you would want to identify the system entities before you could draw a context diagram, so Task 6 cannot begin until Task 3 is completed, as Figure 5-47 shows.

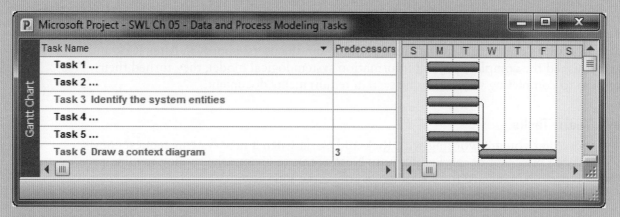

**FIGURE 5-47** Tasks 1, 2, 3, 4, and 5 are concurrent tasks that could be performed at the same time. Task 6 is a dependent task that cannot be performed until Task 3 has been completed.

Chapter 3 describes project management tools, techniques, and software. To learn more, you can use the Features section on your Student Study Tool CD-ROM, or visit the Management Information Systems CourseMate Web site at **www.cengagebrain.com** and locate the project management resources library for this book. On the Web, Microsoft offers demo versions, training, and tips for using Project 2010. You also can visit the OpenWorkbench.org site to learn more about this free, open-source software.

# Ready for a Challenge?

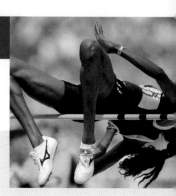

In additional to technical skills, IT professionals need critical thinking skills such as perception, organization, analysis, problem-solving, and decision-making. The Ready for a Challenge feature can help you learn, practice, and apply critical thinking skills that you can take to the workplace.

The IT team at Game Technology is moving forward with the new Customer Contact Care information system, or $C^3$.

Your next assignment is to develop a set of data flow diagrams (DFDs). To be sure you can handle the tasks, you decide to review Chapter 5 of your systems analysis textbook. Based on previous requirements modeling, you know that the new $C^3$ system will have three external entities, with the following data flows:

| Entity | Data Flow from the Entity | Data Flow to the Entity |
|---|---|---|
| Customer | Contact Information | Sales Specials |
| Sales Records System | Customer Sales History | None |
| Marketing Rep | Suggested Contact Plan | Sales Feedback |

You also know that the $C^3$ system will have three subsystems: **Analyze Customer Data**, **Analyze Sales History**, and **Manage Contact Plan**, and a data store called **Customer Profile**. The data flows are as follows:

| Data Flow | From | To |
|---|---|---|
| Contact Information | Customer entity | Analyze Customer Data process |
| Sales Specials | Manage Contact Plan process | Customer entity |
| Customer Sales History | Sales Records System entity | Analyze Sales History process |
| Suggested Contact Plan | Marketing Rep entity | Develop Contact Plan process |
| Sales Feedback | Analyze Sales History process | Marketing Rep entity |
| Customer Data (two-way) | Analyze Customer Data process | Customer Profile data store |
| Customer Data (two-way) | Customer Profile data store | Analyze Customer Data process |
| Profile Data | Customer Profile data store | Manage Contact Plan process |
| Sales Data | Analyze Sales History process | Customer Profile data store |

## Practice Tasks
A. Draw a context diagram for the new $C^3$ system.
B. Draw a DFD diagram 0 that shows the three processes, the data store, and the data flows.

After you complete the Practice Tasks, to check your work and view sample answers, visit the Management Information Systems CourseMate Web site at **www.cengagebrain.com**, navigate to the resources for this chapter, and locate Ready for a Challenge?.

## The Challenge
Your context diagram and DFD diagram 0 were accurate, but there have been some design changes. Management has decided to connect the external **Accounts Receivable System** directly to the $C^3$ system as a fourth entity. A two-way data flow called **AR Data** will connect this entity to the $C^3$ system. Inside the $C^3$ system, **AR Data** will connect to the **Analyze Sales History** process.

Also, another new two-way data flow called **Billing Data** will connect to the **Analyze Sales History** process and the **Customer Profile** data store.

## Challenge Tasks
A. Draw a context diagram for the new $C^3$ system that shows the revised design.
B. Draw a DFD diagram 0 that shows the revised design.

# CHAPTER 6 Object Analysis

**Chapter 6** is the third of four chapters in the systems analysis phase of the SDLC. This chapter discusses object modeling techniques that analysts use to create a logical model. In addition to structured analysis, object-oriented analysis is another way to represent and design an information system.

## INTRODUCTION

## OBJECTIVES

*When you finish this chapter, you will be able to:*

- Explain how object-oriented analysis can be used to describe an information system

- Define object modeling terms and concepts, including objects, attributes, methods, messages, classes, and instances

- Explain relationships among objects and the concept of inheritance

- Draw an object relationship diagram

- Describe Unified Modeling Language (UML) tools and techniques, including use cases, use case diagrams, class diagrams, sequence diagrams, state transition diagrams, and activity diagrams

- Explain the advantages of using CASE tools in developing the object model

- Explain how to organize an object model

In Chapter 5, you learned how to use structured analysis techniques to develop a data and process model of the proposed system. Now, in Chapter 6, you learn about object-oriented analysis, which is another way to view and model system requirements. In this chapter, you use object-oriented techniques to document, analyze, and model the information system. In Chapter 7, which concludes the systems analysis phase, you will evaluate alternatives, develop the system requirements document, learn about prototyping, and prepare for the systems design phase of the SDLC.

## CHAPTER INTRODUCTION CASE:   Mountain View College Bookstore

**Background:** Wendy Lee, manager of college services at Mountain View College, wants a new information system that will improve efficiency and customer service at the three college bookstores.

In this part of the case, Tina Allen (systems analyst) and David Conroe (student intern) are talking about object-oriented concepts, tools, and techniques.

| | |
|---|---|
| **Participants:** | Tina and David |
| **Location:** | Mountain View College Cafeteria, Wednesday afternoon, November 2, 2011. |
| **Project status:** | Tina and David have completed data and processing modeling, and are discussing object-oriented techniques that they can use to develop an object model of the new system. |
| **Discussion topics:** | Object-oriented concepts, tools, and techniques |

**Tina:**   Hi, David. I want to chat with you about object-oriented analysis before we finish the systems analysis phase. Would this be a good time to talk?

**David:**   *Sure. I know that object-oriented analysis is another way of viewing the system, but I don't know much about it.*

**Tina:**   Well, object-oriented analysis describes an information system by identifying things called objects.  An object represents a real person, place, event, or transaction. For example, in the bookstore, when a student purchases a textbook, the student is an object, the textbook is an object, and the purchase transaction itself is an object.

**David:**   *That sounds a little like the entities we identify in structured analysis.*

**Tina:**   Yes, but there's a major difference! In structured analysis we treat data and the processes that affect the data separately. Objects, on the other hand, contain the data *and* the processes, called methods, that can add, modify, or change the data. To make it even more interesting, one object can send a message to another object to request some action or response. For example, a driver object adjusts the cruise control, which sends one or more messages to the car object telling it to maintain a steady speed.

**David:**   *I get it. So objects can be people, things, or events?*

**Tina:**   Yes. To show how the system works, we use a special modeling language called the UML. We even show human actors as stick figures that interact with business functions called use cases.

**David:**   *I'd like to give it a try.*

**Tina:**   No problem. Although we'll still use structured analysis, it will be interesting to model the system in object-oriented terms. Let's get started on our task list:

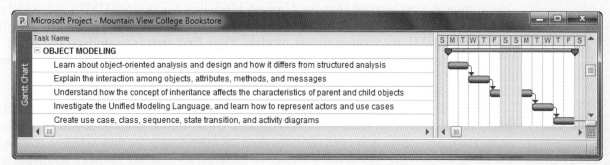

**FIGURE 6-1** Typical object modeling task list.

## OVERVIEW OF OBJECT-ORIENTED ANALYSIS

As you learned in Chapter 1, the most popular systems development options are structured analysis, object-oriented analysis (O-O), and agile methods, also called adaptive methods. The table in Figure 1-25 on page 21 shows the three alternatives and describes some pros and cons for each approach. As the table indicates, O-O methodology is popular because it integrates easily with object-oriented programming languages such as Java, Smalltalk, C++, and Perl. Programmers also like O-O code because it is modular, reusable, and easy to maintain.

**Object-oriented (O-O) analysis** describes an information system by identifying things called objects. An **object** represents a real person, place, event, or transaction. For example, when a patient makes an appointment to see a doctor, the patient is an object, the doctor is an object, and the appointment itself is an object.

Object-oriented analysis is a popular approach that sees a system from the viewpoint of the objects themselves as they function and interact. The end product of object-oriented analysis is an **object model**, which represents the information system in terms of objects and object-oriented concepts.

## VIDEO LEARNING SESSION: OBJECT-ORIENTED TERMS AND CONCEPTS

Video Learning Sessions can help you understand key concepts, practice your skills, and check your work. To access the sessions, visit the Management Information Systems CourseMate Web site at **www.cengagebrain.com** and navigate to the **Video Learning Sessions** for this book. In this session you'll learn basic object modeling terms and concepts, how to use symbols to create object models, and how you can use a CASE tool to create object models.

### Object-Oriented Terms and Concepts

In Chapter 4, you learned that the **Unified Modeling Language** (UML) is a widely used method of visualizing and documenting an information system. In this chapter, you use the UML to develop object models. Your first step is to understand basic object-oriented terms, including objects, attributes, methods, messages, classes, and instances. In this chapter, you will learn how systems analysts use those terms to describe an information system.

An object represents a person, place, event, or transaction that is significant to the information system. In Chapter 5, you created DFDs that treated data and processes separately. An object, however, includes data *and* the processes that affect that data. For example, a customer object has a name, an address, an account number, and a current balance. Customer objects also can perform specific tasks, such as placing an order, paying a bill, and changing their address.

An object has certain **attributes**, which are characteristics that describe the object. For example, if you own a car, it has attributes such as make, model, and color. An object also has **methods**, which are tasks or functions that the object performs when it receives a **message**, or command, to do so. For example, your car performs a method called OPERATE WIPERS when you send a message by moving the proper control. Figure 6-2 shows examples of attributes, methods, and messages for a car object.

A **class** is a group of similar objects. For example, Ford Fiestas belong to a class called CAR. An **instance** is a specific member of a class. *Your* Ford Fiesta, therefore, is an instance of the CAR class. At an auto dealership, like the one shown in Figure 6-3, you might observe many instances of the CAR class, the TRUCK class, the MINIVAN class, and the SPORT UTILITY VEHICLE class, among others. Although the term "object" usually refers to a particular instance, systems analysts sometimes use the term to refer to a class of objects. Usually the meaning is understood from the context and the way the term is used.

## Objects

Consider how the UML describes a family with parents and children. The UML represents an object as a rectangle with the object name at the top, followed by the object's attributes and methods.

Figure 6-4 shows a PARENT object with certain attributes such as name, age, sex, and hair color. If there are two parents, then there are two instances of the PARENT object. The PARENT object can perform methods, such as reading a bedtime story, driving the car pool van, or preparing a school lunch. When a PARENT object receives a message, it performs an action, or method.

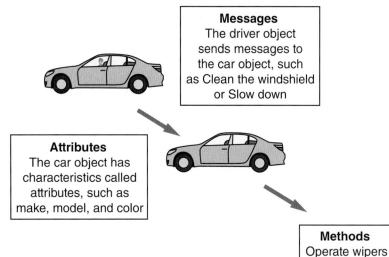

**Examples of Interaction Between Objects**

**Messages**
The driver object sends messages to the car object, such as Clean the windshield or Slow down

**Attributes**
The car object has characteristics called attributes, such as make, model, and color

**Methods**
Operate wipers
Apply brakes

**FIGURE 6-2** Objects have attributes, can send and receive messages, and perform actions called methods.

**FIGURE 6-3** At an auto dealership, you can observe the CAR class, the TRUCK class, the MINIVAN class, and the SPORT UTILITY VEHICLE class.

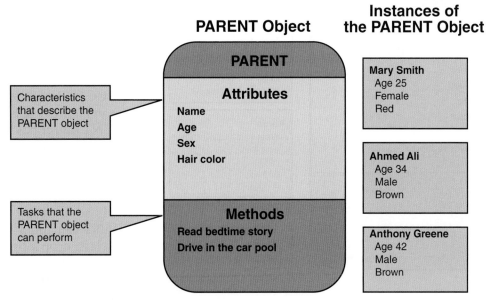

**PARENT Object**

**Instances of the PARENT Object**

Characteristics that describe the PARENT object

**PARENT**

**Attributes**
Name
Age
Sex
Hair color

Tasks that the PARENT object can perform

**Methods**
Read bedtime story
Drive in the car pool

**Mary Smith**
Age 25
Female
Red

**Ahmed Ali**
Age 34
Male
Brown

**Anthony Greene**
Age 42
Male
Brown

**FIGURE 6-4** The PARENT object includes four attributes and two methods. Mary Smith, Ahmed Ali, and Anthony Greene are instances of the PARENT object.

For example, the message GOOD NIGHT from a child might tell the PARENT object to read a bedtime story, while the message DRIVE from another parent signals that it is the PARENT object's turn to drive in the car pool.

Continuing with the family example, the CHILD object in Figure 6-5 possesses the same attributes as the PARENT object and an additional attribute that shows the number of siblings. A CHILD object performs certain methods, such as picking up toys, eating dinner, playing, cooperating, and getting ready for bed. To signal the CHILD object to perform those tasks, a parent can send certain messages that the CHILD object will understand. For example, the DINNER'S READY message tells a CHILD object to come to the table, while the SHARE WITH YOUR BROTHER/SISTER message tells a CHILD object to cooperate with other CHILD objects.

The family also might have a DOG object, as shown in Figure 6-6. That object can have attributes such as name, breed, age, color, sex, and favorite food. The DOG object can perform methods such as wagging its tail, eating, fetching, and sleeping. The message GOOD DOG, when directed to the DOG object, signals it to wag its tail. Similarly, the DINNER'S READY message signals the DOG object to run to its food bowl.

Now consider an example of a fitness center, as shown in Figure 6-7, and the objects that interact with the fitness center's enrollment system. A typical fitness center might have students, instructors, fitness-class schedules, and a registration process.

STUDENT and INSTRUCTOR objects are shown in Figure 6-8. Each STUDENT object has the following attributes: student number, name, address, telephone, date of birth, fitness record, and status. In addition, a STUDENT can add a fitness-class; drop a fitness-class; change an address, telephone, or status; and update his or her fitness record.

**CHILD Object**

**Instances of the CHILD Object**

Characteristics that describe the CHILD object

**CHILD**

**Attributes**
Name
Age
Sex
Hair color
Number of siblings

Tasks that the CHILD object can perform

**Methods**
Pick up toys
Eat dinner
Play
Cooperate
Get ready for bed

James Smith
Age 3
Male
Red

Amelia Ali
Age 1
Female
Brown

Misty Greene
Age 12
Female
Blonde

FIGURE 6-5 The CHILD object includes five attributes and five methods. James Smith, Amelia Ali, and Misty Greene are instances of the CHILD object.

**DOG Object**

**Instances of the DOG Object**

Characteristics that describe the DOG object

**DOG**

**Attributes**
Name
Breed
Age
Color
Sex
Favorite food

Tasks that the DOG object can perform

**Methods**
Wag tail
Eat
Fetch
Sleep

Buddy
Terrier mix
Age 12
White
Male
Kibbles and Bits

Annie
West Highland Terrier
Age 1
White
Female
ProPlan

Megan
Poodle mix
Age 8
Tan
Female
Purina Dog Chow

FIGURE 6-6 The DOG object includes six attributes and four methods. Buddy, Annie, and Megan are instances of the DOG object.

**FIGURE 6-7** A typical fitness center might have students, instructors, fitness-class schedules, and a registration process.

The INSTRUCTOR object in Figure 6-8 has the following attributes: instructor number, name, address, telephone, fitness-classes taught, availability, private lesson fee, and status. An INSTRUCTOR object can teach a fitness-class, and change his or her availability, address, telephone, private lesson fee, or status.

The FITNESS-CLASS SCHEDULE object shown in Figure 6-9 on the next page includes data about fitness classes, including fitness-class number, date, time, type, location, instructor number, and maximum enrollment. The FITNESS-CLASS SCHEDULE object includes the methods that can add or delete a fitness class, or change a fitness-class date, time, instructor, location, or enrollment.

The REGISTRATION RECORD object shown in Figure 6-10 on the next page includes the student number, fitness-class number, registration date, fee, and status. The REGISTRATION RECORD

**STUDENT Object**

| STUDENT |
| --- |
| **Attributes** |
| Student number |
| Name |
| Address |
| Telephone |
| Date of birth |
| Fitness record |
| Status |
| **Methods** |
| Add fitness-class |
| Drop fitness-class |
| Change address |
| Change telephone |
| Change status |
| Update fitness record |

**INSTRUCTOR Object**

| INSTRUCTOR |
| --- |
| **Attributes** |
| Instructor number |
| Name |
| Address |
| Telephone |
| Fitness-classes taught |
| Availability |
| Private lesson fee |
| Status |
| **Methods** |
| Teach fitness-class |
| Change availability |
| Change address |
| Change telephone |
| Change private lesson fee |
| Change status |

**FIGURE 6-8** The STUDENT object includes seven attributes and six methods. The INSTRUCTOR object includes eight attributes and six methods.

object includes methods to add a REGISTRATION instance when a student enrolls, or drop a REGISTRATION instance if the fitness class is canceled or for nonpayment. Notice that if a student registers for three fitness classes, the result is three instances of the REGISTRATION RECORD object. The REGISTRATION RECORD object also includes a method of notifying students and instructors of information.

## FITNESS-CLASS SCHEDULE Object

### FITNESS-CLASS SCHEDULE

**Attributes**

Fitness-class number
Date
Time
Type
Location
Instructor number
Maximum enrollment

**Methods**

Add fitness-class
Delete fitness-class
Change date
Change time
Change instructor
Change location
Change enrollment

**FIGURE 6-9** The FITNESS-CLASS SCHEDULE object includes seven attributes and seven methods.

## REGISTRATION RECORD Object

### REGISTRATION RECORD

**Attributes**

Student number
Fitness-class number
Registration date
Fee
Status

**Methods**

Add student
Drop student
Notify instructor of add
Notify instructor of drop
Notify all of fitness-class cancellations

**FIGURE 6-10** The REGISTRATION object includes five attributes and five methods.

## Attributes

If objects are similar to nouns, attributes are similar to adjectives that describe the characteristics of an object. How many attributes are needed? The answer depends on the business requirements of the information system and its users. Even a relatively simple object, such as an inventory item, might have a part number, description, supplier, quantity on hand, minimum stock level, maximum stock level, reorder time, and so on. Some objects might have a few attributes; others might have dozens.

Systems analysts define an object's attributes during the systems design process. In an object-oriented system, objects can inherit, or acquire, certain attributes from other objects. When you learn about relationships between objects and classes, you will understand how that occurs.

Objects can have a specific attribute called a **state**. The state of an object is an adjective that describes the object's current status. For example, depending on the state, a student can be a future student, a current student, or a past student. Similarly, a bank account can be active, inactive, closed, or frozen.

## Methods

A method defines specific tasks that an object can perform. Just as objects are similar to nouns and attributes are similar to adjectives, methods resemble verbs that describe *what* and *how* an object does something.

Consider a server who prepares fries in a fast-food restaurant, as shown in Figure 6-11. A systems analyst might describe the operation as a method called MORE FRIES, as shown in

**FIGURE 6-11** In a fast-food restaurant, preparing more fries is a common task.

FIGURE 6-12 The MORE FRIES method requires the server to perform seven specific steps.

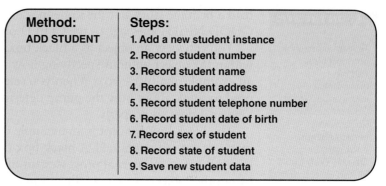

FIGURE 6-13 In the fitness center example, the ADD STUDENT method requires the STUDENT object to perform nine specific steps.

Figure 6-12. The MORE FRIES method includes the steps required to heat the oil, fill the fry basket with frozen potato strips, lower it into the hot oil, check for readiness, remove the basket when ready and drain the oil, pour the fries into a warming tray, and add salt.

Figure 6-13 shows another example of a method. At the fitness center, an ADD STUDENT method adds a new instance of the STUDENT class. Notice that nine steps are required to add the new instance and record the necessary data.

## Messages

A message is a command that tells an object to perform a certain method. For example, the message ADD STUDENT directs the STUDENT class to add a STUDENT instance. The STUDENT class understands that it should add the student number, name, and other data about that student, as shown in Figure 6-14. Similarly, a message named DELETE STUDENT tells the STUDENT class to delete a STUDENT instance.

The same message to two different objects can produce different results. The concept that a message gives different meanings to different objects is called **polymorphism**. For example, in Figure 6-15, the message GOOD NIGHT signals the PARENT object to

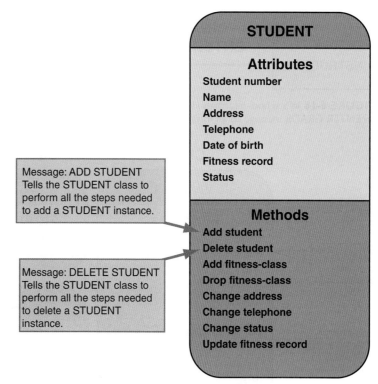

FIGURE 6-14 The message ADD STUDENT signals the STUDENT class to perform the ADD STUDENT method. The message DELETE STUDENT signals the STUDENT class to perform the DELETE STUDENT method.

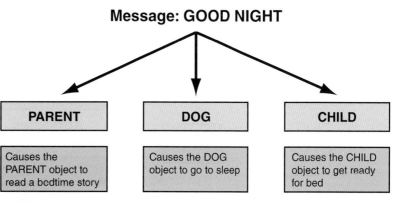

FIGURE 6-15 In an example of polymorphism, the message GOOD NIGHT produces different results, depending on which object receives it.

read a bedtime story, but the same message to the DOG object tells the dog to sleep. The GOOD NIGHT message to the CHILD object signals it to get ready for bed.

You can view an object as a **black box**, because a message to the object triggers changes within the object without specifying how the changes must be carried out. A gas pump is an example of a black box. When you select the economy grade at a pump, you do not need to think about how the pump determines the correct price and selects the right fuel, as long as it does so properly.

The black box concept is an example of **encapsulation**, which means that all data and methods are self-contained. A black box does not want or need outside interference. By limiting access to internal processes, an object prevents its internal code from being altered by another object or process. Encapsulation allows objects to be used as modular components anywhere in the system, because objects send and receive messages but do not alter the internal methods of other objects.

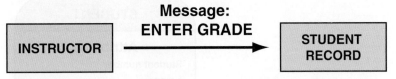

**FIGURE 6-16** In a school information system, an INSTRUCTOR object sends an ENTER GRADE message to an instance of the STUDENT RECORD class.

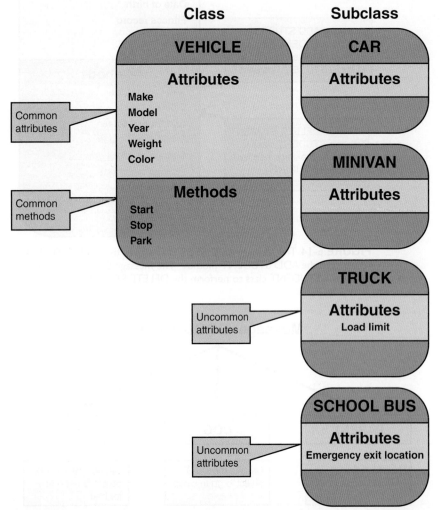

**FIGURE 6-17** The VEHICLE class includes common attributes and methods. CAR, TRUCK, MINIVAN, and SCHOOL BUS are instances of the VEHICLE class.

Object-oriented designs typically are implemented with object-oriented programming languages. A major advantage of O-O designs is that systems analysts can save time and avoid errors by using modular objects, and programmers can translate the designs into code, working with reusable program modules that have been tested and verified. For example, in Figure 6-16, an INSTRUCTOR object sends an ENTER GRADE message to an instance of the STUDENT RECORD class. Notice that the INSTRUCTOR object and STUDENT RECORD class could be reused, with minor modifications, in other school information systems where many of the attributes and methods would be similar.

**Classes**

An object belongs to a group or category called a class. All objects within a class share common attributes and methods, so a class is like a blueprint, or template for all the objects within the class. Objects within a class can be grouped into **subclasses**, which are more specific categories within a class. For example, TRUCK objects represent a subclass within the VEHICLE class, along with other subclasses called CAR, MINIVAN, and SCHOOL BUS, as shown in Figure 6-17. Notice that all four subclasses share common traits of the VEHICLE class, such as make, model, year, weight, and color. Each subclass also can possess traits that are uncommon, such as a load limit for the TRUCK or an emergency exit location for the SCHOOL BUS.

In the fitness center example shown in Figure 6-18, INSTRUCTOR objects represent a subclass within the EMPLOYEE class. The EMPLOYEE class also can contain MANAGER and OFFICE STAFF subclasses, because a manager and staff members are employees. All INSTRUCTOR, MANAGER, and OFFICE STAFF objects contain similar information (such as employee name, title, and pay rate) and perform similar tasks (such as getting hired and changing an address or telephone number).

A class can belong to a more general category called a **superclass**. For example, a NOVEL class belongs to a superclass called BOOK, because all novels are books.

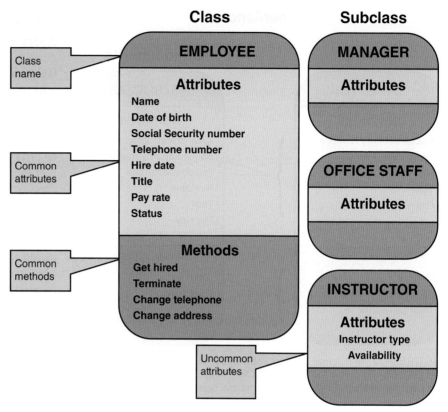

**FIGURE 6-18** The fitness center EMPLOYEE class includes common attributes and methods. INSTRUCTOR, MANAGER, and OFFICE STAFF are subclasses within the EMPLOYEE class.

The NOVEL class can have subclasses called HARDCOVER and PAPERBACK. Similarly, as shown in Figure 6-19, the EMPLOYEE class belongs to the PERSON superclass, because every employee is a person, and the INSTRUCTOR class is a subclass of EMPLOYEE.

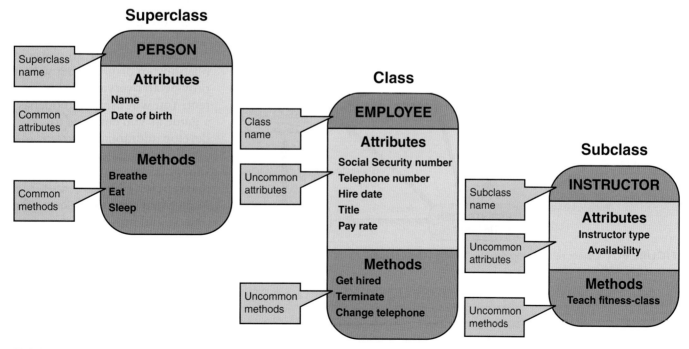

**FIGURE 6-19** At the fitness center, the PERSON superclass includes common attributes and methods. EMPLOYEE is a class within the PERSON superclass. INSTRUCTOR is a subclass within the EMPLOYEE class.

## Inheritance

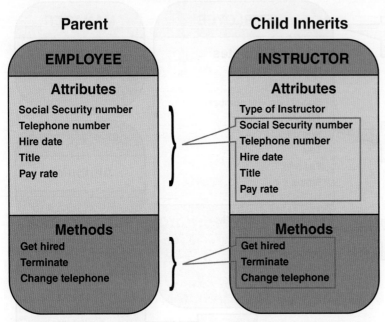

**FIGURE 6-20** An inheritance relationship exists between the INSTRUCTOR and EMPLOYEE objects. The INSTRUCTOR (child) object inherits characteristics from the EMPLOYEE (parent) class and can have additional attributes of its own.

# RELATIONSHIPS AMONG OBJECTS AND CLASSES

**Relationships** enable objects to communicate and interact as they perform business functions and transactions required by the system. Relationships describe what objects need to know about each other, how objects respond to changes in other objects, and the effects of membership in classes, superclasses, and subclasses. Some relationships are stronger than others (just as a relationship between family members is stronger than one between casual acquaintances). The strongest relationship is called inheritance. **Inheritance** enables an object, called a **child**, to derive one or more of its attributes from another object, called a **parent**. In the example in Figure 6-20, the INSTRUCTOR object (child) inherits many traits from the EMPLOYEE object (parent), including SOCIAL SECURITY NUMBER, TELEPHONE NUMBER, and HIRE DATE. The INSTRUCTOR object also can possess additional attributes, such as TYPE OF INSTRUCTOR. Because all employees share certain attributes, those attributes are assumed through inheritance and do not need to be repeated in the INSTRUCTOR object.

## Object Relationship Diagram

After you identify the objects, classes, and relationships, you are ready to prepare an object relationship diagram that will provide an overview of the system. You will use that model as a guide as you continue to develop additional diagrams and documentation. Figure 6-21 shows an object relationship diagram for a fitness center. Notice that the model shows the objects and how they interact to perform business functions and transactions.

**FIGURE 6-21** Object relationship diagram for the fitness center.

## OBJECT MODELING WITH THE UNIFIED MODELING LANGUAGE

Just as structured analysis uses DFDs to model data and processes, systems analysts use the Unified Modeling Language (UML) to describe object-oriented systems.

In Chapter 4, you learned that the UML is a popular technique for documenting and modeling a system. The UML uses a set of symbols to represent graphically the various components and relationships within a system. Although the UML can be used for business process modeling and requirements modeling, it mainly is used to support object-oriented system analysis and to develop object models.

## VIDEO LEARNING SESSION: OBJECT-ORIENTED DIAGRAMS AND MODELS

Video Learning Sessions can help you understand key concepts, practice your skills, and check your work. To access the sessions, visit the Management Information Systems CourseMate Web site at **www.cengagebrain.com** and navigate to the **Video Learning Sessions** for this book. In this session you'll learn how to create various types of object diagrams, including use-case, class, sequence, state-transition, and activity diagrams, and how you can use a CASE tool to create object models.

### Use Case Modeling

A **use case** represents the steps in a specific business function or process. An external entity, called an **actor**, initiates a use case by requesting the system to perform a function or process. For example, in a medical office system, a PATIENT (actor) can MAKE APPOINTMENT (use case), as shown in Figure 6-22.

Notice that the UML symbol for a use case is an oval with a label that describes the action or event. The actor is shown as a stick figure, with a label that identifies the actor's role. The line from the actor to the use case is called an association, because it links a particular actor to a use case. Figure 6-23 shows use case examples of a passenger making an airline reservation, a customer placing an order, and a bus dispatcher changing a student's pickup address.

Use cases also can interact with other use cases. When the outcome of one use case is incorporated by another use case, we say that the second case *uses* the first case. The UML

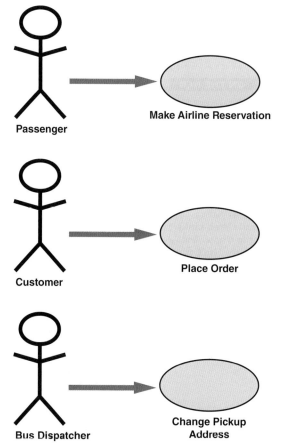

**FIGURE 6-23** Three use case examples. The UML symbol for a use case is an oval. The actor is shown as a stick figure.

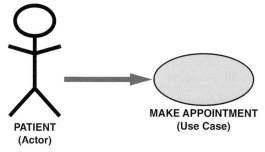

**FIGURE 6-22** In a medical office system, a PATIENT (actor) can MAKE APPOINTMENT (use case).

indicates the relationship with a hollow-headed arrow that *points at* the use case being used. Figure 6-24 shows an example where a student adds a fitness class and PRODUCE FITNESS-CLASS ROSTER *uses* the results of ADD FITNESS-CLASS to generate a new fitness-class roster. Similarly, if an instructor changes his or her availability, UPDATE INSTRUCTOR INFORMATION *uses* the CHANGE AVAILABILITY use case to update the instructor's information.

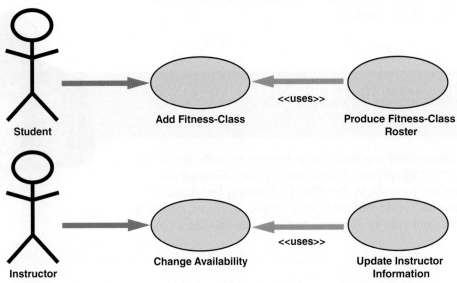

**FIGURE 6-24** When a student adds a class, PRODUCE FITNESS-CLASS ROSTER uses the results of ADD CLASS to generate a new class roster. When an instructor changes his or her availability, UPDATE INSTRUCTOR INFORMATION uses the CHANGE AVAILABILITY use case to update the instructor's information.

To create use cases, you start by reviewing the information that you gathered during the requirements modeling phase. Your objective is to identify the actors and the functions or transactions they initiate. For each use case, you also develop a **use case description** in the form of a table. A use case description documents the name of the use case, the actor, a description of the use case, a step-by-step list of the tasks and actions required for successful completion, a description of alternative courses of action, preconditions, postconditions, and assumptions. Figure 6-25 shows an example of the ADD NEW STUDENT use case.

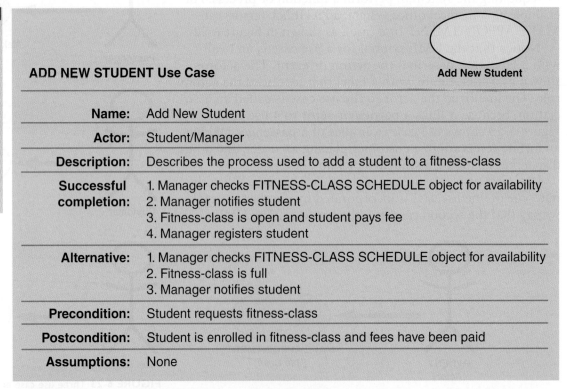

**ADD NEW STUDENT Use Case**                                          Add New Student

| | |
|---|---|
| **Name:** | Add New Student |
| **Actor:** | Student/Manager |
| **Description:** | Describes the process used to add a student to a fitness-class |
| **Successful completion:** | 1. Manager checks FITNESS-CLASS SCHEDULE object for availability<br>2. Manager notifies student<br>3. Fitness-class is open and student pays fee<br>4. Manager registers student |
| **Alternative:** | 1. Manager checks FITNESS-CLASS SCHEDULE object for availability<br>2. Fitness-class is full<br>3. Manager notifies student |
| **Precondition:** | Student requests fitness-class |
| **Postcondition:** | Student is enrolled in fitness-class and fees have been paid |
| **Assumptions:** | None |

**FIGURE 6-25** The ADD NEW STUDENT use case description documents the process used to add a current student into an existing class.

When you identify use cases, try to group all the related transactions into a single use case. For example, when a hotel customer reserves a room, the reservation system blocks a room, updates the occupancy forecast, and sends the customer a confirmation. Those events are all part of a single use case called RESERVE ROOM, and the specific actions are step-by-step tasks within the use case.

## CASE IN POINT 6.1: HILLTOP MOTORS

You have been hired by Hilltop Motors as a consultant to help the company plan a new information system. Hilltop is an old-line dealership, and the prior owner was slow to change. A new management team has taken over, and they are eager to develop a first-class system. Right now, you are reviewing the service department, which is going though a major expansion. You decide to create a model of the service department in the form of a use case diagram. The main actors in the service operation are customers, service writers who prepare work orders and invoices, and mechanics who perform the work. You are meeting with the management team tomorrow morning. Create an initial draft of the diagram to present to them at that time.

### Use Case Diagrams

A **use case diagram** is a visual summary of several related use cases within a system or subsystem. Consider a typical auto service department, as shown in Figure 6-26. The service department involves customers, service writers who prepare work orders and invoices, and mechanics who perform the work. Figure 6-27 on the next page shows a possible use case diagram for the auto service department.

**ON THE WEB**

To learn more about use case diagrams, visit the Management Information Systems CourseMate Web site at **www. cengagebrain. com**, navigate to **On the Web Links** for this chapter, and locate the Use Case Diagrams link.

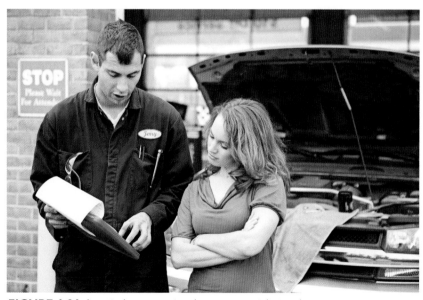
**FIGURE 6-26** A typical auto service department might involve customers, service writers who prepare work orders, and mechanics who perform the work.

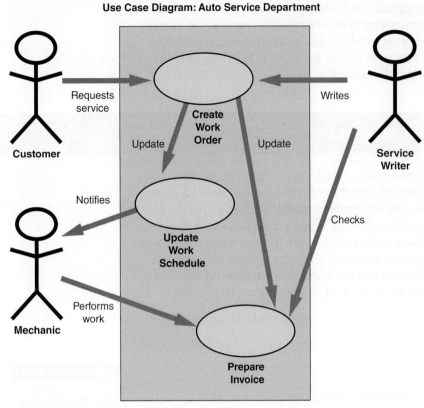

**Use Case Diagram: Auto Service Department**

**FIGURE 6-27** A use case diagram to handle work at an auto service department.

When you create a use case diagram, the first step is to identify the system boundary, which is represented by a rectangle. The **system boundary** shows what is included in the system (inside the rectangle) and what is not included in the system (outside the rectangle). After you identify the system boundary, you place the use cases on the diagram, add the actors, and show the relationships. Figure 6-28 shows a use case diagram for a school bus system that creates a new bus route.

## Class Diagrams

A **class diagram** shows the object classes and relationships involved in a use case. Like a DFD, a class diagram is a logical model, which evolves into a physical model and finally becomes a functioning information system. In structured analysis, entities, data stores, and processes are transformed into data structures and program code. Similarly, class diagrams evolve into code modules, data objects, and other system components.

In a class diagram, each class appears as a rectangle, with the class name at the top, followed by the class's attributes and methods. Lines show relationships between classes and have labels identifying the action that relates the two classes. To create a class diagram, you review the use case and identify the classes that participate in the underlying business process.

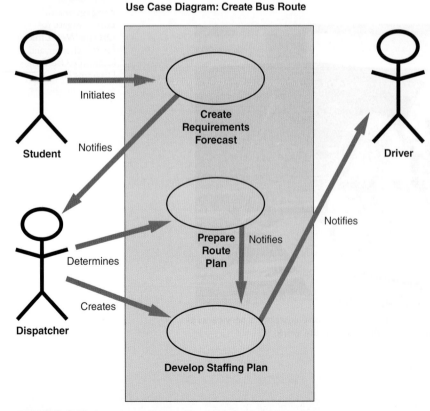

**Use Case Diagram: Create Bus Route**

**FIGURE 6-28** A use case diagram to create a school bus route.

The class diagram also includes a concept called **cardinality**, which describes how instances of one class relate to instances of another class. For example, an employee might have earned no vacation days or one vacation day or many vacation days. Similarly, an employee might have no spouse or one spouse. Figure 6-29 shows various UML notations and cardinality examples. Notice that in Figure 6-29, the first column shows a UML notation symbol that identifies the relationship shown in the second column. The third column provides a typical example of the relationship, which is described in the last column. In the first row of the figure, the UML notation $0..*$ identifies a *zero or many* relation. The example is that an employee can have no payroll deductions or many deductions.

| UML Notation | Nature of the Relationship | Example | | Description |
|---|---|---|---|---|
| 0..* | Zero or many | Employee — Payroll Deduction <br> 1    0..* | | An employee can have no payroll deductions or many deductions. |
| 0..1 | Zero or one | Employee — Spouse <br> 1    0..1 | | An employee can have no spouse or one spouse. |
| 1 | One and only one | Office Manager — Sales Office <br> 1    1 | | An office manager manages one and only one office. |
| 1..* | One or many | Order — Item Ordered <br> 1    1..* | | One order can include one or many items ordered. |

**FIGURE 6-29** Examples of UML notations that indicate the nature of the relationship between instances of one class and instances of another class.

You will learn more about cardinality in Chapter 9, which discusses data design.

Figure 6-30 shows a class diagram for a sales order use case. Notice that the sales office has one sales manager who can have anywhere from zero to many sales reps. Each sales rep can have anywhere from zero to many customers, but each customer has only one sales rep.

**FIGURE 6-30** Class diagram for a sales order use case (attributes and methods omitted for clarity).

## CASE IN POINT 6.2:  TRAIN THE TRAINER, INC.

Train the Trainer develops seminars and workshops for corporate training managers, who in turn train their employees. Your job at Train the Trainer is to put together the actual training materials. Right now, you are up against a deadline. The new object modeling seminar has a chapter on cardinality, and the client wants you to come up with at least three more examples for each of the four cardinality categories listed in Figure 6-29 on the previous page. The four categories are *zero or many*, *zero or one*, *one and only one*, and *one or many*. Even though you are under pressure, you are determined to use examples that are realistic and familiar to the students. What examples will you submit?

### Sequence Diagrams

A **sequence diagram** is a dynamic model of a use case, showing the interaction among classes during a specified time period. A sequence diagram graphically documents the use case by showing the classes, the messages, and the timing of the messages. Sequence diagrams include symbols that represent classes, lifelines, messages, and focuses. These symbols are shown in Figure 6-31.

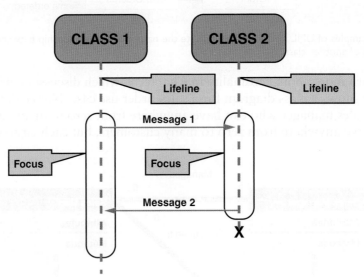

**FIGURE 6-31** A sequence diagram with two classes. Notice the X that indicates the end of the CLASS 2 lifeline. Also notice that each message is represented by a line with a label that describes the message, and that each class has a focus that shows the period when messages are sent or received.

**CLASSES**   A class is identified by a rectangle with the name inside. Classes that send or receive messages are shown at the top of the sequence diagram.

**LIFELINES**   A lifeline is identified by a dashed line. The **lifeline** represents the time during which the object above it is able to interact with the other objects in the use case. An X marks the end of the lifeline.

**MESSAGES**   A message is identified by a line showing direction that runs between two objects. The label shows the name of the message and can include additional information about the contents.

**FOCUSES** A focus is identified by a narrow vertical shape that covers the lifeline. The **focus** indicates when an object sends or receives a message.

The fitness center example shown in Figure 6-32 shows a sequence diagram for the ADD NEW STUDENT use case. Notice that the vertical position of each message indicates the timing of the message.

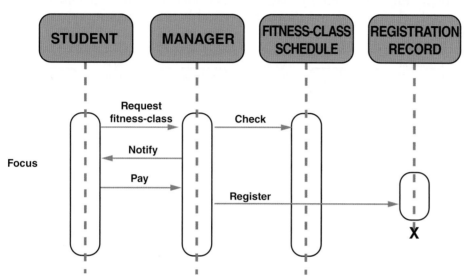

**FIGURE 6-32** The sequence diagram for the ADD NEW STUDENT use case. The use case description for ADD NEW STUDENT is shown in Figure 6-25 on page 260.

## State Transition Diagrams

Earlier in this chapter you learned that state refers to an object's current status. A **state transition diagram** shows how an object changes from one state to another, depending on events that affect the object. All possible states must be documented in the state transition diagram, as shown in Figure 6-33. A bank account, for example, could be opened as a NEW account, change to an ACTIVE or EXISTING account, and eventually become a CLOSED or FORMER account. Another possible state for a bank account could be FROZEN, if the account's assets are legally attached.

In a state transition diagram, the states appear as rounded rectangles with the state names inside. The small circle to the left is the initial state, or the point where the object first interacts with the system. Reading from left to right, the lines show direction and describe the action or event that causes a transition from one state to another. The circle at the right with a hollow border is the final state.

**FIGURE 6-33** An example of a state transition diagram for a bank account.

## Activity Diagrams

An **activity diagram** resembles a horizontal flowchart that shows the actions and events as they occur. Activity diagrams show the order in which the actions take place and identify the outcomes. Figure 6-34 shows an activity diagram for a cash withdrawal at an ATM machine. Notice that the customer initiates the activity by inserting an ATM card and requesting cash. Activity diagrams also can display multiple use cases in the form of a grid, where classes are shown as vertical bars and actions appear as horizontal arrows.

**FIGURE 6-34** An activity diagram shows the actions and events involved in withdrawing cash from an ATM machine.

Sequence diagrams, state transition diagrams, and activity diagrams are dynamic modeling tools that can help a systems analyst understand how objects behave and interact with the system.

# CASE IN POINT 6.3: TRAVELBIZ

Jack Forester and Lisa Turner are systems analysts in the IT department of TravelBiz, a nationwide travel agency that specializes in business travel. TravelBiz has decided to expand into the vacation travel market by launching a new business division called TravelFun. The IT director assigned Jack and Lisa to create a flexible, efficient information system for the new division. Jack wants to use traditional analysis and modeling techniques for the project. Lisa, on the other hand, wants to use an object-oriented methodology. Which approach would you suggest and why?

The CASE tools in Appendix B can help you develop and maintain complex information systems. To learn more about these tools, turn to Appendix B.

## CASE Tools

Object modeling requires many types of diagrams to represent the proposed system. Creating the diagrams by hand is time consuming and tedious, so systems analysts rely on CASE tools to speed up the process and provide an overall framework for documenting the system components. In addition, CASE tools ensure consistency and provide common links so that once objects are described and used in one part of the design, they can be reused multiple times without further effort.

## ORGANIZING THE OBJECT MODEL

In this chapter, you learned how to use object-oriented tools and techniques to build a logical model of the information system. Now you are ready to organize your diagrams and documentation so the object model is easily read and understood. If you used a CASE tool to develop the design, much of this work will be performed automatically by the CASE software.

There are many ways to proceed with the task of organizing the object model, and experience will be your best teacher. After you identify the system's objects, classes, and relationships, you should develop an object relationship diagram that provides an overview of the system. If you do not use a CASE-generated model, each diagram or object definition should be supported by clear, relevant documentation that can be accessed easily by anyone who reviews the object model. For example, you should organize your use cases and use case diagrams so they can be linked to the appropriate class, state transition, sequence, and activity diagrams. Your diagrams and documentation are the foundation for the system's design, so accuracy is important. Remember that it is much easier to repair a diagram now than to change the software later.

## CASE IN POINT 6.4: CYBER ASSOCIATES

One of your responsibilities at Cyber Associates, an IT consulting firm, is to assign new systems analysts to various tasks and projects. Some of the senior people believe that inexperienced analysts should start with object-oriented techniques, which are easier to learn and apply. Others think that an analyst should learn structured analysis first, and then proceed to object-oriented skills. What is your viewpoint, and why?

## A QUESTION OF ETHICS

Last month, your company launched a peer review process for IT projects. At the end of each project, team members rate the performance of the overall team, and his or her co-workers individually. The stated goal was to obtain honest, peer-based feedback. Unfortunately, like many good ideas, there was a downside. Although the input is anonymous, the results are submitted to the entire team. Some members, including you, are uncomfortable with the new process because it could encourage cliques and actually undermine a team-based culture. Others see it as an opportunity for honest input.

One team member, who is a close friend of yours, is not very popular with her teammates. To make matters worse, she recently had some personal problems that affected her work, and she is worried that her ratings will be quite negative. She has not specifically asked you about your feedback, but you know she is hoping for a favorable review from you. Even though her work was not great, you don't want to see her get hurt by a process that you yourself are not comfortable with.

Is this a question of ethics versus friendship? Would it be wrong to tilt the scales in her favor just a bit?

## CHAPTER SUMMARY

This chapter introduces object modeling, which is a popular technique that describes a system in terms of objects. Objects represent real people, places, events, and transactions. Unlike structured analysis, which treats data and processes separately, objects include data and processes that can affect the data. During the implementation process, systems analysts and programmers transform objects into program code modules that can be optimized, tested, and reused as often as necessary.

Object-oriented terms include classes, attributes, instances, messages, and methods. Classes include objects that have similar attributes, or characteristics. Individual members of a class are called object instances. Objects within a class can be grouped into subclasses, which are more specific categories within the class. A class also can belong to a more general category called a superclass.

Objects can send messages, or commands, that require other objects to perform certain methods, or tasks. The concept that a message gives different meanings to different objects is called polymorphism. An object resembles a black box, with encapsulated, or self-contained, data and methods. The strongest relationship between objects is inheritance.

After you identify the objects, classes, and relationships, you prepare an object relationship diagram that shows the objects and how they interact to perform business functions and transactions.

The Unified Modeling Language (UML) is a widely used method of visualizing and documenting an information system. UML techniques include use cases, use case diagrams, class diagrams, sequence diagrams, state transition diagrams, and activity diagrams.

A use case describes a business situation initiated by an actor, who interacts with the information system. Each use case represents a specific transaction, or scenario. A use case diagram is a visual summary of related use cases within a system or subsystem. A class diagram represents a detailed view of a single use case, showing the classes that participate in the underlying business transaction, and the relationship among class instances, which is called cardinality. A sequence diagram is a dynamic model of a use case, showing the interaction among classes during a specified time period. Sequence diagrams include lifelines, messages, and focuses. A state transition diagram shows how an object changes from one state to another, depending on events that affect the object. An activity diagram resembles a horizontal flowchart that shows actions and events as they occur in a system.

CASE tools provide an overall framework for system documentation. CASE tools can speed up the development process, ensure consistency, and provide common links that enable objects to be reused.

At the end of the object modeling process, you organize your use cases and use case diagrams and create class, sequence, state transition, and activity diagrams.

# Key Terms and Phrases

activity diagram 266
actor 259
attributes 250
black box 256
cardinality 263
child 258
class 251
class diagram 262
encapsulation 256
focus 265
inheritance 258
instance 251
lifeline 264
message 250
methods 250
object 250

object model 250
object-oriented (O-O) analysis 250
parent 258
polymorphism 255
relationships 258
sequence diagram 264
state 254
state transition diagram 265
subclass 256
superclass 257
system boundary 262
Unified Modeling Language (UML) 250
use case 259
use case description 260
use case diagram 261

# Learn It Online

**Instructions:**   To complete the Learn It Online exercises, visit the Management Information Systems CourseMate Web site at **www.cengagebrain.com**, navigate to the resources for this chapter, and click the link for the exercise you want to complete.

## 1  Chapter Reinforcement

### TF, MC, and SA

Click one of the Chapter Reinforcement links for Multiple Choice, True/False, or Short Answer. Answer each question and submit to your instructor.

## 2  Flash Cards

Click the Flash Cards link and read the instructions. Type 20 (or a number specified by your instructor) in the Number of Playing Cards text box, type your name in the Enter your Name text box, and then click the Flip Card button. When the flash card is displayed, read the question and then click the ANSWER box arrow to select an answer. Flip through the Flash Cards. If your score is 15 (75%) correct or greater, click Print on the File menu to print your results. If your score is less than 15 (75%) correct, then redo this exercise by clicking the Replay button.

## 3  Practice Test

Click the Practice Test link. Answer each question, enter your first and last name at the bottom of the page, and then click the Grade Test button. When the graded practice test is displayed on your screen, click Print on the File menu to print a hard copy. Continue to take practice tests until you score 80% or better.

## 4  Who Wants To Be a Computer Genius?

Click the Computer Genius link. Read the instructions, enter your first and last name at the bottom of the page, and then click the Play button. When your score is displayed, click the PRINT RESULTS link to print a hard copy.

## 5  Wheel of Terms

Click the Wheel of Terms link. Read the instructions, and then enter your first and last name and your school name. Click the PLAY button. When your score is displayed on the screen, right-click the score and then click Print on the shortcut menu to print a hard copy.

## 6  Crossword Puzzle Challenge

Click the Crossword Puzzle Challenge link. Read the instructions, and then click the Continue button. Work the crossword puzzle. When you are finished, click the Submit button. When the crossword puzzle is redisplayed, submit it to your instructor.

## Overview

The SCR Associates case study is a Web-based simulation that allows you to practice your skills in a real-world environment. The case study transports you to SCR's intranet, where you complete 12 work sessions, each aligning with a chapter. As you work on the case, you will receive e-mail and voice mail messages, obtain information from SCR's online libraries, and perform various tasks.

## How do I use the case?

- Review the SCR background material in Chapter 1.
- Read the Preview for this session and study the Task List.
- Visit the Management Information Systems CourseMate Web site at **www.cengagebrain.com**, navigate to the **SCR Case Simulation**, and locate the intranet link.
- Enter your name and the password **sad9e**. An opening screen will display the 12 sessions.
- Select this session. Check your e-mail and voice mail carefully, and then work on the tasks.

## Preview: Session 6

In the last session, you used data and process modeling techniques to develop a logical model of the new system. Now you will apply your object modeling skills to create various diagrams and documentation for the new TIMS system. You will review the background material and develop an object-oriented model that includes several types of diagrams.

## Task List

| Task List |
|---|
| 1. I need to review Jesse's e-mail message regarding object modeling and the JAD session summary. Then she wants me to identify possible use cases and actors, and create a use case diagram for the TIMS system. |
| 2. She also wants me to select one of the use cases and create a class diagram. |
| 3. I will need a sequence diagram for the selected use case. |
| 4. Jesse asked for a state transition diagram that describes typical student states and how they change based on certain actions and events. |

**FIGURE 6-35** Task list: Session 6.

# Chapter Exercises

## Review Questions

1. What is object-oriented analysis, and what are some advantages of using this technique?
2. Define an object, and give an example.
3. Define an attribute, and give an example.
4. Define a method, and give an example.
5. Define encapsulation, and explain the benefits it provides.
6. Define polymorphism, and give an example.
7. Define a class, subclass, and superclass, and give examples.
8. Define an actor, and give an example.
9. Define a use case and a use case diagram, and give examples.
10. Define the term *black box*, and explain why it is an important concept in object-oriented analysis.

## Discussion Topics

1. The chapter mentioned that systems analysts and programmers transform objects into program code modules that can be optimized, tested, and reused. Modular design is a very popular design concept in many industries. What other examples of modular design can you suggest?
2. You are an IT consultant, and you are asked to create a new system for a small real estate brokerage firm. Your only experience is with traditional data and process modeling techniques. This time, you decide to try an object-oriented approach. How will you begin? How are the tasks different from traditional structured analysis?
3. You are creating a system for a bowling alley to manage information about its leagues. During the modeling process, you create a state transition diagram for an object called LEAGUE BOWLERS. What are the possible states of a league bowler, and what happens to a bowler who quits the league and rejoins the following season?
4. A debate is raging at the IT consulting firm where you work. Some staff members believe that it is harder for experienced analysts to learn object-modeling techniques, because the analysts are accustomed to thinking about data and processes as separate entities. Others believe that solid analytical skills are easily transferable and do not see a problem in crossing over to the newer approach. What do you think, and why?

# Apply Your Knowledge

The Apply Your Knowledge section contains four mini-cases. Each case describes a situation, explains your role in the case, and asks you to respond to questions. You can answer the questions by applying knowledge you learned in the chapter.

## 1 | Hertford Post Office

**Situation:**

Hertford has a typical small town post office that sells stamps, rents post office boxes, and delivers mail to postal customers.

1. Identify possible actors and use cases involved in the post office functions.
2. Create a use case diagram for the post office operation.
3. Select one of the use cases and create a class diagram.
4. Create a sequence diagram for the use case you selected.

## 2 | New Branch School District

**Situation:**

The New Branch School District operates a fleet of 40 buses that serve approximately 1,000 students in grades K–12. The bus operation involves 30 regular routes, plus special routes for activities, athletic events, and summer sessions. The district employs 12 full-time drivers and 25 to 30 part-time drivers. A dispatcher coordinates the staffing and routes and relays messages to drivers regarding students and parents who call about pickup and drop-off arrangements.

1. Identify possible actors and use cases involved in school bus operations.
2. Create a use case diagram for the school bus system.
3. Create a sequence diagram for the use case you selected.
4. Create a state transition diagram that describes typical student states and how they change based on specific actions and events.

**3** **Pleasant Creek Community College Registration System**

**Situation:**

Pleasant Creek Community College has a typical school registration process. Student support services include faculty advisors and tutors. The administration has asked you, as IT manager, to develop an object-oriented model for a new registration system.

1. List possible objects in the new registration system, including their attributes and methods.
2. Identify possible use cases and actors.
3. Create a use case diagram that shows how students register.
4. Create a state transition diagram that describes typical student states and how they change based on specific actions and events.

**4** **Student Bookstore at Pleasant Creek Community College**

**Situation:**

The bookstore staff at Pleasant Creek Community College works hard to satisfy students, instructors, and the school's business office. Instructors specify textbooks for particular courses, and the bookstore orders the books and sells them to students. The bookstore wants you to develop an object-oriented model for a new bookstore information management system.

1. List possible objects in the bookstore operation, including their attributes and methods.
2. Identify possible use cases and actors.
3. Select one of the use cases that you identified in step 2 and create a sequence diagram.
4. Create an object relationship diagram that provides an overview of the system, including how textbooks are selected by instructors, approved by a department head, and sold to students by the bookstore.

# Case Studies

Case studies allow you to practice specific skills learned in the chapter. Each chapter contains several case studies that continue throughout the textbook, and a chapter capstone case.

## New Century Health Clinic

New Century Health Clinic offers preventive medicine and traditional medical care. In your role as an IT consultant, you will help New Century develop a new information system.

### Background

You began the systems analysis phase at New Century Health Clinic by completing a series of interviews, reviewing existing reports, and observing office operations. Then, in Chapter 5, you acquired more information and developed a set of DFDs, process descriptions, and a data dictionary.

Now you decide to practice the object modeling skills you learned in this chapter. Before you begin, go back to Chapter 5 and review the New Century background material and fact-finding results. Also, your instructor may provide you with a complete set of interview summaries that you can use to perform your assignments. Then complete the following tasks.

### Assignments

1. Identify possible use cases and actors, and create a use case diagram for the New Century Health Clinic system.
2. Select one of the use cases and create a class diagram.
3. Create a sequence diagram for the use case that you selected.
4. Create a state transition diagram that describes typical patient states and how they change based on specific actions and events.

## PERSONAL TRAINER, INC.

Personal Trainer, Inc., owns and operates fitness centers in a dozen Midwestern cities. The centers have done well, and the company is planning an international expansion by opening a new "supercenter" in the Toronto area. Personal Trainer's president, Cassia Umi, hired an IT consultant, Susan Park, to help develop an information system for the new facility. During the project, Susan will work closely with Gray Lewis, who will manage the new operation.

### Background

Working as an IT consultant for Personal Trainer, Susan Park used data and process modeling tools to create a logical model of the proposed information system. Now she wants to build an object-oriented view of the system using O-O tools and techniques.

### Assignments

Before you perform the following tasks, you should review the information and background in Chapters 1 and 2, and the fact-finding summary of the case provided in Chapter 4.

1. Identify possible use cases and actors, and create a use case diagram for the Personal Trainer information system.
2. Select one of the use cases and create a class diagram.
3. Create an object relationship diagram for the system.
4. Create a state transition diagram that describes typical member states and how they change based on specific actions and events.

# CHAPTER CAPSTONE CASE: SoftWear, Limited

**SWL**

SoftWear, Limited (SWL), is a continuing case study that illustrates the knowledge and skills described in each chapter. In this case study, the student acts as a member of the SWL systems development team and performs various tasks.

## Background

Rick Williams, a systems analyst, and Carla Moore, a programmer/analyst, completed a set of DFDs representing a data and process model of the SWL payroll system project. Rick had recently attended a workshop on object modeling techniques, and suggested that he and Carla should experiment with object-oriented analysis. After he explained the concepts and techniques to Carla, she agreed that it was a good opportunity to gain some experience, and they decided to give it a try.

Rick and Carla began by reviewing the data they had collected earlier, during requirements modeling. They studied the DFDs and the data dictionary to identify the people, events, and transactions that would show as classes. They identified employees, human resources transactions, time sheet entries, payroll actions, and stock transfers. They defined attributes and methods for each of those classes, as shown in Figure 6-36. When they were finished, they reviewed the results. They noticed that the structured DFDs did not show a department head as an entity. Rick remembered that department heads submitted time sheets to the payroll department, and the payroll clerks actually entered the data into the system. Because they were looking at the system in a different way, they decided to include department heads as a subclass of the EMPLOYEE class.

**EMPLOYEE**

Employee number
Employee name
Address
Telephone number
Date of birth
Sex
Title, rate of pay
Deductions
State

Add new
Change name
Change address
Change telephone
Change deductions
Change state

**HR TRANSACTION**

Employee number
Employee name
State

Add new
Change state
Notify

**TIME SHEET ENTRY**

Employee number
Week ending date
Hours worked

Add new
Correct hours
Generate report

**PAYROLL ACTION**

Employee number
Hours worked
Overtime hours
Rate of pay
Overtime rate
Deductions
Contributions
Federal tax withheld
State tax withheld
Local tax withheld

Generate checks
Change deductions
Change contributions
Change federal rate
Change local rate
Change state rate
Change rate of pay
Generate W-2
Notify
Calculate

**STOCK TRANSFER**

Employee number
Stock holdings
Stock contribution

Purchase stock
Sell stock
Change contribution
Generate report

**DEPT HEAD**

Employee number
Employee name
Address
Telephone number
Date of birth
Sex
Title, rate of pay
Deductions
State

Add new
Change name
Change address
Change telephone
Change deductions
Change state
Manages work
Submits time sheets

FIGURE 6-36 SWL payroll system classes.

## Use Cases

The next step was for Rick and Carla to define the use cases. They tried to think of all the situations that involve an EMPLOYEE object. For example, employees might get hired, promoted, receive a raise, terminate, retire, change their names, or change their payroll contributions.

## CHAPTER CAPSTONE CASE:   SoftWear, Limited (continued)                    SWL

They also decided to create use cases that involved the PAYROLL ACTION object. The examples included these: Change an employee's deductions, change an employee's contributions, change the federal tax rate, change the state tax rate, change the local tax rate, calculate weekly gross pay, calculate weekly taxes, calculate weekly contributions, generate weekly paychecks, and notify the stock transfer department of change in contributions.

After they defined the use cases and the actors, they created a description for each use case showing the use case name, actors, description, successful completion, alternatives, preconditions, postconditions, and assumptions.

Creating use case descriptions was hard work, and they found that they had to return frequently to their documentation and fact-finding results. First, they created descriptions for the RECEIVE RAISE and RECEIVE PROMOTION use cases, as shown in Figure 6-37.

**RECEIVE RAISE Use Case**

| | |
|---|---|
| **Name:** | RECEIVE RAISE |
| **Actor:** | Employee |
| **Description:** | Describes the change to an employee's pay rate |
| **Successful completion:** | 1. Employee gets a raise<br>2. Human resources department changes employee data to the employee object and the human resources records |
| **Alternative:** | None |
| **Precondition:** | Employee has been approved for a raise |
| **Postcondition:** | Employee's pay rate is changed on all records |
| **Assumptions:** | None |

**RECEIVE PROMOTION Use Case**

| | |
|---|---|
| **Name:** | RECEIVE PROMOTION |
| **Actor:** | Employee |
| **Description:** | Describes the change to employee title |
| **Successful completion:** | 1. Employee gets promoted<br>2. Human resources department changes employee data and completes HR transaction |
| **Alternative:** | None |
| **Precondition:** | Employee has been approved for promotion |
| **Postcondition:** | Employee title is changed |
| **Assumptions:** | Employee accepts position |

**FIGURE 6-37** Descriptions for the RECEIVE RAISE and RECEIVE PROMOTION use cases.

Now they were ready to create a use case diagram to show several related use cases. To keep it simple, Carla suggested that they show no more than three use cases per diagram.

They decided to create a use case diagram to describe how the payroll is generated. The diagram, shown in Figure 6-38, includes three use cases: CREATE TIMESHEET, CALCULATE PAYROLL, and GENERATE PAYCHECK. In the diagram, the DEPARTMENT HEAD actor creates a new instance of the TIMESHEET ENTRY object, which notifies the CALCULATE PAYROLL use case, which is initiated by the PAYROLL CLERK. The GENERATE PAYCHECK use case then issues a paycheck to the EMPLOYEE actor.

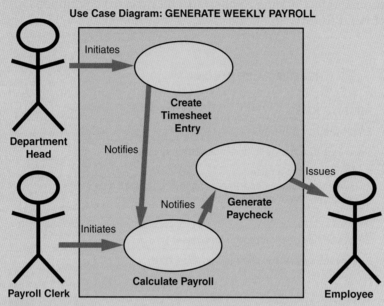

**FIGURE 6-38** Use case diagram for the GENERATE WEEKLY PAYROLL scenario.

## Class Diagrams

The use case diagram gave Rick and Carla a valuable snapshot of the business processes involved in GENERATE WEEKLY PAYROLL. To document the relationships and interaction in more detail, they created the class diagram shown in Figure 6-39. The diagram includes five different classes and various types of cardinality.

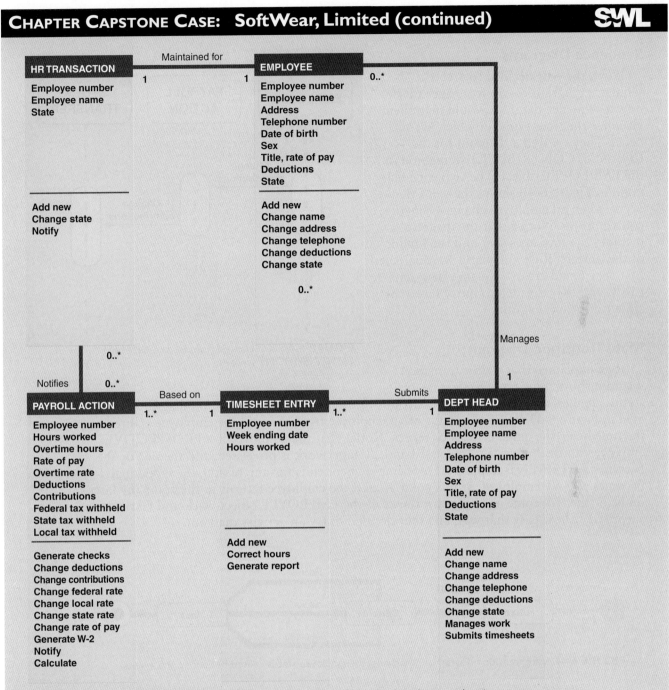

**HR TRANSACTION**

Employee number
Employee name
State
_____
Add new
Change state
Notify

Maintained for

1                    1

**EMPLOYEE**

Employee number
Employee name
Address
Telephone number
Date of birth
Sex
Title, rate of pay
Deductions
State
_____
Add new
Change name
Change address
Change telephone
Change deductions
Change state

0..*

0..*

Manages

1

0..*

0..*

Notifies

**PAYROLL ACTION**

Employee number
Hours worked
Overtime hours
Rate of pay
Overtime rate
Deductions
Contributions
Federal tax withheld
State tax withheld
Local tax withheld
_____
Generate checks
Change deductions
Change contributions
Change federal rate
Change local rate
Change state rate
Change rate of pay
Generate W-2
Notify
Calculate

Based on

1..*      1

**TIMESHEET ENTRY**

Employee number
Week ending date
Hours worked
_____
Add new
Correct hours
Generate report

1..*        1

Submits

**DEPT HEAD**

Employee number
Employee name
Address
Telephone number
Date of birth
Sex
Title, rate of pay
Deductions
State
_____
Add new
Change name
Change address
Change telephone
Change deductions
Change state
Manages work
Submits timesheets

**FIGURE 6-39** The GENERATE WEEKLY PAYROLL class diagram includes five classes and various types of relationships among the classes.

**CHAPTER CAPSTONE CASE:   SoftWear, Limited (continued)**                          SWL

## Sequence Diagrams

Next, the pair decided to create a sequence diagram. Carla was eager to see how a sequence diagram would help them visualize the time frame in which events occur. They created a diagram for the CHANGE CONTRIBUTIONS method in the EMPLOYEE object. The sequence diagram in Figure 6-40 shows the steps that occur when an employee changes benefits contributions. Notice that the diagram includes the messages sent and the lifeline of the objects. Rick and Carla were satisfied that they could create sequence diagrams easily, and they decided to move on to the state transition diagram.

| EMPLOYEE | PAYROLL ACTION | STOCK TRANSFER |
|---|---|---|

Change contributions →

Change contributions →

**FIGURE 6-40** Sequence diagram for the CHANGE CONTRIBUTIONS scenario.

## State Transition Diagram

Rick explained that a state transition diagram shows how an object's state, or status, changes as a result of various actions or events. The state transition diagram they created in Figure 6-41 shows the status of an employee from the time the employee is hired to the time he or she quits, is fired, or retires. Notice that the employee is a PROSPECTIVE employee until all physicals are passed and all paperwork is processed, and then he or she becomes a CURRENT employee. Once employment ends for any reason, the individual becomes a PAST employee. At this point, even if the employee returns to the company later on he or she will come in as a new instance of the EMPLOYEE object. Rick and Carla were surprised at how easy that was, and they decided to try an activity diagram.

**FIGURE 6-41** State transition diagram shows changes in employee status caused by actions and events.

## Activity Diagram

Rick suggested that they create an activity diagram showing some of the situations they had explored in detail. Their diagram showed the interaction between objects during certain scenarios and enabled them to visualize system activity, as shown in Figure 6-42. They agreed that the technique gave them additional object modeling experience that would be valuable in the future. At that point, they packaged all the diagrams in a folder and saved the overall object model for future reference.

## CHAPTER CAPSTONE CASE:   SoftWear, Limited (continued)                    SWL

**FIGURE 6-42** Activity diagram shows the RECEIVE PROMOTION scenario and the CHANGE CONTRIBUTIONS scenario.

## Team Tasks

1. Rick is interested in your views on the future of object-oriented analysis and design. He is scheduled to make a presentation on the topic next week at a meeting of IT professionals. He asked you to do some research, using the Internet and industry publications, and send him an e-mail message describing the current use of object-oriented analysis and trends for the future.

2. As a team member, you know how important it can be to have a well-organized object model. The team has asked you to handle this task. How will you go about it?

3. When you worked on the class diagrams, you had to understand and apply the concept of cardinality. How would you explain this concept to a new team member?

4. List all the different types of diagrams you used to create the object model, with a brief explanation of each diagram.

## Manage the SWL Project

You have been asked to manage SWL's new information system project. One of your most important activities will be to identify project tasks and determine when they will be performed. Before you begin, you should review the SWL case in this chapter. Then list and analyze the tasks, as follows:

**LIST THE TASKS** Start by listing and numbering at least 10 tasks that the SWL team needs to perform to fulfill the objectives of this chapter. Your list can include SWL Team Tasks and any other tasks that are described in this chapter. For example, Task 3 might be to Identify the actors, and Task 6 might be to Draw a use case diagram.

**ANALYZE THE TASKS** Now study the tasks to determine the order in which they should be performed. First identify all concurrent tasks, which are not dependent on other tasks. In the example shown in Figure 6-43 on the next page, Tasks 1, 2, 3, 4, and 5 are concurrent tasks, and could begin at the same time if resources were available.

Other tasks are called dependent tasks, because they cannot be performed until one or more earlier tasks have been completed. For each dependent task, you must identify specific tasks that need to be completed before this task can begin. For example, you would want to identify the actors before you could draw a use case diagram, so Task 6 cannot begin until Task 3 is completed, as Figure 6-43 shows.

## CHAPTER CAPSTONE CASE:   SoftWear, Limited (continued)

**FIGURE 6-43** Tasks 1, 2, 3, 4, and 5 are concurrent tasks that could be performed at the same time. Task 6 is a dependent task that cannot be performed until Task 3 has been completed.

Chapter 3 describes project management tools, techniques, and software. To learn more, you can use the Features section on your Student Study Tool CD-ROM, or visit the Management Information Systems CourseMate Web site at **www.cengagebrain.com** and locate the project management resources library for this book. On the Web, Microsoft offers demo versions, training, and tips for using Project 2010. You also can visit the OpenWorkbench.org site to learn more about this free, open-source software.

## Ready for a Challenge?

In additional to technical skills, IT professionals need critical thinking skills such as perception, organization, analysis, problem-solving, and decision-making. The Ready for a Challenge feature can help you learn, practice, and apply critical thinking skills that you can take to the workplace.

The IT team at Game Technology prepared DFDs for the new Customer Contact Care system ($C^3$). Now, you will help the team develop a set of object models. To be sure you can handle the tasks you decide to review Chapter 6 of your systems analysis textbook.

The $C^3$ system model will include use cases that represent various business processes and functions. The customer and sales rep entities will be shown as actors, with the following methods:

| Entity | Methods |
|---|---|
| Customer | • Request product information<br>• Place order<br>• Respond to Web promotion<br>• Sign up on game blog |
| Sales Rep | • Initiate sales call to customer<br>• Respond to customer inquiry<br>• Follow up after prior order<br>• Follow up after prior information request |

You also learned that customers will fall into one of four categories. Customers move from one category to another when certain conditions occur, as shown:

| Customer Category | Conditions |
|---|---|
| Potential | Has not placed an order in the last 24 months, but *has*<br>• Responded to a Web promotion, or<br>• Requested product information, or<br>• Signed up on our game blog |
| Active | Placed at least one order in the last 24 months |
| Preferred | Placed at least three orders in the last 24 months |
| Former | Any **Active** or **Preferred** customer who placed no orders in the last 24 months |

### Practice Tasks

A. Draw a use case diagram that includes the entities and the use cases.
B. Draw a state transition diagram that shows the customer categories and the conditions for each category.

After you complete the Practice Tasks, to check your work and view sample answers, visit the Management Information Systems CourseMate Web site at **www.cengagebrain.com**, navigate to the resources for this chapter, and locate Ready for a Challenge?.

### The Challenge

The marketing group decided to add a new marketing technician position to provide IT support for sales reps. Specifically, the marketing tech will track customer response times, prepare contact management plans for sales reps, and develop surveys to measure customer satisfaction.

Marketing also decided to update the customer categories. The **Potential** and **Former** categories are not affected. The new categories are **Silver**, which replaces the **Active** category; **Gold**, which replaces the **Preferred** category; and **Platinum**, which includes any customer whose orders total at least $1,000 in the last 24 months.

### Challenge Tasks

A. Draw a new version of the use case diagram that adds the new marketing technician.
B. Draw a state transition diagram that shows the new customer categories and the conditions for each category.

# CHAPTER 7
# Options for Development

**Chapter 7** is the final chapter in the systems analysis phase of the SDLC. This chapter describes software trends, acquisition and development strategies, traditional versus Web-based development, outsourcing versus in-house development, the system requirements document, prototyping, and preparing for the transition to the next SDLC phase — systems design.

## INTRODUCTION

## OBJECTIVES

*When you finish this chapter, you will be able to:*

- Describe the concept of Software as a Service
- Define Web 2.0 and cloud computing
- Explain software acquisition alternatives, including traditional and Web-based software development strategies
- Describe software outsourcing options, including offshore outsourcing and the role of service providers
- Explain advantages and disadvantages of in-house software development
- Discuss cost-benefit analysis and financial analysis tools
- Describe a request for proposal (RFP) and a request for quotation (RFQ)
- Describe the system requirements document
- Explain the transition from systems analysis to systems design
- Discuss systems design guidelines
- Describe software development trends

The main objective of the systems analysis phase is to build a logical model of the new information system. In Chapters 4, 5, and 6, you learned about requirements modeling, data and process modeling, and object modeling. Chapter 7 describes the remaining activities in the systems analysis phase, which include evaluation of alternative solutions, preparation of the system requirements document, and presentation of the system requirements document to management. The chapter also describes the transition to systems design, prototyping, and systems design guidelines. The chapter concludes with a discussion of trends in software development.

# CHAPTER INTRODUCTION CASE:   Mountain View College Bookstore

**Background:** Wendy Lee, manager of college services at Mountain View College, wants a new information system that will improve efficiency and customer service at the three college bookstores.

In this part of the case, Tina Allen (systems analyst) and David Conroe (student intern) are talking about development strategies for the new system.

| | |
|---|---|
| **Participants:** | Tina and David |
| **Location:** | Tina's office, Wednesday morning, November 16, 2011 |
| **Project status:** | Tina and David developed a logical model that includes data flow diagrams, a data dictionary, and process descriptions. They also created an object model. Now they are ready to discuss development strategies for the new bookstore system. |
| **Discussion topics:** | Web-based versus traditional development, cost-benefit analysis, steps in purchasing a software package, transition to systems design, and systems design guidelines |

**Tina:**   Good morning, David.  Are you ready for the next step?

**David:**   *Sure. Now that we have a logical model of the bookstore system, what comes next?*

**Tina:**   We're at a transition point between the logical design, which describes what the new system will do, and the physical design phase, which describes how it will be done, including the user interface and physical components. Before we start the physical design, we have to study various systems development options and make a recommendation to Wendy.

**David:**   *What are the options?*

**Tina:**   Well, some large organizations use Web-based systems hosted by outside vendors who supply and maintain the software. In a sense, the customer rents the application. I checked with our IT director, and she feels we're not ready for that approach. She wants us to implement a system on the college network and migrate to a Web-based system later. That brings us to the next set of questions.

**David:**   *Such as?*

**Tina:**   We need to consider our role in the development process. We can build the system ourselves, which is called in-house development. Or we can purchase a software package, which might need some degree of modification to meet our needs. Or we could consider outsourcing options, including hiring an IT consultant to help with development tasks. Either way, we need to do a cost-benefit study.

**David:**   *What about the transition from logical to physical design that you mentioned?*

**Tina:**   The idea is to take our logical design, which is similar to an architect's proposal, and translate it into a physical design, which is more like a working blueprint. If we decide to develop the system in-house, we'll probably build a prototype, or working model of the system. If we decide to purchase a package, we'll follow a series of steps that will help us select the best product. We'll also talk about systems design guidelines.

**David:**   *When you mention the idea of a blueprint, it sounds like we're getting ready to pick up our tools and go to work.*

**Tina:**   We sure are. Here's a task list to get us started:

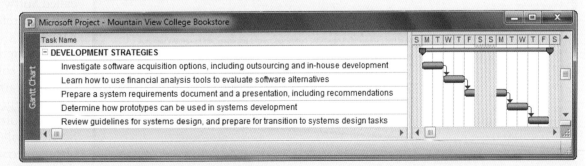

**FIGURE 7-1** Typical development strategies task list.

## DEVELOPMENT STRATEGIES OVERVIEW

Just a few years ago, a typical company either developed software itself, purchased a software package (which might need some modification), or hired consultants or outside resources to perform the work. Today, a company has many more choices, including application service providers, Web-hosted software options, and firms that offer a variety of enterprise-wide software solutions.

Selecting the best development path is an important decision that requires companies to consider three key topics: the impact of the Internet, software outsourcing options, and in-house software development alternatives. These topics are reviewed in the following sections.

## THE IMPACT OF THE INTERNET

The Internet has triggered enormous changes in business methods and operations, and software acquisition is no exception. This section examines a trend that views Software as a Service, the changing marketplace for software, and how Web-based development compares to traditional methods. The section concludes with a description of Internet-related trends, including Web 2.0 and cloud computing.

### Software as a Service

In the traditional model, software vendors develop and sell application packages to customers. Typically, customers purchase licenses that give them the right to use the software under the terms of the license agreement. Although this model still accounts for most software acquisition, a new model, called **Software as a Service (SaaS)**, is changing the picture dramatically.

SaaS is a model of software deployment where an application is hosted as a service provided to customers over the Internet. SaaS reduces the customer's need for software maintenance, operation, and support.

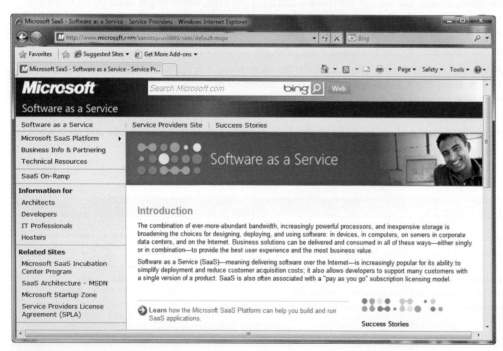

FIGURE 7-2 Microsoft's SaaS platform promises better value and a new concept called Software + Services.

In a highly competitive marketplace, major vendors constantly strive to deliver new and better solutions. For example, as shown in Figure 7-2, Microsoft claims that its SaaS platform offers the best solution and business value. Microsoft also promotes a broader vision, called Software + Services. The term refers to Microsoft's strategy for cloud computing, which integrates software applications, platforms and infrastructure. According to Microsoft, Software + Services will allow seamless connection of smart devices to the tremendous power of the Web.

The Web Host Industry Review shown in Figure 7-3 is an online source of information about SaaS products, trends, and events. In a published report, the Review quoted a Gartner, Inc. prediction that 25% of all new business software will be deployed as a service by 2011, while the value of the SaaS industry will grow to $40 billion.

## Traditional vs. Web-Based Systems Development

As a systems analyst, you must consider whether development will take place in a Web-centric framework, or in a traditional environment. This section provides an overview of some of the similarities and differences.

**FIGURE 7-3** The Web Host Industry Review (WHIR) is a clearinghouse for SaaS information.

In an Internet-based system, the Web becomes an integral part of the application, rather than just a communication channel, and systems analysts need new application development tools and solutions to handle the new systems. Two major Web-based development environments are Microsoft's **.NET** and IBM's **WebSphere,** which are shown in Figure 7-4 on the next page. Microsoft regards .NET as a platform-independent software environment. IBM describes WebSphere as a set of products specifically designed to support e-business applications across multiple computing platforms.

Although there is a major trend toward Web-based architecture, many firms rely on traditional systems, either because they are legacy applications that are not easily replaced, or because they do not require a Web component to satisfy user needs. If you need to choose, you should consider some key differences between traditional and Web-based system development. Building the application in a Web-based environment can offer greater benefits, and sometimes greater risks, compared to a traditional environment. The following sections list some characteristics of traditional versus Web-based development.

**TRADITIONAL DEVELOPMENT**  In a traditional systems development environment:

- Systems design is influenced by compatibility issues, including existing hardware and software platforms and legacy system requirements.

- Systems are designed to run on local and wide-area company networks.

- Systems often utilize Internet links and resources, but Web-based features are treated as enhancements rather than core elements of the design.

- Development typically follows one of three main paths: in-house development, purchase of a software package with possible modification, or use of outside consultants.

- Scalability can be affected by network limitations and constraints.
- Many applications require substantial desktop computing power and resources.
- Security issues usually are less complex than with Web-based systems, because the system operates on a private company network, rather than the Internet.

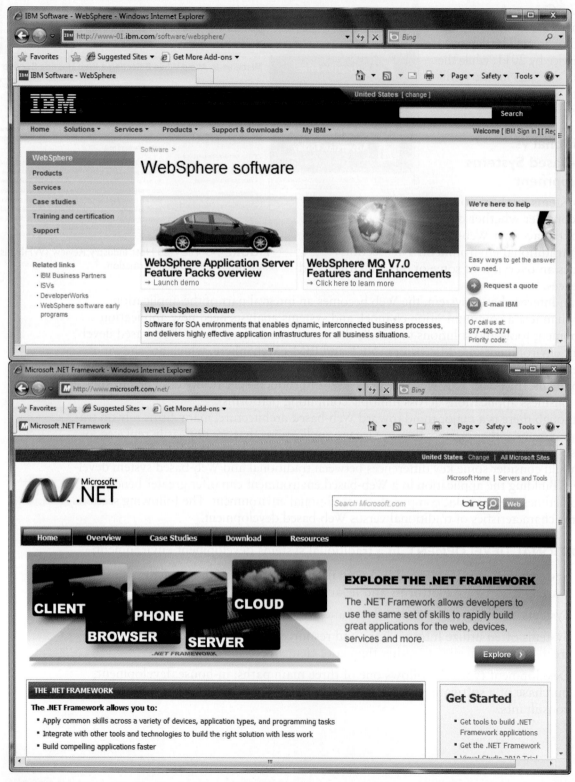

**FIGURE 7-4** Microsoft's .Net Framework and IBM's WebSphere are comprehensive software development environments.

**WEB-BASED DEVELOPMENT**  In a Web-based systems development environment:

- Systems are developed and delivered in an Internet-based framework such as .NET or WebSphere.

- Internet-based development treats the Web *as* the platform, rather than just a communication channel.

- Web-based systems are easily scalable, and can run on multiple hardware environments.

- Large firms tend to deploy Web-based systems as enterprise-wide software solutions for applications such as customer relationship management, order processing, and materials management.

- Web-based software treats the software application as a service that is less dependent on desktop computing power and resources.

- When companies acquire Web-based software as a *service* rather than a *product* they purchase, they can limit in-house involvement to a minimum and have the vendor install, configure, and maintain the system by paying agreed-upon fees.

- Web-based software usually requires additional layers, called **middleware**, to communicate with existing software and legacy systems.

**ON THE WEB**

To learn more about Web 2.0, visit the Management Information Systems CourseMate Web site at **www. cengagebrain.com**, navigate to **On the Web Links** for this chapter, and locate the Web 2.0 link.

## Looking to the Future: Web 2.0 and Cloud Computing

In the constantly changing world of IT, no area is more dynamic than Internet technology. Two examples of evolving trends are Web 2.0 and cloud computing. Systems analysts should be aware of these concepts and consider them as they plan large-scale systems. Web 2.0 and cloud computing are discussed in more detail in Chapter 10, System Construction Planning.

**ON THE WEB**

To learn more about cloud computing, visit the Management Information Systems CourseMate Web site at **www. cengagebrain. com**, navigate to **On the Web Links** for this chapter, and locate the Cloud Computing link.

Many IT professionals use the term **Web 2.0** to describe a second generation of the Web that will enable people to collaborate, interact, and share information much more effectively. This new environment is based on continuously available user applications rather than static HTML Web pages, without limitations regarding the number of users or how they will be able to access, modify, and exchange data. The Web 2.0 platform will enhance interactive experiences, including wikis and blogs, and social-networking applications such as Twitter, MySpace and Facebook.

The term **cloud computing** refers to the cloud symbol that indicates a network, or the Internet. Some industry leaders predict that cloud computing will offer an overall online software and data environment supported by supercomputer technology. If so, cloud computing would be an ultimate form of SaaS, delivering services and data to users who would need only an Internet connection and a browser. However, as the *InfoWorld* article shown in Figure 7-5 points out, no standard definition of cloud computing exists, and the concept means different things to different people.

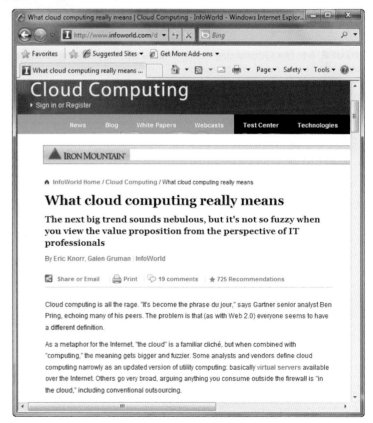

**FIGURE 7-5** Cloud computing holds the promise of a new generation of powerful Web applications and services. This is an evolving technology, and at this point, the term means different things to different people.

# OUTSOURCING

**Outsourcing** is the transfer of information systems development, operation, or maintenance to an outside firm that provides these services, for a fee, on a temporary or long-term basis. Outsourcing can refer to relatively minor programming tasks, the rental of software from a service provider, the outsourcing of a basic business process (often called **business process outsourcing,** or **BPO**), or the handling of a company's entire IT function. Numerous firms and organizations offer information about outsourcing topics and issues. For example, the Outsourcing Center, shown in Figure 7-6, provides free research, case studies, database directories, market intelligence, and updates on trends and best practices in outsourcing as a strategic business solution.

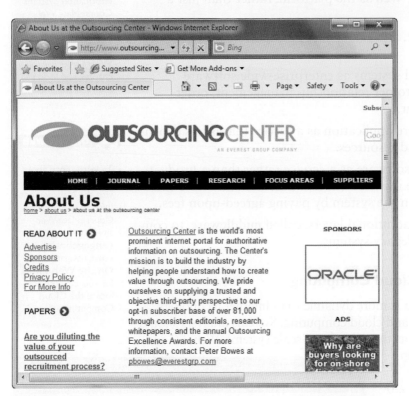

**FIGURE 7-6** The Outsourcing Center is dedicated to providing information about outsource trends and practices.

## The Growth of Outsourcing

Traditionally, firms outsourced IT tasks as a way of controlling costs and dealing with rapid technological change. While those reasons still are valid, outsourcing has become part of an overall IT strategy for many organizations. The outsourcing trend also has affected software vendors, who have adjusted their marketing accordingly. For example, Oracle Corporation offers a service called Oracle On Demand, which provides e-business applications, as shown in Figure 7-7. Oracle also cites data that shows that businesses spend up to 80% of their IT budgets maintaining existing software and systems, which forces IT managers "... to spend time managing tedious upgrades instead of revenue-generating IT projects."

A firm that offers outsourcing solutions is called a **service provider**. Some service providers concentrate on specific software applications; others offer business services such as order processing and customer billing. Still others offer enterprise-wide software solutions that integrate and manage functions such as accounting, manufacturing, and inventory control.

Two popular outsourcing options involve application service providers and firms that offer Internet business services. These terms are explained in the following sections.

**FIGURE 7-7** Oracle Corporation offers a fixed-fee outsourcing plan called Oracle On Demand.

**APPLICATION SERVICE PROVIDERS**  An **application service provider (ASP)** is a firm that delivers a software application, or access to an application, by charging a usage or subscription fee. An ASP provides more than a license to use the software; it *rents* an operational package to the customer. ASPs typically provide commercially available software such as databases and accounting packages. If a company uses an ASP to supply a data management package, for example, the company does not have to design, develop, implement, or maintain the package. ASPs represent a rapidly growing trend, using the Internet as the primary delivery channel.

**ON THE WEB**

To learn more about application service providers, visit the Management Information Systems CourseMate Web site at **www. cengagebrain. com**, navigate to **On the Web Links** for this chapter, and locate the Application Service Providers link.

**INTERNET BUSINESS SERVICES**  Some firms offer **Internet business services (IBS)**, which provide powerful Web-based support for transactions such as order processing, billing, and customer relationship management. Another term for IBS is **managed hosting**, because system operations are managed by the outside firm, or host.

An IBS solution is attractive to customers because it offers online data center support, mainframe computing power for mission-critical functions, and universal access via the Internet. Many firms, such as Rackspace, compete in the managed hosting market, as shown in Figure 7-8.

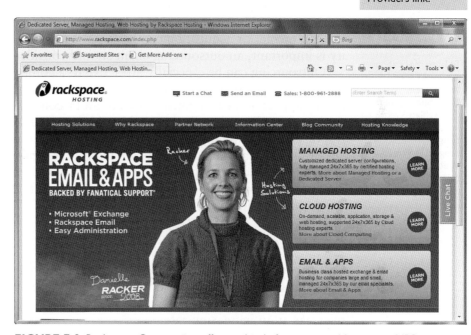

## Outsourcing Fees

Firms that offer Software as a Service, rather than a product, have developed fee structures that are based on how the application is used by customers during a specific time period. Several models exist,

**FIGURE 7-8**  Rackspace Corporation offers multi-platform managed hosting and IBS services.

including fixed fee, subscription, and usage or transaction. A **fixed fee model** uses a set fee based on a specified level of service and user support. An example of a fixed fee model is Oracle's On Demand service. A **subscription model** has a variable fee based on the number of users or workstations that have access to the application. Finally, a **usage model** or **transaction model** charges a variable fee based on the volume of transactions or operations performed by the application.

When a company considers outsourcing, it should estimate usage characteristics to determine which fee structure would be most desirable, and then attempt to negotiate a service provider contract based on that model.

## Outsourcing Issues and Concerns

When a company decides to outsource IT functions, it takes an important step that can affect the firm's resources, operations, and profitability. Mission-critical IT systems should be outsourced only if the result is a cost-attractive, reliable, business solution that fits the company's long-term business strategy and involves an acceptable level of risk. Moving IT work overseas raises even more issues, including potential concerns about control, culture, communication, and security.

In addition to long-term strategic consequences, outsourcing also can raise some concerns. For example, a company must turn over sensitive data to an external service provider and trust the provider to maintain security, confidentiality, and quality. Also, before outsourcing, a company must carefully review issues relating to insurance, potential liability, licensing and information ownership, warranties, and disaster recovery.

Most important, a company considering outsourcing must realize that the solution can be only as good as the outsourcing firm that provides the service. A dynamic economy can give rise to business failures and uncertainty about the future. In this climate, it is especially important to review the history and financial condition of an outsourcing firm before making a commitment.

Mergers and acquisitions also can affect outsourcing clients. For example, after their merger, Compaq and Hewlett-Packard restructured and streamlined the products and services offered by the new company. Even with large, financially healthy firms such as these, a merger or acquisition can have some impact on clients and customers. If stability is important, an outsourcing client should consider these issues.

Outsourcing can be especially attractive to a company whose volume fluctuates widely, such as a defense contractor. In other situations, a company might decide to outsource application development tasks to an IT consulting firm if the company lacks the time or expertise to handle the work on its own. Outsourcing relieves a company of the responsibility of adding IT staff in busy times and downsizing when the workload lightens. A major disadvantage of outsourcing is that it raises employee concerns about job security. Talented IT people usually prefer positions where the firm is committed to in-house IT development — if they do not feel secure, they might decide to work directly for the service provider.

**ON THE WEB**

To learn more about outsourcing, visit the Management Information Systems CourseMate Web site at **www. cengagebrain.com**, navigate to **On the Web Links** for this chapter, and locate the Outsourcing link.

## Offshore Outsourcing

**Offshore outsourcing**, or **global outsourcing**, refers to the practice of shifting IT development, support, and operations to other countries. In a trend similar to the outflow of manufacturing jobs over a several-decade period, many firms are sending IT work overseas at an increasing rate.

For example, Dartmouth professor Matthew Slaughter has noted that IT work will move offshore even faster than manufacturing, because it is easier to ship work across networks and telephone lines and put consultants on airplanes than it is to ship bulky raw materials, build factories, and deal with tariffs and transportation issues. Several years ago, the IT consulting firm Gartner, Inc., accurately forecast the steady growth of offshore outsourcing, and predicted that outsourcing would evolve from labor-intensive maintenance and support to higher-level systems development and software design.

In addition to exporting IT jobs, many large multinational firms, including Microsoft and IBM, have opened technical centers in India and other countries. Some observers believe that India might gain as many as 2 million IT jobs in the next decade.

The main reason for offshore outsourcing is the same as domestic outsourcing: lower bottom-line costs. Offshore outsourcing, however, involves some unique risks and concerns. For example, workers, customers, and shareholders in some companies have protested this trend, and have raised public awareness of possible economic impact. Even more important, offshore outsourcing involves unique concerns regarding project control, security issues, disparate cultures, and effective communication with critical functions that might be located halfway around the globe.

## CASE IN POINT 7.1: TURNKEY SERVICES

Turnkey Services is an application service provider that offers payroll and tax preparation services for hundreds of businesses in the Midwest. The firm is considering a major expansion into accounting and financial services, and is looking into the possibility of supporting this move by hiring IT subcontractors in several foreign countries. Peter Belmont, Turnkey's president, has asked you to help him reach a decision. Specifically, he wants you to cite the pros and cons of offshore outsourcing. He expects you to perform Internet research on this topic, and he wants you to present your views at a meeting of Turnkey managers next week.

## IN-HOUSE SOFTWARE DEVELOPMENT OPTIONS

In addition to numerous outsourcing options, a company can choose to develop its own systems, or purchase, possibly customize, and implement a software package. These development alternatives are shown in Figure 7-9. Although many factors influence this decision, the most important consideration is the total cost of ownership (TCO), which was explained in Chapter 4. In addition to these options, companies also develop user applications designed around commercial software packages, such as Microsoft Office, to improve user productivity and efficiency.

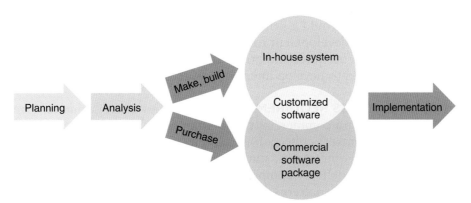

**FIGURE 7-9** Instead of outsourcing, a company can choose to develop a system in-house, or purchase and possibly customize a commercial package.

### Make or Buy Decision

The choice between developing versus purchasing software often is called a **make or buy**, or **build or buy** decision. The company's IT department makes, builds, and develops **in-house software**. A **software package** is obtained from a vendor or application service provider.

The package might be a standard commercial program or a customized package designed specifically for the purchaser. Companies that develop software for sale are called **software vendors**. A firm that enhances a commercial package by adding custom features and configuring it for a particular industry is called a **value-added reseller (VAR)**.

Software packages are available for every type of business activity. A software package that can be used by many different types of organizations is called a **horizontal application**. An accounting package is a good example of a horizontal application because it can be utilized by many different businesses, or separate divisions that exist in large, diversified companies.

 **ON THE WEB**

To learn more about value-added resellers, visit the Management Information Systems CourseMate Web site at **www. cengagebrain. com**, navigate to **On the Web Links** for this chapter, and locate the Value-Added Resellers link.

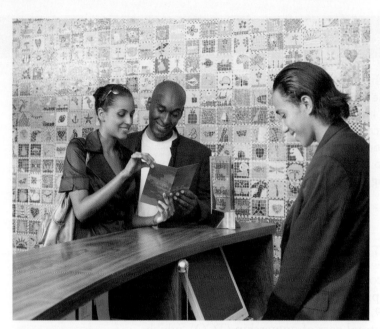

FIGURE 7-10 Hotel chains require vertical applications to support reservation systems and information needs that are unique to the hotel industry.

In contrast, a software package developed to handle information requirements for a specific type of business is called a **vertical application**. For example, organizations with special system requirements include colleges, banks, hospitals, insurance companies, construction companies, real estate firms, and airlines. A hotel chain might require a vertical application for its guest reservation system, as shown in Figure 7-10, and use horizontal applications for basic business needs, such as payroll processing and accounts payable.

Of the in-house software acquisition options — developing a system, buying a software package, or customizing a software package — each has advantages, disadvantages, and cost considerations, as shown in Figure 7-11. These software acquisition options are described in detail in the following sections.

## Developing Software In-House

With an enormous variety of software packages available to handle horizontal and vertical business operations, why would a firm choose to develop its own software? Typically, companies choose in-house development to satisfy unique business requirements, to minimize changes in business procedures and policies, to meet constraints of existing systems and existing technology, and to develop internal resources and capabilities.

**SATISFY UNIQUE BUSINESS REQUIREMENTS** Companies often decide to develop software in-house because no commercially available software package can meet their unique business requirements. A college, for example, needs a course scheduling system based on curriculum requirements, student demand, classroom space, and available instructors. A package delivery company needs a system to identify the best combination of routes and loading patterns for the company's fleet of delivery trucks. If existing software packages cannot handle those requirements, then in-house developed software might be the only choice.

| REASONS FOR IN-HOUSE DEVELOPMENT | REASONS FOR PURCHASING A SOFTWARE PACKAGE |
| --- | --- |
| Satisfy unique business requirements | Lower costs |
| Minimize changes in business procedures and policies | Requires less time to implement |
| Meet constraints of existing systems | Proven reliability and performance benchmarks |
| Meet constraints of existing technology | Requires less technical development staff |
| Develop internal resources and capabilities | Future upgrades provided by the vendor |
| Satisfy unique security requirements | Obtain input from other companies |

FIGURE 7-11 Companies consider various factors when comparing in-house development with the purchase of a software package.

**MINIMIZE CHANGES IN BUSINESS PROCEDURES AND POLICIES** A company also might choose to develop its own software if available packages will require changes in current business operations or processes. Installing a new software package almost always requires some degree of change in how a company does business; however, if the installation of a purchased package will be too disruptive, the organization might decide to develop its own software instead.

**MEET CONSTRAINTS OF EXISTING SYSTEMS** Any new software installed must work with existing systems. For example, if a new budgeting system must interface with an existing accounting system, finding a software package that works correctly with the existing accounting system might prove difficult. If so, a company could develop its own software to ensure that the new system will interface with the old system.

**MEET CONSTRAINTS OF EXISTING TECHNOLOGY** Another reason to develop software in-house is that the new system must work with existing hardware and legacy systems. That could require a custom design not commercially available. Some companies have older microcomputer workstations that cannot handle graphics-intensive software or high-speed Internet access. In that situation, the company either must upgrade the environment or must develop in-house software that can operate within the constraints of the existing hardware. As a systems analyst, you addressed the issue of technical feasibility during the preliminary investigation. Now, in the systems analysis phase, you must examine the advantages and disadvantages of in-house software development to decide whether it is justifiable.

**DEVELOP INTERNAL RESOURCES AND CAPABILITIES** By designing a system in-house, companies can develop and train an IT staff that understands the organization's business functions and information support needs. Many firms feel that in-house IT resources and capabilities provide a competitive advantage because an in-house team can respond quickly when business problems or opportunities arise. For example, if a company lacks internal resources, it must depend on an outside firm for vital business support. Also, outsourcing options might be attractive, but a series of short-term solutions would not necessarily translate into lower TCO over the long term. Top managers often feel more comfortable with an internal IT team to provide overall guidance and long-term stability.

## Purchasing a Software Package

If a company decides not to outsource, a commercially available software package might be an attractive alternative to developing its own software. Advantages of purchasing a software package over developing software in-house include lower costs, less time to implement a system, proven reliability and performance benchmarks, less technical development staff, future upgrades that are provided by the vendor, and the ability to obtain input from other companies who already have implemented the software.

**LOWER COSTS** Because many companies use software packages, software vendors spread the development costs over many customers. Compared with software developed in-house, a software package almost always is less expensive, particularly in terms of initial investment.

**REQUIRES LESS TIME TO IMPLEMENT** When you purchase a package, it already has been designed, programmed, tested, and documented. The in-house time normally spent on those tasks, therefore, is eliminated. Of course, you still must install the software and integrate it into your systems environment, which can take a significant amount of time.

**PROVEN RELIABILITY AND PERFORMANCE BENCHMARKS** If the package has been on the market for any length of time, any major problems probably have been detected already and corrected by the vendor. If the product is popular, it almost certainly has been rated and evaluated by independent reviewers.

**REQUIRES LESS TECHNICAL DEVELOPMENT STAFF** Companies that use commercial software packages often are able to reduce the number of programmers and systems analysts on the IT staff. Using commercial software also means that the IT staff can concentrate on systems whose requirements cannot be satisfied by software packages.

**FUTURE UPGRADES PROVIDED BY THE VENDOR** Software vendors regularly upgrade software packages by adding improvements and enhancements to create a new version or release. A new release of a software package, for example, can include drivers to support a new laser printer or a new type of data storage technology. In many cases, the vendor receives input and suggestions from current users when planning future upgrades.

**INPUT FROM OTHER COMPANIES** Using a commercial software package means that you can contact users in other companies to obtain their input and impressions. You might be able to try the package or make a site visit to observe the system in operation before making a final decision.

### Customizing a Software Package

If the standard version of a software product does not satisfy a company's requirements, the firm can consider adapting the package to meet its needs. Three ways to customize a software package are:

1. You can purchase a basic package that vendors will customize to suit your needs. Many vendors offer basic packages in a standard version with add-on components that are configured individually. A vendor offers options when the standard application will not satisfy all customers. A human resources information system is a typical example, because each company handles employee compensation and benefits differently. If you need assistance in making a determination, firms such as Ideas International offer services to help you select and configure a system, as shown in Figure 7-12.

**FIGURE 7-12** Firms such as Ideas International offer services to help customers select and configure a system.

2. You can negotiate directly with the software vendor to make enhancements to meet your needs by paying for the changes.

3. You can purchase the package and make your own modifications, if this is permissible under the terms of the software license. A disadvantage of this approach is that systems analysts and programmers might be unfamiliar with the software and will need time to learn the package and make the modifications correctly.

Additionally, some advantages of purchasing a standard package disappear if the product must be customized. If the vendor does the customizing, the modified package probably will cost more and take longer to obtain. Another issue is future support: Although vendors regularly upgrade their standard software packages, they might not upgrade a customized version. In addition, if the modifications are done by the company purchasing the software, when a new release of the package becomes available, the company might have to modify the new version.

## Creating User Applications

Business requirements sometimes can be fulfilled by a user application, rather than a formal information system or commercial package. User applications are examples of user productivity systems, which were discussed in Chapter 1.

A **user application** utilizes standard business software, such as Microsoft Word or Microsoft Excel, which has been configured in a specific manner to enhance user productivity. For example, to help a sales rep respond rapidly to customer price requests, an IT support person can set up a form letter with links to a spreadsheet that calculates incentives and discounts. In addition to configuring the software, the IT staff can create a **user interface**, which includes screens, commands, controls, and features that enable users to interact more effectively with the application. User interface design is described in Chapter 8.

In some situations, user applications offer a simple, low-cost solution. Most IT departments have a backlog of projects, and IT solutions for individuals or small groups do not always receive a high priority. At the same time, application software is more powerful, flexible, and user-friendly than ever. Companies such as Microsoft and Corel offer software suites and integrated applications that can exchange data with programs that include tutorials, wizards, and Help features to guide less experienced users who know what they need to do but do not know how to make it happen.

Many companies empower lower-level employees by providing more access to data and more powerful data management tools. The main objective is to allow lower-level employees more access to the data they require to perform their jobs, with no intervention from the IT department. This can be accomplished by creating effective user interfaces for company-wide applications such as accounting, inventory, and sales systems. Another technique is to customize standard productivity software, such as Microsoft Word or Microsoft Excel, to create user applications. In either case, empowerment makes the IT department more productive because it can spend less time responding to the daily concerns and data needs of users and more time on high-impact systems development projects that support strategic business goals.

Empowerment reduces costs and makes good business sense, but companies that adopt this approach must provide the technical support that empowered users require. In most large and medium-sized companies, a **help desk**, or **information center (IC)**, within the IT department is responsible for providing user support. The IC staff offers services such as hotline assistance, training, and guidance to users who need technical help.

Once they learn an application, many users can perform tasks that once required a programmer. Some user applications have powerful **screen generators** and **report generators** that allow users to design their own data entry forms and reports. For example, as shown in Figure 7-13, Microsoft Access includes a Form Wizard and a Report Wizard, which are menu-driven tools that can create screen forms and reports. These design tools allow users to design specific input and output views that meet their operational needs — with little or no assistance required from the IT staff.

Users typically require spreadsheets, database management programs, and other software packages to meet their information needs. If user applications access corporate data, you must provide appropriate controls to ensure data security and integrity. For example, some files should be hidden totally from view; others should have **read-only properties** so users can view, but not change, the data.

## ROLE OF THE SYSTEMS ANALYST

At some point in the systems development process, the company must decide whether to use an outsourcing option, develop software in-house, acquire a software package, develop user applications, or select some combination of these solutions. The decision will affect the remaining SDLC phases and your involvement as a systems analyst. The decision to develop software in-house, for example, will require more participation from the systems analyst than outsourcing or choosing a commercial package. Management usually makes a determination after receiving written recommendations from the IT staff and a formal presentation, which is described later in this chapter.

Even a single system can use a mix of software alternatives. For example, a company might purchase a standard software package to process its payroll, and then develop its own software to handle the interface between the payroll package and the company's in-house manufacturing cost analysis system.

The evaluation and selection of alternatives is not a simple process. The objective is to obtain the product with the lowest total cost of ownership, but actual cost and performance can be difficult to forecast. With a large number of choices, how do you select the best alternative?

**FIGURE 7-13** Microsoft Access includes Form Wizard and Report Wizard tools that ask a series of questions, and then create the form or report.

When selecting hardware and software, systems analysts often work as an **evaluation and selection team**. A team approach ensures that critical factors are not overlooked and that a sound choice is made. The evaluation and selection team also must include users, who will participate in the selection process and feel a sense of ownership in the new system.

The primary objective of the evaluation and selection team is to eliminate system alternatives that will not meet requirements, rank the alternatives that are feasible, and present the viable alternatives to management for a final decision. The process begins with a careful study of the costs and benefits of each alternative, as explained in the following section.

## ANALYZING COST AND BENEFITS

In Chapter 2, you learned that economic feasibility is one of the four feasibility measurements that are made during the preliminary investigation of a systems request. Now, at the end of the systems analysis phase of the SDLC, you must apply financial analysis tools and techniques to evaluate development strategies and decide how the project will move forward. Appendix C describes three popular tools, which are payback analysis, return on investment (ROI), and net present value (NPV). These tools, and others, can be used to determine total cost of ownership (TCO), which was described in Chapter 4. At this stage, you will identify specific systems development strategies and choose a course of action. For example, a company might find that its total cost of ownership will be higher if it develops a system in-house, compared with outsourcing the project or using an ASP.

An accurate forecast of TCO is critical, because nearly 80% of total costs occur *after* the purchase of the hardware and software, according to Gartner, Inc. An IT department can develop its own TCO estimates, or use TCO calculation tools offered by vendors. For example, as shown in Figure 7-14 on the next page, HP and Oracle offer an online TCO calculator that includes a questionnaire and a graphical display of results.

### Financial Analysis Tools

Appendix C explains how to use three main cost analysis tools: payback analysis, return on investment (ROI), and net present value (NPV). **Payback analysis** determines how long it takes an information system to pay for itself through reduced costs and increased benefits. **Return on investment (ROI)** is a percentage rate that compares the total net benefits (the return) received from a project to the total costs (the investment) of the project. The **net present value (NPV)** of a project is the total value of the benefits minus the total value of the costs, with both costs and benefits adjusted to reflect the point in time at which they occur.

**ON THE WEB**

To learn more about financial analysis tools, visit the Management Information Systems CourseMate Web site at **www.cengagebrain.com**, navigate to **On the Web Links** for this chapter, and locate the Financial Analysis Tools link.

**VIDEO LEARNING SESSIONS**

To learn more about financial analysis tools, visit the Management Information Systems CourseMate Web site at **www.cengagebrain.com** and navigate to the Video Learning Sessions for this book. These sessions can help you understand key concepts, practice your skills, and check your work.

## CASE IN POINT 7.2: STERLING ASSOCIATES

Joan Sterling is CEO and principal stockholder of Sterling Associates, which specializes in advising clients on IT projects and information systems development. Joan is creating a brochure for prospective new clients. She wants you to develop a section that describes payback analysis, ROI, and NPV in simple terms, and mentions the pros and cons of each financial analysis tool. She suggested that you start by viewing the Video Learning Sessions on financial analysis tools, and reviewing the material in Appendix C.

**FIGURE 7-14** HP and Oracle offer an online TCO calculator.

## Cost-Benefit Analysis Checklist

Companies use all three financial analysis tools to evaluate various development strategies. The best way to apply the tools is to develop a cost-benefit checklist with the following steps:

- List each development strategy being considered.
- Identify all costs and benefits for each alternative. Be sure to indicate when costs will be incurred and benefits realized.
- Consider future growth and the need for scalability.
- Include support costs for hardware and software.
- Analyze various software licensing options, including fixed fees and formulas based on the number of users or transactions.
- Apply the financial analysis tools to each alternative.
- Study the results and prepare a report to management.

# THE SOFTWARE ACQUISITION PROCESS

Although each situation is different, the following section describes a typical example of the issues and tasks involved in software acquisition.

## Step 1: Evaluate the Information System Requirements

Based on your analysis of the system requirements, you must identify the system's key features; consider network and Web-related issues; estimate volume and future growth; specify any hardware, software, or personnel constraints; and prepare a request for proposal or quotation.

**IDENTIFY KEY FEATURES** Whether you are considering in-house development or out-sourcing options, you must develop a clear, detailed list of features that can serve as an overall specification for the system. Using the data you gathered during fact-finding, which was discussed in Chapter 4, you must list all system requirements and critical features. This information will be included in the system requirements document, which is the end product of the SDLC systems analysis phase.

**CONSIDER NETWORK AND WEB-RELATED ISSUES** As you evaluate the system requirements, you must consider network and Web-related issues. You must decide whether the system will run on a network, the Internet, or a company intranet, and build these requirements into the design. Also, you must determine whether the system will exchange data with vendor or customer systems, and ensure that the system will be compatible.

**ESTIMATE VOLUME AND FUTURE GROWTH** You need to know the current volume of transactions and forecast future growth. Figure 7-15 shows volume estimates for an order processing system. In addition to current levels, the figure displays two forecasts, one based on the existing order processing procedures and another that assumes a new Web site is operational.

## Online Order Processing System Estimated Activity During Next 12-Month Period

| | CURRENT LEVEL | FUTURE GROWTH (based on existing procedures) | FUTURE GROWTH (assuming new Web site is operational) |
|---|---|---|---|
| Customers | 36,500 | 40,150 | 63,875 |
| Daily Orders | 1,435 | 1,579 | 2,811 |
| Daily Order Lines | 7,715 | 7,893 | 12,556 |
| Sales Reps | 29 | 32 | 12 |
| Order Processing Support Staff | 2 | 4 | 3 |
| Products | 600 | 650 | 900 |

**FIGURE 7-15** Volume estimate for an order processing system showing current activity levels and two forecasts: one based on the existing order processing procedures and another that assumes a new Web site is operational.

A comparison of the two forecasts shows that the Web site will generate more new customers, process almost 80% more orders, and substantially reduce the need for sales reps and support staff. If you are considering in-house development, you must make sure that your software and hardware can handle future transaction volumes and data storage requirements. Conversely, if you are considering outsourcing, volume and usage data is essential to analyze ASP fee structures and develop cost estimates for outsourcing options.

**SPECIFY HARDWARE, SOFTWARE, OR PERSONNEL CONSTRAINTS**  You must determine whether existing hardware, software, or personnel issues will affect the acquisition decision. For example, if the firm has a large number of legacy systems or if an ERP strategy has been adopted, these factors will have an impact on the decision. Also, you must investigate the company's policy regarding outsourcing IT functions, and whether outsourcing is part of a long-term strategy. With regard to personnel issues, you must define in-house staffing requirements to develop, acquire, implement, and maintain the system — and determine whether the company is willing to commit to those staffing levels versus an outsourcing option.

**PREPARE A REQUEST FOR PROPOSAL OR QUOTATION**  To obtain the information you need to make a decision, you should prepare a request for proposal or a request for quotation. The two documents are similar but used in different situations, based on whether or not you have selected a specific software product.

A **request for proposal (RFP)** is a document that describes your company, lists the IT services or products you need, and specifies the features you require. An RFP helps ensure that your organization's business needs will be met. An RFP also spells out the service and support levels you require. Based on the RFP, vendors can decide if they have a product that will meet your needs. RFPs vary in size and complexity, just like the systems they describe. An RFP for a large system can contain dozens of pages with unique requirements and features. You can use an RFP to designate some features as essential and others as desirable. An RFP also requests specific pricing and payment terms.

Figure 7-16 shows an example of a ready-made RFP template offered by Infotivity Technologies. Notice that the vendor can choose from a range of responses, and also add comments. Figure 7-17 shows the RFP Evaluation Centers site. This organization offers samples of RFP templates, cover letters, and other resources.

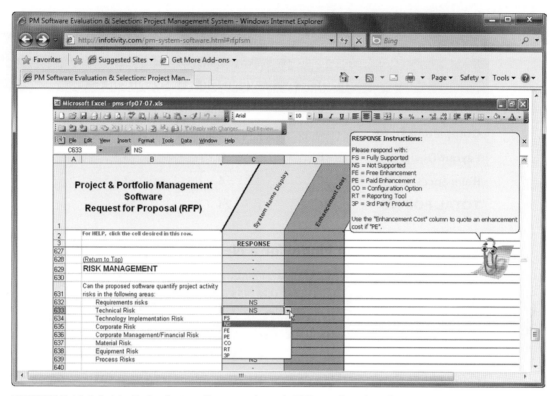

**FIGURE 7-16** Infotivity Technologies offers a ready-made RFP template that allows a wide range of reponses and comments.

When you evaluate several responses to an RFP, you might find it helpful to use an evaluation model. An **evaluation model** is a technique that uses a common yardstick to measure and compare vendor ratings.

Figure 7-18 on the next page shows two evaluation models for a network project. The evaluation model at the top of the figure simply lists the key elements and each vendor's score. The model at the bottom of the figure adds a weight factor. In this example, each element receives a rating based on its relative importance. Although the initial scores are the same in both models, notice that vendor A has the highest point total in the top example, but vendor C emerges as the best in the weighted model.

**FIGURE 7-17** The RFP Evaluation Centers site offers samples of RFP templates, cover letters, and other resources.

## Unweighted Evaluation Model for a Network Project

| | VENDOR A | VENDOR B | VENDOR C |
|---|---|---|---|
| **Instructions:** Rate each vendor on a scale from 1(low) to 10 (high), then add vendor scores to calculate total points. | | | |
| **Price** | 6 | 5 | 9 |
| **Completion Date** | 2 | 5 | 8 |
| **Layout/Design** | 8 | 8 | 5 |
| **References** | 10 | 6 | 3 |
| **TOTAL POINTS** | 26 | 24 | 25 |

## Weighted Evaluation Model for a Network Project

| | WEIGHT FACTOR | VENDOR A | VENDOR B | VENDOR C |
|---|---|---|---|---|
| **Instructions:** Rate each vendor on a scale from 1(low) to 10 (high), then multiply the vendor's score by the weight factor. Add vendor scores to calculate total points. | | | | |
| **Price** | 25 | 6 * 25 = 150 | 5 * 25 = 125 | 9 * 25 = 225 |
| **Completion Date** | 25 | 2 * 25 = 50 | 5 * 25 = 125 | 8 * 25 = 200 |
| **Layout/Design** | 35 | 8 * 35 = 280 | 8 * 35 = 280 | 5 * 35 = 175 |
| **References** | 15 | 10 * 15 = 150 | 6 * 15 = 90 | 3 * 15 = 45 |
| **TOTAL POINTS** | 100 | 630 | 620 | 645 |

**FIGURE 7-18** The three vendors have the same initial ratings, but the two evaluation models produce different results. In the unweighted model at the top of the figure, vendor A has the highest total points. However, after applying weight factors, vendor C is the winner, as shown in the model at the bottom of the figure.

Evaluation models can be used throughout the SDLC, and you will find them a valuable tool. You can use a spreadsheet program to build an evaluation model, experiment with different weighting factors, and graph the results.

A **request for quotation (RFQ)** is more specific than an RFP. When you use an RFQ, you already know the specific product or service you want and you need to obtain price quotations or bids. RFQs can involve outright purchase or a variety of leasing options and can include maintenance or technical support terms. Many vendors provide convenient RFQ forms on their Web sites, as shown in Figure 7-19. RFPs and RFQs have the same objective: to obtain vendor replies that are clear, comparable, and responsive so you can make a well-informed selection decision.

In today's fast-paced IT marketplace, traditional methods for obtaining RFPs often are too slow. The Web site shown in Figure 7-20 offers an online meeting place where customers can post RFPs and vendors can reply with solutions and bids.

### Step 2: Identify Potential Vendors or Outsourcing Options

The next step is to identify potential vendors or outsourcing providers. The Internet is a primary marketplace for all IT products and services, and you can find descriptive information on the Web about all major products and acquisition alternatives.

If you need to locate vertical applications for specific industries, you can research industry trade journals or Web sites to find reviews for industry-specific software. Industry trade groups often can direct you to companies that offer specific software solutions.

Another approach is to work with a consulting firm. Many IT consultants offer specialized services that help companies select software packages. A major advantage of using a consultant is that you can tap into broad experience that is difficult for any one company to acquire. Consultants can be located by contacting professional organizations or industry sources, or simply by searching the Internet. Using a consultant involves additional expense but can prevent even more costly mistakes.

Another valuable resource is the Internet bulletin board system that contains thousands of forums, called **newsgroups**, that cover every imaginable topic. Newsgroups are excellent sources of information and good places to exchange ideas with other analysts and IT professionals. You can search the Web for newsgroups that interest you, or you can visit the sites of specific companies, such as Microsoft, that provide a valuable source of information for IT professionals, including blogs, technical chats, newsgroups, Webcasts, and other resources, as shown in Figure 7-21 on the next page.

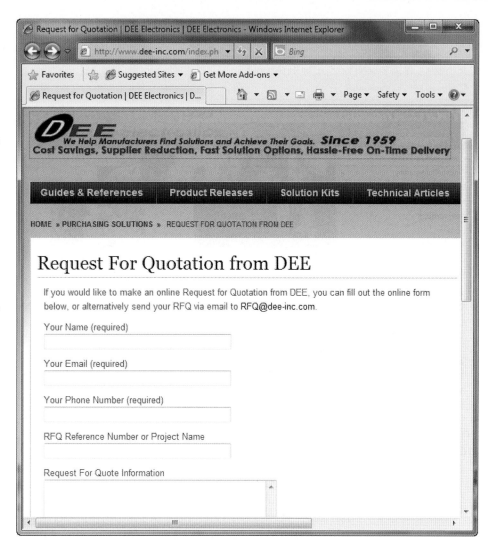

**FIGURE 7-19** Many vendors provide convenient RFQ forms on their Web sites, as shown in this example.

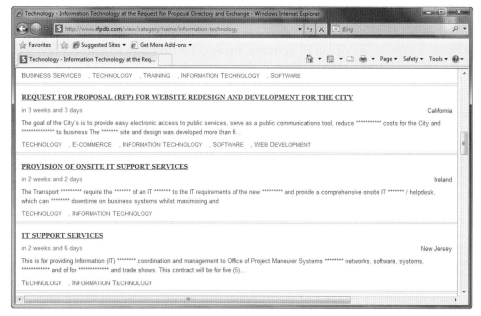

**FIGURE 7-20** The rfpDB site offers an online meeting place where customers post RFPs and vendors can respond.

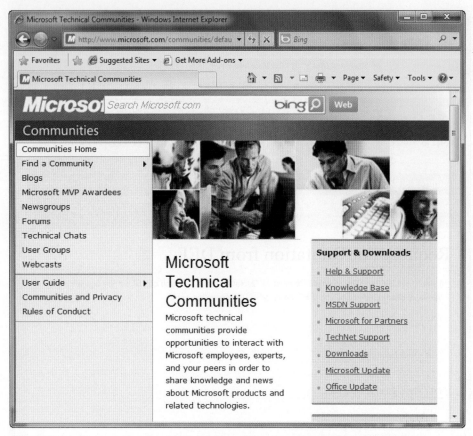

**FIGURE 7-21** Microsoft Communities is an excellent resource for IT professionals.

## Step 3: Evaluate the Alternatives

After identifying the alternatives, you must select the one that best fits the company's needs. You should obtain information about the options from as many sources as possible, including vendor presentations and literature, product documentation, trade publications, and companies that perform software testing and evaluation. To learn more about particular software packages, search the Internet using keywords that describe the application. Web sites maintained by consultants and software publishers often include product references and links to vendors. As part of the evaluation process, you should try to obtain information from existing users, test the application, and benchmark the package.

**EXISTING USERS** You can contact existing users to obtain feedback and learn about their experiences. For large-scale software packages, ASPs and vendors typically supply user references. User references are important because you need to know whether the software package has worked well for companies like yours. Be aware that some vendors limit their reference lists to satisfied clients, so you can expect mostly positive feedback from those firms.

**APPLICATION TESTING** If a software package is one of the options, find out if it is possible for users in your organization to try the product. For horizontal applications or small systems, using a demo copy to enter a few sample transactions could be an acceptable test. For vertical applications or large systems, a team of IT staff and users might need several days or weeks to perform tests.

**ON THE WEB**

To learn more about benchmark tests, visit the Management Information Systems CourseMate Web site at **www. cengagebrain.com**, navigate to **On the Web Links** for this chapter, and locate the Benchmark Tests link.

**BENCHMARKING** To determine whether a package can handle a certain transaction volume efficiently, you can perform a benchmark test. A **benchmark** measures the time a package takes to process a certain number of transactions. For example, a benchmark test can measure the time needed to post 1,000 sales transactions.

If you use benchmarks, remember that a benchmark test is conducted in a controlled environment, which might not resemble the actual day-to-day situation at your company. Although benchmarking cannot predict your specific results, benchmark testing is a good way to measure relative performance of two or more competing products in a standard environment.

Many IT publications publish regular reviews of individual packages, including benchmark tests, and often have annual surveys covering various categories of software. Some of the publications shown in Figure 7-22 also offer online versions and additional Web-based features, search capability, and IT links.

You also can obtain information from independent firms that benchmark various software packages and sell comparative analyses of the results, as shown in Figure 7-23 on the next page. The Transaction Processing Performance Council (TPC) is an example of a non-profit organization that publishes standards and reports for its members and the general public, while InfoSizing is an IT consulting firm that offers analysis of performance benchmarks.

Finally, you should match each package against the RFP features and rank the choices. If some features are more important than others, give them a higher weight using an evaluation model similar to the one shown in Figure 7-18 on page 304.

**FIGURE 7-22** Many IT publications test and review software packages. Although an enormous amount of information is available on the Web, many IT professionals enjoy reading traditional magazines like these.

## Step 4: Perform Cost-Benefit Analysis

Review the suggestions in this chapter and in Appendix C, and develop a spreadsheet to identify and calculate TCO for each option you are considering. Be sure to include all costs, using the volume forecasts you prepared. If you are considering outsourcing options, carefully study the alternative fee structure models described earlier. If possible, prepare charts to show the results graphically, and build in what-if capability so you can gauge the impact if one or more variables change.

If you are considering a software package, be sure to consider acquisition options. When you purchase software, what you are buying is a **software license** that gives you the right to use the software under certain terms and conditions. For example, the license could allow you to use the software only on a single computer, a specified number of computers, a network, or an entire site, depending on the terms of the agreement. Other license restrictions could prohibit you from making the software available to others or modifying the program. For desktop applications, software license terms and conditions usually cannot be modified. For large-scale systems, license agreement terms often can be negotiated.

Also consider user support issues, which can account for a significant part of TCO. If you select an outsourcing alternative, the arrangement probably will include certain technical support and maintenance. If you choose in-house development, you must consider the cost of providing these services on your own. If you purchase a software package, consider a supplemental **maintenance agreement**, which offers additional support and assistance from the vendor. The agreement might provide full support for a period of time or list specific charges for particular services. Some software packages provide free technical support for a period of time. Afterward, support is offered with a charge per occurrence, or per minute or hour of technical support time. Some software vendors contact registered owners whenever a new release is available and usually offer the new release at a reduced price.

> The Financial Analysis tools in Appendix C can help you analyze project costs, benefits, and economic feasibility. To learn more about these tools, turn to Appendix C.

## Step 5: Prepare a Recommendation

You should prepare a recommendation that evaluates and describes the alternatives, together with the costs, benefits, advantages, and disadvantages of each option. At this point, you may be required to submit a formal system requirements document and deliver a presentation. You should review the suggestions for presenting written

**FIGURE 7-23** The Transaction Processing Performance Council is a non-profit organization that publishes standards and reports for its members and the general public, while InfoSizing is an IT consulting firm that offers analysis of performance benchmarks.

proposals and oral presentations in Appendix A. Additional suggestions about preparing the system requirements document and the management presentation are contained in the following section.

## Step 6: Implement the Solution

Implementation tasks will depend on the solution selected. In-house options will require more time and effort than outsourcing alternatives. For large systems or network installations, the process can require considerable time and effort. Your installation strategy should be planned well in advance, especially if any disruption of normal business operations is expected. If the software package is customized, then the task will be more complex and difficult.

Before the new software becomes operational, you must complete all implementation steps, including loading, configuring, and testing the software; training users; and converting data files to the new system's format. Chapter 11 discusses implementation strategies and techniques in more detail.

## CASE IN POINT 7.3: DOUG'S SPORTING GOODS

Doug's Sporting Goods sells hiking and camping supplies. The company has grown considerably in the last two years. Doug Sawyer, the company's founder and president, wants to develop a customer order entry system and hired your IT consulting firm to advise him about software alternatives. Doug is leaning toward in-house development because he does not want to depend on outside vendors and suppliers for technical support and upgrades. Doug also says that he is not interested in selling on the Web, but that could change in the future.

Doug wants to meet with you tomorrow to make a decision. What will you say to Doug at the meeting?

## COMPLETION OF SYSTEMS ANALYSIS TASKS

To complete the systems analysis phase, you must prepare the system requirements document and your presentation to management.

> The Communication Tools in Appendix A can help you develop better documents, reports, and presentations. To learn more about these tools, turn to Appendix A.

### System Requirements Document

The **system requirements document**, or **software requirements specification**, contains the requirements for the new system, describes the alternatives that were considered, and makes a specific recommendation to management. This important document is the starting point for measuring the performance, accuracy, and completeness of the finished system before entering the systems design phase.

The system requirements document is like a contract that identifies what the system developers must deliver to users. Recall that system requirements are identified during the fact-finding process, and a system requirements checklist is created at that time. Various examples of system requirements are listed on pages 153–155 in Chapter 4. You should write the system requirements document in language that users can understand so they can offer input, suggest improvements, and approve the final version.

Because the system requirements document can be lengthy, you should format and organize it so it is easy to read and use. The system requirements document should include a cover page and a detailed table of contents. You also can add an index and a glossary of terms to make the document easier to use. The content of the system requirements document will depend on the company and the complexity of the system.

### Presentation to Management

The presentation to management at the end of the systems analysis phase is one of the most critical milestones in the systems development process. At this point, managers make key decisions that affect the future development of the system.

Prior to the management presentation, you might give two other presentations: one to the principal individuals in the IT department to keep them posted, and another presentation to users to answer their questions and invite feedback. The system requirements document is the basis for all three presentations, and you should distribute the document (or a summary) in advance so the recipients can review it.

When preparing your presentation, you should review the suggestions in Appendix A, which will help you design and deliver a successful presentation. If you plan a slide presentation, you should review the Appendix guidelines for effective presentations. In addition to the techniques found in the Appendix, also keep the following suggestions in mind:

- Begin your presentation with a brief overview of the purpose and primary objectives of the system project, the objectives of this presentation, and what decisions need to be made.

- Summarize the primary viable alternatives. For each alternative, describe the costs, advantages, and disadvantages.

- Explain why the evaluation and selection team chose the recommended alternative.

- Allow time for discussion and for questions and answers.

- Obtain a final decision from management or agree on a timetable for the next step in the process.

The object of the management presentation is to obtain approval for the development of the system and to gain management's full support, including necessary financial resources. Management probably will choose one of five alternatives: develop an in-house system, modify a current system, purchase or customize a software package, perform additional systems analysis work, or stop all further work. Depending on their decision, your next task as a systems analyst will be one of the following:

1. Implement an outsourcing alternative. If outsourcing is selected, you will work with representatives of the service provider to achieve a smooth transition to the new environment.

2. Develop an in-house system. Begin systems design tasks, as described in Chapters 8, 9, and 10.

3. Purchase or customize a software package. Negotiate the purchase terms with the software vendor for management approval. Then, if the package will be used without modification, you can begin planning the systems implementation phase. If you must make modifications to the package, your next step is to start the systems design phase. If the vendor will make the modifications, then your next step is to start planning the testing and documentation of the modifications as part of the systems implementation phase, which is described in Chapter 11.

4. Perform additional systems analysis work. Management might want you to investigate certain alternatives further, explore alternatives not examined, develop a prototype, reduce the project scope because of cost constraints, or expand the project scope based on new developments. If necessary, you will perform the additional work and schedule a follow-up presentation.

5. Stop all further work. The decision might be based on your recommendation, a shift in priorities or costs, or for other reasons. Whatever the reason, if that is management's decision, then you have no additional tasks for the project other than to file all your research in a logical location so it can be retrieved if the project is reopened in the future.

After the presentation and management decision, you will begin a transition to the systems design phase of the SDLC. If you are developing an in-house system or modifying a package, you will build a model of the proposed system and start designing the system's output, input, files, and data structures. The following sections describe several tools and techniques that can assist you in that process, including prototyping, CASE tools, and alternative graphical tools.

## TRANSITION TO SYSTEMS DESIGN

In a traditional SDLC environment, systems design usually started when the systems analysis phase was done. Using the system requirements specification as a blueprint, developers transformed the logical design into a working model that could be tested, reviewed by users, and implemented. Today, the process is much more dynamic. In general, systems development is faster, more flexible, and more user-oriented. The introduction of adaptive methods such as agile development and extreme programming has changed the landscape significantly. Depending on the project, system developers often blend traditional and cutting-edge development methods, because what works in one situation might not work in another.

This textbook discusses systems analysis in Chapters 4, 5, 6, and 7, and systems design in Chapters 8, 9, and 10. However, in a typical IT workplace, all these tasks — and more — are integrated and managed together.

This section discusses preparation for systems design and the relationship between logical and physical design. The chapter concludes with a description of systems design guidelines, prototyping methods, and software development trends.

## Preparing for Systems Design

Regardless of the development method, systems design requires accurate documentation. Traditionally, a system requirements document provided detailed specifications for output, input, data, processes, and whatever else was needed. Although agile methods do not require a particular form of documentation, a successful development team must understand and record user requirements as they evolve during the project.

## Logical and Physical Design

A **logical design** defines *what* must take place, not *how* it will be accomplished. Logical designs do not address the actual methods of implementation. In contrast, a **physical design** is like a set of blueprints for the actual construction of a building. Typically, a physical design describes the actual processes of entering, verifying, and storing data; the physical layout of data files and sorting procedures, the format of reports, and so on. Because logical and physical designs are related so closely, good systems design is impossible without careful, accurate systems analysis. For example, you might return to fact-finding if you discover that you overlooked an important issue, if users have significant new needs, or if legal or governmental requirements change.

## SYSTEMS DESIGN GUIDELINES

Because the components of a system are interdependent, the design phase is not a series of clearly defined steps. Although you might start in one area, you could find yourself working with several different elements at the same time. For example, a decision to change a report format might require changes in data design or input screens. Your design checklist will include the user interface, input and output procedures, data design, and system architecture. As shown in Figure 7-24, the final steps are to prepare a systems design specification and present the results to management.

| STEP | ACTIVITY | DESCRIPTION |
| --- | --- | --- |
| 1 | Review system requirements. | Study the system requirements document carefully to understand the logical design. |
| 2 | Design the system.<br>• User interface, output, and input issues | Design an overall user interface, including screens, commands, controls, and features that enable users to interact with an application. Determine how data will enter the system, and design necessary source documents. Design the physical layout for input and output forms and reports, including screens and printed reports. |
| | • Data issues | Determine how data will be organized, stored, maintained, updated, accessed, and used. |
| | • System architecture issues | Determine processing strategies and methods, client/server interaction, network configuration, and Internet/intranet interface issues. |
| 3 | Create a system design specification. | Develop a systems design specification that describes and documents the proposed design. |
| 4 | Deliver a management presentation. | Include a progress report, a budget update, and a timetable for system implementation and operation. |

**FIGURE 7-24** Systems design tasks typically are performed in a four-step process.

## Overview

The goal of **systems design** is to build a system that satisfies business requirements. A successful system must be effective, reliable, and maintainable:

- A system is effective if it supports business requirements and meets user needs.

- A system is reliable if it handles input errors, processing errors, hardware failures, or human mistakes. A good design will anticipate errors, detect them as early as possible, make it easy to correct them, and prevent them from damaging the system itself.

- A system is maintainable if it is flexible, scalable, and easily modified. Changes might be needed to correct problems, adapt to user requirements, or take advantage of new technology.

Although each project is different, design considerations usually involve users, data, and system architecture.

**USER CONSIDERATIONS**  The most important goal is to make the system user-friendly. Here are some suggestions to keep in mind:

- **Carefully consider any point where users receive output or provide input.** The user interface must be easy to learn. Input processes should be easy to follow, intuitive, and forgiving of errors. Output should be attractive and easy to understand, with an appropriate level of detail.

- **Anticipate future needs.** Suppose that a parts inventory database contains a one-character field for category, such as electrical, mechanical, or hydraulic. The design works well, but what if the company decides to break these overall groups down into more specific segments? Why should there be a limitation of just one character? A better design would anticipate possible expansion to two or more characters. For example, many people recall the concern called the **Y2K issue**, when some older programs that used only two characters to store the year might not adjust properly to the new century.

- **Provide flexibility.** Suppose that a user wants a screen display of all customer balances that exceed $5,000 in an accounts receivable system. How should you design that feature? The program could be coded to check customer balances against a fixed value of 5000, which is a simple solution for both the programmer and the user because no extra keystrokes are required to produce the display. However, that approach is inflexible. For instance, if a user later needs a list of customers whose balances exceed $7,500 rather than $5,000, more programming would be needed. A better approach might be to allow the user to enter the amount. For example, if a user wants to display customers with balances of more than $7,500, he or she can enter that figure in a parameter query. A **parameter** is a value that the user enters whenever the query is run, which provides flexibility, enables users to access information easily, and costs less. A good systems design can combine both approaches. For example, you could design the program to accept a variable amount entered by the user, but start with a **default** value of 5000 that the system displays automatically. Users can press the ENTER key to accept the default value, or enter another value. Often the best design strategy is to come up with several alternatives, so users can decide what will work best for them.

## CASE IN POINT 7.4: DOWNTOWN!

Downtown! is a rapidly growing Web-based retailer with about 100 management and technical support employees at its headquarters office in Florida. Mary Estrada, the firm's IT manager, is planning a new information system that will give users better access to sales and marketing data and trends. She has a concern, however. She knows that users often request reports but use only a small portion of the data. In many offices she sees inboxes filled with printed reports gathering dust. Mary asked for your opinion: What if new system users could design most of their own reports without assistance from the IT staff, by using a powerful, user-friendly report writer program? Do you think they would request as many reports or the same types of reports? What are the pros and cons of giving users total control over output?

**DATA CONSIDERATIONS** Data entry and storage are important in every system. Here are some suggestions to keep in mind:

- **Enter data as soon as possible.** For example, employees in the receiving department should enter data about incoming shipments when the shipments arrive, and sales clerks should enter data about new orders when they take the orders.

- **Verify data as it is entered.** The input design should specify a data type, such as alphabetic, numeric, or alphanumeric, and a range of acceptable values for each data item. If an incorrect value is entered, the system should recognize and flag it immediately. The system also should allow corrections at any time. Some errors, for example, can be easily corrected while the original source documents are at hand or the customer is on the phone. Other errors may need further investigation, so users must be able to correct errors at a later time.

- **Use automated methods of data entry whenever possible.** For example, receiving department employees can use scanners to capture data about merchandise received. Automated data entry methods, such as the RFID scanner shown in Figure 7-25, can reduce input errors and improve employee productivity.

- **Control data entry access and report all entries or changes to critical values.** Dollar fields and volume fields are critical data fields. Examples of critical volumes might include the number of checks processed, the number of medical prescriptions dispensed, or the number of insurance premium payments received. Reports that trace the data entry and changes to critical data values are called **audit trails** and are essential in every system.

- **Log every instance of data entry and changes.** For example, the system should record when a customer's credit limit was established, by whom, and any other information necessary to construct the history of a transaction.

**FIGURE 7-25** Automated data entry methods, such as the RFID scanner shown above, reduce input errors and improve employee productivity.

- **Enter data once.** If input data for a payroll system also is needed for a human resources system, you should design a program interface between the systems so data can be transferred automatically. For example, an employee's date of birth should be entered only once, but the data should be accessible by multiple systems or authorized users.

- **Avoid data duplication.** In an inventory database, vendor addresses should not be stored with every part record. Otherwise, the address of a vendor who supplies 100 different parts will be repeated 100 times. Additionally, if the vendor's address changes, all 100 parts records must be updated. Data duplication also can produce inconsistencies. If the 100 stored addresses for the vendor are not identical, how would a user know which version is correct? In Chapter 9, you will learn about data design and a technique called normalization, which is a set of rules that can help you identify and avoid data design problems when you create a database.

**ARCHITECTURE CONSIDERATIONS** In addition to the issues affecting users and data, you should consider the overall architecture. Here are some suggestions to keep in mind:

- **Use a modular design.** In a modular design, you create individual components, called modules, which connect to a higher-level program or process. In a structured design, each module represents a specific process, which is shown on a DFD and documented in a process description. If you are using an object-oriented design, as described in Chapter 6, object classes are represented by code modules. You will learn more about modular design in Chapter 11, which describes systems implementation.

- **Design modules that perform a single function.** Independent modules provide greater flexibility because they can be developed and tested individually, and then combined or reused later in the development process. Modular design is especially important in designing large-scale systems, because separate teams of analysts and programmers can work on different areas and then integrate the results.

## Design Trade-Offs

You will find that design goals often conflict, and you must consider alternatives and trade-offs. To make a system easier to use, for example, programming requirements might be more complex. Making a system more flexible might increase maintenance requirements. Meeting one user's requirements could make it harder to satisfy another user's needs.

Most design trade-off decisions that you will face come down to the basic issue of quality versus cost. Although every project has budget and financial constraints, you should avoid decisions that achieve short-term savings but might mean higher costs later. For example, if you try to reduce implementation costs by cutting back on system testing or user training, you can create higher operational costs in the future. If necessary, you should document and explain the situations carefully to management and discuss the possible risks. Each trade-off must be considered individually, and the final result must be acceptable to users, the systems staff, and company management.

# PROTOTYPING

**Prototyping** produces an early, rapidly constructed working version of the proposed information system, called a **prototype**. Prototyping, which involves a repetitive sequence of analysis, design, modeling, and testing, is a common technique that can be used to design anything from a new home to a computer network. For example, engineers use a prototype to evaluate an aircraft design before production begins, as shown in the wind tunnel testing in Figure 7-26.

User input and feedback is essential at every stage of the systems development process. Prototyping allows users to examine a model that accurately represents system outputs, inputs, interfaces, and processes. Users can

**FIGURE 7-26** Wind tunnel testing is a typical example of prototyping.

"test-drive" the model in a risk-free environment and either approve it or request changes. In some situations, the prototype evolves into the final version of the information system; in other cases, the prototype is intended only to validate user requirements and is discarded afterward.

Perhaps the most intense form of prototyping occurs when agile methods are used. As you learned in Chapter 1, agile methods build a system by creating a series of prototypes and constantly adjusting them to user requirements. As the agile process continues, developers revise, extend, and merge earlier versions into the final product. An agile approach emphasizes continuous feedback, and each incremental step is affected by what was learned in the prior steps.

## Prototyping Methods

Systems analysts use two different prototyping methods: system prototyping and design prototyping. **System prototyping** produces a full-featured, working model of the information system. As Figure 7-27 shows, a system prototype is ready for the implementation phase of the SDLC.

**FIGURE 7-27** The end product of system prototyping is a working model of the information system, ready for implementation.

While agile methods represent the latest approach to system prototyping, rapid application development (RAD), which is described in Chapter 4, remains a popular strategy. Using RAD methods, a team of users, managers, and IT staff members works together to develop a model of the information system that evolves into the completed system. The RAD team defines, analyzes, designs, and tests prototypes using a highly interactive process, which is shown in Figure 4-5 on page 146.

Systems analysts also use prototyping to verify user requirements, after which the prototype is discarded and implementation continues, as shown in Figure 7-28 on the next page. The approach is called **design prototyping**, or **throwaway prototyping**. In this case, the prototyping objectives are more limited, but no less important. The end product of design prototyping is a user-approved model that documents and benchmarks the features of the finished system.

**FIGURE 7-28** The end product of design prototyping is a user-approved model that documents and benchmarks the features of the finished system.

Design prototyping makes it possible to capture user input and approval while continuing to develop the system within the framework of the SDLC. Systems analysts typically use design prototyping as they construct outputs, inputs, and user interfaces, as discussed in Chapter 8.

Whenever possible, you should allow users to experiment with a prototype and provide feedback on how well it meets their needs. This approach can increase development costs, but the expense will be offset by lower costs during subsequent SDLC phases. Prototyping offers many benefits, including the following:

- Users and systems developers can avoid misunderstandings.

- System developers can create accurate specifications for the finished system based on the prototype.

- Managers can evaluate a working model more effectively than a paper specification.

- Systems analysts can use a prototype to develop testing and training procedures before the finished system is available.

- Prototyping reduces the risk and potential financial exposure that occur when a finished system fails to support business needs.

Although most systems analysts believe that the advantages of prototyping far outweigh any disadvantages, you should consider the following potential problems:

- The rapid pace of development can create quality problems, which are not discovered until the finished system is operational.

- Other system requirements, such as reliability and maintainability, cannot be tested adequately using a prototype.

- In very complex systems, the prototype becomes unwieldy and difficult to manage.

## Prototyping Tools

The CASE Tools in Appendix B can help you document business functions and processes, develop graphical models, and provide an overall framework for information system development. To learn more about these tools, turn to Appendix B.

Systems analysts can use powerful tools to develop prototypes. Most prototyping is done using CASE tools, application generators, report generators, screen generators, and fourth-generation languages (4GLs). In a **fourth-generation language (4GL)**, the commands tend to resemble natural statements that people use. For example, a 4GL statement might be PRINT ALL PRODUCTS WHERE CODE = IN STOCK AND STATUS = OK.

In combination, the tools provide a framework for rapid, efficient software development, called a **fourth-generation environment**.

Appendix B describes CASE tools in more detail and explains how systems analysts can use them to speed the development process, reduce costs, and avoid design errors. In a fourth-generation environment, the development tools are highly interactive. For example, systems analysts use CASE tools to create a series of diagrams and definitions, which generate a data dictionary automatically. The data dictionary organizes and documents all data elements and interacts with application, screen, and report generators to produce a system prototype.

## Limitations of Prototypes

The final version of the system typically demands higher-level performance than the prototype can provide. A prototype is a functioning system, but it is less efficient than a fully developed system. Because it is a model, rather than a completed system, the prototype will have slower processing speeds and response times. The prototype also might lack security requirements, exception and error-handling procedures, and other required functions. Despite those limitations, systems developers can upgrade the prototype into the final information system by adding the necessary capability. Otherwise, the prototype is discarded and the remaining SDLC phases are completed.

Even when it does not evolve into the finished system, a prototype helps to ensure that the final product will meet all requirements. Satisfying system requirements is the ultimate goal of systems development, and prototyping is an extremely valuable tool during the process.

**ON THE WEB**

To learn more about software development trends, visit the Management Information Systems CourseMate Web site at **www. cengagebrain.com**, navigate to **On the Web Links** for this chapter, and locate the Software Development Trends link.

## SOFTWARE DEVELOPMENT TRENDS

Whether you are a student, an entry-level IT professional, or a seasoned veteran, you need to be aware of technology trends and developments. Because the digital world changes so rapidly, if you have a personal development plan, you can take advantage of future changes and opportunities. This section describes software development trends to consider.

### Views from the IT Community

As senior vice president of the Developer Division at Microsoft, Dr. S. Somasegar supports software developers and the technical computing community. His team handles Visual Studio, Expression Studio, the .NET Framework, Silverlight, and related development technologies. Dr. Somasegar mentions six key software development trends in his February, 2010 blog, which are summarized in Figure 7-29.

Many IT professionals try to stay in touch with key issues and trends. For most people, this is not a scientific research project, but rather an effort to keep up with developments and avoid surprises. A sampling of current articles and blogs includes some predictions and forecasts for the next few years:

- Software quality will be more important than ever, and intense modeling will support the quality assurance process. Software testing also will receive more emphasis. In the post-9/11 environment, many firms will

FIGURE 7-29 In his blog, Dr. S. Somasegar mentions six key software development trends.

The Internet Resource tools in Appendix D can help you in using the Internet to stay abreast of current IT trends and to build your systems analysis skills. To learn more about these tools, turn to Appendix D.

need to do more testing to ensure that their systems are not vulnerable to physical attack or electronic intrusion.

- Project management will be a major focus of IT managers. With increased pressure for quality software that meets budget, schedule, and quality requirements, project managers will be key players. In this environment, there will be even more emphasis on project management training and credentials.

- Service-oriented architecture (SOA) will become an important factor in future development. **Service-oriented architecture (SOA)** is an architectural style whose goal is to achieve loose coupling among interacting software objects that provide services. **Loose coupling** means that objects can interact, but are essentially independent. A common example is a DVD and a DVD player— if you want to watch your DVD, you put it into a DVD player and watch your video, because the player provides a DVD playing service. But loose coupling allows you to you to replace your DVD player with another, or to play your videos on more than one player.

- Growth in open-source software such as Linux has increased demand for powerful open-source development tools, while traditional development languages such as C and C++ are becoming less popular. There is a growing open-source community that supports and promotes vendor-neutral open-source development.

- Developers will use more **Web services**, which are modular applications such as currency converters or language translators. Most Web services are based on a combination of HTML and XML. You learned in Chapter 1 that HTML is a platform-independent language that controls the way information is presented on a browser, and that Extensible Markup Language (XML) provides a common data description language that allows easy Web-based communication between different types of hardware and software.

- Programmers will continue to use dynamic languages such as Java, Python, Perl, Ruby, and Visual Basic, among others, and new languages will evolve.

As a systems analyst, you will be affected by rapidly changing technology, and you will want to know about IT trends and developments. Appendix D contains tips and techniques that you can use to access Web-based information and use it to help build your skills and success.

# A QUESTION OF ETHICS

Sally works as a junior analyst for a medium-sized IT consulting firm. Her manager, Bob, has asked her to draft a response to an RFP from a large company that is seeking IT consulting services in connection with a new accounting system.

As Sally worked on the RFP, she noticed a specific question about her firm's recent experience on this type of system. To the best of her knowledge, the firm has only worked on one other accounting project in the last three years. When Bob saw Sally's draft response, he was upset about the way she answered the question. "You don't have to be quite that candid," he said. "Even though we only had one *formal* project, we do have several people who worked on accounting systems before they came here."

"Yes," Sally replied, "But that isn't what the question is asking." As he left her office, Bob's final comment was, "If we want that job, we'll have to come up with a better answer." Thinking about it, Sally isn't comfortable with anything but a straight answer. Is this an ethical question? What are Sally's options?

# CHAPTER SUMMARY

This chapter describes system development strategies, the preparation and presentation of the system requirements document, and the transition to the systems design phase of the SDLC.

An important trend that views Software as a Service (SaaS), rather than a product, has created new software acquisition options. Systems analysts must consider Web-based development environments such as .NET and WebSphere, and various outsourcing options, including application service providers and Internet business services. Application service providers (ASPs) charge subscription fees for providing application software packages. Internet business services (IBSs) offer powerful Web-based servers, software hosting, and IT support services to customers.

Traditional systems must function in various hardware and software environments, be compatible with legacy systems, and operate within the constraints of company networks and desktop computing capability. Such systems utilize Internet links and resources as enhancements. In contrast, Internet-based systems treat the Web *as* the platform, rather than just a communication channel. Many large companies use Web-based systems to handle enterprise-wide applications. Compared to traditional systems, Web-based systems are more scalable, less dependent on specific hardware and software, and more adaptable to outsourcing the operation and support of a software application.

The new Web generation is called Web 2.0, and it is fueling the expansion of information sharing, user collaboration, and social-networking applications such as Twitter, MySpace and Facebook. Another development, called cloud computing because of the commonly used cloud symbol for the Internet, describes an overall online software and data environment, powered by supercomputer technology, that will be an ultimate form of Software as a Service.

If a company chooses to handle its own software development needs, it can create in-house systems, or purchase (and possibly customize) commercially available software packages from a software vendor or value-added reseller (VAR).

Compared with developing an in-house system, an existing commercial software package can be an attractive alternative, because a package generally costs less, takes less time to implement, has a proven track record, and is upgraded frequently. In-house development or customizing a software package might be the best choice when a standard software package cannot meet specific business requirements or constraints. In addition to customizing software packages, companies can create user applications based on standard software that has been specially configured to enhance user productivity.

The systems analyst's role in the software development process depends on the specific development strategy. In-house development requires much more involvement than outsourcing or choosing a commercial package.

The most important factor in choosing a development strategy is total cost of ownership (TCO). Financial analysis tools include payback analysis, which determines how long it takes for a system to pay for itself through reduced costs and increased benefits; return on investment (ROI), which compares a project's total return with its total costs; and net present value (NPV), which analyzes the value of a project by adjusting costs and benefits to reflect the time that they occur.

The process of acquiring software involves a series of steps: evaluate the system requirements, consider network and Web-related issues, identify potential software vendors or outsourcing options, evaluate the alternatives, perform cost-benefit analysis, prepare a recommendation, and implement the solution. During software acquisition, a company can use a request for proposal (RFP) or a request for quotation (RFQ). An RFP invites vendors to respond to a list of system requirements and features; an RFQ seeks bids for a specific product or service.

The system requirements document is the deliverable, or end product, of the systems analysis phase. The document details all system requirements and constraints, recommends the best solution, and provides cost and time estimates for future development work. The system requirements document is the basis for the management presentation. At this point, the firm might decide to develop an in-house system, modify the current system, purchase or customize a software package, perform additional systems analysis work, or stop all further work.

As you prepared for the transition from the systems analysis to systems activities, you learned that a prototype is a working model of the proposed system that you can use to verify the system requirements with users or as a basis for the new system.

You learned that a set of interactive tools, called a fourth-generation environment, can help you construct the prototype. A fourth-generation environment includes screen generators, report writers, application or code generators, and fourth-generation languages, all of which interact with a data dictionary developed with CASE tools. You also reviewed a set of systems design guidelines and suggestions, including user considerations, data considerations, and processing considerations. Finally, you learned about trends in software development, including outsourcing, agile development, and various other topics.

# Key Terms and Phrases

application service provider (ASP) *291*

audit trail *313*

benchmark *306*

build or buy *293*

business process outsourcing (BPO) *290*

cloud computing *289*

default *312*

design prototyping *315*

evaluation and selection team *299*

evaluation model *303*

fixed fee model *291*

fourth-generation environment *316*

fourth-generation language (4GL) *316*

global outsourcing *292*

help desk *297*

horizontal application *293*

in-house software *293*

information center (IC) *297*

Internet business services (IBS) *291*

logical design *311*

loose coupling *318*

maintenance agreement *307*

make or buy *293*

managed hosting *291*

middleware *289*

.NET *287*

net present value (NPV) *299*

newsgroup *305*

offshore outsourcing *292*

outsourcing *290*

parameter *312*

payback analysis *299*

physical design *311*

prototype *315*

prototyping *315*

read-only properties *298*

report generator *297*

request for proposal (RFP) *302*

request for quotation (RFQ) *304*

return on investment (ROI) *299*

screen generator *297*

service-oriented architecture (SOA) *318*

service provider *290*

Software as a Service (SaaS) *286*

software license *307*

software package *293*

software requirements specification *309*

software vendor *293*

subscription model *291*

system prototyping *315*

system requirements document *309*

systems design *312*

throwaway prototyping *315*

transaction model *291*

usage model *291*

user application *297*

user interface *297*

value-added reseller (VAR) *293*

vertical application *294*

Web 2.0 *289*

WebSphere *287*

Web services *318*

Y2K issue *312*

# Learn It Online

**Instructions:** To complete the Learn It Online exercises, visit the Management Information Systems CourseMate Web site at **www.cengagebrain.com**, navigate to the resources for this chapter, and click the link for the exercise you want to complete.

## 1   Chapter Reinforcement

### TF, MC, and SA

Click one of the Chapter Reinforcement links for Multiple Choice, True/False, or Short Answer. Answer each question and submit to your instructor.

## 2   Flash Cards

Click the Flash Cards link and read the instructions. Type 20 (or a number specified by your instructor) in the Number of playing cards text box, type your name in the Enter your Name text box, and then click the Flip Card button. When the flash card is displayed, read the question and then click the ANSWER box arrow to select an answer. Flip through the Flash Cards. If your score is 15 (75%) correct or greater, click Print on the File menu to print your results. If your score is less than 15 (75%) correct, then redo this exercise by clicking the Replay button.

## 3   Practice Test

Click the Practice Test link. Answer each question, enter your first and last name at the bottom of the page, and then click the Grade Test button. When the graded practice test is displayed on your screen, click Print on the File menu to print a hard copy. Continue to take practice tests until you score 80% or better.

## 4   Who Wants To Be a Computer Genius?

Click the Computer Genius link. Read the instructions, enter your first and last name at the bottom of the page, and then click the Play button. When your score is displayed, click the PRINT RESULTS link to print a hard copy.

## 5   Wheel of Terms

Click the Wheel of Terms link. Read the instructions, and then enter your first and last name and your school name. Click the PLAY button. When your score is displayed on the screen, right-click the score and then click Print on the shortcut menu to print a hard copy.

## 6   Crossword Puzzle Challenge

Click the Crossword Puzzle Challenge link. Read the instructions, and then click the Continue button. Work the crossword puzzle. When you are finished, click the Submit button. When the crossword puzzle is redisplayed, submit it to your instructor.

## SCR Associates Case Simulation Session 7: Development Strategies

### Overview

The SCR Associates case study is a Web-based simulation that allows you to practice your skills in a real-world environment. The case study transports you to SCR's intranet, where you complete 12 work sessions, each aligning with a chapter. As you work on the case, you will receive e-mail and voice mail messages, obtain information from SCR's online libraries, and perform various tasks.

### How do I use the case?

- Review the SCR background material in Chapter 1.
- Read the Preview for this session and study the Task List.
- Visit the Management Information Systems CourseMate Web site at **www.cengagebrain. com**, navigate to the **SCR Case Simulation**, and locate the intranet link.
- Enter your name and the password sad9e. An opening screen will display the 12 sessions.
- Select this session. Check your e-mail and voice mail carefully, and then work on the tasks.

### Preview: Session 7

As you consider various development strategies for the TIMS system, you receive specific directions from your supervisor, Jesse Baker. She wants you to determine whether vertical software packages exist, and she wants you to explore outsourcing options for the new system. She also expects you to conduct a cost-benefit analysis of developing TIMS in-house, and she wants your input on outsourcing and prototyping.

### Task List

| |
|---|
| 1. Determine whether vertical software packages exist for training operations management. Search the Internet and draft a message describing the results. |
| 2. Investigate the possibility of outsourcing the TIMS system. List the options, together with advantages and disadvantages of each. |
| 3. Follow Jesse's e-mail instructions about calculating payback, ROI, and NPV for the TIMS system. |
| 4. Jesse wants my thoughts on how we can use prototyping for TIMS. She also wants me to prepare a system requirements document and a management presentation. |

**FIGURE 7-30** Task list: Session 7.

## Chapter Exercises

### Review Questions

1. Describe the trend that views software as a service rather than a product. What effect has this trend had on software acquisition options?
2. Explain the difference between horizontal and vertical application software.
3. What is the most common reason for a company to choose to develop its own information system? Give two other reasons why a company might choose the in-house approach.
4. What is an RFP, and how does it differ from an RFQ?
5. What is the purpose of a benchmark test?
6. Explain software licenses and maintenance agreements.
7. What decisions might management reach at the end of the systems analysis phase, and what would be the next step in each case?
8. What is a prototype, and how do systems developers use prototyping?
9. What is a fourth-generation environment?
10. Explain the relationship between logical and physical design.

### Discussion Topics

1. As more companies outsource systems development, will there be less need for in-house systems analysts? Why or why not?
2. Suppose you tried to explain the concept of throwaway prototyping to a manager, and she responded by asking, "So, is throwaway prototyping a waste of time and money?" How would you reply?
3. Select a specific type of vertical application software to investigate. Visit local computer stores and use the Internet to determine what software packages are available. Describe the features of those packages.
4. Select a specific type of horizontal application software to investigate. Visit local computer stores and use the Internet to determine what software packages are available. Describe the features of those packages.

# Apply Your Knowledge

The Apply Your Knowledge section contains four mini-cases. Each case describes a situation, explains your role in the case, and asks you to respond to questions. You can answer the questions by applying knowledge you learned in the chapter.

## 1  Top Sail Realty

**Situation:**

Top Sail Realty is one of the largest time-sharing and rental brokers for vacation cottages along the North Carolina coast. After 10 successful years of matching up owners and renters, Top Sail decided to acquire a computerized reservation and booking system. Top Sail's owner read an article about software packages, and she asked you, as an IT consultant, for your advice.

1. Should Top Sail implement a Web-based system? Why or why not?
2. What software acquisition options are available to Top Sail?
3. Do you consider the reservations system to be a horizontal or a vertical application? Give reasons for your answer.
4. When you evaluate software packages, what steps will you follow?

## 2  One Way Movers, Inc.

**Situation:**

As IT manager at One Way, you scheduled a management presentation next week. You prepared and distributed a system requirements document, and you anticipate some intense questioning at the meeting.

1. When planning your presentation, what are some techniques you will use?
2. Based on the suggestions in Appendix A, what visual aids could you use during your presentation?
3. In deciding on your proposal, what options does management have?
4. If management decides to purchase or customize a software package, what steps will you take?

**3** **Tangible Investments Corporation**

**Situation:**

Tangible Investments Corporation needs a new customer billing system. As project leader, you decided to create a prototype that users can evaluate before the final design is implemented. You plan to use a traditional structured analysis methodology. To prepare for your meeting with top management tomorrow, you need to review the following topics.

1. Explain the main purpose of prototyping.
2. Explain why a prototype might or might not evolve into the final version of the system.
3. Describe the tools typically used in developing prototypes.
4. List three advantages and three disadvantages of prototyping.

**4** **IT Flash Magazine**

**Situation:**

You are a staff writer at IT Flash Magazine, a popular online newsletter aimed at IT professionals. Your editor has asked you to prepare a special report for next week's edition. Specifically, she wants you to research the subject of software outsourcing, and other significant trends that might affect software development in the future. If possible, she wants you to cite specific sources for your information, including IT employment statistics and employment forecasts from the Bureau of Labor Statistics.

1. Search for information about software outsourcing generally, using the search techniques described in Appendix D.
2. Visit the Bureau of Labor Statistics site at bls.gov and search for information about employment trends affecting systems analysts, computer programmers, and software engineers.
3. Does the Bureau of Labor Statistics offer any comments or insights into the subject of outsourcing generally? What conclusions does it reach?
4. In your report, comment on whether the offshore outsourcing of IT jobs is just another step in the progression that began with manufacturing jobs, or represents a whole new trend. Be sure to cite Web research sources and your own reasons.

# Case Studies

Case studies allow you to practice specific skills learned in the chapter. Each chapter contains several case studies that continue throughout the textbook, and a chapter capstone case.

## New Century Health Clinic

New Century Health Clinic offers preventive medicine and traditional medical care. In your role as an IT consultant, you will help New Century develop a new information system.

### Background

Based on your earlier recommendations, New Century decided to continue the systems development process for a new information system that would improve operations, decrease costs, and provide better service to patients.

Now, at the end of the systems analysis phase, you are ready to prepare a system requirements document and give a presentation to the New Century associates. Many of the proposed system's advantages were described during the fact-finding process. Those include smoother operation, better efficiency, and more user-friendly procedures for patients and New Century staff.

You also must examine tangible costs and benefits to determine the economic feasibility of several alternatives. If New Century decides to go ahead with the development process, the main options are to develop the system in-house or purchase a vertical package and configure it to meet New Century's needs. You have studied those choices and put together some preliminary figures.

You know that New Century's current workload requires three hours of office staff overtime per week at a base rate of $8.50 per hour. In addition, based on current projections, New Century will need to add another full-time clerical position in about six months. Neither the overtime nor the additional job will be needed if New Century implements the new system. The current manual system also causes an average of three errors per day, and each error takes about 20 minutes to correct. The new system should eliminate those errors.

Based on your research, you estimate by working full-time you could complete the project in about 12 weeks. Your consulting rate, which New Century agreed to, is $30 per hour. If you design the new system as a database application, you can expect to spend about $2,500 for a networked commercial package. After the system is operational and the staff is trained, New Century should be able to handle routine maintenance tasks without your assistance.

As an alternative to in-house development, a vertical software package is available for about $9,000. The vendor offers a lease-purchase package of $3,000 down, followed by two annual installments of $3,000 each. If New Century buys the package, it would take you about four weeks to install, configure, and test it, working full-time. The vendor provides free support during the first year of operation, but then New Century must sign a technical support agreement at an annual cost of $500. Although the package contains many of the features that New Century wants, most of the reports are pre-designed and it would be difficult to modify their layouts.

No matter which approach is selected, New Century probably will need you to provide about 10 hours of initial training and support each week for the first three months of operation. After the new system is operational, it will need routine maintenance, file backups, and updating. These tasks will require about four hours per week and can be performed by a clinic staff member. In both cases, the necessary hardware and network installation will cost about $5,000.

In your view, the useful life of the system will be about five years, including the year in which the system becomes operational.

## Assignments

You scheduled a presentation to New Century in one week, and you must submit a system requirements document during the presentation. Prepare both the written documentation and the presentation. (To give a successful presentation, you will need to learn the skills described in Appendix A.) Your oral and written presentation must include the following tasks:

1. Provide an overview of the proposed system, including costs and benefits, with an explanation of the various cost-and-benefit types and categories.
2. Develop an economic feasibility analysis, using payback analysis, ROI, and present value (assume a discount rate of 10%).
3. Prepare a context diagram and diagram 0 for the new system.
4. Provide a brief explanation of the various alternatives that should be investigated if development continues, including in-house development and any other possible strategies.

You may wish to include other material to help your audience understand the new system and make a decision on the next step.

## Presentation Rules

The following presentation rules should be considered:

- Use suitable visual aids.
- Use presentation software, if possible.
- Distribute handouts before, during, or after the presentation.
- Follow the guidelines in Appendix A.
- Keep your presentation to 30 minutes, including 5 minutes for questions.

## Rules for the System Requirements Document

Consider the following rules while preparing the system requirements document:

- Follow the guidelines in Appendix A.
- Include charts, graphs, or other helpful visual information in the document.
- Spell check and carefully proofread the entire document.

# PERSONAL TRAINER, INC.

Personal Trainer, Inc., owns and operates fitness centers in a dozen Midwestern cities. The centers have done well, and the company is planning an international expansion by opening a new "supercenter" in the Toronto area. Personal Trainer's president, Cassia Umi, hired an IT consultant, Susan Park, to help develop an information system for the new facility. During the project, Susan will work closely with Gray Lewis, who will manage the new operation.

## Background

During data and process modeling, Susan Park developed a logical model of the proposed system. She drew an entity-relationship diagram and constructed a set of leveled and balanced DFDs. Now Susan is ready to consider various development strategies for the new system. She will investigate traditional and Web-based approaches and weigh the advantages and disadvantages of in-house development versus other alternatives. As she moves ahead to the systems design phase, she will review design guidelines, consider the use of prototypes, and analyze the possible use of codes.

**Before You Begin ...**

Review the facts presented in the Personal Trainer case study in Chapters 2, 4, and 5. Use that information to complete the following tasks.

**Assignments**

1. Should the new system be designed as a Web-based system? Why or why not? What are some specific issues and options that Susan should consider in making a decision?

2. Assume that Cassia Umi, Personal Trainer's president, has asked Susan to prepare a system requirements document and deliver a presentation to the management team. What should be the main elements of the system requirements document? Also, based on the suggestions in Appendix A, what visual aids should Susan use during her presentation?

3. Should Susan use a prototype during systems design? What options does she have, and how would you advise her?

4. Susan wants to prepare a presentation that will calculate the total cost of ownership for the system. What financial analysis tools are available to her, and what are the advantages (and possible disadvantages) of each tool?

## CHAPTER CAPSTONE CASE:    SoftWear, Limited          SWL

SoftWear, Limited (SWL), is a continuing case study that illustrates the knowledge and skills described in each chapter. In this case study, the student acts as a member of the SWL systems development team and performs various tasks.

### Background

Systems analyst Rick Williams and programmer/analyst Carla Moore continued to work on a logical model of the payroll system. Meanwhile, the information systems department recently purchased and installed Visible Analyst, a CASE toolkit that supports logical and physical modeling. Rick and Carla traveled to Massachusetts to attend a one-week workshop to learn how to use the package.

After returning from their trip, Rick and Carla decided to create the logical model for the payroll system with Visible Analyst. They felt that the time spent now would pay off in later phases of the project. Rick and Carla used the manual DFDs they created in Chapter 5 to create computerized DFDs using Visible Analyst. Now all related items for the new system are stored in the CASE tool.

Over the next month, Rick and Carla looked at various alternatives and spent their time evaluating the potential solutions. They determined that the best solution was to purchase a payroll package, but the ESIP processing was so unique that none of the available software packages would handle SWL's specific requirements. They concluded that SWL should purchase a payroll package and develop the ESIP system in-house. Jane Rossman and Ann Hon agreed with their recommendation.

The systems analysts completed work on the logical model, alternative evaluations, and cost and time estimates and then prepared the system requirements document for the payroll system. The document was printed and distributed and a management presentation was scheduled at the end of the following week.

At this point, the IT team members were confident that they had done a good job. They had worked closely with SWL users throughout the development process and received user approval on important portions of the document as it was being prepared. They developed visual aids, rehearsed the presentation, and then tried to anticipate questions that management might ask.

Carla gave the management presentation. She recommended that SWL purchase a payroll package sold by Pacific Software Solutions and that ESIP processing be developed in-house to interface with the payroll package.

During the presentation, Carla and Rick answered questions on several points, including the economic analysis they had done. Michael Jeremy, vice president of finance, was especially interested in the method they used to calculate payback analysis, return on investment, and net present value for the new system.

Robert Lansing, SWL's president, arrived for the last part of the presentation. When the presentation ended, he asked the top managers how they felt about the project, and they indicated support for the proposal made by the IT department. The next step was to negotiate a contract with Pacific Software Solutions and for Rick and Carla to begin systems design for the ESIP processing component.

### SWL Team Tasks

1. Although the presentation was successful, Rick and Carla ask you to create a checklist of presentation dos and don'ts that would be helpful for IT staff people who deliver presentations.

2. Rick and Carla also want you to review the DFDs that they prepared to see if you have any suggestions for improvement. If you have access to a copier, make a copy of the DFDs shown in Chapter 5 and then write your notes directly on the diagrams.

## CHAPTER CAPSTONE CASE:  SoftWear, Limited (continued)                  SWL

3. Michael Jeremy, vice president of finance, was interested in the financial analysis tools that Rick and Carla used in the presentation. Rick has asked you to write a memo to Mr. Jeremy explaining each tool, with a specific description of how it is used, and what results can be obtained. Before you do this, you should review the material in Appendix C.

4. Although SWL decided to develop the ESIP system in-house, Ann Hon, director of information technology, has requested a report on the trend toward outsourcing software development. Perform Internet research to get up-to-date information about this topic, and prepare a memo for Ms. Hon. Be sure to cite your sources of information.

### Manage the SWL Project

You have been asked to manage SWL's new information system project. One of your most important activities will be to identify project tasks and determine when they will be performed. Before you begin, you should review the SWL case in this chapter. Then list and analyze the tasks, as follows:

**LIST THE TASKS** Start by listing and numbering at least ten tasks that the SWL team needs to perform to fulfill the objectives of this chapter. Your list can include SWL Team Tasks and any other tasks that are described in this chapter. For example, Task 3 might be to Evaluate system requirements, and Task 6 might be to Prepare an RFP.

**ANALYZE THE TASKS** Now study the tasks to determine the order in which they should be performed. First identify all concurrent tasks, which are not dependent on other tasks. In the example shown in Figure 7-31, Tasks 1, 2, 3, 4, and 5 are concurrent tasks, and could begin at the same time if resources were available.

Other tasks are called dependent tasks, because they cannot be performed until one or more earlier tasks have been completed. For each dependent task, you must identify specific tasks that need to be completed before this task can begin. For example, you would want to evaluate system requirements before you could prepare an RFP, so Task 6 cannot begin until Task 3 is completed, as Figure 7-31 shows.

**FIGURE 7-31** Tasks 1, 2, 3, 4, and 5 are concurrent tasks that could be performed at the same time. Task 6 is a dependent task that cannot be performed until Task 3 has been completed.

Chapter 3 describes project management tools, techniques, and software. To learn more, you can use the Features section on your Student Study Tool CD-ROM, or visit the Management Information Systems CourseMate Web site at **www.cengagebrain.com** and locate the project management resources library for this book. On the Web, Microsoft offers demo versions, training, and tips for using Project 2010. You also can visit the OpenWorkbench.org site to learn more about this free, open-source software.

# Ready for a Challenge?

You are helping the IT team at Game Technology study several software acquisition options for their Customer Contact Care system ($C^3$). First, you review Chapter 7 of your systems analysis textbook and the material on financial analysis tools, including the Video Learning Sessions. The IT team is considering two commercial software packages and an in-house development option. They prepared the following summary.

| Option | Description | Costs | Benefits |
|---|---|---|---|
| Software Solutions, Inc. | Software package<br>Four-year useful life<br>Less flexible than in-house system<br>Some customizing needed | $8,000 to purchase<br>$1,500 to install and configure<br>$2,500 to load existing data<br>$1,000 additional hardware needed<br>$2,000 annual support fee after first year free | $9,000/yr through positive customer response. Cannot predict other specific savings. Increased sales, improved customer care, and better productivity are expected. |
| CRM Corp. | Software package<br>Five-year useful life<br>Less flexible than in-house system<br>Moderate customizing needed<br>Runs slower than other options | $7,000 to purchase<br>$2,500 to install and configure<br>$2,000 to load existing data<br>$4,000 additional hardware needed<br>$1,200 annual support fee in all five years | Same as above |
| Develop $C^3$ system in-house | In-house system<br>Six-year useful life, can use our software and hardware<br>Easiest to update and maintain | $15,000 to develop, install, and configure<br>$1,000 to load existing data<br>Existing staff can handle support | Same as above |

### Practice Tasks

Study the summary carefully and prepare spreadsheet templates, or navigate to the Forms Library at the MIS CourseMate for this book at **www.cengagebrain.com**. You should assume that all three options require a six-month period for acquisition or development, installation, configuration, and data loading. This period is called Year 0. Actual operation begins in Year 1. Now complete these tasks:

A. Perform ROI **and** NPV analysis of the Software Solutions package. Use an 8% discount factor.

B. Perform ROI analysis of the in-house development option.

After you complete the Practice Tasks, to check your work and view sample answers, visit the Management Information Systems CourseMate Web site at **www.cengagebrain.com**, navigate to the resources for this chapter, and locate Ready for a Challenge?.

### The Challenge

Now you will work on your own to finish up the remaining financial analysis tasks. Again, you can prepare spreadsheet templates, or navigate to the Forms Library (see above).

### Challenge Tasks

A. Perform ROI and NPV analysis of the CRM package. Use an 8% discount factor.

B. Perform NPV analysis of the in-house option. Use an 8% discount factor.

# PHASE 3 SYSTEMS DESIGN

**DELIVERABLE**
System design specification

**SUPPORT**
Primary tools: Communications and CASE tools

**VIDEO LEARNING SESSIONS**
Entity Relationship Diagrams, Data Normalization

As the Dilbert cartoon suggests, you should understand a problem before you decide that a database is the solution. You will learn more about systems design topics, including database design, in the systems design phase.

Systems design is the third of five phases in the systems development life cycle. In the previous phase, systems analysis, you developed a logical model of the new system. Now you will work on a physical design that will meet the specifications described in the system requirements document. Your tasks will include user interface design, data design, and system architecture. The deliverable for this phase is the system design specification.

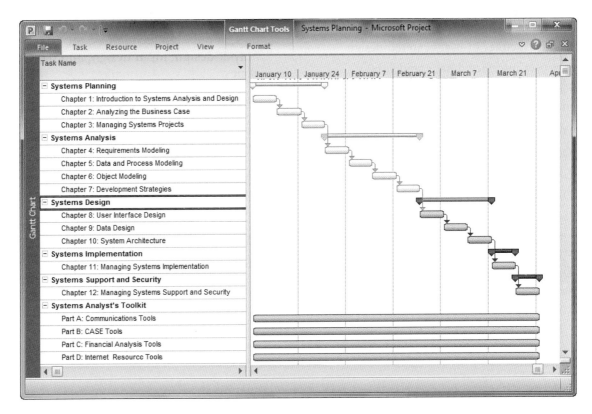

# CHAPTER 8 Designing the Interface

**Chapter 8** is the first of three chapters in the systems design phase of the SDLC. This chapter explains how to design an effective user interface, and how to handle data output, input, and security issues. The chapter stresses the importance of user feedback and involvement in all design decisions.

## INTRODUCTION

### OBJECTIVES

*When you finish this chapter, you will be able to:*

- Explain the concept of user interface design and human-computer interaction, including basic principles of user-centered design

- List user interface design guidelines

- Describe user interface components, including screen elements and controls

- Discuss output design and technology issues

- Design effective source documents

- Explain input design and technology issues

- Discuss guidelines for data entry screen design

- Use input masks and validation rules to reduce input errors

- Describe output and input controls and security

User interface design is the first task in the systems design phase of the SDLC. Designing the interface is extremely important, because everyone wants a system that is easy to learn and use.

After discussing user interface evolution, principles, and design techniques, the chapter describes output design, input design, and data security issues.

## CHAPTER INTRODUCTION CASE:    Mountain View College Bookstore

**Background:** Wendy Lee, manager of college services at Mountain View College, wants a new information system that will improve efficiency and customer service at the three college bookstores.

In this part of the case, Tina Allen (systems analyst) and David Conroe (student intern) are talking about user interface design issues.

| | |
|---|---|
| **Participants:** | Tina and David |
| **Location:** | Mountain View College Cafeteria, Monday afternoon, November 28, 2011 |
| **Project status:** | Tina and David have examined development strategies for the new bookstore system. After performing cost-benefit analysis, they recommended in-house development of the new bookstore system. Now they are ready to begin the systems design phase by working on user interface design for the new system. |
| **Discussion topics:** | User interface design concepts and principles |

**Tina:**   Hi, David. Ready to start work on user interface design?

**David:**   *Sure. Will we start with output, because it's important to users?*

**Tina:**   Output is very important, but the *most* important issue for users is the interface itself. For example, is it easy to learn? Is it easy to work with? We'll try to design everything — output, input, and all the other elements — from a user's point of view.

**David:**   *How do we do that?*

**Tina:**   Well, many sources of information about effective design concepts and principles are available. We'll study those, and then ask our own users for their input and suggestions.

**David:**   *What about input and data entry?*

**Tina:**   Good question. You've heard the old saying, "garbage in, garbage out." User interface principles apply to user input generally, but repetitive data entry deserves special attention. We need to create screen forms that are logical and easy to understand, as well as input masks and data entry validation rules. We also need to review any source documents that will be filled in manually.

**David:**   *Anything else?*

**Tina:**   Yes. The bookstore system probably will have some confidential data regarding budgets and markup policies, so we'll have to consider output and input control and security. If you're ready, here's a task list to get us started:

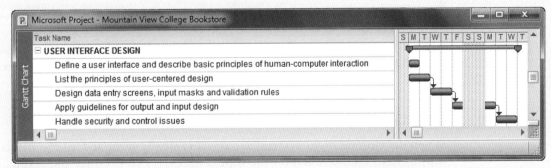

**FIGURE 8-1** Typical user interface design tasks.

**ON THE WEB**

To learn more about user interface design, visit the Management Information Systems CourseMate Web site at **www.cengagebrain.com**, navigate to **On the Web Links** for this chapter, and locate the User Interface Design link.

# WHAT IS A USER INTERFACE?

A **user interface (UI)** describes how users interact with a computer system, and consists of all the hardware, software, screens, menus, functions, output, and features that affect two-way communications between the user and the computer.

Figure 8-2 suggests an interesting viewpoint that interface designers should keep in mind: Industry leader IBM believes that the best interfaces are the ones that users do not even notice — they make sense because they do what users expect them to do.

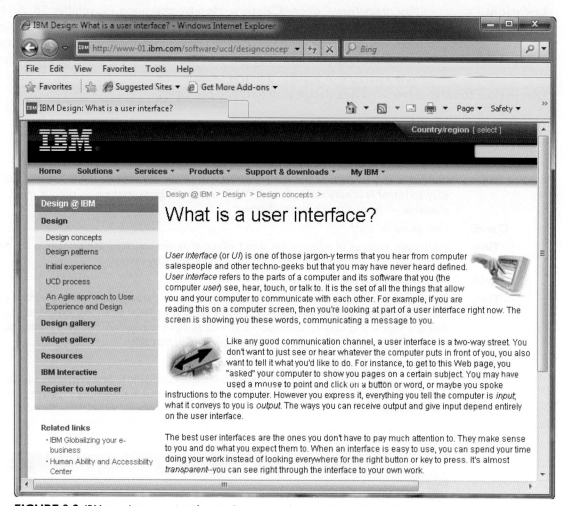

**FIGURE 8-2** IBM says that a user interface is what you see, hear, touch, or talk to when you use a computer.

## Evolution of the User Interface

When developing older systems, analysts typically designed all the printed and screen output first, then worked on the inputs necessary to produce the results. Often, the user interface mainly consisted of **process-control** screens that allowed the user to send commands to the system. That approach worked well with traditional systems that simply transformed input data into structured output.

As information management evolved from centralized data processing to dynamic, enterprise-wide systems, the primary focus also shifted — from the IT department to the users themselves. The IT group became a supplier of information technology, rather than a supplier of information. Today, the main focus is on users within and outside the company, how they communicate with the information system, and how the system supports the firm's business operations. Figure 8-3 compares a traditional, processing-centered information system with a modern, user-centered system. Notice that the IT department, which was the main interface for user information requests, has become a system facilitator that maintains and supports the system for its users.

In a **user-centered** system, the distinction blurs between input, output, and the interface itself. Most users work with a varied mix of input, screen output, and data queries as they perform their day-to-day job functions. Because all those tasks require interaction with the computer system, the user interface is a vital element in the systems design phase. Ergosoft laboratories is one of many firms that offer consulting services and software solutions to help companies develop successful user interfaces, as shown in Figure 8-4 on the next page.

User interface design requires an understanding of human-computer interaction and user-centered design principles, which are discussed in the next section. Input and output design topics are covered later in this chapter.

**Traditional, Processing-Centered Information System Model**

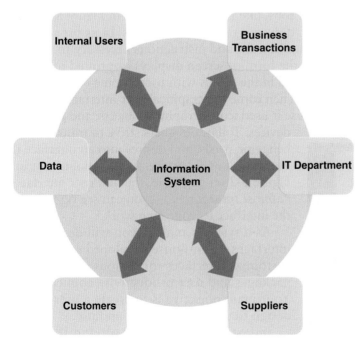

**Modern, User-Centered Information System Model**

**FIGURE 8-3** Compare the traditional, processing-centered system at the top of the figure with the modern, user-centered information system at the bottom. Notice the change in the role of the IT department.

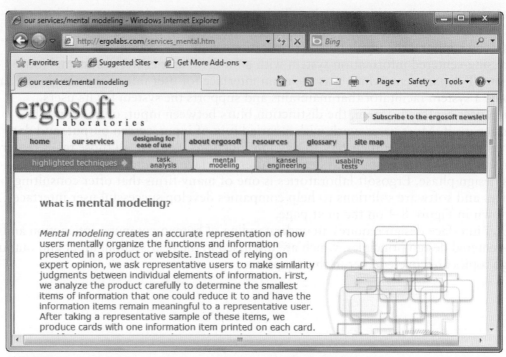

**FIGURE 8-4** Ergosoft laboratories is an example of a firm that offers consulting services and software solutions to help companies develop successful user interfaces.

## Human-Computer Interaction

A user interface is based on basic principles of human-computer interaction. **Human-computer interaction (HCI)** describes the relationship between computers and people who use them to perform their jobs, like the worker shown in Figure 8-5. HCI concepts apply to everything from PC desktops to global networks. In its broadest sense, a user interface includes all the communications and instructions necessary to enter input to the system and to obtain output in the form of screen displays or printed reports.

The human-computer interface started in the 1980s with users typing complex commands in green text on a black screen. Then came the **graphical user interface (GUI)**, which was a huge improvement, because it used icons, graphical objects, and pointing devices. Today, designers strive to translate user behavior, needs, and desires into an interface that users don't really notice. As IBM points out in Figure 8-2 on page 336, the best user interfaces are *"almost transparent — you can see right though the interface to your own work."*

As a systems analyst, you will design user interfaces for in-house developed software and customize interfaces for various commercial packages and user productivity applications. Your main objective is to create a user-friendly design that is easy to learn and use.

Industry leaders Microsoft and IBM both devote considerable resources to user interface research. Figure 8-6 describes Microsoft's Redmond labs, where engineers observe volunteers who participate in software usability studies.

**FIGURE 8-5** HCI is essential to employee productivity, whether the work is done in a traditional office setting, or on a construction site like the one shown here.

At its Almaden Research Center, IBM conducts usability testing and studies human-computer interaction, as shown in Figure 8-7. According to IBM, its User Sciences & Experience Research (USER) lab focuses on improving ease of use and exploring new ways of using computers.

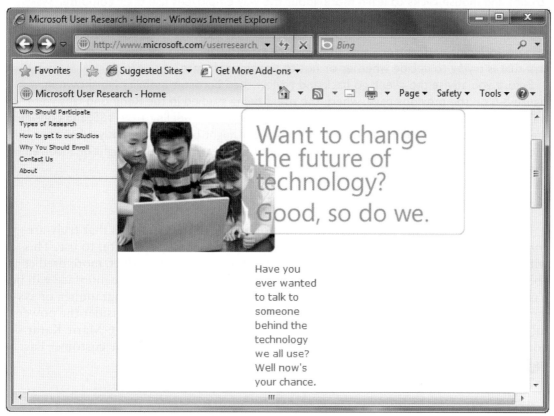

**FIGURE 8-6**  Microsoft invites people to participate in software usability studies at its labs.

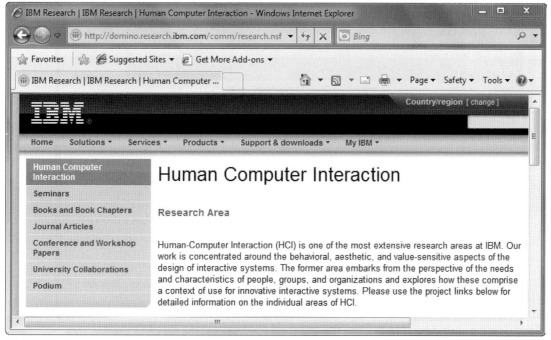

**FIGURE 8-7**  According to IBM, human-computer interaction (HCI) is one of the most extensive research areas at the company.

## CASE IN POINT 8.1:  CASUAL OBSERVER SOFTWARE

Casual Observer Software's main product is a program that monitors and analyzes user keystrokes and mouse clicks to learn more about the way employees use their computer systems. The problem is that some users feel this is an unwarranted intrusion into their privacy, and they prefer not to be observed. Some even fear that the data would be used for other reasons, including performance appraisal. You are a consultant who has been hired by a client firm that is trying to decide whether or not to use this software.

Before you advise the client, go back and review the Microsoft usability lab shown in Figure 8-6 on the previous page, where the users being studied in the Redmond labs were willing participants. Then, refer to Chapter 4, Requirements Modeling, page 165, and consider the Hawthorne Effect, which suggests that employees might behave differently when they know they are being observed. Finally, think about the ethical issues that might be involved in this situation. What will you advise your client, and why?

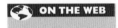
**ON THE WEB**

To learn more about human-computer interaction, visit the Management Information Systems CourseMate Web site at **www. cengagebrain. com**, navigate to **On the Web Links** for this chapter, and locate the Human-Computer Interaction link.

IBM believes that the user interface evolution will lead to computers that truly are *consumer products* that are simple and natural for the general population to use. This will occur, in IBM's view, because computers will function in a friendlier, more predictable way — much like a telephone or video player. Most important, the interface will be based on the perspective of a user rather than a computer engineer, programmer, or systems analyst. To understand the magnitude of this shift in thinking, consider the powerful statement shown in Figure 8-8, where IBM usability expert Dr. Clare-Marie Karat notes that "in this new computer age, the customer is not only right, the customer has rights." Those rights are listed in Figure 8-9.

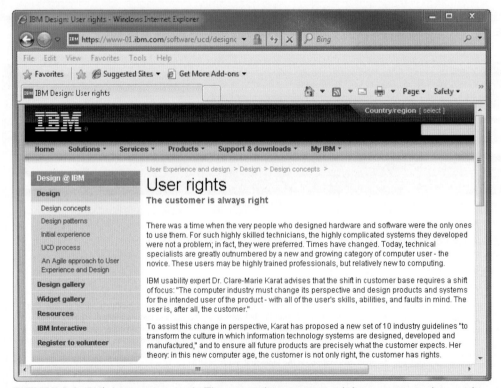

**FIGURE 8-8** IBM's logic is very simple: The user is the customer, and the customer is always right.

**User Rights**

1. **Perspective:** The user always is right. If there is a problem with the use of the system, the system is the problem, not the user.
2. **Installation:** The user has the right to install and uninstall software and hardware systems easily without negative consequences.
3. **Compliance:** The user has the right to a system that performs exactly as promised.
4. **Instruction:** The user has the right to easy-to-use instructions (user guides, online or contextual help, and error messages) for understanding and utilizing a system to achieve desired goals and recover efficiently and gracefully from problem situations.
5. **Control:** The user has the right to be in control of the system and to be able to get the system to respond to a request for attention.
6. **Feedback:** The user has the right to a system that provides clear, understandable, and accurate information regarding the task it is performing and the progress toward completion.
7. **Dependencies:** The user has the right to be informed clearly about all systems requirements for successfully using software or hardware.
8. **Scope:** The user has the right to know the limits of the system's capabilities.
9. **Assistance:** The user has the right to communicate with the technology provider and receive a thoughtful and helpful response when raising concerns.
10. **Usability:** The user should be the master of software and hardware technology, not vice versa. Products should be natural and intuitive to use.

**FIGURE 8-9** User rights suggested by IBM's Dr. Clare-Marie Karat.

## PRINCIPLES OF USER-CENTERED DESIGN

Although IT professionals have different views about interface design, most would agree that good design depends on seven basic principles, which are described in the following sections.

### Understand the Business

The interface designer must understand the underlying business functions and how the system supports individual, departmental, and enterprise goals. The overall objective is to design an interface that helps users to perform their jobs. A good starting point might be to analyze a functional decomposition diagram (FDD). As you learned in Chapter 4, an FDD is a graphical representation of business functions that starts with major functions, and then breaks them down into several levels of detail. An FDD can provide a checklist of user tasks that you must include in the interface design.

### Maximize Graphical Effectiveness

Studies show that people learn better visually. The immense popularity of Apple Mac OS and Microsoft Windows is largely the result of their graphical user interfaces that are easy to learn and use. A well-designed interface can help users learn a new system rapidly, and be more productive. Also, in a graphical environment, a user can display and work with multiple windows on a single screen and transfer data between programs. If the interface supports data entry, it must follow the guidelines for data entry screen design that are discussed later in this chapter.

### Think Like a User

A systems analyst should understand user experience, knowledge, and skill levels. If a wide range of capability exists, the interface should be flexible enough to accommodate novices as well as experienced users.

To develop a user-centered interface, the designer must learn to think like a user and see the system through a user's eyes. The interface should use terms and metaphors that are familiar to users. Users are likely to have real-world experience with many other

**VIDEO LEARNING SESSIONS**

To learn more about FDDs, visit the Management Information Systems CourseMate Web site at **www. cengagebrain. com** and navigate to the **Video Learning Sessions** for this book. These sessions can help you understand key concepts, practice your skills, and check your work.

machines and devices that provide feedback, such as automobiles, ATM machines, and microwave ovens. Based on that experience, users will expect useful, understandable feedback from a computer system.

## Use Models and Prototypes

From a user's viewpoint, the interface is the most critical part of the system design because it is where he or she interacts with the system — perhaps for many hours each day. It is essential to construct models and prototypes for user approval. An interface designer should obtain as much feedback as possible, as early as possible. You can present initial screen designs to users in the form of a **storyboard,** which is a sketch that shows the general screen layout and design. The storyboard can be created with software, or drawn freehand. Users must test all aspects of the interface design and provide feedback to the designers. User input can be obtained in interviews, via questionnaires, and by observation. Interface designers also can obtain data, called **usability metrics,** by using software that can record and measure user interaction with the system.

## Focus on Usability

The Communication Tools in Appendix A can help you communicate effectively with users. To learn more about these tools, turn to Appendix A.

The user interface should include all tasks, commands, and communications between users and the information system. The screen in Figure 8-10 shows the main options for a student registration system. Each screen option leads to another screen, with more options. The objective is to offer a reasonable number of choices that a user easily can comprehend. Too many options on one screen can confuse a user — but too few options increase the number of submenu levels and complicate the navigation process. Often, an effective strategy is to present the most common choice as a default, but allow the user to select other options.

## Invite Feedback

Even after the system is operational, it is important to monitor system usage and solicit user suggestions. You can determine if system features are being used as intended by observing and surveying users. Sometimes, full-scale operations highlight problems that were not apparent when the prototype was tested. Based on user feedback, Help screens might need revision and design changes to allow the system to reach its full potential.

## Document Everything

You should document all screen designs for later use by programmers. If you are using a CASE tool or screen generator, number the screen designs and save them in a hierarchy similar to a menu tree. User-approved sketches and storyboards also can be used to document the user interface.

By applying basic user-centered design principles, a systems analyst can plan, design, and deliver a successful user interface.

## DESIGNING THE USER INTERFACE

It is important to design a user interface that is easy to use, attractive, and efficient. When you create a user interface, you should follow eight basic guidelines. These guidelines also apply to data entry screen design, which is discussed later in this chapter.

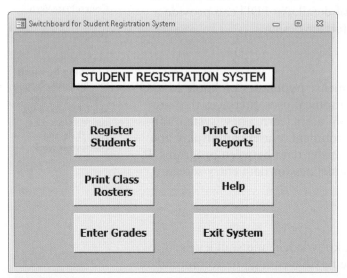

**FIGURE 8-10** The opening screen displays the main options for a student registration system. A user can click an option to see lower-level actions and menu choices.

1. Design a transparent interface.
2. Create an interface that is easy to learn and use.
3. Enhance user productivity.
4. Make it easy for users to obtain help or correct errors.
5. Minimize input data problems.
6. Provide feedback to users.
7. Create an attractive layout and design.
8. Use familiar terms and images.

Good user interface design is based on a combination of ergonomics, aesthetics, and interface technology. **Ergonomics** describes how people work, learn, and interact with computers; **aesthetics** focuses on how an interface can be made attractive and easy to use; and **interface technology** provides the operational structure required to carry out the design objectives. As shown in Figure 8-11, Cognetics Corporation offers user interface design services. Cognetics stresses that an interface must be effective, efficient, engaging, error tolerant, and easy to learn.

The following sections provide examples of the basic user interface design guidelines. As mentioned earlier, many of the specific points also apply to data entry screen design, which is discussed later in this chapter.

### Design a Transparent Interface

- Facilitate the system design objectives, rather than calling attention to the interface.
- Create a design that is easy to learn and remember.
- Design the interface to improve user efficiency and productivity.
- Write commands, actions, and system responses that are consistent and predictable.
- Minimize data entry problems.
- Allow users to correct errors easily.
- Create a logical and attractive layout.

**FIGURE 8-11** Cognetics Corporation offers user interface design services and training.

Data overload! Please start over.

Data is not suitable.

Check the instructions for this task and the previous task!

Not enough data to proceed.

The data is incorrect.

Please use the proper format: Three letters followed by three numbers, with no spaces. Example: CTS285

**FIGURE 8-12** In the example at the top, the icons do not have a clear message. In the Help text examples at the bottom, only one message is understandable. The others would frustrate and annoy most users.

## Create an Interface that Is Easy to Learn and Use

- Clearly label all controls, buttons, and icons.
- Select only those images that users can understand easily, and provide on-screen instructions that are logical, concise, and clear. Users become very frustrated when they see images or messages that are confusing or misleading. For example, the top screen in Figure 8-12 shows four control buttons, but many of them do not have an obvious meaning. In the bottom screen, notice the difference in the messages: The first five provide little or no information. The last message is the only one that is easy to understand.
- Show all commands in a list of menu items, but dim any commands that are not currently available.
- Make it easy to navigate or return to any level in the menu structure.

## Enhance User Productivity

- Organize tasks, commands, and functions in groups that resemble actual business operations. You should group functions and submenu items in a multilevel menu hierarchy, or tree, that is logical and reflects how users typically perform the tasks. Figure 8-13 shows an example of a menu hierarchy for an order tracking system.
- Create alphabetical menu lists or place the selections used frequently at the top of the menu list. No universally accepted approach to menu item placement exists. The best strategy is to design a prototype and obtain feedback from users. Some applications even allow menus to show recently used commands first. Some users like that feature, but others might find it distracting. The best approach is to offer a choice, and let users decide.
- Provide shortcuts so experienced users can avoid multiple menu levels. You can create shortcuts using hot keys that allow a user to press the ALT key + the underlined letter of a command.
- Use default values if the majority of values in a field are the same. For example, if 90% of the firm's customers live in Albuquerque, use *Albuquerque* as the default value in the City field.
- Use a duplicate value function that enables users to insert the value from the same field in the previous record.
- Provide a fast-find feature that displays a list of possible values as soon as users enter the first few letters.
- Use a **natural language** feature that allows users to type commands or requests in normal English phrases. For example, many applications allow users to request Help by typing a question into a dialog box. The software then uses natural language technology to retrieve a list of topics that match the request. Most users like natural language features because they do not have to memorize a series of complex commands and syntax. According to the American Association for Artificial Intelligence (AAAI), the value of being able to communicate with computers in everyday "natural" language cannot be overstated. Natural language technology is used in speech recognition systems, text-to-speech synthesizers, automated voice response systems, Web search engines, text editors, and language instruction materials.

## Make It Easy for Users to Obtain Help or Correct Errors

- Ensure that help is always available. Help screens should provide information about menu choices, procedures, shortcuts, and errors.

- Provide user-selected help and context-sensitive help. **User-selected** help displays information when the user requests it. By making appropriate choices through the menus and submenus, the user eventually reaches a screen with the desired information. Figure 8-14 shows the main Help screen for the student registration system. **Context-sensitive** help offers assistance for the task in progress. Figure 8-15 on the next page shows a Help dialog box that is displayed if a user requests help while entering data into the ADVISOR ASSIGNED field. Clicking the Close button returns the user to the current task.

- Provide a direct route for users to return to the point from where help was requested. Title every help screen to identify the topic, and keep help text simple and concise. Insert blank lines between paragraphs to make Help easier to read, and provide examples where appropriate.

- Include contact information, such as a telephone extension or e-mail address if a department or help desk is responsible for assisting users.

- Require user confirmation before data deletion (*Are you sure?*) and provide a method of recovering data that is deleted inadvertently. Build in safeguards that prevent critical data from being changed or erased.

- Provide an Undo key or a menu choice that allows the user to eradicate the results of the most recent command or action.

- When a user-entered command contains an error, highlight the erroneous part and allow the user to make the correction without retyping the entire command.

- Use hypertext links to assist users as they navigate through help topics.

**Customer Order Tracking System**

**FIGURE 8-13** This menu hierarchy shows tasks, commands, and functions organized into logical groups and sequences. The structure resembles a functional decomposition diagram (FDD), which is a model of business functions and processes.

**FIGURE 8-14** The main Help screen for a student registration system.

**FIGURE 8-15** A context-sensitive dialog box displays if a user requests help while entering data into the ADVISOR ASSIGNED field. Clicking the Close button returns the user to the task.

## Minimize Input Data Problems

- Create **input masks,** which are templates or patterns that make it easier for users to enter data. Also use data validation rules, which limit the acceptable values that users can enter. More information on input masks and data validation rules is provided in the section on input design later in the chapter.

- Display event-driven messages and reminders. Just as context-sensitive help is important to users, it is desirable to display an appropriate message when it is time for the user to perform a certain task. For example, when exiting the system, a message might ask users if they want a printed report of the data entered during the recent session.

- Establish a list of predefined values that users can click to select. Predefined values prevent spelling errors, avoid inappropriate data in a field, and make the user's job easier — the input screen displays a list of acceptable values and the user simply points and clicks the choice.

- Build in rules that enforce data integrity. For example, if the user tries to enter an order for a new customer, the customer must be added before the system will accept the order data.

## Provide Feedback to Users

- Display messages at a logical place on the screen, and be consistent.

- Alert users to lengthy processing times or delays. Give users an on-screen progress report, especially if the delay is lengthy.

- Allow messages to remain on the screen long enough for users to read them. In some cases, the screen should display messages until the user takes some action.

- Let the user know whether the task or operation was successful or not. For example, use messages such as Update completed, All transactions have been posted, or ID Number not found.

- Provide a text explanation if you use an icon or image on a control button. This helps the user to identify the control button when moving the mouse pointer over the icon or image.

- Use messages that are specific, understandable, and professional. Avoid messages that are cute, cryptic, or vague, such as: *ERROR — You have entered an unacceptable value,* or *Error DE4-16.* Better examples are: *Enter a number between 1 and 5; Customer number must be numeric. Please re-enter a numeric value;* or *Call the Accounting Department, Ext. 239 for assistance.*

## Create an Attractive Layout and Design

- Use appropriate colors to highlight different areas of the screen; avoid gaudy and bright colors.

- Use special effects sparingly. For example, animation and sound might be effective in some situations, but too many special effects can be distracting and annoying to a user, especially if he or she must view them repeatedly.

- Use hyperlinks that allow users to jump to related topics.

- Group related objects and information. Visualize the screen the way a user will see it, and simulate the tasks that the user will perform.

- Screen density is important. Keep screen displays uncluttered, with enough white space to create an attractive, readable design.

- Display titles, messages, and instructions in a consistent manner and in the same general locations on all screens.

- Use consistent terminology. For example, do not use the terms *delete*, *cancel*, and *erase* to indicate the same action. Similarly, the same sound always should signal the same event.

- Ensure that commands always will have the same effect. For example, if the *BACK* control button returns a user to the prior screen, the *BACK* command always should perform that function throughout the application.

- Ensure that similar mouse actions will produce the same results throughout the application. The results of pointing, clicking, and double-clicking should be consistent and predictable.

- When the user enters data that completely fills the field, do not move automatically to the next field. Instead, require the user to confirm the entry by pressing the ENTER key or TAB key at the end of every fill-in field.

## Use Familiar Terms and Images

- Remember that users are accustomed to a pattern of *red = stop*, *yellow = caution*, and *green = go*. Stick to that pattern and use it when appropriate to reinforce on-screen instructions.

- Provide a keystroke alternative for each menu command, with easy-to-remember letters, such as File, Exit, and Help.

- Use familiar commands if possible, such as Cut, Copy, and Paste.

- Provide a Windows look and feel in your interface design if users are familiar with Windows-based applications.

- Avoid complex terms and technical jargon; instead, select terms that come from everyday business processes and the vocabulary of a typical user.

## Add Control Features

The designer can include many features, such as menu bars, toolbars, dialog boxes, text boxes, toggle buttons, list boxes, scroll bars, drop-down list boxes, option buttons, check boxes, command buttons, and calendar controls, among others. Figure 8-16 on the next page shows a data entry screen for the student registration system. The screen design uses several features that are described in the following section.

The **menu bar** at the top of the screen displays the main menu options. Some software packages allow you to create customized menu bars and toolbars. You can add a shortcut feature that lets a user select a menu command either by clicking the desired choice or by pressing the ALT key + the underlined letter. Some forms also use a **toolbar** that contains icons or buttons that represent shortcuts for executing common commands.

A **command button** initiates an action such as printing a form or requesting help. For example, when a user clicks the Find Student command button in Figure 8-16, a dialog box opens with instructions, as shown in Figure 8-17.

Other design features include dialog boxes, text boxes, toggle buttons, list boxes, scroll bars, drop-down list boxes, option or radio buttons, check boxes, and calendar controls. These features are described as follows:

- A **dialog box** allows a user to enter information about a task that the system will perform.

- A **text box** can display messages or provide a place for a user to enter data.

- A **toggle button** is used to represent on or off status — clicking the toggle button switches to the other status.

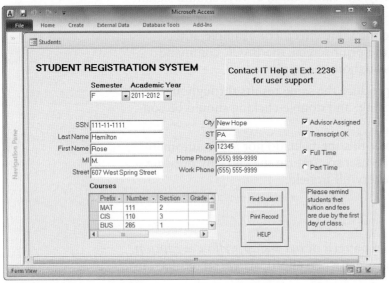

FIGURE 8-16 A data entry screen for the student registration system. This screen uses several design features that are described in the text.

FIGURE 8-17 When a user clicks the Find Student command button, a dialog box is displayed with instructions.

- A **list box** displays a list of choices that the user can select. If the list does not fit in the box, a **scroll bar** allows the user to move through the available choices.

- A **drop-down list box** displays the current selection; when the user clicks the arrow, a list of the available choices displays.

- An **option button**, or **radio button**, represents one choice in a set of options. The user can select only one option at a time, and selected options show a black dot.

- A **check box** is used to select one or more choices from a group. Selected options are represented by a checkmark or an X.

- A **calendar control** allows the user to select a date that the system will use as a field value.

Screen design requires a sense of aesthetics as well as technical skills. You should design screens that are attractive, easy to use, and workable. You also should obtain user feedback early and often as the design process continues.

The opening screen is especially important because it introduces the application and allows users to view the main options. When designing an opening screen, you can use a main form that functions as a switchboard. A **switchboard** uses command buttons that enable users to navigate the system and select from groups of related tasks. Figure 8-18 shows the switchboard and a data entry screen for a project management system. Notice the drop-down list box that allows users to enter a status code simply by clicking a selection.

**FIGURE 8-18** An example of a switchboard and data entry screen for a project management system.

## CASE IN POINT 8.2: BOOLEAN TOYS

When should a systems analyst decide a design issue, and when should users be allowed to select what works best for them? The field of ergonomics is concerned with improving the work environment and studying how users interact with their environment.

Suppose you are a systems analyst studying the order processing system at Boolean Toys, a fast-growing developer of software for preschool children. You know that many data entry users have complained about the input screens. Some users would prefer to rearrange the order of the fields; others would like to change the background color on their screens; still others want shortcuts that would allow them to avoid a series of introductory screens.

What if Boolean's users could customize their own data entry screens without assistance from the IT staff by using a menu-driven utility program? What would be the pros and cons of such an approach?

## OUTPUT DESIGN

Before designing output, ask yourself several questions:

- What is the purpose of the output?
- Who wants the information, why is it needed, and how will it be used?
- What specific information will be included?
- Will the output be printed, viewed on-screen, or both? What type of device will the output go to?
- When will the information be provided, and how often must it be updated?
- Do security or confidentiality issues exist?

The design process should not begin until you have answered those questions. Some of the information probably was gathered during the systems analysis phase. To complete your understanding, you should meet with users to find out exactly what kind of output is needed. You can use prototypes and mock-ups to obtain feedback throughout the design process. Your answers will affect your output design strategies, as you will see in the next section.

In today's interconnected world, output from one system often becomes input for another system. For example, within a company, production data from the manufacturing system becomes input to the inventory system. The same company might transmit employee W-2 tax data to the IRS system electronically. A company employee might use tax preparation software to file a tax return online, receive a refund deposited directly into his or her bank account, and see the deposit reflected on the bank's information system.

Although digital technology has opened new horizons in business communications, printed material still is a common type of output, and specific considerations apply to it. For those reasons, printed and screen reports are discussed in a separate section, which follows.

### Overview of Report Design

Although many organizations strive to reduce the flow of paper and printed reports, few firms have been able to eliminate printed output totally. Because they are portable, printed reports are convenient, and even necessary in some situations. Many users find it handy to view screen output, then print the information they need for a discussion or business meeting. Printed output also is used in **turnaround documents**, which are output documents that are later entered back into the same or another information system. In some areas, your telephone or utility bill, for example, might be a turnaround document printed by the company's billing system. When you return the required portion of the bill with your check, the bill is scanned into the company's accounts receivable system to record the payment accurately.

Designers use a variety of styles, fonts, and images to produce reports that are attractive and user friendly. Whether printed or viewed on-screen, reports must be easy to read and well organized. Rightly or wrongly, some managers judge an entire project by the quality of the reports they receive.

Database programs such as Microsoft Access include a variety of report design tools, including a Report Wizard, which is a menu-driven feature that designers can use to create reports quickly and easily. Microsoft Access also provides a comprehensive guide to designing reports, as shown in Figure 8-19.

In addition to built-in design tools, popular software packages such as Crystal Reports offer powerful features that help designers deal with professional-level design issues across the enterprise, as shown in Figure 8-20.

**FIGURE 8-19** Microsoft offers suggestions, tips, and a video that can help you design better forms and reports.

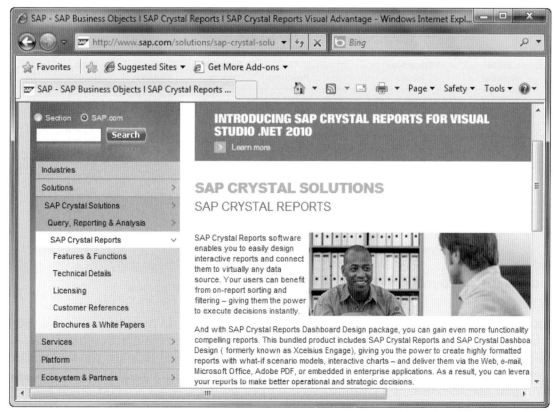

**FIGURE 8-20** Crystal Reports is a popular, powerful, report design package.

Although the vast majority of reports are designed graphically, some systems still produce one or more **character-based reports** that use a character set with fixed spacing. Printing character-based reports on high-speed impact printers is a fast, inexpensive method for producing large-scale reports, such as payroll or inventory reports, or registration rosters at a school. This is especially true if multiple copies are required.

## Types of Reports

To be useful, a report must include the information that a user needs. From a user's point of view, a report with too little information is of no value. Too much information, however, can make a report confusing and difficult to understand. When designing reports, the essential goal is to match the report to the user's specific information needs. Depending on their job functions, users might need one or more of the reports described in the following sections.

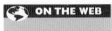

To learn more about printed output, visit the Management Information Systems CourseMate Web site at **www. cengagebrain. com**, navigate to **On the Web Links** for this chapter, and locate the Printed Output link.

**DETAIL REPORTS**  A **detail report** produces one or more lines of output for each record processed. Each line of output printed is called a **detail line**. Figure 8-21 shows a simple detail report of employee hours for a chain of retail stores. Notice that one detail line prints for each employee. All the fields in the record do not have to be printed, nor do the fields have to be printed in the sequence in which they appear in the record. An employee paycheck that has multiple output lines for a single record is another example of a detail report.

Because it contains one or more lines for each record, a detail report can be quite lengthy. Consider, for example, a large auto parts business. If the firm stocks 3,000 parts, then the detail report would include 3,000 detail lines on approximately 50 printed pages. A user who wants to locate any part in short supply has to examine 3,000 detail lines to find the critical items. A much better alternative is to produce an exception report.

| Store Number | Employee Name | Position | Regular Hours | Overtime Hours | Total Hours |
|---|---|---|---|---|---|
| | | | | | Employee Hours<br>week ending date: 6/24/11 — Page 1 | |

| Store Number | Employee Name | Position | Regular Hours | Overtime Hours | Total Hours |
|---|---|---|---|---|---|
| 8 | Andres, Marguerite | Clerk | 20.0 | 0.0 | 20.0 |
| 8 | Bogema, Michelle | Clerk | 12.5 | 0.0 | 12.5 |
| 8 | Davenport, Kim | Asst Mgr | 40.0 | 5.0 | 45.0 |
| 8 | Lemka, Susan | Clerk | 32.7 | 0.0 | 32.7 |
| 8 | Ramirez, Rudy | Manager | 40.0 | 8.5 | 48.5 |
| 8 | Ullery, Ruth | Clerk | 20.0 | 0.0 | 20.0 |
| 17 | De Martini, Jennifer | Clerk | 40.0 | 8.4 | 48.4 |
| 17 | Haff, Lisa | Manager | 40.0 | 0.0 | 40.0 |
| 17 | Rittenbery, Sandra | Clerk | 40.0 | 11.0 | 51.0 |
| 17 | Wyer, Elizabeth | Clerk | 20.0 | 0.0 | 20.0 |
| 17 | Zeigler, Cecille | Clerk | 32.0 | 0.0 | 32.0 |

detail lines

**FIGURE 8-21** A detail report with one printed line per employee.

**EXCEPTION REPORTS**  An **exception report** displays only those records that meet a specific condition or conditions. Exception reports are useful when the user wants information only on records that might require action, but does not need to know the details. For example, a credit manager might use an exception report to identify only those customers with past due accounts, or a customer service manager might want a report on all packages that were not delivered within a specified time period. Figure 8-22 shows an exception report that includes information only for those employees who worked overtime, instead of listing information for all employees.

| Store Number | Position | Employee Name | Overtime Hours |
|---|---|---|---|
| | | Overtime Report | Page 1 |
| | | week ending date: 6/24/11 | |
| 8 | Asst Mgr | Davenport, Kim | 5.0 |
| | Manager | Ramirez, Rudy | 8.5 |
| | | Store 8 totals: | 13.5 |
| 17 | Clerk | De Martini, Jennifer | 8.4 |
| | Clerk | Rittenbery, Sandra | 11.0 |
| | | Store 17 totals: | 19.4 |
| | | Grand total: | 32.9 |

FIGURE 8-22 An exception report that shows information *only* for employees who worked overtime.

**SUMMARY REPORTS** Upper-level managers often want to see total figures and do not need supporting details. A sales manager, for example, might want to know total sales for each sales representative, but not want a detail report listing every sale made by them. In that case, a **summary report** is appropriate. Similarly, a personnel manager might need to know the total regular and overtime hours worked by employees in each store but might not be interested in the number of hours worked by each employee. For the personnel manager, a summary report such as the one shown in Figure 8-23 would be useful. Generally, reports used by individuals at higher levels in the organization include less detail than reports used by lower-level employees.

| Store Number | | Regular Hours | Overtime Hours | Total Hours |
|---|---|---|---|---|
| | Employee Hours Summary | | | Page 1 |
| | week ending date: 6/24/11 | | | |
| 8 | | 181.2 | 13.5 | 194.7 |
| 17 | | 172.0 | 19.4 | 191.4 |
| | Totals: | 337.2 | 32.9 | 370.1 |

FIGURE 8-23 A summary report displays totals without showing details.

## User Involvement in Report Design

Printed reports are an important way of delivering information, so users should approve all report designs in advance. The best approach is to submit each design for approval as you complete it, rather than waiting until you finish all report designs.

When designing a report, you should prepare a sample report, called a **mock-up**, or prototype, for users to review. The sample should include typical field values and contain enough records to show all the design features. Depending on the type of printed output, you can create a Word document or use a report generator to create mock-up reports. After a report design is approved, you should document the design by creating **a report analysis form**, which contains information about the layout, fields, frequency, distribution, data security considerations, and other issues.

## Report Design Principles

Printed reports must be attractive, professional, and easy to read. For example, a well-designed detail report should provide totals for numeric fields. Notice that the report shown in Figure 8-21 on page 352 lacked subtotals and grand totals for regular hours, overtime hours, and total hours. Figure 8-24 shows the same report with subtotals and grand totals added. In the example, the Store Number field is called a **control field** because it controls the output.

When the value of a control field changes, a **control break** occurs. A control break usually causes specific actions, such as printing subtotals for a group of records. That type of detail report is called a **control break report**. To produce a control break report, the records must be arranged, or sorted, in **control field order**. The sorting can be done by the report program itself, or in a previous procedure.

Good report design requires effort and attention to detail. To produce a well-designed report, the analyst must consider design features such as report headers and footers, page headers and footers, column headings and alignment, column spacing, field order, and grouping of detail lines. The report shown in Figure 8-24 shows examples of these design features.

**REPORT HEADERS AND FOOTERS** Every report should have a report header and a report footer. The **report header**, which appears at the beginning of the report, identifies the report, and contains the report title, date, and other necessary information. The **report footer**, which appears at the end of the report, can include grand totals for numeric fields and other end-of-report information, as shown in Figure 8-24.

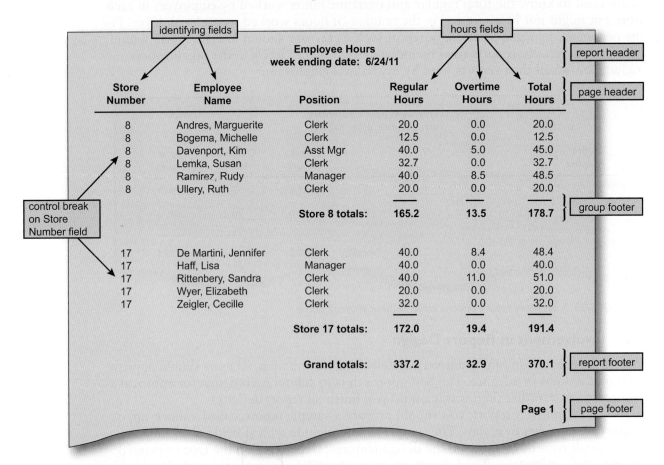

**FIGURE 8-24** The Employee Hours report is a detail report with control breaks, subtotals, and grand totals. Notice that a report header identifies the report, a page header contains column headings, a group footer contains subtotals for each store, a report footer contains grand totals, and a page footer identifies the page number.

**PAGE HEADERS AND FOOTERS** Every page should include a **page header**, which appears at the top of the page and includes the column headings that identify the data. The headings should be short but descriptive. Avoid abbreviations unless you know that users will understand them clearly. Either a page header or a **page footer**, which appears at the bottom of the page, is used to display the report title and the page number.

**COLUMN HEADING ALIGNMENT** Figure 8-25 shows several column heading alignment options. In Example 1, the left-justified column headings do not work well with numeric fields because the amount 1.25 would print past the right edge of the AMOUNT heading. In Example 2, the right-justified headings cause a problem with alphanumeric fields, because none of the characters in a short name would print under any part of the NAME heading. Centering headings over *maximum* field widths, as shown in Example 3, is not ideal when many of the actual values are shorter than the maximum width. Many designers prefer Example 4, where headings are left-justified over alphanumeric fields and right-justified over numeric fields.

| | | |
|---|---|---|
| Example 1: Column headings are left-justified over maximum field widths. | NAME                                                     NUMBER      AMOUNT<br>XXXXXXXXXXXXXXXXXXXXXXXXX         ZZZ9      ZZZ,ZZ9.99 | |
| Example 2: Column headings are right-justified over maximum field widths. |                                                  NAME   NUMBER      AMOUNT<br>XXXXXXXXXXXXXXXXXXXXXXXXX         ZZZ9      ZZZ,ZZ9.99 | |
| Example 3: Column headings are centered over maximum field widths. |                          NAME                   NUMBER      AMOUNT<br>XXXXXXXXXXXXXXXXXXXXXXXXX         ZZZ9      ZZZ,ZZ9.99 | |
| Example 4: Column headings are left-justified over alphanumeric fields and right-justified over numeric fields. | NAME                                                     NUMBER      AMOUNT<br>XXXXXXXXXXXXXXXXXXXXXXXXX         ZZZ9      ZZZ,ZZ9.99 | |

**FIGURE 8-25** Four different column heading alignment options.

**COLUMN SPACING** You should space columns of information carefully. A crowded report is hard to read, and large gaps between columns make it difficult for the eye to follow a line. Columns should stretch across the report, with uniform spacing and suitable margins at top, bottom, right, and left. Some report designers use landscape orientation when working with a large number of columns; others prefer to break the information into more than one report. In some cases, a smaller point size will solve the problem, but the report must remain readable and acceptable to users.

**FIELD ORDER** Fields should be displayed and grouped in a logical order. For example, the report shown in Figure 8-24 shows the detail lines printed in alphabetical order within store number, so the store number is in the left column, followed by the employee name. The employee position relates to the employee's name, so the items are adjacent. The three hours fields also are placed together.

**GROUPING DETAIL LINES** Often, it is meaningful to arrange detail lines in groups, based on a control field. For example, using the department number as a control field, individual employees can be grouped by department. You can print a **group header**

above the first detail line and a **group footer** after the last detail line in a group, as shown in Figure 8-24.

Database programs such as Microsoft Access make it easy to create groups and subgroups based on particular fields. You also can have the report calculate and display totals, averages, record counts, and other data for any group or subgroup. For example, in a large company, you might want to see total sales and number of sales broken down by product within each of the 50 states. The screen shown in Figure 8-26 is an Access Help screen that refers to a step-by-step process for creating multilevel grouping.

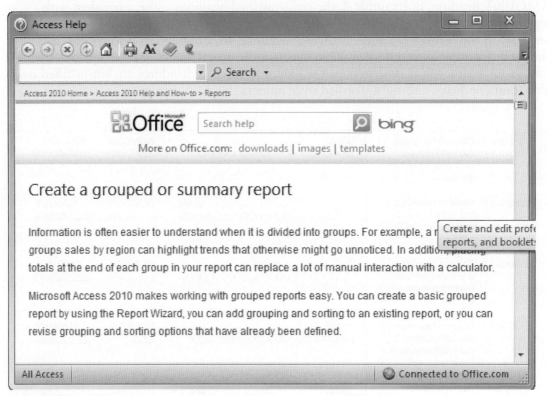

**FIGURE 8-26** Microsoft Access includes an easy-to-use tool for grouping data.

**REPEATING FIELDS**  Report design is an art, not a science. User involvement is essential, but users often don't know what they want without seeing samples. For example, consider the issue of repeating fields. The sample report in Figure 8-21 on page 352 repeats the store number on every row. Is that a good thing? The best advice is to ask users what they think, and be guided accordingly. A similar issue exists with regard to the overtime hours column. Is it better to print the zero overtime data, or only print actual hours, so the data stands out clearly? Again, the best answer is usually the one that works best for users.

**CONSISTENT DESIGN**  Look and feel are important to users, so reports should be uniform and consistent. When a system produces multiple reports, each report should share common design elements. For example, the date and page numbers should print in the same place on each report page. Abbreviations used in reports also should be consistent. For example, when indicating a numeric value, it is confusing for one report to use #, another *NO*, and a third *NUM*. Items in a report also should be consistent. If one report displays the inventory location as a shelf number column followed by a bin number column, that same layout should be used on all inventory location reports.

## CASE IN POINT 8.3:   LAZY EDDIE

Lynn Jennings is the IT manager at Lazy Eddie, a chain that specializes in beanbag chairs and recliners. She asked Jan Lauten, a senior systems analyst, to review the large number of printed reports that are distributed to Lazy Eddie's 35 store managers. "Jan, I just can't believe that our people really read all of those reports," Lynn said. "We constantly add new reports, and we never seem to eliminate the old ones. Sometimes I think all we're doing is keeping the paper companies in business!" Jan replied, "I agree, but what can we do? The managers say they want the reports, but I always see them stacked on top of file cabinets. I've never seen anyone read a report."

"I have an idea," Lynn said. "I want you to come up with a procedure that requires users to review and justify their information needs to see if they really use the reports we send them. You could design a form that asks if the information still is required, and why. Try to get users to decide if a report is worth the cost of producing it. Do you think you can do it?"

"Sure I can," Jan replied. When Jan returned to her office, she wondered where to begin. What advice would you give to Jan?

### Output Technology

Although business information systems still provide most output as screen displays and printed matter, technology is having an enormous impact on how people communicate and obtain information. This trend is especially important to firms that use information technology to lower their costs, improve employee productivity, and communicate effectively with their customers.

In addition to screen output and printed matter, output can take many forms. The system requirements document probably identified user output needs. Now, in the systems design phase, you will create the actual forms, reports, documents, and other types of output. During this process, you must consider the format and how it will be delivered, stored, and retrieved. The following sections explain various output types and the technologies that are available to systems developers.

**INTERNET-BASED INFORMATION DELIVERY**   Millions of firms use the Internet to reach new customers and markets around the world. To support the explosive growth in e-commerce, Web designers must provide user-friendly screen interfaces that display output and accept input from customers. For example, a business can link its inventory system to its Web site so the output from the inventory system is displayed as an online catalog. Customers visiting the site can review the items, obtain current prices, and check product availability.

Another example of Web-based output is a system that provides customized responses to product or technical questions. When a user enters a product inquiry or requests technical support, the system responds with appropriate information from an on-site knowledge base. Web-based delivery allows users to download a universe of files and documents to support their information needs. For example, the Web provides consumers with instant access to brochures, product manuals, and parts lists; while prospective home buyers can obtain instant quotes on mortgages, insurance, and other financial services.

To reach prospective customers and investors, companies also use a live or prerecorded **Webcast**, which is an audio or video media file distributed over the Internet. Radio and TV stations also use this technique to broadcast program material to their audiences.

**E-MAIL**   E-mail is an essential means of internal and external business communication. Employees send and receive e-mail on local or wide area networks, including the Internet. Companies send new product information to customers via e-mail, and financial services

ON THE WEB

To learn more about e-mail, visit the Management Information Systems CourseMate Web site at **www. cengagebrain.com**, navigate to **On the Web Links** for this chapter, and locate the E-Mail link.

companies use e-mail messages to confirm online stock trades. Employees use e-mail to exchange documents, data, and schedules and to share business-related information they need to perform their jobs. In many firms, e-mail has virtually replaced traditional memos and printed correspondence.

**BLOGS** Web-based logs, called **blogs**, are another form of Web-based output. Because blogs are journals written from a particular point of view, they not only deliver facts to Web readers, but also provide opinions. Blogs are useful for posting news, reviewing current events, and promoting products.

**INSTANT MESSAGING** This popular form of communication is another way for individuals and companies to communicate effectively over the Internet. Although some users feel that it can be a distraction, others like the constant flow of communication, especially as a team member in a collaborative situation.

**WIRELESS DEVICES** Messages and data can be transmitted to a wide array of mobile devices, including PDAs, handheld computers, smart cell phones, and similar wireless products that combine portable computing power, multimedia capability, and Internet access.

**DIGITAL AUDIO, IMAGES, AND VIDEO** Sounds, images, and video clips can be captured, stored in digital format, and transmitted as output to users who can reproduce the content.

Audio or video output can be attached to an e-mail message or inserted as a clip in a Microsoft Word document, as shown in Figure 8-27. Businesses also use automated systems to handle voice transactions and provide information to customers. For example, using a telephone keypad, a customer can confirm an airline seat assignment, check a credit card balance, or determine the current price of a mutual fund.

If a picture is worth a thousand words, then digital images and video clips certainly are high-value output types that offer a whole new dimension. For example, an insurance adjuster with a digital camera phone can take a picture, submit the image via a wireless device, and receive immediate authorization to pay a claim on the spot. If images are a valuable form of output, video clips are even better in some situations. For example, video clips provide online virtual tours that allow realtors to show off the best features of homes they are marketing. The user can zoom in or out, and rotate the image in any direction.

**PODCASTS** A **podcast** is a specially formatted digital audio file that can be downloaded by Internet users from a variety of content providers. Many firms use podcasts as sales and marketing tools, and to communicate with their own employees. Using software such as iTunes, you can receive a podcast, launch the file on your computer, and store it on your portable player. Podcasts can include images, sounds, and video.

**AUTOMATED FACSIMILE SYSTEMS** An **automated facsimile** or **faxback** system allows a customer to request a fax using e-mail, via the company Web site, or by telephone. The response is transmitted in a matter of seconds back to the user's fax machine. Although most users prefer to download documents from the Web, many organizations, including the U.S. Department of Transportation, still offer an automated faxback service as another way to provide immediate response 24 hours a day.

**COMPUTER OUTPUT TO MICROFILM (COM)** Computer output to microfilm (COM) is often used by large firms to scan and store images of original documents to provide high-quality records management and archiving. COM systems are especially important for legal reasons, or where it is necessary to display a signature, date stamp, or other visual features of a document.

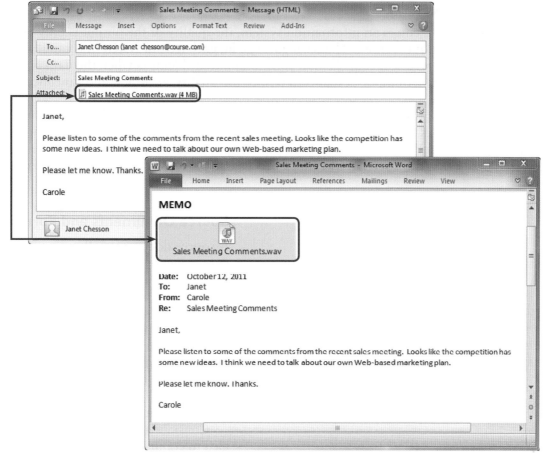

**FIGURE 8-27** Audio or video clips can be attached to an e-mail message or inserted in a document. The recipient can double-click the link or icon and a media player opens the file.

**COMPUTER OUTPUT TO DIGITAL MEDIA** This process is used when many paper documents must be scanned, stored in digital format, and retrieved quickly. For example, if an insurance company stores thousands of paper application forms, special software can treat the documents as data and extract information from a particular column or area on the form. Digital storage media can include magnetic tape, CDs, DVDs, and high-density laser disks.

**SPECIALIZED FORMS OF OUTPUT** An incredibly diverse marketplace requires many forms of specialized output and devices such as these:

- Portable, Web-connected devices that can run applications, handle multimedia output, and provide powerful, multipurpose communication for users

- Retail point-of-sale terminals that handle computer-based credit card transactions, print receipts, and update inventory records

- Automatic teller machines (ATMs) that can process bank transactions and print deposit and withdrawal slips

- Special-purpose printers that can produce labels, employee ID cards, driver's licenses, gasoline pump receipts, and, in some states, lottery tickets

- Plotters that can produce high-quality images such as blueprints, maps, and electronic circuit diagrams

- Electronic detection of data embedded in credit cards, bank cards, and employee identification cards

# INPUT DESIGN

No matter how data enters an information system, the quality of the output is only as good as the quality of the input. The term **garbage in, garbage out** (**GIGO**), is familiar to IT professionals, who know that the best time to avoid problems is when the data is entered. The objective of input design is to ensure the quality, accuracy, and timeliness of input data.

Good input design requires attention to human factors as well as technology issues. This section includes a discussion of source documents, data entry screen design, input masks, and data validation rules. The final topic, input technology, examines devices and techniques that can speed up the input process, reduce costs, and handle new forms of data.

## Source Documents and Forms

A **source document** collects input data, triggers or authorizes an input action, and provides a record of the original transaction. During the input design stage, you develop source documents that are easy to complete and use for data entry. Source documents generally are paper-based, but also can be provided online. Either way, the design considerations are the same.

Consider a time when you struggled to complete a poorly designed form. You might have encountered insufficient space, confusing instructions, or poor organization, all symptoms of incorrect **form layout**. Good form layout makes the form easy to complete and provides enough space, both vertically and horizontally, for users to enter the data. A form should indicate data entry positions clearly using blank lines or boxes and descriptive captions. Figure 8-28 shows several techniques for using line and boxed captions in source documents, and an example of check boxes, which are effective when a user must select choices from a list.

The placement of information on a form also is important. Source documents typically include most of the zones shown in Figure 8-29. The **heading zone** usually contains the company name or logo and the title and number of the form. The **control zone** contains codes, identification information, numbers, and dates that are used for storing completed forms.

**FIGURE 8-28** Examples of caption techniques for source documents.

The **instruction zone** contains instructions for completing the form. The main part of the form, called the **body zone**, usually takes up at least half of the space on the form and contains captions and areas for entering variable data. If totals are included on the form, they appear in the **totals zone**. Finally, the **authorization zone** contains any required signatures.

Information should flow on a form from left to right and top to bottom to match the way users read documents naturally. That layout makes the form easy to use for the individual who completes the form, and for users who enter data into the system using the completed form. You can review samples of source document design that appear in the SWL case study on pages 382–387.

The same user-friendly design principles also apply to printed forms such as invoices and monthly statements, except that heading information usually is preprinted. You should make column headings short but descriptive, avoid nonstandard abbreviations, and use reasonable spacing between columns for better readability.

The order and placement of printed fields should be logical, and totals should be identified clearly. When designing a preprinted form, you should contact the form's vendor for

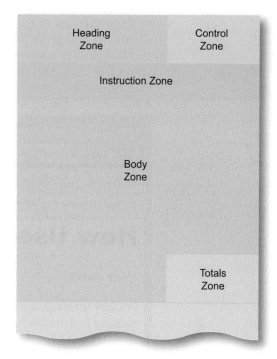

**FIGURE 8-29** Source document zones.

advice on paper sizes, type styles and sizes, paper and ink colors, field placement, and other important form details. Your goal is to design a form that is attractive, readable, and effective.

Layout and design also are important on Web-based forms, and you can find many resources that will help you design efficient, user-friendly forms. For example, Figure 8-30 describes a book by Luke Wroblewski, a well-known author and consultant. His Web site offers valuable suggestions, guidelines, and examples.

A major challenge of Web-based form design is that most people read and interact differently with on-screen information compared to paper forms. In the view of Dr. Jakob Nielsen, a pioneer in Web usability design, users simply do not read on the Web,

**FIGURE 8-30** Luke Wroblewski's Web site is a good source of information about form design.

as shown in Figure 8-31. Dr. Nielsen believes that users *scan* a page, picking out individual words and sentences. As a result, Web designers must use **scannable text** to capture and hold a user's attention. On his site, Dr. Nielson offers several suggestions for creating scannable text. Also notice that Dr. Nielsen employs various usability metrics to measure user responses, comprehension, and recall.

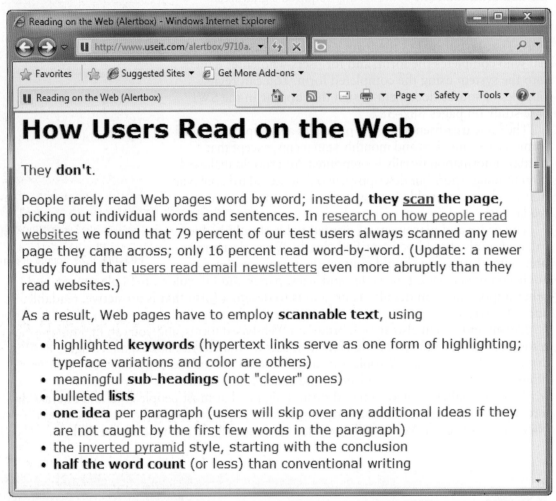

**FIGURE 8-31**  Dr. Jakob Nielsen believes that users scan Web material rather than reading it. He suggests that Web designers must use scannable text and employ usability metrics to measure the results.

## CASE IN POINT 8.4:  TRUSTWORTHY INSURANCE COMPANY

Trustworthy Insurance maintains its headquarters in a large Midwestern city. Right now, a debate is raging in the IT department. Several analysts want to use standard, company-wide desktop screen layouts and icons. Others want to allow users to set up their screens any way they choose. Those who argue for standardization point out that Trustworthy employs a number of part-time employees, who fill in for employees on vacation. Without a standard interface, these people would have to reorient to every workstation, and the proponents of standardization claim that would reduce productivity and increase costs. Those opposed to standardization believe that employees are most productive when they have control over their workplace, including the ability to design an interface they feel is attractive, even if no one else does.

   You are on a committee that was charged with resolving this issue, and yours is the tie-breaking vote. What will you decide, and why?

## Data Entry Screens

To learn more about data entry, visit the Management Information Systems CourseMate Web site at **www. cengagebrain.com**, navigate to **On the Web Links** for this chapter, and locate the Data Entry link.

During input design, you determine how data will be captured and entered into the system. **Data capture** uses an automated or manually operated device to identify source data and convert it into computer-readable form. Examples of data capture devices include credit card scanners and bar code readers. **Data entry** is the process of manually entering data into the information system, usually in the form of keystrokes, mouse clicks, touch screens, or spoken words.

Some users work with many features of the user interface; others spend most of their time entering data. This section discusses design guidelines and concepts that primarily relate to repetitive data entry. Notice that many of the guidelines are based on general principles of interface design discussed in this chapter.

The most effective method of online data entry is **form filling**, in which a blank form that duplicates or resembles the source document is completed on the screen. The user enters the data and then moves to the next field. The following guidelines will help you design data entry screens that are easy to learn and use.

1. Restrict user access to screen locations where data is entered. For example, when the screen in Figure 8-32 appears, the system should position the insertion point in the first data entry location. After the operator enters a Customer ID, the insertion point should move automatically to the entry location for the next field (Item). A user should be able to position the insertion point only in places where data is entered on the form.

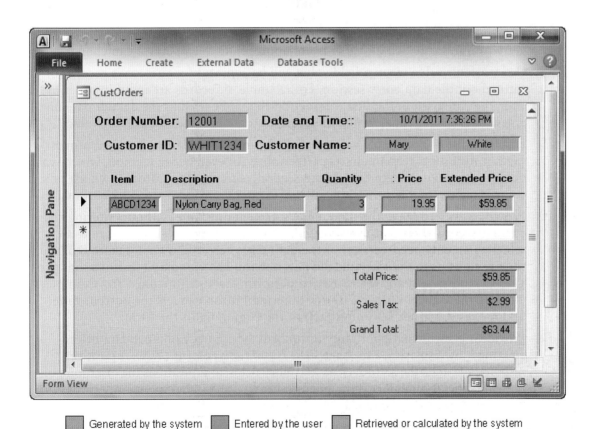

**FIGURE 8-32** In this data screen for customer orders, the system generates an order number and logs the current date and time. The user enters a customer ID. If the entry is valid, the system displays the customer name so the user can verify it. The user then enters the item and quantity. Note that the description, price, extended price, total price, sales tax, and grand total are retrieved automatically or calculated by the system.

2. Provide a descriptive caption for every field, and show the user where to enter the data and the required or maximum field size. Typically, white boxes show the location and length of each field. Other methods used to indicate field locations are video highlighting, underscores, special symbols, or a combination of these features.

3. Display a sample format if a user must enter values in a field in a specific format. For example, provide an on-screen instruction to let users know that the date format is MMDDYY, and provide an example if the user must enter **separators**, such as slashes. It is better to use an input mask, so users simply can enter 112711 to represent November 27, 2011.

4. Require an ending keystroke for every field. Pressing the ENTER key or the TAB key should signify the end of a field entry. Avoid a design that moves automatically to the next item when the field is full. The latter approach requires an ending keystroke *only* when the data entered is less than the maximum field length. It is confusing to use two different data entry procedures.

5. Do not require users to type leading zeroes for numeric fields. For example, if a three-digit project number is 045, the operator should be able to type 45 instead of 045 before pressing the ENTER key. An exception to that rule might occur when entering a date, where a leading zero is needed to identify single-digit months or days, such as 06-04-2011.

6. Do not require users to type trailing zeroes for numbers that include decimals. For example, when a user types a value of 98, the system should interpret the value as 98.00 if the field has been formatted to include numbers with two decimal places. The decimal point is needed *only* to indicate nonzero decimal places, such as 98.76.

7. Display default values so operators can press the ENTER key to accept the suggested value. If the default value is not appropriate, the operator can change it.

8. Use a default value when a field value will be constant for successive records or throughout the data entry session. For example, if records are input in order by date, the date used in the first transaction should be used as the default date until a new date is entered, at which time the new date becomes the default value.

9. Display a list of acceptable values for fields, and provide meaningful error messages if the user enters an unacceptable value. An even better method, which was described in the user interface design section, is to provide a drop-down list box containing acceptable values that allows the user to select a value by clicking.

10. Provide a way to leave the data entry screen at any time without entering the current record. This feature is available in the screen shown in Figure 8-33, which is an enhanced version of the data entry screen shown in Figure 8-32 on the previous page. Notice that the new version has command buttons that provide flexibility and allow the user to perform various functions. For example, clicking the Cancel Order Without Entering button cancels the current order and moves the insertion point back to the beginning of the form.

11. Provide users with an opportunity to confirm the accuracy of input data before entering it by displaying a message such as, *Add this record? (Y/N)*. A positive response *(Y)* adds the record, clears the entry fields, and positions the insertion point in the first field so the user can input another record. If the response is negative *(N)*, the current record is not added and the user can correct the errors.

12. Provide a means for users to move among fields on the form in a standard order or in any order they choose. For example, when a user opens the form shown in Figure 8-33, the insertion point automatically will be in the first field. After the user fills in each field and confirms the entry, the insertion point moves to the next field, in a

**FIGURE 8-33** This is an enhanced version of the data entry screen shown in Figure 8-32. The new version has command buttons that allow the user to perform various functions.

predetermined order. In a graphical user interface (GUI), the user can override the standard field order and select field locations using the mouse or arrow keys.

13. Design the screen form layout to match the layout of the source document. If the source document fields start at the top of the form and run down in a column, the input screen should use the same design.

14. Allow users to add, change, delete, and view records. Figure 8-33 shows a screen that can be used for entering orders, finding items, and finding customers. After the operator enters a customer identification code, the order form displays current values for all appropriate fields. Then the operator can view the data, make changes, enter the order, or cancel without ordering. Messages such as: *Apply these changes? (Y/N)* or *Delete this record? (Y/N)* should require users to confirm the actions. Highlighting the letter *N* as a default response will avoid problems if the user presses the ENTER key by mistake.

15. Provide a method to allow users to search for specific information, as shown in Figure 8-33.

## Input Masks

Use **input masks,** which are templates or patterns that restrict data entry and prevent errors. Microsoft Access 2010 provides standard input masks for fields such as dates, telephone numbers, postal codes, and Social Security numbers. In addition, you can create custom input masks for any type of data, as shown in Figure 8-34 on the next page. Notice that a mask can manipulate the input data and apply a specific format. For example, if a user enters text in lowercase letters, the input mask >L<???????????? will automatically capitalize the first letter.

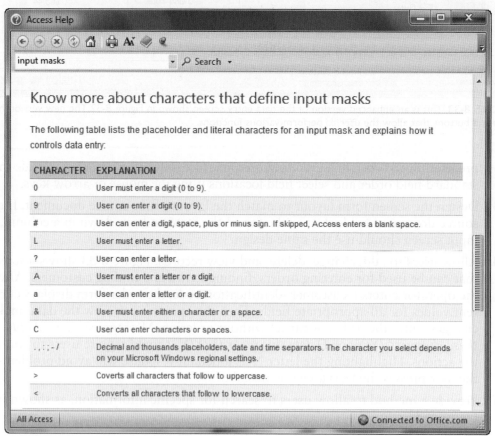

**FIGURE 8-34** Microsoft Access 2010 provides various input masks for dates, phone numbers, and postal codes, among others. In addition, it is easy to create a custom mask using the characters shown here.

## Validation Rules

Reducing the number of input errors improves data quality. One way to reduce input errors is to eliminate unnecessary data entry. For example, a user cannot misspell a customer name if it is not entered, or is entered automatically based on the user entering the customer ID. Similarly, an outdated item price cannot be used if the item price is retrieved from a master file instead of being entered manually.

The best defense against incorrect data is to identify and correct errors before they enter the system by using data validation rules, as shown in Figure 8-35. A **data validation rule** improves input quality by testing the data and rejecting any entry that fails to meet specified conditions. You can design at least eight types of data validation rules. For example:

1. A **sequence check** is used when the data must be in some predetermined sequence. If the user must enter work orders in numerical sequence, for example, then an out-of-sequence order number indicates an error, or if the user must enter transactions chronologically, then a transaction with an out-of-sequence date indicates an error.

2. An **existence check** is used for mandatory data items. For example, if an employee record requires a Social Security number, an existence check would not allow the user to save the record until he or she enters a suitable value in the Social Security number field.

3. A **data type check** tests to ensure that a data item fits the required data type. For example, a numeric field must have only numbers or numeric symbols, and an alphabetic field can contain only the characters A through Z (or a through z).

4. A **range check** tests data items to verify that they fall between a specified minimum and maximum value. The daily hours worked by an employee, for example, must fall within the range of 0 to 24. When the validation check involves a minimum or a maximum value, but not both, it is called a **limit check**. Checking that a payment amount is greater than zero, but not specifying a maximum value, is an example of a limit check.

5. A **reasonableness check** identifies values that are questionable, but not necessarily wrong. For example, input payment values of $.05 and $5,000,000.00 both pass a simple limit check for a payment value greater than zero, and yet both values could be errors. Similarly, a daily hours worked value of 24 passes a 0 to 24 range check; however, the value seems unusual, and the system should verify it using a reasonableness check.

6. A **validity check** is used for data items that must have certain values. For example, if an inventory system has 20 valid item classes, then any input item that does not match one of the valid classes will fail the check. Verifying that a customer number on an order matches a customer number in the customer file is another type of validity check. Because the value entered must refer to another value, that type of check also is called **referential integrity**, which is explained in Chapter 9, Designing the Data. Another validity check might verify that a new customer number does *not* match a number already stored in the customer master file.

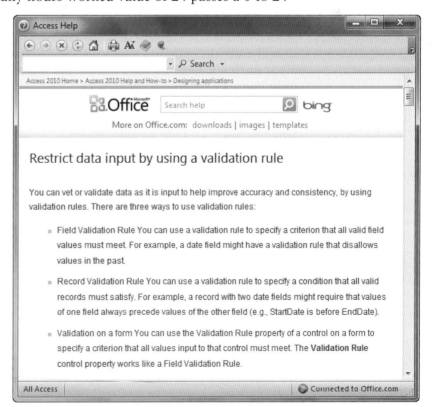

**FIGURE 8-35** Validation rules can improve data quality by requiring the input to meet specific requirements or conditions.

7. A **combination check** is performed on two or more fields to ensure that they are consistent or reasonable when considered together. Even though all the fields involved in a combination check might pass their individual validation checks, the combination of the field values might be inconsistent or unreasonable. For example, if an order input for 30 units of a particular item has an input discount rate applicable only for purchases of 100 or more units, then the combination is invalid; either the input order quantity or the input discount rate is incorrect.

8. **Batch controls** are totals used to verify batch input. Batch controls might check data items such as record counts and numeric field totals. For example, before entering a batch of orders, a user might calculate the total number of orders and the sum of all the order quantities. When the batch of orders is entered, the order system also calculates the same two totals. If the system totals do not match the input totals, then a data entry error has occurred. Unlike the other validation checks, batch controls do not identify specific errors. For example, if the sum of all the order quantities does not match the batch control total, you know only that one or more orders in that batch were entered incorrectly or not input. The batch control totals often are called **hash totals**, because they are not meaningful numbers themselves, but are useful for comparison purposes.

**ON THE WEB**

To learn more about input devices, visit the Management Information Systems CourseMate Web site at **www. cengagebrain. com**, navigate to **On the Web Links** for this chapter, and locate the Input Devices link.

## Input Technology

Input technology has changed dramatically in recent years. In addition to traditional devices and methods, there has been a rapid expansion of new hardware and ways to capture and enter data into a system, some of which are shown in Figure 8-36. Businesses are using the new technology to speed up the input process, reduce costs, and capture data in new forms, such as the digital signature shown in Figure 8-37.

The following sections discuss input and data entry methods, and the impact of input volume reduction.

Input methods should be cost-efficient, timely, and as simple as possible. Systems analysts study transactions and business operations to determine how and when data should enter the system. Usually, the first decision is whether to use batch or online input methods. Each method has advantages and disadvantages, and the systems analyst must consider the following factors.

**BATCH INPUT** Using **batch input**, data entry usually is performed on a specified time schedule, such as daily, weekly, monthly, or longer. For example, batch input occurs when a payroll department collects time cards at the end of the week and enters the

| INPUT TECHNOLOGY | | |
|---|---|---|
| **Traditional** | **Evolving** | **Emerging** |
| Keyboard | Body motion detection | Brain-Computer Interface (BCI) |
| Mouse | Advanced voice recognition | Neural networks |
| Pointing devices | Biological feedback | Artificial intelligence (AI) |
| Microphone | Embedded magnetic data | Advanced motion sensors |
| OCR (optical character recognition) | RFID | Two-way satellite interface |
| MICR (magnetic ink character recognition) | Advanced optical recognition | Virtual environments |
| Graphic input devices | Physical adaptation devices | 3-D technology |

**FIGURE 8-36** Input devices can be very traditional, or based on the latest technology.

**FIGURE 8-37** When a customer's signature is stored in digital form, it becomes input to the information system.

data as a **batch**. Another example is a school that enters all grades for the academic term in a batch.

**ONLINE INPUT** Although batch input is used in specific situations, most business activity requires **online data entry**. The online method offers major advantages, including the immediate validation and availability of data. A popular online input method is **source data automation**, which combines online data entry and automated data capture using input devices such as **RFID tags** or **magnetic data strips**. Source data automation is fast and accurate, and minimizes human involvement in the translation process.

Many large companies use a combination of source data automation and a powerful communication network to manage global operations instantly. Some common examples of source data automation are:

- Businesses that use point-of-sale (POS) terminals equipped with bar code scanners and magnetic swipe scanners to input credit card data.

- Automatic teller machines (ATMs) that read data strips on bank cards.

- Factory employees who use magnetic ID cards to clock on and off specific jobs so the company can track production costs accurately.

- Hospitals that imprint bar codes on patient identification bracelets and use portable scanners when gathering data on patient treatment and medication.

- Retail stores that use portable bar code scanners to log new shipments and update inventory data.

- Libraries that use handheld scanners to read optical strips on books.

**TRADEOFFS** Although online input offers many advantages, it does have some disadvantages. For example, unless source data automation is used, manual data entry is slower and more expensive than batch input because it is performed at the time the transaction occurs and often done when computer demand is at its highest.

The decision to use batch or online input depends on business requirements. For example, hotel reservations must be entered and processed immediately, but hotels can enter their monthly performance figures in a batch. In fact, some input occurs naturally in batches. A cable TV provider, for example, receives customer payments in batches when the mail arrives.

## Input Volume Reduction

To reduce input volume, you must reduce the number of data items required for each transaction. Data capture and data entry require time and effort, so when you reduce input volume, you avoid unnecessary labor costs, get the data into the system more quickly, and decrease the number of errors. The following guidelines will help reduce input volume:

1. Input necessary data only. Do not input a data item unless it is needed by the system. A completed order form, for example, might contain the name of the clerk who took the order. If that data is not needed by the system, the user should not enter it.

2. Do not input data that the user can retrieve from system files or calculate from other data. In the order system example shown in Figure 8-33 on page 365, the system generates an order number and logs the current date and time. Then the user enters a customer ID. If the entry is valid, the system displays the customer name so the user can verify it. The user then enters the item and quantity. Note that the description, price, extended price, total price, sales tax, and grand total are retrieved automatically or calculated by the system.

3. Do not input constant data. If orders are in batches with the same date, then a user should enter the order date only once for the first order in the batch. If orders are entered online, then the user can retrieve the order date automatically using the current system date.

4. Use codes. Codes are shorter than the data they represent, and coded input can reduce data entry time. You will learn more about various types of codes in Chapter 9, Designing the Data.

## SECURITY AND CONTROL ISSUES

A company must do everything in its power to protect its data. This includes not only the firm's own information, but that of its customers, employees, and suppliers. Most assets have a value, but corporate data is priceless, because without safe, secure, accurate data, a company cannot function.

The following sections discuss output and input data security and control.

### Output Security and Control

Output must be accurate, complete, current, and secure. Companies use various **output control** methods to maintain output integrity and security. For example, every report should include an appropriate title, report number or code, printing date, and time period covered. Reports should have pages that are numbered consecutively, identified as *Page nn of nn*, and the end of the report should be labeled clearly. Control totals and record counts should be reconciled against input totals and counts. Reports should be selected at random for a thorough check of correctness and completeness. All processing errors or interruptions must be logged so they can be analyzed.

**Output security** protects privacy rights and shields the organization's proprietary data from theft or unauthorized access. To ensure output security, you must perform several important tasks. First, limit the number of printed copies and use a tracking procedure to account for each copy. When printed output is distributed from a central location, you should use specific procedures to ensure that the output is delivered to authorized recipients only. That is especially true when reports contain sensitive information, such as payroll data. All sensitive reports should be stored in secure areas. All pages of confidential reports should be labeled appropriately.

ON THE WEB

To learn more about output control and security, visit the Management Information Systems CourseMate Web site at **www. cengagebrain. com**, navigate to **On the Web Links** for this chapter, and locate the Output Control and Security link.

As shown in Figure 8-38, it is important to shred sensitive reports, out-of-date reports, and output from aborted print runs. Blank check forms must be stored in a secure location and be inventoried regularly to verify that no forms are missing. If signature stamps are used, they must be stored in a secure location away from the forms storage location.

In most organizations, the IT department is responsible for output control and security measures. Systems analysts must be concerned with security issues as they design, implement, and support information systems. Whenever possible, security should be designed into the system by using passwords, shielding sensitive data, and controlling user access. Physical security always will be necessary, especially in the case of printed output that is tangible and can be viewed and handled easily.

Enterprise-wide data access creates a whole new set of security and control issues. Many firms have responded to those concerns by installing diskless workstations. A **diskless workstation** is a network terminal that supports a full-featured user interface, but limits the printing or copying of data, except to certain network resources that can be monitored and controlled. This concept worked well with terminals that had limited hardware and software features.

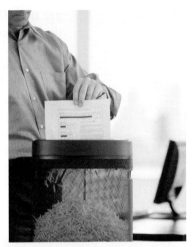
FIGURE 8-38 To maintain output security, it is important to shred sensitive material.

However, over time, the number of removable media devices has expanded greatly, along with a wide variety of physical interfaces such as USB, FireWire, and PCMCIA, as well as wireless interfaces such as Wi-Fi and Bluetooth. A popular security solution is the use of a network-based application, often called a **port protector**, that controls access to and from workstation interfaces. The SafeGuard® PortProtector is shown in Figure 8-39.

## Input Security and Control

**Input control** includes the necessary measures to ensure that input data is correct, complete, and secure. You must focus on input control during every phase of input design, starting with source documents that promote data accuracy and quality. When a batch input method is used, the computer can produce an input log file that identifies and documents the data entered.

Every piece of information should be traceable back to the input data that produced it. That means that you must provide an **audit trail** that records the source of each data item and when it entered the system. In addition to recording the original source, an audit trail must show how and when data is accessed or changed, and by whom. All those actions must be logged in an audit trail file and monitored carefully.

A company must have procedures for handling source documents to ensure that data is not lost before it enters the system. All source documents that originate from outside the organization should be logged when they are received. Whenever source documents pass between departments, the transfer should be recorded.

**Data security** policies and procedures protect data from loss or damage, which is a vital goal in every organization. If the safeguards

FIGURE 8-39 In addition to being diskless, like the lab terminal shown here, a workstation should have a port protector to control input and output access.

are not 100% effective, data recovery utilities should be able to restore lost or damaged data. Once data is entered, the company should store source documents in a safe location for some specified length of time. The company should have a **records retention policy** that meets all legal requirements and business needs.

Audit trail files and reports should be stored and saved. Then, if a data file is damaged, you can use the information to reconstruct the lost data. Data security also involves protecting data from unauthorized access. System sign-on procedures should prevent unauthorized individuals from entering the system, and users should change their passwords regularly. Having several levels of access also is advisable. For example, a data entry person might be allowed to *view* a credit limit, but not *change* it. Sensitive data can be **encrypted**, or coded, in a process called **encryption**, so only users with decoding software can read it.

## A QUESTION OF ETHICS

Jacob thought that he did a good job of designing the company's tech support Web page, but Emily, his supervisor, isn't so sure. She is concerned that Jacob's design is very similar to a page used by the company's major competitor, and she asked him whether he had used any HTML code from that site in his design. Although Jacob didn't copy any of the code, he did examine it in his Web browser to see how they handled some design issues.

Emily asked Jacob to investigate Web page copyright issues, and report back to her. In his research, he learned that outright copying would be a copyright violation, but merely viewing other sites to get design ideas would be permissible. What is not so clear is the gray area in the middle. Jacob asked you, as a friend, for your opinion on this question: Even if no actual copying is involved, are there ethical constraints on how far you should go in using the creative work of others? How would you answer Jacob?

## CHAPTER SUMMARY

The purpose of systems design is to create a physical model of the system that satisfies the design requirements that were defined during the systems analysis phase. The chapter began with a discussion of user interface design and human-computer interaction (HCI) concepts. A graphical user interface (GUI) uses visual objects and techniques that allow users to communicate effectively with the system. User-centered design principles include: understanding the business, maximizing graphic effectiveness, thinking like a user, using models and prototypes, focusing on usability, inviting feedback, and documenting everything.

When you design the interface itself, you should try to make it transparent; create an interface that is easy to learn and use; enhance user productivity; make it easy to obtain help or correct errors; minimize input data problems; provide feedback; create an attractive layout and design; and use familiar terms and images. You also can add control features, such as menu bars, toolbars, drop-down list boxes, dialog boxes, toggle buttons, list boxes, option buttons, check boxes, and command buttons. Controls are placed on a main switchboard, which is like a graphical version of a main menu.

The chapter described various types of printed reports, including detail, exception, and summary reports. You learned about the features and sections of reports, including control fields, control breaks, report headers and footers, page headers and footers, and group headers and footers. You also learned about other types of output, such as Web-based information delivery, audio output, instant messaging, podcasts, e-mail, and other specialized forms of output.

The discussion of input design began with a description of source documents and the various zones in a document, including the heading zone, the control zone, the instruction zone, the body zone, the totals zone, and the authorization zone. The discussion of data entry screen design explained the use of input masks and validation rules to reduce data errors. Input masks are like templates that only permit certain combinations of characters, and data validation rules can provide checks to ensure that inappropriate data is prevented from entering the system. These checks can include data sequence, existence, range and limit, reasonableness, and validity, among others.

You also learned about batch and online input methods, input media and procedures, and input volume. Input methods include data capture and data entry. Data capture, which may be automated, involves identifying and recording source data. Data entry involves converting source data into a computer-readable form and entering it into the system. New technology offers optical and voice recognition systems, biological feedback devices, motion sensors, and a variety of graphical input devices.

Finally, you learned about security and control. Output control includes physical protection of data and reports, and control of unauthorized ports or devices that can extract data from the system. Input controls include audit trails, encryption, password security, data security, and the creation of access levels to limit persons authorized to view or use data.

# Key Terms and Phrases

aesthetics *343*
audit trail *371*
authorization zone *361*
automated facsimile *358*
batch *369*
batch control *368*
batch input *368*
blog *358*
body zone *361*
calendar control *348*
character-based report *352*
check box *348*
combination check *368*
command button *348*
computer output to microfilm (COM) *358*
context-sensitive *345*
control break *354*
control break report *354*
control field *354*
control field order *354*
control zone *360*
data capture *363*
data entry *363*
data security *371*
data type check *367*
data validation rule *367*
detail line *352*
detail report *352*
dialog box *348*
diskless workstation *371*
drop-down list box *348*
encrypted *374*
encryption *374*
ergonomics *343*
exception report *352*
existence check *367*
faxback *358*
form filling *363*
form layout *360*
garbage in, garbage out (GIGO) *360*
graphical user interface (GUI) *338*
group footer *355*
group header *355*
hash totals *368*
heading zone *360*
human-computer interaction (HCI) *338*
input control *371*

input masks *346*
instruction zone *361*
interface technology *343*
limit check *367*
list box *348*
magnetic data strip *369*
menu bar *348*
mock-up *353*
natural language *344*
online data entry *369*
option button *348*
output control *370*
output security *370*
page footer *355*
page header *355*
podcast *358*
port protector *371*
process-control *336*
radio button *348*
range check *367*
reasonableness check *367*
records retention policy *372*
referential integrity *367*
report analysis form *353*
report footer *354*
report header *354*
RFID tag *369*
scannable text *362*
scroll bar *348*
separator *364*
sequence check *367*
source data automation *369*
source document *360*
storyboard *342*
summary report *353*
switchboard *348*
text box *348*
toggle button *348*
toolbar *348*
totals zone *361*
turnaround document *350*
usability metrics *342*
user-centered *337*
user interface (UI) *336*
user-selected *345*
validity check *367*
Webcast *357*

# Learn It Online

**Instructions:**  To complete the Learn It Online exercises, visit the Management Information Systems CourseMate Web site at **www.cengagebrain.com**, navigate to the resources for this chapter, and click the link for the exercise you want to complete.

## 1  Chapter Reinforcement

### TF, MC, and SA

Click one of the Chapter Reinforcement links for Multiple Choice, True/False, or Short Answer. Answer each question and submit to your instructor.

## 2  Flash Cards

Click the Flash Cards link and read the instructions. Type 20 (or a number specified by your instructor) in the Number of playing cards text box, type your name in the Enter your Name text box, and then click the Flip Card button. When the flash card is displayed, read the question and then click the ANSWER box arrow to select an answer. Flip through the Flash Cards. If your score is 15 (75%) correct or greater, click Print on the File menu to print your results. If your score is less than 15 (75%) correct, then redo this exercise by clicking the Replay button.

## 3  Practice Test

Click the Practice Test link. Answer each question, enter your first and last name at the bottom of the page, and then click the Grade Test button. When the graded practice test is displayed on your screen, click Print on the File menu to print a hard copy. Continue to take practice tests until you score 80% or better.

## 4  Who Wants To Be a Computer Genius?

Click the Computer Genius link. Read the instructions, enter your first and last name at the bottom of the page, and then click the Play button. When your score is displayed, click the PRINT RESULTS link to print a hard copy.

## 5  Wheel of Terms

Click the Wheel of Terms link. Read the instructions, and then enter your first and last name and your school name. Click the PLAY button. When your score is displayed on the screen, right-click the score and then click Print on the shortcut menu to print a hard copy.

## 6  Crossword Puzzle Challenge

Click the Crossword Puzzle Challenge link. Read the instructions, and then click the Continue button. Work the crossword puzzle. When you are finished, click the Submit button. When the crossword puzzle is redisplayed, submit it to your instructor.

## SCR Associates Case Simulation   Session 8: User Interface Design

### Overview

The SCR Associates case study is a Web-based simulation that allows you to practice your skills in a real-world environment. The case study transports you to SCR's intranet, where you complete 12 work sessions, each aligning with a chapter. As you work on the case, you will receive e-mail and voice mail messages, obtain information from SCR's online libraries, and perform various tasks.

### How do I use the case?

- Review the SCR background material in Chapter 1.
- Read the Preview for this session and study the Task List.
- Visit the Management Information Systems CourseMate Web site at **www.cengagebrain.com**, navigate to the **SCR Case Simulation**, and locate the intranet link.
- Enter your name and the password **sad9e**. An opening screen will display the 12 sessions.
- Select this session. Check your e-mail and voice mail carefully, and then work on the tasks.

### Preview: Session 8

Now that the overall data design is complete, Jesse Baker wants you to work on output and user interface design. You will consider user needs, and apply principles of human-computer interaction to build a user-centered interface that is easy to learn and use. You also will consider data validation checks, source documents, forms, and reports.

### Task List

| |
|---|
| 1. Create a detail report that will display all SCR courses in alphabetical order, with the course name and the instructor name in a group header; the Social Security number, name, and telephone number of each current student in the detail section; and the student count in a group footer. |
| 2. Create a switchboard design with control buttons that lead to students, instructors, courses, course schedules, and course rosters. Allow a user to add, update, or delete records in each area. Jesse wants to see storyboards that show the proposed screens. |
| 3. Suggest data validation checks for data entry screens. |
| 4. Create a source document for an SCR mail-in registration form. Also need a design for a Web-based course registration form. |

**FIGURE 8-40** Task list: Session 8.

## Chapter Exercises

**Review Questions**

1. Explain the concept of human-computer interaction (HCI).
2. Explain the concept of a GUI and a switchboard. How does a GUI design differ from a character-based screen design?
3. Describe seven principles for a user-centered interface design.
4. Describe six types of user interface controls, and provide an example of how you could use each type in a data entry screen.
5. Define detail reports, exception reports, and summary reports. Explain the concept of a control field and how it is used to produce a control-break report.
6. List and describe various types of output, including technology-based forms of information delivery.
7. Explain each of the data validation rules mentioned in this chapter.
8. What are the main principles of source document design?
9. Explain batch and online input methods. Define source data automation and provide an example.
10. Provide four guidelines for reducing input volume.

**Discussion Topics**

1. Some systems analysts maintain that source documents are unnecessary. They say that all input can be entered directly into the system, without wasting time in an intermediate step. Do you agree? Can you think of any situations where source documents are essential?
2. Some systems analysts argue, "Give users what they ask for. If they want lots of reports and reams of data, then that is what you should provide. Otherwise, they will feel that you are trying to tell them how to do their jobs." Others say, "Systems analysts should let users know what information can be obtained from the system. If you listen to users, you'll never get anywhere, because they really don't know what they want and don't understand information systems." What do you think of these arguments?
3. Suppose your network support company employs 75 technicians who travel constantly and work at customer sites. Your task is to design an information system that provides technical data and information to the field team. What types of output and information delivery would you suggest for the system?
4. A user interface can be quite restrictive. For example, the interface design might not allow a user to exit to a Windows desktop or to log on to the Internet. Should a user interface include such restrictions? Why or why not?

# Apply Your Knowledge

The Apply Your Knowledge section contains four mini-cases. Each case describes a situation, explains your role in the case, and asks you to respond to questions. You can answer the questions by applying knowledge you learned in the chapter.

## North Shore Boat Sales

**Situation:**

North Shore Boat Sales sells new and used boats and operates a Web-based boat brokerage business in Toronto. The company has grown, and North Shore needs a new information system to manage the inventory, the brokerage operation, and information about prospective buyers and sellers. Dan Robeson, the owner, asked you to design samples of computer screens and reports that the new system might produce.

1. Design a switchboard that includes the main information management functions that North Shore might require. Create a storyboard with a design layout that allows customers to perform the following functions: Obtain information about new boats, obtain information about used boats, send an e-mail to North Shore, learn more about the company, or review links to other marine-related sites.
2. Prospective buyers might want to search for boats by type, size, price range, or manufacturer. Develop a screen design that would permit those choices.
3. Suggest reports that might be useful to North Shore's management.
4. Suggest the general layout for a Web-based source document that prospective sellers could use to describe their boats. The information should include boat type (sail or power), manufacturer, year, length, type of engine, hull color, and asking price.

## 2  Terrier News

**Situation:**

Terrier News is a monthly newsletter devoted to various breeds of terriers and topics of interest to terrier owners and breeders. Annie West, the editor and publisher, asked you to help her design a system to enter and manage the hundreds of classified ads that Terrier News publishes. Some ads are for dogs wanted; some are for dogs for sale; and some offer products and services.

1. Design a suitable source document for ads that are telephoned or mailed in.
2. Explain user-centered design principles in a brief memo to Annie.
3. Suggest at least four user interface design guidelines that could be used for the new system.
4. Suggest several types of controls that might be used on the switchboard you plan to design. Explain why you chose each control, and create a storyboard that shows the switchboard layout.

### 3  Sky-High Internet Services

**Situation:**

Sky-High Internet Services is a leading Internet service provider in a metropolitan area. The new customer billing system has caused an increase in complaints. Tammy Jones, the office manager, asked you to investigate the situation. After interviewing data entry operators and observing the online data input process, you are fairly certain that most errors occur when data is entered.

1. Write a brief memo to Tammy explaining the importance of data validation during the input process.
2. Suggest at least three specific data validation checks that might help reduce input errors.
3. Would a batch input system offer any advantages? Write a brief memo to Tammy stating your views.
4. Suppose that Sky-High is predicting 25% annual growth, on a current base of 90,000 customers. If the growth pattern holds, how many customers will Sky-High have in three years? If it takes about 12 minutes to enter a new customer into the system, how many additional data entry operators will be needed to handle the growth next year? Assume that an operator works about 2,000 hours per year. Also assume a 30% annual attrition rate for existing customers.

### 4  Castle Point Antique Auction

**Situation:**

Castle Point Antique Auction operates a successful Web site that offers an auction forum for buyers and sellers of fine antiques. Monica Creighton, the owner, asked you to help her design some new documents and reports.

1. Suggest the general layout for a Web-based source document that prospective bidders would submit. The information should include user ID, password, name, address, telephone, e-mail address, item number, bid offered, and method of payment (money order, check, American Express, MasterCard, or Visa).
2. Suggest the general layout for a Web-based source document that prospective sellers could use to describe their antiques. The information should include the user ID, password, item, dimensions, origin, condition, and asking price.
3. Write a brief memo to Monica explaining the difference between detail reports, exception reports, and summary reports. Suggest at least one example of each type of report that she might want to consider.
4. Suggest several types of data validation checks that could be used when input data is entered.

# Case Studies

Case studies allow you to practice specific skills learned in the chapter. Each chapter contains several case studies that continue throughout the textbook, and a chapter capstone case.

## New Century Health Clinic

The associates at New Century Health Clinic approved your recommendations for a new computer system. Your next step is to develop a design for the new system, including output and user interface issues.

### Background

To complete the output and user interface design for the new information system at New Century, you should review the DFDs and object-oriented diagrams you prepared previously, and the rest of the documentation from the systems analysis phase. Perform the following tasks.

### Assignments

1. Dr. Jones has asked you to create a monthly Claim Status Summary report. He wants you to include the insurance company number, the patient number and name, the procedure date, the procedure code and description, the fee, the date the claim was filed, the amount of the claim, the amount of reimbursement, and the amount remaining unpaid. He wants you to group the data by insurance company number, with subtotals by company and grand totals for each numeric field. When you design the report, make sure to include a mock-up report and a report analysis form.

2. Design the daily appointment list and a monthly statement to make it readable and visually attractive. Include a mock-up report and a report analysis form for each report.

3. Determine the data required for a new patient. Design an input source document that will be used to capture the data and a data entry screen to input the information.

4. What data validation checks would the clinic need for the new patient data entry screen? Write a brief memo with your recommendations.

## PERSONAL TRAINER, INC.

Personal Trainer, Inc., owns and operates fitness centers in a dozen Midwestern cities. The centers have done well, and the company is planning an international expansion by opening a new "supercenter" in the Toronto area. Personal Trainer's president, Cassia Umi, hired an IT consultant, Susan Park, to help develop an information system for the new facility. During the project, Susan will work closely with Gray Lewis, who will manage the new operation.

### Background

Following the decision to use an in-house team to develop a design prototype, Susan began to work on the physical design for Personal Trainer's new information system. At this stage, she is ready to begin working with Gray on the output and user interface design. Together, Susan and Gray will seek to develop a user-centered design that is easy to learn and use. Personal Trainer users will include managers, fitness instructors, support staff, and members themselves.

## Assignments

1.  Create a detail report that will display all Personal Trainer courses in alphabetical order, with the course name and the instructor name in a group header; the Social Security number, name, and telephone number of each current student in the detail section; and the student count in a group footer.

2.  Create a switchboard design with control buttons that lead to members, fitness instructors, activities and services, schedules, and fitness class rosters. Allow a user to add, update, or delete records in each area.

3.  Suggest context-sensitive and specific Help for the switchboard and lower-level menus and forms. Prepare storyboards that show the proposed screens. Also suggest at least six types of data validation rules for data entry screens.

4.  Design a mail-in source document that members can use to register for fitness classes. Also design a Web-based registration form.

## VIDEO SUPERSTORE

Video Superstore has hired you to design two online data entry screens. Based on what you know about the operation of a video rental store, complete the following assignments.

## Assignments

1.  Design a weekly operations summary report that will include overall data on rentals, new customers, late charges, and anything else you think a store manager might want to review. Be sure to include numeric activity and dollar totals.

2.  Design a data entry screen for entering new members.

3.  Design a video rental input screen. In addition to the video data, the video rental form must include the following fields: Member Number, Name, and Date.

4.  Suggest at least three data validation rules that might help reduce input errors for the video rental system.

# CHAPTER CAPSTONE CASE:   SoftWear, Limited                          SWL

SoftWear, Limited (SWL), is a continuing case study that illustrates the knowledge and skills described in each chapter. In this case study, the student acts as a member of the SWL systems development team and performs various tasks.

## Background

SoftWear, Limited, decided to use the payroll package developed by Pacific Software Solutions and customize it by adding its own ESIP system to handle SWL's Employee Savings and Investment Plan.

Because most of the payroll requirements would be handled by Pacific's payroll package, the IT team decided that Carla Moore would work on the new ESIP modules, and Rick Williams would concentrate on the rest of the payroll system. A new systems analyst, Becky Evans, was assigned to help Rick with the payroll package.

Pacific Software Solutions offered free training for new customers, so Rick and Becky attended a three-day train-the-trainer workshop at Pacific's site in Los Angeles. When they returned, they began developing a one-day training session for SWL users, including people from the accounting, payroll, and human resources departments. The initial training would include the features and processing functions of the new payroll package that was scheduled to arrive the following week.

Carla's first task was to work on the ESIP outputs. She had to design several reports: the ESIP Deduction Register, the ESIP Payment Summary, and the checks that SWL sends to the credit union and the stock purchase plan. Carla also needed to develop an ESIP Accounting Summary as a data file to be loaded into the accounting system.

Carla learned that standard SWL company checks were used to make the payments to the credit union and stock purchase department. In addition, the output entry to the accounting system had been specified by the accounting department in a standard format for all entries into that system.

To prepare the new ESIP Deduction Register, Carla reviewed the documentation from the systems analysis phase to make sure that she understood the logical design and the available data fields.

Carla decided to use a monthly format because accounting would apply some deductions on a monthly cycle. She started her design with a standard SWL report heading. Then she added a control heading and footing for each employee's Social Security number. The total of employee deductions would be compared with the transferred ESIP funds to make sure that they matched. After preparing a rough layout, Carla prepared the mock-up report shown in Figure 8-41, using test data for the month of May 2011.

During the systems analysis phase, Carla learned that the accounting department required a control report to show the ESIP deduction amounts that were not yet applied. The control report is used to verify the amount of the checks or fund transfers SWL makes to the credit union and stock purchase plan. The accounting department needs the control report to verify the accounting system outputs and balance the ESIP deduction totals against the payroll system's Payroll Register report.

Figure 8-42 on page 384 shows a mock-up of the ESIP Payment Summary report. Carla met with Buddy Goodson, director of accounting, to review the design. Buddy was pleased with the report and felt it would be acceptable to the company's outside auditors. Buddy met with the auditing firm later that week and secured the team's approval.

As Carla turned her attention to the user interface for the ESIP system, she realized that she would need to develop two new source documents: an ESIP Option Form and an ESIP Deduction Authorization Form. She also planned to design a main switchboard and all necessary screen forms.

## CHAPTER CAPSTONE CASE:   SoftWear, Limited (continued)

| SoftWear, Ltd. | ESIP Deduction Register | | | |
|---|---|---|---|---|
| Month | Employee SSN | Period Ending | ESIP Option | Deduction |
| **May 2011** | | | | |
| | 111-11-1111 | | | |
| | | 5/6/2011 | Stock Purchase Plan | $15.00 |
| | | 5/6/2011 | Credit Union | $20.00 |
| | | 5/13/2011 | Credit Union | $25.00 |
| | | 5/13/2011 | Stock Purchase Plan | $15.00 |
| | | 5/20/2011 | Stock Purchase Plan | $15.00 |
| | | 5/20/2011 | Credit Union | $20.00 |
| | | 5/27/2011 | Stock Purchase Plan | $15.00 |
| | | 5/27/2011 | Credit Union | $20.00 |
| | | | *Employee Total* | *$145.00* |
| | 123-45-6789 | | | |
| | | 5/6/2011 | Stock Purchase Plan | $10.00 |
| | | | *Employee Total* | *$10.00* |
| | 222-22-2222 | | | |
| | | 5/6/2011 | Stock Purchase Plan | $10.00 |
| | | 5/6/2011 | Credit Union | $30.00 |
| | | 5/13/2011 | Stock Purchase Plan | $10.00 |
| | | 5/13/2011 | Credit Union | $30.00 |
| | | 5/20/2011 | Stock Purchase Plan | $10.00 |
| | | 5/20/2011 | Credit Union | $30.00 |
| | | 5/27/2011 | Credit Union | $30.00 |
| | | 5/27/2011 | Stock Purchase Plan | $10.00 |
| | | | *Employee Total* | *$160.00* |
| | 333-33-3333 | | | |
| | | 5/6/2011 | ESIP: Option 1 | $9.99 |
| | | 5/13/2011 | ESIP: Option 1 | $9.99 |
| | | 5/18/2011 | ESIP: Option 1 | $9.99 |
| | | 5/25/2011 | ESIP: Option 1 | $9.99 |
| | | | *Employee Total* | *$39.96* |
| *Summary for Period Ending 5/25/2011 (21 detail records)* | | | | |
| | | | *Monthly Total* | *$354.96* |

**FIGURE 8-41**  Mock-up for the ESIP Deduction Register.

Carla started by designing an ESIP Option Form that could be used for adding new ESIP options and modifying existing ones when authorized by the vice president of human resources.

**CHAPTER CAPSTONE CASE:   SoftWear, Limited (continued)**          **SWL**

---

### SoftWear, Ltd.        ESIP Payment Summary Report

Last Deduction Period in Month:            5/27/2011

| ESIP Code | Name | Deduction |
|-----------|------|-----------|
| CREDUN | Credit Union | $205.00 |
| ESIP01 | ESIP: Option 1 | $39.96 |
| SWLSTK | Stock Purchase Plan | $110.00 |
| | **Grand Total:** | **$354.96** |

**FIGURE 8-42** Mock-up of the ESIP Payment Summary Report.

Next, Carla worked on a data entry screen based on the ESIP Option Form. Using SWL's existing screen design standards, she quickly developed the screen mock-up shown in Figure 8-43. Her design allowed users to add, delete, save, clear, or find a record by clicking the appropriate command button.

**ESIP Options**

| | |
|---|---|
| ESIP ID | CREDUN |
| Name | Credit Union |
| Description | SWL Employee Credit Union |
| Deduction Cycle | EW |
| Application Cycle | EW |
| Minimum Service | 3M |
| Minimum Amt ($) | $10.00 |
| Maximum Amt (%) | 20 |

Add Record | Delete Record | Save Record | Clear Record | Find Record | STOP  Exit to System

Use the arrow keys to move from field to field.

If you need assistance, call the IT Help Desk at ext. 239 or send an e-mail message to help.swl

**FIGURE 8-43** Carla's ESIP data entry screen form design.

The ESIP Deduction Authorization Form required more data and several signatures. Carla divided the form into three sections: The employee completes the information in the top section; human resources completes the middle section; and payroll representatives complete the bottom section.

Carla designed a data entry screen based on the ESIP Deduction Authorization Form shown in Figure 8-44 and made the screen consistent with the other ESIP screen designs. Now a user could add, delete, save, clear, or find a record by clicking the appropriate command buttons. Carla also provided instructions to the operator for exiting from the system.

Carla decided to create a series of mock-ups to show users how the new ESIP deduction screen would work. In Figure 8-45 on the next page, the system has retrieved the employee's name, Joseph J. Smith, so the user can verify it against the source document.

The users approved the new design, with one suggestion — the system date should be added automatically as the entry date. Carla made the change and then designed the switchboard shown in Figure 8-46 on the next page, based on comments that users made during the design process. Now that she had a working model, Carla went back to the users to show them the complete package.

**SWL**   Employee Saving and Investment Plan
ESIP Deduction Authorization Form

**Name**

**Social Security Number**

☐☐☐ - ☐☐ - ☐☐☐☐

**Option (Check One):**

SWL Credit Union                ☐
Employee Stock Purchase   ☐
Other _____    ☐

**Deduction Amount:**

$_____

I want to select the ESIP option and deduction amount specified above, and I authorize the company to make this deduction from my regular earnings. I have read the plan description and I understand that SWL's ESIP plan is subject to company policies and various federal and state regulations that might change in the future.

Signed _____ Date _____

**Human Resources Department Approval:**

By _____ Date _____

**Payroll Department Verification:**

By _____ Date _____

Effective Date _____

FIGURE 8-44 The ESIP Deduction Authorization Form.

## SWL Team Tasks

1. Review the mock-up report shown in Figure 8-41 on page 383. When Carla showed this report design to Mike Feiner, director of human resources, he said that he wanted to see the data grouped by the type of ESIP deduction with the appropriate subtotals. Carla wants you to modify the report design to satisfy his request. You can use Microsoft Access, a report generator, or simply construct a sample layout using any word processing or drawing program. Be sure to show the placement and grouping of all fields.

2. Carla Moore also wants employees to have an online information request form that they can use to learn more about ESIP options and request up-to-date balances for their ESIP accounts. Follow the guidelines and suggestions in this chapter, and design an online screen form for Carla.

3. In addition to being available online, Carla wants the information request form to be available as a paper source document, which can be used by employees who do not have easy access to the online form. Follow the guidelines and suggestions in this chapter, and design a paper source document for Carla.

4. Carla wants an update on usability, how users read on the Web. Review the material in this chapter and visit the Web to learn more about this topic. Summarize the results of your research in a memo to Carla.

FIGURE 8-45 After the user presses the ENTER key, the system retrieves the employee name and displays it so the user can verify it. Notice that the user must check a box to verify that the form has been signed properly.

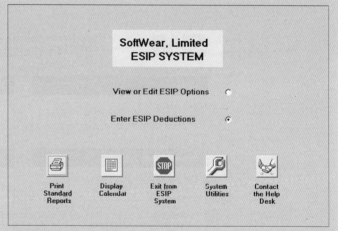

FIGURE 8-46 The ESIP switchboard includes option buttons and command buttons to select various processing choices.

## Manage the SWL Project

You have been asked to manage SWL's new information system project. One of your most important activities will be to identify project tasks and determine when they will be performed. Before you begin, you should review the SWL case in this chapter. Then list and analyze the tasks, as follows:

LIST THE TASKS Start by listing and numbering at least 10 tasks that the SWL team needs to perform to fulfill the objectives of this chapter. Your list can include SWL Team Tasks and any other tasks that are described in this chapter. For example, Task 3 might be to Find out what output is needed, and Task 6 might be to Design an output screen.

**CHAPTER CAPSTONE CASE:  SoftWear, Limited (continued)**

**ANALYZE THE TASKS** Now study the tasks to determine the order in which they should be performed. First identify all concurrent tasks, which are not dependent on other tasks. In the example shown in Figure 8-47, Tasks 1, 2, 3, 4, and 5 are concurrent tasks, and could begin at the same time if resources were available.

Other tasks are called dependent tasks, because they cannot be performed until one or more earlier tasks have been completed. For each dependent task, you must identify specific tasks that need to be completed before this task can begin. For example, you would want to find out what output is needed before you could design an output screen, so Task 6 cannot begin until Task 3 is completed, as Figure 8-47 shows.

Chapter 3 describes project management tools, techniques, and software. To learn more, you can use the Features section on your Student Study Tool CD-ROM, or visit the Management Information Systems CourseMate Web site at **www.cengagebrain.com** and locate the project management resources library for this book. On the Web, Microsoft offers demo versions, training, and tips for using Project 2010. You also can visit the OpenWorkbench.org site to learn more about this free, open-source software.

**FIGURE 8-47** Tasks 1, 2, 3, 4, and 5 are concurrent tasks that could be performed at the same time. Task 6 is a dependent task that cannot be performed until Task 3 has been completed.

# Ready for a Challenge?

In additional to technical skills, IT professionals need critical thinking skills such as perception, organization, analysis, problem-solving, and decision-making. The Ready for a Challenge feature can help you learn, practice, and apply critical thinking skills that you can take to the workplace.

This week, the IT team is working on user interface design for the new C³ system. One goal is to reduce input errors by using validation rules and input masks. The team leader has assigned you to do research and develop a recommendation. To perform these tasks, you must navigate to the Microsoft Access Help area, where you will see examples of validation rules and input masks. You should also review Chapter 8 of your systems analysis textbook.

Based on requirements modeling, you know that the new C³ system will store personal data about customers, their buying habits, and their interests. To reduce errors, the C³ user interface will use input masks where possible.

Here are five sample data items, with specific descriptions and examples:

| Data Item | Description | Examples |
| --- | --- | --- |
| First Name | Must start with a capital letter followed by at least one, and up to 9 more lowercase letters. | Li<br>Stephanie |
| Middle Initial | May have up to one capital letter, or none. | J |
| Last Name | Must start with a capital letter followed by at least one, and up to 11 more lowercase letters. | Steinbrenner<br>Ho |
| Category | Must start with two capital letters followed by two digits. | AB12<br>XY01 |
| Postal Code | Must have five digits, and may be followed by a hyphen and four more digits. | 12345<br>12345-9999 |

In addition to input masks, the team leader wants you to learn about validation rules and text. Specifically, she wants you to go back to the Microsoft Access Help area and review the explanation of validation rules, and the examples.

## Practice Tasks

A. Create an input mask for each data item shown in the table.
B. Develop a brief handout that explains the concept of validation rules. Include an example of a validation rule that will only accept the letters A or B.

After you complete the Practice Tasks, to check your work and view sample answers, visit the Management Information Systems CourseMate Web site at **www.cengagebrain.com**, navigate to the resources for this chapter, and locate Ready for a Challenge?.

## The Challenge

Now that you are familiar with input masks and validation rules, your team leader wants you to review two more data items, as follows:

| Customer ID | Must include the first capital letter of the customer's last name, followed by the last four digits of the customer's Social Security Number. | R0118<br>B1234 |
| --- | --- | --- |
| Password | Must include at least six, and no more than 12 letters or digits. | 1X2y3Z<br>123456789999 |

## Challenge Tasks

A. Create input masks for the two additional data items shown in the table.
B. Create a validation rule that will only accept numbers greater than 10 **and** less than 20.

# CHAPTER 9 Designing the Data

**Chapter 9** is the second of three chapters in the systems design phase of the SDLC. In this chapter, you will focus on data design skills that are necessary to construct the physical model of the information system.

## INTRODUCTION

### OBJECTIVES

*When you finish this chapter, you will be able to:*

- Explain file-oriented systems and how they differ from database management systems
- Explain data design terminology, including entities, fields, common fields, records, files, tables, and key fields
- Describe data relationships, draw an entity-relationship diagram, define cardinality, and use cardinality notation
- Explain the concept of normalization
- Explain the importance of codes and describe various coding schemes
- Explain data warehousing and data mining
- Differentiate between logical and physical storage and records
- Explain data control measures

During the systems analysis phase, you created a logical model of the system. Now, you must decide how data will be organized, stored, and managed. These are important issues that affect data quality and consistency.

This chapter begins with a review of data design concepts and terminology, then discusses file-based systems and database systems, including Web-based databases. You will learn how to create entity-relationship diagrams that show the relationships among data elements, and you will learn how to use normalization concepts. You also will learn about using codes to represent data items. The chapter concludes with a discussion of data storage and access issues, including data warehousing and data mining, physical design, logical and physical records, data storage formats, and data control.

## CHAPTER INTRODUCTION CASE:    Mountain View College Bookstore

**Background:** Wendy Lee, manager of college services at Mountain View College, wants a new information system that will improve efficiency and customer service at the three college bookstores.

In this part of the case, Tina Allen (systems analyst) and David Conroe (student intern) are talking about data design issues.

| | |
|---|---|
| **Participants:** | Tina and David |
| **Location:** | Mountain View College Cafeteria, Monday morning, December 5, 2011 |
| **Project status:** | Tina and David have completed their user interface design tasks and are ready to work on data design for the new system. |
| **Discussion topics:** | Data design terms and concepts, cardinality, relational databases, normalization, Web-based design, codes, and physical design issues |

**Tina:**    Good morning, David. Now that we have a logical model of the bookstore information system, we're ready for the next step. We have to select an overall data design strategy. I think we should start by looking at a relational database, rather than a file processing design.

**David:**    *What are the pros and cons?*

**Tina:**    Well, in some situations file processing systems are better, especially when you have to process large numbers of records in a sequence. But in our case, I think a relational database would be more powerful and flexible.

**David:**    *I know what a database is, but what do you mean by the term relational?*

**Tina:**    In a relational database, all the entities — the individual people, places, events, and transactions — are stored in separate locations called tables, which are related or linked together. That means you have to enter an item of data only once, and you can access all the data items just as if they were all stored in a single location.

**David:**    *That makes sense. How do we decide what data goes where?*

**Tina:**    We'll start by creating an entity-relationship diagram. Then we'll develop a set of table designs that follow a set of rules called normalization.

**David:**    *I've heard that term before. Aren't there several different levels of normalization, called normal forms?*

**Tina:**    Yes, and we want our data to be in what's called third normal form, which is what most business-related systems use. We also will consider using various codes to represent data items.

**David:**    *I know that we decided to build the system to run on the college network and then migrate to a Web-based system in the future. But shouldn't we use a design that will make it easy to migrate to the Web?*

**Tina:**    Yes, and a relational database will be the most flexible approach.

**David:**    *Sounds good. Any other issues?*

**Tina:**    Well, we need to consider some physical design issues, too. Here's a task list to get us started:

**FIGURE 9-1**  Typical data design task list.

## DATA DESIGN CONCEPTS

Before constructing an information system, a systems analyst must understand basic data design concepts, including data structures and the characteristics of file-oriented and database management systems, including Web-based database design.

### Data Structures

A **data structure** is a framework for organizing, storing, and managing data. Data structures consist of files or tables that interact in various ways. Each **file** or **table** contains data about people, places, things, or events. For example, one file or table might contain data about customers, and other files or tables might store data about products, orders, suppliers, or employees. Depending on how the files and tables are designed, an information system is called a file-oriented system or a database management system (DBMS).

Figure 9-2 shows a typical auto repair shop that handles tune-ups, brakes, and alignment. The following sections describe how this shop might manage its business data.

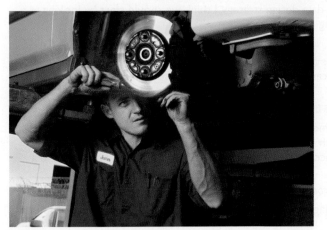

**FIGURE 9-2**   In the example shown here, data about the mechanic, the customer, and the brake job might be stored in a file-oriented system or in a database system.

**FILE-ORIENTED SYSTEM**   A **file-oriented system**, sometimes called a file processing system, stores data in one or more separate files. For example, Figure 9-3 shows the auto repair shop with two separate file-oriented systems: A Job Records system that uses a JOB data file, and an Employee Records system that uses a MECHANIC data file. In the example, the JOB file contains the data necessary to answer inquiries and generate reports about work performed at the shop. Similarly, the MECHANIC file stores the data necessary to answer inquiries and generate reports about the shop's employees.

Notice that the same data is stored in more than one location. For example, three items of information (Mechanic No, Name, and Pay Rate) are stored in both data files. This redundancy is a major disadvantage of file-oriented systems, because it reduces efficiency and data quality.

**DATABASE MANAGEMENT SYSTEM**   In a **database management system (DBMS)**, all the tables are connected by common fields. A typical common field might be a Customer Number, which could be used to locate information about that customer in other tables. A common field that connects two tables is said to *link*, *join*, or *relate* the tables.

In a DBMS, the linked tables form a unified data structure that greatly improves data quality and access. This design, also called a **relational database** or **relational model**, was introduced in the 1970s and continues to be the most popular approach for organizing, storing, and managing business data.

Now consider Figure 9-4, which shows how the same auto repair shop might use a relational database instead of a file-oriented system. Notice that the two tables are linked by the Mechanic No field. This link allows information to be accessed from either table as if the two tables were one large table, making it unnecessary to store duplicate information.

### Overview of File Processing

Although file processing is an older approach, you should understand how these systems were designed, constructed, and maintained. Some companies still use file processing to handle large volumes of structured data on a regular basis. Many older legacy systems

**File-Oriented Design**
The two systems use separate data files. This results in the redundancy shown.

Job Records System                    Employee Records System

JOB
  Job No
  Work Code
  Hours
  Date
  Mechanic No
  Name
  Pay Rate

MECHANIC
  Mechanic No
  Name
  Pay Rate
  Hire Date
  Status
  Insurance

| Mechanic No | Name | Pay Rate | Hire Date | Status | Insurance |
|---|---|---|---|---|---|
| 12 | Lear, Robert | $15.00 | 4/17/2010 | Part-time | No |
| 17 | Jones, Jim | $17.50 | 1/15/1998 | Full-time | Yes |
| 23 | Smith, Stacy | $20.00 | 7/1/1996 | Full-time | Yes |

JOB

| Job No | Work Code | Hours | Date | Mechanic No | Name | Pay Rate |
|---|---|---|---|---|---|---|
| 198 | TUNE | 3.2 | 12/6/2011 | 12 | Lear, Robert | $15.00 |
| 110 | BRAKES | 4.0 | 12/5/2011 | 17 | Jones, Jim | $17.50 |
| 134 | ALIGN | 3.0 | 12/6/2011 | 23 | Smith, Stacy | $20.00 |

**FIGURE 9-3**   This auto repair shop uses two separate systems: a Job Records system and an Employee Records system. This design requires the same data to be entered in two different places.

**Database Management System**
Data is stored in separate tables, which are linked by a common field. Data is stored in only one physical location, as shown.

Relationships

JOB
  Job No
  Work Code
  Hours
  Date
  Mechanic No

MECHANIC
  Mechanic No
  Name
  Pay Rate
  Hire Date
  Status
  Insurance

JOB - MECHANIC DATABASE

| Job No | Work Code | Hours | Date | Mechanic No | Name | Pay Rate | Hire Date | Status | Insurance |
|---|---|---|---|---|---|---|---|---|---|
| 110 | BRAKES | 4.0 | 12/5/2011 | 17 | Jones, Jim | $17.50 | 1/15/1998 | Full-time | Yes |
| 134 | ALIGN | 3.0 | 12/6/2011 | 23 | Smith, Stacy | $20.00 | 7/1/1996 | Full-time | Yes |
| 198 | TUNE | 3.2 | 12/6/2011 | 12 | Lear, Robert | $15.00 | 4/17/2010 | Part-time | No |

The linked tables behave as if they were one large table, no matter where the data is stored physically.

**FIGURE 9-4**   This is how the same repair shop could use a database design that avoids duplication. A common field joins the tables, and the data behaves like one large table, regardless of where it physically is stored.

utilized file processing designs because that method worked well with mainframe hardware and batch input. Although much less common today, file processing can be efficient and cost-effective in certain situations. For example, consider a credit card company that posts thousands of daily transactions from a TRANSACTION file to customer balances stored in a CUSTOMER file, as shown in Figure 9-5. For that relatively simple process, file processing is highly effective.

**TRANSACTION file**

| Customer No: | S3914 |
| Date: | 10-13-2011 |
| Code: | Charge |
| Amount: | $10.00 |

| Customer No: | S3914 |
| Date: | 10-27-2011 |
| Code: | Charge |
| Amount: | $15.00 |

**CUSTOMER file**

| Customer No: | S3914 |
| Customer Name: | Mary Smith |
| Balance Due: | $25.00 |

**FIGURE 9-5**  A credit card company might use a file processing system to post daily sales transactions from a TRANSACTION file to the CUSTOMER file.

In a typical file processing environment, a company might have three departments, each with its own information system and data files. Three potential problems exist in a file processing environment. The first problem is **data redundancy**, which means that data common to two or more information systems is stored in several places. Data redundancy requires more storage space, and maintaining and updating data in several locations is expensive.

Second, **data integrity** problems can occur if updates are not applied in every file. Changing the data in only one of the systems will cause inconsistent data and result in incorrect information in the second system.

The third problem is the rigid data structure of a typical file processing environment. Businesses must make decisions based on company-wide data, and managers often require information from multiple business units and departments. In a file processing environment, that means retrieving information from independent, file-based systems, which is slow and inefficient.

A file-oriented information system can contain various types of files, including master files, table files, transaction files, work files, security files, and history files.

- A **master file** stores relatively permanent data about an entity. For example, a PRODUCT master file contains one logical record for each product the company sells. The quantity field in each record might change daily, but other data, such as the product's code, name, and description, would not change.

- A **table file** contains reference data used by the information system. As with master files, table files are relatively static and are not updated by the information system. Examples of table files include tax tables and postage rate tables.

- A **transaction file** stores records that contain day-to-day business and operational data. A transaction file is an input file that updates a master file; after the update is completed, the transaction file has served its purpose. An example of a transaction file is a charges and payments file that updates a customer balance file.

- A **work file** is a temporary file created by an information system for a single task. Examples of work files include sorted files and report files that hold output reports until they are printed.

- A **security file** is created and saved for backup and recovery purposes. Examples of security files include audit trail files and backups of master, table, and transaction files. New security files must be created regularly to replace outdated files.

- A **history file** is a file created for archiving purposes. For example, students who have not registered for any course in the last two semesters might be deleted from the active student master file and added to an inactive student file, which is a history file that can be used for queries or reports.

These problems do not exist in a database system, which is explained in the following section.

## The Evolution from File Systems to Database Systems

A properly designed database system offers a solution to the problems of file processing. A database provides an overall framework that avoids data redundancy and supports a real-time, dynamic environment, two potential problems of a file processing system.

In a file processing environment, data files are designed to fit individual business systems. In contrast, in a database environment, several systems can be built around a single database. Figure 9-6 shows a database environment with a database serving four separate information systems.

A **database management system (DBMS)** is a collection of tools, features, and interfaces that enables users to add, update, manage, access, and analyze the contents of a set of data. From a user's point of view, the main advantage of a DBMS is that it offers timely, interactive, and flexible data access. Specific DBMS advantages include the following:

**FIGURE 9-6**  In this example, a sales database can support four separate business systems.

- **Scalability**, which means that a system can be expanded, modified, or downsized easily to meet the rapidly changing needs of a business enterprise. For example, if a company decides to add data about secondary suppliers of material it uses, a new table can be added to the relational database and linked with a common field.

- Better support for client/server systems. In a **client/server** system, processing is distributed throughout the organization. Client/server systems require the power and flexibility of a database design. You will learn more about client/server systems in Chapter 10.

- Economy of scale. Database design allows better utilization of hardware. If a company maintains an enterprise-wide database, processing is less expensive using a powerful mainframe server instead of using several smaller computers. The inherent efficiency of high-volume processing on larger computers is called **economy of scale**.

- Flexible data sharing. Data can be shared across the enterprise, allowing more users to access more data. A database can be highly flexible, allowing users to view the same information in different ways. Users are empowered because they have access to the information they need to do their jobs.

- Enterprise-wide application. Typically, a DBMS is managed by a person called a **database administrator (DBA)**, who assesses overall requirements and maintains the database for the benefit of the entire organization rather than a single department or user. Database systems can support enterprise-wide applications more effectively than file processing systems.

- Stronger standards. Effective database administration helps ensure that standards for data names, formats, and documentation are followed uniformly throughout the organization.

- Controlled redundancy. Redundancy means storing data in more than one place, which can result in inconsistency and data errors. Because the data is stored in a set of related tables, data items do not need to be duplicated in multiple locations. Even where some duplication is desirable for performance reasons, or disaster recovery, the database approach allows control of the redundancy.

- Better security. The DBA can define authorization procedures to ensure that only legitimate users can access the database and can allow different users to have different levels of access. Most DBMSs provide sophisticated security support.

- Increased programmer productivity. Programmers do not have to create the underlying file structure for a database. That allows them to concentrate on logical design and, therefore, a new database application can be developed more quickly than in a file-oriented system.

- Data independence. Systems that interact with a DBMS are relatively independent of how the physical data is maintained. That design provides the DBA flexibility to alter data structures without modifying information systems that use the data.

Although the trend is toward enterprise-wide database design, many companies still use a combination of centralized DBMSs and smaller, department-level database systems. Why is this so? Most large businesses view data as a company-wide resource that must be accessible to users throughout the company. At the same time, other factors encourage a decentralized design, including network expense; a reluctance to move away from smaller, more flexible systems; and a realization that enterprise-wide DBMSs can be highly complex and expensive to maintain. The compromise, in many cases, is a client/server design, where processing is shared among several computers. Client/server systems are described in detail in Chapter 10. As with many design decisions, the best solution depends on the individual circumstances.

# DBMS COMPONENTS

A DBMS provides an interface between a database and users who need to access the data. Although users are concerned primarily with an easy-to-use interface and support for their business requirements, a systems analyst must understand all of the components of a DBMS. In addition to interfaces for users, database administrators, and related systems, a DBMS also has a data manipulation language, a schema and subschemas, and a physical data repository, as shown in Figure 9-7.

**FIGURE 9-7** In addition to interfaces for users, database administrators, and related information systems, a DBMS also has a data manipulation language, a schema and subschemas, and a physical data repository.

## Interfaces for Users, Database Administrators, and Related Systems

When users, database administrators, and related information systems request data and services, the DBMS processes the request, manipulates the data, and provides a response.

**USERS** Users typically work with predefined queries and switchboard commands, but also use query languages to access stored data. A **query language** allows a user to specify a task without specifying how the task will be accomplished. Some query languages use natural language commands that resemble ordinary English sentences. With a **query by example (QBE)** language, the user provides an example of the data requested. Many database programs also generate **SQL** (**Structured Query Language**), which is a language that allows client workstations to communicate with servers and mainframe computers. Figure 9-8 shows a QBE request for all Red Candy Metallic or Blue Flame Metallic 2011 Ford Fusions with navigation. The QBE request generates the SQL commands shown at the bottom of Figure 9-8.

**DATABASE ADMINISTRATORS** A DBA is responsible for DBMS management and support. DBAs are concerned with data security and integrity, preventing unauthorized access, providing backup and recovery, audit trails, maintaining the database, and supporting user needs. Most DBMSs provide utility programs to assist the DBA in creating and updating data structures, collecting and reporting patterns of database usage, and detecting and reporting database irregularities.

**RELATED INFORMATION SYSTEMS** A DBMS can support several related information systems that provide input to, and require specific data from, the DBMS. Unlike a user interface, no human intervention is required for two-way communication between the DBMS and the related systems.

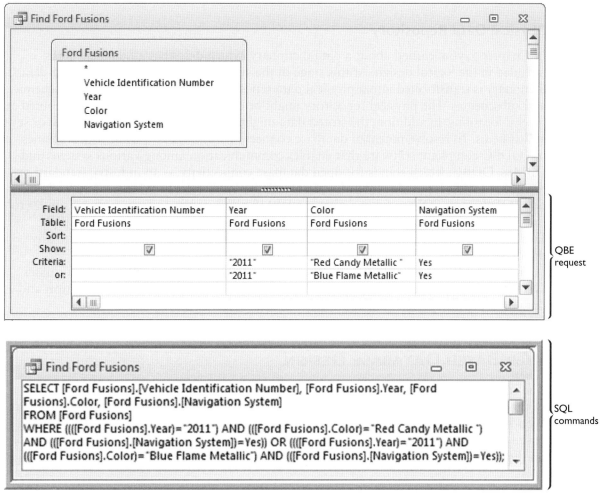

**FIGURE 9-8**  Using QBE, a user can request a list of all Red Candy Metallic or Blue Flame Metallic 2011 Ford Fusions with navigation.

## Data Manipulation Language

A **data manipulation language** (DML) controls database operations, including storing, retrieving, updating, and deleting data. Most commercial DBMSs, such as Oracle and IBM's DB/2, use a DML. Some database products, such as Microsoft Access, also provide an easy-to-use graphical environment that enables users to control operations with menu-driven commands.

## Schema

The complete definition of a database, including descriptions of all fields, tables, and relationships, is called a **schema**. You also can define one or more subschemas. A **subschema** is a view of the database used by one or more systems or users. A subschema defines only those portions of the database that a particular system or user needs or is allowed to access. For example, to protect individual privacy, you might not want to allow a project management system to retrieve employee pay rates. In that case, the project management system subschema would not include the pay rate field. Database designers also use subschemas to restrict the level of access permitted. For example, specific users, systems, or locations might be permitted to create, retrieve, update, or delete data, depending on their needs and the company's security policies.

## Physical Data Repository

In Chapter 5, you learned about a data dictionary, which describes all data elements included in the logical design. At this stage of the systems development process, the data dictionary is transformed into a physical data repository, which also contains the schema and subschemas. The physical repository might be centralized, or it might be distributed at several locations. In addition, the stored data might be managed by a single DBMS, or several systems. To resolve potential database connectivity and access problems, companies use ODBC-compliant software that enables communication among various systems and DBMSs. **ODBC**, which stands for **open database connectivity**, is an industry-standard protocol that makes it possible for software from different vendors to interact and exchange data. ODBC uses SQL statements that the DBMS understands and can execute, similar to the ones shown in Figure 9-7 on page 396. Another common standard is called **JDBC**, or **Java database connectivity**. JDBC enables Java applications to exchange data with any database that uses SQL statements and is JDBC-compliant.

You will learn more about physical design issues in Chapter 10, which discusses system architecture, and in Chapter 11, which discusses system implementation and data conversion.

## WEB-BASED DATABASE DESIGN

The concept of Web-based systems was discussed in Chapter 7, Options for Development. In this chapter, you will revisit this concept and examine the main components of a Web-based database system. The following sections discuss the characteristics of Web-based design, Internet terminology, connecting a database to the Web, and data security on the Web.

### Characteristics of Web-Based Design

Figure 9-9 on the next page lists some major characteristics of Web-based database design. In a Web-based design, the Internet serves as the front end, or interface, for the database management system. Internet technology provides enormous power and flexibility because the system is not tied to any specific combination of hardware and software. Access to the database requires only a Web browser and an Internet connection. Web-based systems are popular because they offer ease of access, cost-effectiveness, and worldwide connectivity — all of which are vital to companies that must compete in a global economy.

## Web-Based Database Design Characteristics

| CHARACTERISTIC | EXPLANATION |
| --- | --- |
| Global access | The Internet enables worldwide access, using existing infrastructure and standard telecommunications protocols. |
| Ease of use | Web browsers provide a familiar interface that is user-friendly and easily learned. |
| Multiple platforms | Web-based design is not dependent on a specific combination of hardware or software. All that is required is a browser and an Internet connection. |
| Cost effectiveness | Initial investment is relatively low because the Internet serves as the communication network. Users require only a browser, and Web-based systems do not require powerful workstations. Flexibility is high because numerous outsourcing options exist for development, hosting, maintenance, and system support. |
| Security issues | Security is a universal issue, but Internet connectivity raises special concerns. These can be addressed with a combination of good design, software that can protect the system and detect intrusion, stringent rules for passwords and user identification, and vigilant users and managers. |
| Adaptability issues | The Internet offers many advantages in terms of access, connectivity, and flexibility. Migrating a traditional database design to the Web, however, can require design modification, additional software, and some added expense. |

**FIGURE 9-9**   Web-based design characteristics include global access, ease of use, multiple platforms, cost effectiveness, security issues, and adaptability issues. In a Web-based design, the Internet serves as the front end, or interface, for the database management system. Access to the database requires only a Web browser and an Internet connection.

## Internet Terminology

To understand Web-based data design, it is helpful to review some basic Internet terms and concepts. To access information on the Internet, a person uses a **Web browser**, which is an application that enables the user to navigate, or browse, the Internet and display Web pages on his or her local computer. A **Web page** is a text document written in **HTML (Hypertext Markup Language)**. HTML uses formatting codes called **tags**, which specify how the text and visual elements will be displayed in a Web browser. Web pages are stored on a **Web server**, which is a computer that receives requests and makes Web pages available to users. Together, the Web server and the Web pages are referred to as a **Web site**.

In addition to maintaining a Web site, many companies use intranets and extranets to support business operations and communications. An **intranet** is a private, company-owned

ON THE WEB

To learn more about HTML, visit the Management Information Systems CourseMate Web site at **www. cengagebrain. com**, navigate to **On the Web Links** for this chapter, and locate the HTML link.

network to provide Web-based access to internal users. An **extranet** is an extension of a company intranet that allows access by external users, such as customers and suppliers. Extranets are typical examples of B2B (business-to-business) data sharing and EDI (electronic data interchange), which were discussed in Chapter 1, where you also learned about Extensible Markup Language (XML). XML is a flexible data description language that allows Web-based communication between different hardware and software environments. Because intranets and extranets use the same **protocols**, or data transmission standards, as the Internet, they are called **Web-centric**.

The Internet and company intranets/extranets are forms of client/server architecture. In a client/server design, tasks are divided between **clients**, which are workstations that users interact with, and **servers**, which are computers that supply data, processing, and services to the client workstations. Client/server architecture is discussed in more detail in Chapter 10, System Construction Planning.

## Connecting a Database to the Web

To access data in a Web-based system, the database must be connected to the Internet or intranet. The database and the Internet speak two different languages, however. Databases are created and managed by using various languages and commands that have nothing to do with HTML, which is the language of the Web. The objective is to connect the database to the Web and enable data to be viewed and updated.

To bridge the gap, it is necessary to use **middleware**, which is software that integrates different applications and allows them to exchange data. Middleware can interpret client requests in HTML form and translate the requests into commands that the database can execute. When the database responds to the commands, middleware translates the results into HTML pages that can be displayed by the user's browser, as shown in Figure 9-10. Notice that the four steps in the process can take place using the Internet or a company intranet as the communications channel.

**FIGURE 9-10**   When a client workstation requests a Web page (1), the Web server uses middleware to generate a data query to the database server (2). The database server responds (3) and middleware translates the retrieved data into an HTML page that can be sent by the Web server and displayed by the user's browser (4).

A popular example of middleware is Adobe ColdFusion, which is shown in Figure 9-11. Middleware is discussed in more detail in Chapter 10.

**FIGURE 9-11**    Adobe ColdFusion is a popular example of middleware.

## Data Security

Web-based data must be secure, yet easily accessible to authorized users. To achieve this goal, well-designed systems provide security at three levels: the database itself, the Web server, and the telecommunication links that connect the components of the system.

Data security is discussed in this chapter and in Chapter 12, Securing and Supporting the System.

## DATA DESIGN TERMINOLOGY

Using the concepts discussed in the previous section, a systems analyst can select a design approach and begin to construct the system. The first step is to understand data design terminology.

## Definitions

Data design terms include entity, table, file, field, record, tuple, and key field. These terms are explained in the following sections.

**ENTITY**   An **entity** is a person, place, thing, or event for which data is collected and maintained. For example, an online sales system may include entities named CUSTOMER, ORDER, PRODUCT, and SUPPLIER. When you prepared DFDs during the systems analysis phase, you identified various entities and data stores. Now you will consider the relationships among the entities.

**TABLE OR FILE** Data is organized into tables or files. A table, or file, contains a set of related records that store data about a specific entity. Tables and files are shown as two-dimensional structures that consist of vertical columns and horizontal rows. Each column represents a field, or characteristic of the entity, and each row represents a record, which is an individual instance, or occurrence of the entity. For example, if a company has 10,000 customers, the CUSTOMER table will include 10,000 records, each representing a specific customer.

Although they can have different meanings in a specific context, the terms *table* and *file* often can be used interchangeably.

**FIELD** A **field**, also called an **attribute**, is a single characteristic or fact about an entity. For example, a CUSTOMER entity might include the Customer ID, First Name, Last Name, Address, City, State, Zip, and E-mail Address.

A **common field** is an attribute that appears in more than one entity. Common fields can be used to link entities in various types of relationships.

**RECORD** A **record**, also called a **tuple** (rhymes with couple), is a set of related fields that describes one instance, or occurrence of an entity, such as one customer, one order, or one product. A record might have one or dozens of fields, depending on what information is needed.

## Key Fields

During the systems design phase, you use **key fields** to organize, access, and maintain data structures. The four types of keys are primary keys, candidate keys, foreign keys, and secondary keys.

**PRIMARY KEY** A **primary key** is a field or combination of fields that uniquely and minimally identifies a particular member of an entity. For example, in a customer table the customer number is a unique primary key because no two customers can have the same customer number. That key also is minimal because it contains no information beyond what is needed to identify the customer. In a CUSTOMER table, a Customer ID might be used as a unique primary key. Customer ID is an example of a primary key based on a single field.

A primary key also can be composed of two or more fields. For example, if a student registers for three courses, his or her student number will appear in three records in the registration system. If one of those courses has 20 students, 20 separate records will exist for that course number — one record for each student who registered.

In the registration file, neither the student number nor the course ID is unique, so neither field can be a primary key. To identify a specific student in a specific course, the primary key must be a combination of student number and course ID. In that case, the primary key is called a **combination key**. A combination key also can be called a **composite key**, a **concatenated key**, or a **multivalued key**.

Figure 9-12 shows four different tables. The first three tables have single-field primary keys. Notice that in the fourth table, however, the primary key is a combination of two fields: STUDENT-NUMBER and COURSE-ID.

**CANDIDATE KEY** Sometimes you have a choice of fields or field combinations to use as the primary key. Any field that could serve as a primary key is called a **candidate key**. For example, if every employee has a unique employee number, then you could use either the employee number or the Social Security number as a primary key. Because you can designate only one field as a primary key, you should select the field that contains the least amount of data and is the easiest to use. Any field that is not a primary key or a candidate key is called a **nonkey field**.

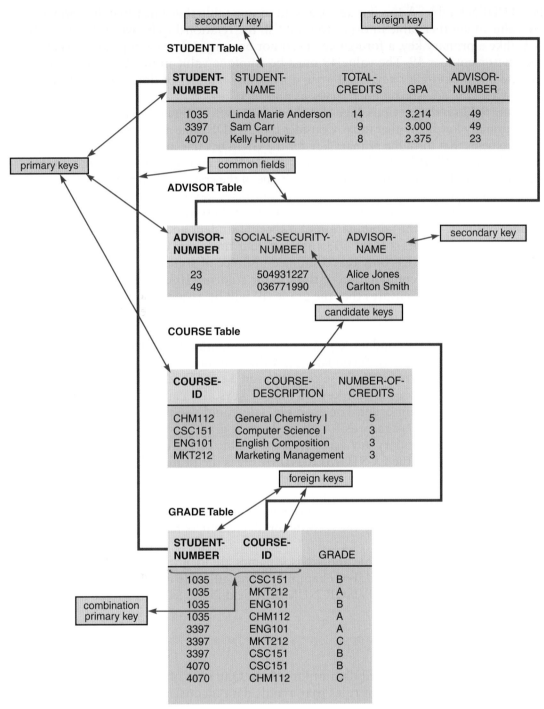

**FIGURE 9-12** Examples of common fields, primary keys, candidate keys, foreign keys, and secondary keys.

The primary keys shown in Figure 9-12 also are candidate keys. Two other candidate keys exist: the SOCIAL-SECURITY-NUMBER field in the ADVISOR table and the COURSE-DESCRIPTION field in the COURSE table.

**FOREIGN KEY** Recall that a common field exists in more than one table and can be used to form a relationship, or link, between the tables. For example, in Figure 9-12, the ADVISOR-NUMBER field appears in both the STUDENT table and the ADVISOR table and joins the tables together. Notice that ADVISOR-NUMBER is a primary key in the ADVISOR table, where it uniquely identifies each advisor, and is a foreign key in the STUDENT table. A **foreign key** is a field in one table that must match a primary key value in another table in order to establish the relationship between the two tables.

Unlike a primary key, a foreign key need not be unique. For example, Carlton Smith has advisor number 49. The value 49 must be a unique value in the ADVISOR table because it is the primary key, but 49 can appear any number of times in the STUDENT table, where the advisor number serves as a foreign key.

Figure 9-12 on the previous page also shows how two foreign keys can serve as a composite primary key in another table. Consider the GRADE table at the bottom of the figure. The two fields that form the primary key for the GRADE table are both foreign keys: the STUDENT-NUMBER field, which must match a student number in the STUDENT table, and the COURSE-ID field, which must match one of the course IDs in the COURSE table.

How can these two foreign keys serve as a primary key in the GRADE table? When you study the table, you will notice that student numbers and course IDs can appear any number of times, but the *combination* of a specific student and a specific course occurs only once. For example, student 1035 appears four times and course CSC151 appears three times — but there is only *one* combined instance of student 1035 *and* course CSC151. Because the combination of the specific student (1035) and the specific course (CSC151) is unique, it ensures that the grade (B) will be assigned to the proper student in the proper course.

**SECONDARY KEY** A **secondary key** is a field or combination of fields that can be used to access or retrieve records. Secondary key values are not unique. For example, if you need to access records for only those customers in a specific ZIP code, you would use the ZIP code field as a secondary key. Secondary keys also can be used to sort or display records in a certain order. For example, you could use the GPA field in a STUDENT file to display records for all students in grade point order.

The need for a secondary key arises because a table can have only one primary key. In a CUSTOMER file, the CUSTOMER-NUMBER is the primary key, so it must be unique. You might know a customer's name, but not the customer's number. For example, you might want to access a customer named James Morgan, but you do not know his customer number. If you search the table using the CUSTOMER-NAME field as a secondary key, you can retrieve the records for all customers named James Morgan and then select the correct one.

In Figure 9-12, student name and advisor names are identified as secondary keys, but other fields also could be used. For example, to find all students who have a particular advisor, you could use the ADVISOR-NUMBER field in the STUDENT file as a secondary key.

## Referential Integrity

Validity checks can help avoid data input errors. One type of validity check, called **referential integrity**, is a set of rules that avoids data inconsistency and quality problems. In a relational database, referential integrity means that a foreign key value cannot be entered in one table unless it matches an existing primary key in another table. For example, referential integrity would prevent you from entering a customer order in an order table unless that customer already exists in the customer table. Without referential integrity, you might have an order called an **orphan**, because it had no related customer.

In the example shown in Figure 9-12 on page 403, referential integrity will not allow a user to enter an advisor number (foreign key value) in the STUDENT table unless a valid advisor number (primary key value) already exists in the ADVISOR table.

**ON THE WEB**

To learn more about referential integrity, visit the Management Information Systems CourseMate Web site at **www.cengagebrain.com**, navigate to **On the Web Links** for this chapter, and locate the Referential Integrity link.

Referential integrity also can prevent the deletion of a record if the record has a primary key that matches foreign keys in another table. For example, suppose that an advisor resigns to accept a position at another school. You cannot delete the advisor from the ADVISOR table while records in the STUDENT file still refer to that advisor number. Otherwise, the STUDENT records would be orphans. To avoid the problem, students must be reassigned to other advisors by changing the value in the ADVISOR-NUMBER field; then the advisor record can be deleted.

When creating a relational database, you can build referential integrity into the design. Figure 9-13 shows a Microsoft Access screen that identifies a common field and allows the user to enforce referential integrity rules.

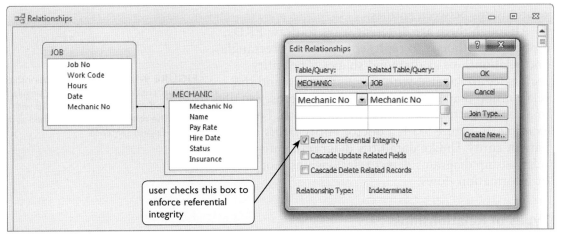

**FIGURE 9-13** Microsoft Access allows a user to specify that referential integrity rules will be enforced in a relational database design.

## VIDEO LEARNING SESSION: ENTITY-RELATIONSHIP DIAGRAMS

Video Learning Sessions can help you understand key concepts, practice your skills, and check your work. To access the sessions, visit the Management Information Systems CourseMate Web site at **www.cengagebrain.com** and navigate to the **Video Learning Sessions** for this book. In this session, you'll learn how to create an entity-relationship diagram (ERD) that shows the system entities and the nature of their relationships.

## ENTITY-RELATIONSHIP DIAGRAMS

Recall that an entity is a person, place, thing, or event for which data is collected and maintained. For example, entities might be customers, sales regions, products, or orders. An information system must recognize the relationships among entities. For example, a *customer* entity can have several instances of an *order* entity, and an *employee* entity can have one instance, or none, of a *spouse* entity.

**ON THE WEB**

To learn more about entity-relationship diagrams, visit the Management Information Systems CourseMate Web site at **www. cengagebrain. com**, navigate to **On the Web Links** for this chapter, and locate the Entity-Relationship Diagrams link.

An **entity-relationship diagram (ERD)** is a model that shows the logical relationships and interaction among system entities. An ERD provides an overall view of the system and a blueprint for creating the physical data structures.

## Drawing an ERD

The first step is to list the entities that you identified during the systems analysis phase and to consider the nature of the relationships that link them. At this stage, you can use a simplified method to show the relationships between entities.

Although there are different ways to draw ERDs, a popular method is to represent entities as rectangles and relationships as diamond shapes. The entity rectangles are labeled with singular nouns, and the relationship diamonds are labeled with verbs, usually in a top-to-bottom and left-to-right fashion. For example, in Figure 9-14, a doctor entity *treats* a patient entity. Unlike data flow diagrams, entity-relationship diagrams depict relationships, not data or information flows.

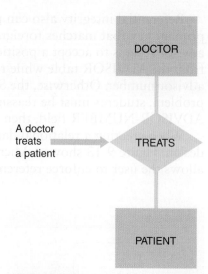

**FIGURE 9-14** In an entity-relationship diagram, entities are labeled with singular nouns and relationships are labeled with verbs. The relationship is interpreted as a simple English sentence.

## Types of Relationships

Three types of relationships can exist between entities: one-to-one, one-to-many, and many-to-many.

A **one-to-one relationship**, abbreviated **1:1**, exists when exactly one of the second entity occurs for each instance of the first entity. Figure 9-15 shows examples of several 1:1 relationships. A number 1 is placed alongside each of the two connecting lines to indicate the 1:1 relationship.

A **one-to-many relationship**, abbreviated **1:M**, exists when one occurrence of the first entity can relate to many instances of the second entity, but each instance of the second entity can associate with only one instance of the first entity. For example, the relationship between DEPARTMENT and EMPLOYEE is one-to-many: One department can have many employees, but each employee works in only one department at a time. Figure 9-16 shows several 1:M relationships. The line connecting the *many* entity is labeled with the letter M, and the number 1 labels the other connecting line. How many is *many*? The first 1:M relationship shown in Figure 9-16 shows the entities INDIVIDUAL and AUTOMOBILE. One individual might own five automobiles, or one, or none. Thus, *many* can mean any number, including zero.

**FIGURE 9-15** Examples of one-to-one (1:1) relationships.

A **many-to-many relationship**, abbreviated **M:N**, exists when one instance of the first entity can relate to many instances of the second entity, and one instance of the second entity can relate to many instances of the first entity. The relationship between STUDENT and CLASS, for example, is many-to-many — one student can take many classes, and one class can have many students enrolled. Figure 9-17 shows several M:N entity-relationships. One of the connecting lines is labeled with the letter M, and the letter N labels the other connection.

Notice that an M:N relationship is different from 1:1 or 1:M relationships because the event or transaction that links the two entities is actually a third entity, called an **associative entity** that has its own characteristics. In the first example in Figure 9-17,

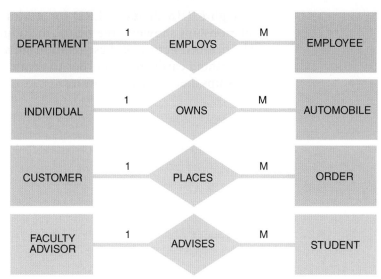

**FIGURE 9-16** Examples of one-to-many (1:M) relationships.

the ENROLLS IN symbol represents a REGISTRATION entity that records each instance of a specific student enrolling in a specific course. Similarly, the RESERVES SEAT ON symbol represents a RESERVATION entity that records each instance of a specific passenger reserving a seat on a specific flight. In the third example, the LISTS symbol represents an ORDER-LINE entity that records each instance of a specific product listed in a specific customer order.

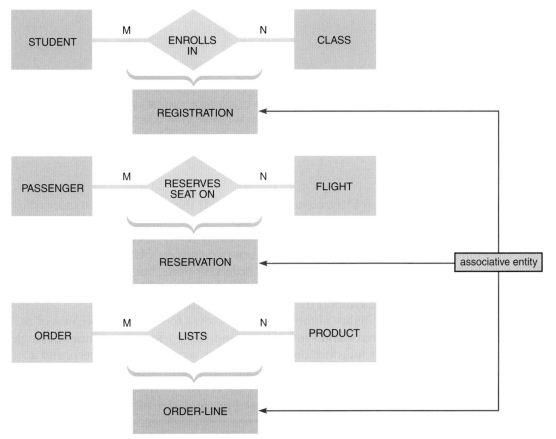

**FIGURE 9-17** Examples of many-to-many (M:N) relationships. Notice that the event or transaction that links the two entities is an associative entity with its own set of attributes and characteristics.

Figure 9-18 shows an ERD for a sales system. Notice the various entities and relationships shown in the figure, including the associative entity named ORDER-LINE. The detailed nature of these relationships is called cardinality. As an analyst, you must understand cardinality in order to create a data design that accurately reflects all relationships among system entities.

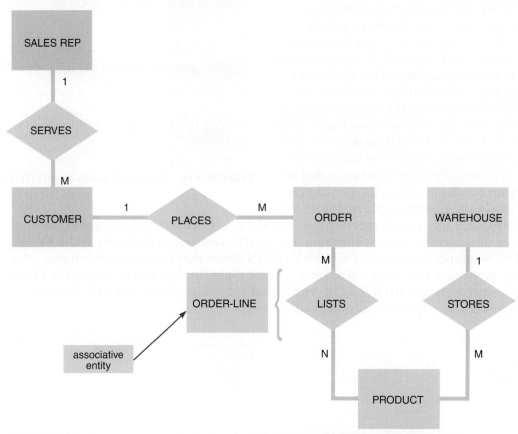

**FIGURE 9-18** An entity-relationship diagram for SALES REP, CUSTOMER, ORDER, PRODUCT, and WAREHOUSE. Notice that the ORDER and PRODUCT entities are joined by an associative entity named ORDER-LINE.

## Cardinality

**ON THE WEB**

To learn more about cardinality, visit the Management Information Systems CourseMate Web site at **www. cengagebrain. com**, navigate to **On the Web Links** for this chapter, and locate the Cardinality link.

After an analyst draws an initial ERD, he or she must define the relationships in more detail by using a technique called cardinality. **Cardinality** describes the numeric relationship between two entities and shows how instances of one entity relate to instances of another entity. For example, consider the relationship between two entities: CUSTOMER and ORDER. One customer can have one order, many orders, or none, but each order must have one and only one customer. An analyst can model this interaction by adding **cardinality notation**, which uses special symbols to represent the relationship.

A common method of cardinality notation is called **crow's foot notation** because of the shapes, which include circles, bars, and symbols, that indicate various possibilities. A single bar indicates one, a double bar indicates one and only one, a circle indicates zero, and a crow's foot indicates many. Figure 9-19 shows various cardinality symbols, their meanings, and the UML representations of the relationships. As you learned in Chapter 4, the **Unified Modeling Language (UML)** is a widely used method of visualizing and documenting software systems design.

In Figure 9-20, four examples of cardinality notation are shown. In the first example, one and only one CUSTOMER can place anywhere from zero to many of the ORDER entity. In the second example, one and only one ORDER can include one ITEM ORDERED or many. In the third example, one and only one EMPLOYEE can have one SPOUSE or none. In the fourth example, one EMPLOYEE, or many employees, or none, can be assigned to one PROJECT, or many projects, or none.

Most CASE products support the drawing of ERDs from entities in the data repository. Figure 9-21 on the next page shows part of a library system ERD drawn using the Visible Analyst CASE tool. Notice that crow's foot notation is used to show the nature of the relationships, which are described in both directions.

Now that you understand database elements and their relationships, you can start designing tables. The first step is the normalization of your table designs, which is described next.

**FIGURE 9-19**   Crow's foot notation is a common method of indicating cardinality. The four examples show how you can use various symbols to describe the relationships between entities.

**FIGURE 9-20**   In the first example of cardinality notation, one and only one CUSTOMER can place anywhere from zero to many of the ORDER entity. In the second example, one and only one ORDER can include one ITEM ORDERED or many. In the third example, one and only one EMPLOYEE can have one SPOUSE or none. In the fourth example, one EMPLOYEE, or many employees, or none, can be assigned to one PROJECT, or many projects, or none.

**FIGURE 9-21** An ERD for a library system drawn with Visible Analyst. Notice that crow's foot notation has been used and relationships are described in both directions.

## CASE IN POINT 9.1: TopText Publishing

TopText Publishing is a textbook publishing company with a headquarters location, a warehouse, and three sales offices that each have a sales manager and sales reps. TopText sells to schools, colleges, and individual customers. Many authors write more than one book for TopText, and some books are written by more than one author. TopText maintains an active list of more than 100 books, each identified by a universal code called an ISBN number. You have been asked to draw an ERD for the TopText information system, and to include cardinality notation.

## NORMALIZATION

**Normalization** is the process of creating table designs by assigning specific fields or attributes to each table in the database. A **table design** specifies the fields and identifies the primary key in a particular table or file. Working with a set of initial table designs, you use normalization to develop an overall database design that is simple, flexible, and free of data redundancy. Normalization involves applying a set of rules that can help you identify and correct inherent problems and complexities in your table designs. The concept of normalization is based on the work of Edgar Codd, a British computer scientist who formulated the basic principles of relational database design.

The normalization process typically involves four stages: unnormalized design, first normal form, second normal form, and third normal form. The three normal forms constitute a progression in which third normal form represents the best design. Most business-related databases must be designed in third normal form.

## Standard Notation Format

Designing tables is easier if you use a **standard notation format** to show a table's structure, fields, and primary key. The standard notation format in the following examples starts with the name of the table, followed by a parenthetical expression that contains the field names separated by commas. The primary key field(s) is underlined, like this:

NAME (<u>FIELD 1</u>, FIELD 2, FIELD 3)

## Repeating Groups and Unnormalized Designs

During data design, you must be able to recognize a repeating group of fields. A **repeating group** is a set of one or more fields that can occur any number of times in a single record, with each occurrence having different values.

Repeating groups often occur in manual documents prepared by users. For example, consider a school registration form with the student's information at the top of the form, followed by a list of courses the student is taking. If you were to design a table based on this registration form, the courses would represent a repeating group of values for each student.

An example of a repeating group is shown in Figure 9-22. The first two records in the ORDER table contain multiple products, which represent a repeating group of fields. Notice that in addition to the order number and date, the records with multiple products contain repetitions of the product number, description, and number ordered. You can think of a repeating group as a set of child (subsidiary) records contained within the parent (main) record.

A table design that contains a repeating group is called **unnormalized**. The standard notation method for representing an unnormalized design is to enclose the repeating group of fields within a second set of parentheses. An example of an unnormalized table would look like this:

NAME (<u>FIELD 1</u>, FIELD 2, FIELD 3, (REPEATING FIELD 1, REPEATING FIELD 2))

Now review the unnormalized ORDER table design shown in Figure 9-22. Following the notation guidelines, you can describe the design as follows:

ORDER (<u>ORDER-NUM</u>, ORDER-DATE, (<u>PRODUCT-NUM</u>, PRODUCT-DESC, NUM-ORDERED))

The notation indicates that the ORDER table design contains five fields, which are listed within the outer parentheses. The ORDER-NUM field is underlined to show that it is the primary key. The PRODUCT-NUM, PRODUCT-DESC, and NUM-ORDERED fields are enclosed within an inner set of parentheses to indicate that they are fields within a repeating group. Notice that PRODUCT-NUM also is underlined because it acts as the

| | | | | primary key | | |
| | | | | | for repeating group | |

**ORDER (UNNORMALIZED)**

| RECORD# | ORDER-NUM | ORDER-DATE | PRODUCT-NUM | PRODUCT-DESC | NUM-ORDERED | |
|---|---|---|---|---|---|---|
| 1 | 40311 | 03112011 | 304 | All-purpose gadget | 7 | |
| | | | 633 | Assembly | 1 | }  repeating groups |
| | | | 684 | Super gizmo | 4 | |
| 2 | 40312 | 03112011 | 128 | Steel widget | 12 | } |
| | | | 304 | All-purpose gadget | 3 | |
| 3 | 40313 | 03122011 | 304 | All-purpose gadget | 144 | |

**FIGURE 9-22**   In the ORDER table design, records 1 and 2 have repeating groups because they contain several products. ORDER-NUM is the primary key for the ORDER table, and PRODUCT-NUM serves as a primary key for the repeating group. Because it contains a repeating group, the ORDER table design is unnormalized.

primary key of the repeating group. If a customer orders three different products in one order, then the fields PRODUCT-NUM, PRODUCT-DESC, and NUM-ORDERED repeat three times, as shown in Figure 9-22 on the previous page.

# VIDEO LEARNING SESSION:  FIRST NORMAL FORM

Video Learning Sessions can help you understand key concepts, practice your skills, and check your work. To access the sessions, visit the Management Information Systems CourseMate Web site at **www.cengagebrain.com** and navigate to the **Video Learning Sessions** for this book. This is the first of three Video Learning Sessions about data normalization. In this session, you'll learn how to transform unnormalized data into first normal form (1NF).

### First Normal Form

A table is in **first normal form (1NF)** if it does not contain a repeating group. To convert an unnormalized design to 1NF, you must expand the table's primary key to include the primary key of the repeating group.

For example, in the ORDER table shown in Figure 9-22, the repeating group consists of three fields: PRODUCT-NUM, PRODUCT-DESC, and NUM-ORDERED. Of the three fields, only PRODUCT-NUM can be a primary key because it uniquely identifies each instance of the repeating group. The product description cannot be a primary key because it might or might not be unique. For example, a company might sell a large number of parts with the same descriptive name, such as *washer*, relying on a coded part number to identify uniquely each washer size.

When you expand the primary key of ORDER table to include PRODUCT-NUM, you eliminate the repeating group and the ORDER table is now in 1NF, as shown:

ORDER (<u>ORDER-NUM</u>, ORDER-DATE, <u>PRODUCT-NUM</u>, PRODUCT-DESC, NUM-ORDERED)

Figure 9-23 shows the ORDER table in 1NF. Notice that when you eliminate the repeating group, additional records emerge — one for each combination of a specific order and a specific product. The result is more records, but a greatly simplified design. In the new version, the repeating group for order number 40311 has become three separate records, and the repeating group for order number 40312 has become two separate records. Therefore, when a table is in 1NF, each record stores data about a single instance of a specific order and a specific product.

Also notice that the 1NF design shown in Figure 9-23 has a combination primary key. The primary key of the 1NF design cannot be the ORDER-NUM field alone, because the order number does not uniquely identify each product in a multiple-item order. Similarly, PRODUCT-NUM cannot be the primary key, because it appears more than once if several orders include the same product. Because each record must reflect a specific product in a specific order, you need *both* fields, ORDER-NUM and PRODUCT-NUM, to identify a single record uniquely. Therefore, the primary key is the *combination* of two fields: ORDER-NUM and PRODUCT-NUM.

**ORDER IN 1NF**

combination
primary key

| RECORD# | ORDER-NUM | ORDER-DATE | PRODUCT-NUM | PRODUCT-DESC | NUM-ORDERED |
|---------|-----------|------------|-------------|--------------|-------------|
| 1 | 40311 | 03 11 2011 | 304 | All-purpose gadget | 7 |
| 2 | 40311 | 03 11 2011 | 633 | Assembly | 1 |
| 3 | 40311 | 03 11 2011 | 684 | Super gizmo | 4 |
| 4 | 40312 | 03 11 2011 | 128 | Steel widget | 12 |
| 5 | 40312 | 03 11 2011 | 304 | All-purpose gadget | 3 |
| 6 | 40313 | 03 12 2011 | 304 | All-purpose gadget | 144 |

repeating groups have been eliminated

**FIGURE 9-23** The ORDER table as it appears in 1NF. The repeating groups have been eliminated. Notice that the repeating group for order 40311 has become three separate records, and the repeating group for order 40312 has become two separate records. The 1NF primary key is a combination of ORDER-NUM and PRODUCT-NUM, which uniquely identifies each record.

# VIDEO LEARNING SESSION: SECOND NORMAL FORM

Video Learning Sessions can help you understand key concepts, practice your skills, and check your work. To access the sessions, visit the Management Information Systems CourseMate Web site at **www.cengagebrain.com** and navigate to the **Video Learning Sessions** for this book. This is the second of three Video Learning Sessions about data normalization. In this session, you'll learn how to transform data from first normal form (1NF) to second normal form (2NF).

## Second Normal Form

To understand second normal form (2NF), you must understand the concept of functional dependence. For example, *Field A* is **functionally dependent** on *Field B* if the value of *Field A* depends on *Field B*. For example, in Figure 9-23, the ORDER-DATE value is functionally dependent on the ORDER-NUM, because for a specific order number, there can be only one date. In contrast, a product description is *not* dependent on the order number. For a particular order number, there might be several product descriptions — one for each item ordered.

A table design is in **second normal form (2NF)** if it is in 1NF *and* if all fields that are not part of the primary key are functionally dependent on the *entire* primary key. If any field in a 1NF table depends on only one of the fields in a combination primary key, then the table is not in 2NF.

Notice that if a 1NF design has a primary key that consists of only one field, the problem of partial dependence does not arise — because the entire primary key is a single field. Therefore, a 1NF table with a single-field primary key is automatically in 2NF.

Now reexamine the 1NF design for the ORDER table shown in Figure 9-23:

ORDER (<u>ORDER-NUM</u>, ORDER-DATE, <u>PRODUCT-NUM</u>, PRODUCT-DESC, NUM-ORDERED)

Recall that the primary key is the combination of the order number and the product number. The NUM-ORDERED field depends on the *entire* primary key, because NUM-ORDERED refers to a specific product number *and* a specific order number. In contrast, the ORDER-DATE field depends on the order number, which is only a part of the primary key. Similarly, the PRODUCT-DESC field depends on the product number, which also is only a part of the primary key. Because some fields are not dependent on the *entire* primary key, the design is not in 2NF.

A standard process exists for converting a table from 1NF to 2NF. The objective is to break the original table into two or more new tables and reassign the fields so that each nonkey field will depend on the entire primary key in its table. To accomplish this, you follow these steps:

1. First, create and name a separate table for each field in the existing primary key. For example, in Figure 9-23 on the previous page, the ORDER table's primary key has two fields, ORDER-NUM and PRODUCT-NUM, so you must create two tables. The ellipsis (...) indicates that fields will be assigned later. The result is:

   ORDER (<u>ORDER-NUM</u>,...)

   PRODUCT (<u>PRODUCT-NUM</u>,...)

2. Next, create a new table for each possible combination of the original primary key fields. In the Figure 9-23 example, you would create and name a new table with a combination primary key of ORDER-NUM and PRODUCT-NUM. This table describes individual lines in an order, so it is named ORDER-LINE, as shown:

   ORDER-LINE (<u>ORDER-NUM</u>, <u>PRODUCT-NUM</u>,...)

3. Finally, study the three tables and place each field with its appropriate primary key, which is the minimal key on which it functionally depends. When you finish placing all the fields, remove any table that did not have any additional fields assigned to it. The remaining tables are the 2NF version of your original table. In the Figure 9-23 example, the three tables would be shown as:

   ORDER (<u>ORDER-NUM</u>, ORDER-DATE)

   PRODUCT (<u>PRODUCT-NUM</u>, PRODUCT-DESC)

   ORDER-LINE (<u>ORDER-NUM</u>, <u>PRODUCT-NUM</u>, NUM-ORDERED)

Figure 9-24 shows the 2NF table designs. By following the steps, you have converted the original 1NF table into three 2NF tables.

Why is it important to move from 1NF to 2NF? Four kinds of problems are found with 1NF designs that do not exist in 2NF:

- Consider the work necessary to change a particular product's description. Suppose 500 current orders exist for product number 304. Changing the product description involves modifying 500 records for product number 304. Updating all 500 records would be cumbersome and expensive.

- 1NF tables can contain inconsistent data. Because someone must enter the product description in each record, nothing prevents product number 304 from having different product descriptions in different records. In fact, if product number 304 appears in a large number of order records, some of the matching product descriptions might be inaccurate or improperly spelled. Even the presence or absence of a hyphen in the orders for *All-purpose gadget* would create consistency problems. If a data entry person must enter a term such as *IO1 Queue Controller* numerous times, it certainly is possible that some inconsistency will result.

- Adding a new product is a problem. Because the primary key must include an order number and a product number, you need values for both fields in order to add a record. What value do you use for the order number when you want to add a new product that has not been ordered by any customer? You could use a dummy order number, and then replace it with a real order number when the product is ordered to solve the problem, but that solution also creates difficulties.

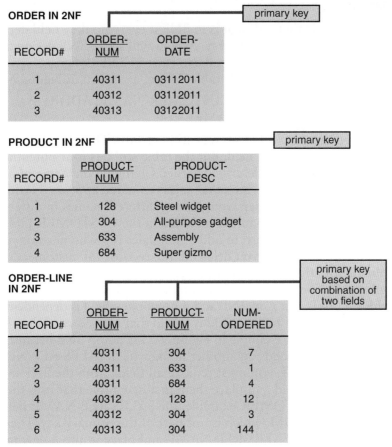

**FIGURE 9-24** ORDER, PRODUCT, and ORDER-LINE tables in 2NF. All fields are functionally dependent on the primary key.

- Deleting a product is a problem. If all the related records are deleted once an order is filled and paid for, what happens if you delete the only record that contains product number 633? The information about that product number and its description is lost.

Has the 2NF design eliminated all potential problems? To change a product description, now you can change just one PRODUCT record. Multiple, inconsistent values for the product description are impossible because the description appears in only one location. To add a new product, you simply create a new PRODUCT record, instead of creating a dummy order record. When you remove the last ORDER-LINE record for a particular product number, you do not lose that product number and its description because the PRODUCT record still exists. The four potential problems are eliminated, and the three 2NF designs are superior to both the original unnormalized table and the 1NF design.

## VIDEO LEARNING SESSION: THIRD NORMAL FORM

Video Learning Sessions can help you understand key concepts, practice your skills, and check your work. To access the sessions, visit the Management Information Systems CourseMate Web site at **www.cengagebrain.com** and navigate to the **Video Learning Sessions** for this book. This is the third of three Video Learning Sessions about data normalization. In this session, you'll learn how to transform data from second normal form (2NF) to third normal form (3NF).

### Third Normal Form

A popular rule of thumb is that a design is in 3NF if every nonkey field depends on *the key, the whole key, and nothing but the key*. As you will see, a 3NF design avoids redundancy and data integrity problems that still can exist in 2NF designs.

Consider the following CUSTOMER table design, as shown in Figure 9-25:

CUSTOMER (<u>CUSTOMER-NUM</u>, CUSTOMER-NAME, ADDRESS, SALES-REP-NUM, SALES-REP-NAME)

The table is in 1NF because it has no repeating groups. The design also is in 2NF because the primary key is a single field. But the table still has four potential problems similar to the four 1NF problems described earlier. Changing the name of a sales rep still requires changing every record in which that sales rep name appears. Nothing about the design prohibits a particular sales rep from having different names in different records. In addition, because the sales rep name is included in the CUSTOMER table, you must create a dummy CUSTOMER record to add a new sales rep who has not yet been assigned any customers. Finally, if you delete all the records for customers of sales rep number 22, you will lose that sales rep's number and name.

Those potential problems are caused because the design is not in 3NF. A table design is in **third normal form** (3NF) if it is in 2NF and if no nonkey field is dependent on another nonkey field. Remember that a nonkey field is a field that is not a candidate key for the primary key. The CUSTOMER example in Figure 9-25 is not in 3NF because one nonkey field, SALES-REP-NAME, depends on another nonkey field, SALES-REP-NUM.

To convert the table to 3NF, you must remove all fields from the 2NF table that depend on another nonkey field and place them in a new table that uses the nonkey field as a primary key. In the CUSTOMER example, the SALES-REP-NAME field depends on another field, SALES-REP-NUM, which is not part of the primary key. Therefore, to reach 3NF, you must remove SALES-REP-NAME and place it into a new table that uses SALES-REP-NUM as the primary key. As shown in Figure 9-26, the third normal form produces two separate tables:

CUSTOMER (<u>CUSTOMER-NUM</u>, CUSTOMER-NAME, ADDRESS, SALES-REP-NUM)

SALES-REP (<u>SALES-REP-NUM</u>, SALES-REP-NAME)

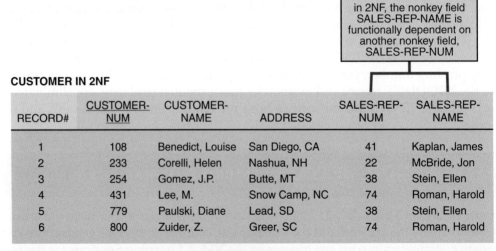

in 2NF, the nonkey field SALES-REP-NAME is functionally dependent on another nonkey field, SALES-REP-NUM

**CUSTOMER IN 2NF**

| RECORD# | CUSTOMER-NUM | CUSTOMER-NAME | ADDRESS | SALES-REP-NUM | SALES-REP-NAME |
|---------|--------------|---------------|---------|---------------|----------------|
| 1 | 108 | Benedict, Louise | San Diego, CA | 41 | Kaplan, James |
| 2 | 233 | Corelli, Helen | Nashua, NH | 22 | McBride, Jon |
| 3 | 254 | Gomez, J.P. | Butte, MT | 38 | Stein, Ellen |
| 4 | 431 | Lee, M. | Snow Camp, NC | 74 | Roman, Harold |
| 5 | 779 | Paulski, Diane | Lead, SD | 38 | Stein, Ellen |
| 6 | 800 | Zuider, Z. | Greer, SC | 74 | Roman, Harold |

**FIGURE 9-25**  2NF design for the CUSTOMER table.

**CUSTOMER IN 3NF**

| RECORD# | CUSTOMER-NUM | CUSTOMER-NAME | ADDRESS | SALES-REP-NUM |
|---------|-------------|---------------|---------|---------------|
| 1 | 108 | Benedict, Louise | San Diego, CA | 41 |
| 2 | 233 | Corelli, Helen | Nashua, NH | 22 |
| 3 | 254 | Gomez, J.P. | Butte, MT | 38 |
| 4 | 431 | Lee, M. | Snow Camp, NC | 74 |
| 5 | 779 | Paulski, Diane | Lead, SD | 38 |
| 6 | 800 | Zuider, Z. | Greer, SC | 74 |

in 3NF, no nonkey field is dependent on another nonkey field

**SALES-REP IN 3NF**

| RECORD# | SALES-REP-NUM | SALES-REP-NAME |
|---------|--------------|----------------|
| 1 | 22 | McBride, Jon |
| 2 | 38 | Stein, Ellen |
| 3 | 41 | Kaplan, James |
| 4 | 74 | Roman, Harold |

**FIGURE 9-26** When the CUSTOMER table is transformed from 2NF to 3NF, the result is two tables: CUSTOMER and SALES-REP.

## A Normalization Example

To show the normalization process, consider the familiar situation in Figure 9-27, which depicts several entities in a school advising system: ADVISOR, COURSE, and STUDENT. The relationships among the three entities are shown in the ERD in Figure 9-28 on the next page. The following sections discuss normalization rules for these three entities.

Before you start the normalization process, you notice that the STUDENT table contains fields that relate to the ADVISOR and COURSE entities, so you decide to begin with the initial design for the STUDENT table, which is shown in Figure 9-29. Notice that the table design includes the student number, student name, total credits taken, grade point average (GPA), advisor number, advisor name, and, for every course the student has taken, the course number, course description, number of credits, and grade received.

The STUDENT table in Figure 9-29 on the next page is unnormalized, because it has a repeating group. The STUDENT table design can be written as:

STUDENT (<u>STUDENT-NUMBER</u>, STUDENT-NAME, TOTAL-CREDITS, GPA, ADVISOR-NUMBER, ADVISOR-NAME, (<u>COURSE-NUMBER</u>, COURSE-DESC, NUM-CREDITS, GRADE))

To convert the STUDENT record to 1NF, you must expand the primary key to include the key of the repeating group, producing:

STUDENT (<u>STUDENT-NUMBER</u>, STUDENT-NAME, TOTAL-CREDITS, GPA, ADVISOR-NUMBER, ADVISOR-NAME, <u>COURSE-NUMBER</u>, COURSE-DESC, NUM-CREDITS, GRADE)

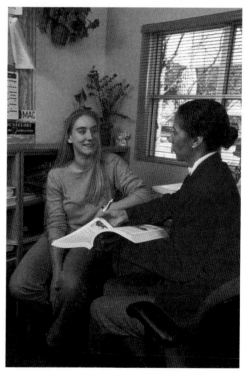

**FIGURE 9-27** A faculty advisor, who represents an entity, can advise many students, each of whom can register for one or many courses.

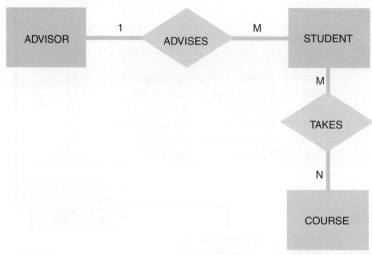

**FIGURE 9-28**   An initial entity-relationship diagram for ADVISOR, STUDENT, and COURSE.

**STUDENT**

| STUDENT-NUMBER | STUDENT-NAME | TOTAL-CREDITS | GPA | ADVISOR-NUMBER | ADVISOR-NAME | COURSE-NUMBER | COURSE-DESC | NUM-CREDITS | GRADE |
|---|---|---|---|---|---|---|---|---|---|
| 1035 | Linda | 47 | 3.647 | 49 | Smith | CSC151 | Computer Science I | 4 | B |
| | | | | | | MKT212 | Marketing Management | 3 | A |
| | | | | | | ENG101 | English Composition | 3 | B |
| | | | | | | CHM112 | General Chemistry I | 4 | A |
| | | | | | | BUS105 | Introduction to Business | 2 | A |
| 3397 | Sam | 29 | 3.000 | 49 | Smith | ENG101 | English Composition | 3 | A |
| | | | | | | MKT212 | Marketing Management | 3 | C |
| | | | | | | CSC151 | Computer Science I | 4 | B |
| 4070 | Kelly | 14 | 2.214 | 23 | Jones | CSC151 | Computer Science I | 4 | B |
| | | | | | | CHM112 | General Chemistry I | 4 | C |
| | | | | | | ENG101 | English Composition | 3 | C |
| | | | | | | BUS105 | Introduction to Business | 2 | C |

repeating groups

**FIGURE 9-29**   The STUDENT table is unnormalized because it contains a repeating group that represents the courses each student has taken.

Figure 9-30 shows the 1NF version of the sample STUDENT data. Do any of the fields in the 1NF STUDENT record depend on only a portion of the primary key? The student name, total credits, GPA, advisor number, and advisor name all relate only to the student number and have no relationship to the course number. The course description depends on the course number, but not on the student number. Only the GRADE field depends on the entire primary key.

Following the 1NF – 2NF conversion process described earlier, you would create a new table for each field and combination of fields in the primary key, and place the other fields with their appropriate key. The result is:

STUDENT (<u>STUDENT-NUMBER</u>, STUDENT-NAME, TOTAL-CREDITS, GPA, ADVISOR-NUMBER, ADVISOR-NAME)

COURSE (<u>COURSE-NUMBER</u>, COURSE-DESC, NUM-CREDITS)

GRADE (<u>STUDENT-NUMBER</u>, <u>COURSE-NUMBER</u>, GRADE)

You now have converted the original 1NF STUDENT table to three tables, all in 2NF. In each table, every nonkey field depends on the entire primary key.

Figure 9-31 on page 420 shows the 2NF STUDENT, COURSE, and GRADE designs and sample data. Are all three tables in 3NF? The COURSE and GRADE are in 3NF. STUDENT is not in 3NF, however, because the ADVISOR-NAME field depends on the

**STUDENT**

| STUDENT-NUMBER | STUDENT-NAME | TOTAL-CREDITS | GPA | ADVISOR-NUMBER | ADVISOR-NAME | COURSE-NUMBER | COURSE-DESC | NUM-CREDITS | GRADE |
|---|---|---|---|---|---|---|---|---|---|
| 1035 | Linda | 47 | 3.647 | 49 | Smith | CSC151 | Computer Science I | 4 | B |
| 1035 | Linda | 47 | 3.647 | 49 | Smith | MKT212 | Marketing Management | 3 | A |
| 1035 | Linda | 47 | 3.647 | 49 | Smith | ENG101 | English Composition | 3 | B |
| 1035 | Linda | 47 | 3.647 | 49 | Smith | CHM112 | General Chemistry I | 4 | A |
| 1035 | Linda | 47 | 3.647 | 49 | Smith | BUS105 | Introduction to Business | 2 | A |
| 3397 | Sam | 29 | 3.000 | 49 | Smith | ENG101 | English Composition | 3 | A |
| 3397 | Sam | 29 | 3.000 | 49 | Smith | MKT212 | Marketing Management | 3 | C |
| 3397 | Sam | 29 | 3.000 | 49 | Smith | CSC151 | Computer Science I | 4 | B |
| 4070 | Kelly | 14 | 2.214 | 23 | Jones | CSC151 | Computer Science I | 4 | B |
| 4070 | Kelly | 14 | 2.214 | 23 | Jones | CHM112 | General Chemistry I | 4 | C |
| 4070 | Kelly | 14 | 2.214 | 23 | Jones | ENG101 | English Composition | 3 | C |
| 4070 | Kelly | 14 | 2.214 | 23 | Jones | BUS105 | Introduction to Business | 2 | C |

**FIGURE 9-30** The STUDENT table in 1NF. Notice that the primary key has been expanded to include STUDENT-NUMBER and COURSE-NUMBER. Also, the repeating group has been eliminated.

ADVISOR-NUMBER field, which is not part of the STUDENT primary key. To convert STUDENT to 3NF, you remove the ADVISOR-NAME field from the STUDENT table and place it into a table with ADVISOR-NUMBER as the primary key.

Figure 9-32 on page 421 shows the 3NF versions of the sample data for STUDENT, ADVISOR, COURSE, and GRADE. The final 3NF design is:

STUDENT (<u>STUDENT-NUMBER</u>, STUDENT NAME, TOTAL-CREDITS, GPA, ADVISOR-NUMBER)

ADVISOR (<u>ADVISOR-NUMBER</u>, ADVISOR-NAME)

COURSE (<u>COURSE-NUMBER</u>, COURSE-DESC, NUM-CREDITS)

GRADE (<u>STUDENT-NUMBER</u>, <u>COURSE-NUMBER</u>, GRADE)

Figure 9-33 on page 422 shows the complete ERD after normalization. Now there are four entities: STUDENT, ADVISOR, COURSE, and GRADE, which is an associative entity. If you go back to Figure 9-28 on page 418, which was drawn before you identified GRADE as an entity, you can see that the M:N relationship between STUDENT and COURSE has been converted into two 1:M relationships: one relationship between STUDENT and GRADE and the other relationship between COURSE and GRADE.

To create 3NF designs, you must understand the nature of first, second, and third normal forms. In your work as a systems analyst, you will encounter designs that are much more complex than the examples in this chapter. You also should know that normal forms beyond 3NF exist, but they rarely are used in business-oriented systems.

# CASE IN POINT 9.2: CyberToys

You handle administrative support for CyberToys, a small chain that sells computer hardware and software and specializes in personal service. The company has four stores located at malls and is planning more. Each store has a manager, a technician, and between one and four sales reps.

Bruce and Marcia Berns, the owners, want to create a personnel records database, and they asked you to review a table that Marcia designed. She suggested fields for store number, location, store telephone, manager name, and manager home telephone. She also wants fields for technician name and technician home telephone and fields for up to four sales rep names and sales rep home telephones.

Draw Marcia's suggested design and analyze it using the normalization concepts you learned in the chapter. What do you think of Marcia's design and why? What would you propose?

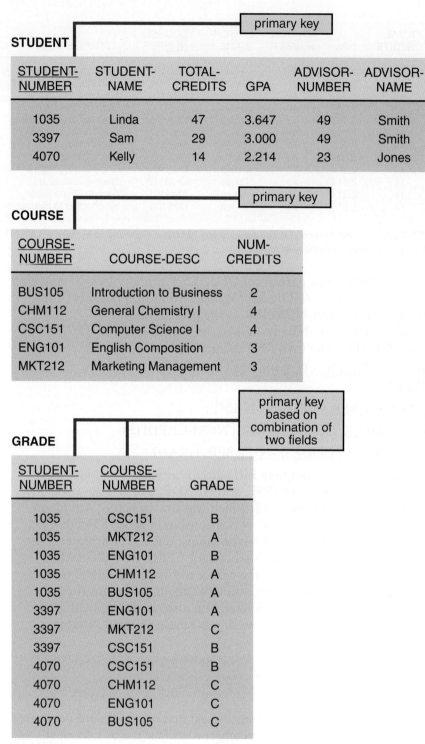

**FIGURE 9-31** STUDENT, COURSE, and GRADE tables in 2NF. Notice that all fields are functionally dependent on the entire primary key of their respective tables.

**STUDENT**

| STUDENT-NUMBER | STUDENT-NAME | TOTAL-CREDITS | GPA | ADVISOR-NUMBER |
|---|---|---|---|---|
| 1035 | Linda | 47 | 3.647 | 49 |
| 3397 | Sam | 29 | 3.000 | 49 |
| 4070 | Kelly | 14 | 2.214 | 23 |

in 3NF, no nonkey field is dependent on another nonkey field

**ADVISOR**

| ADVISOR-NUMBER | ADVISOR-NAME |
|---|---|
| 23 | Jones |
| 49 | Smith |

**COURSE**

| COURSE-NUMBER | COURSE-DESC | NUM-CREDITS |
|---|---|---|
| BUS105 | Introduction to Business | 2 |
| CHM112 | General Chemistry I | 4 |
| CSC151 | Computer Science I | 4 |
| ENG101 | English Composition | 3 |
| MKT212 | Marketing Management | 3 |

**GRADE**

| STUDENT-NUMBER | COURSE-NUMBER | GRADE |
|---|---|---|
| 1035 | CSC151 | B |
| 1035 | MKT212 | A |
| 1035 | ENG101 | B |
| 1035 | CHM112 | A |
| 1035 | BUS105 | A |
| 3397 | ENG101 | A |
| 3397 | MKT212 | C |
| 3397 | CSC151 | B |
| 4070 | CSC151 | B |
| 4070 | CHM112 | C |
| 4070 | ENG101 | C |
| 4070 | BUS105 | C |

**FIGURE 9-32**   STUDENT, ADVISOR, COURSE, and GRADE tables in 3NF. When the STUDENT table is transformed from 2NF to 3NF, the result is two tables: STUDENT and ADVISOR.

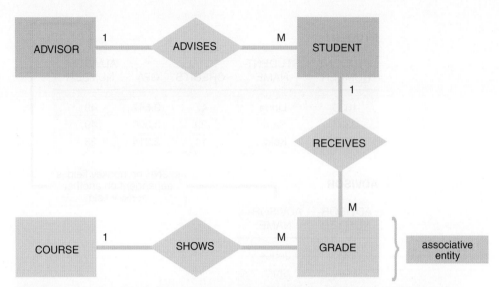

**FIGURE 9-33** The entity-relationship diagram for STUDENT, ADVISOR, and COURSE after normalization. The GRADE entity was identified during the normalization process. GRADE is an associative entity that links the STUDENT and COURSE tables.

## USING CODES DURING DATA DESIGN

A **code** is a set of letters or numbers that represents a data item. Codes can be used to simplify output, input, and data formats. During the data design process, you review existing codes and develop new ones that will be used to store and access data efficiently.

### Overview of Codes

Because codes often are used to represent data, you encounter them constantly in your everyday life. Student numbers, for example, are unique codes to identify students in a school registration system. Three students with the name John Turner might be enrolled at your school, but only one is student number 268960.

Your ZIP code is another common example. A ZIP code contains multiple items of information compressed into nine digits. The first digit identifies one of ten geographical areas of the United States. The combination of the next three digits identifies a major city or major distribution point. The fifth digit identifies an individual post office, an area within a city, or a specific delivery unit. The last four digits identify a post office box or a specific street address.

For example, consider the ZIP code 27906-2624 shown in Figure 9-34. The first digit, 2, indicates a broad geographical area in the eastern United States. The digits, 790, indicate Elizabeth City, North Carolina. The fifth digit, 6, identifies the post office that services the College of the Albemarle. The last four digits, 2624, identify the post office box for the college.

**FIGURE 9-34** A ZIP code is an example of a significant digit code that uses subgroups to provide information.

As you can imagine, codes serve many useful purposes. Because codes often are shorter than the data they represent, they save storage space and costs, reduce data transmission time, and decrease data entry time. For example, ZIP codes are used to classify and sort mail efficiently. Codes also can be used to reveal or conceal information. The last two digits of a seven-digit part number, for example, can represent the supplier number. The coded wholesale price on a retail price tag is known to salespeople but generally not to customers.

Finally, codes can reduce data input errors in situations when the coded data is easier to remember and enter than the original source data, when only certain valid codes are allowed, and when something within the code itself can provide immediate verification that the entry is correct.

## Types of Codes

Companies use many different coding methods. Because information system users must work with coded data, the codes should be easy to learn and apply. If you plan to create new codes or change existing ones, you first should obtain comments and feedback from users. The following section describes eight common coding methods.

1.  **Sequence codes** are numbers or letters assigned in a specific order. Sequence codes contain no additional information other than an indication of order of entry into the system. For example, a human resource system issues consecutive employee numbers to identify employees. Because the codes are assigned in the order in which employees are hired, you can use the code to see that employee number 584 was hired after employee number 433. The code, however, does not indicate the starting date of either person's employment.

2.  **Block sequence codes** use blocks of numbers for different classifications. College course numbers usually are assigned using a block sequence code. 100-level courses, such as Chemistry 110 and Mathematics 125, are freshman-level courses, whereas course numbers in the 200s indicate sophomore-level courses. Within a particular block, the sequence of numbers can have some additional meaning, such as when English 151 is the prerequisite for English 152.

3.  **Alphabetic codes** use alphabet letters to distinguish one item from another based on a category, an abbreviation, or an easy-to-remember value, called a mnemonic code. Many classification codes fit more than one of the following definitions:

    a.  **Category codes** identify a group of related items. For example, a local department store uses a two-character category code to identify the department in which a product is sold: GN for gardening supplies, HW for hardware, and EL for electronics.

    b.  **Abbreviation codes** are alphabetic abbreviations. For example, standard state codes include NY for New York, ME for Maine, and MN for Minnesota. Some abbreviation codes are called **mnemonic codes** because they use a specific combination of letters that are easy to remember. Many three-character airport codes such as those pictured in Figure 9-35 on the next page are mnemonic codes: BOS represents Boston, SEA represents Seattle, and ANC represents Anchorage. Some airport codes are not mnemonic, such as ORD, which designates Chicago O'Hare International Airport, or HPN, which identifies the White Plains, New York Airport.

**FIGURE 9-35**  Airline baggage tags include three-letter codes that identify airports, and machine-readable bar codes that contain information about the passenger, the flight number, and other pertinent information.

4. **Significant digit codes** distinguish items by using a series of subgroups of digits. ZIP codes, for example, are significant digit codes. Other such codes include inventory location codes that consist of a two-digit warehouse code, followed by a one-digit floor number code, a two-digit section code, a one-digit aisle number, and a two-digit bin number code. Figure 9-36 illustrates the inventory location code 11205327. What looks like a large eight-digit number is actually five separate numbers, each of which has significance.

5. **Derivation codes** combine data from different item attributes, or characteristics, to build the code. Most magazine subscription codes are derivation codes. One popular magazine's subscriber code consists of the subscriber's five-digit ZIP code, followed by the first, third, and fourth letters of the subscriber's last name, the last two digits of the subscriber's house number, and the first, third, and fourth letters of the subscriber's street name. The magazine's subscriber code for one particular subscriber is shown in Figure 9-37.

**FIGURE 9-36**  Sample of a code that uses significant digits to pinpoint the location of an inventory item.

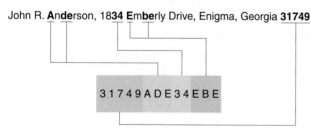

**FIGURE 9-37**  A magazine subscriber code is derived from various parts of the name and address.

6. **Cipher codes** use a keyword to encode a number. A retail store, for example, might use a 10-letter word, such as CAMPGROUND, to code wholesale prices, where the letter C represents 1, A represents 2, and so on. Thus, the code, GRAND, indicates that the store paid $562.90 for the item.

7. **Action codes** indicate what action is to be taken with an associated item. For example, a student records program might prompt a user to enter or click an action code such as *D* (to display a record), *A* (to add a record), and *X* (to exit the program).

### Developing a Code

Devising a code with too many features makes it difficult to remember, decipher, and verify. Keep the following suggestions in mind when developing a code:

1. Keep codes concise. Do not create codes that are longer than necessary. For example, if you need a code to identify each of 250 customers, you will not need a six-digit code.

2. Allow for expansion. A coding scheme must allow for reasonable growth in the number of assigned codes. If the company currently has eight warehouses, you should not use a one-digit code for the warehouse number. If three more warehouses are added, the code must be increased to two digits or changed to a character code in order to identify each location. The rule also applies to using a single letter as a character code; you might need more than 26 codes in the future. Of course, you can add more characters, which is just what the airline industry has done. Airlines now use six-character locator codes, which allow more than 300 million combinations.

3. Keep codes stable. Changes in codes can cause consistency problems and require data updates. During the changeover period, you will have to change all the stored occurrences of a particular code and all documents containing the old code, as users switch to the new code. Usually, both the old and new codes are used for an interim period, and special procedures are required to handle the two codes. For example, when area codes change, you can use either area code for a certain time period.

4. Make codes unique. Codes used for identification purposes must be unique to have meaning. If the code HW can indicate hardware or houseware, the code is not very useful.

5. Use sortable codes. If products with three-digit codes in the 100s or the 300s are of one type, while products with codes in the 200s are a different type, a simple sort will not group all the products of one type together. In addition, be careful that single-digit character codes will sort properly with double-digit codes — in some cases you must add a leading zero (01, 02, 03, and so on) to ensure that codes sort correctly.

6. Avoid confusing codes. Do not code some part numbers with two letters, a hyphen, and one digit, and others with one letter, a hyphen, and two digits. Avoid allowing both letters and numbers to occupy the same positions within a code because some of those are easily confused. It is easy to confuse the number zero (0) and the uppercase letter O, or the number one (1) with the lowercase letter L (l) or uppercase letter I. For example, the five-character code 5Z081 easily can be misread as 5ZO8I, or 52081, or even totally incorrectly as S2OBI.

7. Make codes meaningful. Codes must be easy to remember, useful for users, convenient to use, and easy to encode and interpret. Using SW as a code for the southwest sales region, for example, has far more meaning than the code 14. Using ENG as the code for the English department is easier to interpret and remember than either XVA or 132.

8. Use a code for a single purpose. Do not use a single code to classify two or more unrelated attributes. For example, if you use a single code to identify the combination of an employee's department *and* the employee's insurance plan type, users will have difficulty identifying all the subscribers of a particular plan, or all the workers in a particular department, or both. A separate code for each separate characteristic makes much more sense.

9. Keep codes consistent. For example, if the payroll system already is using two-digit codes for departments, do not create a new, different coding scheme for the personnel system. If the two systems already are using different coding schemes, you should try to convince the users to adopt a consistent coding scheme.

## CASE IN POINT 9.3: DOTCOM TOOLS

DotCom Tools operates a small business that specializes in hard-to-find woodworking tools. The firm advertises in various woodworking magazines, and currently accepts mail and telephone orders. DotCom is planning a Web site that will be the firm's primary sales channel. The site will feature an online catalog, powerful search capabilities, and links to woodworking information and resources.

DotCom has asked you, an IT consultant, whether a set of codes would be advantageous and if so, what codes you would suggest. Provide at least two choices for a customer code and at least two choices for a product code. Be sure to describe your choices and provide some specific examples. Also include an explanation of why you selected these particular codes and what advantages they might offer.

## DATABASE DESIGN: ONE STEP AT A TIME

After normalizing your table designs, you are ready to create a physical database. The following steps will help you construct a database that is user-friendly, efficient, maintainable, and meets IT industry design standards:

**Step 1:** Create an initial ERD. Start by reviewing your DFDs and class diagrams to identify all system entities. Also consider any data stores shown on the DFDs to see whether they might represent entities. For example, a data store called JOB APPLICANTS will need a table to store the information and attributes of each applicant.

**Step 2:** Next, create an ERD. Carefully analyze each relationship to determine if it is 1:1, 1:M, or M:N.

**Step 3:** During modeling, you created a data dictionary. Now, review all the data elements to be sure that each one is assigned to an appropriate entity.

**Step 4:** Review the 3NF designs for all tables, and verify that all primary, secondary, and foreign keys are identified properly. If you added any associative entities during the design process, now is the time to update your ERD.

**Step 5:** Double-check all data dictionary entries. Make sure that the entries for data stores, records, and data elements are documented completely and correctly. Also be sure that all codes that were developed or identified during the data design process are documented in the data dictionary.

After creating your final ERD and normalized table designs, you can transform them into a database. You might work with applications such as Microsoft Access, Oracle, IBM's DB2, or other DBMS development tools — or the design might be coded in-house, using one of the popular programming languages.

In the next section, you will work with examples of relational design and apply skills that you learned earlier in the chapter. At this point, it makes no difference whether you used traditional modeling or object-oriented methods to create your model. Either way, you must transform the logical model into a physical data structure that will support user needs and business requirements.

# DATABASE MODELS

Whether traditional or object-oriented development methods are used, the relational database model is universally accepted as the best way to organize, store, and access large amounts of data. Relational databases can run on many platforms, including personal computers, and are well suited to client/server computing because they are so powerful and flexible. Other models exist, but they are less common, and generally are found on older, mainframe-based systems. At the other end of the spectrum, researchers are exploring **neural architectures** that resemble human brain functions, and some observers believe that this research could change the way we think about database design.

## A Real-World Business Example

Imagine a company that provides on-site service for electronic equipment, including parts and labor. Figure 9-38 shows the overall database design that such a firm might use. If you study the figure carefully, you will see examples of many concepts described earlier. The database consists of seven separate tables, all joined by common fields so they form an integral data structure.

Figure 9-39 on the next page shows even more detail, including sample data, primary keys, and common fields. Notice that the entities include customers, technicians, service calls, and parts. Other tables store data about labor and parts that are used on specific service calls. Also notice that all tables use a single field as a primary key, except the SERVICE-LABOR-DETAIL and SERVICE-PARTS-DETAIL tables, where the primary key requires a combination of two fields to uniquely identify each record.

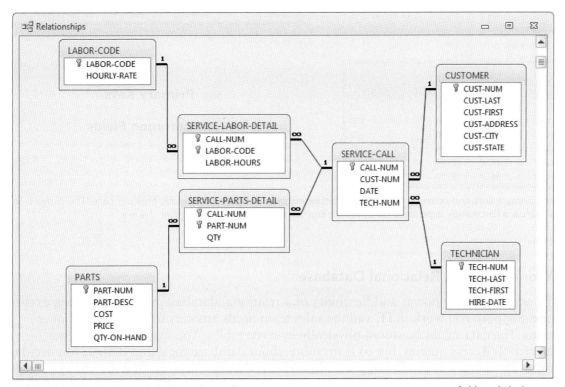

**FIGURE 9-38** A relational database design for a computer service company uses common fields to link the tables and form an overall data structure. Notice the one-to-many notation symbols, and the primary keys, which are shown in bold.

**FIGURE 9-39**   Sample data, primary keys, and common fields for the database shown in Figure 9-38 on the previous page. The design is in 3NF. Notice that all nonkey fields are functionally dependent on a primary key, the whole key, and nothing but the key.

## Working with a Relational Database

To understand the power and flexibility of a relational database, try the following exercise. Suppose you work in IT, and the sales team needs answers to three specific questions. The data might be stored physically in seven tables. You know how to create Microsoft Access queries, but to learn more about database logic and design, you decide to study Figure 9-39, and then pretend to tell the database how to find the answers, step by step. The questions are shown in Figures 9-40, 9-41, and 9-42 on pages 429 and 430.

---

**Question 1:    Did any customers receive service after 12/14/2011? If so, who were they?**

**Steps:** To identify service dates after 12/14/2011, go to the SERVICE-CALL table and look in the DATE field for dates later than *12/14/2011*. Three service call records meet that condition: *10799*, *10800*, and *10801*. Each record has a CUST-NUM field, which shows that two of the calls were made to customer *1456*, and one call was made to customer *6321*. To obtain the customer names, go to the CUSTOMER table, look up the customer numbers, and identify the two customers as Albert Jones and Mary Belli.

**Access Query:**

**Query Results:**

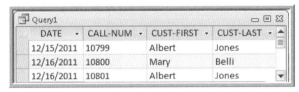

FIGURE 9-40    Question 1

---

**Question 2:    Did technician Marie Johnson put in more than six hours of labor on any service calls? If so, which ones?**

**Steps:** To locate Marie Johnson, find her name in the TECHNICIAN table and locate her technician number, which is *21*. Then, go to the SERVICE-CALL table and seek matching values of *21* in the TECH-NUM field. Marie's two service calls are shown as call numbers *10798* and *10800*. Finally, go to the SERVICE-LABOR-DETAIL table and use those two values to see if either service call showed more than six hours of labor. In the example, only service call *10798* meets the conditions.

**Access Query:**

**Query Results:**

| TECH-FIRST | TECH-LAST | TECH-NUM | CALL-NUM | LABOR-HOURS |
|---|---|---|---|---|
| Marie | Johnson | 21 | 10798 | 5.0 |

FIGURE 9-41    Question 2

**Question 3:  Were any parts used on service calls in Washington? If so, what were the part numbers, descriptions and quantities?**

**Steps:**  To identify Washington customers, go to the CUSTOMER table and locate all records with the value of **WA** in the CUST-STATE field. This shows a record for Juan Gonzalez, customer number **2836**. Next, to see whether he received service, look for the value **2836** in the SERVICE-CALL table. This produces one record: service call **10797**. Then, to find out what, if any, parts were used, go to the SERVICE-PARTS-DETAIL table, and look for service record **10797**. It appears part **AB-6784** was used on service call **10797**. Finally, to get a description for part **AB-6784**, go to the PARTS table, look for part number **AB-6784**, and retrieve the description. The final result indicates that six meters with part number **AB-6784** were sold to Washington customers.

**Access Query:**

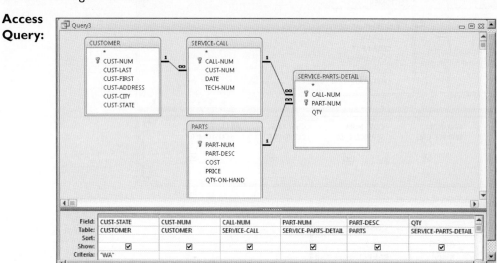

**Query Results:**

| CUST-STATE | CUST-NUM | CALL-NUM | PART-NUM | PART-DESC | QTY |
|---|---|---|---|---|---|
| WA | 2836 | 10797 | AB-6784 | METER | 6 |

**FIGURE 9-42**  Question 3

# DATA STORAGE AND ACCESS

Data storage and access involve strategic business tools, such as data warehousing and data mining software, as well as logical and physical storage issues, selection of data storage formats, and special considerations regarding storage of date fields.

## Strategic Tools for Data Storage and Access

**ON THE WEB**

To learn more about data warehousing, visit the Management Information Systems CourseMate Web site at **www.cengagebrain.com**, navigate to **On the Web Links** for this chapter, and locate the Data Warehousing link.

Companies use data warehousing and data mining as strategic tools to help manage the huge quantities of data they need for business operations and decisions. A large number of software vendors compete for business in this fast-growing IT sector.

**DATA WAREHOUSING**  Large firms maintain many databases, which might or might not be linked together into an overall structure. To provide rapid access to this information, companies use software packages that organize and store data in special configurations called data warehouses. A **data warehouse** is an integrated collection of data that can include seemingly unrelated information, no matter where it is stored in the company. Because it can link various information systems and databases, a data warehouse provides an enterprise-wide view to support management analysis and decision making.

A data warehouse allows users to specify certain **dimensions**, or characteristics. By selecting values for each characteristic, a user can obtain multidimensional information from the stored data. For example, in a typical company, most data is generated by transaction-based systems, such as order processing systems, inventory systems, and payroll systems. If a user wants to identify the customer on sales order 34071, he or she can retrieve the data easily from the order processing system by entering an order number.

On the other hand, suppose that a user wants to see November, 2011 sales results for Sally Brown, the sales rep assigned to Jo-Mar Industries. The data is stored in two different systems: the sales information system and the human resources information system, as shown in Figure 9-43. Without a data warehouse, it would be difficult for a user to extract data that spans several information systems and time frames. Rather than accessing separate systems, a data warehouse stores transaction data in a format that allows users to retrieve and analyze the data easily.

While a data warehouse typically spans the entire enterprise, many firms prefer to use a **data mart**, which is designed to serve the needs of a specific department, such as sales, marketing, or finance. Each data mart includes only the data that users in that department require to perform their jobs. There are pros and cons to both approaches, and the best solution usually depends on the specific situation.

As the article in Figure 9-44 on the next page points out, storing large quantities of data is like building a house — it doesn't just happen. A well-constructed data warehouse needs an architecture that includes detailed planning and specifications.

**FIGURE 9-43** A data warehouse stores data from several systems. By selecting data dimensions, a user can retrieve specific information without having to know how or where the data is stored.

**DATA MINING** **Data mining** software looks for meaningful data patterns and relationships. For example, data mining software could help a consumer products firm identify potential customers based on their prior purchases. Information about customer behavior is valuable, but data mining also raises serious ethical and privacy issues, such as the example in the Question of Ethics feature on page 436. Figure 9-45 on the next page shows North Carolina State University's Ethics in Computing site, which offers many articles and research papers on this subject.

The enormous growth in e-commerce has focused attention on data mining as a marketing tool. In an article in *New Architect*, a Web-based magazine, Dan R. Greening noted that Web hosts typically possess a lot of information about visitors, but most of it is of little value. His article mentions that smart marketers and business analysts are using data mining techniques, which he describes as "machine learning algorithms that find buried patterns in databases, and report or act on those findings." He concludes by saying that "The great advantage of Web marketing is that you can measure visitor interactions more effectively than in brick-and-mortar stores or direct mail. Data mining works best when you have clear, measurable goals." Some of the goals he suggests are:

- Increase the number of pages viewed per session
- Increase the number of referred customers

**ON THE WEB**

To learn more about data mining, visit the Management Information Systems CourseMate Web site at **www. cengagebrain. com**, navigate to **On the Web Links** for this chapter, and locate the Data Mining link.

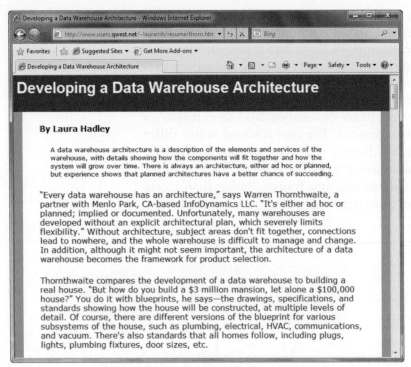

**FIGURE 9-44**  As the author points out, without an overall architecture, a data warehouse would be difficult to manage and change.

- Reduce **clicks to close**, which means average page views to accomplish a purchase or obtain desired information
- Increase checkouts per visit
- Increase average profit per checkout

This type of data gathering is sometimes called **clickstream storage**. Armed with this information, a skillful Web designer could build a profile of typical new customers, returning customers, and customers who browse but do not buy. Although this information would be very valuable to the retailer, clickstream storage could raise serious legal and privacy issues if an unscrupulous firm sought to link a customer's Web behavior to a specific name or e-mail address, and then sell or otherwise misuse the information.

Because it can detect patterns and trends in large amounts of data, data mining is a valuable tool for managers. The popular Wikipedia site contains an interesting example of data mining. According to the Wikipedia article, a hypothetical chain of supermarkets performed a detailed analysis of purchases, and found that beer and diapers were often purchased together. Without attempting to explain this correlation, the obvious tactic for a retailer would be to display these items in the same area of the store. Wikipedia states that this data mining technique is often called **market basket analysis**.

**FIGURE 9-45**  The Ethics in Computing site at North Carolina State University offers many articles about ethical and privacy issues associated with data mining.

## Logical and Physical Storage

It is important to understand the difference between logical storage and physical storage. **Logical storage** refers to data that a user can view, understand, and access, regardless of how or where that information actually is organized or stored. In contrast, **physical storage** is strictly hardware-related, because it involves the process of reading and writing binary data to physical media such as a hard drive, CD-ROM, or network-based storage device. For example, portions of a document might be stored in different physical locations on a hard drive, but the user sees the document as a single logical entity on the computer screen.

**LOGICAL STORAGE**  Logical storage consists of alphabetic and numeric **characters**, such as the letter *A* or the number 9. As you learned earlier in this chapter, a set of related characters forms a field, which describes a single characteristic, or attribute, of a person, place, thing, or event. A field also is called a **data element** or a **data item**.

When designing fields, you should provide space for the largest values that can be anticipated, without allocating unnecessarily large storage capacities that will not be used. For example, suppose you are designing a customer order entry system for a firm with 800 customers. It would be a mistake to limit the customer number field to three, or even four characters. Instead, you might consider a five-character field with leading zeros that could store customer numbers from *00001* to *99999*.

You also might consider a mix of alphabetic and numeric characters, which many people find easier to view and use. Alphabetic characters expand the storage capacity, because there are 26 possible values for each character position. Most airlines now use six alphabetic characters as a record locator, which has over 300 million possible values.

A **logical record** is a set of field values that describes a single person, place, thing, or event. For example, a logical customer record contains specific field values for a single customer, including the customer number, name, address, telephone number, credit limit, and so on. Application programs see a logical record as a group of related fields, regardless of how or where the data is stored physically.

The term *record* usually refers to a logical record. Whenever an application program issues a read or write command, the operating system supplies one logical record to the program or accepts one logical record from the program. The physical data might be stored on one or more servers, in the same building or thousands of miles away, but all the application program sees is the logical record — the physical storage location is irrelevant.

**PHYSICAL STORAGE**  Physical storage involves a **physical record**, or **block**, which is the smallest data unit that can be handled by the operating system. The system reads or writes one physical record at a time. When the system *reads* a physical record, it loads the data from storage into a **buffer**, which is a segment of computer memory.

The physical storage location can be local, remote, or Web-based. Similarly, when the system *writes* a physical record, all data in the memory buffer is saved physically to a storage location. A physical record can contain more than one logical record, depending on the **blocking factor**. For example, a blocking factor of two means that each physical record will consist of two logical records. Some database programs, such as Microsoft Access, automatically write a physical record each time that a logical record is created or updated.

## Data Coding and Storage

Computers represent data as **bits**, or **binary digits**, that have only two possible values: 1 (which indicates an electrical signal) and 0 (which indicates the absence of a signal). A computer understands a group of bits as a digital code that can be transmitted, received, and stored. Computers use various data coding and storage schemes, such as EBCDIC, ASCII, and binary. A more recent coding standard called Unicode also is popular. Also, the storage of dates raises some design issues that must be considered.

**EBCDIC, ASCII, AND BINARY**  EBCDIC (pronounced EB-see-dik), which stands for Extended Binary Coded Decimal Interchange Code, is a coding method used on mainframe computers and high-capacity servers. **ASCII** (pronounced ASK-ee), which stands for American Standard Code for Information Interchange, is a coding method used on most personal computers. EBCDIC and ASCII both require eight bits, or one **byte**, for each character. For example, the name Ann requires three bytes of storage, the number *12,345* requires five bytes of storage, and the number *1,234,567,890* requires ten bytes of storage.

Compared with character-based formats, a **binary storage format** offers a more efficient storage method because it represents numbers as actual binary values, rather than as coded numeric digits. For example, an **integer format** uses only 16 bits, or two bytes, to represent the number *12,345* in binary form. A **long integer format** uses 32 bits, or four bytes, to represent the number *1,234,567,890* in binary form.

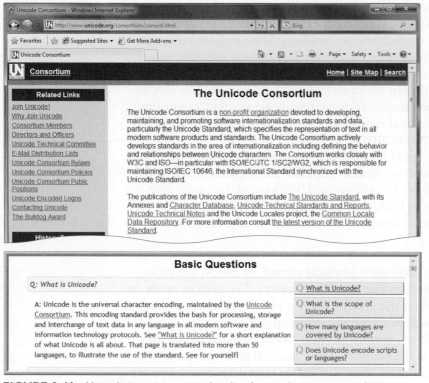

**FIGURE 9-46**  Unicode is an international coding format that represents characters as integers, using 16 bits per character. The Unicode Consortium maintains standards and support for Unicode.

**UNICODE**  Unicode is a more recent coding standard that uses two bytes per character, rather than one. This expanded scheme enables Unicode to represent more than 65,000 unique, multilingual characters. Why is this important? Consider the challenge of running a multinational information system, or developing a program that will be sold in Asia, Europe, and North America. Because it supports virtually all languages, Unicode has become a global standard.

Traditionally, domestic software firms developed a product in English, then translated the program into one or more languages. This process was expensive, slow, and error-prone. In contrast, Unicode creates translatable content right from the start. Today, most popular operating systems support Unicode, and the Unicode Consortium maintains standards and support, as shown in Figure 9-46. Although Unicode has many advantages, it also has some disadvantages. In fact, because of its size and certain typographical issues, Microsoft recommends that you use its Arial Unicode font " ... only when you can't use multiple fonts tuned for different writing systems."

**STORING DATES**  What is the best way to store dates? The answer depends on how the dates will be displayed and whether they will be used in calculations.

At the beginning of the 21st century, many firms that used only two digits to represent the year were faced with a major problem called the **Y2K issue**. Based on that experience, most date formats now are based on the model established by the **International Organization for Standardization (ISO)**, which requires a format of four digits for the year, two for the month, and two for the day (YYYYMMDD). A date stored in that format can be sorted easily and used in comparisons. If a date in ISO form is larger than another date in the same form, then the first date is later. For example, 20120927 (September 27, 2012) is later than 20110713 (July 13, 2011).

But, what if dates must be used in calculations? For example, if a manufacturing order placed on June 23 takes three weeks to complete, when will the order be ready? If a payment due on August 13 is not paid until April 27 of the following year, exactly how late is the payment and how much interest is owed? In these situations, it is easier to use absolute dates.

An **absolute date** is the total number of days from some specific base date. To calculate the number of days between two absolute dates, you subtract one date from the other. For example, if the base date is January 1, 1900, then September 27, 2012 has an absolute date value of 41179. Similarly, July 13, 2011 has an absolute date of 40737. If you subtract the earlier date value from the later one, the result is 442 days. You can use a spreadsheet to determine and display absolute dates easily, as shown in Figure 9-47.

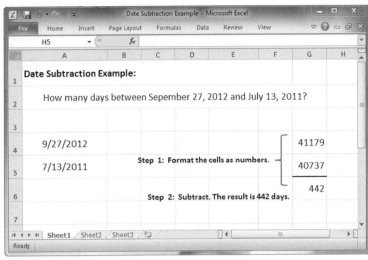

**FIGURE 9-47**  Microsoft Excel uses absolute dates in calculations. For example, January 1, 1900, has a numeric value of 1. In the example shown, September 27, 2012 is displayed as 41179, and July 13, 2011 is displayed as 40737. The difference between the dates is 442 days.

## DATA CONTROL

Just as it is important to secure the physical part of the system, as shown in Figure 9-48, file and database control must include all measures necessary to ensure that data storage is correct, complete, and secure. File and database control also is related to input and output techniques discussed earlier.

A well-designed DBMS must provide built-in control and security features, including subschemas, passwords, encryption, audit trail files, and backup and recovery procedures to maintain data. Your main responsibility is to ensure that the DBMS features are used properly.

Earlier in this chapter, you learned that a subschema can be used to provide a limited view of the database to a specific user, or level of users. Limiting access to files and databases is the most common way of protecting stored data. Users must furnish a proper **user ID** and **password** to access a file or database. Different privileges, also called **permissions,** can be associated with different users, so some employees can be limited to read-only access, while other users might be allowed to update or delete data. For highly sensitive data, additional access codes can be established that restrict specific records or fields within records. Stored data also can be encrypted to prevent unauthorized access. **Encryption** is the process of converting readable data into unreadable characters to prevent unauthorized access to the data.

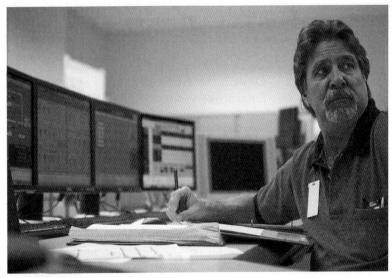

**FIGURE 9-48**  In addition to network monitoring, system security includes access codes, data encryption, passwords, and audit trails.

All system files and databases must be backed up regularly and a series of **backup copies** must be retained for a specified period of time. In the event of a file catastrophe, **recovery procedures** can be used to restore the file or database to its current state at the time of the last backup. **Audit log files**, which record details of all accesses and changes to the file or database, can be used to recover changes made since the last backup. You also can include **audit fields**, which are special fields within data records to provide additional control or security information. Typical audit fields include the date the record was created or modified, the name of the user who performed the action, and the number of times the record has been accessed.

## CASE IN POINT 9.4: SOCCERMOM

SoccerMom Company sells a patented seat that spectators can take to youth soccer games. The seat folds so it is small enough to fit in the glove box of most vehicles. The company operates a factory in Kansas and also contracts its manufacturing projects to small firms in Canada and Mexico.

An unusual problem has occurred for this small multinational company: People are getting confused about dates in internal memos, purchase orders, and e-mail. Towson Hopkins handles all IT functions for SoccerMom. When he designed the company's database, he was not aware that the format for dates in Canada and Mexico was different from the format used in the United States. For example, in Canada and Mexico, the notation 7/1/11 indicates January 7, 2011, whereas in the United States the same notation indicates July 1, 2011. Although it seems like a small point, the date confusion has resulted in several order cancellations.

Towson has asked for your advice. You could suggest writing a simple program to convert the dates automatically or designing a switchboard command that would allow users to select a date format as data is entered. You realize, however, that SoccerMom might want to do business in other countries in the future. What would be the best course of action? Should SoccerMom adapt to the standard of each country, or should it maintain a single international format? What are the arguments for each option?

## A QUESTION OF ETHICS

Olivia is the database manager at Tip Top Toys, a relatively small division of Worldwide Enterprises. Worldwide has nine other divisions, which include insurance, health care products, and financial planning services, to name a few.

Riccardo, corporate marketing director for Worldwide, has requested Tip Top's customer shopping data to target people who might be likely to purchase items or services from other Worldwide divisions. Olivia is not totally comfortable with this, and pointed out Tip Top's Web privacy policy, which states that "Tip Top Toys, a division of Worldwide Enterprises, will not share personal data with other companies without a customer's consent."

Riccardo replied that the statement only applies to outside companies – not other Worldwide divisions. He said he checked with the corporate legal department, and they agreed. Emily responded "Even if it is legally OK, it's not the *right* thing to do. Many people take our statement to mean that their data does not leave Tip Top. At the very least, we should give customers a choice, and share the data only with their consent."

Do you agree with Olivia? Why or why not?

## CHAPTER SUMMARY

In this chapter, you continued your study of the systems design phase of the SDLC. You learned that files and tables contain data about people, places, things, or events that affect the information system. File-oriented systems, also called file processing systems, manage data stored in separate files, including master files, table files, transaction files, work files, security files, and history files.

A database consists of linked tables that form an overall data structure. A database management system (DBMS) is a collection of tools, features, and interfaces that enable users to add, update, manage, access, and analyze data in a database.

DBMS designs are more powerful and flexible than traditional file-oriented systems. A database environment offers scalability, support for organization-wide access, economy of scale, data sharing among user groups, balancing of conflicting user requirements, enforcement of standards, controlled redundancy, effective security, flexibility, better programmer productivity, and data independence. Large-scale databases are complex and require extensive security and backup/recovery features.

DBMS components include interfaces for users, database administrators, and related systems; a data manipulation language; a schema; and a physical data repository. Other data management techniques include data warehousing, which stores data in an easily accessible form for user access, and data mining, which looks for meaningful patterns and relationships among data. Data mining also includes clickstream storage, which records how users interact with a site, and market basket analysis, which can identify product relationships and consumer buying patterns.

In an information system, an entity is a person, place, thing, or event for which data is collected and maintained. A field, or attribute, is a single characteristic of an entity. A record, or tuple, is a set of related fields that describes one instance of an entity. Records are grouped into files (in a file-oriented system) and tables (in a database environment).

A primary key is the field or field combination that uniquely and minimally identifies a specific record; a candidate key is any field that could serve as a primary key. A foreign key is a field or field combination that must match the primary key of another file or table. A secondary key is a field or field combination used as the basis for sorting or retrieving records.

An entity-relationship diagram (ERD) is a graphic representation of all system entities and the relationships among them. The ERD is based on entities and data stores in DFDs prepared during the systems analysis phase. The three basic relationships represented in an ERD are one-to-one (1:1), one-to-many (1:M), and many-to-many (M:N). In a M:N relationship, the two entities are linked by an associative entity.

The relationship between two entities also is referred to as cardinality. A common form of cardinality notation is called crow's foot notation, which uses various symbols to describe the characteristics of the relationship.

Normalization is a process for avoiding problems in data design. A first normal form (1NF) record has no repeating groups. A record is in second normal form (2NF) if it is in 1NF and all nonkey fields depend on the entire primary key. A record is in third normal form (3NF) if it is in 2NF and if no field depends on a nonkey field.

Data design tasks include creating an initial ERD; assigning data elements to an entity; normalizing all table designs; and completing the data dictionary entries for files, records, and data elements. Files and database tables should be sized to estimate the amount of storage space they will require.

You learned that a code is a set of letters or numbers used to represent data in a system. By using codes, you can speed up data entry, reduce data storage space, and reduce transmission time. Codes also can be used to reveal or to conceal information. The main types of codes are sequence codes, block sequence codes, classification codes, alphabetic codes (including category codes, abbreviation codes, and mnemonic codes), significant digit codes, derivation codes, cipher codes, and action codes.

Logical storage is information seen through a user's eyes, regardless of how or where that information actually is organized or stored. Physical storage is hardware-related and involves reading and writing blocks of binary data to physical media. A logical record is a related set of field values that describes a single person, place, thing, or event. A physical record consists of one or more logical records, depending on the blocking factor. Data storage formats include EBCDIC, ASCII, binary, and Unicode. Dates can be stored in several formats, including ISO and absolute format.

File and database control measures include limiting access to the data, data encryption, backup/recovery procedures, audit-trail files, and internal audit fields.

# Key Terms and Phrases

# Learn It Online

**Instructions:** To complete the Learn It Online exercises, visit the Management Information Systems CourseMate Web site at **www.cengagebrain.com**, navigate to the resources for this chapter, and click the link for the exercise you want to complete.

**1 Chapter Reinforcement**

**TF, MC, and SA**

Click one of the Chapter Reinforcement links for Multiple Choice, True/False, or Short Answer. Answer each question and submit to your instructor.

**2 Flash Cards**

Click the Flash Cards link and read the instructions. Type 20 (or a number specified by your instructor) in the Number of playing cards text box, type your name in the Enter your Name text box, and then click the Flip Card button. When the flash card is displayed, read the question and then click the ANSWER box arrow to select an answer. Flip through the Flash Cards. If your score is 15 (75%) correct or greater, click Print on the File menu to print your results. If your score is less than 15 (75%) correct, then redo this exercise by clicking the Replay button.

**3 Practice Test**

Click the Practice Test link. Answer each question, enter your first and last name at the bottom of the page, and then click the Grade Test button. When the graded practice test is displayed on your screen, click Print on the File menu to print a hard copy. Continue to take practice tests until you score 80% or better.

**4 Who Wants To Be a Computer Genius?**

Click the Computer Genius link. Read the instructions, enter your first and last name at the bottom of the page, and then click the Play button. When your score is displayed, click the PRINT RESULTS link to print a hard copy.

**5 Wheel of Terms**

Click the Wheel of Terms link. Read the instructions, and then enter your first and last name and your school name. Click the PLAY button. When your score is displayed on the screen, right-click the score and then click Print on the shortcut menu to print a hard copy.

**6 Crossword Puzzle Challenge**

Click the Crossword Puzzle Challenge link. Read the instructions, and then click the Continue button. Work the crossword puzzle. When you are finished, click the Submit button. When the crossword puzzle is redisplayed, submit it to your instructor.

## SCR Associates Case Simulation  Session 9: Data Design

### Overview

The SCR Associates case study is a Web-based simulation that allows you to practice your skills in a real-world environment. The case study transports you to SCR's intranet, where you complete 12 work sessions, each aligning with a chapter. As you work on the case, you will receive e-mail and voice mail messages, obtain information from SCR's online libraries, and perform various tasks.

### How do I use the case?

- Review the SCR background material in Chapter 1.
- Read the Preview for this session and study the Task List.
- Visit the Management Information Systems CourseMate Web site at **www.cengagebrain.com**, navigate to the **SCR Case Simulation**, and locate the intranet link.
- Enter your name and the password **sad9e**. An opening screen will display the 12 sessions.
- Select this session. Check your e-mail and voice mail carefully, and then work on the tasks.

### Preview: Session 9

Your supervisor, Jesse Baker, has asked you to begin working on data design tasks for the new information system, which will be implemented as a relational database. You will need to identify the entities, draw an ERD, design tables, and add sample data to each table.

### Task List

| |
|---|
| 1. List all the entities that interact with the TIMS system. Start by reviewing the data library, previous e-mail messages, DFDs, and other documentation. |
| 2. Draw an ERD that shows cardinality relationships among the entities. Send the diagram to Jesse. |
| 3. For each entity, Jesse wants to see table designs in 3NF. Use standard notation format to show the primary key and the other fields in each table. |
| 4. Jesse wants to use sample data to populate fields for at least three records in each table. Better get started on this right away. |

**FIGURE 9-49**  Task list: Session 9.

# Chapter Exercises

## Review Questions

1. Explain the main differences between a file processing system and a database system.
2. What is a DBMS? Briefly describe the components of a DBMS.
3. Describe a primary key, candidate key, secondary key, foreign key, and common field.
4. What are entity-relationship diagrams and how are they used? What symbol is used to represent an entity in an ERD? What symbol is used for a relationship? What is cardinality, and what symbols do you use in the crow's foot notation method?
5. What are data warehousing and data mining? Are the terms related?
6. What is the criterion for a table design to be in first normal form? How do you convert an unnormalized design to 1NF?
7. What are the criteria for a table design to be in second normal form? How do you convert a 1NF design to 2NF?
8. What are the criteria for a table design to be in third normal form? How do you convert a 2NF design to 3NF?
9. Explain the difference between a logical record and a physical record.
10. How would a specific date, such as September 1, 2011, be represented as an absolute date?

## Discussion Topics

1. Are there ethical issues to consider when planning a database? For example, should sensitive personal data (such as medical information) be stored in the same DBMS that manages employee salary and benefits data? Why or why not?
2. Suggest three typical business situations where referential integrity avoids data problems.
3. Consider an automobile dealership with three locations. Data fields exist for stock number, vehicle identification number, make, model, year, color, and invoice cost. Identify the possible candidate keys, the likely primary key, a probable foreign key, and potential secondary keys.
4. In the example shown in Figures 9-25 and 9-26 on pages 416 and 417, the 2NF customer table was converted to two 3NF tables. Verify that the four potential problems identified for 2NF tables were eliminated in the 3NF design.

# Apply Your Knowledge

The Apply Your Knowledge section contains four mini-cases. Each case describes a situation, explains your role in the case, and asks you to respond to questions. You can answer the questions by applying knowledge you learned in the chapter.

## 1 Pick and Shovel Construction Company

**Situation:**

Pick and Shovel Construction Company is a multistate building contractor specializing in medium-priced town homes. C. T. Scott, the owner, is in your office for the third time today to see how the new relational database project is coming along. Unfortunately, someone mentioned to C. T. that the delay had something to do with achieving *normalization*.

"Why is all this normalization stuff so important?" he asks. "The old system worked OK most of the time, and now you are telling me that we need all these special rules. Why is this necessary?"

1. How should you respond to C. T.? Write him a brief memo with your views.

2. Assume that the Pick and Shovel's main entities are its customers, employees, projects, and equipment. A customer can hire the company for more than one project, and employees sometimes work on more than one project at a time. Equipment, however, is assigned only to one project. Draw an ERD showing those entities.

3. Add cardinality notation to your ERD.

4. Create 3NF table designs.

## 2 Puppy Palace

**Situation:**

Puppy Palace works with TV and movie producers who need dogs that can perform special tricks, such as headstands, somersaults, ladder climbs, and various dog-and-pony tricks. Puppy Palace has about 16 dogs and a list of 50 tricks from which to choose. Each dog can perform one or more tricks, and many tricks can be performed by more than one dog. When a dog learns a new trick, the trainer assigns a skill level. Some customers insist on using dogs that score a 10, which is the highest skill level. As an IT consultant, you have been asked to suggest 3NF table designs. You are fairly certain that a M:N relationship exists between dogs and tricks.

1. Draw an ERD for the Puppy Palace information system.

2. Indicate cardinality.

3. Identify all fields you plan to include in the dogs and tricks tables. For example, in the dogs table, you might want breed, size, age, name, and so on. In the tricks table, you might want the trick name and description. You will need to assign a primary key in each table. *Hint*: Before you begin, review some database design samples in this chapter. You might spot a similar situation that requires an associative entity that you can use as a pattern. In addition, remember that numeric values work well in primary key fields.

4. Create 3NF table designs.

3   **Mayville Public Library**

**Situation:**

Mayville is a rural village with a population of 900. Until now, Mayville was served by a bookmobile from a larger town. The Mayville Village Council has authorized funds for a small public library, and you have volunteered to set up an information system for the library. Assume that the library will have multiple copies of certain books.

1. Draw an ERD for the Mayville library system.
2. Indicate cardinality.
3. Identify all fields you plan to include in the tables.
4. Create 3NF table designs.

4   **Western Wear Outfitters**

**Situation:**

Western Wear is a mail-order firm that offers an extensive selection of casual clothing for men and women. Western Wear plans to launch a new Web site, and the company wants to develop a new set of product codes. Currently, 650 different products exist, with the possibility of adding more in the future. Many products come in various sizes, styles, and colors. The marketing manager asked you to develop an individualized product code that can identify a specific item and its characteristics. Your initial reaction is that it can be done, but the code might be fairly complex. Back in your office, you give the matter some thought.

1. Design a code scheme that will meet the marketing manager's stated requirements.
2. Write a brief memo to the marketing manager suggesting at least one alternative to the code she proposed, and state your reasons.
3. Suggest a code scheme that will identify each Western Wear customer.
4. Suggest a code scheme that will identify each specific order.

# Case Studies

Case studies allow you to practice specific skills learned in the chapter. Each chapter contains several case studies that continue throughout the textbook, and a chapter capstone case.

## New Century Health Clinic

New Century Health Clinic offers preventive medicine and traditional medical care. In your role as an IT consultant, you will help New Century develop a new information system.

### Background

After completing the user interface, input, and output design for the new information system at New Century, you will consider data design issues. Begin by studying the DFDs and object-oriented diagrams you prepared previously and the rest of the documentation from the systems analysis phase. Perform the following tasks:

### Assignments

1. Create an initial entity-relationship diagram for the New Century Health Clinic system.
2. Normalize your table designs.
3. If you identified any new entities during normalization, create a final entity-relationship diagram for the system.
4. Write a memo for your documentation file that contains your recommendation about whether a file processing or a database environment should be used. Attach copies of your ERD(s) and normalized designs.

## PERSONAL TRAINER, INC.

Personal Trainer, Inc., owns and operates fitness centers in a dozen Midwestern cities. The centers have done well, and the company is planning an international expansion by opening a new "supercenter" in the Toronto area. Personal Trainer's president, Cassia Umi, hired an IT consultant, Susan Park, to help develop an information system for the new facility. During the project, Susan will work closely with Gray Lewis, who will manage the new operation.

### Background

After evaluating various development strategies, Susan prepared a system requirements document and submitted her recommendations to Cassia Umi, Personal Trainer's president. During her presentation, Susan discussed several development strategies, including in-house development and outsourcing. She did not feel that a commercial software package would meet Personal Trainer's needs.

Based on her research, Susan felt it would be premature to select a development strategy at this time. Instead, she recommended to Cassia that an in-house team should develop a design prototype, using a relational database as a model. Susan said that the prototype would have two main objectives: It would represent a user-approved model of the new system, and it would identify all systems entities and the relationships among them. Susan explained that it would be better to design the basic system first, and then address other issues, including Web enhancements and implementation options. She proposed a three-step plan: data design, user interface design, and application architecture. She explained that systems analysts refer to this as the systems design phase of a development project.

Cassia agreed with Susan's recommendation, and asked her to go forward with the plan.

**Assignments**

1. Review the Personal Trainer fact-finding summary in Chapter 4 and draw an ERD with cardinality notation. Assume that system entities include members, activities and services, and fitness instructors.

2. Design tables in 3NF. As you create the database, include various codes for at least three of the fields.

3. Use sample data to populate the fields for at least three records in each table.

4. Recommend a date format for the new system. Should Personal Trainer adopt a single international standard, or should the format be determined by the country in which the center is located? Write a message to Susan with your recommendation.

## Fastflight Airlines

FastFlight Airlines is a small air carrier operating in three northeastern states. FastFlight is computerizing its passenger reservation system. The data items must include reservation number, flight number, flight date, origin, destination, departure time, arrival time, passenger name, and seat number. For example, flight number 303 leaves Augusta, Maine, daily at 9:23 a.m. and arrives in Nashua, New Hampshire, at 10:17 a.m. A typical reservation code might be AXQTBC, for passenger Lisa Lane, in seat 4A, on flight 303 on 11/12/2011.

**Assignments**

1. Create an ERD for the reservations system.
2. Create 3NF table designs for the system.
3. For each of the entities identified, design tables and identify the possible candidate keys, the primary key, a probable foreign key, and potential secondary keys.
4. Use sample data to populate the fields for three records.

## CHAPTER CAPSTONE CASE: SoftWear, Limited

SoftWear, Limited (SWL), is a continuing case study that illustrates the knowledge and skills described in each chapter. In this case study, the student acts as a member of the SWL systems development team and performs various tasks.

### Background

Work continued on the ESIP system. Rick said that the system would be a client/server design that could support SWL's current and future business requirements. He also said that Ann Hon wanted to use the ESIP system as a prototype for developing other SWL systems in the future. Ann said that the new design would have to be powerful, flexible, and scalable. With that in mind, the team decided that a DBMS strategy was the best solution for SWL's future information systems requirements.

### ERDs and Normalization

Rick asked Tom and Becky to draw an entity-relationship diagram with normalized designs. Tom and Becky used the Visible Analyst, a CASE tool, to produce the diagram shown in Figure 9-50. Rick noticed that only two entities were shown: EMPLOYEE and DEDUCTION. Rick suggested that the ESIP-OPTION and HUMAN RESOURCES entities should be added. Tom and Becky agreed. The second version of their ERD is shown in Figure 9-51 on the next page.

With the ERD completed, Tom turned to the design of the EMPLOYEE table. He suggested the following design:

EMPLOYEE (<u>SSN</u>, EMPLOYEE-NAME, HIRE-DATE)

"The table obviously is in 1NF, because it has no repeating groups," Tom said. "It's also in 2NF, because it has a single field as the primary key. And I'm sure it's in 3NF, because the

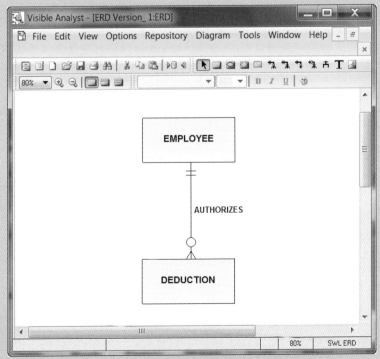

**FIGURE 9-50** The initial ERD shows two entities: EMPLOYEE and DEDUCTION. Notice that crow's foot notation indicates that one and only one employee can authorize anywhere from zero to many deductions.

employee name and the hire date both depend on the Social Security number." Everyone agreed that this was the correct design. Tom and Becky turned their attention to designing the ESIP-OPTION table and later suggested the following design:

ESIP-OPTION (<u>OPTION-CODE</u>, OPTION-NAME, DESCRIPTION, DEDUCTION-CYCLE, APPLICATION-CYCLE, MIN-SERVICE, MIN-DEDUCTION, MAX-DEDUCTION)

The design appeared to meet the test for 3NF. Although seven fields existed in addition to the primary key, each field seemed to depend on the entire primary key. Finally, Becky proposed the following design for the DEDUCTION record:

DEDUCTION (<u>SSN</u>, <u>ESIP-OPTION</u>, <u>DATE</u>, EMPLOYEE-NAME, AMOUNT)

This time, Rick felt that the table was in 1NF, but not in 2NF because the EMPLOYEE-NAME field was dependent on only a part of the key rather than the entire key. Becky agreed with him and suggested that the EMPLOYEE-NAME field could be removed and accessed using the EMPLOYEE table. The SSN field could be used as a foreign key to match values in the EMPLOYEE table's primary key. To put the table into 2NF, she revised the DEDUCTION table design as follows:

DEDUCTION (<u>SSN</u>, <u>ESIP-OPTION</u>, <u>DATE</u>, AMOUNT)

With that change, everyone agreed that the table also was in 3NF because the AMOUNT field depended on the entire primary key. The next step was to work on a system design to interface with the payroll system and provide support for SWL's long-term information technology goals.

While Rick, Tom, and Becky were working on ERDs and normalization, Pacific Software delivered the payroll package that SWL ordered. Tom was assigned to work on installing and configuring the package and training users on the new payroll system.

Meanwhile, Rick felt that SWL should get more information about client/server design. With Ann Hon's approval, he contacted several IT consulting firms that advertised their client/server design expertise on the Internet. Rick and Becky met with three firms and recommended that SWL work with True Blue Systems, a consulting group with a local office in Raleigh, not far from SWL's headquarters. In addition to the design for the ESIP system, Rick suggested that the agenda should include the possibility that employees could access their ESIP accounts from home via the Internet.

**FIGURE 9-51** Second version of the ERD. Now, the DEDUCTION entity has relationships to two other entities: EMPLOYEE and ESIP-OPTION.

### SWL Team Tasks

1. Rick asked you to help him put together a brief progress update for Michael Jeremy and several other top managers. Specifically, Rick wants you to explain the concept of normalization without using a lot of technical jargon. Rick wants you to summarize the concept using plain English and simple examples.

2. At SWL, each employee is assigned to a specific department. Employees from several departments often are assigned to special project teams, however, when a new product is launched or for major marketing events. Carla wants to develop a project management system to track the projects, employees assigned, and accumulated project hours. She believes that employees and projects are in a M:N relationship. She showed you an initial design where all data is stored in a single table:

   PROJECT DATA (PROJECT-NUMBER, PROJECT-NAME, START-DATE, PROJECT-STATUS, (EMPLOYEE-NUMBER, EMPLOYEE-NAME, JOB-TITLE, DEPT-NUMBER, DEPT-NAME, PROJECT-HOURS))

   How would you describe Carla's design?

3. Carla wants you to create an ERD, including cardinality, for the project management system. She says that you probably will need to add an associative entity.

4. After you create the ERD in the previous step, design a table for each entity, in third normal form.

### Manage the SWL Project

You have been asked to manage SWL's new information system project. One of your most important activities will be to identify project tasks and determine when they will be performed. Before you begin, you should review the SWL case in this chapter. Then list and analyze the tasks, as follows:

**LIST THE TASKS** Start by listing and numbering at least 10 tasks that the SWL team needs to perform to fulfill the objectives of this chapter. Your list can include SWL Team Tasks and any other tasks that are described in this chapter. For example, Task 3 might be to Identify all entities, and Task 6 might be to Create an initial ERD.

**ANALYZE THE TASKS** Now study the tasks to determine the order in which they should be performed. First identify all concurrent tasks, which are not dependent on other tasks. In the example shown in Figure 9-52 on the next page, Tasks 1, 2, 3, 4, and 5 are concurrent tasks, and could begin at the same time if resources were available.

Other tasks are called dependent tasks, because they cannot be performed until one or more earlier tasks have been completed. For each dependent task, you must identify specific tasks that need to be completed before this task can begin. For example, you would want to identify all the entities before you could create an initial ERD, so Task 6 cannot begin until Task 3 is completed, as Figure 9-52 shows.

**CHAPTER CAPSTONE CASE:   SoftWear, Limited (continued)**                    SWL

**FIGURE 9-52**  Tasks 1, 2, 3, 4, and 5 are concurrent tasks that could be performed at the same time. Task 6 is a dependent task that cannot be performed until Task 3 has been completed.

Chapter 3 describes project management tools, techniques, and software. To learn more, you can use the Features section on your Student Study Tool CD-ROM, or visit the Management Information Systems CourseMate Web site at **www.cengagebrain.com** and locate the project management resources library for this book. On the Web, Microsoft offers demo versions, training, and tips for using Project 2010. You also can visit the OpenWorkbench.org site to learn more about this free, open-source software.

# Ready for a Challenge?

In additional to technical skills, IT professionals need critical thinking skills such as perception, organization, analysis, problem-solving, and decision-making. The Ready for a Challenge feature can help you learn, practice, and apply critical thinking skills that you can take to the workplace.

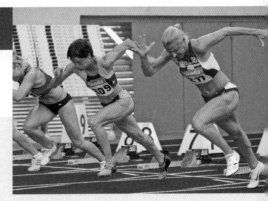

This week, the IT team at Game Technology is working on database design and codes. Your job is to develop a recommendation for keeping track of individual games and their authors. You will be expected to create an ERD and table designs. Here is what you know so far:

- Every game has a product ID, name, version number, category code, and category description.
- Every author has an author ID, name, mailing address, and e-mail address.
- An individual author can develop one or more games.
- A game also can be developed by several authors. In this case, each author receives a specific percentage of the royalty that the game earns.

This information must be stored in the database. Your plan is to develop an overall design, list all the individual data items, and then include them as fields in the tables you create. Your design must be in the form of an ERD that shows all the entities, including any associative entities, and their relationships. Also, all table designs must be in third normal form (3NF).

The IT team also discussed data codes. You read somewhere that six-letter codes can have over 300 million unique combinations, but you don't know the exact number. Your friend, a math major, said that you could figure out the answer on your own, and she gave you a hint by saying it was 26 to the sixth power.

## Practice Tasks

A. Draw an ERD showing all entities and their relationships, and create table designs that include all necessary fields.

B. Calculate the exact number of unique combinations that are possible using a six-letter code.

After you complete the Practice Tasks, to check your work and view sample answers, visit the Management Information Systems CourseMate Web site at **www.cengagebrain.com**, navigate to the resources for this chapter, and locate Ready for a Challenge?.

## The Challenge

Your recommended design ran into a snag. The team leader said it wasn't bad, but it did not go far enough. The specific comment was that it was not in third normal form.

Also, the team finally decided on a code for the customer ID field, which is a primary key. The code will be a combination code, with four letters followed by four digits. The letters would be the first four letters of the customer's last name, which might make it easier for customers to remember.

## Challenge Tasks

A. Review the sample ERD and table designs, and convert them to third normal form (3NF).

B. Calculate the exact number of possible combinations with a code composed of four letters followed by four numbers. Does this seem like a good choice? Why or why not? What would you suggest?

# CHAPTER 10

# System Construction Planning

**Chapter 10** is the final chapter in the systems design phase of the SDLC. This chapter describes system architecture, which translates the logical design of an information system into a physical blueprint, or architecture. As you plan the system architecture, you will learn about servers, clients, processing methods, networks, and related issues.

## INTRODUCTION

## OBJECTIVES

*When you finish this chapter, you will be able to:*

- Provide a checklist of issues to consider when selecting a system architecture

- Describe servers, server-based processing, clients, and client-based processing

- Explain client/server architecture, including tiers, cost-benefit issues, and performance

- Compare in-house e-commerce development with packaged solutions

- Discuss the potential impact of cloud computing and Web 2.0

- Explain the difference between online and batch processing

- Define network topology, including hierarchical, bus, ring, and star models

- Explain network protocols and licensing issues

- Describe wireless networking, including wireless standards, topologies, and trends

- Describe the system design specification

At this point in the SDLC, your objective is to determine an overall architecture to implement the information system. You learned in Chapter 1 that an information system requires hardware, software, data, procedures, and people to accomplish a specific set of functions. An effective system combines those elements into an architecture, or design, that is flexible, cost-effective, technically sound, and able to support the information needs of the business. This chapter covers a wide range of topics that support the overall system design, just as a plan for a new home would include a foundation plan, building methods, wiring and plumbing diagrams, traffic flows, and costs.

**System architecture** translates the logical design of an information system into a physical structure that includes hardware, software, network support, processing methods, and security. The end product of the systems design phase is the system design specification. If this document is approved, the next step is systems implementation.

## CHAPTER INTRODUCTION CASE:    Mountain View College Bookstore

**Background:** Wendy Lee, manager of college services at Mountain View College, wants a new information system that will improve efficiency and customer service at the three college bookstores.

In this part of the case, Tina Allen (systems analyst) and David Conroe (student intern) are talking about system architecture issues.

| | |
|---|---|
| **Participants:** | Tina and David |
| **Location:** | Mountain View College cafeteria, Monday afternoon, January 9, 2012 |
| **Project status:** | The team has completed data design tasks and user interface, output, and input design work. The last step in the systems design phase is to consider a system architecture for the bookstore system. |
| **Discussion topics:** | System architecture checklist, client/server architecture, processing methods, network issues, and system management tools |

**Tina:** Hi, David. Did you enjoy the holiday break?

**David:** *I sure did. Now I'm ready to get back to work.*

**Tina:** Good. As the last step in the systems design phase of the SDLC, we need to study the physical structure, or architecture, of the bookstore system. Our checklist includes enterprise resource planning, total cost of ownership, scalability, Web integration, legacy systems, processing methods, and security issues that could affect the system design.

**David:** *Where do we start?*

**Tina:** Well, the bookstore interfaces with many publishers and vendors, so we'll consider supply chain management, which is part of enterprise resource planning, or ERP for short.

**David:** *What happens after we finish the checklist?*

**Tina:** Then we'll define a client/server architecture. As I see it, the bookstore client workstations will share the processing with a server in the IT department. Also, we may need to look at middleware software to connect the new system with existing legacy systems, such as the college accounting system.

**David:** *Anything else?*

**Tina:** Yes. We need to select a network plan, or topology, so we'll know how to plan the physical cabling and connections — or possibly use wireless technology. When we're done, we'll submit a system design specification for approval.

**David:** *Sounds good to me.*

**Tina:** Good. Here's a task list to get us started:

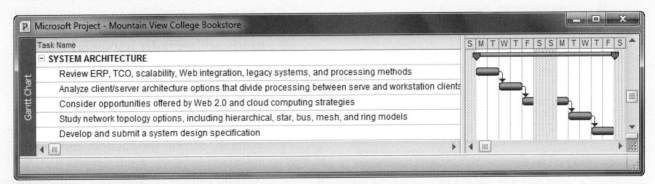

**FIGURE 10-1**   Typical system architecture tasks.

## System Architecture Checklist

Just as an architect begins a project with a list of the owner's requirements, a systems analyst must approach system architecture with an overall checklist. Before making a decision, the analyst must consider seven specific issues that will affect the architecture choice:

- Enterprise resource planning (ERP)
- Initial and total cost of ownership (TCO)
- Scalability
- Web integration
- Legacy system interface requirements
- Processing options
- Security issues

### Enterprise Resource Planning (ERP)

Many companies use **enterprise resource planning** (**ERP**) software, which was described in Chapter 1. The objective of ERP is to establish a company-wide strategy for using IT resources. ERP defines a specific architecture, including standards for data, processing, network, and user interface design. A main advantage of ERP is that it describes a specific hardware and software **environment**, also called a **platform**, that ensures connectivity and easy integration of future systems, including in-house software and commercial packages.

In the article in *CIO* magazine shown in Figure 10-2, Thomas Wailgum remarks that ERP is like watching the TV series *Lost*, because both have subplots, crashes, and interesting characters. In an earlier article, Mr. Wailgum pointed out that ERP isn't really about resources or planning — it is about the *enterprise*, and the concept of integrating departmental systems into an overall application, with a central database that can be shared and used effectively.

Many companies are extending internal ERP systems to their suppliers and customers, using a concept called **supply chain management** (**SCM**). For example, in a totally integrated supply chain system, a customer order could cause a manufacturing system to schedule a work order, which in turn triggers a call for more parts from one or more suppliers. In a dynamic, highly competitive economy, SCM can help companies achieve faster response, better customer service, and lower operating costs. Most supply chain management systems depend on RFID technology for real-time input data. As you learned in Chapter 1, RFID allows companies to track incoming material, current production, and finished inventory by using small devices that respond to radio frequency signals.

Microsoft offers an ERP solution called Microsoft Dynamics, as shown in Figure 10-3. The company claims that the software can integrate financial management, customer relationship management (CRM),

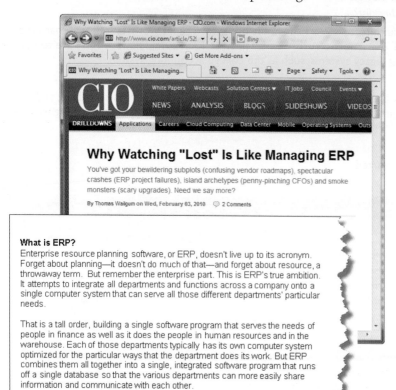

**FIGURE 10-2**   The article by Thomas Wailgum makes an interesting comparison between ERP and a popular TV series.

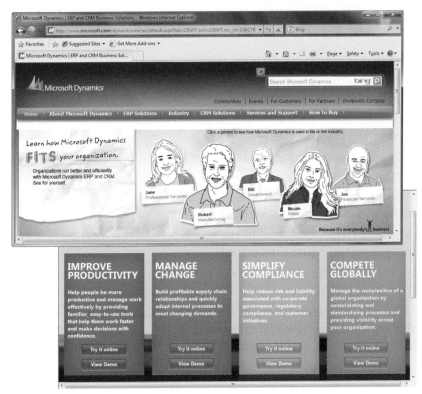

**FIGURE 10-3**  Microsoft Dynamics is an ERP strategy that can integrate separate systems and improve productivity throughout the organization.

supply chain management (SCM), project management, human resources, and business intelligence reporting.

## CASE IN POINT 10.1:  ABC SYSTEMS

You are a systems analyst at ABC Systems, a fast-growing IT consulting firm that provides a wide range of services to companies that want to establish e-commerce operations. During the last 18 months, ABC acquired two smaller firms and set up a new division that specializes in supply chain management. Aligning ABC's internal systems was quite a challenge, and top management was not especially happy with the integration cost or the timetable. To avoid future problems, you have decided to suggest an ERP strategy, and you plan to present your views at the staff meeting tomorrow. ABC's management team is very informal and prefers a loose, flexible style of management. How will you persuade them that ERP is the way to go?

### Initial Cost and TCO

You learned earlier about the importance of considering economic feasibility and TCO during systems planning and analysis. As Figure 10-4 on the next page suggests, TCO includes tangible purchases, fees, and contracts called *hard* costs. However, additional *soft* costs of management, support, training, and downtime are just as important, but more difficult to measure. As the pie chart shows, the combination of user-related and operational costs exceeds hardware and software acquisition costs.

A TCO analysis should include the the following questions.

- If in-house development was selected as the best alternative initially, is it still the best choice? Is the necessary technical expertise available, and does the original cost estimate appear realistic?

- If a specific package was chosen initially, is it still the best choice? Are newer versions or competitive products available? Have any changes occurred in pricing or support?
- Have any new types of outsourcing become available?
- Have any economic, governmental, or regulatory events occurred that could affect the proposed project?
- Have any significant technical developments occurred that could affect the proposed project?
- Have any major assumptions changed since the company made the build versus buy decision?
- Are there any merger or acquisition issues to consider, whereby the company might require compatibility with a specific environment?
- Have any new trends occurred in the marketplace? Are new products or technologies on the verge of being introduced?
- Have you updated the original TCO estimate? If so, are there any significant differences?

The answers to these questions might affect the initial cost and TCO for the proposed system. You should review system requirements and alternatives now, before proceeding to design the system architecture.

### Scalability

A network is composed of individual nodes. A **node** represents a physical device, wired or wireless, that can send, receive, or manage network data. For example, nodes can be servers, workstations, shared printers, mass storage devices, wireless access points, or mobile computers.

**Scalability**, also called **extensibility**, refers to a system's ability to expand, change, or downsize easily to meet the changing needs of a business enterprise. Scalability is especially important in implementing systems that are volume-related, such as transaction processing systems. A scalable system is necessary to support a dynamic, growing business. For example, a scalable network could handle anywhere from a few dozen nodes to thousands of nodes; a scalable DBMS could support the acquisition of a new sales division. When investing large amounts of money in a project, management is especially concerned about scalability issues that could affect the system's life expectancy.

### Web Integration

An information system includes **applications**, which are programs that handle the input, manage the processing logic, and provide the required output. The systems analyst must know if a new application will be part of an e-commerce strategy and the

**FIGURE 10-4** The Micromation site suggests that *soft* costs are very significant, but are more difficult to measure.

degree of integration with other Web-based components. As you learned earlier, a **Web-centric** architecture follows Internet design protocols and enables a company to integrate the new application into its e-commerce strategy. Even where e-commerce is not involved, a Web-centric application can run on the Internet or a company intranet or extranet. A Web-based application avoids many of the connectivity and compatibility problems that typically arise when different hardware environments are involved. In a Web-based environment, a firm's external business partners can use standard Web browsers to import and export data.

Figure 10-5 shows IBM's WebSphere software. WebSphere offers Java-based ERP solutions as well as software development tools that customers can use to build their own Web-centric applications.

## Legacy System Interface Requirements

A new system might have to interface with one or more **legacy systems**, which are older systems that use outdated technology, but still are functional. For example, a new marketing information system might need to report sales data to a server-based accounting system and obtain product cost data from a legacy manufacturing system.

Interfacing a new system with a legacy system involves analysis of data formats and compatibility. In some cases, a company will need to convert legacy file data, which can be an expensive and time-consuming process. Middleware, which is discussed later in this chapter, might be needed to pass data between new systems and legacy systems. Finally, to select the best architecture, the analyst must know if the new application eventually will replace the legacy system.

**ON THE WEB**

To learn more about TCO, visit the Management Information Systems CourseMate Web site at **www. cengagebrain. com**, navigate to **On the Web Links** for this chapter, and locate the TCO link.

**ON THE WEB**

To learn more about legacy systems, visit the Management Information Systems CourseMate Web site at **www. cengagebrain. com**, navigate to **On the Web Links** for this chapter, and locate the Legacy Systems link.

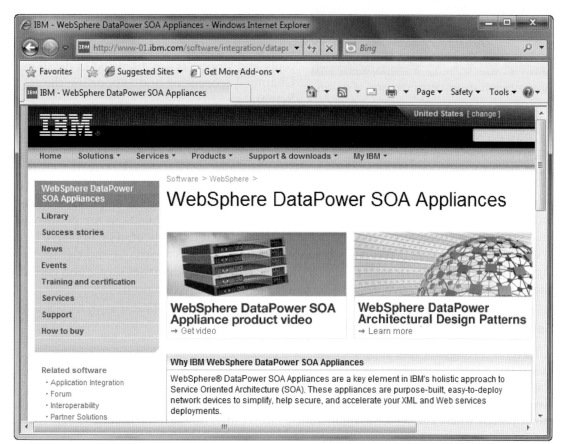

**FIGURE 10-5**   WebSphere offers ERP solutions and development tools.

## Processing Options

In planning the architecture, designers also must consider how the system will process data — online or in batches. For example, a high-capacity transaction processing system, such as an order entry system, requires more network, processing, and data storage resources than a monthly billing system that handles data in batches. Also, if the system must operate online, 24 hours a day and seven days a week (24/7), provision must be made for backup and speedy recovery in the event of system failure.

The characteristics of online and batch processing methods are described later in this chapter, with examples of each type.

## Security Issues

From the password protection shown in Figure 10-6 to complex intrusion detection systems, security threats and defenses are a major concern to a systems analyst. As the physical design is translated into specific hardware and software, the analyst must consider security issues and determine how the company will address them. Security is especially important when data or processing is performed at remote locations, rather than at a centralized facility. In mission-critical systems, security issues will have a major impact on system architecture and design.

Web-based systems introduce additional security concerns, as critical data must be protected in the Internet environment. Also, firms that use e-commerce applications must assure customers that their personal data is safe and secure. System security concepts and strategies are discussed in detail in Chapter 12, Securing and Supporting the System.

**FIGURE 10-6**   User IDs and passwords are important elements of system security.

## PLANNING THE ARCHITECTURE

Every information system involves three main functions: data storage and access methods, application programs to handle the processing logic, and an interface that allows users to interact with the system. Depending on the architecture, the three functions are performed on a server, on a client, or are divided between the server and the client. As you plan the system design, you must determine where the functions will be carried out and the advantages and disadvantages of each design approach. This section discusses server and client characteristics and how each design alternative handles system functions.

### Servers

A **server** is a computer that supplies data, processing services, or other support to one or more computers, called **clients**. A system design where the server performs *all* the processing sometimes is described as **mainframe architecture**. Although the actual server does not have to be a mainframe, the term mainframe architecture typically describes a multiuser environment where the server is significantly more powerful than the clients. A systems analyst should know the history of mainframe architecture to understand the server's role in modern system design.

**MAINFRAME HISTORY** In the 1960s, mainframe architecture was the *only* system design available. In addition to centralized data processing, early systems performed all data input and output at a central location, often called a **data processing center**. Physical data was delivered or transmitted in some manner to the data processing center, where it was entered into the system. Users in the organization had no input or output capability, except for printed reports that were distributed by a corporate IT department.

**SERVER-BASED PROCESSING** As network technology advanced and became affordable, companies installed terminals at remote locations, so that users could enter and access data from anywhere in the organization, regardless of where the centralized computer was located. A **terminal** included a keyboard and display screen to handle input and output, but lacked independent processing capability. In a centralized design, as shown in Figure 10-7, the remote user's keystrokes are transmitted from his or her terminal to the mainframe, which responds by sending screen output back to the user's screen.

**FIGURE 10-7** In a centralized design, the remote user's keystrokes are transmitted to the mainframe, which responds by sending screen output back to the user's screen.

A main advantage of server-based processing is that various types of terminals can communicate with the mainframe, and the design is not tied to a specific hardware platform. A disadvantage is that server-based processing typically uses character-based terminals that provide a limited interface for users. In a server-based system, all data storage, access, and application programs are located on the mainframe.

Today, mainframe architecture still is used in industries that require large amounts of data processing that can be done in batches at a central location. For example, a credit card company might run monthly statements in a batch, or a bank might use mainframe servers to update customer balances each night. In a blend of old and new technology, an Internet-based retail operation might use centralized data management at a customer service center to support and manage its online sales activity, as shown in Figure 10-8.

As server technology evolved, terminals also changed dramatically. Instead of simple input–output devices, a company might use a mix of PCs, handheld computers, and other specialized hardware that allows users to interact with a centralized server. In most companies, workstations that use powerful GUIs have replaced character-based terminals.

## Clients

As PC technology exploded in the 1980s and 1990s, powerful microcomputers quickly appeared on corporate desktops. Users found that they could run their own word processing, spreadsheet, and database applications, without assistance from the IT group, in a mode called stand-alone computing. Before long, companies linked the stand-alone computers into networks that enabled the user clients to exchange data and perform local processing.

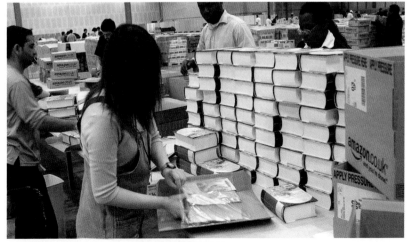

**FIGURE 10-8** Internet-based retail operations such as Amazon.com use customer service centers to support online sales activity.

**STAND-ALONE COMPUTING** When an individual user works in **stand-alone** mode, the workstation performs all the functions of a server by storing, accessing, and processing data, as well as providing a user interface. Although stand-alone PCs improved employee productivity and allowed users to perform tasks that previously required IT department assistance, stand-alone computing was inefficient and expensive. Even worse, maintaining data on individual workstations raised major concerns about data security, integrity, and consistency. Without a central storage location, it was impossible to protect and back up valuable business data, and companies were exposed to enormous risks. In some cases, users who were frustrated by a lack of support and services from the IT department created and managed their own databases. In addition to security concerns, this led to data inconsistency and unreliability.

**LOCAL AND WIDE AREA NETWORKS** As technology became available, companies resolved the problems of stand-alone computing by joining clients into a **local area network (LAN)** that allows sharing of data and hardware resources, as shown in Figure 10-9. One or more LANs, in turn, can connect to a centralized server. Further advances in technology made it possible to create powerful networks that could use satellite links, high-speed fiber-optic lines, or the Internet to share data.

A **wide area network (WAN)** spans long distances and can connect LANs that are continents apart, as shown in Figure 10-10. When a user accesses data on a LAN or WAN, the network is **transparent** because a user sees the data as if it were stored on his or her own workstation. Company-wide systems that connect one or more LANs or WANs are called **distributed systems**. The capabilities of a distributed system depend on the power and capacity of the underlying data communication network. Compared to mainframe architecture, distributed systems increase concerns about data secu-

**FIGURE 10-9**  A LAN allows sharing of data and hardware, such as printers and scanners.

rity and integrity because many individual clients require access to perform processing.

**CLIENT-BASED PROCESSING** In a typical LAN, clients share data stored on a local server that supports a group of users or a department. As LANs became popular, the most common LAN configuration was a file server design, as shown in Figure 10-11. In a **file server** design, also called a **file sharing architecture**, an individual LAN client has a copy of the application program installed locally, while the data is stored on a central file server. The client requests a copy of the data file and the server responds by transmitting the entire data file to the client. After performing

ON THE WEB

To learn more about local and wide area networks, visit the Management Information Systems CourseMate Web site at **www. cengagebrain. com**, navigate to **On the Web Links** for this chapter, and locate the Local and Wide Area Networks link.

**FIGURE 10-10**  A WAN can connect many LANs and link users who are continents apart.

the processing locally, the client returns the data file to the central file server where it is stored. File sharing designs are efficient only if the number of networked users is low and the transmitted data file sizes are relatively small. Because the entire data file is sent to each requesting client, a file server design requires significant network resources.

**Client**
- Handles user interface
- Sends data request to server
- Receives data files from server
- Runs application program locally to process data
- Sends data file back to server

**File server**
- Receives data requests from client
- Sends data files to client
- Stores data files
- Manages multiuser access
- Generates a substantial amount of LAN traffic
- Manages data backup

**FIGURE 10-11**   Example of a LAN file server design. The server stores and manages the data, while the clients run the application program and perform all the processing.

## CLIENT/SERVER ARCHITECTURE

Today's interconnected world requires an information architecture that spans the entire enterprise. Whether you are dealing with a departmental network or a multinational corporation, as a systems analyst you will work with a distributed computing strategy called client/server architecture.

### Overview

Although no standard definition exists, the term **client/server architecture** generally refers to systems that divide processing between one or more networked clients and a central server. In a typical client/server system, the client handles the entire user interface, including data entry, data query, and screen presentation logic. The server stores the data and provides data access and database management functions. Application logic is divided in some manner between the server and the clients. In a client/server interaction, the client submits a request for information from the server, which carries out the operation and responds to the client. As shown in Figure 10-12 on the next page, the data file is not transferred from the server to the client — only the request and the result are transmitted across the network. To fulfill a request from a client, the server might

**ON THE WEB**

To learn more about client/server architecture, visit the Management Information Systems CourseMate Web site at **www. cengagebrain. com**, navigate to **On the Web Links** for this chapter, and locate the Client/ Server Architecture link.

**FIGURE 10-12** A file server design compared to a client/server design.

contact other servers for data or processing support, but that process is transparent to the client. The analogy can be made to a restaurant where the customer gives an order to a server, who relays the request to a cook, who actually prepares the meal.

Figure 10-13 lists some major differences between client/server and traditional mainframe systems. Many early client/server systems did not produce expected savings because few clear standards existed, and development costs often were higher than anticipated. Implementation was expensive because clients needed powerful hardware and software to handle shared processing tasks. In addition, many companies had an installed base of data, called **legacy data**, which was difficult to access and transport to a client/server environment.

As large-scale networks grew more powerful, client/server systems became more cost-effective. Many companies invested in client/server systems to achieve a unique combination of computing power, flexibility, and support for changing business operations. Today, client/server architecture is the dominant form of systems design, using Internet protocols and network models such as the ones described on pages 477–480. As businesses form new alliances with customers and suppliers, the client/server concept continues to expand to include clients and servers outside the organization.

| Comparison of Client/Server and Mainframe Systems | | |
|---|---|---|
| **Characteristics** | **Client/Server** | **Mainframe** |
| Basic architecture | Very flexible | Very rigid |
| Application development | Flexible<br>Fast<br>Object-oriented | Highly structured<br>Slow<br>Traditional |
| User environment | PC-based<br>GUI<br>Empowers the user<br>Improves productivity | Uses terminals<br>Text interface<br>Constrains the user<br>Limited options |
| Security and control features | Decentralized<br>Difficult to control | Centralized<br>Easier to control |
| Processing options | Can be shared and configured in any form desired | Cannot be modified |
| Data storage options | Can be distributed to place data closer to users | All data is stored centrally |
| Hardware/software integration | Very flexible<br>Multivendor model | Very rigid<br>Single proprietary vendor |

**FIGURE 10-13** Comparison of the characteristics of client/server and mainframe systems.

## Client/Server Design Styles

Client/server designs can take many forms, depending on the type of server and the relationship between the server and the clients. Figure 10-14 shows the client/server interaction for a database server, a transaction server, an object server, and a Web server. Notice that in each case, the processing is divided between the server and the clients. The nature of the communication depends on the type of server: A database server processes individual SQL commands, a transaction server handles a set of SQL commands, an object server exchanges object messages with clients, and a Web server sends and receives Internet-based communications.

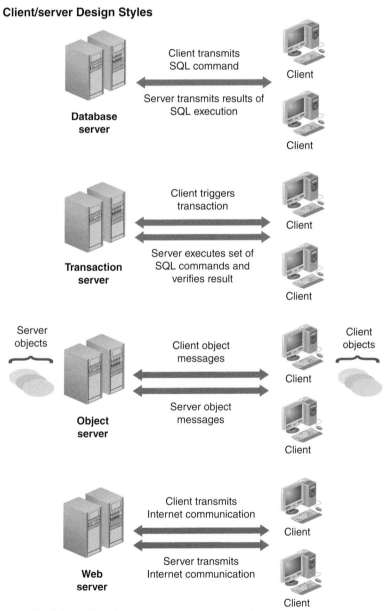

**FIGURE 10-14**    Client/server interaction for a database server, a transaction server, an object server, and a Web server.

## Fat and Thin Clients

Client/server designs can be based on fat or thin clients. A **fat client**, also called a **thick client**, design locates all or most of the application processing logic at the client. A **thin client** design locates all or most of the processing logic at the server. What are the advantages and disadvantages of each design? Most IT experts agree that thin client designs provide better performance, because program code resides on the server, near the data. In contrast, a fat client handles more of the processing and must access and update the data more often. Compared with maintaining a central server, fat client TCO also is higher, because of initial hardware and software requirements and the ongoing expense of supporting and updating remote client computers. A fat client design, however, is simpler and less expensive to develop, because the architecture resembles traditional file server designs where all processing is performed at the client. Figure 10-15 compares the characteristics of fat and thin clients.

| Characteristic | Fat Client | Thin Client |
|---|---|---|
| Network traffic | Higher, because the fat client must communicate more often with the server to access data and update processing results | Lower, because most interaction between code and data takes place at the server |
| Performance | Slower, because more network traffic is required | Faster, because less network traffic is required |
| Initial cost | Higher, because more powerful hardware is required | Lower, because workstation hardware requirements are not as stringent |
| Maintenance cost | Higher, because more program code resides on the client | Lower, because most program code resides on the central server |
| Ease of development | Easier, because systems resemble traditional file-server designs where all processing was performed at the client | More difficult, because developers must optimize the division of processing logic |

**FIGURE 10-15**   Characteristics of fat and thin clients.

## Client/Server Tiers

Early client/server designs were called two-tier designs. In a **two-tier** design, the user interface resides on the client, all data resides on the server, and the application logic can run either on the server or on the client, or be divided between the client and the server.

More recently, another form of client/server design, called a three-tier design, has become popular. In a **three-tier** design, the user interface runs on the client and the data is stored on the server, just as with a two-tier design. A three-tier design also has a middle layer between the client and server that processes the client requests and translates them into data access commands that can be understood and carried out by the server, as shown in Figure 10-16. You can think of the middle layer as an **application server**, because it provides the **application logic**, or **business logic**, required by the system. Three-tier designs also are called **n-tier** designs, to indicate that some designs use more than one intermediate layer.

The advantage of the application logic layer is that a three-tier design enhances overall performance by reducing

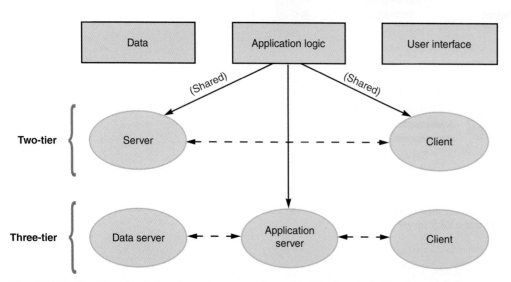

**FIGURE 10-16**   Characteristics of two-tier versus three-tier client/server design.

the data server's workload. The separate application logic layer also relieves clients of complex processing tasks. Because it can run on a minicomputer that is much more powerful than the typical client workstations, the middle layer is more efficient and cost-effective in large-scale systems. Figure 10-17 shows where the data, the application logic, and the user interface are located on various architectures. In a client/server system, the tiers communicate using software called middleware, which is described in the following section.

| Architecture | | Data | Application Logic | User Interface |
|---|---|---|---|---|
| Central data processing center | Server | X | X | X |
| | Client | | | |
| Central server with remote terminals | Server | X | X | |
| | Client | | | X |
| Stand-alone client | Server | | | |
| | Client | X | X | X |
| Two-tier client/server | Server | X | X | |
| | Client | | X | X |
| Three-tier client/server | Data server | X | | |
| | Application server | | X | |
| | Client | | | X |

**FIGURE 10-17**  The location of the data, the application logic, and the user interface depend on the type of architecture.

## Middleware

In an n-tier system, special software called **middleware** enables the tiers to communicate and pass data back and forth. Some IT professionals refer to middleware as the glue that holds clients and servers together. The broader definition shown in Figure 10-18 on the next page states that middleware is software that mediates between an application program and a network.

Middleware provides a transparent interface that enables system designers to integrate dissimilar software and hardware. For example, middleware can link a departmental database to a Web server, which can be accessed by client computers via the Internet or a company intranet. Middleware also can integrate legacy systems and Web-based applications. For example, when a user enters a customer number on a Web-based inquiry form, middleware accesses a legacy accounting system and returns the results.

**ON THE WEB**

To learn more about middleware, visit the Management Information Systems CourseMate Web site at **www. cengagebrain. com**, navigate to **On the Web Links** for this chapter, and locate the Middleware link.

## Cost-Benefit Issues

To support business requirements, information systems need to be scalable, powerful, and flexible. For most companies, client/server systems offer the best combination of features to meet those needs. Whether a business is expanding or downsizing, client/server systems enable the firm to scale the system in a rapidly changing environment. As the size of the business changes, it is easier to adjust the number of clients and the processing functions they perform than it is to alter the capability of a large-scale central server.

Client/server computing also allows companies to transfer applications from expensive mainframes to less-expensive client platforms. In addition, using common languages such as SQL, clients and servers can communicate across multiple platforms. That difference is important because many businesses have substantial investments in a variety of hardware and software environments.

Finally, compared to file server designs, client/server systems reduce network load and improve response times. For example, consider a user at a company headquarters who wants information about total sales figures. In a file server design, the system might need to transmit three separate sales transaction files from three regional offices in order to provide sales data that the client would process; in a client/server system, the server locates the data, performs the necessary processing, and responds immediately to the client's request. The data retrieval and processing functions are transparent to the client because they are done on the server, not the client.

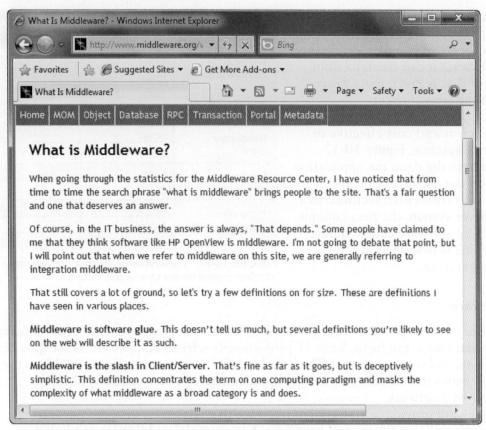

**FIGURE 10-18** Middleware connects dissimilar applications and enables them to communicate and exchange data. Middleware also can integrate legacy systems and Web-based applications.

## Client/Server Performance Issues

While it provides many important advantages over file-based systems, client/server architecture does involve performance issues that relate to the separation of server-based data and networked clients that must access the data.

Consider the difference between client/server design and a centralized environment, where a server-based program issues a command that is executed by the server's own CPU. Processing speed is enhanced because program instructions and data both travel on an internal system bus, which moves data more efficiently than an external network.

In contrast to the centralized system, a client/server design separates applications and data. Networked clients submit data requests to the server, which responds by sending data back to the clients. When the number of clients and the demand for services increases beyond a certain level, network capacity becomes a constraint, and system performance declines dramatically.

In the article shown in Figure 10-19, IBM states that the performance characteristics of a client/server system are not the same as a centralized processing environment. Client/server response times increase gradually as more requests are made, but then rise dramatically when the system nears its capacity. To deliver and maintain acceptable performance, system developers must anticipate the number of users, network traffic, server size and location, and design a client/server architecture that can support current and future business needs.

What is the answer to enhancing client/server performance? According to IBM, client/server systems must be designed so the client contacts the server only when necessary and makes as few trips as possible.

Another issue that affects client/server performance is data storage. Just as processing can be done at various places, data can be stored in more than one location using a **distributed database management system (DDBMS)**.

**FIGURE 10-19**   According to IBM, client/server response times increase gradually, and then rise dramatically when the system nears its capacity. That point is referred to as *the knee of the curve.*

Using a DDBMS offers several advantages: Data stored closer to users can reduce network traffic; the system is scalable, so new data sites can be added without reworking the system design; and with data stored in various locations, the system is less likely to experience a catastrophic failure. A potential disadvantage of distributed data storage involves data security. It can be more difficult to maintain controls and standards when data is stored in various locations. In addition, the architecture of a DDBMS is more complex and difficult to manage. From a system design standpoint, the challenge is that companies often want it both ways — they want the control that comes with centralization *and* the flexibility associated with decentralization.

## INTERNET-BASED ARCHITECTURE

The Internet has had an enormous impact on system architecture. The Internet has become more than a communication channel — many IT observers see it as a fundamentally different environment for system development.

Recall that in a traditional client/server system, the client handles the user interface, as shown in Figure 10-16 on page 464, and the server (or servers in a multi-tier system) handles the data and application logic. In a sense, part of the system runs on the client, part on the server. In contrast, in an Internet-based architecture, in addition to data and application logic, the entire user interface is provided by the Web server in the form of HTML coded documents that are interpreted and displayed by the client's browser. Shifting the responsibility for the interface from the client to the server simplifies the process of data transmission and results in lower hardware costs and complexities.

The trend toward Internet-based e-business is reshaping the IT landscape as more firms use the Web to build efficient, reliable, and cost-effective solutions. When planning new systems, analysts can use available and emerging technology to meet their company's business requirements.

The advantages of Internet-based architecture are changing fundamental ideas about how computer systems should be designed, and many IT experts are shifting their focus to a total online environment. At the same time, large numbers of individual users are seeking Web-based collaboration and social networking services to accomplish tasks that used to be done in person, over the phone, or by more traditional Internet channels. As you learned in Chapter 7, cloud computing and Web 2.0 are important concepts that reflect this online shift.

The following sections examine Web-based architecture, including in-house development, packaged solutions, e-business service providers, corporate portals, cloud computing, and Web 2.0. It is important to be aware of these trends, as they may predict where the IT industry is headed.

### Developing E-Commerce Solutions In-House

In Chapter 7, you learned how to analyze advantages and disadvantages of in-house development versus purchasing a software package. The same basic principles apply to system design.

If you decide to proceed with an in-house solution, you must have an overall plan to help achieve your goals. How should you begin? Figure 10-20 offers guidelines for companies developing e-commerce strategies. An in-house solution usually requires a greater initial investment, but provides more flexibility for a company that must adapt quickly in a dynamic e-commerce environment. By working in-house, a company has more freedom to integrate with customers and suppliers and is less dependent on vendor-specific solutions.

| Guidelines for In-house E-commerce Site Development |
|---|
| Analyze the company's business needs and develop a clear statement of your goals. Consider the experience of other companies with similar projects. |
| Obtain input from users who understand the business and technology issues involved in the project. Plan for future growth, but aim for ease of use. |
| Determine whether the IT staff has the necessary skills and experience to implement the project. Consider training, additional resources, and the use of consultants if necessary. |
| Consider integration requirements for existing legacy systems or enterprise resource planning. Select a physical infrastructure carefully, so it will support the application, now and later. |
| Develop the project in modular form so users can test and approve the functional elements as you go along. |
| Connect the application to existing in-house systems and verify interactivity. |
| Test every aspect of the site exhaustively. Consider a preliminary rollout to a pilot group to obtain feedback before a full launch. |

**FIGURE 10-20**  Guidelines for companies developing e-commerce strategies.

For smaller companies, the decision about in-house Web development is even more critical, because this approach will require financial resources and management attention that many small companies might be unable or unwilling to commit. An in-house strategy, however, can provide valuable benefits, including the following:

- A unique Web site, with a look and feel consistent with the company's other marketing efforts

- Complete control over the organization of the site, the number of pages, and the size of the files

- A scalable structure to handle increases in sales and product offerings in the future

- More flexibility to modify and manage the site as the company changes

- The opportunity to integrate the firm's Web-based business systems with its other information systems, creating the potential for more savings and better customer service

Whether a firm uses an in-house or a packaged design, the decision about Web hosting is a separate issue. Although internal hosting has some advantages, such as greater control and security, the expense would be much greater, especially for a small- to medium-sized firm.

## CASE IN POINT 10.2:   SMALL POTATOES, INC.

Small Potatoes is a family-operated seed business that has grown rapidly. Small Potatoes specializes in supplying home gardeners with the finest seeds and gardening supplies. Until now, the firm has done all its business by placing ads in gardening and health magazines, and taking orders using a toll-free telephone number.

Now, the family has decided to establish a Web site and sell online, but there is some disagreement about the best way to proceed. Some say it would be better to develop the site on their own, and Betty Lou Jones, a recent computer science graduate, believes she can handle the task. Others, including Sam Jones, Betty's grandfather, feel it would be better to outsource the site and focus on the business itself. Suppose the family asked for your opinion. What would you say? What additional questions would you ask?

## Packaged Solutions and E-Commerce Service Providers

If a small company is reluctant to take on the challenge and complexity of developing an Internet commerce site in-house, an alternative can be a packaged solution or an e-commerce service provider. This is true even for medium- to large-sized firms. Many vendors, including Microsoft and Intershop, offer turnkey systems for companies that want to get an e-business up and running quickly, as shown in Figure 10-21.

For large-scale systems that must integrate with existing applications, packaged solutions might be less attractive. Another alternative is to use an application service provider (ASP). As explained in Chapter 7, an ASP provides applications, or access to applications, by charging a usage or subscription fee. Today, many ASPs offer full-scale Internet business services for companies that decide to outsource those functions.

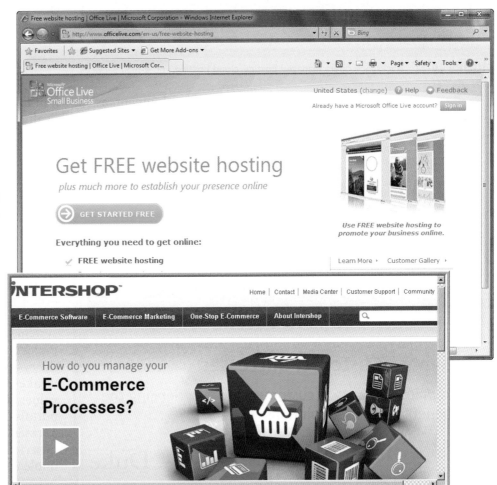

**FIGURE 10-21**   Microsoft and Intershop offer software solutions for companies that want to get an e-business up and running quickly.

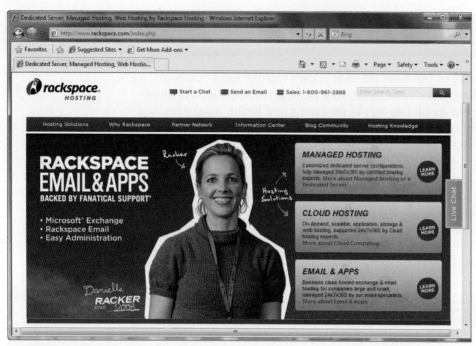

**FIGURE 10-22** Rackspace offers managed hosting, cloud hosting, and e-mail services.

Another option is managed hosting, which also was discussed in Chapter 7. As shown in Figure 10-22, a solution provider such as Rackspace can host and maintain a corporate Web site. Rackspace states that its customers will "never have to implement, update, troubleshoot, patch, monitor, administer, backup data, or worry again."

A systems analyst confronts a bewildering array of products and strategies when implementing Internet-based systems. A good starting point might be to consider the experience of other companies in the same industry. Many firms, including Sybase, offer success stories and case studies of successful systems development, as shown in Figure 10-23. Although each situation is different, this type of research can provide valuable information about a vendor's products and services.

**FIGURE 10-23** Success stories and case studies can provide valuable information about a vendor's products and services.

## Corporate Portals

A **portal** is an entrance to a multi-function Web site. After entering a portal, a user can navigate to a destination using various tools and features provided by the portal designer. A corporate portal can provide access for customers, employees, suppliers, and the public. In a Web-based system, portal design provides an important link between the user and the system, and poor design can weaken system effectiveness and value. Figure 10-24 shows enterprise portals offered by HP and SAP. As partners, the firms use their global IT experience and skills to design and implement portal solutions.

## Cloud Computing

**Cloud computing** refers to the cloud symbol that often is used to represent the Internet. The cloud computing concept envisions a *cloud* of remote computers that provide a total online

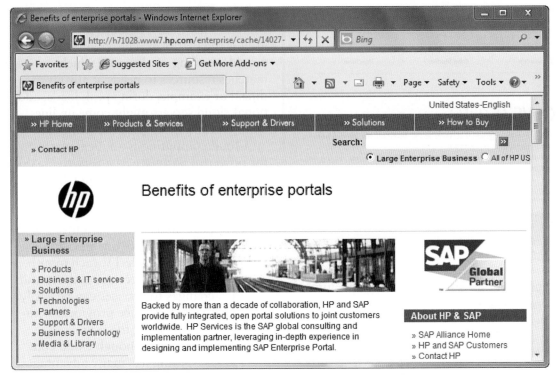

**FIGURE 10-24**   HP and SAP offer enterprise portal solutions to their customers worldwide.

software and data environment that is hosted by third parties. A user's computer does not perform processing or computing tasks — the cloud does. This concept is in contrast to today's computing model, which is based on networks that strategically distribute processing and data across the enterprise. In a sense, the cloud of computers acts as one giant computer that performs tasks for users. As shown in Figure 10-25, a user logs into a local computer and is connected to the cloud, which performs the computing work. Instead of requiring specific hardware and software on the user's computer, cloud computing

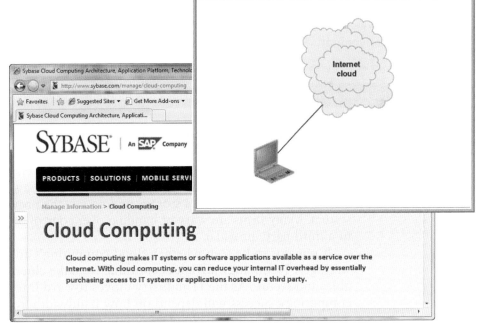

**FIGURE 10-25**   In cloud computing, users connect to the Internet cloud to access personal content and services through an online software and data environment.

spreads the workload to powerful remote systems that are part of the cloud. The user appears to be working on a local system, but all computing is actually performed in the cloud. No updates or maintenance are required of the user, and there are no compatibility issues.

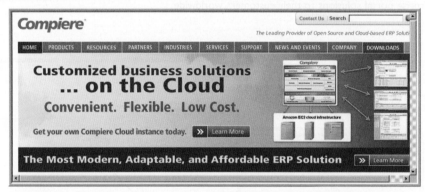

**FIGURE 10-26**   Three popular examples of cloud computing platforms.

Cloud computing effectively eliminates compatibility issues, because the Internet itself is the platform. This architecture also provides **scaling on demand**, which matches resources to needs at any given time. For example, during peak loads, additional cloud servers might come on line automatically to support the workload.

Cloud computing is an ideal platform for powerful Software as a Service (SaaS) applications. As you learned in Chapter 7, SaaS is a popular deployment method where software is not purchased but is paid for as a service, much like one pays for electricity or cable TV each month. In this architecture, updates and changes to services can be easily made by service providers without involving the users.

Even though cloud computing has many advantages, some concerns exist. First, cloud computing requires significantly more **bandwidth** (the amount of data that can be transferred in a fixed time period) than today's networks. Second, because cloud computing is Internet-based, if a user's Internet connection becomes unavailable, he or she will be unable to access any cloud-based services. In addition, there are security concerns associated with sending large amounts of data over the Internet, as well as concerns about storing it securely. Finally, there is the issue of control. Because a service provider hosts the resources and manages data storage and access, the provider has complete control of the system. Many firms are wary of handing over control of mission-critical data and systems to a third-party provider.

It remains to be seen whether cloud computing's advantages will outweigh its disadvantages. Technology advances continue to make cloud computing more feasible, desirable, and secure. As the IT industry moves toward Internet-based architectures, cloud computing's success will depend on how bandwidth, reliability, and security are addressed and how well cloud computing is received by users. As shown in Figure 10-26, examples of popular cloud computing platforms include Windows Azure, Amazon's Elastic Compute Cloud, and Compiere.

## Web 2.0

The shift to Internet-based collaboration has been so powerful and compelling that it has been named **Web 2.0**. Web 2.0 is not a reference to a more technically advanced version of the current Web. Rather, Web 2.0 envisions a second generation of the Web that will enable people to collaborate, interact, and share information more dynamically.

Leading Web 2.0 author Tim O'Reilly has suggested that the strong interest in Web 2.0 is driven by the concept of the *Internet as a platform*. O'Reilly sees future Web 2.0 applications delivering software as a continuous service with no limitations on the number of users that can connect or how users can consume, modify, and exchange data.

Figure 10-27 shows examples of popular social networking sites, which are seeing explosive growth in the Web 2.0 environment. Another form of social collaboration is called a wiki. A **wiki** is a Web-based repository of information that anyone can access, contribute to, or modify. In a sense, a wiki represents the collective knowledge of a group of people. One of the best-known wikis is Wikipedia.org, but smaller-scale wikis are growing rapidly at businesses, schools, and other organizations that want to compile and share information.

One of the goals of Web 2.0 is to enhance creativity, interaction, and shared ideas. In this regard, the Web 2.0 concept resembles the agile development process and the open-source software movement. Web 2.0 communities and services are based on a body of data created by users. As users collaborate, new layers of information are added in an overall environment known as the **Internet operating system**. These layers can contain text, sound bytes, images, and video clips that are shared with the user community.

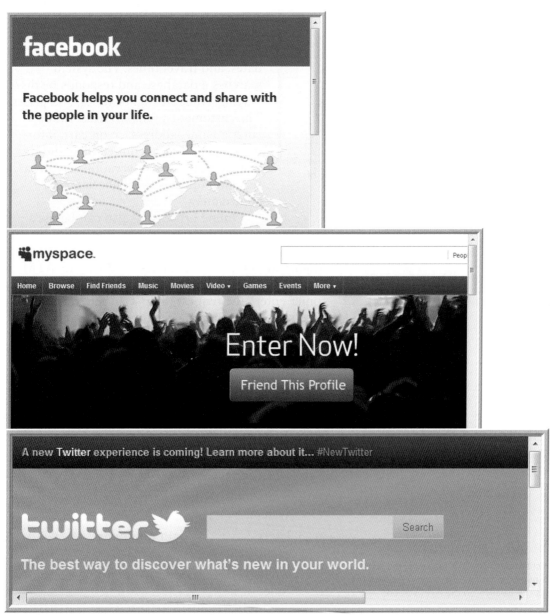

**FIGURE 10-27**  Facebook, MySpace, and Twitter are popular examples of Web 2.0 social networking.

## PROCESSING METHODS

In selecting an architecture, the systems analyst must determine whether the system will be an online system, a batch processing system, or a combination of the two.

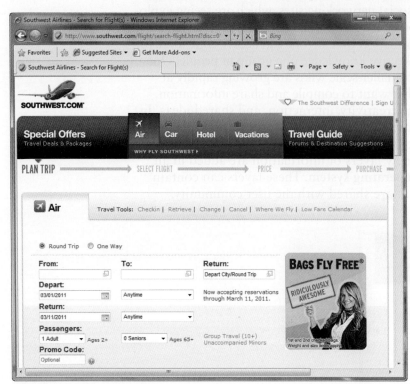

**FIGURE 10-28** The Southwest Airlines reservation system is an example of Web-based online processing.

### ATM QUERY PROCESS

**Step 1:**  Customer enters his or her account number and requests an account balance

**Step 2:**  Retrieves current account balance

**Step 3:**  Verifies bank account number and displays balance on ATM screen

**FIGURE 10-29** When a customer requests a balance, the ATM system verifies the account number, submits the query, retrieves the current balance, and displays the balance on the ATM screen.

### Online Processing

Early computer systems relied mainly on batch processing, but the vast majority of systems today use online processing. An **online system** handles transactions when and where they occur and provides output directly to users. Because it is interactive, online processing avoids delays and allows a constant dialog between the user and the system.

An airline reservations system is a familiar example of online processing. When an online customer views the screen shown in Figure 10-28, he or she can enter the origin, destination, travel dates, and travel times. The system searches a database and responds by displaying available flights, times, and prices. The customer can make a reservation, enter a name, address, credit card information, and other required data and the system creates the reservation, assigns a seat, and updates the flight database immediately.

Online processing also can be used with file-oriented systems. Figure 10-29 shows what happens when a customer uses an ATM to inquire about an account balance. After the ATM verifies the customer's card and password, the customer enters the request (Step 1). Then, the system accesses the account master file using the account number as the primary key and retrieves the customer's record (Step 2). The system verifies the account number and displays the balance (Step 3). Data is retrieved and the system transmits the current balance to the ATM, which prints it for the customer. Online processing systems have four typical characteristics:

1. The system processes transactions completely when and where they occur.

2. Users interact directly with the information system.

3. Users can access data randomly.

4. The information system must be available whenever necessary to support business functions.

## Batch Processing

In a **batch processing** system, data is collected and processed in groups, or batches. Although online processing is used for interactive business systems that require immediate data input and output, batch processing can handle other situations more efficiently. For example, batch processing typically is used for large amounts of data that must be processed on a routine schedule, such as paychecks or credit card transactions.

In batch processing, input transactions are grouped into a single file and processed together. For example, when a firm produces customer statements at the end of the month, a batch application might process many thousands of records in one run of the program. A batch processing system has several main characteristics: collect, group, and process transactions periodically; the IT operations group can run batch programs on a predetermined schedule, without user involvement, during regular business hours, at night, or on weekends; and batch programs require significantly fewer network resources than online systems.

## CASE IN POINT 10.3: R/WAY TRUCKING COMPANY

You are the new IT manager at R/Way, a small but rapidly growing trucking company headquartered in Cleveland, Ohio. The company slogan is "Ship It R/Way — State-of-the-Art in Trucking and Customer Service." R/Way's information system currently consists of a file server and three workstations where freight clerks enter data, track shipments, and prepare freight bills. To perform their work, the clerks obtain data from the server and use database and spreadsheet programs stored on their PCs to process the data.

Unfortunately, your predecessor did not design a relational database. Instead, data is stored in several files, including one for shippers, one for customers, and one for shipments. The system worked well for several years, but cannot handle current volume or support online links for R/Way shippers and customers. The company president is willing to make changes, but he is reluctant to spend money on major IT improvements unless you can convince him that they are necessary.

What would you recommend and why?

## Combined Online and Batch Processing

Even an online system can use batch processing to perform certain routine tasks. Online processing also can be used with file-oriented systems. Figure 10-30 shows a familiar **point-of-sale (POS)** terminal, and Figure 10-31 on the next page shows how a retail chain uses POS terminals to drive online and batch processing methods. Notice that the system uses online processing to handle data entry and inventory updates, while reports and accounting entries are performed in a batch.

**FIGURE 10-30**  Retail point-of-sale terminals provide customer sales support and transaction processing capability.

The retail store system illustrates both online processing and batch processing of data. During business hours, the salesperson enters a sale on a POS terminal, which is part of an information system that handles daily sales transactions and maintains the online inventory file. When the salesperson enters the transaction, online processing occurs. The system performs calculations, updates the inventory file, and produces output on the POS terminal in the

**POINT OF SALE (POS) PROCESSING**

**FIGURE 10-31** Many retailers use a combination of online and batch processing. When a salesperson enters the sale on the POS terminal, the online system retrieves data from the item file, updates the quantity in stock, and produces a sales transaction record. At the end of the day, a batch processing program produces a daily sales report and updates the accounting system.

form of a screen display and a printed receipt. At the same time, each sales transaction creates input data for day-end batch processing.

When the store closes, the system uses the sales transactions to produce the daily sales report and related accounting entries using batch processing. Performing the processing online before all sales transactions are completed does not make sense. In that situation, a batch method provides better routine transaction processing, while an online approach supports point-of-sale processing, which must be done as it occurs.

In the retail store example, both online and batch processing are integral parts of the information system. Online processing offers an inherent advantage because data is entered and validated as it occurs, so the stored data is available sooner and always is up to date. Online processing is more expensive, however, and the effect of computer system downtime or slowdown while transactions are processed causes far more disruption than in batch processing. In addition, backup and recovery for online processing are more difficult. In many situations, batch processing is cost-effective, less vulnerable to system disruption, and less intrusive to normal operations. Many information systems will continue to use a combination of online and batch processing for some time to come.

## NETWORK MODELS

A network allows the sharing of hardware, software, and data resources in order to reduce expenses and provide more capability to users. When planning a network design, you must consider network terms and concepts, including the OSI model, network modeling tools, network topology, network protocols, licensing issues, and wireless networks, which are covered in this section. Other important issues, such as network performance and security, are covered in Chapter 12, Securing and Supporting the System.

### The OSI Reference Model

Based on the discussion of system architecture earlier in this chapter, you already understand basic network terms such as client, server, LAN, WAN, file server design, client/server architecture, tiers, and middleware.

Before you study network topology, you should be familiar with the **OSI (Open Systems Interconnection) model**, which describes how data actually moves from an application on one computer to an application on another networked computer. The OSI model consists of seven layers. Each layer performs a specific function, as shown in Figure 10-32.

**ON THE WEB**

To learn more about the OSI reference model, visit the Management Information Systems CourseMate Web site at **www. cengagebrain. com**, navigate to **On the Web Links** for this chapter, and locate the OSI Reference Model link.

| LAYER NUMBER | NAME | DESCRIPTION |
|---|---|---|
| 7 | Application layer | Provides network services requested by a local workstation |
| 6 | Presentation layer | Ensures that data is uniformly structured and formatted for network transmission |
| 5 | Session layer | Defines control structures that manage the communications link between computers |
| 4 | Transport layer | Provides reliable data flow and error recovery |
| 3 | Network layer | Defines network addresses and determines how data packets are routed over the network |
| 2 | Data link layer | Defines specific methods of transmitting data over the physical layer, such as defining the start and end of a data frame |
| 1 | Physical layer | Contains physical components that carry data, such as cabling and connectors |

**FIGURE 10-32**  In the OSI model, data proceeds down through the layers on the transmitting computer, then up through the layers on the receiving computer. Along the way, data may pass through one or more network routers that control the path from one network address to another.

It is important to understand that OSI is a conceptual model and is not tied to any specific physical environment or hardware. However, the OSI model does provide design standards that assure seamless interchange and connectivity for network hardware and software.

## Network Protocols

In all cases, the network must use a **protocol**, which is a set of standards that govern network data transmission. A popular network protocol is **Transmission Control Protocol/ Internet Protocol (TCP/IP)**. Originally developed by the U.S. Department of Defense to permit interconnection of military computers, today TCP/IP is the backbone of the Internet. Other older network protocols include NetBIOS, which was popular for LANs, and IPX, which is a protocol used by Novell Corporation for older NetWare products.

TCP/IP actually consists of many individual protocols that control the handling of files, mail, and Internet addresses, among others. A familiar example of a TCP/IP protocol is the **File Transfer Protocol (FTP)**, which provides a reliable means of copying files from one computer to another over a TCP/IP network, such as the Internet or an intranet.

**ON THE WEB**

To learn more about network protocols, visit the Management Information Systems CourseMate Web site at **www. cengagebrain. com**, navigate to **On the Web Links** for this chapter, and locate the Network Protocols link.

## Network Topology

The way a network is configured is called the **network topology**. Topology can refer to a physical or a logical view of the network. For example, **physical topology** describes the actual network cabling and connections, while **logical topology** describes the way the components interact. It is important to understand the distinction, because a specific physical topology might be able to support more than one logical topology. For example, it is not uncommon to run cabling in a certain pattern because of physical installation and cost issues, but to use a different pattern for the logical topology.

The workstations in Figure 10-33 on the next page are arranged in a circular shape, but that might or might not reflect the network topology. The examples shown in Figures 10-34 to 10-38 on pages 478 to 481 represent a logical topology, as seen by network users, who do not know or care about the physical cabling pattern.

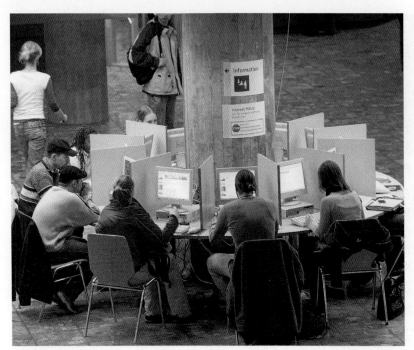

**FIGURE 10-33** Although these workstations form a circle physically, the layout has no bearing on the network topology, which might be a bus, ring, star, or other logical design.

LAN and WAN networks typically are arranged in four patterns: hierarchical, bus, ring, and star. The concepts are the same regardless of the size of the network, but the physical implementation is different for a large-scale WAN that spans an entire business enterprise compared with a small LAN in a single department. The four topologies are described in the following sections.

**HIERARCHICAL NETWORK** In a **hierarchical network**, as shown in Figure 10-34, one or more powerful servers control the entire network. Departmental servers control lower levels of processing and network devices. An example of a hierarchical network might be a retail clothing chain, with a central computer that stores data about sales activity and inventory levels and local computers that handle store-level operations.

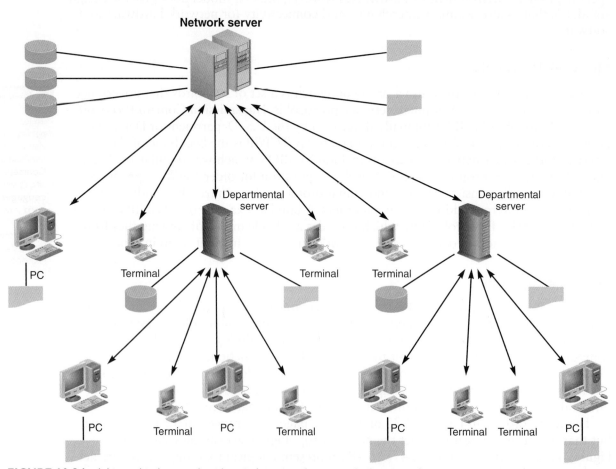

**FIGURE 10-34** A hierarchical network with a single server that controls the network.

The stores transmit data to the central computer, which analyzes sales trends, determines optimum stock levels, and coordinates a supply chain management system. In this situation, a hierarchical network might be used, because it mirrors the actual operational flow in the organization.

One disadvantage of a hierarchical network is that if a business adds additional processing levels, the network becomes more complex and expensive to operate and maintain. Hierarchical networks were often used in traditional mainframe-based systems, but are much less common today.

**BUS NETWORK** In a **bus network**, as shown in Figure 10-35, a single communication path connects the central server, departmental servers, workstations, and peripheral devices. Information is transmitted in either direction between networked devices, and all messages travel over the same central bus. Bus networks require less cabling than other topologies, because only a single cable is used. Devices can also be attached or detached from the network at any point without disturbing the rest of the network. In addition, a failure in one workstation on the network does not necessarily affect other workstations on the network.

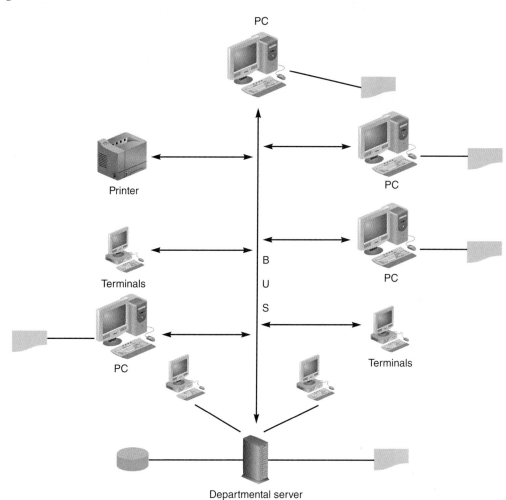

**FIGURE 10-35** A bus network with all devices connected to a single communication path.

One major disadvantage of a bus network is that if the central bus becomes damaged or defective, the entire network shuts down. Another disadvantage is that overall performance declines as more users and devices are added, because all message traffic must flow along the central bus. This does not occur in the treelike structure of a hierarchical network or the hub-and-spoke design of a star network, where network paths are more isolated and independent.

The bus network is one of the oldest LAN topologies, and is a simple way to connect multiple workstations. Before the proliferation of star networks, bus networks were very common. Today, the bus design is much less popular, but some firms have retained bus networks to avoid the expense of new wiring and hardware.

**RING NETWORK** A **ring network**, as shown in Figure 10-36 on the next page, resembles a circle where the data flows in only one direction from one device to the next. In function, a ring network can be thought of as a bus network with the ends connected. One disadvantage of a ring network is that if a network device (such as a PC or a

**FIGURE 10-36** A ring network with a set of computers that send and receive data flowing in one direction.

server) fails, the devices downstream from the failed device cannot communicate with the network. Although ring networks are less common than other topologies, they sometimes are used to tie local processing sites together. For example, workstations and servers in the accounting, sales, and shipping departments might perform local processing and then use a ring network to exchange data with other divisions within the company.

It is interesting to note that in a ring network implementation, the physical wiring can resemble a star pattern, using a central device called a **Multistation Access Unit (MAU)**. This unit internally wires the workstations into a logical ring, and manages the flow of data from one device to the next.

**STAR NETWORK** Because of its speed and versatility, the star network is by far the most popular LAN topology today. A **star network** has a central networking device called a **switch**, which manages the network and acts as a communications conduit for all network traffic. In the past, a device known as a **hub** was used to connect star networks, but a switch offers advanced technology and much better performance. A hub functions like a familiar multi-socket power strip, but with network devices such as servers, workstations, and printers plugged in rather than electrical appliances. The hub broadcasts network traffic, called **data frames**, to all connected devices. In contrast, a switch enhances network performance by sending traffic only to specific network devices that need to receive the data.

A star configuration, as shown in Figure 10-37, provides a high degree of network control, because all traffic flows into and out of the switch. An inherent disadvantage of the star design is that the entire network is dependent on the switch. However, in most large star networks, backup switches are available immediately in case of hardware failure.

**FIGURE 10-37** A typical star network with a switch, departmental server, and connected workstations.

**MESH NETWORK** In the **mesh network** shown in Figure 10-38, each node connects to every other node. While this design is extremely reliable, it also is very expensive to install and maintain. A mesh network resembles the Internet in that a message can travel on more than one path. Originally developed for military applications, the primary advantage of a mesh network is redundancy, because multiple paths provide backup if communication problems arise or some nodes become inoperable.

## Routers

Networks such as LANs or WANs can be interconnected using devices called routers. A **router** is a device that connects network segments, determines the most efficient data path, and guides the flow of data. Routers differ from switches in that they work at a higher OSI level (layer 3), dealing with IP packets, while switches handle data frames (layer 2).

Using a router, any network topology can connect to a larger, dissimilar network, such as the Internet. This connection is called a **gateway**. The example in Figure 10-39 shows a star topology, where the router links the network to the Internet. A device called a **proxy server** provides Internet connectivity for internal LAN users. The vast majority of business networks use routers to integrate the overall network architecture.

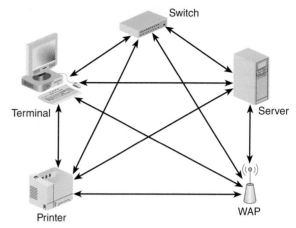

**FIGURE 10-38** Mesh networks are used in situations where a high degree of redundancy is needed, such as military applications. The redundant design provides alternate data paths, but is expensive to install and maintain.

**FIGURE 10-39** Routers can be used to connect LANs and WANs to other networks, such as the Internet.

## Network Modeling Tools

The OSI's multilayer concept makes it easier to understand and work with the individual components. As you translate the OSI conceptual model into a physical version of the system, you can use software tools, such as Microsoft Visio, which is a multipurpose drawing tool, to represent the physical structure and network components. Visio offers a wide variety of drawing types, styles, templates, and shapes. For example, Visio supplies templates for basic network designs, plus manufacturer-specific symbols for firms such as Cisco, IBM, Bay Systems, and Hewlett-Packard, among others.

Visio is an example of a CASE tool that can help you plan, analyze, design, and implement an information system. Visio can be used to create a simple network model, either by using drag-and-drop shapes displayed on the left of the screen, or by using provided wizards to walk through a step-by-step network design process. Figure 10-40 on the next page shows a simple network model created using the drag-and-drop feature.

The CASE Tools in Appendix B can help you document business functions and processes, develop graphical models, and provide an overall framework for information system development. To learn more about these tools, turn to Appendix B.

**FIGURE 10-40** Microsoft Visio can be used to create a network drawing using drag-and-drop shapes displayed in the panel at the left of the screen.

## Network Licensing Issues

When considering a network design, it is important to take into account software licensing restrictions. Various types of individual and site licenses are available from software vendors. Some vendors limit the number of users or the number of computers that can access the program simultaneously. You also must carefully investigate the capabilities of network software to ensure that it can handle the anticipated system traffic.

## WIRELESS NETWORKS

Although a LAN provides enormous flexibility, the initial cabling cost can be substantial, as well as the inevitable wiring changes that occur in a dynamic organization. Many companies find wireless technology to be an attractive alternative. A **wireless local area network**, or **WLAN**, is relatively inexpensive to install and is well-suited to workgroups and users who are not anchored to a specific desk or location. Most notebook computers are equipped with built-in wireless capability, and it is relatively simple to add this feature to existing desktop computers and workstations in order to set up a wireless network.

Like their wired counterparts, wireless networks have certain standards and topologies, which are discussed in the following sections.

### Wireless Network Standards

Wireless networks are based on various standards and protocols that still are evolving. The most popular of these is called IEEE **802.11**, which is a family of standards developed by the **Institute of Electrical and Electronics Engineers (IEEE)** for wireless LANs.

Current wireless networks are based on variations of the original 802.11 standard. Several versions, or **amendments**, were intended to improve bandwidth, range, and security. The table in Figure 10-41 contains a brief comparison of the IEEE 802.11 amendments. Note that maximum speed is measured in **Mbps (megabits per second)**.

| STANDARD | ADOPTED | MAXIMUM SPEED | APPROXIMATE RANGE | COMPATIBILITY |
|---|---|---|---|---|
| 802.11b | 1999 | 11 Mbps | 100–300 feet | Early 802.11 version |
| 802.11a | 1999 | 54 Mbps | 50–100 feet | Incompatible with 802.11b and 802.11g |
| 802.11g | 2003 | 54 Mbps | 50–100 feet | Compatible with 802.11b |
| 802.11n | 2009 | 200+ Mbps | 150–300 feet | Compatible with all 802.11 standards |

(Source: Wikipedia.org and IEEE.org)

**FIGURE 10-41** This table shows various Wi-Fi standards and characteristics. Maximum speed is measured in Mbps (megabits per second).

Early IEEE 802.11 standards had limited transmission capacity and were not popular. Later versions, such as **802.11g**, offered increased bandwidth and were widely accepted by the IT industry. The more recent **802.11n** uses **multiple input/multiple output (MIMO)** technology to boost performance. MIMO relies on multiple data paths, also called **multipath design,** to increase bandwidth and range. An even newer MIMO version, called **802.11y**, is currently being tested. If wireless capacity continues to expand and security issues can be overcome, WLANs could replace wired networks in many situations. Wireless security is discussed in detail in Chapter 12, Securing and Supporting the System.

## Wireless Network Topologies

Like wired networks, wireless networks also can be arranged in different topologies. The three major network topologies available for IEEE 802.11 WLANs are the Basic Service Set, the Extended Service Set, and the Independent Service Set.

The **Basic Service Set (BSS)**, also called the **infrastructure mode,** is shown is Figure 10-42. In this configuration, a central wireless device called an **access point** or **wireless access point (WAP)**, is used to serve all wireless clients. The access point is similar to a hub in the LAN star topology, except it provides network services to wireless clients instead of wired clients. Because access points use a single communications medium, the air, they broadcast all traffic to all clients, just as a hub would do in a wired network. Typically, the access point itself is connected to a wired network, so wireless clients can access the wired network.

The second wireless topology is the **Extended Service Set (ESS)**, as shown in Figure 10-43 on the next page. An Extended Service Set is made up of two or more Basic Service Set networks. Thus, using an ESS topology, wireless access can be expanded over a wide area. Each access point provides wireless services over a limited range. As a client moves away from one access point and closer to another, a process called **roaming** automatically allows the client to associate with the stronger access point, allowing for undisrupted service.

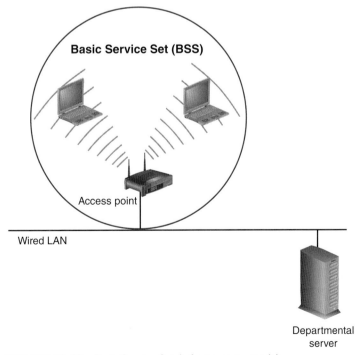

**FIGURE 10-42**  Basic Service Set (infrastructure mode).

Extended Service Set (ESS)

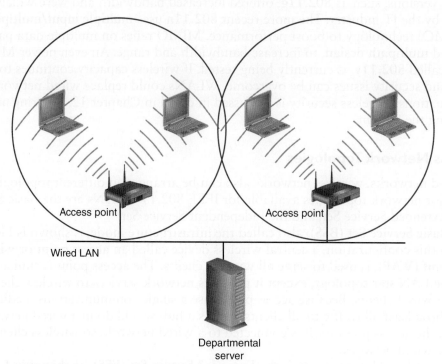

Wired LAN

Departmental
server

**FIGURE 10-43**   Extended Service Set.

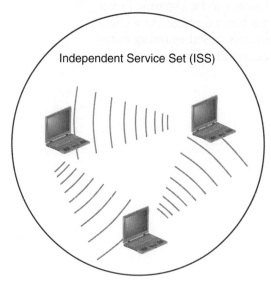

**FIGURE 10-44**   Independent Service Set (peer-to-peer mode).

The third wireless topology is the **Independent Service Set (ISS)**, as shown in Figure 10-44. In the ISS, also called **peer-to-peer mode**, no access point is used. Instead, wireless clients connect to each other directly. Most business WLANs use access points to provide wireless services, and do not utilize the Independent Service Set. However, ISS is well-suited to situations requiring quick data transfer among clients.

## Wireless Trends

Wireless technology has brought explosive change to the IT industry, and will continue to affect businesses, individuals, and society. Even in the ever-changing world of IT, it would be difficult to find a more dynamic area than wireless technology.

With the growing popularity of 802.11, many firms offer networking products, services, and information. One of the most significant groups is the **Wi-Fi Alliance**, which maintains a Web site at *www.wi-fi.org*. According to the site, the Alliance is a nonprofit international association formed in 1999 to certify interoperability of wireless network products based on IEEE 802.11 specifications. Products that meet the requirements are certified as **Wi-Fi (wireless fidelity)** compatible. Currently the Wi-Fi Alliance has over 300 member companies from around the world, and over 4,200 products have received Wi-Fi certification. The stated goal of the Wi-Fi Alliance is to enhance the user experience through product interoperability.

Even though they have many advantages, wireless networks also have limitations and disadvantages. For example, because 802.11b and 802.11g devices use the 2.4 GHz band, these devices can pick up interference from appliances such as microwave ovens and cordless telephones that use the same band. More important, wireless networks pose major security concerns because wireless transmissions are much more susceptible to interception and intrusion than wired networks. These issues are discussed in detail in Chapter 12, Securing and Supporting the System.

In addition to Wi-Fi, another form of wireless transmission called **Bluetooth** is very popular for short-distance wireless communication that does not require high power. Examples of Bluetooth devices include wireless keyboards, mice, printers, cell phone headsets, and digital cameras, among others. People with Bluetooth-equipped phones or PDAs can even beam information to each other and exchange digital notes.

Although the expansion of Wi-Fi has been dramatic, future technology promises even greater wireless speed, range, and compatibility. For example, in addition to 802.11 protocols for LANs, IEEE is working on **802.16** standards, which are broadband wireless communications protocols for **MANs (metropolitan area networks)**. These specifications, which IEEE calls **WiMAX**, are expected to enable wireless multimedia applications with a range of up to 30 miles.

## CASE IN POINT 10.4:   SPIDER IT SERVICES

Spider IT Services specializes in custom network design and installation. Firms hire Spider to do an overall analysis of their network needs, including a detailed cost-benefit study. Recently, a problem arose. One of Spider's clients complained that the relatively new network was too slow and lacked sufficient capacity. Reviewing the case, Spider's top management realized that the rapidly growing client had simply outgrown the network much earlier than anticipated.

Could this problem have been avoided? Note that IBM, in the article shown in Figure 10-19 on page 467, commented that performance can "degrade exponentially" in certain kinds of network situations. Consider the IBM article and other material in this chapter, and offer your views.

## SYSTEMS DESIGN COMPLETION

System architecture marks the end of the systems design phase of the SDLC. Recall that back in the systems analysis phase, all functional primitives were identified and documented with process descriptions. The objective then was to identify the system's functions and determine *what* each logical module would do, without attempting to determine *how* that function would be carried out. Moving from analysis to design tasks, the development process continued with consideration of output and user interface design, data design, and system architecture issues. Now, based on a clear definition of system requirements and design, software applications can be developed, documented, and tested as part of the systems implementation phase of the SDLC, which is described in Chapter 11, Making the System Operational.

Developers must also consider system management and support tools that can monitor system performance, deal with fault management, handle backup, and provide for disaster recovery. These topics are covered in detail in Chapter 12, Securing and Supporting the System.

The final activities in the systems design phase are preparing a system design specification, obtaining user approval, and delivering a presentation to management.

## System Design Specification

The **system design specification** is a document that presents the complete design for the new information system, along with detailed costs, staffing, and scheduling for completing the next SDLC phase — systems implementation.

The system design specification is the baseline against which the operational system will be measured. Unlike the system requirements document, which is written for users to understand, the system design specification is oriented toward the programmers who will use it to create the necessary programs. Some sections of the system requirements document are repeated in the system design specification, such as process descriptions, data dictionary entries, and data flow diagrams.

The system design specification varies in length, so you must organize it carefully and number all pages in sequence. You should include a cover page, a detailed table of contents, and an index. The contents of the system design specification depend on company standards and the complexity of the system. A typical system design specification typically includes the following sections.

1. *Management Summary.* This is a brief overview of the project for company managers and executives. It outlines the development efforts to date, provides a current status report, summarizes project costs, reviews the benefits of the new system, presents the systems implementation schedule, and highlights any issues that management will need to address.

2. *System Components.* This section contains the complete design for the new system, including the user interface, outputs, inputs, files, databases, and network specifications. You should include source documents, report and screen layouts, DFDs, and all other relevant documentation. You also should include the requirements for all support processing, such as backup and recovery, start-up processing, and file retention. If the purchase of a software package is part of the strategy, you must include any interface information required between the package and the system you are developing. If you use a CASE design tool, you can print design diagrams and most other documentation directly from the tool.

3. *System Environment.* This section describes the constraints, or conditions, affecting the system, including any requirements that involve operations, hardware, systems software, or security. Examples of operational constraints include transaction volumes that must be supported, data storage requirements, processing schedules, reporting deadlines, and online response times.

4. *Implementation Requirements.* In this section, you specify start-up processing, initial data entry or acquisition, user training requirements, and software test plans.

5. *Time and Cost Estimates.* This section provides detailed schedules, cost estimates, and staffing requirements for the systems development phase and revised projections for the remainder of the SDLC. You also present total costs-to-date for the project and compare those costs with your prior estimates.

6. *Additional Material.* Other material can be included at the end of the system design specification. In this section, you might insert documents from earlier phases if they would be helpful to readers.

## User Approval

Users must review and approve the interface design, report and menu designs, data entry screens, source documents, and other areas of the system that affect them. The review and approval process continues throughout the systems design phase. When you complete the design for a report, you should meet with users to review the prototype, adjust the design if necessary, and obtain written approval. Chapter 8 contains guidelines and suggestions about report design.

Securing approvals from users throughout the design phase is very important. That approach ensures that you do not have a major task of obtaining approvals at the end, it keeps the users involved with the system's development, and it gives you feedback about whether or not you are on target. Some sections of the system design specification might not interest users, but anything that does affect them should be approved as early as possible.

Other IT department members also need to review the system design specification. IT management will be concerned with staffing, costs, hardware and systems software requirements, network impact, and the effect on the operating environment when the new system is added. The programming team will want to get ready for its role, and the operations group will be interested in processing support, report distribution, network loads, integration with other systems, and any hardware or software issues for which they need to prepare. You must be a good communicator to keep people up to date, obtain their input and suggestions, and obtain necessary approvals.

When the system design specification is complete, you distribute the document to a target group of users, IT department personnel, and company management. You should distribute the document at least one week before your presentation to allow the recipients enough time to review the material.

## Presentations

Usually, you will give several presentations at the end of the systems design phase. The presentations give you an opportunity to explain the system, answer questions, consider comments, and secure final approval. Appendix A can provide valuable guidelines and tips about oral presentations.

The first presentation is to the systems analysts, programmers, and technical support staff members who will be involved in future project phases or operational support for the system. Because of the audience, the presentation is technically oriented.

Your next presentation is to department managers and users from departments affected by the system. As in the first presentation, your primary objective is to obtain support and approval for the systems design. This is not a technical presentation; it is aimed at user interaction with the system and management's interest in budgets, schedules, staffing, and impact on the production environment.

The final presentation is delivered to management. By the time you give this presentation, you should have obtained all necessary approvals from prior presentations, and you should have the support of users and the IT department. Just like the management presentation at the end of the systems analysis phase, this presentation has a key objective: to obtain management's approval and support for the next development step — systems implementation — including a solid commitment for financial and other resources needed.

Based on the presentation and the data you submitted, management might reach one of three decisions: proceed with systems development, perform additional work on the systems design phase, or terminate the project.

The Communication Tools in Appendix A can help you develop better reports and presentations. To learn more about these tools, turn to Appendix A.

# A QUESTION OF ETHICS

The new accounting system is operational, but feedback from users has been negative. The most common complaint is that the system is not user-friendly. Some people in the IT department think that more user training would solve the problem. However, Sam, the IT manager, is opposed to a fresh round of training. "Let's just set up the network to monitor the users' keystrokes and mouse clicks, and see what the patterns are," he suggested. "We can analyze the data and come up with tips and suggestions that would make the system easier to use."

Your initial reaction is that Sam is wrong, for two reasons. First, you believe that monitoring would not be an effective method to learn what users really want. In your view, that should have been done in the system requirements phase. Second, you are bothered by an ethical question: Even though the proposed monitoring would involve company business, the company network, and company time, you feel that many users would resent the unannounced monitoring, and might feel that their performance or other computing activities were being appraised without their knowledge.

Sam has asked to you to write up a recommendation. What will you say about the ethical question that troubles you?

## CHAPTER SUMMARY

An information system combines hardware, software, data, procedures, and people into a system architecture. The architecture translates the system's logical design into a physical structure that includes hardware, software, and processing methods. The software consists of application programs, also called applications, that handle the input, manage the processing logic, and provide the required output.

Before selecting an architecture, the analyst must consider enterprise resource planning, initial cost and TCO, scalability, Web integration, legacy interface requirements, processing options, and security issues.

Enterprise resource planning (ERP) establishes an enterprise-wide strategy for IT resources and specific standards for data, processing, network, and user interface design. Companies can extend ERP systems to suppliers and customers in a process called supply chain management. A systems analyst must assess initial cost and TCO and ensure that the design is scalable. Scalability means that a system can be expanded, modified, or downsized easily to meet business needs. The analyst also must consider if the system will be Web-centric and follow Internet design protocols, and if it must interface with existing systems, called legacy systems. System security is an important concern throughout the design process, especially for e-commerce applications that involve credit card and personal data. Processing options affect system design and resources required.

An architecture requires servers and clients. Servers are computers that supply data, processing services, or other support to one or more computers called clients. In mainframe architecture, the server performs all processing, and terminals communicate with the centralized system. Clients can be connected in distributed systems to form local area networks (LANs) or wide area networks (WANs). A typical LAN design involves file server design, where the client requests a copy of a data file and the server responds by transmitting the entire file to the client.

Client/server architecture divides processing between one or more clients and a central server. In a typical client/server system, the client handles the entire user interface, including data entry, data query, and screen presentation logic. The server stores the data and provides data access and database management functions. Application logic is divided in some manner between the server and the clients. In a typical client/server interaction, the client submits a request for information from the server, which carries out the operation and responds to the client. Compared to file server designs, client/server systems are more scalable and flexible.

A fat, or thick, client design places all or most of the application processing logic at the client. A thin client design places all or most of the processing logic at the server. Thin client designs provide better performance, because program code resides on the server, near the data. In contrast, a fat client handles more of the processing, and must access and update the data more often. Compared with maintaining a central server, fat client TCO also is higher, because of initial hardware and software requirements and the ongoing expense of maintaining and updating remote client computers. The fat client design is simpler to develop, because the architecture resembles traditional file server designs where all processing is performed at the client.

Client/server designs can be two-tier or three-tier (also called n-tier). In a two-tier design, the user interface resides on the client, all data resides on the server, and the application logic can run either on the server or on the client, or be divided between the client and the server. In a three-tier design, the user interface runs on the client and the data is stored on the server, just as with a two-tier design. A three-tier design also has a middle layer between the client and server that processes the client requests and translates them into data access commands that can be understood and carried out by the server. The middle layer is called an application server, because it provides the application logic, or business logic. Middleware is software that connects dissimilar applications and enables them to communicate and pass data. In planning the system design, a systems analyst also must consider cost-benefit and performance issues.

The Internet has had an enormous impact on system architecture. In implementing a design, an analyst should consider e-commerce strategies, the availability of packaged solutions, and corporate portals, which are entrances to a multifunction Web site. The analyst also should understand the concepts of cloud computing and Web 2.0, which are shaping the future of Internet computing.

The primary processing methods are online and batch processing. Users interact directly with online systems that continuously process their transactions when and where they occur and continuously update files and databases. In contrast, batch systems process transactions in groups and execute them on a predetermined schedule. Many online systems also use batch processing to perform routine tasks, such as handling reports and accounting entries.

Networks allow the sharing of hardware, software, and data resources in order to reduce expenses and provide more capability to users. The network is represented by a seven-layer logical model called the OSI (Open Systems Interconnection) model. Various OSI layers handle specific functions as data flows down from the sending computer and up into the receiving computer.

The way a network is configured is called the network topology. Networks typically are arranged in four patterns: hierarchical, bus, ring, and star. A single mainframe computer usually controls a hierarchical network, a bus network connects workstations in a single-line communication path, a ring network connects workstations in a circular communication path, and a star network connects workstations to a central computer or networking device called a switch. Wireless networks, or WLANs, based on IEEE 802.11 standards, have seen explosive growth, especially in situations where the flexibility of wireless is important. The IEEE 802.11n standard uses MIMO, or multipath technology, which has increased wireless network speed and range. WLANs have three major topologies: BSS, ESS, and ISS. Although wireless networks are very popular, they do have some limitations and disadvantages, including interference and security concerns.

The system design specification presents the complete systems design for an information system and is the basis for the presentations that complete the systems design phase. Following the presentations, the project either progresses to the systems development phase, requires additional systems design work, or is terminated.

# Key Terms and Phrases

802.11 *482*
802.11g *483*
802.11n *483*
802.11y *483*
802.16 *485*
access point *483*
amendment *482*
application logic *464*
application server *464*
applications *454*
bandwidth *472*
Basic Service Set (BSS) *483*
batch processing *475*
Bluetooth *485*
bus network *479*
business logic *464*
client/server architecture *461*
clients *458*
cloud computing *470*
data frames *480*
data processing center *459*
distributed database management
    system (DDBMS) *466*
distributed systems *460*
enterprise resource planning (ERP) *454*
environment *454*
Extended Service Set (ESS) *483*
extensibility *454*
fat client *464*
file server *460*
file sharing architecture *460*
File Transfer Protocol (FTP) *477*
gateway *481*
hierarchical network *478*
hub *480*
Independent Service Set (ISS) *484*
infrastructure mode *483*
Institute of Electrical and Electronics
    Engineers (IEEE) *482*
Internet operating system *473*
legacy data *462*
legacy systems *457*
local area network (LAN) *460*
logical topology *477*
mainframe architecture *458*
MAN (metropolitan area network) *485*
Mbps (megabits per second) *482*

mesh network *480*
middleware *465*
multipath design *483*
multiple input/multiple output (MIMO) *483*
Multistation Access Unit (MAU) *480*
network topology *477*
n-tier *464*
node *456*
online system *474*
OSI (Open Systems Interconnection)
    model *476*
peer-to-peer mode *484*
physical topology *477*
platform *454*
point-of-sale (POS) *475*
portal *470*
protocol *477*
proxy server *481*
ring network *479*
roaming *483*
router *481*
scalability *454*
scaling on demand *472*
server *458*
stand-alone *460*
star network *480*
supply chain management (SCM) *454*
switch *480*
system architecture *452*
system design specification *486*
terminal *459*
thick client *464*
thin client *464*
three-tier *464*
Transmission Control Protocol/Internet
    Protocol (TCP/IP) *477*
transparent *460*
two-tier *464*
Web 2.0 *472*
Web-centric *457*
Wi-Fi Alliance *484*
Wi-Fi (wireless fidelity) *484*
wide area network (WAN) *460*
wiki *473*
wireless access point (WAP) *483*
wireless local area network (WLAN) *482*
WiMAX *485*

# Learn It Online

**Instructions:** To complete the Learn It Online exercises, visit the Management Information Systems CourseMate Web site at **www.cengagebrain.com**, navigate to the resources for this chapter, and click the link for the exercise you want to complete.

## 1  Chapter Reinforcement

### TF, MC, and SA

Click one of the Chapter Reinforcement links for Multiple Choice, True/False, or Short Answer. Answer each question and submit to your instructor.

## 2  Flash Cards

Click the Flash Cards link and read the instructions. Type 20 (or a number specified by your instructor) in the Number of playing cards text box, type your name in the Enter your Name text box, and then click the Flip Card button. When the flash card is displayed, read the question and then click the ANSWER box arrow to select an answer. Flip through the Flash Cards. If your score is 15 (75%) correct or greater, click Print on the File menu to print your results. If your score is less than 15 (75%) correct, then redo this exercise by clicking the Replay button.

## 3  Practice Test

Click the Practice Test link. Answer each question, enter your first and last name at the bottom of the page, and then click the Grade Test button. When the graded practice test is displayed on your screen, click Print on the File menu to print a hard copy. Continue to take practice tests until you score 80% or better.

## 4  Who Wants To Be a Computer Genius?

Click the Computer Genius link. Read the instructions, enter your first and last name at the bottom of the page, and then click the Play button. When your score is displayed, click the PRINT RESULTS link to print a hard copy.

## 5  Wheel of Terms

Click the Wheel of Terms link. Read the instructions, and then enter your first and last name and your school name. Click the PLAY button. When your score is displayed on the screen, right-click the score and then click Print on the shortcut menu to print a hard copy.

## 6  Crossword Puzzle Challenge

Click the Crossword Puzzle Challenge link. Read the instructions, and then click the Continue button. Work the crossword puzzle. When you are finished, click the Submit button. When the crossword puzzle is redisplayed, submit it to your instructor.

## SCR Associates Case Simulation Session 10: Systems Architecture

### Overview

The SCR Associates case study is a Web-based simulation that allows you to practice your skills in a real-world environment. The case study transports you to SCR's intranet, where you complete 12 work sessions, each aligning with a chapter. As you work on the case, you will receive e-mail and voice mail messages, obtain information from SCR's online libraries, and perform various tasks.

### How do I use the case?

- Review the SCR background material in Chapter 1.
- Read the Preview for this session and study the Task List.
- Visit the Management Information Systems CourseMate Web site at **www.cengagebrain. com**, navigate to the **SCR Case Simulation**, and locate the intranet link.
- Enter your name and the password **sad9e**. An opening screen will display the 12 sessions.
- Select this session. Check your e-mail and voice mail carefully, and then work on the tasks.

### Preview: Session 10

Your supervisor, Jesse Baker, wants you to be familiar with the main issues that a systems analyst should consider when selecting an architecture, including enterprise resource planning, initial costs and TCO, scalability, Web integration, legacy interface requirements, processing options, and security issues.

### Task List

| |
|---|
| 1.  Jesse wants me to recommend a vendor who offers an ERP strategy. I need to review the SAP and Oracle Web sites, and at least two others that offer ERP solutions, and reply to her with the results and the reasons for my recommendations. |
| 2.  Visit SCR's data library to review SCR's network configuration and then send Jesse a recommendation for the TIMS system architecture. She wants me to suggest an overall client/server design, number of tiers, and network topology. She also asked me to comment on these issues: legacy data, Web-centricity, scalability, security, and batch processing that might be needed. Jesse said it was OK to make reasonable assumptions in my proposal to her. |
| 3.  Perform research on the Internet to learn more about TCO, and develop a TCO checklist that includes the five most important elements of TCO, because of their magnitude or potential impact on TIMS. |
| 4.  Prepare a system design specification as Jesse requested. |

**FIGURE 10-45**   Task list: Session 10.

# Chapter Exercises

## Review Questions

1. Define the term system architecture. Define the term scalability, and explain why it is important to consider scalability in system design.
2. When selecting an architecture, what items should a systems analyst consider as part of the overall design checklist?
3. What is enterprise resource planning (ERP)? What is supply chain management?
4. Explain the term server and provide an example of server-based processing; explain the term client and provide an example of client-based processing.
5. Describe client/server architecture, including fat and thin clients, client/server tiers, and middleware.
6. Describe the impact of the Internet on system architecture. Include examples.
7. Explain the difference between online processing and batch processing and provide an example of each type.
8. Explain the difference between a LAN and a WAN, define the term topology, and draw a sketch of each wired and wireless network model. Also describe the IEEE 802.11g and 802.11n amendments, and multiple input-multiple output (MIMO) technology.
9. Explain the differences between the BSS, ESS, and ISS wireless topologies. Which is rarely used in business? To what kind of network do the 802.16 standards apply?
10. List the sections of a system design specification, and describe the contents.

## Discussion Topics

1. Information technology has advanced dramatically in recent years. At the same time, enormous changes in the business world have occurred as companies reflect global competition and more pressure for quality, speed, and customer service. Did the new technology inspire the business changes, or was it the other way around?
2. Internet-based sales have shown explosive growth in recent years. How does B2B interaction differ from consumer-based Internet marketing, and why is it growing so rapidly?
3. This chapter described seven guidelines that a systems analyst might use when considering an architecture. In your view, are all the items of equal weight and importance, or should some be ranked higher? Justify your position.
4. One manager states, "When a new system is proposed, I want a written report, not an oral presentation, which is like a sales pitch. I only want to see the facts about costs, benefits, and schedules." Do you agree with that point of view?

# Apply Your Knowledge

The Apply Your Knowledge section contains four mini-cases. Each case describes a situation, explains your role in the case, and asks you to respond to questions. You can answer the questions by applying knowledge you learned in the chapter.

## 1 Digital Dynamics

**Situation:**

After three years as a successful Web design firm in Southern California, Digital Dynamics has decided to add two new business ventures: a group that specializes in supplying qualified employees to high-tech firms and a training division that offers online courses in advanced Web design and e-commerce skills. As a senior systems analyst, you have been asked to study the situation and make recommendations.

1. Should Digital Dynamics adopt ERP? What specific advantages would ERP offer?
2. How could the concept of supply chain management apply to a company's service-based division? Provide some specific suggestions.
3. Should Digital Dynamics use separate portals for employees, customers, and suppliers?
4. Is the experience of other companies relevant? Use the Internet to locate examples of Web-based firms that offer personnel services and technical training. How would you evaluate the Web sites you visited? What specific features impressed you favorably or unfavorably?

## 2 R/Way Trucking

**Situation:**

As you learned earlier in this chapter, R/Way is a small but rapidly growing trucking company headquartered in Cleveland, Ohio. R/Way's information system currently consists of a file server and three workstations where freight clerks enter data, track shipments, and prepare freight bills. To perform their work, the clerks obtain data from a file server and use database and spreadsheet programs stored on stand-alone PCs to process the data. At your meeting yesterday, R/Way's president approved your recommendation to create a relational database to handle R/Way operations and provide links for R/Way shippers and customers.

1. Review the concept of supply chain management. Although R/Way offers services rather than products, could that concept apply to the design of R/Way's new system? If so, how?
2. What would be the advantages of selecting an Internet-based architecture for R/Way's system?
3. Should R/Way's new system be based on file-server or client/server architecture? Why?
4. What would be the pros and cons of selecting in-house development versus a packaged solution for the R/Way system?

## 3 Nothing But Net

**Situation:**

Nothing But Net is an IT consulting firm that specializes in e-commerce solutions. As a newly hired systems analyst, you have been asked to research some current topics.

1. Obtain at least two estimates of how much consumers are projected to spend on Internet purchases during the next three years. Are the estimates similar? If not, which forecast do you believe, and why?

2. Many of Nothing But Net's customers are start-up firms that must fight hard to attract investment capital, and many traditional lending institutions are skeptical of new Web-based firms. Perform research to determine the mortality rate of new e-commerce firms that use the Web as their primary marketing channel, and write a brief memo that describes the results of your research.

3. Some IT professionals predict that traditional companies will increase their Internet marketing efforts, making it even harder for new Web-based firms to compete. Perform research to find out more about the topic and share your results with the class.

4. Suppose you were asked to draft a sales brochure for Nothing But Net. List all the services in which potential customers might be interested.

## 4 Aunt Ann's Kitchen

**Situation:**

Aunt Ann's Kitchen offers a line of specialty food products to institutional customers and restaurant chains. The firm prides itself on using only the finest ingredients and preparation methods. The owner, Ann Rose, hired you as an IT consultant to help her plan the system architecture for a new WLAN that will connect employee computers to the main (wired) network. She asked you to start with the following questions:

1. What possible IEEE 802.11 amendments could be used for the new system? What are the pros and cons of each amendment?

2. Choose an amendment to implement and explain your choice.

3. Suppose that microwave ovens and cordless telephones are used extensively in some parts of the facility. Would that affect your IEEE 802.11 amendment choice? If so, why?

4. Suppose that the new WLAN will also provide roaming services for employees with portable notebook computers. Which wireless topology will be required?

# Case Studies

Case studies allow you to practice specific skills learned in the chapter. Each chapter contains several case studies that continue throughout the textbook, and a chapter capstone case.

## New Century Health Clinic

New Century Health Clinic offers preventive medicine and traditional medical care. In your role as an IT consultant, you will help New Century develop a new information system.

### Background

The New Century clinic associates accepted your interface, output, input, and data designs and your recommendation to install a server and four personal computers as clients on a local area network. The network will include a tape backup unit and Internet access via a modem that can exchange data with insurance companies. A high-speed laser printer and an impact printer for multipart forms will be accessible by any of the four PCs. Now you will determine system architecture for the New Century system.

When you created ERDs and record designs for New Century during the data design process in Chapter 9, you considered whether to use a file-processing or database approach. As you know, each strategy has advantages and disadvantages, depending on the specific hardware and software environment and business requirements. At this point, you must decide which way to proceed, and Dr. Jones will accept your recommendation (with your instructor's approval). You should start by reviewing the DFDs and object-oriented diagrams that you prepared in the systems analysis phase, and the ERDs and table designs that you created in the systems design phase. Then, review the system architecture checklist at the beginning of this chapter.

### Assignments

1. What would be the advantages of selecting an Internet-based architecture for the New Century system?
2. Should the New Century system be based on file-server or client/server architecture? Why?
3. Could the New Century system use both online and batch processing? How?
4. Prepare an outline for a system design specification and describe the contents of each section.

## PERSONAL TRAINER, INC.

Personal Trainer, Inc., owns and operates fitness centers in a dozen Midwestern cities. The centers have done well, and the company is planning an international expansion by opening a new "supercenter" in the Toronto area. Personal Trainer's president, Cassia Umi, hired an IT consultant, Susan Park, to help develop an information system for the new facility. During the project, Susan will work closely with Gray Lewis, who will manage the new operation.

### Background

Susan and Gray finished their work on the user interface, input, and output design. They developed a user-centered design that would be easy to learn and use. Now Susan turned her attention to the architecture for the new system.

Susan wanted to consider enterprise resource planning, total cost of ownership, scalability, Web integration, legacy systems, processing methods, and security issues. She also needed to select a network plan, or topology, that would dictate the physical cabling and network connections, or consider a wireless network. When all these tasks were completed, she would submit a system design specification for approval.

### Assignments

1. Would an ERP strategy work well for Personal Trainer? Investigate ERP strategies and products available from Internet vendors and submit a recommendation based on your research.

2. If Susan chooses a client/server architecture, what issues must she consider? Prepare a checklist for her that includes the main topics and issues she should consider.

3. What would be the benefits of using a wireless network? What would be the drawbacks?

4. Prepare an outline for a system design specification and describe the contents of each section.

## CHAPTER CAPSTONE CASE:   SoftWear, Limited                            SWL

SoftWear, Limited (SWL), is a continuing case study that illustrates the knowledge and skills described in each chapter. In this case study, the student acts as a member of the SWL systems development team and performs various tasks.

### Background

Jane Rossman, manager of applications, and Rick Williams, systems analyst, had several meetings with True Blue Systems, the consulting firm hired to assist SWL in implementing the new ESIP system. Michael Jeremy, SWL's finance vice president, requested that True Blue also make recommendations about a possible SWL intranet to link all SWL locations and support client/server architecture.

The initial report from True Blue indicated that the new ESIP system should be designed as a DBMS so it could interface with the new mainframe payroll package. True Blue suggested that the ESIP system be implemented on a server in the payroll department and developed as a Microsoft Access application. They felt that this approach provided a relational database environment, client/server capability, and SQL command output to communicate with the mainframe. Figure 10-46 shows the proposed design of the system.

Jane Rossman met with Ann Hon to review True Blue's report and get her approval for training IT staff members. Jane had some prior experience in Access application development, but Rick had none, so Jane suggested that Rick and Becky Evans, another systems analyst, should attend a one-week workshop. Ann agreed.

Ann, Jane, and Rick met with Michael Jeremy to get his approval before proceeding further. He asked them to develop a specific budget and timetable including all necessary hardware, software, and training costs. They had most of the information, but they needed some help from True Blue to estimate the cost of network implementation, installation, and physical cabling.

The first phase of the project would use a local area network to link the various headquarter departments to the mainframe. A second phase, proposed by True Blue, would connect all SWL locations to a wide area network, with the possibility that employees could access their individual ESIP accounts over the internal network or from outside the company using the Internet.

A week later, Ann received a memo from Michael Jeremy that said he had approved the project and that she should start work immediately.

### System Architecture

The ESIP development team included Jane, Rick, and Becky. The group discovered that the Microsoft Access application consists of interactive objects such as tables, queries, forms, reports, macros, and code modules.

**FIGURE 10-46**   Diagram of the proposed ESIP system.

They decided to begin by reviewing the entity-relationship diagrams they prepared previously to determine the overall structure of the DBMS design. Then they identified the tables, reviewed the relationships among them, and analyzed the record designs they had developed.

**CHAPTER CAPSTONE CASE:   SoftWear, Limited (continued)**

They also reviewed output requirements, input screen designs, processing considerations, backup and recovery procedures, and controls that must be built into the new system.

As recommended by True Blue Systems, the new ESIP system would be implemented as a client/server design, with the data stored on the payroll department server, which would be linked to clients in the payroll and human resources department.

### Planning the System

In their first meeting, Jane asked the team to define all the tasks that the new system would perform, including a list of all reports and other required output. Jane explained that ESIP data would be stored on the server, but the application logic and objects such as forms, queries, and reports would be located on client workstations. Separating the objects from the data would provide better security and reduce the network loads, she explained.

### Security Issues

In their next planning session, Jane asked the group to consider all security issues affecting the new system design. Because the system contains payroll data, it is important to control user access and updates. The team decided to use the security features in Access for control, including passwords and user and workgroup accounts for employees authorized to use the ESIP application. Each user would be assigned a permission level that grants access only to certain objects.

Jane explained her plan for system security by saying, "We'll create a comprehensive security plan later that will cover all the operational security issues for the new system. Meanwhile, let's go back to the department heads, Michael Jeremy and Rob King, to get their input on what the security levels should be." She added that "Users will be allowed to create and modify certain forms and reports, but most other actions will be permitted only by authorized IT department members."

### Creating the Database Objects

Before creating the database objects, the team reviewed the ERDs and verified that the records designs were in 3NF. In addition, they verified that the new payroll system permitted cross-platform access because the ESIP system required data from the payroll master file. They discovered that the payroll package used a standard data format called open database connectivity (ODBC) that supported links to the Access database. After planning the system, they started creating the objects.

### Planning the User Interface

From earlier interviews, the IT team knew that users in the payroll and human resources departments wanted an interface that would be easy to learn and simple to operate. Jane asked Becky to start designing a main form, or switchboard, that would display automatically when the ESIP application started. All ESIP screen forms would use buttons, menus, and icons as shown in Figure 10-47.

Becky created a prototype of the input screens to show to users. After securing user approval, the screen designs were added to the system specification document for the ESIP system.

## CHAPTER CAPSTONE CASE:   SoftWear, Limited (continued)

### Using Visual Basic and Macros

Because she was a programmer before her assignment as a systems analyst, Becky wanted to know if they would be using Visual Basic as a program development language. Jane told her that they would write many of the procedures in Visual Basic because it allows more powerful data manipulation than macros and makes it easier to customize error messages. They would use macros, however, to speed up the development process and handle simple tasks such as opening and closing forms and running reports.

**FIGURE 10-47**   Sample of a main switchboard that displays when the ESIP system starts.

### Completing the Systems Design Phase

The IT team completed the systems design phase by writing the documentation and designing backup and recovery, file retention, and start-up procedures. The final step was to develop a system design specification for the ESIP system.

Rick and Becky showed a draft of the system design specification to Jane and Ann. After incorporating their changes, they e-mailed copies to a distribution list of users, IT staff members, and managers. Their presentations to users and IT staff members went well, and at the management presentation, they received final approval to implement the ESIP system.

### SWL Team Tasks

1. Rick Williams asked you to suggest software products that can provide network management features suitable for a network with 25–50 users. You can use the Internet to research the topic.

2. In the Background section of the SWL case, you learned that True Blue Systems had recommended a local area network to link the various headquarters departments to the SWL mainframe. Should a wireless network have been considered? Your task is to research wireless network products and submit a recommendation for a WLAN installation, supported by an explanation of wireless advantages and possible limitations. Be sure to consider flexibility, scalability, and security issues.

3. Assume that the recommendation you made in the preceding task was accepted. Now you have been asked to develop a specific budget for a WLAN that would consist of 50 workstations. You need to research the TCO of this project, including the cost of hardware, software, installation, and maintenance. You can make reasonable assumptions where you might not have specific facts, but you should state those assumptions clearly.

4. Michael Jeremy, finance vice president, has been reading about cloud computing in his favorite IT magazine, and he is considering the possibility of using the concept at SWL. He asked you to answer the following questions: What would be the benefits of a cloud computing architecture? What would be the disadvantages? What are examples of cloud computing services currently available? Perform research on the Internet and prepare a brief report for him.

**CHAPTER CAPSTONE CASE:   SoftWear, Limited (continued)**

## Manage the SWL Project

You have been asked to manage SWL's new information system project. One of your most important activities will be to identify project tasks and determine when they will be performed. Before you begin, you should review the SWL case in this chapter. Then list and analyze the tasks, as follows:

**LIST THE TASKS** Start by listing and numbering at least 10 tasks that the SWL team needs to perform to fulfill the objectives of this chapter. Your list can include SWL Team Tasks and any other tasks that are described in this chapter. For example, Task 3 might be to Review the logical design, and Task 6 might be to Begin the physical design process.

**ANALYZE THE TASKS** Now study the tasks to determine the order in which they should be performed. First identify all concurrent tasks, which are not dependent on other tasks. In the example shown in Figure 10-48. Tasks 1, 2, 3, 4, and 5 are concurrent tasks, and could begin at the same time if resources were available.

Other tasks are called dependent tasks, because they cannot be performed until one or more earlier tasks have been completed. For each dependent task, you must identify specific tasks that need to be completed before this task can begin. For example, you would want to review the logical design before you could begin the physical design process, so Task 6 cannot begin until Task 3 is completed, as Figure 10-48 shows.

**FIGURE 10-48**   Tasks 1, 2, 3, 4, and 5 are concurrent tasks that could be performed at the same time. Task 6 is a dependent task that cannot be performed until Task 3 has been completed.

Chapter 3 describes project management tools, techniques, and software. To learn more, you can use the Features section on your Student Study Tool CD-ROM, or visit the Management Information Systems CourseMate Web site at **www.cengagebrain.com** and locate the project management resources library for this book. On the Web, Microsoft offers demo versions, training, and tips for using Project 2010. You also can visit the OpenWorkbench.org site to learn more about this free, open-source software.

# Ready for a Challenge?

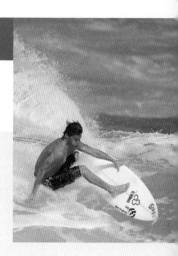

In additional to technical skills, IT professionals need critical thinking skills such as perception, organization, analysis, problem-solving, and decision-making. The Ready for a Challenge feature can help you learn, practice, and apply critical thinking skills that you can take to the workplace.

The IT team at Game Technology is working on an overall architecture for the new C3 system. They solicited RFPs from several hardware vendors, and decided to work with Network Illusions, a well-known local firm. Your job is to help analyze the server test results, and to draw network diagrams when requested.

The Network Illusions sales rep recommended a Model DX server for the C3 network, and submitted the following data, which shows projected network response times for various numbers of Game Technology users:

| Projected Data: Server Model DX | Number of Users | | | | |
|---|---|---|---|---|---|
| | 10 | 20 | 30 | 40 | 50 |
| Response Time (sec) | .01 | .015 | .02 | .025 | .03 |

## Practice Tasks

A. Using the data provided, create an XY chart that shows Response Time on the Y (vertical) axis and Number of Users on the X (horizontal) axis. You learned about XY charts in Chapter 2 of your textbook. Describe the results and your interpretation of the data.

B. Draw a bus network with a server, six workstations, a printer, a scanner, and a wireless access point (WAP). Also, determine how many separate data paths are needed in a mesh network with four nodes. Five nodes?

After you complete the Practice Tasks, to check your work and view sample answers, visit the Management Information Systems CourseMate Web site at **www.cengagebrain.com**, navigate to the resources for this chapter, and locate Ready for a Challenge?.

## The Challenge

Although the spec was for a Model XP server, Network Illusions delivered a newer model, called the DX+. The vendor sales rep said that performance would be the same or better, but the IT team decided to run a series of response time tests. The results are as follows:

| Actual Data: Server Model DX+ | Number of Users | | | | |
|---|---|---|---|---|---|
| | 10 | 20 | 30 | 40 | 50 |
| Response Time (sec) | .01 | .015 | .02 | .03 | .05 |

## Challenge Tasks

A. Use the actual test data to create another XY chart, similar to the first one. Describe the results and your interpretation of the data.

B. Draw the same network as a star topology with a central switch. Also determine how many separate data paths are needed in a mesh network that has six nodes.

# PHASE **4** SYSTEMS IMPLEMENTATION

DELIVERABLE
A functioning information system

SUPPORT
Primary tools: Communications and CASE tools

VIDEO LEARNING SESSION
Structure Charts

As the Dilbert cartoon suggests, successful systems implementation requires effective methods, a capable team, and management support. You will learn more about these topics in the systems implementation phase.

Systems implementation is the fourth of five phases in the systems development life cycle. In the previous phase, systems design, you created a physical model of the system. Now you will implement that design. Your tasks will include application development, documentation, testing, training, data conversion, and system changeover. The deliverable for this phase is a completely functioning information system.

CHAPTER **11** Making the System Operational

**Chapter 11** describes the systems implementation phase of the SDLC. This chapter describes application development, installation, and evaluation.

## INTRODUCTION

### OBJECTIVES

*When you finish this chapter, you will be able to:*

- Explain the importance of software quality assurance and software engineering
- Describe application development using structured, object-oriented, and agile methods
- Draw a structure chart showing top-down design, modular design, cohesion, and coupling
- Explain the coding process
- Explain unit, integration, and system testing
- Differentiate between program, system, operations, and user documentation
- List the main steps in system installation and evaluation
- Develop training plans for various user groups, compare in-house and outside training, and describe effective training techniques
- Describe data conversion and changeover methods
- Explain post-implementation evaluation and the final report to management

Managing systems implementation involves application development, testing, documentation, training, data conversion, system changeover, and post-implementation evaluation of the results.

During systems implementation, the system design specification serves as a blueprint for constructing the new system. The initial task is application development, which requires systems analysts and programmers to work together to construct the necessary programs and code modules. Before a changeover, the system must be tested and documented carefully, users must be trained, and existing data must be converted. After the new system is operational, a formal evaluation of the results takes place as part of a final report to management.

## CHAPTER INTRODUCTION CASE:  Mountain View College Bookstore

**Background:** Wendy Lee, manager of college services at Mountain View College, wants a new information system that will improve efficiency and customer service at the three college bookstores.

In this part of the case, Tina Allen (systems analyst) and David Conroe (student intern) are talking about implementation tasks for the new system.

| | |
|---|---|
| **Participants:** | Wendy, Tina, and David |
| **Location:** | Wendy Lee's office, Monday morning, February 6, 2012 |
| **Project status:** | The system design specification was approved, and Tina and David are ready to implement the new bookstore information system. |
| **Discussion topics:** | Implementation tasks, including quality assurance, structure charts, testing, training, data conversion process, system changeover, and post-implementation evaluation |

| | |
|---|---|
| **Tina:** | Good morning, Wendy. We're ready to start the implementation process, and I'd like to go over our plans. David will be assisting me, so I asked him to join us. |
| **Wendy:** | *I'm glad you did. I met David during the interviews several months ago.* |
| **David:** | Hi, Wendy, good to see you again. What's next? |
| **Tina:** | Let's talk about quality assurance. We'll also discuss various implementation options, including agile methods, but we'll continue with a structured approach for now. |
| **Wendy:** | *Sounds good. What are the major tasks on your list?* |
| **Tina:** | Well, the biggest task is to translate the design into program code and produce a functioning system. We'll develop structure charts that the programmers can use as blueprints, and David will help me coordinate with the programmers. |
| **David:** | It will be great to see all the design work finally turn into a functioning system. |
| **Tina:** | It sure will. Anyway, we'll proceed to do several types of testing, and we'll document everything we do. When we're ready, we'll put the new system into what's called a test environment until we're ready to go online with the operational environment. |
| **Wendy:** | *What about training?* |
| **Tina:** | We'll consider several kinds of training — from vendors or we might do our own. |
| **Wendy:** | *Then what?* |
| **Tina:** | The final steps will be data conversion and system changeover. After the new system is up and running, we'll schedule a formal evaluation and submit a final report. Here's a task list to get us started: |

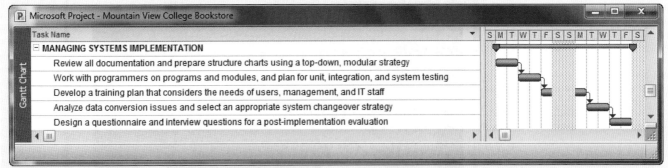

**FIGURE 11-1**  Typical systems implementation task list.

# SOFTWARE QUALITY ASSURANCE

In today's competitive business environment, companies are intensely concerned with the quality of their products and services. A successful organization must improve quality in every area, including its information systems. Top management must provide the leadership, encouragement, and support needed for high-quality IT resources.

No matter how carefully a system is designed and implemented, problems can occur. Rigorous testing can detect errors during implementation, but it is much less expensive to correct mistakes earlier in the development process. The main objective of **quality assurance** is to avoid problems or to identify them as soon as possible. Poor quality can result from inaccurate requirements, design problems, coding errors, faulty documentation, and ineffective testing.

To improve the finished product, software systems developers should consider software engineering and internationally recognized quality standards.

## Software Engineering

Because quality is so important, you can use an approach called software engineering to manage and improve the quality of the finished system. **Software engineering** is a software development process that stresses solid design, accurate documentation, and careful testing.

The Web site for the Software Engineering Institute (SEI) at Carnegie Mellon University is shown in Figure 11-2. SEI is a leader in software engineering and provides quality standards and suggested procedures for software developers and systems analysts. SEI's primary objective is to find better, faster, and less-expensive methods of software development. To achieve that goal, SEI designed a set of software development standards called the **Capability Maturity Model (CMM)**®, which has been used successfully by thousands of organizations around the globe. The purpose of the model, which was introduced in 1991, was to improve software quality, reduce development time, and cut costs. More recently, SEI established a new model, called **Capability Maturity Model Integration (CMMI)**®, that integrates software and systems development into a much

**FIGURE 11-2**  The Software Engineering Institute represents the cutting edge of software design and development technology.

larger framework called **process improvement**. The CMMI® regards software as part of a larger quality improvement process, rather than as an end in itself. The CMMI® tracks an organization's processes, using five maturity levels, from Level 1, which is referred to as unpredictable, poorly controlled, and reactive, to Level 5, in which the optimal result is process improvement. The five maturity levels are shown in Figure 11-3.

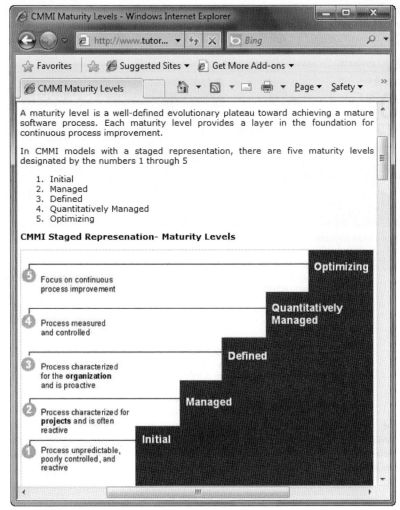

**FIGURE 11-3**  The CMMI® includes five maturity levels, from Level 1, which is referred to as unpredictable, poorly controlled, and reactive, to Level 5, in which the optimal result is process improvement.

## International Organization for Standardization (ISO)

You learned in Chapter 9 that the International Organization for Standardization (ISO) is a worldwide body that establishes quality standards for products and services, as shown in Figure 11-4 on the next page. ISO standards include everything from internationally recognized symbols, such as those shown in Figure 11-5, to the ISBN numbering system that identifies this textbook. In addition, ISO seeks to offer a global consensus of what constitutes good management practices — practices that can help firms deliver consistently high-quality products and services.

Because software is so important to a company's success, many firms seek assurance that software systems, either purchased or developed in-house, will meet rigid quality standards. In 1991, ISO established a set of guidelines called ISO 9000-3, which provided a quality assurance framework for developing and maintaining software.

**FIGURE 11-4**  The International Organization for Standardization (ISO) is an international body that establishes standards for many products and services, including software development. ISO states that standards, which provide product quality, compatibility, and safety, often are taken for granted, and noticed only when they are absent.

**ON THE WEB**

To learn more about ISO, visit the Management Information Systems CourseMate Web site at **www. cengagebrain. com**, navigate to **On the Web Links** for this chapter, and locate the ISO link.

**FIGURE 11-5**  ISO standards include internationally recognized symbols.

The standard was updated in 2004 and is now referred to as **ISO 90003:2004.** A company can specify ISO standards when it purchases software from a supplier or use ISO guidelines for in-house software development to ensure that the final result measures up to ISO standards. ISO requires a specific development plan, which outlines a step-by-step process for transforming user requirements into a finished product. ISO standards can be quite detailed. For example, ISO requires that a software supplier document all testing and maintain records of test results. If problems are found, they must be resolved, and any modules affected must be retested. Additionally, software and hardware specifications of all test equipment must be documented and included in the test records.

# OVERVIEW OF APPLICATION DEVELOPMENT

**Application development** is the process of constructing the programs and code modules that serve as the building blocks of the information system. In Chapter 1, you learned that structured analysis, object-oriented (O-O) analysis, and agile methods are three popular development options. Regardless of the method, the objective is to translate the design into program and code modules that will function properly. Because systems implementation usually is very labor-intensive, developers often use project management tools and techniques to control schedules and budgets.

## Review the System Design

At this point, it might be helpful to review the tasks involved in the creation of the system design.

- In Chapter 4, you learned about requirements modeling and how to use functional decomposition diagrams (FDDs) to break complex business operations down into smaller units, or functions.

- In Chapter 5, you learned about structured data and process modeling, and you created data flow diagrams (DFDs). You also developed process descriptions for functional primitive processes that documented the business logic and processing requirements.

- In Chapter 6, you developed an object-oriented model of the new system that included use case diagrams, class diagrams, sequence diagrams, state transition diagrams, and activity diagrams.

- In Chapter 7, you selected a development strategy.

- In Chapter 8, you designed the user interface.

- In Chapter 9, you worked with data design issues, analyzed relationships between system entities, and constructed entity-relationship diagrams (ERDs).

- In Chapter 10, you considered an overall system architecture.

Taken together, this set of tasks produced an overall design and a plan for physical implementation.

## Application Development Tasks

If you used traditional structured or object-oriented (O-O) methods, you now are ready to translate the design into a functioning application. If you selected an agile development method, you will plan the project, lay the groundwork, assemble the team, and prepare to interact with the customers.

**TRADITIONAL METHODS** Building a new system requires careful planning. After an overall strategy is established, individual modules must be designed, coded, tested, and documented. A **module** consists of related program code organized into small units that are easy to understand and maintain. After the modules are developed and tested individually, more testing takes place, along with thorough documentation of the entire system, as shown in Figure 11-6 on the next page.

When you create program modules using structured or object-oriented methods, you start by reviewing documentation from prior SDLC phases and creating a set of program designs. If you built a documentation file early in the development process and updated it regularly, you now have a valuable repository of information. The centerpiece of your documentation is the system design specification, accompanied by diagrams, source documents, screen layouts, report designs, data dictionary entries, and user comments. If you used a CASE tool during the systems analysis and design process, your job will be much

**FIGURE 11-6** The main steps in application development.

easier. At this point, coding and testing tasks begin. Although programmers typically perform the actual coding, IT managers usually assign systems analysts to work with them as a team.

**AGILE METHODS** If you decided to use an agile approach, intense communication and collaboration will now begin between the IT team and the users or customers. The objective is to create the system through an iterative process of planning, designing, coding, and testing. Agile projects use various models, including the spiral model shown in Figure 1-30 on page 26, or the Extreme Programming (XP) example shown in Figure 11-7. Agile development and XP are discussed in detail later in this chapter.

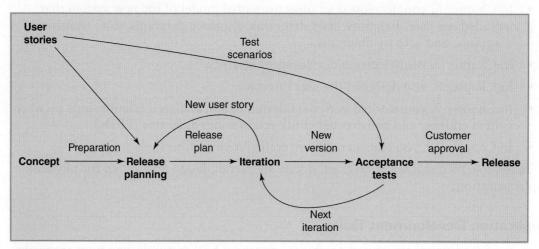

**FIGURE 11-7** Simplified model of an Extreme Programming (XP) project. Note the emphasis on iteration and testing.

## Systems Development Tools

Each systems development approach has its own set of tools that has worked well for that method. For example, structured development relies heavily on DFDs and structure charts; object-oriented methods use a variety of diagrams, including use case, class, sequence, and transition state diagrams; and agile methods tend to use spiral or other iterative models such as the example in Figure 11-7.

System developers also can use multipurpose tools to help them translate the system logic into properly functioning program modules. These generic tools include entity-relationship diagrams, flowcharts, pseudocode, decision tables, and decision trees.

**ENTITY-RELATIONSHIP DIAGRAMS** During data design, in Chapter 9, you learned how to use entity-relationship diagrams to show the interaction among system entities and objects. An ERD is a useful tool regardless of which methodology you are using, because the various relationships (one-to-one, one-to-many, and many-to-many) must be understood and implemented in the application development process.

**FLOWCHARTS** As you learned in Chapter 5, flowcharts can be used to describe program logic, and are very useful in visualizing a modular design. A **flowchart** represents logical rules and interaction graphically, using a series of symbols connected by arrows. Using flowcharts, programmers can break large systems into subsystems and modules that are easier to understand and code.

**PSEUDOCODE** Pseudocode is a technique for representing program logic. Pseudocode is similar to structured English, which was explained in Chapter 5. Pseudocode is not language-specific, so you can use it to describe a software module in plain English without requiring strict syntax rules. Using pseudocode, a systems analyst or a programmer can describe program actions that can be implemented in any programming language. Figure 11-8 illustrates an example of pseudocode that documents a sales promotion policy.

**ON THE WEB**

To learn more about pseudocode, visit the Management Information Systems CourseMate Web site at **www. cengagebrain. com**, navigate to **On the Web Links** for this chapter, and locate the Pseudocode link.

---

**SAMPLE OF A SALES PROMOTION POLICY**

- Preferred customers who order more than $1,000 are entitled to a 5% discount, and an additional 5% discount if they used our charge card.

- Preferred customers who do not order more than $1,000 receive a $25 bonus coupon.

- All other customers receive a $5 bonus coupon.

---

**PSEUDOCODE VERSION OF THE SALES PROMOTION POLICY**

```
IF customer is a preferred customer, and
        IF customer orders more than $1,000 then
                Apply a 5% discount, and
                IF customer uses our charge card, then
                        Apply an additional 5% discount
        ELSE
                        Award a $25 bonus coupon
ELSE
        Award a $5 bonus coupon
```

**FIGURE 11-8** Sample of a sales promotion policy with logical rules, and a pseudocode version of the policy. Notice the alignment and indentation of the logic statements.

---

**DECISION TABLES AND DECISION TREES** As you learned in Chapter 5, decision tables and decision trees can be used to model business logic for an information system. In addition to being used as modeling tools, analysts and programmers can use decision tables and decision trees during system development, as they develop code modules that implement the logical rules. Figure 11-9 shows an example of a decision tree that documents the sales promotion policy shown in Figure 11-8. Notice that the decision tree accurately reflects the sales promotion policy, which has three separate conditions, and four possible outcomes.

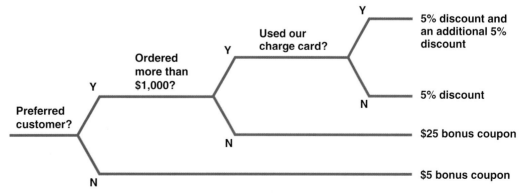

**FIGURE 11-9** Sample decision tree that reflects the sales promotion policy in Figure 11-8. Like a decision table, a decision tree shows the action to be taken based on certain conditions.

## Project Management

Regardless of whether structured analysis, object-oriented design, or agile methods are used, even a modest-sized project might have hundreds or even thousands of modules. For this reason, application development can become quite complex and difficult to manage. At this stage, project management is especially important. Users and managers are looking forward to the new system, and it is very important to set realistic schedules, meet project deadlines, control costs, and maintain quality. To achieve these goals, the systems analyst or project manager should use project management tools and techniques similar to those described in Chapter 3 to monitor and control the development effort.

The following sections describe the application development process. Structured development techniques and tools are discussed first, followed by object-oriented and agile development methods.

## VIDEO LEARNING SESSION:  STRUCTURE CHARTS

Video Learning Sessions can help you understand key concepts, practice your skills, and check your work. To access the sessions, visit the Management Information Systems CourseMate Web site at **www.cengagebrain.com** and navigate to the **Video Learning Sessions** for this book. This session is about structure charts. You'll learn about structure charts and why they are important modeling tools, how to draw structure charts, and how you can use a CASE tool to create structure charts.

## STRUCTURED APPLICATION DEVELOPMENT

Structured application development usually involves a **top-down approach**, which proceeds from a general design to a detailed structure. After a systems analyst documents the system's requirements, he or she breaks the system down into subsystems and modules in a process called **partitioning**. This approach also is called **modular design** and is similar to constructing a leveled set of DFDs. By assigning modules to different programmers, several development areas can proceed at the same time. As explained in Chapter 3, you can use project management software to monitor work on each module, forecast overall development time, estimate required human and technical resources, and calculate a critical path for the project.

Because all the modules must work together properly, an analyst must proceed carefully, with constant input from programmers and IT management to achieve a sound, well-integrated structure. The analyst also must ensure that integration capability is built into each design and thoroughly tested.

### Structure Charts

Structure charts show the program modules and the relationships among them. A **structure chart** consists of rectangles that represent the program modules, with arrows and other symbols that provide additional information. Typically, a higher-level module, called a **control module**, directs lower-level modules, called **subordinate modules**. In a structure chart, symbols represent various actions or conditions. Structure chart symbols represent modules, data couples, control couples, conditions, and loops.

**MODULE** A rectangle represents a module, as shown in Figure 11-10. Vertical lines at the edges of a rectangle indicate that module 1.3 is a library module. A **library module** is reusable code and can be invoked from more than one point in the chart.

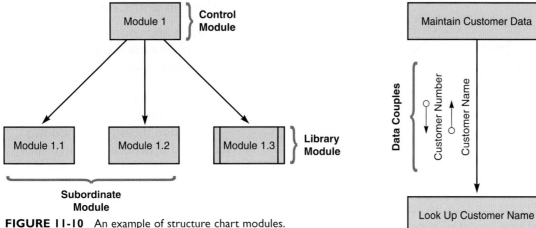

FIGURE 11-10 An example of structure chart modules.

FIGURE 11-11 An example of a structure chart data.

**DATA COUPLE** An arrow with an empty circle represents a data couple. A **data couple** shows data that one module passes to another. In the data couple example shown in Figure 11-11, the *Look Up Customer Name* module exchanges data with the *Maintain Customer Data* module.

**CONTROL COUPLE** An arrow with a filled circle represents a control couple. A **control couple** shows a message, also called a **status flag**, which one module sends to another. In the example shown in Figure 11-12, the *Update Customer File* module sends an *Account Overdue* flag back to the *Maintain Customer Data* module. A module uses a flag to signal a specific condition or action to another module.

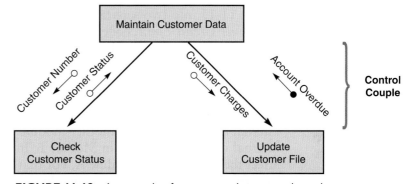

FIGURE 11-12 An example of a structure chart control couple.

**CONDITION** A line with a diamond on one end represents a condition. A **condition** line indicates that a control module determines which subordinate modules will be invoked, depending on a specific condition. In the example shown in Figure 11-13, *Sort Inventory Parts* is a control module with a condition line that triggers one of the three subordinate modules.

**LOOP** A curved arrow represents a loop. A **loop** indicates that one or more modules are repeated. In the example shown in Figure 11-14 on the next page, the *Get Student Grades* and *Calculate GPA* modules are repeated.

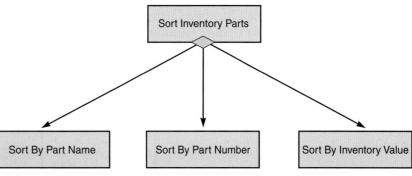

FIGURE 11-13 The diagram shows a control module that triggers three subordinate modules.

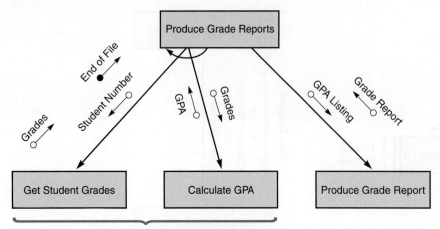

The curved arrow indicates that these modules are repeated.

**FIGURE 11-14**  The diagram shows a structure chart loop with two repeating modules.

## Cohesion and Coupling

Cohesion and coupling are important tools for evaluating the overall design. As explained in the following sections, it is desirable to have modules that are highly cohesive and loosely coupled.

**Cohesion** measures a module's scope and processing characteristics. A module that performs a single function or task has a high degree of cohesion, which is desirable. Because it focuses on a single task, a cohesive module is much easier to code and reuse. For example, a module named *Verify Customer Number* is more cohesive than a module named *Calculate and Print Statements*. If you notice the word *and* in a module name, you know that more than one task is involved.

If a module must perform multiple tasks, more complex coding is required and the module will be more difficult to create and maintain. If you need to make a module more cohesive, you can split it into separate units, each with a single function. For example, by splitting the module *Check Customer Number and Credit Limit* in Figure 11-15 into two separate modules, *Check Customer Number* and *Check Customer Credit Limit*, cohesion is greatly improved.

**Coupling** describes the degree of interdependence among modules. Modules that are independent are **loosely coupled**, which is desirable. Loosely coupled modules are easier to maintain and modify, because the logic in one module does not affect other modules. If a programmer needs to update a loosely coupled module, he or she can accomplish the task in a single location. If modules are **tightly coupled**, one module is linked to internal logic contained in another module. For example, Module A might refer to an internal variable contained in Module B. In that case, a logic error in the Module B will affect the processing in Module A. For that reason, passing a status flag down as a message from a control module is generally regarded as poor design. It is better to have subordinate modules handle processing tasks as independently as possible, to avoid a cascade effect of logic errors in the control module.

In Figure 11-16, the tightly coupled example on the left shows that the subordinate module *Calculate Current Charges* depends on a status flag sent down from the control module *Update Customer Balance*. It would be preferable to have the modules loosely coupled and logically independent. In the example on the right, a status flag is not needed because the subordinate module *Apply Discount* handles discount processing independently. Any logic errors are confined to a single location: the *Apply Discount* module.

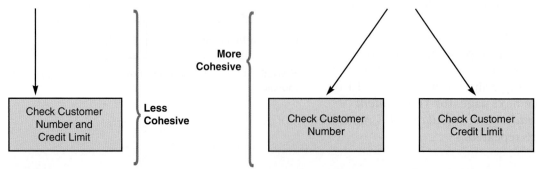

**FIGURE 11-15**  Two examples of cohesion. Notice that the single module on the left is less cohesive than the two modules on the right.

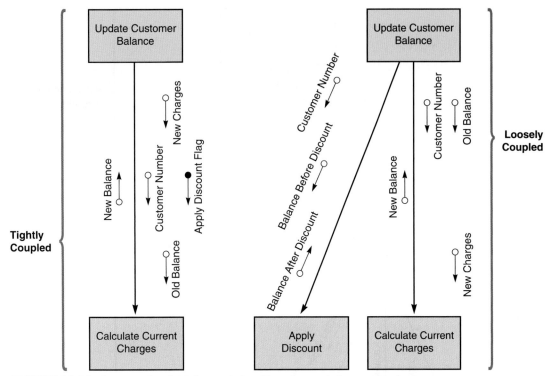

**FIGURE 11-16**  An example of tightly coupled and loosely coupled structure charts.

## Drawing a Structure Chart

If you used a structured analysis method, your structure charts will be based on the DFDs you created during data and process modeling.

Typically, you follow four steps when you create a structure chart. You review DFDs to identify the processes and methods, identify the program modules and determine control-subordinate relationships, add symbols for couples and loops, and analyze the structure chart to ensure that it is consistent with your system documentation.

**STEP 1: REVIEW THE DFDS**  Your first step is to review all DFDs for accuracy and completeness, especially if changes have occurred since the systems analysis phase. If object models also were developed, you should analyze them to identify the objects, the methods that each object must perform, and the relationships among the objects. A method is similar to a functional primitive, and requires code to implement the necessary actions.

**STEP 2: IDENTIFY MODULES AND RELATIONSHIPS**  Working from the logical model, you transform functional primitives or object methods into program modules. When analyzing a set of DFDs, remember that each DFD level represents a processing level. If you are using DFDs, you would work your way down from the context diagram to the lower-level diagrams, identifying control modules and subordinate modules, until you reach functional primitives. If more cohesion is desired, you can divide processes into smaller modules that handle a single task. Figure 11-17 on the next page shows a structure chart based on the order system shown in Figures 5-16, 5-17, and 5-18 on pages 212–214. Notice how the three-level structure chart relates to the three DFD levels.

**STEP 3: ADD COUPLES, LOOPS, AND CONDITIONS**  Next, you add couples, loops, and conditions to the structure chart. If you are working with DFDs, you can review the data flows and the data dictionary to identify the data elements that pass from one module to another. In addition to adding the data couples, you add control couples where a module is sending a control parameter, or flag, to another module. You also add loops and condition

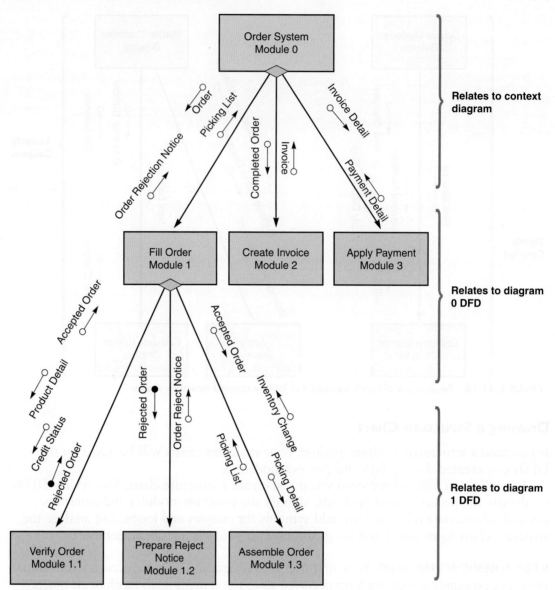

**FIGURE 11-17**  A structure chart based on the order system DFDs on pages 212–214. The three-level structure chart relates to the three DFD levels.

lines that indicate repetitive or alternative processing steps, as shown in Figure 11-17. If you also developed an object model, you can review the class diagrams and object relationship diagrams to be sure that you understand the interaction among the objects.

**STEP 4: ANALYZE THE STRUCTURE CHART AND THE DATA DICTIONARY**  At this point, the structure chart is ready for careful analysis. You should check each process, data element, or object method to ensure that the chart reflects all previous documentation and that the logic is correct. You also should determine that modules are strongly cohesive and loosely coupled. Often, you must draw several versions of the chart. Some CASE tools can help you analyze the chart and identify problem areas.

## OBJECT-ORIENTED APPLICATION DEVELOPMENT

When you studied the object-oriented methods described in Chapter 6, you learned that O-O analysis makes it easier to translate an object model directly into an object-oriented programming language. This process is called **object-oriented development**, or **OOD**. Although many structured design concepts also apply to object-oriented methodology, there are some differences.

## Characteristics of Object-Oriented Application Development

When implementing a structured design, a structure chart is used to describe the interaction between program modules, as explained earlier. In contrast, when implementing an object-oriented design, relationships between objects already exist. Because object interaction is defined during the O-O analysis process, the application's structure is represented by the object model itself.

As Chapter 6 explains, objects contain both data and program logic, called methods. Individual object instances belong to classes of objects with similar characteristics. The relationship and interaction among classes are described using a class diagram, such as the one shown in Figure 11-18. A class diagram includes the class **attributes**, which describe the characteristics of objects in the class, and **methods**, which represent program logic. For example, the Customer class describes customer objects. Customer attributes include Number, Name, Address, and so on. Methods for the Customer class include Place order, Modify order, and Pay invoice, among others. The Customer class can exchange messages with the Order class.

In addition to class diagrams, programmers get an overview of object interaction by using object relationship diagrams that were developed during the O-O analysis process. For example, Figure 11-19 shows an object relationship diagram for a fitness center. Notice that the model shows the objects and how they interact to perform business functions and transactions.

Properly implemented, object-oriented development can speed up projects, reduce costs, and improve overall quality. However, these results are not always achieved. Organizations sometimes have unrealistic expectations, and do not spend enough time learning about, preparing for, and implementing the OOD process. For example, no one would build a bridge without a analysis of needs, supporting data, and a detailed blueprint — and the bridge would not be opened for traffic until it had been carefully inspected and checked to ensure that all specifications were met. O-O software developers sometimes forget that the basic rules of architecture also apply to their projects.

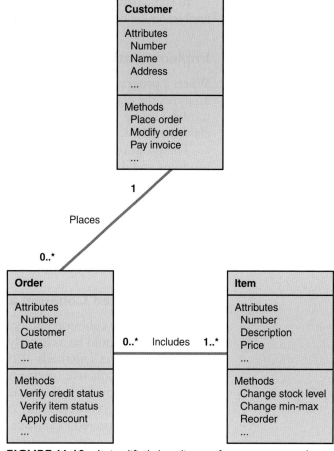

**FIGURE 11-18**  A simplified class diagram for a customer order processing system.

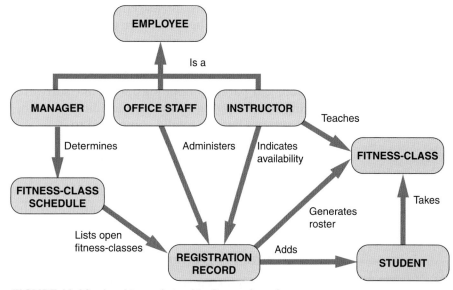

**FIGURE 11-19**  An object-relationship diagram for a fitness center.

In summary, to secure the potential benefits of object-oriented development, systems analysts must carefully analyze, design, implement, test, and document their O-O projects.

## Implementation of Object-Oriented Designs

When a programmer translates an object-oriented design into an application, he or she analyzes the classes, attributes, methods, and messages that are documented in the object model. During this process, the programmer makes necessary revisions and updates to class diagrams, sequence diagrams, state transition diagrams, and activity diagrams.

The programmer's main objective is to translate object methods into program code modules and determine what event or message will trigger the execution of each module. To accomplish the task, the programmer analyzes sequence diagrams and state transition diagrams that show the events and messages that trigger changes to an object. O-O applications are called event-driven, because each event, transaction, or message triggers a corresponding action. The programmer can represent the program steps in pseudocode initially, or use CASE tools and code generators to create object-oriented code directly from the object model.

## Object-Oriented Cohesion and Coupling

The principles of cohesion and coupling also apply to object-oriented application development. Classes should be as loosely coupled (independent of other classes) as possible. In addition, an object's methods also should be loosely coupled (independent of other methods) and highly cohesive (perform closely related actions). By following these principles, classes and objects are easier to understand and edit. O-O programmers who ignore cohesion and coupling concepts may end up creating a web of code that is difficult to maintain. When code is scattered in various places, editing becomes complicated and expensive.

## AGILE APPLICATION DEVELOPMENT

As you learned in Chapter 1, agile development is a distinctly different systems development method. It shares many of the steps found in traditional development, but uses a highly iterative process. The development team is in constant communication with the primary user, who is called the **customer**, shaping and forming the system to match the customer's specifications. Agile development is aptly named because it is based on a quick and nimble development process that easily adapts to change. Agile development focuses on small teams, intense communication, and rapid development iterations.

As agile methods become more popular, many software firms are offering packages that teams can use to manage and document the agile process. For example, as shown in Figure 11-20, Serena claims that its Agile on Demand software can help teams be more effective in dealing with multiple stakeholders. The figure also notes the well-known agile development parable about pigs, who, like software developers, are totally committed to writing and delivering software, and chickens, who, like some stakeholders, are involved in the process but not totally committed to it.

You also learned in Chapter 1 about Extreme Programming (XP), which is one of the newest agile methods. XP is an iterative approach, as shown in Figure 11-21 on page 522, where a team of users and developers immerse themselves in systems development. XP supporters emphasize values such as simplicity, communication, feedback, respect, and courage. Success requires strong commitment to the process, corporate support, and dedicated team members. The following section describes a typical XP project.

## An Extreme Programming (XP) Example

Suppose that a customer has requested a sales tracking system. The first step in the XP process, like any other development method, would be to define the system requirements.

**ON THE WEB**

To learn more about extreme programming (XP), visit the Management Information Systems CourseMate Web site at **www. cengagebrain. com**, navigate to **On the Web Links** for this chapter, and locate the Extreme Programming (XP) link.

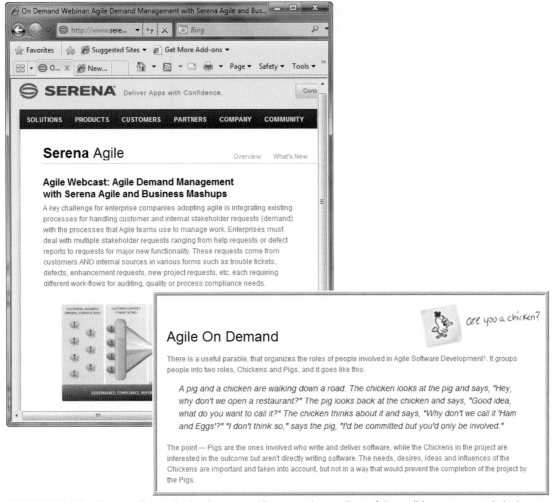

**FIGURE 11-20**   Serena offers agile development software, and a retelling of the well-known pigs and chickens story.

The customer begins by meeting with programmers and providing user stories. A **user story** is a short, simple requirements definition. Programmers use user stories to determine the project's requirements, priorities, and scope.

In our example, suppose we have the following user stories:

- *As the sales manager, I want to identify fast or slow moving items so I can manage our inventory more effectively.*

- *As a store manager, I need enough lead time to replenish my stock so I don't run out of hot items.*

- *As a sales representative, I want to offer the best selection of fast selling items and clear out the old stock that is not moving.*

User stories do not deal with technical details and are so short that they are often written on index cards. Each user story is given a priority by the customer, so the requirements can be ranked. In addition, programmers assign a score to each user story that indicates the estimated difficulty of implementation. This information helps the team form a plan and assign its resources. Projects are often composed of many user stories, from which programmers can estimate the scope, time requirements, and difficulty of the project. In addition to the user stories, frequent face-to-face meetings with customers provide a higher level of detail as the project progresses.

The team must also develop a **release plan,** which specifies when user stories will be implemented and the timing of the releases. Releases are relatively frequent, and each system release is like a prototype that can be tested and modified as needed.

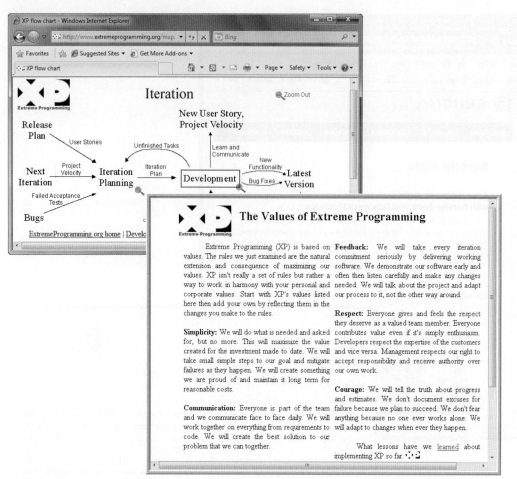

**FIGURE 11-21**  Extreme Programming is based on iteration, values, and a different approach to systems development.

User stories are implemented in a series of iteration cycles. An **iteration cycle** includes planning, designing, coding, and testing of one or more features based on user stories. At the beginning of each iteration cycle, which is often two weeks long, the team holds an **iteration planning meeting** to break down the user stories into specific tasks that are assigned to team members. As new user stories or features are added, the team reviews and modifies the release plan.

As with any development process, success is determined by the customer's approval. The programming team regularly meets with the customer, who tests prototype releases as they become available. This process usually results in additional user stories, and changes are implemented in the next iteration cycle. As the project's code changes during each iteration, obsolete code is removed and remaining code is restructured to keep the system up to date. The iteration cycles continue until all user stories have been implemented, tested, and accepted.

Extreme Programming uses an interesting concept called parallel programming. In **parallel programming**, two programmers work on the same task on the same computer; one drives (programs) while the other navigates (watches). The onlooker examines the code strategically to see the *forest* while the driver is concerned with the individual *trees* immediately in front of him or her. The two discuss their ideas continuously throughout the process.

Another important concept in XP is that unit tests are designed *before* code is written. This **test-driven design** focuses on end results from the beginning and prevents programmers from straying from their goals. Because of the magnitude and intensity of the multicycle process, agile testing relies heavily on automated testing methods and software.

Programmers can use popular agile-friendly languages such as Python, Ruby, and Perl. However, agile methods do not require a specific programming language, and programmers also use various object-oriented languages such as Java, C++, and C#.

## The Future of Agile Development

Agile methodology is becoming very popular for software projects. Its supporters boast that it speeds up software development and delivers precisely what the customer wants, when the customer wants it, while fostering teamwork and empowering employees. However, there are drawbacks to this adaptive rather than predictive method. Critics of agile development often claim that because it focuses on quick iterations and fast releases, it lacks discipline and produces systems of questionable quality. In addition, agile methodology may not work as well for larger projects because of their complexity and the lack of focus on a well-defined end product.

Before implementing agile development, the proposed system and development methods should be examined carefully. As experienced IT professionals know, a one-size-fits-all solution does not exist. For more information on agile methods, refer to the discussion of systems development methods that begins on page 21 in Chapter 1.

**ON THE WEB**

To learn more about the future of agile development, visit the Management Information Systems CourseMate Web site at **www. cengagebrain. com**, navigate to **On the Web Links** for this chapter, and locate the Future of Agile Development link.

## CODING

**Coding** is the process of turning program logic into specific instructions that the computer system can execute. Working from a specific design, a programmer uses a programming language to transform program logic into code statements. An individual programmer might create a small program, while larger programs typically are divided into modules that several individuals or groups can work on simultaneously.

## Programming Environments

Each IT department has its own programming environment and standards. Visual Basic, Python, Ruby, and SQL are examples of commonly used programming languages, and many commercial packages use a proprietary set of commands. As the trend toward Internet-based applications continues, HTML/XML, Java, and other Web-centric languages will be used extensively.

To simplify the integration of system components and reduce code development time, many programmers use an **integrated development environment (IDE)**. IDEs can make it easier to program interactive software products by providing built-in tools and advanced features, such as real-time error detection, syntax hints, highlighted code, class browsers, and version control. As you learned in Chapter 7, IBM WebSphere and Microsoft .NET are popular IDEs. In addition to these commercial packages, programmers can use open-source IDEs such as Java-based NetBeans IDE and Eclipse. You can learn more about IDEs in Appendix B.

The CASE tools in Appendix B can help you understand IDEs. To learn more about these tools, turn to Appendix B.

## Generating Code

You learned in earlier chapters that systems analysts use application generators, report writers, screen generators, fourth-generation languages, and other CASE tools that produce code directly from program design specifications. Some commercial applications can generate editable program code directly from macros, keystrokes, or mouse actions. Figure 11-22 on the next page shows a very simple example of a Visual Basic code module in Microsoft Access that opens a customer order form and produces a beep sound.

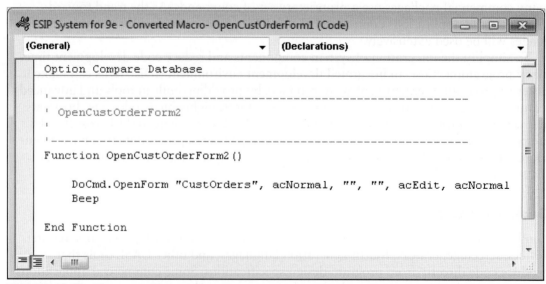

**FIGURE 11-22**   The simple Microsoft Access macro in the upper screen was created using keystrokes and mouse clicks. The macro's editable code is shown in the lower screen.

Note that a macro automatically generated the code, and the macro itself was created by a series of keystrokes and mouse actions. The code module shown in Figure 11-22 includes program commands, comments, and error-handling procedures.

## TESTING THE SYSTEM

After coding, a programmer must test each program to make sure it functions correctly. Later, programs are tested in groups, and finally the development team must test the entire system. The first step is to compile the program using a CASE tool or a language compiler. This process detects **syntax errors**, which are language grammar errors. The programmer corrects the errors until the program executes properly.

Next, the programmer desk checks the program. **Desk checking** is the process of reviewing the program code to spot **logic errors**, which produce incorrect results. This process can be performed by the person who wrote the program or by other programmers. Many organizations require a more formal type of desk checking called a **structured walkthrough**, or **code review**.

Typically, a group of three to five IT staff members participate in code review. The group usually consists of project team members and might include other programmers and analysts who did not work on the project. The objective is to have a peer group identify errors, apply quality standards, and verify that the program meets the requirements of the system design specification. Errors found during a structured walkthrough are easier to fix while coding is still in the developmental stages.

In addition to analyzing logic and program code, the project team usually holds a session with users called a **design walkthrough**, to review the interface with a cross-section of people who will work with the new system and ensure that all necessary features have been included. This is a continuation of the modeling and prototyping effort that began early in the systems development process.

The next step in application development is to initiate a sequence of unit testing, integration testing, and system testing, as shown in Figure 11-23.

**FIGURE 11-23** The first step in testing is unit testing, followed by integration testing, and then system testing.

### Unit Testing

The testing of an individual program or module is called **unit testing**. The objective is to identify and eliminate execution errors that could cause the program to terminate abnormally, and logic errors that could have been missed during desk checking.

## CASE IN POINT 11.1:  YOUR MOVE, INC.

You work for April Olivia, the IT manager at Your Move, Inc., a large retailer specializing in games of all kinds. The company is in the final stages of developing a new inventory management system, and April wants you to handle the testing.

"Be sure you put lots of errors into the test data," she said. "Users are bound to make mistakes, and we need to design built-in safeguards that will catch the mistakes, and either fix them automatically, or alert the user to the problem."

Of course, April's comment makes a lot of sense, but you've never done this before and you wonder how to proceed. Should you try to invent every possible data error? How will you know that you've thought of every situation that could occur? Consider the problem, develop an approach, and write up your plan in a brief memo.

**Test data** should contain both correct data and erroneous data and should test all possible situations that could occur. For example, for a field that allows a range of numeric values, the test data should contain minimum values, maximum values, values outside the acceptable range, and alphanumeric characters. During testing, programmers can use software tools to determine the location and potential causes of program errors.

During unit testing, programmers must test programs that interact with other programs and files individually, before they are integrated into the system. This requires a technique called stub testing. In **stub testing**, the programmer simulates each program outcome or result and displays a message to indicate whether or not the program executed successfully. Each stub represents an entry or exit point that will be linked later to another program or data file.

To obtain an independent analysis, someone other than the programmer who wrote the program usually creates the test data and reviews the results. Systems analysts frequently create test data during the systems design phase as part of an overall test plan. A **test plan** consists of detailed procedures that specify how and when the testing will be performed, who will participate, and what test data will be used. A comprehensive test plan should include scenarios for every possible situation the program could encounter.

Regardless of who creates the test plan, the project manager or a designated analyst also reviews the final test results. Some organizations also require users to approve final unit test results.

### Integration Testing

To learn more about system testing, visit the Management Information Systems CourseMate Web site at **www. cengagebrain. com**, navigate to **On the Web Links** for this chapter, and locate the System Testing link.

Testing two or more programs that depend on each other is called **integration testing**, or **link testing**. For example, consider an information system with a program that checks and validates customer credit status, and a separate program that updates data in the customer master file. The output from the validation program becomes input to the master file update program. Testing the programs independently does not guarantee that the data passed between them is correct. Only by performing integration testing for this pair of programs can you make sure that the programs work together properly. Figure 11-23 on the previous page shows integration testing for several groups of programs. Notice that a program can have membership in two or more groups.

Systems analysts usually develop the data they use in integration testing. As is the case with all forms of testing, integration test data must consider both normal and unusual situations. For example, integration testing might include passing typical records between two programs, followed by blank records, to simulate an unusual event or an operational problem. You should use test data that simulates actual conditions because you are testing the interface that links the programs. A testing sequence should not move to the integration test stage unless it has performed properly in all unit tests.

## System Testing

After completing integration testing, you must perform **system testing**, which involves the entire information system, as shown in Figure 11-23. A system test includes all typical processing situations and is intended to assure users, developers, and managers that the program meets all specifications and that all necessary features have been included.

During a system test, users enter data, including samples of actual, or live, data, perform queries, and produce reports to simulate actual operating conditions. All processing options and outputs are verified by users and the IT project development team to ensure that the system functions correctly. Commercial software packages must undergo system testing similar to that of in-house developed systems, although unit and integration testing usually are not performed. Regardless of how the system was developed, system testing has the following major objectives:

- Perform a final test of all programs

- Verify that the system will handle all input data properly, both valid and invalid

- Ensure that the IT staff has the documentation and instructions needed to operate the system properly and that backup and restart capabilities of the system are adequate (the details of creating this sort of documentation are discussed later in this chapter)

- Demonstrate that users can interact with the system successfully

- Verify that all system components are integrated properly and that actual processing situations will be handled correctly

- Confirm that the information system can handle predicted volumes of data in a timely and efficient manner

Successful completion of system testing is the key to user and management approval, which is why system tests sometimes are called **acceptance tests**. Final acceptance tests, however, are performed during systems installation and evaluation, which is described later in this chapter.

How much testing is necessary? The answer depends on the situation and requires good judgment and input from other IT staff members, users, and management, as shown in Figure 11-24. Unfortunately, IT project managers often are pressured to finish testing quickly and hand the system over to users. Common reasons for premature or rushed testing are demands from users, tight systems development budgets, and demands from top management to finish projects early. Those pressures hinder the testing process and often have detrimental effects on the final product.

You should regard thorough testing as a cost-effective means of providing a quality product. Every error caught during testing eliminates potential expenses and operational problems. No system, however, is 100% error-free. Often, errors go undetected until the system becomes operational. Errors that affect the integrity or accuracy of data must be corrected immediately. Minor errors, such as typographical errors in screen titles, can be corrected later.

Some users want a system that is a completely finished product, while others realize that minor changes can be treated as maintenance items after the system is operational. In the final analysis, you must decide whether or not to postpone system installation if problems are discovered. If conflicting views exist, management will decide whether or not to install the system after a full discussion of the options.

**FIGURE 11-24** System testing requires good judgment and input from other IT staff members, users, and IT management.

## CASE IN POINT 11.2:  WebTest, Inc.

As a new systems analyst, you suspect that testing Web-based systems probably involves a different set of tools and techniques, compared to testing traditional LAN-based systems. Because you've always wanted to run your own IT company, you have decided to launch a start-up firm called WebTest, Inc., that would offer consulting services specifically aimed at testing the performance, integrity, efficiency, and security of Internet-based systems.

Your idea is to identify and purchase various Web site testing tools that currently are available, then use these tools as a Web site testing consultant. No one in your area offers this type of consulting service, so you have high hopes.

Now, you need to perform Internet research to learn more about Web testing software that is available. Review the Internet Resources Tools section, which is Appendix D, and use a search engine to develop a list of at least four products that you might want to use. For each product, write up a brief description of its overall purpose, its features and benefits, its cost, and how it would fit into your business game plan.

## DOCUMENTATION

**Documentation** describes an information system and helps the users, managers, and IT staff who must interact with it. Accurate documentation can reduce system downtime, cut costs, and speed up maintenance tasks. Figure 11-25 shows an example of software that can automate the documentation process and help software developers generate accurate, comprehensive reference material.

Documentation is essential for successful system operation and maintenance. In addition to supporting a system's users, accurate documentation is essential for IT staff members who must modify the system, add a new feature, or perform maintenance. Documentation includes program documentation, system documentation, operations documentation, and user documentation.

**FIGURE 11-25**  In addition to CASE tools, software such as Imagix can automate the task of software documentation.

## Program Documentation

**Program documentation** describes the inputs, outputs, and processing logic for all program modules. The program documentation process starts in the systems analysis phase and continues during systems implementation. Systems analysts prepare overall documentation, such as process descriptions and report layouts, early in the SDLC. This documentation guides programmers, who construct modules that are well supported by internal and external comments and descriptions that can be understood and maintained easily. A systems analyst usually verifies that program documentation is complete and accurate.

System developers also use **defect tracking software**, sometimes called **bug tracking software**, to document

**FIGURE 11-26**   Bugzilla is an example of a defect tracking program that can track bugs and manage software quality assurance.

and track program defects, code changes, and replacement code, called **patches**. One popular example is Bugzilla, shown in Figure 11-26. According to its Web site, Bugzilla is a free, open-source program that can track bugs and manage software quality assurance.

## System Documentation

**System documentation** describes the system's functions and how they are implemented. System documentation includes data dictionary entries, data flow diagrams, object models, screen layouts, source documents, and the systems request that initiated the project. System documentation is necessary reference material for the programmers and analysts who must support and maintain the system.

Most of the system documentation is prepared during the systems analysis and systems design phases. During the systems implementation phase, an analyst must review prior documentation to verify that it is complete, accurate, and up to date, including any changes made during the implementation process. For example, if a screen or report has been modified, the analyst must update the documentation. Updates to the system documentation should be made in a timely manner to prevent oversights.

**ON THE WEB**

To learn more about documentation, visit the Management Information Systems CourseMate Web site at **www.cengagebrain.com**, navigate to **On the Web Links** for this chapter, and locate the Documentation link.

## Operations Documentation

If the information system environment involves a minicomputer, a mainframe, or centralized servers, the analyst must prepare documentation for the IT group that supports centralized operations. A mainframe installation might require the scheduling of batch jobs and the distribution of printed reports. In this type of environment, the IT operations staff serves as the first point of contact when users experience problems with the system.

**Operations documentation** contains all the information needed for processing and distributing online and printed output. Typical operations documentation includes the following information:

- Program, systems analyst, programmer, and system identification
- Scheduling information for printed output, such as report run frequency and deadlines

- Input files and where they originate; and output files and destinations
- E-mail and report distribution lists
- Special forms required, including online forms
- Error and informational messages to operators and restart procedures
- Special instructions, such as security requirements

Operations documentation should be clear, concise, and available online if possible. If the IT department has an operations group, you should review the documentation with them, early and often, to identify any problems. If you keep the operations group informed at every phase of the SDLC, you can develop operations documentation as you go along.

## User Documentation

**User documentation** consists of instructions and information to users who will interact with the system and includes user manuals, Help screens, and tutorials. Programmers or systems analysts usually create program documentation and system documentation. To produce effective and clear user documentation — and hence have a successful project — you need someone with expert skills in this area doing the development, just as you need someone with expert skills developing the software. The skill set required to develop documentation usually is not the same as that to develop a system. This is particularly true as you move into the world of online documentation, which needs to coordinate with print documentation and intranet and Internet information. Technical writing requires specialized skills, and competent technical writers are valuable members of the IT team.

Just as you cannot throw a system together in several days, you cannot add documentation at the end. That is a common misconception and often proves fatal to a project. While that has always been true of software user documentation, this is an even more critical issue now that online Help and context-sensitive Help so often are needed. Context-sensitive Help is part of the program. You must put coded callouts in the text that link to the correct page of information in the documentation. To try to go back and add this after the fact would take a great deal of time; depending on the project size, it could take months! Additionally, it could introduce other coding errors — and it all has to be tested as well.

Systems analysts usually are responsible for preparing documentation to help users learn the system. In larger companies, a technical support team that includes technical writers might assist in the preparation of user documentation and training materials. Regardless of the delivery method, user documentation must be clear, understandable, and readily accessible to users at all levels.

User documentation includes the following:

- A system overview that clearly describes all major system features, capabilities, and limitations
- Description of source document content, preparation, processing, and samples
- Overview of menu and data entry screen options, contents, and processing instructions
- Examples of reports that are produced regularly or available at the user's request, including samples
- Security and audit trail information
- Explanation of responsibility for specific input, output, or processing requirements
- Procedures for requesting changes and reporting problems

- Examples of exceptions and error situations

- Frequently asked questions (FAQs)

- Explanation of how to get help and procedures for updating the user manual

Most users prefer **online documentation**, which provides immediate Help when they have questions or encounter problems. Many users are accustomed to context-sensitive help screens, hints and tips, hypertext, on-screen demos, and other user-friendly features commonly found in popular software packages; they expect the same kind of support for in-house developed software.

If the system will include online documentation, that fact needs to be identified as one of the system requirements. If the documentation will be created by someone other than the analysts who are developing the system, that person or group needs to be involved as early as possible to become familiar with the software and begin developing the required documentation and support material. In addition, system developers must determine whether the documentation will be available from within the program, or as a separate entity in the form of a tutorial, slide presentation, reference manual, or Web site. If necessary, links should be created within the program that will take the user to the appropriate documentation.

Effective online documentation is an important productivity tool because it empowers users

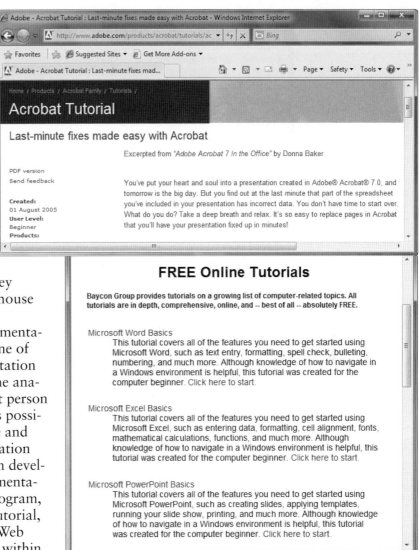

**FIGURE 11-27** Adobe offers interactive tutorials, demos, and seminars for its products, while Baycon Group provides a variety of free tutorials.

and reduces the time that IT staff members must spend in providing telephone, e-mail, or face-to-face assistance. Interactive tutorials are especially popular with users who like to learn by doing. Many software packages include tutorials, and additional tutorials are available online, as shown in Figure 11-27.

In addition to program-based assistance, the Internet offers an entirely new level of comprehensive, immediate support. Many programs include links to Web sites, intranet sites, and Internet-based technical support. For example, the Cisco Systems site shown in Figure 11-28 on the next page offers a wide range of support services, including a wiki that allows Cisco users to collaborate and share their knowledge.

Although online documentation is essential, written documentation material also is valuable, especially in training users and for reference purposes. A sample page from a user manual is shown in Figure 11-29 on page 533. Systems analysts or technical writers usually prepare the manual, but many companies invite users to review the material and participate in the development process.

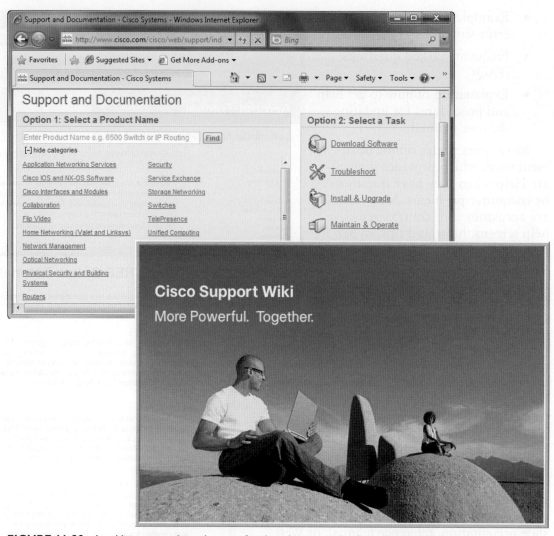

**FIGURE 11-28**  In addition to traditional types of technical support, the Cisco Systems Web site features a support wiki.

No matter what form of user documentation your system will require, you must keep in mind that it can take a good deal of time to develop. The time between finishing software coding and the time when a complete package — including documentation — can be released to users is entirely dependent on how well the documentation is thought out in advance. If the completion of your project includes providing user documentation, this issue needs to be addressed from the very beginning of the project. Determining what the user documentation requirements are and ascertaining who will complete the documents is critical to a timely release of the project.

Neglecting user documentation issues until after all the program is complete often leads to one of two things: (1) The documentation will be thrown together quickly just to get it out the door on time, and it more than likely will be inadequate; or (2) it will be done correctly, and the product release will be delayed considerably.

User training typically is scheduled when the system is installed; the training sessions offer an ideal opportunity to distribute the user manual and explain the procedures for updating it in the future. Training for users, managers, and IT staff is described later in this chapter.

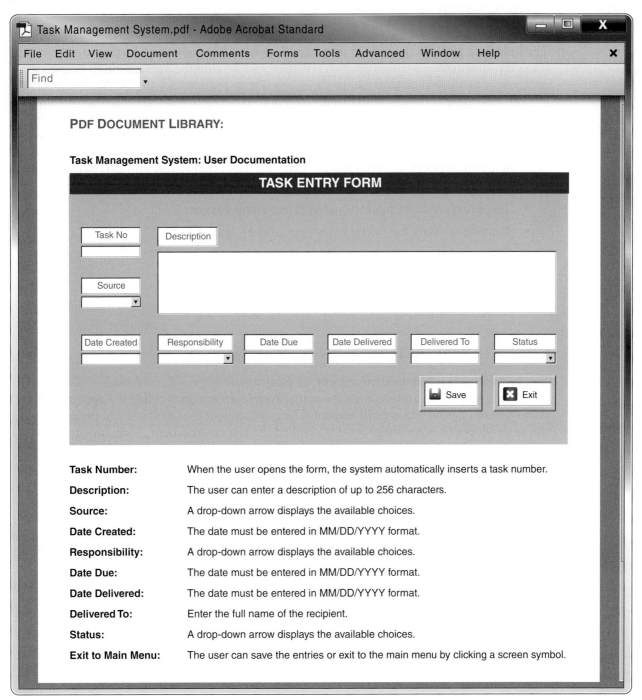

**FIGURE 11-29** A sample page from a user manual. The instructions explain how to add a new task to the system.

## MANAGEMENT APPROVAL

After system testing is complete, you present the results to management. You should describe the test results, update the status of all required documentation, and summarize input from users who participated in system testing. You also must provide detailed time schedules, cost estimates, and staffing requirements for making the system fully operational. If system testing produced no technical, economical, or operational problems, management determines a schedule for system installation and evaluation.

## SYSTEM INSTALLATION AND EVALUATION

The following sections describe system installation and evaluation tasks that are performed for every information systems project, whether you develop the application in-house or purchase it as a commercial package.

The new system now is ready to go to work. Your earlier design activities produced the overall architecture and processing strategy, and you consulted users at every stage of development. You developed and tested programs individually, in groups, and as a complete system. You prepared the necessary documentation and checked it for accuracy, including support material for IT staff and users. Now, you will carry out the remaining steps in systems implementation:

- Prepare a separate operational and test environment
- Provide training for users, managers, and IT staff
- Perform data conversion and system changeover
- Carry out a post-implementation evaluation of the system
- Present a final report to management

## OPERATIONAL AND TEST ENVIRONMENTS

You learned earlier that an environment, or platform, is a specific combination of hardware and software. The environment for the actual system operation is called the **operational environment** or **production environment**. The environment that analysts and programmers use to develop and maintain programs is called the **test environment**. A separate test environment is necessary to maintain system security and integrity and protect the operational environment. Typically, the test environment resides on a limited-access workstation or server located in the IT department.

Access to the operational environment is limited to users and must strictly be controlled. Systems analysts and programmers should not have access to the operational environment except to correct a system problem or to make authorized modifications or enhancements. Otherwise, IT department members have no reason to access the day-to-day operational system.

The test environment for an information system contains copies of all programs, procedures, and test data files. Before making any changes to an operational system, you must verify them in the test environment and obtain user approval. Figure 11-30 shows the differences between test environments and operational environments.

An effective testing process is essential, whether you are examining an information system or a batch of computer chips. Every experienced systems analyst can tell you a story about an apparently innocent program change that was introduced without being tested properly. In those stories, the innocent change invariably ends up causing some unexpected and unwanted changes to the program. After any modification, you should repeat the same acceptance tests you ran

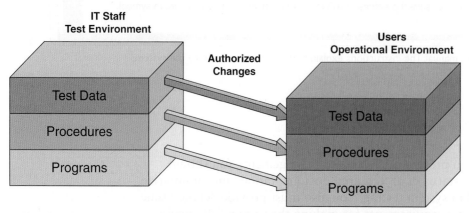

**FIGURE 11-30** The test environment versus the operational environment. Notice that access to the test environment is limited to IT staff, while the operational environment is restricted to users.

when the system was developed. By restricting access to the operational area and performing all tests in a separate environment, you can protect the system and avoid problems that could damage data or interrupt operations.

The operational environment includes hardware and software configurations and settings, system utilities, telecommunications resources, and any other components that might affect system performance. Because network capability is critically important in a client/server environment, you must verify connectivity, specifications, and performance before installing any applications. You should check all communications features in the test environment carefully, and then check them again after loading the applications into the operational environment. Your documentation should identify all network specifications and settings, including technical and operational requirements for communications hardware and software. If you have to build or upgrade network resources to support the new system, you must test the platform rigorously before system installation begins.

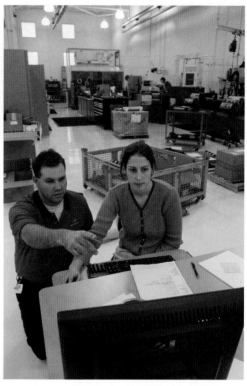

**FIGURE 11-31**  In any situation, training must fit the needs of users and help them carry out their job functions.

## TRAINING

No system can be successful without proper training, whether it involves software, hardware, or manufacturing, as shown in Figure 11-31. A successful information system requires training for users, managers, and IT staff members. The entire systems development effort can depend on whether or not people understand the system and know how to use it effectively.

### Training Plan

You should start to consider a **training plan** early in the systems development process. As you create documentation, you should think about how to use the material in future training sessions. When you implement the system, it is essential to provide the right training for the right people at the right time. The first step is to identify who should receive training and what training is needed. You must look carefully at the organization, how the system will support business operations, and who will be involved or affected. Figure 11-32 on the next page shows specific training topics for users, managers, and IT staff. Notice that each group needs a mix of general background and detailed information to understand and use the system.

As shown in Figure 11-32, the three main groups for training are users, managers, and IT staff. A manager does not need to understand every submenu or feature, but he or she does need a system overview to ensure that users are being trained properly and are using the system correctly. Similarly, users need to know how to perform their day-to-day job functions, but do not need to know how the company allocates system operational charges among user departments. IT staff people probably need the most information. To support the new system, they must have a clear understanding of how the system functions, how it supports business requirements, and the skills that users need to operate the system and perform their tasks.

After you identify the objectives, you must determine how the company will provide training. The main choices are to obtain training from vendors, outside training firms, or use IT staff and other in-house resources.

**ON THE WEB**

To learn more about training, visit the Management Information Systems CourseMate Web site at **www.cengagebrain.com**, navigate to **On the Web Links** for this chapter, and locate the Training link.

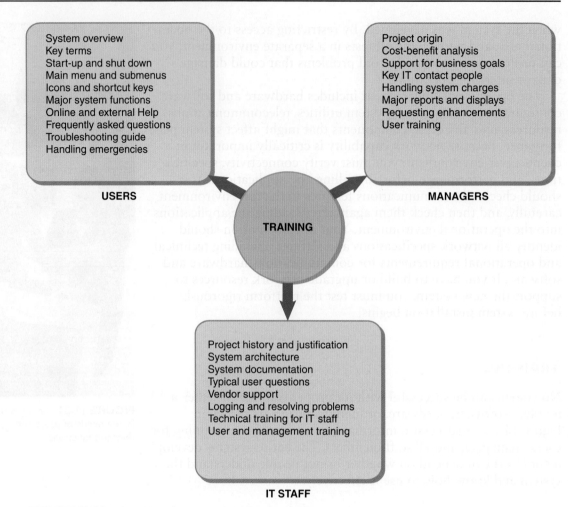

**FIGURE 11-32**   Examples of training topics for three different groups. Users, managers, and IT staff members have different training needs.

## Vendor Training

If the system includes the purchase of software or hardware, then vendor-supplied training is one of the features you should include in the RFPs (requests for proposal) and RFQs (requests for quotation) that you send to potential vendors.

Many hardware and software vendors offer training programs free or at a nominal cost for the products they sell. In other cases, the company might negotiate the price for training, depending on their relationship with the vendor and the prospect of future purchases. The training usually is conducted at the vendor's site by experienced trainers who provide valuable hands-on experience. If a large number of people need training, you might be able to arrange classes at your location.

Vendor training often gives the best return on your training dollars because it is focused on products that the vendor developed. The scope of vendor training, however, usually is limited to a standard version of the vendor's software or hardware. You might have to supplement the training in-house, especially if your IT staff customized the package.

## Webinars, Podcasts, and Tutorials

Many vendors offer Web-based training options, including Webinars, podcasts, and tutorials. Figure 11-33 shows a Webinar and a podcast. A **Webinar**, which combines the words Web and seminar, is an Internet-based training session that provides an interactive experience. Most Webinars are scheduled events with a group of preregistered users and an online presenter or instructor. A pre-recorded Webinar session also can be delivered as a **Webcast**, which is a one-way transmission, whenever a user wants or needs training support.

A **podcast** refers to a Web-based broadcast that allows a user to download multimedia files to a PC or portable device. Podcasts can be prescheduled, made available on demand, or delivered as automatic updates, depending on a user's preference. An advantage of a podcast is that **subscribers** can access the recorded material anywhere, anytime.

**FIGURE 11-33** Vendor training and support can include online tutorials, Webinars, and podcasts.

A **tutorial** is a series of online interactive lessons that present material and provide a dialog with users. Tutorials can be developed by software vendors, or by a company's IT team. A tutorial example is included in the in-house training section.

## Outside Training Resources

You also can look into an independent training firm to provide in-house hardware or software training. If vendor training is not practical and your organization does not have the internal resources to perform the training, you might find that outside training consultants are a desirable alternative.

The rapid expansion of information technology has produced tremendous growth in the computer-training field. Many training consultants, institutes, and firms are available that provide either standardized or customized training packages. IT industry leaders, such as Hewlett-Packard and IBM, offer a wide variety of training solutions, as shown in Figure 11-34 on the next page.

If you decide to investigate outside training resources, you can contact a training provider and obtain references from clients. You also can seek assistance from nonprofit sources with an interest in training, including universities, industry associations, and information management organizations. For example, Figure 11-35 on the next page shows the Web site for Western Illinois University's Center for the Application of Information Technologies (CAIT), which describes a variety of IT education and training resources.

## Training Tips

The IT staff and user departments often share responsibility for developing and conducting training programs for internally developed software. If your organization has a help desk, the staff might be able to handle user training.

Multimedia is an effective training method. Presentation software, such as Microsoft PowerPoint, OpenOffice Impress, or Corel Presentations, allows you to design training sessions that combine slides, animation, and sound. You also can use programs that capture actual keystrokes and mouse actions, and then replay the screens as a demonstration for

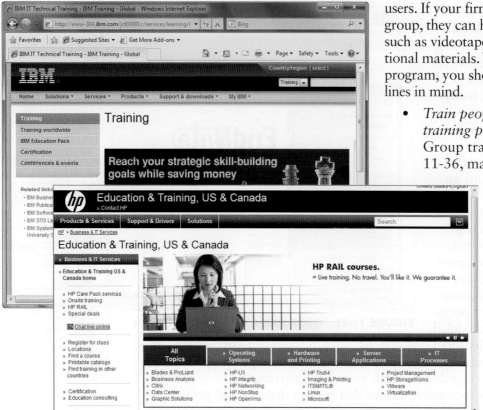

**FIGURE 11-34** IT industry leaders, such as Hewlett-Packard and IBM, offer a wide variety of training solutions.

users. If your firm has a media or graphic arts group, they can help you prepare training aids such as videotapes, charts, and other instructional materials. When developing a training program, you should keep the following guidelines in mind.

- *Train people in groups, with separate training programs for distinct groups.* Group training, as shown in Figure 11-36, makes the most efficient use of time and training facilities. In addition, if the group is small, trainees can learn from the questions and problems of others. A training program must address the job interests and skills of a wide range of participants. For example, IT staff personnel and users require very different information. Problems often arise when some participants have technical backgrounds and others do not. A single program will not meet everyone's needs.

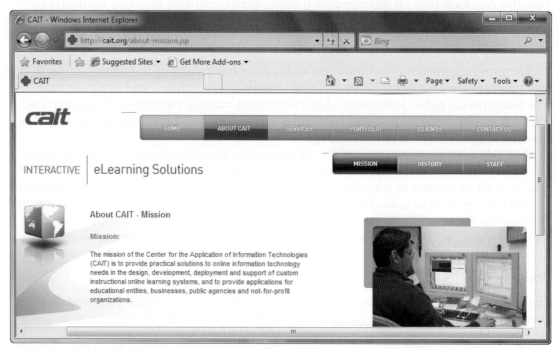

**FIGURE 11-35** Western Illinois University's Center for the Application of Information Technologies (CAIT) helps organizations design, develop, and deploy information technology education and training.

- *Select the most effective place to conduct the training.* Training employees at your company's location offers several advantages. Employees incur no travel expense, they can respond to local emergencies that require immediate attention, and training can take place in the actual environment where the system will operate. You can encounter some disadvantages, however. Employees who are distracted by telephone calls and other duties will not get the full benefit of the training. In addition, using the organization's computer facilities for training can disrupt normal operations and limit the amount of actual hands-on training.

- *Provide for learning by hearing, seeing, and doing.* Some people learn best from lectures, discussions, and question-and-answer sessions. Others learn best from viewing demonstrations or from reading documentation and other material. Most people learn best from hands-on experience. You should provide training that supports each type of learning.

- *Rely on previous trainees.* After one group of users has been trained, they can assist others. Users often learn more quickly from coworkers who share common experience and job responsibilities. Using a **train-the-trainer** strategy, you can select knowledgeable users who then conduct sessions for others. When utilizing train-the-trainer techniques, the initial training must include not only the use of the application or system, but some instruction on how to present the materials effectively.

**FIGURE 11-36**   Users must be trained on the new system. Training sessions might be one-on-one or group situations such as the one shown here. Many vendors provide product training as part of an overall service to customers.

## Interactive Training

Usually, a relationship exists between training methods and costs. Training an airline pilot in a state-of-the-art simulator is quite different from helping corporate users learn a new inventory system. Obviously, training budgets are business decisions, and IT staff sometimes has to work with the resources that are available, rather than the resources they wish they had. Most people prefer hands-on training. However, other less-expensive methods can be used, including training manuals, printed handouts, and online materials. Even the user documentation like that shown in Figure 11-29 on page 533 can be valuable, if users know how to find and use it.

If you are launching a new system and you lack the resources to develop formal training materials, you can design a series of dialog boxes that respond with Help information and suggestions whenever users select various menu topics. A good user interface also includes helpful error messages and hints, as discussed in Chapter 8. However, the most effective training is interactive, self-paced, and multimedia-based. Online training and video tutorials are discussed in the following sections.

**ONLINE TRAINING**   Regardless of the instructional method, training lessons should include step-by-step instructions for using the features of the information system. Training materials should resemble actual screens, and tasks should be typical of a user's daily work — the more realistic, the better. For example, Figure 11-37 on the next page shows a sample tutorial lesson for a sales prospect management system. In Lesson 1, the user learned how to enter and exit the system. In Lesson 2, the user learns how to add a sales prospect and return to the main menu.

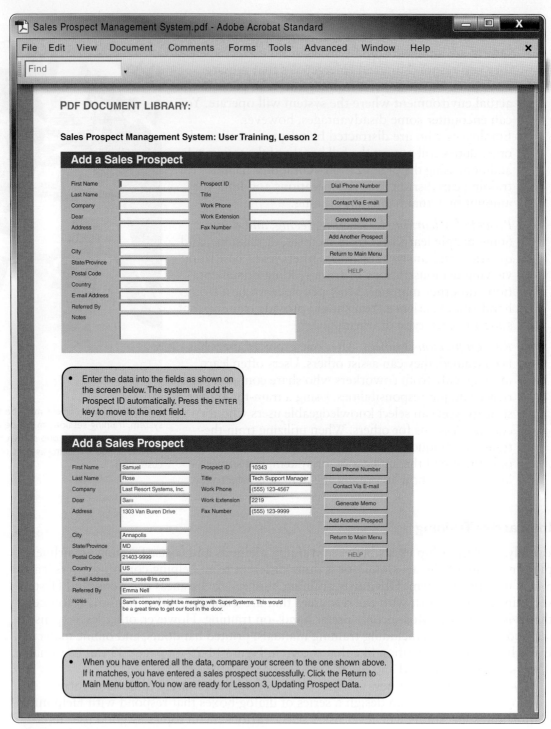

**FIGURE 11-37**   A sample lesson in an online tutorial.

More sophisticated tutorials might offer interactive sessions where users can perform practice tasks and view feedback. Online training materials also should include a reference section that summarizes all options and commands, lists all possible error messages, and what actions the user should take when a problem arises.

**VIDEO TUTORIALS**   You don't have to be a professional video developer to create effective training tutorials. For example, the Video Learning Sessions for this textbook were initially created as classroom teaching tools. Later, they were polished, edited, and transformed into streaming videos.

Suppose you want to develop a tutorial that shows how to create a structure chart, but you have no budget for special multimedia software. You do have Windows 7 and Office 2010, so you could start by creating a set of slides with screen text and graphic images. Then, you could add a live-motion screen capture and an audio narration. Finally, you could import the media into Windows Live Moviemaker where you could edit, save, and publish your training movie. Figure 11-38 shows a step-by-step plan for creating a video tutorial.

| 1. Capture individual screens | Use Windows Snipping Tool to capture full or partial screen images | |
| 2. Integrate screen images and text | Paste the images into Microsoft PowerPoint slides, then add suitable narration text in the Notes section | |
| 3. Capture live-motion video | Use freeware such as Wisdom-Soft Auto Screen Recorder | |
| 4. Record audio narration | Use Windows Sound Recorder to read the narration text | |
| 5. Produce a training video | Use Windows Moviemaker to import media, edit, and produce your training video | |

**FIGURE 11-38**   You can use free software such as Windows Snipping Tool for image capture, Wisdom-Soft Auto Screen Recorder for live-motion video, and Windows Sound Recorder for audio narration. After you create the media, you can import the material into Windows Live Movie Maker.

Figure 11-39 shows a video training session design. The topic is the same Task Management System shown in Figure 11-29 on page 533. There, the focus was on effective documentation. Here, the goal is self-paced, interactive training for users. Figure 11-39 shows a screen design with instructions to the video developer, and a script with instructions to the narrator. At the end of the production process, these materials will be transformed into an integrated multimedia presentation.

| Note to video developer: | Add a red arrow to highlight each bullet of the narration. The first arrow is shown as an example. |
|---|---|
| Note to narrator: | Pause briefly after each bulleted section and speak slowly enough for viewers to follow the steps. |
| Narration text: | Welcome to this video training session. In the session, you will learn how to add a new task to the system. As a reminder, you can pause the session at any time, or go back to review an earlier section. Now let's get started. |

- When you open the Task Entry Form, the system will insert a task number for you.
- Next, click the Description section and enter a description of up to 256 characters.
- Now click the drop-down arrow in the Source section and select one of the choices. Do the same in the Responsibility section.
- In the Date Created section, enter the date in em-em slash dee-dee slash why-why-why-why format. Do the same in the other three date fields.
- Finally, click the drop-down arrow in the Status section and select one of the choices.
- You can save your entries, or exit to the main menu at anytime. Just click the SAVE or EXIT symbols.

**FIGURE 11-39**   A sample video tutorial might include images, narration text, and notes to the video developer and narrator.

In addition to shareware and built-in software, you can use a video editing application such as Camtasia, which offers a powerful, user-friendly interface. Figure 11-40 shows a Camtasia screen, where the user has imported streaming video clip, several images, and a recorded narration. Now the user can crop, split, and extend the video and audio tracks, and can add various special effects.

**FIGURE 11-40**   Camtasia is a moderately-priced video editing tool that can produce professional-quality training videos.

When training is complete, many organizations conduct a full-scale test, or **simulation**, which is a dress rehearsal for users and IT support staff. Organizations include all procedures, such as those that they execute only at the end of a month, quarter, or year, in the simulation. As questions or problems arise, the participants consult the system documentation, help screens, or each other to determine appropriate answers or actions. This full-scale test provides valuable experience and builds confidence for everyone involved with the new system.

## DATA CONVERSION

Data conversion is an important part of the system installation process. During **data conversion**, existing data is loaded into the new system. Depending on the system, data conversion can be done before, during, or after the operational environment is complete. You should develop a data conversion plan as early as possible, and the conversion process should be tested when the test environment is developed.

**ON THE WEB**

To learn more about data conversion, visit the Management Information Systems CourseMate Web site at **www. cengagebrain. com**, navigate to **On the Web Links** for this chapter, and locate the Data Conversion link.

## Data Conversion Strategies

When a new system replaces an existing system, you should automate the data conversion process, if possible. The old system might be capable of **exporting** data in an acceptable format for the new system or in a standard format, such as ASCII or ODBC. **ODBC (Open Database Connectivity)** is an industry-standard protocol that allows DBMSs from various vendors to interact and exchange data. Most database vendors provide ODBC drivers, which are a form of middleware. As you learned in Chapter 10, middleware connects dissimilar applications and enables them to communicate.

If a standard format is not available, you must develop a program to extract the data and convert it to an acceptable format. Data conversion is more difficult when the new system replaces a manual system, because all data must be entered manually unless it can be scanned. Even when you can automate data conversion, a new system often requires additional data items, which might require manual entry.

## Data Conversion Security and Controls

You should maintain strict input controls during the conversion process, when data is extremely vulnerable. You must ensure that all system control measures are in place and operational to protect data from unauthorized access and to help prevent erroneous input.

Even with careful data conversion and input controls, some errors will occur. For example, duplicate customer records or inconsistent part numbers might have been tolerated by the old system, but will cause the new system to crash. Most organizations require that users verify all data, correct all errors, and supply every missing data item during conversion. Although the process can be time-consuming and expensive, it is essential that the new system be loaded with accurate, error-free data.

## SYSTEM CHANGEOVER

**System changeover** is the process of putting the new information system online and retiring the old system. Changeover can be rapid or slow, depending on the method. The four changeover methods are direct cutover, parallel operation, pilot operation, and phased operation. Direct cutover is similar to throwing a switch that instantly changes over from the old system to the new. Parallel operation requires that both systems run simultaneously for a specified period, which is the slowest method. The other methods, pilot and phased operation, fall somewhere between direct cutover and parallel operation. Figure 11-41 illustrates the four system changeover methods.

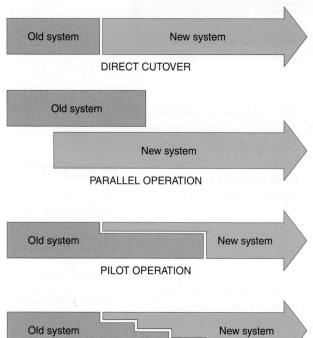

**FIGURE 11-41** The four system changeover methods.

## Direct Cutover

The **direct cutover** approach causes the changeover from the old system to the new system to occur immediately when the new system becomes operational. Direct cutover usually is the least expensive changeover method because the IT group has to operate and maintain only one system at a time.

Direct cutover, however, involves more risk than other changeover methods. Regardless of how thoroughly and carefully you conduct testing and training, some difficulties can arise when the system goes into operation. Problems can result from data situations that were not tested or anticipated or from errors caused by users or operators. A system also can encounter difficulties because live data typically occurs in much larger volumes than test data.

Although initial implementation problems are a concern with all four changeover methods, they are most significant when the direct cutover approach is used. Detecting minor errors also is more difficult with direct cutover because users cannot verify current output by comparing it to output from the old system. Major errors can cause a system process to terminate abnormally, and with the direct cutover method, you cannot revert to the old system as a backup option.

Companies often choose the direct cutover method for implementing commercial software packages because they feel that commercial packages involve less risk of total system failure. Commercial software is certainly not risk-free, but the software vendor usually maintains an extensive knowledge base and can supply reliable, prompt fixes for most problems.

For systems developed in-house, most organizations use direct cutover only for noncritical situations. Direct cutover might be the only choice, however, if the operating environment cannot support both the old and new systems or if the old and new systems are incompatible.

Timing is very important when using a direct cutover strategy. Most systems operate on weekly, monthly, quarterly, and yearly cycles. For example, consider a payroll system that produces output on a weekly basis. Some employees are paid twice a month, however, so the system also operates semimonthly. Monthly, quarterly, and annual reports also require the system to produce output at the end of every month, quarter, and year. When a cyclical information system is implemented in the middle of any cycle, complete processing for the full cycle requires information from both the old and the new systems. To minimize the need to require information from two different systems, cyclical information systems usually are converted using the direct cutover method at the beginning of a quarter, calendar year, or fiscal year.

## Parallel Operation

The **parallel operation** changeover method requires that both the old and the new information systems operate fully for a specified period. Data is input into both systems, and output generated by the new system is compared with the equivalent output from the old system. When users, management, and the IT group are satisfied that the new system operates correctly, the old system is terminated.

The most obvious advantage of parallel operation is lower risk. If the new system does not work correctly, the company can use the old system as a backup until appropriate changes are made. It is much easier to verify that the new system is working properly under parallel operation than under direct cutover, because the output from both systems is compared and verified during parallel operation.

Parallel operation, however, does have some disadvantages. First, it is the most costly changeover method. Because both the old and the new systems are in full operation, the company pays for both systems during the parallel period. Users must work in both systems and the company might need temporary employees to handle the extra workload. In addition, running both systems might place a burden on the operating environment and cause processing delays.

Parallel operation is not practical if the old and new systems are incompatible technically, or if the operating environment cannot support both systems. Parallel operation also is inappropriate when the two systems perform different functions or if the new system involves a new method of business operations. For example, until a company installs data scanners in a factory, it is impractical to launch a new production tracking system that requires such technology.

## Pilot Operation

The **pilot operation** changeover method involves implementing the complete new system at a selected location of the company. A new sales reporting system, for instance, might be implemented in only one branch office, or a new payroll system might be installed in only one department. In these examples, the group that uses the new system first is called the **pilot site**. During pilot operation, the old system continues to operate for the entire organization, including the pilot site. After the system proves successful at the pilot site, it is implemented in the rest of the organization, usually using the direct cutover method. Therefore, pilot operation is a combination of parallel operation and direct cutover methods.

Restricting the implementation to a pilot site reduces the risk of system failure, compared with a direct cutover method. Operating both systems for only the pilot site is less expensive than a parallel operation for the entire company. In addition, if you later use a parallel approach to complete the implementation, the changeover period can be much shorter if the system proves successful at the pilot site.

## Phased Operation

The **phased operation** changeover method allows you to implement the new system in stages, or modules. For example, instead of implementing a new manufacturing system all at once, you first might install the materials management subsystem, then the production control subsystem, then the job cost subsystem, and so on. You can implement each subsystem by using any of the other three changeover methods.

Analysts sometimes confuse phased and pilot operation methods. Both methods combine direct cutover and parallel operation to reduce risks and costs. With phased operation, however, you give a part of the system to all users, while pilot operation provides the entire system, but to only some users.

One advantage of a phased approach is that the risk of errors or failures is limited to the implemented module only. For instance, if a new production control subsystem fails to operate properly, that failure might not affect the new purchasing subsystem or the existing shop floor control subsystem.

Phased operation is less expensive than full parallel operation because you have to work with only one part of the system at a time. A phased approach is not possible, however, if the system cannot be separated easily into logical modules or segments. In addition, if the system involves a large number of separate phases, phased operation can cost more than a pilot approach.

Figure 11-42 shows that each changeover method has risk and cost factors. As a systems analyst, you must weigh the advantages and disadvantages of each method and recommend the best choice in a given situation. The final changeover decision will be based on input from the IT staff, users, and management — and the choice must reflect the nature of the business and the degree of acceptable risk.

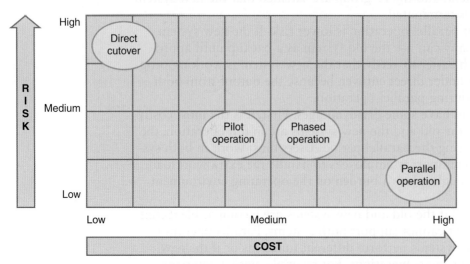

**FIGURE 11-42**   Relative risk and cost characteristics of the four changeover methods.

## CASE IN POINT 11.3: GLOBAL COOLING

You are a systems analyst at Global Cooling, a leading manufacturer of air conditioning units. You are leading a team that is developing a new production scheduling system. The project is now in the application development stage. Unit testing has been completed, and you are in the final stages of integration testing. Your supervisor, Ella Pham, is eager to implement the new application ahead of schedule and asked if you could trim system testing from two weeks to three days, and use a direct cutover method instead of the parallel changeover method that originally was planned. Write a brief memo expressing your views.

## POST-IMPLEMENTATION TASKS

Once the new system is operational, you must perform two additional tasks: Prepare a post-implementation evaluation and deliver a final report to management.

### Post-Implementation Evaluation

A **post-implementation evaluation** assesses the overall quality of the information system. The evaluation verifies that the new system meets specified requirements, complies with user objectives, and produces the anticipated benefits. In addition, by providing feedback to the development team, the evaluation also helps improve IT development practices for future projects.

A post-implementation evaluation should examine all aspects of the development effort and the end product — the developed information system. A typical evaluation includes feedback for the following areas:

- Accuracy, completeness, and timeliness of information system output
- User satisfaction
- System reliability and maintainability
- Adequacy of system controls and security measures
- Hardware efficiency and platform performance
- Effectiveness of database implementation
- Performance of the IT team
- Completeness and quality of documentation
- Quality and effectiveness of training
- Accuracy of cost-benefit estimates and development schedules

You can apply the same fact-finding techniques in a post-implementation evaluation that you used to determine the system requirements during the systems analysis phase. When evaluating a system, you should:

- Interview members of management and key users
- Observe users and computer operations personnel actually working with the new information system
- Read all documentation and training materials
- Examine all source documents, output reports, and screen displays
- Use questionnaires to gather information and opinions from a large number of users
- Analyze maintenance and help desk logs

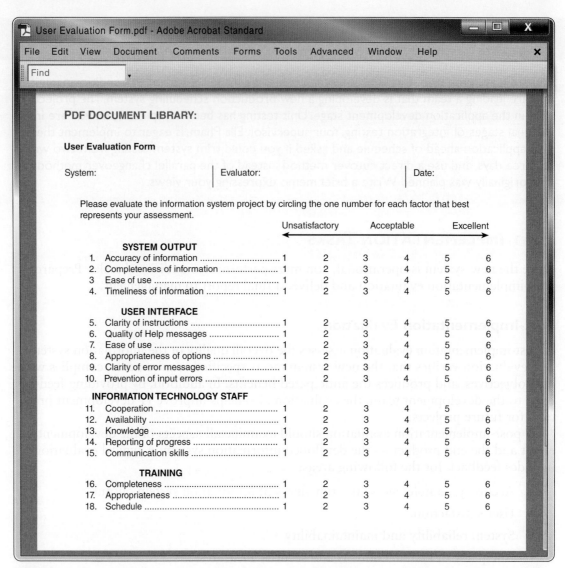

**FIGURE 11-43**   Sample user evaluation form. The numerical scale allows easy tabulation of results. Following this section, the form provides space for open-ended comments and suggestions.

Figure 11-43 shows the first page of a sample user evaluation form for the new information system where users evaluate 18 separate elements on a numerical scale, so the results can be tabulated easily. Following that section, the form provides space for open-ended comments and suggestions.

Whenever possible, people who were not directly involved in developing the system should conduct the post-implementation evaluation. IT staff and users usually perform the evaluation, although some firms use an internal audit group or independent auditors to ensure the accuracy and completeness of the evaluation.

When should post-implementation evaluation occur? Is it better to wait until the new system has been in operation for one month, six months, one year, or longer? Users can forget details of the developmental effort if too much time elapses before the evaluation. After several months or a year, for instance, users might not remember whether they learned a procedure through training, from user documentation, or by experimenting with the system on their own.

Users also might forget their impressions of IT team members over time. An important purpose of the post-implementation evaluation is to improve the quality of IT department functions, including interaction with users, training, and documentation. Consequently, the evaluation team should perform the assessment while users are able to recall specific incidents, successes, and problems so they can offer suggestions for improvement. Post-implementation evaluation primarily is concerned with assessing the quality of the new system. If the team performs the evaluation too soon after implementation, users will not have enough time to learn the new system and appreciate its strengths and weaknesses. Although many IT professionals recommend conducting the evaluation after at least six months of system operation, pressure to finish the project sooner usually results in an earlier evaluation in order to allow the IT department to move on to other tasks.

Ideally, conducting a post-implementation evaluation should be standard practice for all information systems projects. Sometimes, evaluations are skipped because users are eager to work with the new system, or because IT staff members have more pressing priorities. In some organizations, management might not recognize the importance and benefits of a post-implementation evaluation. The evaluations are extremely important, however, because they enable the development team and the IT department to learn what worked and what did not work. Otherwise, developers might commit the same errors in another system.

## CASE IN POINT 11.4:  YORKTOWN INDUSTRIES

Cindy Winslow liked her new job as lead systems analyst at Yorktown Industries. She was pleased that her development team completed the new human resources system ahead of schedule and under budget. Cindy looked forward to receiving the post-implementation evaluation because she was confident that both the system and the development team would receive high marks from users and managers.

After the system operated for one month, Cindy received a call from her supervisor, Ted Haines. Ted told her that she would have to handle the evaluation, even though she headed the development effort. Cindy told Ted that she did not feel comfortable evaluating her own team's work. She explained that someone who was not involved in its development should do an independent evaluation. Ted responded that he had full confidence in Cindy's ability to be objective. He explained that no one else was available and he needed the evaluation quickly so he could move forward with the next stage in the corporate development plan.

Cindy was troubled about the situation and she called you, a professional acquaintance, for your advice. What would you tell her and why?

### Final Report to Management

At the end of each SDLC phase, you submit a report to management, and the systems implementation phase is no exception. Your report should include the following:

The Communication tools in Appendix A can help you develop better reports and presentations. To learn more about these tools, turn to Appendix A.

- Final versions of all system documentation
- Planned modifications and enhancements to the system that have been identified
- Recap of all systems development costs and schedules
- Comparison of actual costs and schedules to the original estimates
- Post-implementation evaluation, if it has been performed

The final report to management marks the end of systems development work. In the next chapter, you will study the role of a systems analyst during systems operation, security, and support, which is the final phase of the SDLC.

# A QUESTION OF ETHICS

Your friend Jill is handling the testing for the new accounting system, and right now she is very upset about the most recent results. "It seems like every time we fix one thing, another issue pops up! After ten days of testing and adjusting, we are meeting over 90% of the goals and benchmarks. If we're looking for perfection, we'll never make the implementation deadline for the new system, and the users will be all over us. Not to mention top management's reaction to a delay. I'm sure we can resolve some of these issues after the system becomes operational."

How would you respond to Jill? Are ethical issues involved? What are your responsibilities, as an employee, as an IT professional, and as a friend?

## CHAPTER SUMMARY

The systems implementation phase consists of application development, testing, installation, and evaluation of the new system. During application development, analysts determine the overall design strategy and work with programmers to complete design, coding, testing, and documentation. Quality assurance is essential during the implementation phase. Many companies utilize software engineering concepts and quality standards established by the International Organization for Standardization (ISO).

Each systems development approach has its own set of tools. For example, structured development relies heavily on DFDs and structure charts. A structure chart consists of symbols that represent program modules, data couples, control couples, conditions, and loops. Object-oriented methods use a variety of diagrams, including use case, class, sequence, and transition state diagrams. Agile methods tend to use a spiral or other iterative model.

System developers also can use more generic tools to help them translate the system logic into properly functioning program modules. These tools include entity-relationship diagrams, flowcharts, pseudocode, decision tables, and decision trees.

If an agile development approach is used, then the customer creates user stories that describe required features and priority levels. In agile methodology, new system releases are made after many iterations and each is test-driven carefully by the customer.

Cohesion measures a module's scope and processing characteristics. A module that performs a single function or task has a high degree of cohesion, which is desirable. Coupling measures relationships and interdependence among modules. Modules that are relatively independent are loosely coupled, which is desirable. Cohesion and coupling concepts are used in structured development, but also are applicable to object-oriented development.

Typically, you follow four steps when you create a structure chart. You review DFDs and object models to identify the processes and methods, identify the program modules and determine control-subordinate relationships, add symbols for couples and loops, and analyze the structure chart to ensure that it is consistent with your system documentation.

Programmers perform desk checking, code review, and unit testing tasks during application development. Systems analysts design the initial test plans, which include test steps and test data for integration testing and system testing. Integration testing is necessary for programs that interact. The final step is system testing for the completed system. System testing includes users in the testing process.

In addition to system documentation, analysts and technical writers also prepare operations documentation and user documentation. Operations documentation provides instructions and information to the IT operations group. User documentation consists of instructions and information for users who interact with the system and includes user manuals, help screens, and tutorials.

During the installation process, you establish an operational, or production, environment for the new information system that is completely separate from the test environment. The operational environment contains live data and is accessible only by authorized users. All future changes to the system must be verified in the test environment before they are applied to the operational environment.

Everyone who interacts with the new information system should receive training appropriate to his or her role and skills. The IT department usually is responsible for training. Software or hardware vendors or professional training organizations also can provide training. When you develop a training program, remember the following guidelines: Train people in groups; utilize people already trained to help train others; develop separate programs for distinct employee groups; and provide for learning by using discussions, demonstrations, documentation, training manuals, tutorials, Webinars, and podcasts. Users learn better with interactive, self-paced training methods.

Data conversion often is necessary when installing a new information system. When a new system replaces a computerized system, you should automate the data conversion process if possible. The old system might be capable of exporting data in a format that the new system can use, or you might have to extract the data and convert it to an acceptable format. Data conversion from a manual system often requires labor-intensive data entry or scanning. Even when data conversion can be automated, a new system often requires additional data items, which might require manual entry. Strict input controls are important during the conversion process to protect data integrity and quality. Typically, data is verified, corrected, and updated during the conversion process.

System changeover is the process of putting the new system into operation. Four changeover methods exist: direct cutover, parallel operation, pilot operation, and phased operation. With direct cutover, the old system stops and the new system starts simultaneously; direct cutover is the least expensive, but the riskiest changeover method. With parallel operation, users operate both the old and new information systems for some period of time; parallel operation is the most expensive and least risky of the changeover methods. Pilot operation and phased operation represent compromises between direct cutover and parallel operation; both methods are less risky than direct cutover and less costly than parallel operation. With pilot operation, a specified group within the organization uses the new system for a period of time, while the old system continues to operate for the rest of the users. After the system proves successful at the pilot site, it is implemented throughout the organization. With phased operation, you implement the system in the entire organization, but only one module at a time, until the entire system is operational.

A post-implementation evaluation assesses and reports on the quality of the new system and the work done by the project team. Although it is best if people who were not involved in the systems development effort perform the evaluation, that is not always possible. The evaluation should be conducted early so users have a fresh recollection of the development effort, but not before users have experience using the new system.

The final report to management includes the final system documentation, describes any future system enhancements that already have been identified, and details the project costs. The report represents the end of the development effort and the beginning of the new system's operational life.

# Key Terms and Phrases

acceptance tests *527*
application development *511*
attributes *519*
bug tracking software *529*
Capability Maturity Model (CMM)® *508*
Capability Maturity Model Integration
   (CMMI)® *508*
code review *525*
coding *523*
cohesion *516*
condition *515*
control couple *515*
control module *514*
coupling *516*
customer *520*
data conversion *543*
data couple *515*
defect tracking software *529*
design walkthrough *525*
desk checking *525*
direct cutover *544*
documentation *528*
exporting *544*
flowchart *513*
integrated development environment
   (IDE) *523*
integration testing *526*
ISO 90003:2004 *510*
iteration cycle *522*
iteration planning meeting *522*
library module *514*
link testing *526*
logic errors *525*
loop *515*
loosely coupled *516*
methods *519*
modular design *514*
module *511*
object-oriented development (OOD) *518*
ODBC (Open Database Connectivity) *544*
online documentation *531*
operational environment *534*

operations documentation *529*
parallel operation *545*
parallel programming *522*
partitioning *514*
patches *529*
phased operation *546*
pilot operation *546*
pilot site *546*
podcast *537*
post-implementation evaluation *547*
process improvement *509*
production environment *534*
program documentation *529*
pseudocode *513*
quality assurance *508*
release plan *521*
simulation *543*
software engineering *508*
status flag *515*
structure chart *514*
structured walkthrough *525*
stub testing *526*
subordinate modules *514*
subscribers *537*
syntax errors *525*
system changeover *544*
system documentation *529*
system testing *527*
test data *526*
test-driven design *522*
test environment *534*
test plan *526*
tightly coupled *516*
top-down approach *514*
training plan *535*
train-the-trainer *539*
tutorial *537*
unit testing *525*
user documentation *530*
user story *521*
Webcast *537*
Webinar *537*

# Learn It Online

**Instructions:**   To complete the Learn It Online exercises, visit the Management Information Systems CourseMate Web site at **www.cengagebrain.com**, navigate to the resources for this chapter, and click the link for the exercise you want to complete.

## 1  Chapter Reinforcement

### TF, MC, and SA

Click one of the Chapter Reinforcement links for Multiple Choice, True/False, or Short Answer. Answer each question and submit to your instructor.

## 2  Flash Cards

Click the Flash Cards link and read the instructions. Type 20 (or a number specified by your instructor) in the Number of playing cards text box, type your name in the Enter your Name text box, and then click the Flip Card button. When the flash card is displayed, read the question and then click the ANSWER box arrow to select an answer. Flip through the Flash Cards. If your score is 15 (75%) correct or greater, click Print on the File menu to print your results. If your score is less than 15 (75%) correct, then redo this exercise by clicking the Replay button.

## 3  Practice Test

Click the Practice Test link. Answer each question, enter your first and last name at the bottom of the page, and then click the Grade Test button. When the graded practice test is displayed on your screen, click Print on the File menu to print a hard copy. Continue to take practice tests until you score 80% or better.

## 4  Who Wants To Be a Computer Genius?

Click the Computer Genius link. Read the instructions, enter your first and last name at the bottom of the page, and then click the Play button. When your score is displayed, click the PRINT RESULTS link to print a hard copy.

## 5  Wheel of Terms

Click the Wheel of Terms link. Read the instructions, and then enter your first and last name and your school name. Click the PLAY button. When your score is displayed on the screen, right-click the score and then click Print on the shortcut menu to print a hard copy.

## 6  Crossword Puzzle Challenge

Click the Crossword Puzzle Challenge link. Read the instructions, and then click the Continue button. Work the crossword puzzle. When you are finished, click the Submit button. When the crossword puzzle is redisplayed, submit it to your instructor.

## SCR Associates Case Simulation **Session 11: Systems Implementation**

### Overview

The SCR Associates case study is a Web-based simulation that allows you to practice your skills in a real-world environment. The case study transports you to SCR's intranet, where you complete 12 work sessions, each aligning with a chapter. As you work on the case, you will receive e-mail and voice mail messages, obtain information from SCR's online libraries, and perform various tasks.

### How do I use the case?

- Review the SCR background material in Chapter 1.
- Read the Preview for this session and study the Task List.
- Visit the Management Information Systems CourseMate Web site at **www.cengagebrain. com**, navigate to the **SCR Case Simulation**, and locate the intranet link.
- Enter your name and the password **sad9e**. An opening screen will display the 12 sessions.
- Select this session. Check your e-mail and voice mail carefully, and then work on the tasks.

### Preview: Session 11

You assisted your supervisor, Jesse Baker, in planning an architecture for the new TIMS system. Now she wants you to work on system implementation tasks and issues. Specifically, she wants you to develop a structure chart, testing and training plans, implementation guidelines, and a post-implementation review.

### Task List

| |
|---|
| 1.  Jesse wants to see a structure chart. She said to use program modules based on the processes we identified earlier. She wants the modules to be cohesive and loosely coupled. |
| 2.  Need a testing plan that includes unit integration and system testing as Jesse requested. Also, need a reminder about careful documentation. |
| 3.  Jesse says it's important to understand the difference between the test and operational environments, and she wants me to draft a message that explains the installation process and includes guidelines for all concerned. Also need to develop a training plan for TIMS, with groups that should receive training, the topics that should be covered, and training methods we might use. |
| 4.  Jesse wants me to recommend a data conversion plan and a changeover method for TIMS. She also wants a plan for post-implementation review, including fact-gathering methods, topics to cover, the timing of the review, and who should perform it. |

**FIGURE 11-44**   Task list: Session 11.

# Chapter Exercises

## Review Questions

1. Where does systems implementation fit in the SDLC, what tasks are performed during this phase, and why is quality assurance so important?
2. How are structured, object-oriented, and agile methods similar? How are they different?
3. Describe structure charts and symbols, and define cohesion and coupling.
4. Define unit testing, integration testing, and system testing.
5. What types of documentation does a systems analyst prepare, and what would be included in each type?
6. What is the purpose of an operational environment and a test environment?
7. Who must receive training before a new information system is implemented?
8. List and describe the four system changeover methods. Which one generally is the most expensive? Which is the riskiest? Explain your answers.
9. Who should be responsible for performing a post-implementation evaluation?
10. List the information usually included in the final report to management.

## Discussion Topics

1. A supervisor states, "Integration testing is a waste of time. If each program is tested adequately, integration testing is not needed. Instead, we should move on to system testing as soon as possible. If modules don't interact properly, we'll handle it then." Do you agree or disagree with this comment? Justify your position.
2. Suppose you are a systems analyst developing a detailed test plan. Explain the testing strategies you will use in your plan. Will you use live or simulated data?
3. Using the Internet, locate an example of training for a software or hardware product. Write a brief summary of the training, the product, the type of training offered, and the cost of training (if available). Discuss your findings with the class.
4. Suppose that you designed a tutorial to train a person in the use of specific software or hardware, such as a Web browser. What specific information would you want to know about the recipient of the training? How would that information affect the design of the training material?

# Apply Your Knowledge

The Apply Your Knowledge section contains four mini-cases. Each case describes a situation, explains your role in the case, and asks you to respond to questions. You can answer the questions by applying knowledge you learned in the chapter.

## 1 Sand and Surf Retailers

### Situation:

Sand and Surf Retailers recently acquired several smaller companies to expand its chain of clothing outlets. To establish consistency for the current organization and future acquisitions, Sand and Surf decided to develop an in-house application called SPS (Standard Purchasing System). The SPS system would standardize purchasing practices for each Sand and Surf subsidiary and manage all purchasing information. System testing will be completed by the end of the week.

1. What types of documentation are needed for this application?
2. During application development, what steps should the IT staff follow to develop a structure chart?
3. What suggestions do you have for help screens and online tutorials?
4. What types of testing should be performed? What types of test data should be used?

## 2 Albatross Airfreight

### Situation:

Albatross Airfreight specializes in shipping cargo via air across North America. In an effort to modernize, the company has begun to computerize manual business processes. The new IT infrastructure includes a computer system that tracks cargo from departure point to destination. At this point, the new system is ready for implementation. Systems analysts are modularizing the system, and programmers are ready to start coding the first modules.

1. What issues should systems analysts and programmers discuss before they proceed with the project?
2. As a systems analyst on this project, how would you describe your primary responsibilities, and how could you contribute to the quality of the finished product?
3. As a programmer, how would you describe your primary responsibilities, and how could you contribute to the quality of the finished product?
4. Will the use of structure charts be beneficial during this stage of development? Discuss the advantages of structure charts compared with flowcharts and pseudocode.

## 3 Victorian Creations

**Situation:**

Victorian Creations is a growing business that specializes in the reproduction of furniture from the Victorian era. Since 2006, sales have increased steadily. The original accounting system was a package from Peachtree Software, which initially ran on a stand-alone PC and later on a LAN. Now, the firm is preparing to install a powerful, scalable accounting package that can support the company's current and future operations. You have been asked to develop a training plan for users.

1. Who should receive training on the new software, and what topics should the training cover?
2. Investigate an accounting package such as Peachtree to learn if the product can convert data from other accounting programs.
3. What changeover strategy would you suggest for the new accounting system? Explain your answer.
4. When should a post-implementation review be scheduled? Explain your answer.

## 4 Calico Prints

**Situation:**

Calico Prints creates a wide range of fabrics and wallpapers. Recently the company updated its payroll software as an in-house development project. Users and IT staff members have completed a comprehensive training curriculum. The system has been in the operational environment for approximately six weeks, and no major problems have occurred. You are responsible for the post-implementation evaluation.

1. What are some techniques you might use to obtain an accurate evaluation?
2. What are some specific questions you would include in a questionnaire? Who should receive the questionnaire?
3. Are there general guidelines that apply to the timing of a post-implementation evaluation? What are they?
4. In your view, should the company schedule a post-implementation evaluation for the payroll system at this time? Give specific reasons for your answer.

# Case Studies

Case studies allow you to practice specific skills learned in the chapter. Each chapter contains several case studies that continue throughout the textbook, and a chapter capstone case.

### New Century Health Clinic

New Century Health Clinic offers preventive medicine and traditional medical care. In your role as an IT consultant, you will help New Century develop a new information system.

#### Background

You completed the systems design for the insurance system at New Century Health Clinic. The associates at the clinic have approved the design specification, and you hired two programmers, Bill Miller and Celia Goldring, to assist you with the programming and testing of the insurance system.

For Assignments 3 and 4, assume that a server and six client workstations have been purchased, installed, and networked in the clinic offices. You now are ready to begin installation and evaluation of the system.

#### Assignments

1. Plan the testing required for the system. You should consider unit, integration, and system testing in your test plan and determine who should participate in the testing. Also design the test data that you will use. Prepare a structure chart that shows the main program functions for the New Century system.

2. You have asked Anita Davenport, New Century's office manager, to contribute to the user manual for the insurance system. She suggested that you include a section of frequently asked questions (FAQs), which you also could include in the online documentation. Prepare 10 FAQs and answers for use in the printed user manual and context-sensitive Help screens. Also identify the specific people who will require training on the new system. Describe the type and level of training you recommend for each person or group.

3. Recommend a changeover method for New Century's system and justify your recommendation. If you suggest phased operation or pilot operation, specify the order in which you would implement the modules or how you would select a pilot workstation or location.

4. Should the associates perform a post-implementation evaluation? If an assessment is done, who should perform it? What options are available and which would you recommend?

### PERSONAL TRAINER, INC.

Personal Trainer, Inc., owns and operates fitness centers in a dozen Midwestern cities. The centers have done well, and the company is planning an international expansion by opening a new "supercenter" in the Toronto area. Personal Trainer's president, Cassia Umi, hired an IT consultant, Susan Park, to help develop an information system for the new facility. During the project, Susan will work closely with Gray Lewis, who will manage the new operation.

#### Background

Susan finished work on system architecture issues, and her system design specification was approved. Now she is ready to address system implementation tasks, including quality assurance, structure charts, testing, training, data conversion, system changeover, and post-implementation evaluation.

## Assignments

1. Identify the specific groups of people who need training on the new system. For each group, describe the type of training you would recommend and list the topics you would cover.

2. Suggest a changeover method for the new billing system and provide specific reasons to support your choice. If you recommend phased operation, specify the order in which you would implement the modules. If your recommendation is for pilot operation, specify the department or area you would select as the pilot site and justify your choice.

3. Develop a data conversion plan that specifies which data items must be entered, the order in which the data should be entered, and which data items are the most time-critical.

4. You decide to perform a post-implementation evaluation to assess the quality of the system. Who would you involve in the process? What investigative techniques would you use and why?

## FANCIFUL CRYSTAL

Fanciful Crystal has produced fine crystal products for many years. The company once dominated the global market, but sales have declined recently. Last year, Fanciful Crystal rushed to implement a new Web-based system to boost sagging sales. Unfortunately, the online system was not tested thoroughly and experienced start-up problems. For example, customers complained about order mix-ups and overcharges for deliveries. You are a new system analyst with the company, and your supervisor asked you to investigate the problems.

1. Based on what you know about e-commerce, how would you have tested a new Web-based system?

2. Should ISO standards have been considered? Explain your answer.

3. What should Fanciful Crystal do in the future to avoid similar problems when developing new systems?

4. Three months after the system changeover, you perform a post-implementation evaluation. Prepare three evaluation forms for the new information system: one for users, one for managers, and one for the IT operations staff.

## CHAPTER CAPSTONE CASE:   SoftWear, Limited

SoftWear, Limited (SWL), is a continuing case study that illustrates the knowledge and skills described in each chapter. In this case study, the student acts as a member of the SWL systems development team and performs various tasks.

### Background

The ESIP development team of Jane Rossman, Tom Adams, and Becky Evans started work on the new system, which they would develop as a Microsoft Access application in a client/server environment. Jane and Tom scheduled additional meetings with the consulting firm, True Blue Systems, while Becky started designing the user interface.

The ESIP system design included a server to interact with various SWL client workstations and an interface to the new payroll package from Pacific Software. The payroll package was implemented successfully on SWL's mainframe, and several payroll cycles were completed without any processing problems.

When the ESIP development team met on Monday morning, the members studied the overview that True Blue submitted, shown in Figure 11-45. Jane said they would use a top-down design approach. Their first step was to partition the system and break it down into a set of modules on a structure chart. Each module would represent a program or function to be performed by macros or Visual Basic procedures.

**FIGURE 11-45**   The ESIP system plan developed by True Blue Systems.

The team reviewed the documentation and DFDs carefully, using the DFDs they prepared during the systems analysis phase. The team determined that the ESIP system would perform five main tasks: Extract the ESIP deductions during payroll processing; apply the extracted deductions to specific ESIP options; update employee deduction selections; update ESIP option choices; and handle fund transfers to internal and external ESIP entities. To accomplish those tasks, the system would need a variety of reports, controls, query and display capabilities, input screens, security provisions, and other features.

## CHAPTER CAPSTONE CASE:  SoftWear, Limited (continued)

Of the five main ESIP processes, only the extracting of payroll deductions would be done on SWL's mainframe. Jane said they would need to develop an interface program to control the extraction processing, but all the other functions would run on the ESIP server and clients. By afternoon, they created a structure chart that showed a top-down model of all functions and processes.

Next, Jane estimated the time needed to design, code, unit test, and document each module. She also estimated the time needed for integration and system testing, completing the ESIP system documentation, and receiving management approval. Jane used Microsoft Project software to create a work breakdown structure and a critical path for the project. The development team decided to meet daily to review their progress.

### Mainframe Interface

Jane met with Rick to discuss the ESIP deduction extraction program that executes when the mainframe runs the weekly payroll. Jane learned that she could write the extract module in Visual Basic.

Working together, Jane and Becky prepared a design, wrote the commands, and unit tested the ESIP program modules with test files. They used stubs to indicate the extraction program files. After verifying the results, Jane created a procedure for downloading the deduction file from the mainframe to the ESIP server in the payroll department. She tested the download procedure and updated the documentation.

### ESIP Server

The team started developing the Access database application that would handle the other ESIP functions. The plan was for Becky to finish the basic switchboard and screen designs, then add features that users had requested, including custom menus and icons for frequently used functions. Becky also would design all the reports documented in the data dictionary.

Meanwhile, Jane and Tom reviewed the ERDs developed in the systems design phase to confirm that the entities and normalized record designs still were valid. Then they started to create objects, including tables, queries, macros, and code modules, using the application design tools in Access.

Jane and Tom defined the data tables, identified primary keys, and linked the tables into a relational structure, as shown in Figure 11-46. They reviewed the designs to ensure that the tables would work properly with Becky's input screens. Jane and Tom used an agreed-upon naming convention for all objects to ensure consistency among the systems.

After they loaded test data, Jane and Tom developed queries that would allow users to retrieve, display, update, and delete records. Some queries affected only individual records, such as ESIP options, while they designed other queries for specific reports, such as the ESIP Deduction Register query shown

**FIGURE 11-46** Relational structure for the ESIP system tables. Notice that the field or fields that comprise the primary key are shown in bold. Common fields link the tables, and referential integrity is indicated by the 1 (one) and ∞ (many) symbols.

## CHAPTER CAPSTONE CASE:   SoftWear, Limited (continued)                SWL

in Figure 11-47, which displays deductions first in date order, then by employee SSN. This query also produces SQL commands shown in the lower screen that will be transmitted to the ESIP server.

Jane and Tom also developed and tested macros that performed specific actions when certain events occurred. The macros later would be linked to various buttons and menus that Becky was designing into her switchboard and input screens. To save coding time, Tom converted several macros to Visual Basic in order to work on additional features and capabilities.

Jane and Tom also completed work on various security features, including password protection and several levels of permission required to view, modify, or delete specific objects. Later, when the system became operational, management would authorize specific permission levels, and Jane would designate a system administrator to maintain security and system policies.

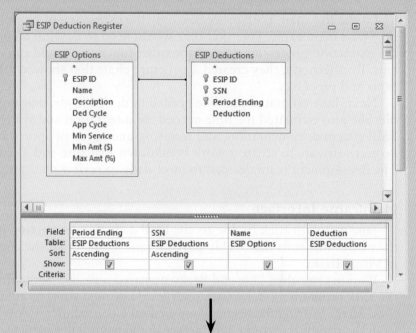

**FIGURE 11-47**   Example of a query that will provide data for the ESIP Deduction Register. Notice that the query sorts deductions by date, then by employee SSN. The query also produces SQL commands shown in the lower screen that will be transmitted to the ESIP server.

### Completing Application Development

In three weeks, the ESIP development team finished unit testing. Becky tested the switchboard, macros, queries, screen forms, menus, submenus, and code modules to ensure that they functioned correctly. Next, they linked the modules and performed integration testing. The testing ran smoothly, and they encountered no significant problems.

After integration testing, the analysts asked several principal users to participate in system testing. During this process, the users suggested some minor changes to screens and reports, which the team implemented.

The team members prepared user documentation as they completed each task. To produce a clear, understandable user manual, they decided to ask Amy Calico, SWL's payroll director, to review their notes and help them write a draft for current and future users. They wanted to explain the system in nontechnical terms, with screen shots and a set of frequently asked questions. Jane said that the entire manual could be put online after SWL's intranet was developed.

### Installation of the ESIP System

After a successful period of parallel operation, SWL fully implemented the payroll package purchased from Pacific Software and was ready to start installation of the ESIP system. In preparation, the IT development team of Jane Rossman, Tom Adams, and Becky Evans confirmed that SWL's existing network could handle the additional traffic generated by the new system, but might need to be upgraded in the future.

Tom's first task was to install the ESIP application on the server in the payroll department and to verify that the system could communicate properly with SWL's mainframe. Then, he installed and tested a new high-speed tape cartridge backup system for the ESIP system.

Next, Tom loaded the ESIP application on a client PC in the human resources department. He checked all hardware and system software settings and used several test files to ensure that the client communicated with the ESIP server in the payroll department.

Meanwhile, Becky Evans and Rick Williams worked together on the interface between the ESIP system and the mainframe. They previously created a module called an extract program that directed the mainframe payroll system to capture the ESIP payroll deductions, store them in a file, and transmit the file back to the ESIP system. They already tested the interface using stubs to represent actual input and output files. Next, they would use a test data file with examples of every possible combination of permissible deductions and several improper deductions that testing should detect.

As soon as Rick confirmed that the payroll package was ready for the interface test, Tom set up the ESIP server and sent the test file to the mainframe. Then, he ran the module that sent processing commands to the payroll system. Everyone was pleased to see that the mainframe handled the test data properly and generated an extracted deduction file.

Becky and Rick were ready to conduct hands-on training with the payroll group, so they arranged an early morning session with Amy Calico, Nelson White, Britton Ellis, and Debra Williams. Becky walked them through the steps, which were described clearly in the user manual, and then answered several questions. The payroll employees seemed pleased with the explanation and commented on how much easier the new system would be for them to use.

Next, Becky went to see Mike Feiner, director of human resources. Mike would be the only person allowed to add, change, or delete any of the ESIP options. Based on written authorization from Rob King, vice president of human resources, Mike would have a special password and permission level to allow him to perform those actions. Becky described to Mike how the system worked and then showed him how to enter, modify, and delete a test option she prepared. For security reasons, the special documentation for those functions would not be printed in the user manual itself, but would be retained in the IT department files.

Becky and Tom met again with the payroll group to show users how to enter the deduction authorizations for individual employees. Although the new payroll system was operational, the company still handled ESIP deductions manually. Using the ESIP server and another networked payroll PC, the payroll clerks were able to enter actual payroll data during a three-day test period. The built-in edit and validation features detected the errors that the team purposely inserted as test data and even identified several invalid authorizations that they had not noticed previously. The group produced printed reports and asked other payroll department members to review and verify the output.

Jane suggested that they could send a notice to all SWL employees to describe the new ESIP system, remind employees how to select options, and invite their questions or comments. Michael Jeremy, vice president of finance, agreed with her suggestion.

Up to that point, the company had made no final decision about the changeover method for the new system. Because the ESIP system replaced a series of manual processing steps, the main question was whether they should run the manual system in parallel operation for a specified period. Managers in the payroll, human resources, and accounting departments all wanted the new system operational as soon as possible, so Jane decided to use a direct cutover method. The cutover was scheduled for the first Friday in May, when the first weekly payroll in May was processed.

Starting on April 23, the IT team met again with each of the users and reviewed a final checklist. No problems appeared, and the system was ready to interface with the mainframe and handle live data in an operational environment. On Friday morning, May 4, the payroll

## CHAPTER CAPSTONE CASE:    SoftWear, Limited (continued)                    SWL

department ran the ESIP module that sent the processing commands to the payroll system. Later that morning, during the weekly processing cycle, the payroll package created a file with the extracted deductions and passed it back to the ESIP server.

With the ESIP system using real input data, IT department members visited each of the recently trained users to make sure they were experiencing no difficulties. They received good reports — users in the payroll and human resources departments seemed pleased with the new system. They were able to access the ESIP data, enter new deductions, and had no problems with screen output or printed reports.

The direct cutover to the ESIP system occurred without major problems. By the end of June, the system had completed nine weekly payroll cycles, produced all required reports and outputs, and properly handled the monthly transfer of funds to the credit union and the SWL stock purchase plan.

During the first part of July, the IT department conducted a post-implementation evaluation with a team that consisted of two people: Katie Barnes, a systems analyst who had not been involved in the ESIP system development, and Ben Mancuso, a member of the finance department designated by Michael Jeremy. The evaluation team reviewed system operations, conducted interviews, and asked users to complete a brief questionnaire. The results were favorable, and it appeared that users were very satisfied with the new ESIP system. When the evaluation was completed in mid-July, Ann Hon sent the e-mail message shown in Figure 11-48 to Michael Jeremy. The systems development effort for the ESIP system was completed successfully.

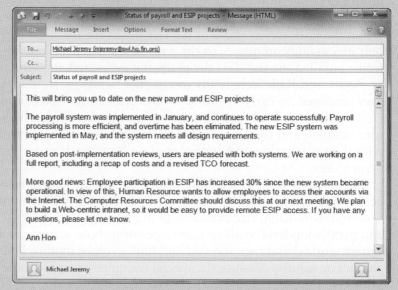

**FIGURE 11-48**   E-mail message from Ann Hon to Michael Jeremy regarding the payroll and ESIP systems.

### SWL Team Tasks

1. Rick has asked you to help him develop a recommendation for future software testing. One of his concerns is that in systems testing, it is virtually impossible to simulate every system transaction and function. Specifically, Rick wants you to suggest some guidelines that will produce the most reliable test results. He suggested that you should consider who should be involved in the testing, what types of transactions should be tested, and when the testing should be done. Based on what you already have learned about the ESIP system in earlier chapters, what would you recommend?

2. Rick also wants you to prepare a list of interview questions for users and design a brief questionnaire that measures the effectiveness of the new system. Develop the interview questions and questionnaire by following the guidelines suggested in this chapter and in Chapter 4, which discusses fact-finding techniques.

3. Rick is interested in using agile development methods for the next SWL project. He asked you to write a "Guide to Agile Methods" for other members of the IT team. The guide should be thorough, easy to understand, and should include your own research on the Internet.

## CHAPTER CAPSTONE CASE:   SoftWear, Limited (continued)                    SWL

4. You know that Jane was under pressure from SWL managers to get the ESIP system up and running. You also know that not everyone on the IT staff agreed with her decision to use a direct cutover method. What are some of the disadvantages of direct cutover? What other methods might have been used? What would you have done?

### Manage the SWL Project

You have been asked to manage SWL's new information system project. One of your most important activities will be to identify project tasks and determine when they will be performed. Before you begin, you should review the SWL case in this chapter. Then list and analyze the tasks, as follows:

**LIST THE TASKS** Start by listing and numbering at least ten tasks that the SWL team needs to perform to fulfill the objectives of this chapter. Your list can include SWL Team Tasks and any other tasks that are described in this chapter. For example, Task 3 might be to Identify training needs, and Task 6 might be to Develop training solutions.

**ANALYZE THE TASKS** Now study the tasks to determine the order in which they should be performed. First identify all concurrent tasks, which are not dependent on other tasks. In the example shown in Figure 11-49, Tasks 1, 2, 3, 4, and 5 are concurrent tasks, and could begin at the same time if resources were available.

Other tasks are called dependent tasks, because they cannot be performed until one or more earlier tasks have been completed. For each dependent task, you must identify specific tasks that need to be completed before this task can begin. For example, you would want to identify training needs before you could develop training solutions, so Task 6 cannot begin until Task 3 is completed, as Figure 11-49 shows.

**FIGURE 11-49**  Tasks 1, 2, 3, 4, and 5 are concurrent tasks that could be performed at the same time. Task 6 is a dependent task that cannot be performed until Task 3 has been completed.

Chapter 3 describes project management tools, techniques, and software. To learn more, you can use the Features section on your Student Study Tool CD-ROM, or visit the Management Information Systems CourseMate Web site at **www.cengagebrain.com** and locate the project management resources library for this book. On the Web, Microsoft offers demo versions, training, and tips for using Project 2010. You also can visit the OpenWorkbench.org site to learn more about this free, open-source software.

## Ready for a Challenge?

In additional to technical skills, IT professionals need critical thinking skills such as perception, organization, analysis, problem-solving, and decision-making. The Ready for a Challenge feature can help you learn, practice, and apply critical thinking skills that you can take to the workplace.

The IT team at Game Technology is working on implementation strategies for the new Customer Contact Care system ($C^3$). You are assigned to help with a structure chart, and to prepare a video tutorial about changeover methods. Before you start, you plan to review Chapter 11 of your textbook, including the Video Learning Session on structure charts.

First, you will work on the structure chart. You know that the system will rate contacts to identify the best sales prospects. The tasks are performed by a control module called Followup, which has three subordinate modules: List Contacts, Rate Contacts, and Produce Reports. Here are some details about the modules, data, and control couples:

| From | Data / Control Couple | To | Comments |
|---|---|---|---|
| Followup | Request Contact Data | List Contacts | |
| List Contacts | Contact Data | Followup | Loop |
| Followup | Contact Data | Rate Contacts | |
| Rate Contacts | Ratings | Followup | |
| Followup | Contact Data | Produce Reports | |
| List Contacts | End of File | Followup | Control Couple |

You also need to work on the video tutorial. To get you started, your team prepared the first three slides, shown here and on the next page.

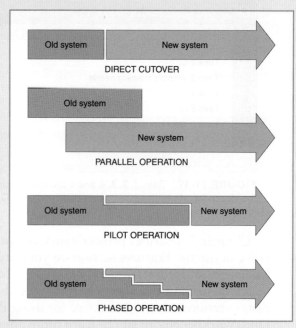

## Which Method Would You Choose?

Examples:

- Mission-critical corporate accounting system
- Franchise operation with 500 locations
- Records archive system for five-year old data

### Practice Tasks

Study the table carefully and decide how to handle each of the data or control couples. Also review the material on video tutorial development. Now complete these tasks:

A. Create a structure chart using the information shown in the table.
B. Using the examples in the chapter, prepare a text narrative for each of the slides shown. Also include notes for the video developer and the narrator.

After you complete the Practice Tasks, to check your work and view sample answers, visit the Management Information Systems CourseMate Web site at **www.cengagebrain.com**, navigate to the resources for this chapter, and locate Ready for a Challenge?.

### The Challenge

You just found out that the structure chart needs a change. The Produce Reports module will have a condition, and can send a Contact Rating to three of its own subordinate modules: High Potential, Medium Potential, and Low Potential.

Also, the team wants you to add a slide and narrative, similar to slide 3, with three additional examples.

### Challenge Tasks

A. Add the necessary changes to the structure chart.
B. Create the additional slide and narrative. Show at least one example where phased changeover would be suitable.

# PHASE 5

# SYSTEMS SUPPORT AND SECURITY

**DELIVERABLE**
An operational system that is properly maintained, supported, and secured

**SUPPORT**
Primary tools: Communications, CASE, and financial analysis tools

As the Dilbert cartoon suggests, users want prompt support, but they might not always receive it. Unhappy users do not bode well for system success. You will learn more about effective user support in this phase.

Systems support and security is the final phase in the systems development life cycle. In the previous phase, systems implementation, you delivered a functioning system. Now, you will support and maintain the system, handle security issues, protect the integrity of the system and its data, and be alert to any signs of obsolescence. The deliverable for this phase is an operational system that is properly maintained, supported, and secured.

# CHAPTER 12

# Securing and Supporting the System

**Chapter 12** describes systems support and security tasks that continue throughout the useful life of the system. In addition to user support, this chapter discusses maintenance, security, backup and disaster recovery, performance measurement, and system obsolescence.

## INTRODUCTION

### OBJECTIVES

*When you finish this chapter, you will be able to:*

- Explain the systems support and security phase
- Describe user support activities, including user training and help desks
- Define the four types of maintenance
- Explain various techniques for managing systems maintenance and support
- Describe techniques for measuring, managing, and planning system performance
- Explain risk management concepts
- Assess system security at six levels: physical security, network security, application security, file security, user security, and procedural security
- Describe backup and disaster recovery
- List factors indicating that a system has reached the end of its useful life
- Assess future challenges and opportunities for IT professionals
- Develop a strategic plan for career advancement and strong IT credentials

Managing systems support and security involves three main concerns: user expectations, system performance, and security requirements.

A systems analyst is like an internal consultant who provides guidance, support, and training. Successful systems often need the most support because users want to learn the features, try all the capabilities, and discover how the system can help them perform their tasks. In most organizations, more than half of all IT department effort goes into supporting existing systems.

This chapter begins with a discussion of systems support, including user training and help desks. You will study the four main types of maintenance: corrective, adaptive, perfective, and preventive. You also will learn how the IT group uses maintenance teams, configuration management, and maintenance releases, and you will examine system performance issues and maintenance tools. You will analyze the security system at each of the six security levels: physical security, network security, application security, file security, user security, and procedural security. You will also learn about data backup and recovery issues. Finally, you will learn how to recognize system obsolescence, and about some of the challenges and opportunities you are likely to face as an IT professional.

# CHAPTER INTRODUCTION CASE:  Mountain View College Bookstore

**Background:** Wendy Lee, manager of college services at Mountain View College, wants a new information system that will improve efficiency and customer service at the three college bookstores.

In this part of the case, Tina Allen (systems analyst) and David Conroe (student intern) are talking about operation, support, and security issues for the new system.

| | |
|---|---|
| **Participants:** | Tina and David |
| **Location:** | Tina's office, Friday afternoon, March 30, 2012 |
| **Project status:** | Tina and David successfully implemented the bookstore information system. Now they will discuss strategies for supporting, maintaining, and securing the new system. |
| **Discussion topics:** | Support activities, training, maintenance, techniques for managing systems operation, enhancing system performance and security, and detecting system obsolescence |

**Tina:** Well, we finally made it. The system is up and running and the users seem satisfied. Now we focus on supporting the system, ensuring that it delivers its full potential, and is properly secured and protected.

**David:** *How do we do that?*

**Tina:** First, we need to set up specific procedures for handling system support and maintenance. We'll set up a help desk that will offer user training, answer technical questions, and enhance user productivity.

**David:** *Sounds good. I'll set up a training package for new users who missed the initial training sessions.*

**Tina:** That's fine. You also should learn about the four types of maintenance. Users typically ask for help that requires corrective maintenance to fix problems or adaptive maintenance to add new features. As IT staff, we will be responsible for perfective maintenance, which makes the system more efficient, and preventive maintenance to avoid problems.

**David:** *Anything else for us to do?*

**Tina:** Yes, we'll need a system for managing maintenance requests from users. Also, we'll need to handle configuration management, maintenance releases, and version control. These tools will help us keep the system current and reduce unnecessary maintenance costs.

**David:** *What about keeping tabs on system performance issues?*

**Tina:** That's important, along with capacity planning to be sure the system can handle future growth.

**David:** *What about system security?*

**Tina:** Good question. We'll look at physical security, network security, application security, file security, user security, and procedural security. We'll also look at backup and disaster recovery issues.

**David:** *Sounds like we'll be busy for quite a while.*

**Tina:** Well, that depends on the system itself and user expectations. Every system has a useful life, including this one. We'll try to get a good return on our investment, but we'll also watch for signs of obsolescence. Here are some tasks we can work on:

**FIGURE 12-1**   Typical systems support and security task list.

## OVERVIEW

The systems support and security phase begins when a system becomes operational and continues until the system reaches the end of its useful life. Throughout the development process, the objective has been to create an information system that is efficient, easy to use, and affordable. After delivering the system, the IT team focuses on support and maintenance tasks.

The first part of this chapter covers four main topics. You will learn how to provide user support, maintain the system, manage the maintenance process, and handle system performance issues.

## USER SUPPORT

Companies provide user support in many forms, including user training and a help desk to provide technical support and assistance.

### User Training

In Chapter 11, you learned about initial training that is performed when a new system is introduced. Additionally, new employees must be trained on the company's information systems. For example, a firm that produces electronic assemblies must train its new employees, as shown in Figure 12-2.

If significant changes take place in the existing system or if a new version is released, the IT department might develop a **user training package**. Depending on the nature of the changes, the package could include online support via e-mail, a special Web site, a revision to the user guide, a training manual supplement, or formal training sessions. Training users about system changes is similar to initial training. The main objective is to show users how the system can help them perform their jobs.

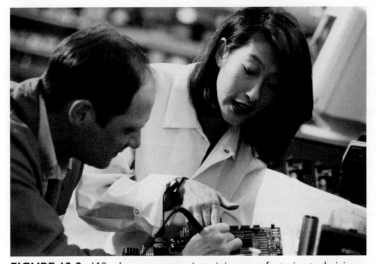

**FIGURE 12-2** Whether a company is training manufacturing technicians, data entry personnel, or customer service representatives, employees need high-quality instruction to perform their jobs efficiently.

### Help Desks

As systems and data structures become more complex, users need constant support and guidance. To make data more accessible and to empower users, many IT departments create help desks. A **help desk** is a centralized resource staffed by IT professionals who provide users with the support they need to do their jobs. A help desk has three main objectives: Show people how to use system resources more effectively, provide answers to technical or operational questions, and make users more productive by teaching them how to meet their own information needs. A help desk often is called an **information center** (IC) because it is the first place users turn when they need information or assistance.

A help desk does not replace traditional IT maintenance and support activities. Instead, help desks enhance productivity and improve utilization of a company's information resources.

Help desk representatives need strong interpersonal and technical skills plus a solid understanding of the business, because they interact with users in many departments.

**ON THE WEB**

To learn more about help desks, visit the Management Information Systems CourseMate Web site at **www.cengagebrain.com**, navigate to **On the Web Links** for this chapter, and locate the Help Desk link.

A help desk should document carefully all inquiries, support tasks, and activity levels. The information can identify trends and common problems and can help build a technical support knowledge base.

A help desk can boost its productivity by using **remote control software**, which allows IT staff to take over a user's workstation and provide support and troubleshooting. Popular examples of remote control software include Microsoft System Center Configuration Manager and DameWare Mini Remote Control.

During a typical day, the help desk staff member shown in Figure 12-3 might have to perform the following tasks:

**FIGURE 12-3** A help desk, also called an information center (IC), provides guidance and assistance to system users. When a user contacts a help desk, the response should be prompt and effective.

- Show a user how to create a data query or report that displays specific business information

- Resolve network access or password problems

- Demonstrate an advanced feature of a system or a commercial package

- Help a user recover damaged data

- Offer tips for better operation

- Explain an undocumented software feature

- Show a user how to use Web conferencing

- Explain how to access the company's intranet or the Internet

- Assist a user in developing a simple database to track time spent on various projects

- Answer questions about software licensing and upgrades

- Provide information about system specifications and the cost of new hardware or software

- Recommend a system solution that integrates data from different locations to solve a business problem

- Provide hardware support by installing or reconfiguring devices such as scanners, printers, network cards, wireless devices, optical drives, backup devices, and multimedia systems

- Show users how to maintain data consistency and integrity among a desktop computer, a notebook computer, and a handheld computer or smart phone

- Troubleshoot software issues via remote control utilities

In addition to functioning as a valuable link between IT staff and users, the help desk is a central contact point for all IT maintenance activities. The help desk is where users report system problems, ask for maintenance, or submit new systems requests. A help desk can utilize many types of automated support, just as outside vendors do, including e-mail responses, on-demand fax capability, an online knowledge base, frequently asked questions (FAQs), discussion groups, bulletin boards, and automated voice mail. Many vendors now provide a live chat feature for online visitors. For example, as shown in Figure 12-4 on the next page, Dell invites its customers to chat interactively with a tech support person.

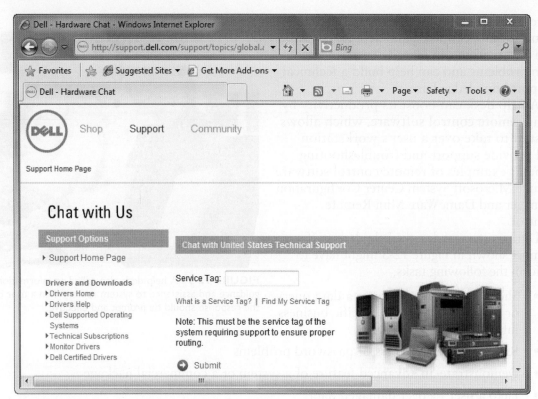

**FIGURE 12-4**   On its support site, Dell offers a variety of technical information and support options for customers.

### Outsourcing Issues

As you learned in Chapter 7, many firms outsource various aspects of application development. This trend also includes outsourcing IT support and help desks. As with most business decisions, outsourcing has pros and cons. Typically, the main reason for outsourcing is cost reduction. Offshore call centers can trim expenses and free up valuable human resources for product development.

However, firms have learned that if tech support quality goes down, customers are likely to notice, and might shop elsewhere. Critical factors might include phone wait times, support staff performance, and online support tools. The real question is whether a company can achieve the desired savings without endangering its reputation and customer base. Risks can be limited, but only if a firm takes an active role in managing and monitoring support quality and consistency.

## MAINTENANCE TASKS

The systems support and security phase is an important component of TCO (total cost of ownership) because ongoing maintenance expenses can determine the economic life of a system.

Figure 12-5 shows a typical pattern of operational and maintenance expenses during the useful life of a system. **Operational costs** include items such as supplies, equipment rental, and software leases. Notice that the lower area shown in Figure 12-5 represents fixed operational expenses, while the upper area represents maintenance expenses.

**Maintenance expenses** vary significantly during the system's operational life and include spending to support maintenance activities. **Maintenance activities** include changing programs, procedures, or documentation to ensure correct system performance; adapting the system to changing requirements; and making the system operate more efficiently. Those needs are met by corrective, adaptive, perfective, and preventive maintenance.

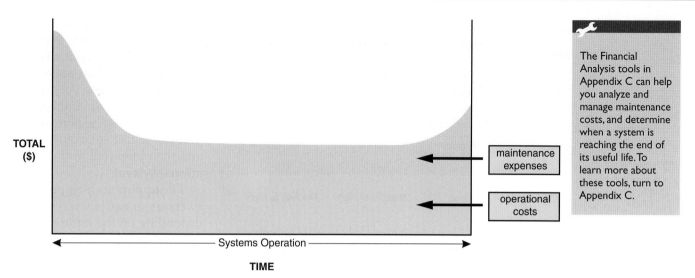

The Financial Analysis tools in Appendix C can help you analyze and manage maintenance costs, and determine when a system is reaching the end of its useful life. To learn more about these tools, turn to Appendix C.

**FIGURE 12-5**  The total cost of operating an information system includes operational and maintenance costs. Operational costs (green) are relatively constant, while maintenance expenses (purple) vary over time.

Although some overlap exists, four types of maintenance tasks can be identified, as shown by the examples in Figure 12-6. **Corrective maintenance** is performed to fix errors, **adaptive maintenance** adds new capability and enhancements, **perfective maintenance** improves efficiency, and **preventive maintenance** reduces the possibility of future system failure. Some analysts use the term *maintenance* to describe only corrective maintenance that fixes problems. It is helpful, however, to view the maintenance concept more broadly and identify the different types of tasks.

Maintenance expenses usually are high when a system is implemented because problems must be detected, investigated, and resolved by corrective maintenance. Once the system becomes stable, costs usually remain low and involve minor adaptive maintenance. Eventually, both adaptive and perfective maintenance activities increase in a dynamic business environment.

Near the end of a system's useful life, adaptive and corrective maintenance expenses increase rapidly, but perfective maintenance typically decreases when it becomes clear that the company plans to replace the system. Figure 12-7 on the next page shows the typical patterns for each of the four classifications of maintenance activities over a system's life span.

**Examples of Maintenance Tasks**

**Corrective Maintenance**
- Diagnose and fix logic errors
- Replace defective network cabling
- Restore proper configuration settings
- Debug program code
- Update drivers
- Install software patch

**Adaptive Maintenance**
- Add online capability
- Create new reports
- Add new data entry field to input screen
- Install links to Web site
- Create employee portal

**Perfective Maintenance**
- Install additional memory
- Write macros to handle repetitive tasks
- Compress system files
- Optimize user desktop settings
- Develop library for code reuse
- Install more powerful network server

**Preventive Maintenance**
- Install new antivirus software
- Develop standard backup schedule
- Implement regular defragmentation process
- Analyze problem report for patterns
- Tighten all cable connections

**FIGURE 12-6**  Corrective maintenance fixes errors and problems. Adaptive maintenance provides enhancements to a system. Perfective maintenance improves a system's efficiency, reliability, or maintainability. Preventive maintenance avoids future problems.

## Corrective Maintenance

Corrective maintenance diagnoses and corrects errors in an operational system. To avoid introducing new problems, all maintenance work requires careful analysis before making changes. The best maintenance approach is a scaled-down version of the SDLC itself, where investigation, analysis, design, and testing are performed before implementing

| | Immediately After Implementation | Early Operational Life | Middle Operational Life | Later Operational Life |
|---|---|---|---|---|
| Corrective Maintenance | High | Low | Low | High |
| Adaptive Maintenance (Minor Enhancements) | None | Medium | Medium | Medium |
| Adaptive Maintenance (Major Enhancements) | None | None | Medium to High | Medium to High |
| Perfective Maintenance | Low | Low to Medium | Medium | Low |
| Preventive Maintenance | Low | Medium | Medium | Low |

**FIGURE 12-7**  Information systems maintenance depends on the type of maintenance and the age of the system.

any solution. Recall that in Chapter 11 you learned about the difference between a test environment and an operational environment. Any maintenance work that could affect the system must be performed first in the test environment, and then migrated to the operational system.

IT support staff respond to errors in various ways, depending on the nature and severity of the problem. Most organizations have standard procedures for minor errors, such as an incorrect report title or an improper format for a data element. In a typical procedure, a user submits a systems request that is evaluated, prioritized, and scheduled by the system administrator or the systems review committee. If the request is approved, the maintenance team designs, tests, documents, and implements a solution.

As you learned in Chapter 2, many organizations use a standard online form for systems requests. In smaller firms, the process might be an informal e-mail message. For more serious situations, such as incorrect report totals or inconsistent data, a user submits a systems request with supporting evidence. Those requests receive a high priority and a maintenance team begins work on the problem immediately.

The worst-case situation is a system failure. If an emergency occurs, the maintenance team bypasses the initial steps and tries to correct the problem immediately. This often requires a **patch**, which is a specially written software module that provides temporary repairs so operations can resume. Meanwhile, a written systems request is prepared by a user or a member of the IT department and added to the maintenance log. When the system is operational again, the maintenance team determines the cause, analyzes the problem, and designs a permanent solution. The IT response team updates the test data files, thoroughly tests the system, and prepares full documentation. Regardless of how the priorities are set, a standard ranking method can be helpful. For example, Figure 12-8 shows a three-level framework for IT support potential impact.

The process of managing system support is described in more detail on page 578, including an overview of maintenance tasks and a procedural flowchart, which is shown in Figure 12-11 on page 581.

### Adaptive Maintenance

Adaptive maintenance adds enhancements to an operational system and makes the system easier to use. An **enhancement** is a new feature or

| PRIORITY | IMPACT | TIMEFRAME |
|---|---|---|
| **Level 1** | Significant impact on IT operations, security, or business activity that requires immediate attention. | Implement patch as soon as possible. |
| **Level 2** | Some impact on IT operations, security, or business activity. Requires prompt attention, but operations can continue. | Patch as necessary and begin implementation prior to next release. |
| **Level 3** | Little or no impact on current IT operations, security, or business activity. | Implement in the next release. |

**FIGURE 12-8**  This three-level ranking framework for IT support considers potential impact and response urgency.

capability. The need for adaptive maintenance usually arises from business environment changes such as new products or services, new manufacturing technology, or support for a new Web-based operation.

The procedure for minor adaptive maintenance is similar to routine corrective maintenance. A user submits a systems request that is evaluated and prioritized by the systems review committee. A maintenance team then analyzes, designs, tests, and implements the enhancement. Although the procedures for the two types of maintenance are alike, adaptive maintenance requires more IT department resources than minor corrective maintenance.

A major adaptive maintenance project is like a small-scale SDLC project because the development procedure is similar. Adaptive maintenance can be more difficult than new systems development because the enhancements must work within the constraints of an existing system.

## Perfective Maintenance

Perfective maintenance involves changing an operational system to make it more efficient, reliable, or maintainable. Requests for corrective and adaptive maintenance normally come from users, while the IT department usually initiates perfective maintenance.

During system operation, changes in user activity or data patterns can cause a decline in efficiency, and perfective maintenance might be needed to restore performance. When users are concerned about performance, you should determine if a perfective maintenance project could improve response time and system efficiency.

Perfective maintenance also can improve system reliability. For example, input problems might cause a program to terminate abnormally. By modifying the data entry process, you can highlight errors and notify the users that they must enter proper data. When a system is easier to maintain, support is less costly and less risky. In many cases, you can simplify a complex program to improve maintainability.

In many organizations, perfective maintenance is not performed frequently enough. Companies with limited resources often consider new systems development, adaptive maintenance, and corrective maintenance more important than perfective maintenance. Managers and users constantly request new projects, so few resources are available for perfective maintenance work. As a practical matter, perfective maintenance can be performed as part of another project. For example, if a new function must be added to a program, you can include perfective maintenance in the adaptive maintenance project.

Perfective maintenance usually is cost effective during the middle of the system's operational life. Early in systems operation, perfective maintenance usually is not needed. Later, perfective maintenance might be necessary, but have a high cost. Perfective maintenance is less important if the company plans to discontinue the system.

When performing perfective maintenance, analysts often use a technique called software reengineering. **Software reengineering** uses analytical techniques to identify potential quality and performance improvements in an information system. In that sense, software reengineering is similar to business process reengineering, which seeks to simplify operations, reduce costs, and improve quality — as you learned in Chapter 1.

Programs that need a large number of maintenance changes usually are good candidates for reengineering. The more a program changes, the more likely it is to become inefficient and difficult to maintain. Detailed records of maintenance work can identify systems with a history of frequent corrective, adaptive, or perfective maintenance.

 **ON THE WEB**

To learn more about software reengineering, visit the Management Information Systems CourseMate Web site at **www. cengagebrain.com**, navigate to **On the Web Links** for this chapter, and locate the Software Reengineering link.

## Preventive Maintenance

To avoid problems, preventive maintenance requires analysis of areas where trouble is likely to occur. Like perfective maintenance, the IT department normally initiates preventive

**FIGURE 12-9**   Regardless of the type of system, high-quality maintenance must be performed by trained professionals.

maintenance. Preventive maintenance often results in increased user satisfaction, decreased downtime, and reduced TCO. Preventive maintenance competes for IT resources along with other projects, and sometimes does not receive the high priority that it deserves.

Regardless of the type of maintenance, computer systems must be supported by trained professionals, just as the aircraft shown in Figure 12-9 must be serviced by skilled technicians. In both cases, the quality of the maintenance will directly affect the organization's success.

## CASE IN POINT 12.1:  OUTBACK OUTSOURCING, INC.

You are a systems analyst at Outback Outsourcing, a firm that handles payroll processing for many large companies. Outback Outsourcing uses a combination of payroll package programs and in-house developed software to deliver custom-made payroll solutions for its clients. Lately, users have flooded you with requests for more new features and Web-based capability to meet customer expectations. Your boss, the IT manager, comes to you with a question. She wants to know when to stop trying to enhance the old software and develop a totally new version better suited to the new marketplace. How would you answer her?

## MAINTENANCE MANAGEMENT

System maintenance requires effective management, quality assurance, and cost control. To achieve these goals, companies use various strategies, such as a maintenance team, a maintenance management program, a configuration management process, and a maintenance release procedure. In addition, firms use version control and baselines to track system releases and analyze the system's life cycle. These concepts are described in the following sections.

### The Maintenance Team

A **maintenance team** includes a system administrator and one or more systems analysts and programmers. The system administrator should have solid technical expertise, and experience in troubleshooting and configuring operating systems and hardware. Successful analysts need a strong IT background, solid analytical abilities, good communication skills, and an overall understanding of business operations.

**SYSTEM ADMINISTRATOR**   A **system administrator** manages computer and network systems. A system administrator must work well under pressure, have good organizational and communication skills, and be able to understand and resolve complex issues in a limited time frame. In most organizations, a system administrator has primary responsibility for the operation, configuration, and security of one or more systems. The system administrator is responsible for routine maintenance, and usually is authorized to take preventive action to avoid an immediate emergency, such as a server crash, network outage, security incident, or hardware failure.

Systems administration is a vital function, and various professional associations, such as SAGE, which is shown in Figure 12-10, offer a wide variety of technical information and support for system administrators. Notice that SAGE members subscribe to a code of ethics that includes professionalism, integrity, privacy, and social responsibility, among other topics.

## THE SYSTEM ADMINISTRATORS' CODE OF ETHICS

*We as professional System Administrators do hereby commit ourselves to the highest standards of ethical and professional conduct, and agree to be guided by this code of ethics, and encourage every System Administrator to do the same.*

PROFESSIONALISM I will maintain professional conduct in the workplace and will not allow personal feelings or beliefs to cause me to treat people unfairly or unprofessionally.

PERSONAL INTEGRITY I will be honest in my professional dealings and forthcoming about my competence and the impact of my mistakes. I will seek assistance from others when required.

I will avoid conflicts of interest and biases whenever possible. When my advice is sought, if I have a conflict of interest or bias, I will declare it if appropriate, and recuse myself if necessary.

PRIVACY I will access private information on computer systems only when it is necessary in the course of my technical duties. I will maintain and protect the confidentiality of any information to which I may have access, regardless of the method by which I came into knowledge of it.

LAWS AND POLICIES I will educate myself and others on relevant laws, regulations, and policies regarding the performance of my duties.

COMMUNICATION I will communicate with management, users, and colleagues about computer matters of mutual interest. I will strive to listen to and understand the needs of all parties.

SYSTEM INTEGRITY I will strive to ensure the necessary integrity, reliability, and availability of the systems for which I am responsible.

I will design and maintain each system in a manner to support the purpose of the system to the organization.

EDUCATION I will continue to update and enhance my technical knowledge and other work-related skills. I will share my knowledge and experience with others.

RESPONSIBILITY TO COMPUTING COMMUNITY I will cooperate with the larger computing community to maintain the integrity of network and computing resources.

SOCIAL RESPONSIBILITY As an informed professional, I will encourage the writing and adoption of relevant policies and laws consistent with these ethical principles.

ETHICAL RESPONSIBILITY I will strive to build and maintain a safe, healthy, and productive workplace.

I will do my best to make decisions consistent with the safety, privacy, and well-being of my community and the public, and to disclose promptly factors that might pose unexamined risks or dangers.

I will accept and offer honest criticism of technical work as appropriate and will credit properly the contributions of others.

I will lead by example, maintaining a high ethical standard and degree of professionalism in the performance of all my duties. I will support colleagues and co-workers in following this code of ethics.

**FIGURE 12-10**  SAGE seeks to establish standards of professional excellence, improve the technical skills of its members, and promote a comprehensive code of ethics.

**SYSTEMS ANALYSTS** Systems analysts assigned to a maintenance team are like skilled detectives who investigate and rapidly locate the source of a problem by using analysis and synthesis skills. *Analysis* means examining the whole in order to learn about the individual elements, while *synthesis* involves studying the parts to understand the overall system. In addition to strong technical skills, an analyst must have a solid grasp of business operations and functions. Analysts also need effective interpersonal and communications skills and they must be creative, energetic, and eager for new knowledge.

**PROGRAMMERS** In a small organization, a programmer might be expected to handle a wide variety of tasks, but in larger firms, programming work tends to be more specialized. For example, typical job titles include an **applications programmer**, who works on new systems development and maintenance; a **systems programmer**, who concentrates on operating system software and utilities; and a **database programmer**, who focuses on creating and supporting large-scale database systems. Many IT departments also use a job title of **programmer/analyst** to designate positions that require a combination of systems analysis and programming skills.

**ORGANIZATIONAL ISSUES** IT managers often divide systems analysts and programmers into two groups: One group performs new system development, and the other group handles maintenance. Some organizations use a more flexible approach and assign IT staff members to various projects as they occur. By integrating development and support work, the people developing the system assume responsibility for maintaining it. Because the team is familiar with the project, additional training or expense is unnecessary, and members are likely to have a sense of ownership from the onset.

Unfortunately, many analysts feel that maintenance is less interesting and creative than developing new systems. In addition, an analyst might find it challenging to troubleshoot and support someone else's work that might have been poorly documented and organized.

Some organizations that have separate maintenance and new systems groups rotate people from one assignment to the other. When analysts learn different skills, the organization is more versatile and people can shift to meet changing business needs. For instance, systems analysts working on maintenance projects learn why it is important to design easily maintainable systems. Similarly, analysts working on new systems get a better appreciation of the development process and the design compromises necessary to meet business objectives.

One disadvantage of rotation is that it increases overhead because time is lost when people move from one job to another. When systems analysts constantly shift between maintenance and new development, they have less opportunity to become highly skilled at any one job.

Newly hired and recently promoted IT staff members often are assigned to maintenance projects because their managers believe that the opportunity to study existing systems and documentation is a valuable experience. In addition, the mini-SDLC used in many adaptive maintenance projects is good training for the full-scale systems development life cycle. For a new systems analyst, however, maintenance work might be more difficult than systems development, and it might make sense to assign a new person to a development team where experienced analysts are available to provide training and guidance.

## CASE IN POINT 12.2:  BRIGHTSIDE INSURANCE, INC.

As IT manager at Brightside Insurance Company, you organized your IT staff into two separate groups — one team for maintenance projects and the other team for new systems work. That arrangement worked well in your last position at another company. Brightside, however, previously made systems assignments with no particular pattern.

At first, the systems analysts in your group did not comment about the team approach. Now, several of your best analysts have indicated that they enjoyed the mix of work and would not want to be assigned to a maintenance team. Before a problem develops, you have decided to rethink your organizational strategy. Should you go back to the way things were done previously at Brightside? Why or why not? Do other options exist? What are they?

### Maintenance Requests

Typically, maintenance requests involve a series of steps, as shown in Figure 12-11. After a user submits a request, a system administrator determines whether immediate action is needed and whether the request is under a prescribed cost limit. In nonemergency requests that exceed the cost limit, a systems review committee assesses the request and either approves it, with a priority, or rejects it. The system administrator notifies affected users of the outcome.

Users submit most requests for corrective and adaptive maintenance when the system is not performing properly, or if they want new features. IT staff members usually initiate requests for perfective and preventive maintenance. To keep a complete maintenance log, all work must be covered by a specific request that users submit in writing or by e-mail.

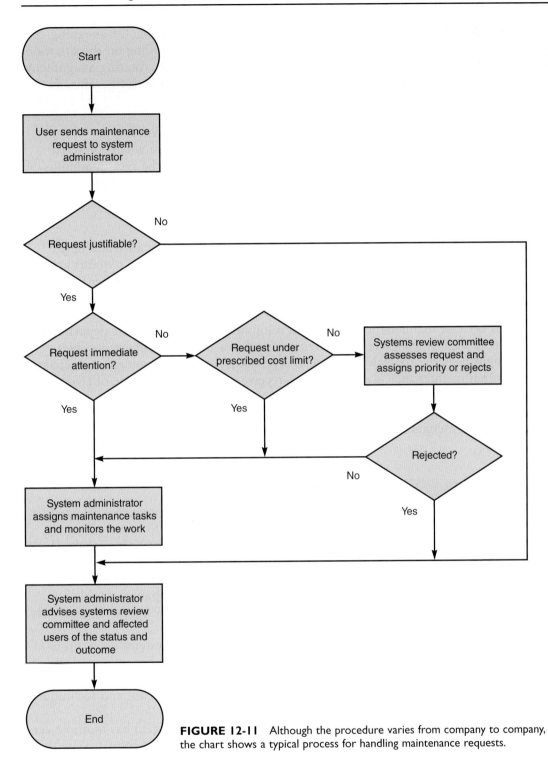

**FIGURE 12-11**  Although the procedure varies from company to company, the chart shows a typical process for handling maintenance requests.

**INITIAL DETERMINATION**  When a user submits a maintenance request, the system administrator makes an initial determination. If the request is justifiable and involves a severe problem that requires immediate attention, the system administrator takes action at once. In justifiable, but noncritical, situations, the administrator determines whether the request can be performed within a preauthorized cost level. If so, he or she assigns the maintenance tasks and monitors the work.

**THE SYSTEMS REVIEW COMMITTEE**  When a request exceeds a predetermined cost level or involves a major configuration change, the systems review committee either approves it and assigns a priority, or rejects it.

**TASK COMPLETION** The system administrator usually is responsible for assigning maintenance tasks to individuals or to a maintenance team. Depending on the situation and the company's policy, the system administrator might consider rotating assignments among the IT staff or limiting maintenance tasks to certain individuals or teams, as explained in the previous section.

**USER NOTIFICATION** Users who initiate maintenance requests expect a prompt response, especially if the situation directly affects their work. Even when corrective action cannot occur immediately, users appreciate feedback from the system administrator and should be kept informed of any decisions or actions that could affect them.

## Establishing Priorities

**ON THE WEB**

To learn more about configuration management, visit the Management Information Systems CourseMate Web site at **www.cengagebrain.com**, navigate to **On the Web Links** for this chapter, and locate the Configuration Management link.

In many companies, the systems review committee separates maintenance and new development requests when setting priorities. In other organizations, all requests are considered together, and the most important project gets top priority, whether it is maintenance or new development.

Some IT managers believe that evaluating all projects together leads to the best possible decisions because maintenance and new development require similar IT department resources. In IT departments where maintenance and new development are not integrated, it might be better to evaluate requests separately. Another advantage of a separate approach is that maintenance is more likely to receive a proportional share of IT department resources.

The most important objective is to have a procedure that balances new development and necessary maintenance work to provide the best support for business requirements and priorities.

## Configuration Management

Configuration management (CM), sometimes referred to as **change control (CC)**, is a process for controlling changes in system requirements during software development. Configuration management also is an important tool for managing system changes and costs after a system becomes operational. Most companies establish a specific process that describes how system changes must be requested and documented.

As enterprise-wide information systems grow more complex, configuration management becomes critical. Industry standards have emerged, and many vendors offer configuration management software and techniques, as shown in Figure 12-12.

CM is especially important if a system has multiple versions that run in different hardware and software environments. Configuration management also helps to organize and handle documentation. An operational system has extensive documentation that covers development, modification, and maintenance for all versions of the installed system. Most documentation material, including the initial systems request, project management data, end-of-phase reports, data dictionary, and the IT operations and user manuals, is stored in the IT department.

Keeping track of all documentation and ensuring that updates are distributed properly are important aspects of configuration management.

**FIGURE 12-12** CM Crossroads provides a source of information and resources for configuration management professionals.

## Maintenance Releases

Keeping track of maintenance changes and updates can be difficult, especially for a complex system. When a **maintenance release methodology** is used, all noncritical changes are held until they can be implemented at the same time. Each change is documented and installed as a new version of the system called a **maintenance release**.

For an in-house developed system, the time between releases usually depends on the level of maintenance activity. A new release to correct a critical error, however, might be implemented immediately rather than saved for the next scheduled release.

When a release method is used, a numbering pattern distinguishes the different releases. In a typical system, the initial version of the system is 1.0, and the release that includes the first set of maintenance changes is version 1.1. A change, for example, from version 1.4 to 1.5 indicates relatively minor enhancements, while whole number changes, such as from version 1.0 to 2.0 or from version 3.4 to 4.0, indicate a significant upgrade.

The release methodology offers several advantages, especially if two teams perform maintenance work on the same system. When a release methodology is used, all changes are tested together before a new system version is released. This approach results in fewer versions, less expense, and less interruption for users. Using a release methodology also reduces the documentation burden, because all changes are coordinated and become effective simultaneously.

A release methodology also has some potential disadvantages. Users expect a rapid response to their problems and requests, but with a release methodology, new features or upgrades are available less often. Even when changes would improve system efficiency or user productivity, the potential savings must wait until the next release, which might increase operational costs.

Commercial software suppliers also provide maintenance releases, often called **service packs**, as shown in Figure 12-13. As Microsoft explains, a service pack contains all the fixes and enhancements that have been made available since the last program version or service pack.

**FIGURE 12-13** A Microsoft service pack provides access to up-to-date drivers, tools, security patches, and customer-requested product changes.

## Version Control

**Version control** is the process of tracking system releases, or versions. When a new version of a system is installed, the prior release is **archived**, or stored. If a new version causes a system to fail, a company can reinstall the prior version to restore operations. In addition to tracking system versions, the IT staff is responsible for configuring systems that have several modules at various release stages. For example, an accounting system might have a one-year old accounts receivable module that must interface with a brand-new payroll module.

As systems grow more complex, version control becomes an essential part of system documentation. In addition to in-house version control procedures, companies can purchase software from vendors such as Serena, as shown in Figure 12-14 on the next page.

**ON THE WEB**

To learn more about version control, visit the Management Information Systems CourseMate Web site at **www. cengagebrain.com**, navigate to **On the Web Links** for this chapter, and locate the Version Control link.

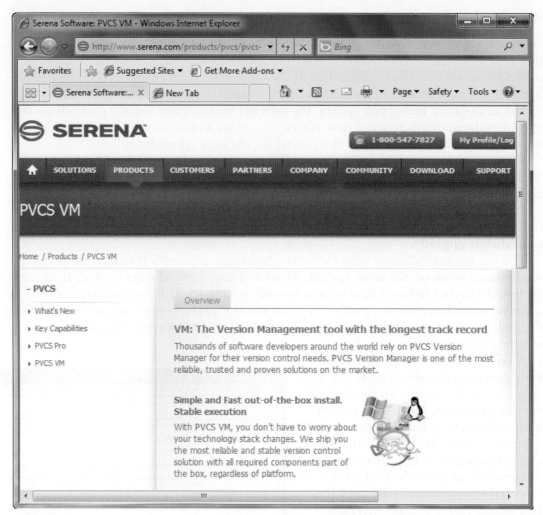

**FIGURE 12-14**  Serena offers software called PVCS Version Manager that developers can use to manage projects.

## Baselines

A **baseline** is a formal reference point that measures system characteristics at a specific time. Systems analysts use baselines as yardsticks to document features and performance during the systems development process. The three types of baselines are functional, allocated, and product.

The **functional baseline** is the configuration of the system documented at the beginning of the project. It consists of all the necessary system requirements and design constraints.

The **allocated baseline** documents the system at the end of the design phase and identifies any changes since the functional baseline. The allocated baseline includes testing and verification of all system requirements and features.

The **product baseline** describes the system at the beginning of system operation. The product baseline incorporates any changes made since the allocated baseline and includes the results of performance and acceptance tests for the operational system.

## SYSTEM PERFORMANCE MANAGEMENT

Years ago, when most firms used a central computer for processing data, it was relatively simple to manage a system and measure its efficiency. Today, companies use complex networks and client/server systems to support business needs. A user at a client workstation often interacts with an information system that depends on other clients, servers, networks, and data located throughout the company. Rather than a single computer, it is the integration of all those components that determines the system's capability and performance. In many situations, IT managers use automated software and CASE tools to manage complex systems.

To ensure satisfactory support for business operations, the IT department must manage system faults and interruptions, measure system performance and workload, and anticipate future needs. The following sections discuss these topics.

## Fault Management

No matter how well it is designed, every system will experience some problems, such as hardware failures, software errors, user mistakes, and power outages. A system administrator must detect and resolve operational problems as quickly as possible. That task, often called **fault management**, includes monitoring the system for signs of trouble, logging all system failures, diagnosing the problem, and applying corrective action.

The more complex the system, the more difficult it can be to analyze symptoms and isolate a cause. In addition to addressing the immediate problem, it is important to evaluate performance patterns and trends. Windows 7 and Vista include a built-in fault management feature called Resource Monitor, which is shown in Figure 12-15. Resource Monitor can evaluate CPU, memory, disk, and network activity in real time, and save the data in a log file. In addition to automated notification, fault management software can identify underlying causes, speed up response time, and reduce service outages.

**FIGURE 12-15** Windows Resource Monitor displays CPU, memory, disk, and network activity in real time.

Although system administrators must deal with system faults and interruptions as they arise, the best strategy is to prevent problems by monitoring system performance and workload.

## Performance and Workload Measurement

In e-business, slow performance can be as devastating as no performance at all. Network delays and application bottlenecks affect customer satisfaction, user productivity, and business results. In fact, many IT managers believe that network delays do more damage than actual stoppages, because they occur more frequently and are difficult to predict, detect, and prevent. Customers expect reliable, fast response 24 hours a day, seven days a week. To support that level of service, companies use performance management software, such as Cisco Network Application Performance Analysis (NAPA), which is shown in Figure 12-16 on the next page.

To measure system performance, many firms use **benchmark testing**, which uses a set of standard tests to evaluate system performance and capacity. In addition to benchmark testing, performance measurements, called **metrics**, can monitor the number of transactions processed in a given time period, the number of records accessed, and the volume of online data. Network performance metrics include response time, bandwidth, throughput, and turnaround time, among others.

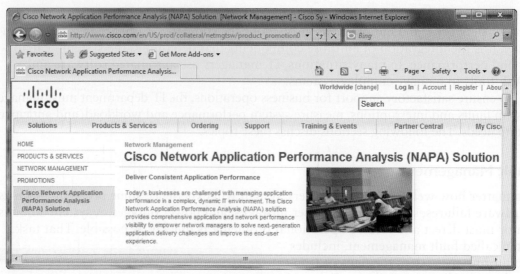

**FIGURE 12-16**   Network managers can use Cisco's NAPA to monitor performance and improve the end-user experience.

**RESPONSE TIME** Response time is the overall time between a request for system activity and the delivery of the response. In the typical online environment, response time is measured from the instant the user presses the ENTER key or clicks a mouse button until the requested screen display appears or printed output is ready. Response time is affected by the system design, capabilities, and processing methods. If the request involves network or Internet access, response time is affected by data communication factors.

Online users expect an immediate response, and they are frustrated by any apparent lag or delay. Of all performance measurements, response time is the one that users notice and complain about most.

**BANDWIDTH AND THROUGHPUT** Bandwidth and throughput are closely related terms, and many analysts use them interchangeably. **Bandwidth** describes the amount of data that the system can transfer in a fixed time period. Bandwidth requirements are expressed in bits per second. Depending on the system, you might measure bandwidth in **Kbps (kilobits per second)**, **Mbps (megabits per second)**, or **Gbps (gigabits per second)**. Analyzing bandwidth is similar to forecasting the hourly number of vehicles that will use a highway in order to determine the number of lanes required.

**Throughput** measures actual system performance under specific circumstances and is affected by network loads and hardware efficiency. Throughput, like bandwidth, is expressed as a data transfer rate, such as Kbps, Mbps, or Gbps. Just as traffic jams delay highway traffic, throughput limitations can slow system performance and response time. That is especially true with graphics-intensive systems and Web-based systems that are subject to Internet-related conditions.

In addition to the performance metrics explained in the previous section, system administrators measure many other performance characteristics. Although no standard set of metrics exists, several typical examples are:

- Arrivals — The number of items that appear on a device during a given observation time.
- Busy — The time that a given resource is unavailable.
- Completions — The number of arrivals that are processed during a given observation period.
- Queue length — The number of requests pending for a service.
- Service time — The time it takes to process a given task once it reaches the front of the queue.

- Think time — The time it takes an application user to issue another request.

- Utilization — How much of a given resource was required to complete a task.

- Wait time — The time that requests must wait for a resource to become available.

The Computer Measurement Group (CMG®) maintains a site, shown in Figure 12-17, that provides support and assistance for IT professionals concerned with performance evaluation and capacity planning.

**FIGURE 12-17**  The Computer Measurement Group is a nonprofit organization that primarily is concerned with performance evaluation and capacity management.

**TURNAROUND TIME** **Turnaround time** applies to centralized batch processing operations, such as customer billing or credit card statement processing. Turnaround time measures the time between submitting a request for information and the fulfillment of the request. Turnaround time also can be used to measure the quality of IT support or services by measuring the time from a user request for help to the resolution of the problem.

The IT department often measures response time, bandwidth, throughput, and turnaround time to evaluate system performance both before and after changes to the system or business information requirements. Performance data also is used for cost-benefit analyses of proposed maintenance and to evaluate systems that are nearing the end of their economically useful lives.

Finally, management uses current performance and workload data as input for the capacity planning process.

## Capacity Planning

**Capacity planning** is a process that monitors current activity and performance levels, anticipates future activity, and forecasts the resources needed to provide desired levels of service.

As the first step in capacity planning, you develop a current model based on the system's present workload and performance specifications. Then you project demand and user requirements over a one- to three-year time period and analyze the model to see what is needed to maintain satisfactory performance and meet requirements. To assist you in the process, you can use a technique called what-if analysis.

**What-if analysis** allows you to vary one or more elements in a model in order to measure the effect on other elements. For example, you might use what-if analysis to answer questions such as: How will response time be affected if we add more PC workstations to the network? Will our client/server system be able to handle the growth in sales from the new Web site? What will be the effect on server throughput if we add more memory?

Powerful spreadsheet tools also can assist you in performing what-if analysis. For example, Microsoft Excel contains a feature called Goal Seek that determines what changes are necessary in one value to produce a specific result for another value. In the example shown in Figure 12-18 on the next page, a capacity planning worksheet indicates that the system can handle 3,840 Web-based orders per day, at 22.5 seconds each. The user wants to know the effect on processing time if the number of transactions increases to 9,000. As the Goal Seek solution in the bottom figure shows, order processing will have to be performed in 9.6 seconds to achieve that goal.

To learn more about capacity planning, visit the Management Information Systems CourseMate Web site at **www. cengagebrain.com,** navigate to **On the Web Links** for this chapter, and locate the Capacity Planning link.

**FIGURE 12-18**   Microsoft Excel provides a Goal Seek feature that permits what-if analysis.

When you plan capacity, you need detailed information about the number of transactions; the daily, weekly, or monthly transaction patterns; the number of queries; and the number, type, and size of all generated reports. If the system involves a LAN, you need to estimate network traffic levels to determine whether or not the existing hardware and software can handle the load. If the system uses a client/server design, you need to examine performance and connectivity specifications for each platform.

Most important, you need an accurate forecast of future business activities. If new business functions or requirements are predicted, you should develop contingency plans based on input from users and management. The main objective is to ensure that the system meets all future demands and provides effective support for business operations. Some firms handle their own capacity planning, while others purchase software and services from companies such as Teamquest, shown in Figure 12-19.

## System Maintenance Tools

You can use automated tools that provide valuable assistance during the operation and support phase. Many CASE tools include system evaluation and maintenance features, including the following examples:

- Performance monitor that provides data on program execution times
- Program analyzer that scans source code, provides data element cross-reference information, and helps evaluate the impact of a program change

The CASE tools in Appendix B can help you document business functions and processes, develop graphical models, and provide an overall framework for information system development. To learn more about these tools, turn to Appendix B.

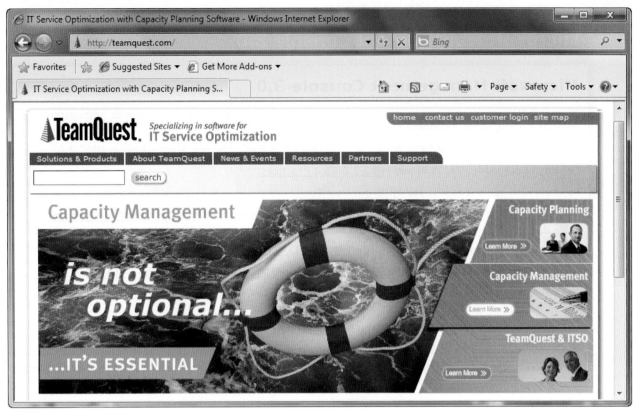

**FIGURE 12-19**  TeamQuest is an example of a firm that offers capacity planning software and services.

- Interactive debugging analyzer that locates the source of a programming error
- Reengineering tools
- Automated documentation
- Network activity monitor
- Workload forecasting tool

In addition to CASE tools, you also can use spreadsheet and presentation software to calculate trends, perform what-if analyses, and create attractive charts and graphs to display the results. Information technology planning is an essential part of the business planning process, and you probably will deliver presentations to management. You can review Appendix A for more information on using spreadsheet and presentation software to help you communicate effectively.

## SYSTEM SECURITY OVERVIEW

Security is a vital part of every information system. **Security** protects the system, and keeps it safe, free from danger, and reliable. In a global environment that includes many types of threats and attacks, security is more important than ever. This section includes a discussion of system security concepts, risk management, and common attacks against the system.

### System Security Concepts

The **CIA triangle** in Figure 12-20 shows the three main elements of system security: confidentiality, integrity, and availability. **Confidentiality** protects information from unauthorized disclosure and safeguards privacy.

**FIGURE 12-20**  System security must provide information confidentiality, integrity, and availability.

## Microsoft Management Console 3.0

### Microsoft Management Console 3.0

Microsoft Management Console (MMC) hosts administrative tools that you can use to administer networks, computers, services, and other system components.

To find features that have been added or changed since MMC 2.0, see What's New in MMC 3.0.

For tips about using MMC 3.0, see MMC 3.0 Best Practices.

For help with specific tasks, see MMC 3.0 How To....

For help using Group Policy settings to configure MMC behavior, see Use Group Policy to Control MMC 3.0 Usage.

For general background information, see MMC 3.0 Concepts.

For information about MMC command-line options, see MMC 3.0 Command-Line Options.

For information about compatibility with 64-bit computing environments or earlier versions of MMC, see MMC 3.0 Compatibility.

For information about accessibility features of MMC, see Accessibility for MMC 3.0.

**FIGURE 12-21**   The Microsoft Management Console (MMC) includes built-in security tools, such as password and lockout policies, audit policies, user rights, and security configurations, among others.

**Integrity** prevents unauthorized users from creating, modifying, or deleting information. **Availability** ensures that authorized users have timely and reliable access to necessary information. The first step in managing IT security is to develop a **security policy** based on these three elements. Although it is beyond the scope of this chapter, the **Microsoft Management Console (MMC)** shown in Figure 12-21 is a portal to a broad array of built-in security tools and techniques.

**Risk Management**

**FIGURE 12-22**   Risk management requires continuous risk identification, assessment, and control.

## Risk Management

In the real world, *absolute* security is not a realistic goal. Instead, managers must balance the value of the assets being protected, potential risks to the organization, and security costs. For example, it might not be worth installing an expensive video camera monitoring system to protect an empty warehouse. To achieve the best results, most firms use a **risk management** approach that involves constant attention to three interactive tasks: risk identification, risk assessment, and risk control, as shown in Figure 12-22.

**Risk identification** analyzes the organization's assets, threats, and vulnerabilities. **Risk assessment** measures risk likelihood and impact. **Risk control** develops safeguards that reduce risks and their impact.

**RISK IDENTIFICATION** The first step in risk identification is to list and classify business assets. An **asset** might include company hardware, software, data, networks, people, or procedures. For each asset, a risk manager rates the impact of an attack and analyzes possible threats. A **threat** is an internal or external entity that could endanger an asset. For example, threat categories might include natural disasters, software attacks, or theft, as shown in Figure 12-23.

## Threat Categories and Examples

ON THE WEB

To learn more
about risk
management, visit
the Management
Information Systems
CourseMate Web
site at **www.
cengagebrain.com**,
navigate to **On the
Web Links** for this
chapter, and locate
the Risk Management
link.

| THREAT | CATEGORY |
|---|---|
| Extortion | Hacker steals trade secrets and threatens to release them if not paid. |
| Hardware and software failures | Router stops functioning, or software causes the application server to crash. |
| Human error or failure | Employee accidentally deletes a file. |
| Natural disasters | Flood destroys company building and networked systems. |
| Service failure | Electricity is disrupted and brings the entire system down for hours. |
| Software attack | A group plants destructive software, a virus, or a worm into a company network. |
| Technical obsolescence | Outdated software is slow, difficult to use, and vulnerable to attacks. |
| Theft of physical or intellectual property | Physical server is stolen, intellectual property is stolen or used without permission; may be physical or electronic. |
| Trespass and espionage | Employee enters unlocked server room and views the payroll data on a forbidden system. |
| Vandalism | Attacker defaces Web site logo, or destroys CEO's hard drive physically or electronically. |

**FIGURE 12-23** System threats can be grouped into several broad categories. Note the examples provided for each category.

Next, the risk manager identifies vulnerabilities and how they might be exploited. A **vulnerability** is a security weakness or soft spot, and an **exploit** is an attack that takes advantage of a vulnerability. To identify vulnerabilities, a risk manager might ask questions like these: *Could hackers break through the proxy server? Could employees retrieve sensitive files without proper authorization? Could people enter the computer room and sabotage our servers?* Each vulnerability is rated and assigned a value. The output of risk identification is a list of assets, vulnerabilities, and ratings.

**RISK ASSESSMENT** In IT security terms, a **risk** is the impact of an attack multiplied by the likelihood of a vulnerability being exploited. For example, an impact value of 2 and a vulnerability rating of 10 would produce a risk of 20. On the other hand, an impact value of 5 and a vulnerability rating of 5 would produce a risk of 25. When risks arecalculated and prioritized, **critical risks** will head the list. Although ratings can be subjective, the overall process provides a consistent approach and framework.

**RISK CONTROL**  After risks are identified and assessed, they must be controlled. Control measures might include the following examples: *We could place a firewall on the proxy server; We could assign permissions to sensitive files; We could install biometric devices to guard the computer room.* Typically, management chooses one of four risk control strategies: avoidance, mitigation, transference, or acceptance. **Avoidance** eliminates the risk by adding protective safeguards. For example, to prevent unauthorized access to LAN computers, a secure firewall might be installed. **Mitigation** reduces the impact of a risk by careful planning and preparation. For example, a company can prepare a disaster recovery plan in case a natural disaster occurs. **Transference** shifts the risk to another asset or party, such as an insurance company. **Acceptance** means that nothing is done. Companies usually accept a risk only when the protection clearly is not worth the expense.

The risk management process is iterative — risks constantly are identified, assessed, and controlled. To be effective, risk managers need a combination of business knowledge, IT skills, and experience with security tools and techniques.

### Attacker Profiles and Attacks

An **attack** is a hostile act that targets the system, or the company itself. Thus, an attack might be launched by a disgruntled employee, or a hacker who is 10,000 miles away. Attackers break into a system to cause damage, steal information, or gain recognition, among other reasons. Attackers can be grouped into categories, as shown in Figure 12-24, while Figure 12-25 describes some common types of attacks.

### Attacker Characteristics

| ATTACKER | DESCRIPTION | SKILL SET |
|---|---|---|
| Cyberterrorist | Attacks to advance political, social, or ideological goals. | High |
| Employee | Uses unauthorized information or privileges to break into computer systems, steal information, or cause damage. | Varies |
| Hacker | Uses advanced skills to attack computer systems with malicious intent (black hat) or to expose flaws and improve security (white hat). | High |
| Hacktivist | Attacks to further a social or political cause; often involves shutting down or defacing Web sites. | Varies |
| Script kiddie | Inexperienced or juvenile hacker who uses readily available malicious software to disrupt or damage computer systems, and gain recognition. | Low |
| Spy | Non-employee who breaks into computer systems to steal information and sell it. | High |

**FIGURE 12-24**   IT security professionals have coined labels for various types of attackers.

## Types of Attacks and Examples

| ATTACK | EXAMPLES |
|---|---|
| Back door | Attacker finds vulnerability in software package and exploits it. |
| Denial of service or distributed denial of service | One or more computers send a stream of connection requests to disable a Web server. |
| DNS poisoning | False DNS (Domain Name Server) information steers the user to the attacker's Web site. Attackers trick users into thinking they are visiting a legitimate site, such as a bank site, then attempt to obtain bank account numbers, usernames, and passwords. |
| Dumpster diving | Attacker scours the trash for valuable information that can be used to compromise the system. |
| Mail bombing | Enormous volumes of e-mail are sent to a target address. |
| Malicious code | Attacker sends infected e-mail to the target system. Attackers may use viruses, worms, Trojan horses, keystroke loggers, spyware, or scripts to destroy data, bog down systems, spy on users, or assume control of infected systems. |
| Man in the middle | The attacker intercepts traffic and poses as the recipient, sending the data to the legitimate recipient but only after reading the traffic or modifying it. |
| Password cracking | Hacker attempts to discover a password to gain entry into a secured system. This can be a dictionary attack, where numerous words are tried, or a brute force attack, where every combination of characters is attempted. |
| Privilege escalation | Employee tricks a computer into raising his or her account to the administrator level. |
| Sniffing | Network traffic is intercepted and scanned for valuable information. |
| Social engineering | An attacker calls the help desk posing as a legitimate user and requests that his or her password be changed. |
| Spam | Unwanted, useless e-mail is sent continuously to business e-mail accounts, wasting time and decreasing productivity. |
| Spoofing | IP address is forged to match a trusted host, and similar content may be displayed to simulate the real site for unlawful purposes. |

**FIGURE 12-25** Attacks can take many forms, as this table shows. IT security managers must be able to detect these attacks and respond with suitable countermeasures.

The following sections discuss how companies combat security threats and challenges by using a multilevel strategy.

Security Levels

Physical

Network

Application

File

Procedural

User

**FIGURE 12-26**
Each security link has a specific focus, and the overall chain is only as strong as the weakest link.

# SECURITY LEVELS

To provide system security, you must consider six separate but interrelated levels: physical security, network security, application security, file security, user security, and procedural security. Like the chain shown in Figure 12-26, system security is only as strong as the weakest link. The following sections describe these security levels, and the issues that must be addressed. Top management often makes the final strategic and budget decisions regarding security, but systems analysts should understand the overall picture in order to make informed recommendations.

## Physical Security

The first level of system security concerns the physical environment, including IT resources and people throughout the company. Special attention must be paid to critical equipment located in operations centers, where servers, network hardware, and related equipment operate. Large companies usually have a dedicated room built specifically for IT operations. Smaller firms might use an office or storage area. Regardless of its size and shape, an operations center requires special protection from unwanted intrusion. In addition to centrally located equipment, all computers on the network must be secure, because each server or workstation can be a potential access point. Physical access to a computer represents an entry point into the system and must be controlled and protected.

**FIGURE 12-27**   Companies use biometric scanning to analyze the features of the eye's iris, which has more than 200 points that can be measured and used for comparison.

**OPERATIONS CENTER SECURITY** Perimeter security is essential in any room or area where computer equipment is operated or maintained. Physical access must be controlled tightly, and each entrance must be equipped with a suitable security device. All access doors should have internal hinges and electromagnetic locks that are equipped with a battery backup system to provide standby power in the event of a power outage. When the battery power is exhausted, the doors should fail in a closed position, but it should be possible for someone locked inside the room to open the door with an emergency release.

To enhance security, many companies are installing **biometric scanning systems**, which map an individual's facial features, fingerprints, handprint, or eye characteristics, as shown in Figure 12-27. These hi-tech authentication systems replace magnetic identification badges, which can be lost, stolen, or altered.

Video cameras and motion sensors can be used to monitor computer room security and provide documentation of all physical activity in the area. A motion sensor uses infrared technology to detect movement, and can be configured to provide audible or silent alarms, and to send e-mail messages when it is triggered. Other types of sensors can monitor temperature and humidity in the computer room. Motion sensor alarms can be activated at times when there is no expected activity in the computer room, and authorized technicians should have codes to enable or disable the alarms.

**SERVERS AND DESKTOP COMPUTERS** If possible, server and desktop computer cases should be equipped with locks. This simple, but important, precaution might prevent an intruder from modifying the hardware configuration of a server, damaging the equipment, or removing a disk drive. Server racks should be locked, to avoid the unauthorized placement and retrieval of keystroke loggers. A **keystroke logger** is a device that can be inserted between a keyboard and a computer. Typically, the device resembles an ordinary cable plug, so it does not call attention to itself.

The device can record everything that is typed into the keyboard, including passwords, while the system continues to function normally. Keystroke loggers can be used legitimately to monitor, back up, and restore a system, but if placed by an intruder, a keystroke logger represents a serious security threat.

In addition to hardware devices, keystroke logging software also exists. A keystroke logging program can be disguised as legitimate software and downloaded from the Internet or a company network. The program remains invisible to the user as it records keystrokes and uploads the information to whoever installed the program. Such malicious software can be removed by antivirus and antispyware software, discussed later in the Application Security section.

**Tamper-evident cases** should be used where possible. A tamper-evident case is designed to show any attempt to open or unlock the case. In the event that a computer case has been opened, an indicator LED remains lit until it is cleared with a password. Tamper-evident cases do not prevent intrusion, but a security breach is more likely to be noticed. Many servers now are offered with tamper-evident cases as part of their standard configuration.

Monitor screen savers that hide the screen and require special passwords to clear should be used on any server or workstation that is left unattended. Locking the screen after a period of inactivity is another safeguard. Microsoft Windows 7 allows an administrator to include this feature in security policies. Also, you can use a **BIOS-level password**, also called a **boot-level password** or a **power-on password**, that must be entered before the computer can be started. A boot-level password can prevent an unauthorized person from booting a computer by using a CD-ROM or USB device.

Finally, companies must consider electric power issues. In mission-critical systems, large-scale backup power sources are essential to continue business operations. In other cases, computer systems and network devices should be plugged into an **uninterruptible power supply (UPS)** that includes battery backup with suitable capacity. The UPS should be able to handle short-term operations in order to permit an orderly backup and system shutdown.

**NOTEBOOK COMPUTERS** When assessing physical security issues, be sure to consider additional security provisions for notebook, laptop, and tablet computers. Because of their small size and high value, these computers are tempting targets for thieves and industrial spies. Although the following suggestions are intended as a checklist for notebook computer security, many of them also apply to desktop workstations.

- Select an operating system, such as Windows 7, that allows secure logons, BIOS-level passwords, and strong firewall protection. You can also select hardware that allows you to require BIOS-level passwords. Also, log on and work with a user account that has limited privileges rather than an administrator account, and mask the administrator account by giving it a different name that would be hard for a casual intruder to guess.

- Mark or engrave the computer's case with the company name and address, or attach a tamper-proof asset ID tag. Many hardware vendors allow corporate customers to add an asset ID tag in the BIOS. For example, after powering up, you might see the message: *Property of SCR Associates – Company Use Only.* These measures might not discourage a professional thief, but might deter a casual thief, or at least make your computer relatively less desirable because it would be more difficult to use or resell. Security experts also recommend that you use a generic carrying case, such as an attaché case, rather than a custom carrying case that calls attention to itself and its contents. Also be sure to complete and submit all manufacturer registration cards.

- Consider notebook models that have a built-in fingerprint reader, as shown in Figure 12-28.

- Many notebook computers have a **Universal Security Slot (USS)** that can be fastened to a cable lock or laptop alarm. Again, while these precautions might not deter professional thieves, they might discourage and deter casual thieves.

**FIGURE 12-28** Some notebook computers feature a fingerprint reader, which is a small metallic sensor located near the keyboard or display.

- Back up all vital data before using the notebook computer outside the office. Also, instead of using your computer's hard drive, save and transport highly sensitive data on removable media, such as a flash memory device.

- Use tracking software that directs your laptop periodically to contact a security tracking center. If your notebook is stolen, the call-in identifies the computer and its physical location. Armed with this information, the security tracking center can alert law enforcement agencies and communications providers. As shown in Figure 12-29, Computrace sells a product called LoJack for Laptops, which offers call-in service, as well as a remote data erase capability. Some versions of the product even provide a payment if the firm does not recover your stolen laptop.

- While traveling, try to be alert to potential high-risk situations, where a thief, or thieves, might attempt to distract your attention and snatch your computer. These situations often occur in crowded, noisy places like airport baggage claim areas, rental car counters, and security checkpoints. Also, when traveling by car, store your computer in a trunk or lockable compartment where it will not be visible.

- Establish stringent password protection policies that require minimum length and complexity, and set a limit on how many times an invalid password can be entered before the system locks itself down. In some situations, you might want to establish file encryption policies to protect extremely sensitive files.

**FIGURE 12-29** Many students use LoJack on their notebook computers. The product offers automated call-in identification and remote data erase capability.

## CASE IN POINT 12.3: OUTER BANKS COUNTY

Outer Banks County is a 200-square-mile area in coastal North Carolina, and you are the IT manager. The county has about a hundred office employees who perform clerical tasks in various departments. A recent budget crisis has resulted in a wage and hiring freeze, and morale has declined. The county manager has asked you to install some type of keystroke logger to monitor employees and determine whether they are fully productive. After your conversation, you wonder whether there might be some potential privacy and security issues involved.

For example, does an employer have a duty to notify its employees that it is monitoring them? Should the employer notify them even if not required to do so? From a human resources viewpoint, what would be the best way to approach this issue? Also, does a potential security issue exist? If an unauthorized person gained possession of the keystroke log, he or she might be able to uncover passwords and other sensitive data.

What are your conclusions? Are these issues important, and how would you respond to the county manager's recommendation? Before you answer, you should go on the Internet and learn more about keystroke loggers generally, and specific products that currently are available.

## Network Security

A **network** is defined as two or more devices that are connected for the purpose of sending, receiving, and sharing data, which is called network traffic. In order to connect to a network, a computer must have a **network interface**, which is a combination of hardware and software that allows the computer to interact with the network. To provide security for network traffic, data can be **encrypted**, which refers to a process of encoding the data so it cannot be accessed without authorization.

**ENCRYPTING NETWORK TRAFFIC** Network traffic can be intercepted and possibly altered, redirected, or recorded. For example, if an **unencrypted**, or **plain text**, password or credit card number is transmitted over a network connection, it can be stolen. When the traffic is encrypted, it still is visible, but its content and purpose are masked.

Figure 12-30 on the next page shows an example of encrypted traffic compared to plain text traffic. In the upper screen, the user has logged on to the SCR Associates case study, using a password of *sad9e*. Notice that anyone who gains access to this data easily could learn the user's password. In the lower screen, the user has logged on to an online bank account and used a password, but the encryption process has made it impossible to decipher the keystrokes.

Two commonly used encryption techniques are private key encryption and public key encryption. **Private key encryption** is symmetric, because a single key is used to encrypt and decrypt information. While this method is simple and fast, it poses a fundamental problem. To use symmetric encryption, both the sender and receiver must possess the same key beforehand, or it must be sent along with the message, which increases the risk of interception and disclosure.

In contrast, **public key encryption** (**PKE**) is asymmetric, because each user has a pair of keys: a public key and a private key, as shown in Figure 12-31 on the next page. Public keys are used to encrypt messages. Users can share their public keys freely, while keeping their private keys tightly guarded. Any message encrypted with a user's public key can only be decrypted with that user's private key. This method is commonly used in secure online shopping systems.

A recent Wikipedia article uses an interesting analogy for public key encryption. The article suggests that PKE is similar to a locked mailbox with a mail slot that is accessible to the public. The mailbox's location (street address) represents the public key. Anyone knowing the street address can drop a message through the slot. However, only a person with a key can open the box and read the message.

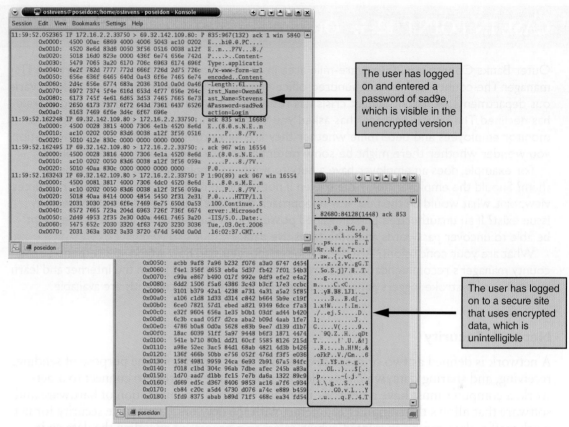

FIGURE 12-30   The upper screen shows an example of unencrypted text, which contains a visible password. In the lower screen, the encrypted text cannot be read.

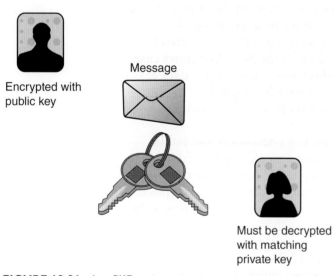

FIGURE 12-31   In a PKE environment, a message encrypted with a public key only can be decrypted with the matching private key.

**WIRELESS NETWORKS** As you learned in Chapter 10, wireless network security is a vital concern, because wireless transmission is much more vulnerable than traffic on a wired network. However, if wireless traffic is encrypted, any data that is intercepted by an unintended recipient will be useless to the intruder.

The earliest form of wireless security, called **Wired Equivalent Privacy (WEP)**, required each wireless client to use a special, preshared key. Although this method was used by many home and small office networks, it provided relatively weak protection.

WEP was replaced by **Wi-Fi Protected Access (WPA)**, which offered major security improvements based on protocols created by the Wi-Fi Alliance. The most recent wireless security enhancement, called **WPA2**, further strengthens the level of wireless protection. WPA2 is an extension of WPA based on a full implementation of the **IEEE 802.11i** standard. According to the WiFi Alliance, the WPA2 standard became mandatory for all new devices seeking Wi-Fi certification after 2006. WPA2 is compatible with WPA, so companies easily can migrate to the new security standard.

**PRIVATE NETWORKS**  It is not always practical to secure all network traffic. Unfortunately, encrypting traffic increases the burden on a network, and can decrease network performance significantly. In situations where network speed is essential, such as a Web server linked to a database server, many firms use a private network to connect the computers. A **private network** is a dedicated connection, similar to a leased telephone line. Each computer on the private network must have a dedicated interface to the network, and no interface on the network should connect to any point outside the network. In this configuration, unencrypted traffic safely can be transmitted because it is not visible, and cannot be intercepted from outside the network.

**VIRTUAL PRIVATE NETWORKS**  Private networks work well with a limited number of computers, but if a company wants to establish secure connections for a larger group, it can create a virtual private network (VPN). A **virtual private network (VPN)** uses a public network, such as the Internet or a company intranet, to connect remote users securely. Instead of using a dedicated connection, a VPN allows remote clients to use a special key exchange that must be authenticated by the VPN. Once authentication is complete, a secure network connection, called a **tunnel**, is established between the client and the access point of the local intranet. All traffic is encrypted through the VPN tunnel, which provides an additional level of encryption and security. As more companies allow employees to work from home, a VPN can provide acceptable levels of security and reliability.

**PORTS AND SERVICES**  A **port**, which is identified by a number, is used to route incoming traffic to the correct application on a computer. In TCP/IP networks, such as the Internet, all traffic received by a computer contains a destination port. Because the destination port determines where the traffic will be routed, the computer sorts the traffic by port number, which is included in the transmitted data. An analogy might be a large apartment building with multiple mailboxes. Each mailbox has the same street address, but a different box number. Port security is critically important, because an attacker could use an open port to gain access to the system.

A **service** is an application that monitors, or listens on, a particular port. For example, a typical e-mail application listens on port 25. Any traffic received by that port is routed to the e-mail application. Services play an important role in computer security, and they can be affected by port scans and denial-of-service attacks.

- Port scans. **Port scans** attempt to detect the services running on a computer by trying to connect to various ports and recording the ports on which a connection was accepted. For example, the result of an open port 25 would indicate that a mail server is running. Port scans can be used to draw an accurate map of a network, and pinpoint possible weaknesses.

- Denial of service. A **denial of service (DoS)** attack occurs when an attacking computer makes repeated requests to a service or services running on certain ports. Because the target computer has to respond to each request, it can become bogged down and fail to respond to legitimate requests. A much more devastating attack based on this method is called a **distributed denial of service (DDoS)** attack. This attack involves multiple attacking computers that can synchronize DOS attacks and immobilize a server, as shown in Figure 12-32 on the next page. The seriousness of a DOS attack is evident in the National Cyber Alert System tip shown in Figure 12-33 on the next page.

**FIREWALLS**  A **firewall** is the main line of defense between a local network, or intranet, and the Internet. A firewall must have at least one network interface with the Internet, and at least one network interface with a local network or intranet. Firewall software examines all network traffic sent to and from each network interface. Preset rules establish certain conditions that determine whether the firewall will allow the traffic to pass. When a

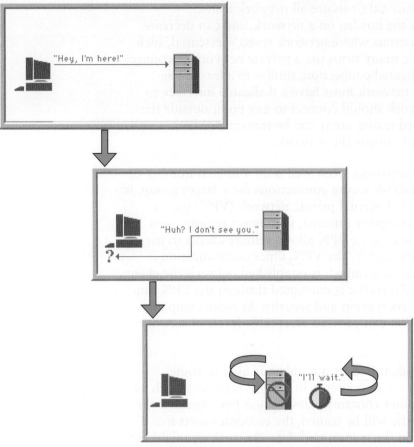

**FIGURE 12-32** In a denial of service attack, an attacker sends numerous authentication requests with false return addresses. The server tries unsuccessfully to send authentication approval, and eventually is disabled by the flood of requests.

matching rule is found, the firewall automatically accepts, rejects, or drops the traffic. When a firewall rejects traffic, it sends a reply indicating that the traffic is not permissible. When a firewall drops traffic, no reply is sent. Firewalls can be configured to detect and respond to denial-of-service attacks, port scans, and other suspicious activity.

Figure 12-34 shows a basic set of firewall rules for a company that has a Web server and a mail server. In this example, the firewall would accept public Web server traffic only on ports 80 and 443, and public mail server traffic only on port 25. The firewall would allow private LAN traffic to any destination and port.

**NETWORK INTRUSION DETECTION** Suppose an intruder attempts to gain access to the system. Obviously, an intrusion alarm should be sounded when certain activity or known attack patterns are detected. A **network intrusion detection system (NIDS)** is like a burglar alarm that goes off when it detects a configuration violation. The NIDS also can alert the administrator when it detects suspicious network traffic patterns. A NIDS requires fine-tuning to detect the difference between legitimate network traffic and an

**FIGURE 12-33** The United States Computer Emergency Readiness Team has published a security tip about DoS threats.

| RULE | INTERFACE | SOURCE | DESTINATION | PORT | ACTION |
|------|-----------|--------|-------------|------|--------|
| 1 | Public | Any | Web Server | 80 | Accept |
| 2 | Public | Any | Web Server | 443 | Accept |
| 3 | Public | Any | Web Server | Any | Reject |
| 4 | Public | Any | Mail Server | 25 | Accept |
| 5 | Public | Any | Mail Server | Any | Reject |
| 6 | Public | Any | Any | Any | Drop |
| 7 | Private | LAN | Any | Any | Accept |

**FIGURE 12-34**  Examples of rules that determine whether the firewall will allow traffic to pass.

attack. It is also important that a NIDS be placed on a switch or other network device that can monitor all network traffic. Although a NIDS requires some administrative overhead, it can be very helpful in documenting the efforts of attackers and analyzing network performance.

## Application Security

In addition to securing the computer room and shielding network traffic, it is necessary to protect all server-based applications. To do so, you must analyze the application's functions, identify possible security concerns, and carefully study all available documentation. Application security requires an understanding of services, hardening, application permissions, input validation techniques, software patches and updates, and software logs.

**SERVICES**  In the network security section, you learned that a service is an application that monitors, or listens, on a particular port. You can determine which services are running by using a port scan utility. If a particular application is not needed, it should be disabled. This will improve system security, performance, and reliability. An unnecessary or improperly configured service could create a vulnerability called a **security hole**. For example, if a loosely configured FTP (File Transfer Protocol) service is available to a hacker, he or she might be able to upload destructive code to the server.

**HARDENING**  The **hardening** process makes a system more secure by removing unnecessary accounts, services, and features. Hardening is necessary because the default configuration of some software packages might create a vulnerability. For example, initial software settings might include relatively weak account permissions or file sharing controls. Hardening can be done manually or by using a configuration template, which speeds up the process in a large organization.

Hardening also includes additional protection such as antivirus and antispyware software. These programs can detect and remove **malware**, which is hostile software designed to infiltrate, damage, or deny service to a computer system. Malware includes worms, Trojan horses, keystroke loggers, and spyware, among others.

**APPLICATION PERMISSIONS**  Typically, an application is configured to be run only by users who have specific rights. For example, an **administrator**, or **superuser** account, allows essentially unrestricted access. Other users might be allowed to enter data, but not to modify or delete existing data. To prevent unauthorized or destructive changes, the application should be configured so that nonprivileged users can access the program, but cannot make changes to built-in functions or configurations. **User rights**, also called **permissions**, are discussed in more detail in the file security section.

**INPUT VALIDATION**  As you learned in Chapter 8, when designing the user interface, input validation can safeguard data integrity and security. For example, if an application requires a number from *1* to *10*, what happens if an alphabetic character or the number *31* is entered? If the application is designed properly, it will respond with an appropriate error message. Chapter 8 also explained data entry and validation checks, which are important techniques that can improve data integrity and quality. Failure to validate input data can result in output errors, increased maintenance expense, and erratic system behavior.

**PATCHES AND UPDATES**  In an operational system, security holes or vulnerabilities might be discovered at any time. Patches can be used to repair these holes, reduce vulnerability, and update the system. Like any other new software, patches must be tested carefully. Before applying a patch, an effort should be made to determine the risks of *not* applying the patch, and the possibility that the patch might affect other areas of the system.

Many firms purchase software packages called **third-party software**. Patches released by third-party software vendors usually are safe, but any patch must be reviewed carefully before it is applied. Because researching and applying patches is time consuming and expensive, many software vendors offer an **automatic update service** that enables an application to contact the vendor's server and check for a needed patch or update. Depending on the configuration, available patches can be downloaded and installed without human intervention, or might require approval by IT managers. Although it is convenient, automatic updating carries substantial risks, and should be used only if changes can readily be undone if unexpected results or problems develop.

**SOFTWARE LOGS**  Operating systems and applications typically maintain a **log** that documents all events, including dates, times, and other specific information. Logs can be important in understanding past attacks and preventing future intrusions. For example, a pattern of login errors might reveal the details of an intrusion attempt. A log also can include system error messages, login histories, file manipulation, and other information that could help track down unauthorized use. Software logs should be monitored constantly to determine if misuse or wrongdoing has occurred. As explained in the network security section, a network intrusion detection system (NIDS) can alert a system administrator whenever suspicious events occur. Windows Event Viewer, shown in Figure 12-35, is an example of a built-in software log.

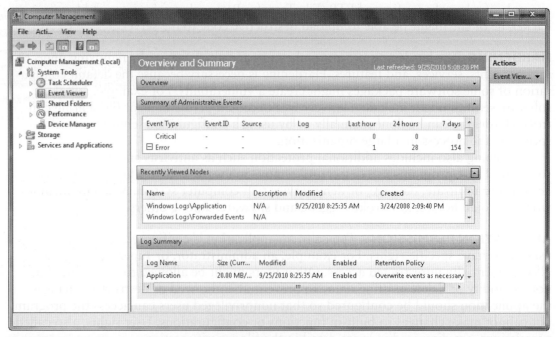

**FIGURE 12-35**  Windows Event Viewer can log application usage, security settings, and system changes.

# File Security

Computer configuration settings, users' personal information, and other sensitive data are stored in files. The safety and protection of these files is a vital element in any computer security program, and a systems analyst needs to consider the importance of encryption, or encoding files to make them unreadable by unauthorized users, and permissions, which can be assigned to individual users or to user groups.

**ENCRYPTION** As you learned in the section on network security, encryption scrambles the contents of a file or document to protect it from unauthorized access. All corporate data must be protected, but encryption is especially important for sensitive material such as personnel or financial records. You can use the **Encrypting File System (EFS)**, which is fully implemented on Windows 7 Professional, to encrypt and limit access to data. EFS can be enabled or disabled at the folder or the document level by simply changing the properties for that folder or document.

**PERMISSIONS** File security is based on establishing a set of permissions, which describe the rights a user has to a particular file or directory on a server. The most common permissions are read, write, and execute. Typical examples of permissions include the following:

- Read a file — The user can read the contents of the file.
- Write a file — The user can change the contents of the file.
- Execute a file — The user can run the file, if it is a program.
- Read a directory — The user can list the contents of the directory.
- Write a directory — The user can add and remove files in the directory.

When assigning file permissions, a system administrator should ensure that each user has only the minimum permissions necessary to perform his or her work — not more. In some firms, the system administrator has broad discretion in assigning these levels; in other companies, an appropriate level of management approval is required for any permissions above a standard user level. In any case, a well-documented and enforced permissions policy is necessary to promote file security and reduce system vulnerability.

**USER GROUPS** Individual users who need to collaborate and share files often request a higher level of permissions that would enable any of them to change file content. A better approach, from a system administrator's viewpoint, might be to create a user group, add specific users, and assign file permissions to the group, rather than to the individuals. Many firms use this approach, because it allows a user's rights to be determined by his or her work responsibilities, rather than by job title or rank. If a person is transferred, he or she leaves certain groups and joins others that reflect current job duties.

# User Security

User security involves the identification of system users and consideration of user-related security issues. Regardless of other security precautions and features, security ultimately depends on system users and their habits, practices, and willingness to support security goals. Unfortunately, many system break-ins begin with a user account that is compromised in some way. Typically, an intruder accesses the system using the compromised account, and may attempt a **privilege escalation attack**, which is an unauthorized attempt to increase permission levels.

User security requires identity management, comprehensive password protection, defenses against social engineering, an effective means of overcoming user resistance, and consideration of new technologies. These topics are discussed in the following sections.

ON THE WEB

To learn more about identity management, visit the Management Information Systems CourseMate Web site at www. cengagebrain.com, navigate to On the Web Links for this chapter, and locate the Identity Management link.

**IDENTITY MANAGEMENT** Identity management refers to controls and procedures necessary to identify legitimate users and system components. An identity management strategy must balance technology, security, privacy, cost, and user productivity. Identity management is an evolving technology that is being pursued intensively by corporations, IT associations, and governments.

The Burton Group, a leading IT security consultant, has described identity management as a "set of electronic records that represent … people, machines, devices, applications, and services." This definition suggests that not just users, but each component in a system, must have a verifiable identity that is based on unique characteristics. For example, user authentication might be based on a combination of a password, a Social Security number, an employee number, a job title, and a physical location.

Because of the devastating consequences of intrusion, IT managers are giving top priority to identity management strategies and solutions.

**PASSWORD PROTECTION** As the section on physical security points out, a secure system must have a password policy that requires minimum length, complexity, and a limit on invalid login attempts. Although passwords are a key element in any security program, users often choose passwords that are easy to recall, and they sometimes resent having to remember complex passwords. Even so, IT managers should insist on passwords that have a minimum length, require a combination of case-sensitive letters and numbers, and must be changed periodically. Unfortunately, any password can be compromised if a user writes it down and stores it in an easily accessible location such as a desk, a bulletin board, or under the keyboard.

During a recent U.S. election campaign, a hacker made global headlines by gaining access to the e-mail account of a vice-presidential candidate. The intruder signed on as the candidate, requested a new password, guessed the answers to the security questions, and was able to enter the account. These actions were totally illegal, and constituted a serious felony under federal law.

**SOCIAL ENGINEERING** Even if users are protecting and securing their passwords, an intruder might attempt to gain unauthorized access to a system using a tactic called social engineering. In a social engineering attack, an intruder uses social interaction to gain access to a computer system. For example, the intruder might pretend to be a new employee, an outside technician, or a journalist. Through a series of questions, the intruder tries to obtain the information that he or she needs to compromise the system. A common ploy is for the attacker to contact several people in the same organization, and use some information from one source to gain credibility and entry to another source.

An intruder also might contact a help desk and say: "Hi. This is Anna Dressler from accounting. I seem to have forgotten my password. Could you give me a new one?" Although this request might be legitimate, it also might be an attacker trying to access the system. A password never should be given based solely on this telephone call. The user should be required to provide further information to validate his or her identity, such as a Social Security number, employee ID, telephone extension, and company e-mail address.

One highly publicized form of social engineering is called **pretexting**, which is a method of obtaining personal information under false pretenses. Pretexting, which is described in the Federal Trade Commission statement shown in Figure 12-36, is a very real threat. The best way to combat social engineering attacks is with employee education, more training, and a high level of awareness during day-to-day operations.

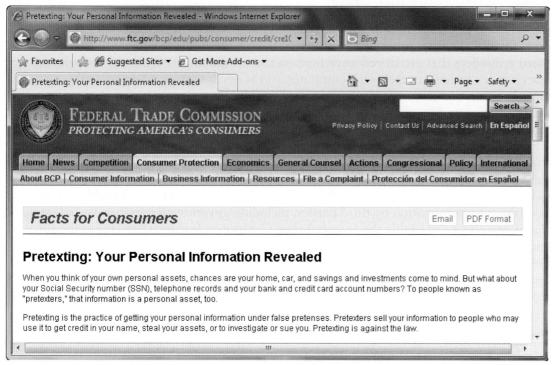

**FIGURE 12-36**   As the Federal Trade Commission points out, pretexting involves obtaining your personal information under false pretenses.

**USER RESISTANCE**   Many users, including some senior managers, dislike tight security measures because they can be inconvenient and time consuming. Systems analysts should remind users that the company owes the best possible security to its customers, who have entrusted personal information to the firm; to its employees, who also have personal information stored in company files; and to its shareholders, who expect the company to have a suitable, effective, and comprehensive security program that will safeguard company assets and resources. When users understand this overall commitment to security and feel that they are part of it, they are more likely to choose better passwords, be more alert to security issues, and contribute to the overall success of the company's security program.

**NEW TECHNOLOGIES**   In addition to traditional measures and biometric devices, technology can enhance security and prevent unauthorized access. For example, a **security token** is a physical device that authenticates a legitimate user. The Wikipedia image in Figure 12-37 shows several types of security tokens. Some firms provide employees with security tokens that generate a numeric validation code, which the employee enters in addition to his or her normal password.

Unfortunately, new technology sometimes creates new risks. For example, Google offers a desktop-based search engine, Google Desktop, with a powerful indexing feature that scans all the files, documents, e-mails, chats, and stored Web pages on a user's computer. Although the program provides a convenient way for users to locate and retrieve their data, it also can make it easier for an

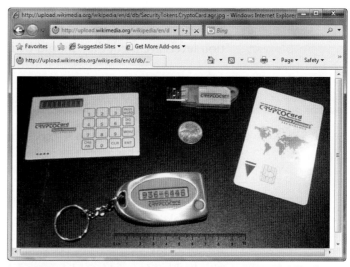

**FIGURE 12-37**   Security tokens, which come is various forms, can provide an additional level of security.

intruder to obtain private information, especially in a multiuser environment, because the program can recall and display almost anything stored on the computer. Also, if an intruder uses the term *password* in a search, the program might be able to find password reminders that are stored anywhere on the computer. According to Google, the search index resides on the user's computer and is never sent or made accessible to Google or anyone else without explicit consent. However, to maintain privacy for multiuser computers, Google strongly recommends that each user have a separate account, with individual usernames and passwords.

Google Desktop also offers a way for users to search across multiple computers, and this option has caused some concern among IT managers and privacy advocates. To perform a multi-computer search, it is necessary to store a user's data temporarily on Google's servers. Some observers feel that this makes the data more vulnerable and possibly subject to examination by third parties, including government agencies. Google states that if you choose to enable the *Search Across Computers* feature, your shared data is encrypted and treated as personal information, in accordance with the Google Privacy Policy. Software such as Google Desktop is powerful, convenient, and fun to use. However, you should understand the possible risks involved before installing this type of software on personal or business workstations.

## Procedural Security

**Procedural security**, also called **operational security**, is concerned with managerial policies and controls that ensure secure operations. In fact, many IT professionals believe that security depends more on managerial issues than technology. Management must work to establish a corporate culture that stresses the importance of security to the firm and its people. Procedural security defines how particular tasks are to be performed, from large-scale data backups to everyday tasks such as storing e-mails or forms. Other procedures might spell out how to update firewall software or how security personnel should treat suspected attackers.

All employees should understand that they have a personal responsibility for security. For example, an employee handbook might require that users log out of their system accounts, clear their desks, and secure all documents before leaving for the day. These policies reduce the risk of **dumpster diving** attacks, in which an intruder raids desks or trash bins for valuable information. In addition, paper shredders should be used to destroy sensitive documents.

Procedural security also includes safeguarding certain procedures that would be valuable to an attacker. The most common approach is a *need-to-know* concept, where access is limited to employees who need the information to perform security-related tasks. Many firms also apply a set of classification levels for access to company documents. For example, highly sensitive technical documents might be available only to the IT support team, while user-related materials would be available to most company employees. If classification levels are used, they should be identified clearly and enforced consistently.

## CASE IN POINT 12.4: CHAIN LINK CONSULTING, INC.

Chain Link Consulting is an IT consulting firm that specializes in system security issues. The company's president has asked you to help her put together a presentation to a group of potential clients at a trade show meeting next month. First, she wants you to review system security issues, considering all six security levels. Then she wants you to come up with a list of ways that Chain Link could test a client's security practices, in order to get a real-world assessment of vulnerability.

To make matters more interesting, she told you it was OK to be creative in your recommendations, but not to propose any action that would be illegal or unethical. For example, it would be OK to pose as a job applicant with false references to see if they were being checked, but it would not be appropriate to pick a lock and enter the computer room.

Your report is due tomorrow. What will you suggest?

Procedural security must be supported by upper management and fully explained to all employees. The organization must provide training to explain the procedures and issue reminders from time to time that will make security issues a priority.

## BACKUP AND RECOVERY

Every system must provide for data backup and recovery. **Backup** refers to copying data at prescribed intervals, or continuously. **Recovery** involves restoring the data and restarting the system after an interruption. An overall backup and recovery plan that prepares for a potential disaster is called a **disaster recovery plan.**

The tragic events of September 11, 2001, and increased concern about global terrorism have led many companies to upgrade their backup and disaster recovery plans. Heightened focus on disaster recovery has spawned a whole new industry, which includes new tools and strategies. Many IT professionals feel that terrorism concerns have raised security awareness throughout the corporate world. Although they are separate topics, backup and disaster recovery issues usually are intertwined. The following sections cover these topics in more detail.

**ON THE WEB**

To learn more backup and disaster recovery, visit the Management Information Systems CourseMate Web site at **www. cengagebrain. com**, navigate to **On the Web Links** for this chapter, and locate the Backup and Disaster Recovery link.

### Backup Policies

The cornerstone of business data protection is a **backup policy**, which contains detailed instructions and procedures. An effective backup policy can help a firm continue business operations and survive a catastrophe. The backup policy should specify backup media, backup types, and retention periods.

**BACKUP MEDIA** Backup media can include tape, hard drives, optical storage, and online storage. Physical backups must be carefully identified and stored in a secure location. **Offsiting** refers to the practice of storing backup media away from the main business location, in order to mitigate the risk of a catastrophic disaster such as a flood, fire, or earthquake. Even if the operating system includes a backup utility, many system administrators prefer to use specialized third-party software that offers more options and better controls for large-scale operations.

In addition to on-site data storage, many companies use Web-based data backup and retrieval services offered by vendors such as Rocky Mountain Software and IBM. For a small- or medium-sized firm, this option can be cost effective and reliable.

**BACKUP TYPES** Backups can be full, differential, incremental, or continuous. A **full backup** is a complete backup of every file on the system. Frequent full backups are time consuming and redundant if most files are unchanged since the last full backup. Instead of performing a full backup, another option is to perform a **differential backup,** which is faster because it backs up *only* the files that are new or changed since the last full backup. To restore the data to its original state, you restore the last full backup, and then restore the last differential backup. Many IT managers believe that a combination of full and differential backups is the best option, because it uses the least amount of storage space and is simple.

The fastest method, called an **incremental backup,** only includes recent files that never have been backed up by any method. This approach, however, requires multiple steps to restore the data — one for each incremental backup.

Most large systems use **continuous backup,** which is a real-time streaming method that records all system activity as it occurs. This method requires expensive hardware, software, and substantial network capacity. However, system restoration is rapid and effective because data is being captured in real time, as it occurs. Continuous backup often uses a **RAID (redundant array of independent disks)** system that mirrors the data. RAID systems are called **fault-tolerant,** because a failure of any one disk does not disable the system. Compared to one large drive, a RAID design offers better performance, greater capacity, and improved reliability. When installed on a server, a RAID array of multiple drives appears to the computer as a single logical drive. Figure 12-38 shows a comparison of various backup methods.

## Comparison of Backup Methods

| BACKUP TYPE | CHARACTERISTICS | PROS AND CONS | TYPICAL FREQUENCY |
|---|---|---|---|
| Full | Backs up all files. | Slowest backup time and requires the most storage space. Rapid recovery because all files are restored in a single step. | Monthly or weekly. |
| Differential | Only backs up files that are new or changed since the last full backup. | Faster than a full backup and requires less storage space. All data can be restored in just two steps by using the last full backup and the last differential backup. | Weekly or daily. |
| Incremental | Only backs up files that are new or changed since the last backup of any kind. | Fastest backup and requires the least storage space because it only saves files that have never been backed up. However, requires many restore steps – one for each incremental backup. | Daily or more often. |
| Continuous | Real-time, streaming method that records all system activity. | Very expensive hardware, software, and network capacity. Recovery is very fast because system can be restored to just before an interruption. | Usually only used by large firms and network-based systems. |

**FIGURE 12-38**   Comparison of full, differential, incremental, and continuous backup methods.

**RETENTION PERIODS**   Backups are stored for a specific **retention period** after which they are either destroyed or the backup media is reused. Retention periods can be a specific number of months or years, depending on legal requirements and company policy. Stored media must be secured, protected, and inventoried periodically.

## Business Continuity Issues

Global concern about terrorism has raised awareness levels and increased top management support for a business continuity strategy in the event of an emergency. A disaster recovery plan describes actions to be taken, specifies key individuals and rescue authorities to be notified, and spells out the role of employees in evacuation, mitigation, and recovery efforts. The disaster recovery plan should be accompanied by a **test plan**, which can simulate various levels of emergencies and record the responses, which can be analyzed and improved as necessary.

secure location. Afterward, the plan should focus on resuming business operations, including the salvaging or replacement of equipment and the recovery of backup data. The main objective of a disaster recovery plan is to restore business operations to pre-disaster levels.

Disaster recovery plans are often part of a larger **business continuity plan (BCP)**, which goes beyond a recovery plan, and defines how critical business functions can continue in the event of a major disruption. Some BCPs specify the use of a hot site. A **hot site** is an alternate IT location, anywhere in the world, that can support critical systems in the event of a power outage, system crash, or physical catastrophe. A hot site requires **data replication**, which means that any transaction on the primary system must be mirrored on the hot site. If the primary system becomes unavailable, the hot site will have the latest data and can function seamlessly, with no downtime.

Although hot sites are attractive backup solutions, they are very expensive. However, a hot site provides the best insurance against major business interruptions. In addition to hot sites, business insurance can be important in a worst-case scenario. Although expensive, business insurance can offset the financial impact of system failure and business interruption.


## SYSTEM OBSOLESCENCE

At some point, every system becomes obsolete. For example, you might not remember punched cards, but they represented the cutting edge of data management back in the 1960s. Data was stored by punching holes at various positions, and was retrieved by machines that could sense the presence or absence of a punched hole. Most full-size cards stored only 80 characters, or bytes, so more than 12,000 cards would be needed to store a megabyte. Punched cards were even used as checks and utility bills. Today, this technology is virtually obsolete.

Constantly changing technology means that every system has a limited economic life span. Analysts and managers can anticipate system obsolescence in several ways and it never should come as a complete surprise.

A system becomes **obsolete** when it no longer supports user needs, or when the platform becomes outmoded. The most common reason for discontinuing a system is that it has reached the end of its economically useful life, as indicated by the following signs:

- The system's maintenance history indicates that adaptive and corrective maintenance are increasing steadily.

- Operational costs or execution times are increasing rapidly, and routine perfective maintenance does not reverse or slow the trend.

- A software package is available that provides the same or additional services faster, better, and less expensively than the current system.

- New technology offers a way to perform the same or additional functions more efficiently.

- Maintenance changes or additions are difficult and expensive to perform.

- Users request significant new features to support business requirements.

Systems operation and support continues until a replacement system is installed. Toward the end of a system's operational life, users are unlikely to submit new requests for adaptive maintenance because they are looking forward to the new release. Similarly, the IT staff usually does not perform much perfective or preventive maintenance because the system will not be around long enough to justify the cost. A system in its final stages requires corrective maintenance only to keep the system operational.

User satisfaction typically determines the life span of a system. The critical success factor for any system is whether or not it helps users achieve their operational and business goals. As an IT staff member, you should expect to receive input from users and managers throughout the systems development process. You should investigate and document all negative feedback, because it can be the first signal of system obsolescence.

At some point in a system's operational life, maintenance costs start to increase, users begin to ask for more features and capability, new systems requests are submitted, and the SDLC begins again.

## FUTURE CHALLENGES AND OPPORTUNITIES

The only thing that is certain about the future is continuous change. Change itself is neither good nor bad — the real issue is how people and companies deal with the challenges and opportunities that are bound to occur.

No one would start a complex journey without a map and a plan. To navigate the future of information technology, companies require strategic plans, which were discussed in Chapter 2. An individual also needs a plan to reach to a specific goal or destination. This section discusses some predictions and stresses the importance of personal planning and development, including the acquisition of professional credentials.

### Predictions

Although no one can foresee the future, it is safe to assume that companies will face intense competition and economic, social, and political uncertainty. Many IT experts believe that in this environment, the highest priorities will be the safety and security of corporate operations, environmental concerns, and bottom-line TCO.

Gartner Inc. is a leading consulting firm that is famous for accurate predictions of IT trends. Here is a summary of predictions that Gartner published in January, 2010:

- By 2012, 50% of traveling workers will use lighter, smaller Internet-centric devices rather than notebook computers. A new class of portable applications will enable users to re-create their work environment across multiple locations or systems.

- By 2012, 80% of commercial software will include open-source components. As open-source applications become mature, stable, and well supported, they will represent significant value opportunities for users.

- By 2012, one-third of business software spending will be for Software as a Service (SaaS).

- By 2012, 20% of businesses will use third parties to supply IT needs and will own no IT assets.

- By 2012, Facebook will become the hub for social network integration and Web socialization.

- By 2012, 60% of a new PC's total greenhouse gas emissions will have occurred before the user first turns the machine on.

- By 2013, mobile phones will overtake PCs as the most common Web access device worldwide.

- By 2014, most IT business cases will include carbon remediation costs.

- By 2014, over 3 billion adults worldwide will perform electronic transactions via mobile or Internet technology.

- By 2015, some aspects of online marketing will be regulated, which will affect more than $250 billion in Internet sales worldwide.

Gartner also predicted that large enterprises will require suppliers to certify their green credentials and sourcing policies. One issue might relate to the explosion of data storage and server farms, such as the one shown in Figure 12-39. In his 2008 book, *Planet Google*, author Randall Stross noted that the enormous amount of energy needed to drive cloud computing, including Google's servers, has raised serious environmental concerns. At the time he wrote the book, the author stated that data centers were already consuming more power in the United States than television sets.

## Strategic Planning for IT Professionals

An IT professional should think of himself or herself as a business corporation that has certain assets, potential liabilities, and specific goals. Individuals, like companies, must have a strategic plan. The starting point is to formulate an answer to the following career planning question: What do I want to be doing three, five, or ten years from now?

Working backwards from your long-term goals, you can develop intermediate milestones and begin to manage your career just as you would manage an IT project. You can even use the project management tools described in Chapter 3 to construct a Gantt chart or a PERT/CPM chart using months (or years) as time units. Once the plan is developed, you would monitor it regularly to see whether you were still on schedule.

**FIGURE 12-39** The rapid growth of data centers and server farms has increased energy consumption significantly and raised environmental concerns.

Planning a career is not unlike planting a tree that takes several years to reach a certain height. Once you know the desired height and the annual growth rate, you can determine when you must plant the tree. Similarly, if you want to possess a particular educational credential two years from now, and the credential takes two years to earn, then you need to start on it immediately if you want to adhere to stay on track.

## IT Credentials and Certification

In recent years, technical credentials and certification have become extremely important to IT employers and employees. In a broad sense, **credentials** include formal degrees, diplomas, or certificates granted by learning institutions to show that a certain level of education has been achieved successfully. The term **certification** also has a special meaning that relates to specific hardware and software skills that can be measured and verified by examination. For example, a person might have a two- or four-year degree in Information Systems and possess an A+ certification, which attests to the person's computer hardware knowledge and skills.

Many IT industry leaders offer certification, including Microsoft, Cisco, Novell, Oracle, and Sun Microsystems.

About.com, shown in Figure 12-40 on the next page, offers hundreds of online guides and solutions for everyday questions and topics. The site includes descriptions of popular computer certifications, suggestions for choosing a certification, and tips on how to prepare for the exams.

## Critical Thinking Skills

In additional to technical skills, IT professionals must have **soft skills**, such as communications, interpersonal, and perceptive abilities. IT professionals also need critical thinking skills to succeed in the workplace.

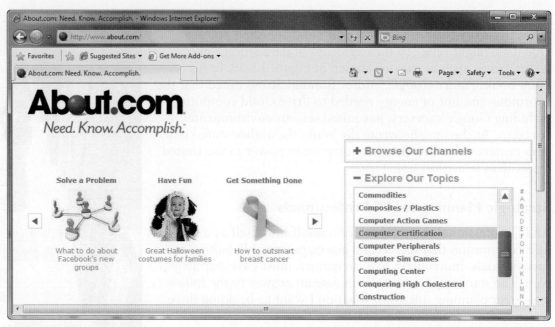

**FIGURE 12-40**   About.com offers online guides and solutions for everyday questions, including a section on computer certification.

Our digital society is inundated with massive amounts of data. Data mining, clever algorithms, and technical innovation are important, but the most valuable asset is an employee who can solve problems. The IT community has become interested in **critical thinking skills** that can help a person find, organize, analyze, and use the information he or she needs on the job. Many employers now seek critical thinkers who can locate data, identify important facts, and apply their knowledge in real-world decisions.

Many training courses exist for technical skills, but how do you develop your critical thinking skills? The best answer is to practice by performing tasks that resemble actual workplace tasks. As a future systems analyst, you already have an advantage — you know how to develop models, organize data, and recognize patterns. You can also complete the 12 *Ready for a Challenge* exercises at the end of each chapter. These exercises require critical thinking skills, and can help you learn, practice, and apply skills that you can take to the workplace.

Many instructors find that individual and team-based exercises can strengthen critical thinking skills. Examples include games, puzzles, brainstorming, creative problem-solving, decision tables, working with ethical questions, Boolean logic, Venn diagrams, and using cause-and-effect tools such as Pareto charts, X-Y diagrams, and fishbone diagrams, all of which can be found in this textbook.

# A QUESTION OF ETHICS

Jamie just completed a routine security audit on the company's information systems, and she found several areas of vulnerability. For example, file permissions have not been updated in some time, no comprehensive password policy exists, and network traffic is not fully encrypted. She noted these areas, among others, in a report to Tamika, her supervisor. The report included specific recommendations to fix the problems.

Tamika responded by saying that budgets are tight right now, and she could not approve Jamie's requests to resolve these issues. As an IT professional, Jamie is very uncomfortable with the risk level, but she has been unable to sway Tamika. When Jamie discussed the situation with her friend, Ethan, he said, "Why worry about it? If it's good enough for Tamika, it should be good enough for you."

What do you think of Ethan's advice, and why? Is this an ethical question? If Jamie still is uncomfortable, what are her options?

## CHAPTER SUMMARY

Systems support and security covers the period from the implementation of an information system until the system no longer is used. A systems analyst's primary involvement with an operational system is to manage and solve user support requests.

Corrective maintenance includes changes to correct errors. Adaptive maintenance satisfies new systems requirements, and perfective maintenance makes the system more efficient. Adaptive and perfective maintenance changes often are called enhancements. Preventive maintenance is performed to avoid future problems.

The typical maintenance process resembles a miniature version of the systems development life cycle. A systems request for maintenance work is submitted and evaluated. If it is accepted, the request is prioritized and scheduled for the IT group. The maintenance team then follows a logical progression of investigation, analysis, design, development, testing, and implementation.

Corrective maintenance projects occur when a user or an IT staff member reports a problem. Standard maintenance procedures usually are followed for relatively minor errors, but work often begins immediately when users report significant errors.

In contrast to corrective maintenance, adaptive, perfective, and preventive maintenance projects always follow the organization's standard maintenance procedures. Adaptive maintenance projects occur in response to user requests for improvements to meet changes in the business or operating environments. The IT staff usually initiates perfective maintenance projects to improve performance or maintainability. Automated program restructuring and reengineering are forms of perfective maintenance. In order to avoid future problems, IT staff performs preventive maintenance, which involves analysis of areas where trouble is likely to occur.

A maintenance team consists of one or more systems analysts and programmers. Systems analysts need the same talents and abilities for maintenance work as they use when developing a new system. Many IT departments are organized into separate new development and maintenance groups where staff members are rotated from one group to the other.

Configuration management is necessary to handle maintenance requests, to manage different versions of the information system, and to distribute documentation changes. Maintenance changes can be implemented as they are completed or a release methodology can be used in which all noncritical maintenance changes are collected and implemented simultaneously. A release methodology usually is cost effective and advantageous for users because they do not have to work with a constantly changing system. Systems analysts use functional, allocated, and product baselines as formal reference points to measure system characteristics at a specific time.

System performance measurements include response time, bandwidth, throughput, and turnaround time. Capacity management uses those measurements to forecast what is needed to provide future levels of service and support. Also, CASE tools that include system evaluation and maintenance features can be used during the systems operation, security, and support phase.

Security is a vital part of every computer system. System security is dependent upon a comprehensive security policy that defines how organizational assets are to be protected and how attacks are to be responded to.

Risk management creates a workable security policy by identifying, analyzing, anticipating, and reducing risks to an acceptable level. Because information systems face a wide array of threats and attacks, six separate but interrelated security levels should be analyzed: physical security, network security, application security, file security, user security, and procedural security. Physical security concerns the physical environment, including critical equipment located in a computer room, as well as safeguards for servers and desktops throughout the company. Network security involves encryption techniques, as well as private networks and other protective measures, especially where wireless transmissions are concerned. Application security requires an understanding of services, hardening, application permissions, input validation techniques, software patches and updates, and software logs. File security involves the use of encryption, and permissions, which can be assigned to individual users or to user groups. User security involves identity management techniques, a comprehensive password protection policy, an awareness of social engineering risks, and an effective means of overcoming user resistance. Procedural security involves managerial controls and policies that ensure secure operations.

Data backup and recovery issues include backup media, backup schedules, and retention periods, as well as backup designs such as RAID and Web-based backups.

All information systems eventually become obsolete. The end of a system's economic life usually is signaled by rapidly increasing maintenance or operating costs, the availability of new software or hardware, or new requirements that cannot be achieved easily by the existing system. When a certain point is reached, an information system must be replaced, and the entire systems development life cycle begins again.

Many IT experts predict intense competition in the future, along with economic, political, and social uncertainty. Facing these challenges, top IT priorities will be the safety and security of corporate operations, environmental concerns, and bottom-line TCO.

An IT professional should have a strategic career plan that includes long-term goals and intermediate milestones. An important element of a personal strategic plan is the acquisition of IT credentials and certifications that document specific knowledge and skills. Many IT industry leaders offer certification. In addition to technical ability, other skills, such as critical thinking skills, also are extremely valuable.

# Key Terms and Phrases

acceptance *592*
adaptive maintenance *575*
administrator *601*
allocated baseline *584*
applications programmer *579*
archived *583*
asset *590*
attack *592*
automatic update service *602*
availability *590*
avoidance *592*
backup *607*
backup media *607*
backup policy *607*
bandwidth *586*
baseline *584*
benchmark testing *585*
biometric scanning systems *594*
BIOS-level password *595*
boot-level password *595*
business continuity plan (BCP) *609*
capacity planning *587*
certification *611*
change control (CC) *582*
CIA triangle *589*
confidentiality *589*
configuration management (CM) *582*
continuous backup *607*
corrective maintenance *575*
credentials *611*
critical risk *591*
critical thinking skills *612*
database programmer *579*
data replication *609*
denial of service (DOS) *599*
differential backup *607*
disaster recovery plan *607*
distributed denial of service (DDOS) *599*
dumpster diving *606*
encrypted *597*
Encrypting File System (EFS) *603*
enhancement *576*
exploit *591*
fault management *585*
fault tolerant *607*

firewall *599*
full backup *607*
functional baseline *584*
Gbps (gigabits per second) *586*
hardening *601*
help desk *572*
hot site *609*
identity management *604*
IEEE 802.11i *598*
incremental backup *607*
information center (IC) *572*
integrity *590*
Kbps (kilobits per second) *586*
keystroke logger *594*
log *602*
maintenance activities *574*
maintenance expenses *574*
maintenance release *583*
maintenance release methodology *583*
maintenance team *578*
malware *601*
Mbps (megabits per second) *586*
metrics *585*
Microsoft Management Console (MMC) *590*
mitigation *592*
network *597*
network interface *597*
network intrusion detection system (NIDS) *600*
obsolete *609*
offsiting *607*
operational costs *574*
operational security *606*
patches *576*
perfective maintenance *575*
permissions *601*
plain text *597*
port *599*
port scan *599*
power-on password *595*
pretexting *604*
preventive maintenance *575*
private key encryption *597*
private network *599*
privilege escalation attack *603*
procedural security *606*
product baseline *584*

programmer/analyst *579*
public key encryption (PKE) *597*
RAID (redundant array of independent disks) *607*
recovery *607*
remote control software *573*
response time *586*
retention period *608*
risk *591*
risk assessment *590*
risk control *590*
risk identification *590*
risk management *590*
security *589*
security hole *601*
security policy *590*
security token *605*
service *599*
service packs *583*
social engineering *604*
soft skills *611*
software reengineering *576*
superuser *601*
system administrator *578*
systems programmer *579*
tamper-evident cases *595*
test plan *608*
third-party software *602*
threat *590*
throughput *586*
transference *592*
tunnel *599*
turnaround time *587*
unencrypted *597*
uninterruptible power supply (UPS) *595*
Universal Security Slot (USS) *595*
user rights *601*
user training package *572*
version control *583*
virtual private network (VPN) *599*
vulnerability *591*
what-if analysis *587*
Wi-Fi Protected Access (WPA) *598*
Wired Equivalent Privacy (WEP) *598*
WPA2 *598*

# Learn It Online

**Instructions:** To complete the Learn It Online exercises, visit the Management Information Systems CourseMate Web site at **www.cengagebrain.com**, navigate to the resources for this chapter, and click the link for the exercise you want to complete.

**1  Chapter Reinforcement**

**TF, MC, and SA**

Click one of the Chapter Reinforcement links for Multiple Choice, True/False, or Short Answer. Answer each question and submit to your instructor.

**2  Flash Cards**

Click the Flash Cards link and read the instructions. Type 20 (or a number specified by your instructor) in the Number of playing cards text box, type your name in the Enter your Name text box, and then click the Flip Card button. When the flash card is displayed, read the question and then click the ANSWER box arrow to select an answer. Flip through the Flash Cards. If your score is 15 (75%) correct or greater, click Print on the File menu to print your results. If your score is less than 15 (75%) correct, then redo this exercise by clicking the Replay button.

**3  Practice Test**

Click the Practice Test link. Answer each question, enter your first and last name at the bottom of the page, and then click the Grade Test button. When the graded practice test is displayed on your screen, click Print on the File menu to print a hard copy. Continue to take practice tests until you score 80% or better.

**4  Who Wants To Be a Computer Genius?**

Click the Computer Genius link. Read the instructions, enter your first and last name at the bottom of the page, and then click the Play button. When your score is displayed, click the PRINT RESULTS link to print a hard copy.

**5  Wheel of Terms**

Click the Wheel of Terms link. Read the instructions, and then enter your first and last name and your school name. Click the PLAY button. When your score is displayed on the screen, right-click the score and then click Print on the shortcut menu to print a hard copy.

**6  Crossword Puzzle Challenge**

Click the Crossword Puzzle Challenge link. Read the instructions, and then click the Continue button. Work the crossword puzzle. When you are finished, click the Submit button. When the crossword puzzle is redisplayed, submit it to your instructor.

## Overview

The SCR Associates case study is a Web-based simulation that allows you to practice your skills in a real-world environment. The case study transports you to SCR's intranet, where you complete 12 work sessions, each aligning with a chapter. As you work on the case, you will receive e-mail and voice mail messages, obtain information from SCR's online libraries, and perform various tasks.

## How do I use the case?

- Review the SCR background material in Chapter 1.
- Read the Preview for this session and study the Task List.
- Visit the Management Information Systems CourseMate Web site at **www.cengagebrain.com**, navigate to the **SCR Case Simulation**, and locate the intranet link.
- Enter your name and the password **sad9e**. An opening screen will display the 12 sessions.
- Select this session. Check your e-mail and voice mail carefully, and then work on the tasks.

## Preview: Session 12

You assisted your supervisor, Jesse Baker, in various implementation tasks, and the TIMS system is up and running. Now she wants you to focus on system operation, support, and security tasks. Specifically, she wants you to work on a help desk, version control, configuration management, capacity planning, and system security issues. She also wants you to create a checklist that will help SCR know when the TIMS system is reaching the end of its useful life.

## Task List

| |
|---|
| 1. Jesse wants a recommendation about creating an SCR help desk. She said that I can find lots of information about help desks on the Internet. |
| 2. At our meeting, Jesse asked me how SCR should manage the TIMS system in the future. I need to search the Internet to learn more about version control, configuration management, and capacity planning, and send her the results of my research. |
| 3. Another important issue: Security! Jesse wants my thoughts on how SCR should manage IT security. She wants me to consider all six levels, and prepare an outline for a corporate security policy. |
| 4. Jesse says that no one likes surprises or problems. She wants me to draft a checklist that SCR can use to detect TIMS obsolescence as early as possible. She also said that I might be receiving some interesting news very soon. Wonder what that's about? |

**FIGURE 12-41**   Task list: Session 12.

# Chapter Exercises

### Review Questions

1. Describe the four classifications of maintenance and provide an example of each type.
2. Why are newly hired systems analysts often assigned to maintenance projects?
3. What is configuration management and why is it important?
4. What is the purpose of capacity planning? How is what-if analysis used in capacity planning?
5. What is a release methodology and what are the pros and cons of this approach? What is the purpose of version control?
6. Define the following terms: response time, bandwidth, throughput, and turnaround time. How are the terms related?
7. What are some key issues that you must address when considering data backup and recovery?
8. Explain the concept of risk management, including risk identification, assessment, and control.
9. What are the six security levels? Name at least three specific issues that apply to each level. Also provide three examples of threat categories, attacker profiles, and types of attacks.
10. List six indications that an information system is approaching obsolescence.

### Discussion Topics

1. Assume that your company uses a release methodology for its sales system. The current version is 4.5. Decide whether each of the following changes would justify a version 5.0 release, or be included in a version 4.6 update: (a) Add a new report, (b) add a Web interface, (c) add data validation checks, (d) add an interface to the marketing system, and (e) change the user interface.
2. The four types of IT system maintenance also apply to other industries. Suppose you were in charge of aircraft maintenance for a small airline. What would be an example of each type of maintenance — corrective, adaptive, perfective, and preventive?
3. An IT manager assigns programmers and systems analysts to maintenance projects if they have less than two years of experience or if they received an average or lower rating in their last performance evaluation. Do you agree with this practice?
4. What are the most important security issues facing companies today? Have these changed in the last five years, and will they continue to change? How should companies prepare themselves for security threats and problems in the future?

# Apply Your Knowledge

The Apply Your Knowledge section contains four mini-cases. Each case describes a situation, explains your role in the case, and asks you to respond to questions. You can answer the questions by applying knowledge you learned in the chapter.

## 1 Premium Publishers

**Situation:**

Premium Publishers is a small publishing firm that specializes in reprinting classic literature. A year ago the IT staff developed a Web-based order entry system. The system has performed well, but the company would like to add more features and improve performance. So far, most of the maintenance has involved correcting minor errors.

1. What types of maintenance have the IT staff performed? What types of maintenance will they perform if the existing system is retained?
2. If new features are added, what methodology should the IT staff use to add new functions and enhancements?
3. What IT security measures should the firm adopt? Prepare a security checklist, and be sure to consider all six security levels.
4. Even though the new system is only a year old, e-commerce changes constantly. At what point should Premium Publishers consider replacing the Web-based system with a new system, and why?

## 2 Oceanside Furniture

**Situation:**

Oceanside Furniture produces indoor and outdoor wicker furniture. The company grew from one store in 2007 to eight locations today. Two years ago, the company's IT department developed an inventory control system to keep track of products and reorder out-of-stock items. The new system was well received by users, and inventory problems have decreased significantly. Since the inventory system became operational, however, users steadily have requested increased functionality and changes in screen forms and reports.

1. Should Oceanside have a specific process to manage future changes and enhancements? What should it be?
2. What about version control? Should Oceanside institute a maintenance release methodology? Why or why not?
3. Suppose that you had to assign specific IT staff members to maintain the inventory control system. How would you accomplish the task? Describe your strategy in a brief memo.
4. What should Oceanside watch for to detect possible obsolescence in the future? Develop a checklist with specific examples that Oceanside management could use.

**3** **Robin Hood Associates**

**Situation:**

Robin Hood Associates is an IT consulting firm that develops new systems and maintains older systems for its clients. Robin Hood recently was awarded a contract to correct problems with an existing system. The system is three years old, and the consulting firm that initially designed the system did a poor job of documentation. The data dictionary, user manuals, and other reference material never have been updated, and no process exists for version control.

1. As one of the Robin Hood team members, how should you proceed? What steps would you take, and what would be your priorities?
2. Are CASE tools available that you could use on this assignment? What are they?
3. What advice would you give to the client regarding capacity planning for the future?
4. What steps should the client take to ensure that the system is secure? Prepare a checklist with at least 15 security items that the client should evaluate and monitor. Be sure to consider all six security levels.

**4** **Economy Travel**

**Situation:**

Economy Travel specializes in personalized travel packages at popular prices, and the firm operates 12 offices in major U.S. cities. A key selling point is the firm's client management database, which includes preferences such as airline seating choices and favorite hotels. Economy Travel purchased the client management software as an off-the-shelf vendor package and modified the program to meet the company's needs. The package has been operational for one year and has performed well. Economy Travel, however, is in the process of expanding its operation to include six additional locations. You have been called in as a consultant to help the company make some decisions about IT support.

1. What performance and workload measurement issues should the company consider at the present time?
2. What capacity planning issues should the company consider at the present time?
3. Should the company establish a system baseline before the integration of the six new sites? Explain your answer.
4. As an IT consultant, you must understand the client's business. From that perspective, consider the impact of the Internet on the travel agency business. Investigate this topic using the Internet and other sources of information, and decide what issues to discuss with Economy Travel.

# Case Studies

Case studies allow you to practice specific skills learned in the chapter. Each chapter contains several case studies that continue throughout the textbook, and a chapter capstone case.

## New Century Health Clinic

New Century Health Clinic offers preventive medicine and traditional medical care. In your role as an IT consultant, you will help New Century develop a new information system.

### Background

You implemented the new system at New Century Health Clinic successfully, and the staff has used the system for nearly four months. New Century is pleased with the improvements in efficiency, office productivity, and patient satisfaction.

Some problems have surfaced, however. The office staff members call you almost daily to request assistance and suggest changes in certain reports and forms. You try to be helpful, but now you are busy with a major project for a local distributor of exercise equipment. Actually, your contract with New Century required you to provide support only during the first three months of operation. Anita Davenport, New Century's office manager, reported that the system seems to slow down at certain times during the day, making it difficult for the staff to keep up with its workload. Also, you increasingly are concerned about system security. A recent article in the local newspaper described an incident where a disgruntled former employee was about to break into the computer system and destroy or alter data.

### Assignments

1. You are willing to charge a lower rate for ongoing support services because you designed the system. You want New Century to use a specific procedure for requesting assistance and changes, however, so that you can plan your activities efficiently. Prepare a complete, written procedure for New Century Health Clinic maintenance change requests. Include appropriate forms with your procedure.
2. What could be causing the periodic slowdowns at New Century? If a problem does exist, which performance and workload measures would you monitor to pinpoint the problem?
3. At the end of the systems analysis phase, you studied the economic feasibility of the system and estimated the future costs and benefits. Now that the system is operational, should those costs and benefits be monitored? Why or why not?
4. You decide to prepare a security checklist for New Century. Prepare a list of security issues that the firm should evaluate and monitor. Be sure to organize the items into categories that match the six security levels.

## PERSONAL TRAINER, INC.

Personal Trainer, Inc., owns and operates fitness centers in a dozen Midwestern cities. The centers have done well, and the company is planning an international expansion by opening a new "supercenter" in the Toronto area. Personal Trainer's president, Cassia Umi, hired an IT consultant, Susan Park, to help develop an information system for the new facility. During the project, Susan will work closely with Gray Lewis, who will manage the new operation.

### Background

System changeover and data conversion were successful for the new Personal Trainer system. The post-implementation evaluation indicated that users were pleased with the system. The evaluation also confirmed that the system was operating properly. Several users commented, however, that system response seemed slow. Susan Park, the project consultant, wants to meet with you to discuss operation, maintenance, and security issues affecting the new system.

### Assignments

1. What might be causing the slow response time? Prepare a brief memo explaining system performance and workload measurement, using nontechnical language that Personal Trainer users can understand easily.

2. Personal Trainer's top management asked you to provide ongoing maintenance for the new system. In order to avoid any misunderstanding, you want to provide a brief description of the various types of maintenance. Prepare a brief memo that does this, and include at least two realistic examples of each type of maintenance.

3. Although the system has been operational for a short time, users already have submitted several requests for enhancements and noncritical changes. Should Personal Trainer use a maintenance release methodology to handle the requests? Why or why not?

4. What are the main security issues that Personal Trainer should address? Prepare a memo that lists the primary concerns and offers a specific recommendation for dealing with each issue.

## TARHEEL INDUSTRIES

Tarheel Industries is a medium-sized sporting goods manufacturer located in North Carolina. Tarheel's online production support system was developed in-house and was implemented two months ago. The system runs 24 hours a day in Tarheel's three manufacturing facilities.

### Background

Last Monday morning, the production support system developed a problem. When a screen display for certain parts was requested, the displayed values were garbled.

When she was alerted to the situation, Marsha Stryker, Tarheel's IT manager, immediately assigned a systems analyst to investigate the problem. Marsha instructed the analyst, Eric Wu, to resolve the problem and get the system up and running as soon as possible. Eric previously worked on two small maintenance projects for the production control system, so he was somewhat familiar with the application.

Eric worked all day on the problem, and by 6:30 p.m., he developed and implemented a fix. After verifying that the production support system was capable of producing correct part displays, Eric went home. Early the following morning, Marsha called Eric and two other members of the applications maintenance group to a meeting in her office, where she briefed them on a new adaptive maintenance project for another high-priority system. She asked them to begin work on the new project immediately.

Several nights later, the production control system crashed shortly after midnight. Every time the system was reactivated, it crashed again. Finally, around 2:30 a.m., all production lines were shut down and third-shift production workers were sent home. The production support system finally was corrected and full production was restored the following day, but by that time, Tarheel Industries had incurred thousands of dollars in lost production costs. The cause of the production support system crash was identified as a side effect of the fix that Eric made to the system.

### Assignments

1. Is the second production support system failure entirely unexpected?
2. Who is most to blame for the second system failure?
3. What might Marsha have done differently to avoid the situation? What might Eric have done differently?
4. Outline a new set of maintenance procedures that will help Tarheel Industries avoid such problems in the future.

## MILLS IMPORTS

Mills Imports is a successful importer of gourmet coffees, cheeses, and specialty foods from around the world. Mills Imports recently developed and implemented an online sales information system.

### Background

Using a client/server design, the PCs in each of the firm's 12 retail stores were networked with a server located in the sales support center at the main office. Salespeople in the retail stores use the customer sales information system to record sales transactions; to open, close, or query customer accounts; and to print sales receipts, daily sales reports by salesperson, and daily sales reports by merchandise code. The sales support staff uses the system to query customer accounts and print various daily, weekly, and monthly reports.

When the customer sales system was implemented, the IT department conducted extensive training for the salespeople and the sales support center staff. One member of the systems development team also prepared a user manual, but users are familiar with the system so the manual rarely is used.

Two weeks ago, Mills opened two additional stores and hired six new sales representatives. A manager gave the user manual to the new sales representatives and asked them to read it and experiment with the system. Now, salespeople in both new stores are having major problems using the sales system. When a representative from the main office visited the stores to investigate the problem, she discovered that the new people could not understand the user manual. When she asked for examples of confusing instructions, several salespeople pointed to the following examples:

- *Obtaining the authorization of the store manager on Form RBK-23 is required before the system can activate a customer charge account.*
- *Care should be exercised to ensure that the BACKSPACE key is not pressed when the key on the numeric keypad with a left-facing arrow is the appropriate choice to accomplish nondestructive backspacing.*
- *To prevent report generation interruption, the existence of sufficient paper stock should be verified before any option that requires printing is selected. If not, the option must be reselected.*
- *The F2 key should be pressed in the event that a display of valid merchandise codes is required. That same key terminates the display.*

### Assignments

1. What could Mills Imports have done to avoid the situation?
2. Should the sales support staff ask the IT department to rewrite the user manual as a maintenance project, or should they request a training session for the new salespeople? Can you offer any other suggestions?
3. Rewrite the user manual instructions so they are clear and understandable for new users. What steps might you take to ensure the accuracy of the new user manual instructions?
4. In the process of rewriting the user manual instructions, you discover that some of the instructions were not changed to reflect system maintenance and upgrade activities. A request form on the firm's intranet, for example, has replaced Form RBK-23. Mills also has phased out printed reports in favor of online reports, which users can view by entering a username and password. Rewrite the user manual instructions to reflect the changes.

## CHAPTER CAPSTONE CASE:   SoftWear, Limited

SoftWear, Limited (SWL), is a continuing case study that illustrates the knowledge and skills described in each chapter. In this case study, the student acts as a member of the SWL systems development team and performs various tasks.

### Background

In mid-December 2012, five months after the post-implementation evaluation, the payroll package and the ESIP system were operating successfully and users seemed satisfied with both systems.

During that time, users requested minor changes in reports and screen displays, which the IT staff handled easily. Jane Rossman, manager of applications, continued to assign a mixture of new systems and maintenance tasks to the IT team, and the members indicated that they enjoyed the variety and challenge of both types of work.

Debra Williams, the payroll clerk who prints the ESIP checks, reported the only operational problem. She could not load and align the special check stock in the printer correctly. Becky Evans visited Debra to study the situation and then wrote a specific procedure to solve the problem.

No overtime had been paid in the payroll department since the new system was implemented, and errors in payroll deductions had stopped. Michael Jeremy, SWL's vice president of finance, who initiated the payroll and ESIP projects, is very pleased with the system's operation and output. He recently visited an IT department staff meeting to congratulate the entire group personally.

Some requests for enhancements also occurred. Mike Feiner recently submitted a systems request for the ESIP system to produce an annual employee benefits statement with the current value of all savings plan deductions, plus information on insurance coverage and other benefits data. Mike also indicated that the company would offer several new ESIP choices, including various mutual funds.

In mid-December, Pacific Software announced the latest release of its payroll package. The new version supported full integration of all payroll and human resources functions and data. Ann Hon, director of information systems, was interested in the announcement because she knew that Rob King, SWL's vice president of human resources, wanted a human resources information system (HRIS) to support SWL's long-term needs. At Ann's request, Jane Rossman assigned Becky Evans to analyze the new payroll package to determine if SWL could implement the latest version as a company-wide client/server application.

Becky began the preliminary investigation by reviewing the current system and meeting with Mike Feiner to learn more about the new ESIP options. Next, she met with Marty Hoctor, a representative from Pacific Software, to review the features of the new release. After describing the new software, Marty mentioned that a large Midwestern retail chain recently implemented the package, and he invited Becky to contact Sean Valine, director of IT at that company, to discuss the new release. Becky spoke with Sean, and he agreed to e-mail her a summary of comments that users had made about the new software.

Becky completed her preliminary investigation, including a cost-benefit analysis, and worked with Jane Rossman and Ann Hon to prepare a report and presentation to SWL's newly formed systems review committee, which was created at Ann's suggestion. In their presentation, the IT team recommended that SWL upgrade to the new release of the payroll package and build a client/server application for all of SWL's payroll and personnel functions, including the ESIP system. They also suggested that a team of IT and human resources people get together to study preliminary economic, technical, and operational factors involved in a human resources information system and report back to the systems review committee. They pointed out that if the project was approved, the same team could handle the systems development using JAD or RAD techniques. After the presentation, the committee approved the request and Ann called an IT department staff meeting for the next morning to start planning the systems analysis phase.

During the meeting, Ann and Jane thanked the entire department for its efforts on the payroll and ESIP projects. Ann pointed out that although the payroll package and the ESIP system support SWL's current needs, the business environment changes rapidly and a successful, growing company must investigate new information management technology constantly. At this point, the systems development life cycle for SWL begins again.

## SWL Team Tasks

1. Now that the new ESIP system is operational, Jane Rossman wants you to track system performance using various measurements. At a minimum, she expects you to monitor operational costs, maintenance frequency, technical issues, and user satisfaction. You can add other items if you choose. Write a proposal for Jane that lists each factor you will measure, and make sure that you explain why the item is important and how you plan to obtain the information.

2. Jane assigned you to the SWL team that will study the feasibility of a human resources information system (HRIS). Using the Internet, identify several commercial packages and the names of firms or consultants who specialize in HRIS implementation. Write a brief memo to Jane with your findings.

3. Jane wants you to prepare a security audit procedure for SWL. Specifically, she wants you to prepare a checklist of security issues that need to be evaluated and rated. She said to consider all six security levels, and to include as many specific items as possible that should be assessed.

4. As Ann Hon pointed out in the last meeting, the business environment changes rapidly and a successful, growing company like SWL must investigate new information management technology constantly. Ann has asked you to describe trends in software and hardware that might affect SWL's future IT plans. Perform research on the Internet to identify several technology issues that might represent potential problems or opportunities for SWL, and present the results in a memo to Ann.

## Manage the SWL Project

You have been asked to manage SWL's new information system project. One of your most important activities will be to identify project tasks and determine when they will be performed. Before you begin, you should review the SWL case in this chapter. Then list and analyze the tasks, as follows:

**LIST THE TASKS** Start by listing and numbering at least 10 tasks that the SWL team needs to perform to fulfill the objectives of this chapter. Your list can include SWL Team Tasks and any other tasks that are described in this chapter. For example, Task 3 might be to Perform necessary corrective maintenance and Task 6 might be to Identify perfective maintenance tasks.

**ANALYZE THE TASKS** Now study the tasks to determine the order in which they should be performed. First identify all concurrent tasks, which are not dependent on other tasks. In the example shown in Figure 12-42, Tasks 1, 2, 3, 4, and 5 are concurrent tasks, and could begin at the same time if resources were available.

**CHAPTER CAPSTONE CASE:    SoftWear, Limited (continued)**

Other tasks are called dependent tasks, because they cannot be performed until one or more earlier tasks have been completed. For each dependent task, you must identify specific tasks that need to be completed before this task can begin. For example, you would to perform any necessary corrective maintenance before you could identify perfective maintenance tasks, so Task 6 cannot begin until Task 3 is completed, as Figure 12-42 shows.

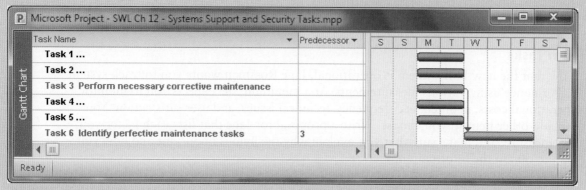

**FIGURE 12-42**   SWL Tasks 1, 2, 3, 4, and 5 are concurrent tasks that could be performed at the same time. Task 6 is a dependent task that cannot be performed until Task 3 has been completed.

Chapter 3 describes project management tools, techniques, and software. To learn more, you can use the Features section on your Student Study Tool CD-ROM, or visit the Management Information Systems CourseMate Web site at **www.cengagebrain.com** and locate the project management resources library for this book. On the Web, Microsoft offers demo versions, training, and tips for using Project 2010. You also can visit the OpenWorkbench.org site to learn more about this free, open-source software.

# Ready for a Challenge?

In additional to technical skills, IT professionals need critical thinking skills such as perception, organization, analysis, problem-solving, and decision-making. The Ready for a Challenge feature can help you learn, practice, and apply critical thinking skills that you can take to the workplace.

Your team leader wants to develop a standard method for rating and ranking maintenance requests for the new C³ system. The idea is to develop some type of grid that could suggest priorities based on the type of maintenance requested and the potential impact on operations. When you review your notes from your systems analysis textbook, you realize that you used a similar approach when you created a risk matrix in Chapter 3, developed an evaluation model in Chapter 7, and selected a changeover method in Chapter 11.

The team leader also wants to test IT security levels with a simulated attack, something like a fire drill. The planned exercise would include realistic threats that will allow the team to evaluate responses and security procedures.

## Practice Tasks

Before you begin, review different techniques for showing multifactor grids. Also review the material on user support and types of maintenance. Then complete these tasks:

A. Develop the maintenance request grid, using the factors listed and any others you want to include. The design should enable requests to be rated or ranked, and the style is not important, as it will be refined later.
B. Draft a plan for the simulated attacks on IT security. Include at least five types of attacks. For each attack, provide an example and suggest a response or action that should be taken to counter the attack.

After you complete the Practice Tasks, to check your work and view sample answers, visit the Management Information Systems CourseMate Web site at **www.cengagebrain.com**, navigate to the resources for this chapter, and locate Ready for a Challenge?.

## The Challenge

Your initial design was good, but the team leader wants you to try another approach. She put these questions to you: "Should corrective maintenance get a higher priority than other types of maintenance? Why or why not? Should cost-benefit issues be considered? If so, how would this be done?"

Also, your security plan was good, but did not go far enough. The team leader wants you to include at least five more types of attacks, with examples and suggested responses.

## Challenge Tasks

A. Consider the team leader's questions carefully. When you reply, include a revised grid design as needed.
B. Revise the simulated attack plan by including five more types of attacks, with examples and suggested responses.

# THE SYSTEMS ANALYST'S APPENDIX

The Systems Analyst's Appendix presents a valuable set of cross-phase skills and knowledge that you can use throughout the systems development process. Appendix A discusses communication tools that can help you write clearly, speak effectively, and deliver powerful presentations. Appendix B describes CASE tools that you can use to design, construct, and document an information system. Appendix C demonstrates financial analysis tools you can use to measure project feasibility, develop accurate cost-benefit estimates, and make sound decisions. Appendix D describes Internet resource tools that you can use to locate information, obtain reference material, and monitor IT trends and developments.

# APPENDIX A Communicating

In **Appendix A**, you will learn about written and oral communication skills that you will need to use as a systems analyst.

## OBJECTIVES

*When you finish this part of the Appendix, you will be able to:*

- List overall guidelines for successful communications
- Write effective letters, memos, and e-mail messages
- Measure the readability of written material
- Organize and prepare written reports that are required during systems development
- Follow guidelines for effective oral communication
- Plan, develop, and deliver a successful presentation
- Use effective speaking techniques to achieve your objectives
- Manage and strengthen your communication skills

A successful systems analyst must have good written and oral communication skills to perform his or her job effectively. Never underestimate the importance of effective communication, whether you are using a memo, e-mail, an oral presentation, or a social networking site to convey your ideas. The following guidelines will help you prepare and deliver effective presentations. Remember, however, that nothing increases your ability to communicate better than practicing these skills.

## APPENDIX INTRODUCTION CASE:   Mountain View College Bookstore

**Background:** Wendy Lee, manager of college services at Mountain View College, wants a new information system that will improve efficiency and customer service at the three college bookstores.

In this part of the case, Tina Allen (systems analyst) and David Conroe (student intern) are talking about communication tools and techniques.

**Participants:**      Tina and David
**Location:**          Mountain View College Cafeteria, at the beginning of the bookstore information system project
**Discussion topics:** Guidelines for successful oral and written communications

| | |
|---|---|
| **Tina:** | David, before we start the project for Wendy, let's talk about written and oral communication tools and techniques. We'll be using these throughout the systems development process. |
| **David:** | *Fine with me. I've always enjoyed my English and writing courses.* |
| **Tina:** | Well, everything you learned in school certainly applies in the workplace. The basic principles of good communications apply everywhere. But in a business environment there are some additional issues to keep in mind. |
| **David:** | *Such as?* |
| **Tina:** | For example, you will be preparing documents, presentations, and training material for users. In each situation, you have to consider the audience very carefully, including their technical knowledge, organizational level, and experience. You'll need to adjust your approach based on those factors, and be aware of the readability of your written work. Also, you'll be using e-mail as a primary communications tool. |
| **David:** | *I understand. Are there any special ground rules for using e-mail?* |
| **Tina:** | Well, e-mail can be more casual than typical business writing — but not *too* casual. We'll talk about that, along with ways to maximize your online effectiveness using software such as Microsoft Outlook. Also, we'll go over some guidelines for preparing presentations. |
| **David:** | *Sounds good to me. When do we start?* |
| **Tina:** | Right now. Here's a task list to get us under way: |

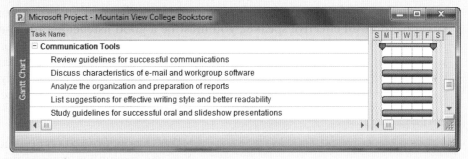

**FIGURE A-1**   Typical communication tasks.

## SUCCESSFUL COMMUNICATION STRATEGIES

Successful communication does not just happen. Usually, it is the result of a specific strategy that includes careful planning, hard work, and practice. To be a successful communicator, you must consider five related questions about yourself, your audience, and your objectives: why, who, what, when, and how. You also must consider the cultural context of your communication. Above all, you must know your subject and have confidence in yourself.

### Why, Who, What, When, and How

The **why, who, what, when, and how of communications** are important questions that you must answer before you communicate. These five questions are described in the following section.

**WHY** Know *why* you are communicating, and what you want to accomplish. Ask yourself the question, "Is this communication necessary, and what specific results am I seeking?" Your entire communication strategy depends on the results that you need.

**WHO** Know *who* your targets are. Chapter 1 describes how information needs of users depend on their organizational and knowledge levels. When communicating with management, for example, sometimes a fine line exists between saying enough and saying too much. Each situation is different, so you must use good judgment and be alert for input from your audience.

**WHAT** Know *what* is expected of you and when to go into detail. This is directly related to knowing who your targets are and the organizational and knowledge levels of your audience. For example, a vice president might expect less detail and more focus on how a project supports the company's strategic business goals. You must design your communications just as carefully as your systems project. For example, will the recipients expect you to address a specific issue or topic? Will they expect cost estimates or charts? Design your communications based on the answers to those questions.

**WHEN** Know *when* to speak and *when* to remain silent and let others continue the discussion. To be an effective speaker, you must be a good listener — and use audience feedback to adjust your presentation. Good timing is an essential part of every presentation. Your delivery must be paced properly — too fast and you will lose your audience; too slow and they might become bored.

**HOW** Know *how* to communicate effectively. You can strengthen your communication skills by using Appendix suggestions, reflecting upon your own experiences, and observing successful and unsuccessful techniques used by others.

### Cultural Context

Communication strategy is affected by the cultural context in which the communication takes place, as shown in Figure A-2. Cultural factors can include geography, background, educational level, and societal differences, among others. These differences must be

**FIGURE A-2**  Every communication takes place within an overall cultural context.

considered when asking and answering the *why*, *who*, *what*, *when*, and *how* questions.

In addition to these factors, you learned in Chapter 1 that corporate culture is very important. A **corporate culture** includes the beliefs, rules, traditions, values, and attitudes that define a company and influence its way of doing business. To be successful, a systems analyst must understand, and work within this culture. For example, if you speak to a group in a company that encourages a highly participative style, you might want to solicit feedback, invite audience comments, or conduct a poll during your presentation. Similarly, if the organization or group is very formal, or very informal, you might want to adjust your style accordingly.

## Know Your Subject

No matter how well you plan your communication, you must know your subject inside and out. Your credibility and effectiveness will depend on whether others believe you and support your views. No one can know everything, so it is important to adopt a specific preparation strategy. For example, before a presentation, consider what others expect you to know and what questions they will ask. No matter how well you prepare, however, you will not have an answer for every question. Remember that it is better to say, "I don't know, but I'll find out and get back to you," rather than to guess.

## WRITTEN COMMUNICATIONS

Good writing is important because others often judge you by your writing. If you make a mistake while speaking, your audience probably will forget it. Your written errors, however, might stay around for a long time. Grammatical, typographical, and spelling errors distract readers from your message. Your written communications will include e-mail messages, memos, letters, workgroup communications, and formal reports.

**ON THE WEB**

To learn more about effective written communications, visit the Management Information Systems CourseMate Web site at **www. cengagebrain. com**, navigate to **On the Web Links** for Appendix A, and locate the Effective Written Communications link.

### Writing Style and Readability

If you have not taken a writing course, you should consider doing so. If you have a choice of courses, select one that focuses on business writing or technical writing. Any writing class, however, is worth the effort. Most bookstores and libraries have excellent books on effective communications, and many Internet sites offer writing guidelines, tips, and grammar rules. As you prepare written documents, keep in mind the following suggestions:

1. Know your audience. If you are writing for nontechnical readers, use terms that readers will understand.
2. Use the **active voice** whenever possible. For example, the active voice sentence "Tom designed the system," is better than, "The system was designed by Tom," which is an example of the **passive voice**.
3. Keep your writing clear, concise, and well-organized. Each paragraph should present a single topic or idea.
4. Use an appropriate style. For example, use a conversational tone in informal documents and a business tone in formal documents.
5. Use lists. If a topic has many subtopics, a list can organize the material and make it easier to understand.
6. Use short, easy-to-understand words. Your objective is not to impress your audience with the size of your vocabulary.
7. Avoid repeating the same word too often. Use a thesaurus to locate synonyms for frequently repeated words. Many word processing programs include a thesaurus and other tools to help you write better.

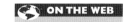

**ON THE WEB**

To learn more about grammar checkers, visit the Management Information Systems CourseMate Web site at **www. cengagebrain.com**, navigate to **On the Web Links** for Appendix A, and locate the Grammar Checkers link.

8. Check your spelling. You can use the spell checker in your word processing program to check your spelling, but remember that a **spell checker** is a tool that identifies only words that do not appear in the program's dictionary. For example, a spell checker will not identify instances when you use the word *their*, instead of the word *there*.

9. Check your grammar. Most word processing programs include a **grammar checker**, which is a tool that can detect usage problems and offer suggestions. When you use a grammar checker, you can set various options to match the level and style of the writing and to highlight or ignore certain types of usage. For example, you can set the grammar checker in Microsoft Word to check grammar rules only, or you can configure it to check writing style, as shown in Figure A-3, including gender-specific words, sentence fragments, and passive sentences.

10. Review your work carefully. Then double-check it for spelling, grammatical, and typographical mistakes. If possible, ask a colleague to proofread your work and suggest improvements.

All writers must consider **readability**, which analyzes ease of comprehension by measuring specific characteristics of syllables, words, and sentences. Two popular readability tools are the Flesch Reading Ease Score and the Flesch-Kincaid Grade Level Score.

The **Flesch Reading Ease score** measures the average sentence length and the average number of syllables per word and rates the text on a 100-point scale using the formula shown in Figure A-4. With this tool, the higher the score, the easier it is to understand. Microsoft suggests that for most standard documents, you should aim for a score of 60-70.

The **Flesch-Kincaid Grade Level score** uses the same variables, but in a different formula that produces a rating keyed to a U.S. grade-school level. For example, a score of 8.0 would indicate material easily understood by a person at an eighth-grade reading level. With this tool, Microsoft suggests that for most standard documents, you should aim for a score of 7.0 to 8.0.

## E-Mail, Memos, and Letters

Because e-mail will be your primary tool for written communication, it is important to use it properly and effectively. E-mail usually is less formal than other written correspondence, but you still must follow the rules of good grammar, correct spelling, and clear writing.

**FIGURE A-3** You can set the grammar checker in Microsoft Word to check grammar rules only, or you can configure it to check your writing style.

Although many authors use a more conversational style for e-mail, you should remember that e-mail messages often are forwarded to other recipients or groups, and so you must consider the users to whom it might be distributed. If you regularly exchange messages with a specific group of users, most e-mail programs allow you to create a distribution list that includes the members and their e-mail addresses. For example, Figure A-5 shows how to use Microsoft Outlook to send an e-mail to a six-person systems development team. Now that e-mail has become the standard method of business communication, it is important that all users know how to use e-mail properly, professionally, and courteously. This topic is discussed in the following section.

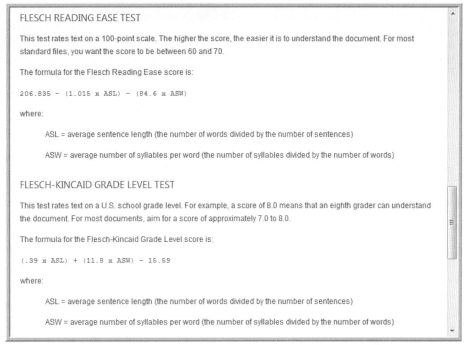

FLESCH READING EASE TEST

This test rates text on a 100-point scale. The higher the score, the easier it is to understand the document. For most standard files, you want the score to be between 60 and 70.

The formula for the Flesch Reading Ease score is:

$$206.835 - (1.015 \times ASL) - (84.6 \times ASW)$$

where:

ASL = average sentence length (the number of words divided by the number of sentences)

ASW = average number of syllables per word (the number of syllables divided by the number of words)

FLESCH-KINCAID GRADE LEVEL TEST

This test rates text on a U.S. school grade level. For example, a score of 8.0 means that an eighth grader can understand the document. For most documents, aim for a score of approximately 7.0 to 8.0.

The formula for the Flesch-Kincaid Grade Level score is:

$$(.39 \times ASL) + (11.8 \times ASW) - 15.59$$

where:

ASL = average sentence length (the number of words divided by the number of sentences)

ASW = average number of syllables per word (the number of syllables divided by the number of words)

FIGURE A-4   Two popular readability measurement tools are the Flesch Reading Ease Score and the Flesch-Kincaid Grade Level Score.

Although e-mail is the main form of internal communication, internal memos and announcements still are important, and external communications often require letters printed on company letterhead. Most companies use a standard format, or template, for internal memos and external letters. If your company stores those on a network, you can download and use the templates. If you want to create your own designs, you can use a word processor to create templates with specific layouts, fonts, and margin settings. A **template** gives your work a consistent look and makes your job easier. Most word processing programs also provide a feature that allows you to design your memos as forms and fill in the blanks as you work.

ON THE WEB

To learn more about readability, locate the **On the Web links** for Appendix A at **www.engagebrain. com** and click the Readability link.

## Netiquette

**Netiquette** is a term that combines the words *Internet* and *etiquette*. With the explosive growth of social networking, netiquette is more important than ever. On the Web, you can find many sources of information about netiquette. One example is the site shown in Figure A-6 on the next page, which offers an excellent source of netiquette guidelines, tips, and links.

All e-mail users should be aware of some simple rules, most of which are nothing more than good manners and common sense. For example, an excellent starting point is to avoid sending material that is personal or confidential, because your messages might be forwarded by others and distributed more

FIGURE A-5   Microsoft Outlook allows users to create distribution lists for sending e-mail messages.

**FIGURE A-6**   This site offers netiquette guidelines, tips, and links.

widely than you intended. Another important rule is never to send or reply to an e-mail when you are tired or upset. Instead, you can write a draft if you want to, but save the unsent message so you can review it later.

Here are some common rules and tips:

- Always fill in the subject field with a brief description of the contents.
- Be brief — in most cases, less is more.
- Be professional. Remember, if it has your name on it, it reflects on you personally and that often is how people will view your messages.
- Be sure to check your spelling.
- Don't forward jokes or chain letters without the permission of the recipient.
- Don't overuse humor or sarcasm that might work in a face-to-face situation, but not in an e-mail context.
- Don't type in all caps — it is like YELLING! It is also hard to read.
- Don't use colored fonts, background, or images in business e-mail messages.
- Don't use the return receipt request feature unless there is a valid business reason to do so.
- If you have large attachment files, try to zip or compress them before sending.
- If you send a message to a group of people, especially if they don't know each other, use a blind copy (Bcc) for all of the recipients in order to shield the addresses from the entire group.
- Never give out personal contact information of others without their specific permission to do so.
- Never include personal information unless you are 100% sure of your recipient and no other means of communication would provide better privacy and security.
- Remember that there are copyright laws. You do not have an unrestricted right to do whatever you please with someone else's e-mail message to you. Laws against discrimination and defamation can also apply to e-mail messages.
- When replying, don't include all the earlier messages unless there is a reason to do so.
- Social networking, instant messaging (IM), and cell-phone texting are popular because they allow informal, interactive, and immediate communication. While IM and texting can be valuable collaboration tools, users should exercise good judgment and common sense, just as they would in any form of business conversation.

In addition to these guidelines, it is important to follow company policy regarding communications at work. Many firms restrict personal communications that involve company time or equipment, and courts have upheld an employer's right to limit or monitor such communications.

## Workgroup Software

Many companies use **workgroup software**, often called **groupware**, because it enhances employee productivity and teamwork. In addition to basic e-mail, workgroup software enables users to manage and share their calendars, task lists, schedules, contact lists, and documents. Popular examples of workgroup software include Microsoft Outlook and Novell's GroupWise, which is shown in Figure A-7.

Google Docs, which is shown in Figure A-8, offers free, Web-based collaboration. Using this application, a team can work on centrally stored documents instead of e-mailing drafts back and forth. Teams also can use powerful multiauthoring software, such as Adobe Acrobat, to add revisions, notes, and comments to PDF documents.

**FIGURE A-7** Workgroup software, such as Novell's GroupWise, allows a user to collaborate with others by sharing documents and folders.

## Reports

You must prepare many reports during systems development, including the preliminary investigation report, the system requirements document at the end of the systems analysis phase, the system design specification at the end of the system design phase, and the final report to management when the system goes into operation. You also might submit other reports, such as status reports, activity reports, proposals, and departmental business plans. You will create your reports as electronic documents, so you can attach them to e-mails. Although most reports are delivered electronically, in some cases you must prepare printed versions. For example, Figure A-9 on the next page shows a binder for a system requirements document, which includes an introduction, an executive summary, findings, recommendations, time and cost estimates, expected benefits, and an appendix containing relevant data.

You can use a cover memo, or an e-mail message similar to the one shown in Figure A-9, when you send a report, and you can set a date, time, and place for an oral presentation. You also can request that the recipients read the report in advance of the presentation.

The introduction usually includes a title page, table of contents, and brief description of the proposal. The title page should be clean and neat and contain the name of the proposal, the subject, the date, and the

**FIGURE A-8** An employee team can use Google Docs to work on centrally stored documents.

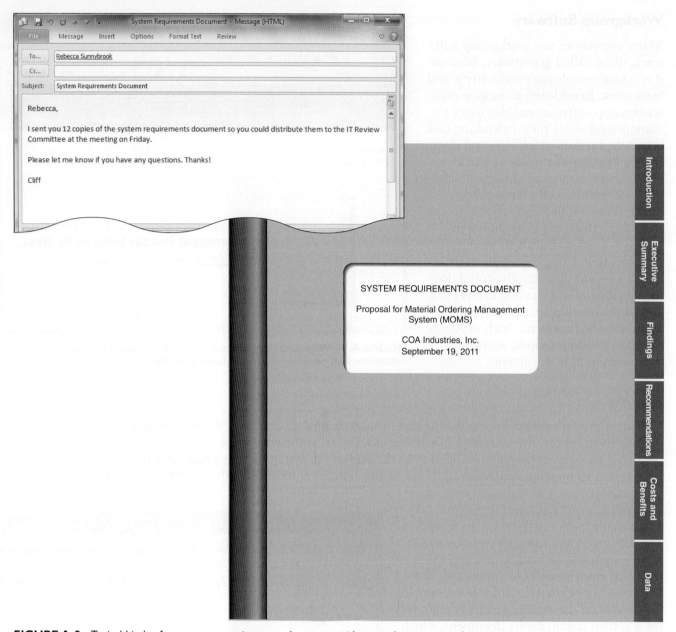

**FIGURE A-9** Typical binder for a system requirements document, with an explanatory e-mail message.

names of the development team members. If the project already has a recognized name or acronym, use it. Include a table of contents when the report is long or includes many exhibits. Many word processing programs include a tool that can generate a table of contents automatically.

The executive summary is used to summarize the entire project, including your recommendations, in several paragraphs. Generally, the executive summary should not exceed 200 words or one page.

Use the findings section to describe the major conclusions that you or the team reached during the systems analysis phase. You can make the findings section detailed or summarized, depending on the project. You must explain the logical design of the new system in a way that nontechnical managers can understand clearly. With a management audience, the most important task is to explain how the proposed system supports the company's business needs.

The recommendations section presents the best system alternative, with a brief explanation that should mention economic, technical, operational, and schedule feasibility.

In the costs and benefits section, you should list the advantages, disadvantages, costs, and benefits of each major system alternative. You should include a clear description of the financial analysis techniques you used. You might want to apply one or more of the financial analysis tools described in Appendix C of the Systems Analyst's Appendix. You can use tables or graphs to support and clarify your alternatives when necessary.

When you have a large number of supporting documents such as questionnaires or sampling results, you should put those items in a data section located at the end of the document. Make sure you include only relevant information, and provide references for interested readers.

## ORAL COMMUNICATIONS

An **oral presentation** is required at the end of the preliminary investigation and again at the conclusion of the systems analysis phase. You might need to give more than one presentation in some situations to present technical material to members of the IT department or to present an overview for top managers. When preparing an oral presentation, you should perform six important tasks: Define the audience, define the objectives for your presentation, organize the presentation, define any technical terms you will use, prepare your presentation aids, and practice your delivery.

 **ON THE WEB**

To learn more about effective presentations, visit the Management Information Systems CourseMate Web site at **www. cengagebrain. com**, navigate to **On the Web Links** for Appendix A, and locate the Effective Presentations link.

### Define the Audience

Before you develop a detailed plan for a management presentation, you must define the audience. Senior managers often prefer an executive summary rather than a detailed presentation, but that is not always the case, especially in smaller companies where top management is more involved in day-to-day activities. If you consider the expectations of your audience and design your presentation accordingly, you will improve your chances of success.

### Define the Objectives

When you communicate, you should focus on your objectives. In the management presentation for the systems analysis phase, your goals are the following:

- Inform management of the status of the current system
- Describe your findings concerning the current system problems
- Explain the alternative solutions that you developed
- Provide detailed cost and time estimates for the alternative solutions
- Recommend the best alternative and explain the reasons for your selection

## Organize the Presentation

Plan your presentation in three stages: the introduction, the information, and the summary. First, you should introduce yourself and describe your objectives. During the presentation, make sure that you discuss topics in a logical order. You should be as specific as possible when presenting facts — your listeners want to hear your views about what is wrong, how it can be fixed, how much it will cost, and when the objectives can be accomplished. In your summary, briefly review the main points, and then ask for questions.

## Define Any Technical Terms

You should avoid specialized or technical terminology whenever possible. If your audience might be unfamiliar with a term that you plan to use, either define the term or find another way to say it so they will understand your material.

## Prepare Presentation Aids

Much of what people learn is acquired visually, so you should use helpful, appropriate visual aids to help the audience follow the logic of your presentation and hold their attention. Visual aids also can direct audience attention away from you, which is helpful if you are nervous when you give the presentation. You can use a visual aid with an outline of topics that will help you stay on track. You can enhance the effect of your presentation with visual aids that use various media and software, as explained in the following sections.

**ON THE WEB**

To learn more about presentation software, visit the Management Information Systems CourseMate Web site at **www. cengagebrain. com**, navigate to **On the Web Links** for Appendix A, and locate the Presentation Software link.

**VISUAL AIDS** Visual aids can help you display a graphical summary of performance trends, a series of cost-benefit examples, or a bulleted list of important points. You can use whiteboards, flip charts, overhead transparencies, slides, films, and videotapes to enhance your presentation. When preparing your visual aids, make sure that the content is clear, readable, and easy to understand. Verify ahead of time that the audience can see the visual material from anywhere in the room. Remember that equipment can fail unexpectedly, so be prepared with an alternate plan.

**PRESENTATION SOFTWARE** With a computer and a projection system, you can use **presentation software**, such as Microsoft PowerPoint, to create a multimedia slide show. As shown in Figure A-10, Microsoft offers free tutorials with advanced tips and techniques that can improve your presentations. The lower screen shows a Microsoft PowerPoint 2010 training video.

Preparing an effective slide presentation requires time and effort, and personal experience is the best teacher. There is no universal agreement about

**FIGURE A-10** Microsoft PowerPoint offers many free online tutorials that demonstrate the full potential of the software.

how to prepare a slide show, and many sources of information exist. Some overall guidelines include the following:

- Your first step (and perhaps the most important) is to prepare an overall outline that will be the foundation of your presentation. You should focus on the content and structure of your presentation before you consider visual issues.

- Remember that a fine line exists between providing too little information and too much.

- Display one topic per slide, and try to follow the rule often called the **7 by 7 rule**: no more than seven items per slide, and no more than seven words per item. Some presenters believe that a **6 by 6 rule** is even more effective.

- When displaying a list of items, consider using a series of slides to add each point sequentially, especially if you want to focus attention on the item being discussed.

- Use bullets rather than numbers, unless you are showing a specific sequence or order.

- Choose easily readable fonts. Use sans serif styles, such as **Arial**, for all body text. If you do use a serif style (such as Times Roman), apply it only in titles.

- Use appropriate point sizes for titles and body text. Your goal is to prepare slides that are readable and visually attractive. Although point size selection depends on individual judgment and experience, here are some suggestions to get you started: For titles, try either 40- or 36-point fonts; for body text, 32- or 24-point fonts usually work well.

- Select special effects carefully — too many graphics, colors, sounds, or other special effects will distract your audience.

- You can include tables or graphics, but keep them simple and easy to understand. Also, you can use a special effect, such as boldface, italic, underlining, or a different color, to highlight an important word or phrase.

- Strive for a consistent look and feel among your slides, and position visual elements in the same place on each slide. You should use a master template to ensure uniformity and conform to company-wide standards that might apply, such as a copyright notice, a confidentiality statement, or placement of the company name and logo. Choose colors carefully, and keep them consistent. Usually, light letters on a dark background are easiest to read. Presentation software normally has predefined color palettes that provide background and text colors that ensure readability. Use these palettes as a guideline for selecting colors when possible.

- Be sure to check spelling and grammar!

- During the presentation, do *not* read your slides to the audience! They can read the slides on their own. Your slide presentation is an outline that provides structure and emphasis — it is not the presentation itself.

- It is important to deliver a presentation that can be viewed easily from anywhere in the room. When setting up, consider the size of the room, the number of people attending, the size and location of your visual aids, and the characteristics of any projection equipment you will be using.

## Practice

The most important part of your preparation is practice. You should rehearse several times to ensure that the presentation flows smoothly and the timing is correct. Practicing will make you more comfortable and build your confidence.

Do not be tempted to write a script. If you read your presentation, you will be unable to interact with your audience and adjust your content based on their reactions. Instead, prepare an outline of your presentation and practice from the outline. Then, when you deliver the actual presentation, you will not have to struggle to remember the exact words you planned to say, and you will be able to establish a good rapport with your audience.

## The Presentation

When you deliver your presentation, the following pointers will help you succeed:

**SELL YOURSELF AND YOUR CREDIBILITY**  As a presenter, you must sell yourself and your credibility. A brilliant presentation will not convince top managers to approve the system if they are not sold on the person who gave the presentation. On the other hand, projects often are approved on the basis of the presenter's knowledge, commitment, and enthusiasm.

Your presentation must show confidence about the subject and your recommendations. You should avoid any conflicts with the people attending the presentation. If you encounter criticism or hostility, remain calm and stay focused on the issues — not the person making the comments. You will have a successful presentation only if you know the material thoroughly, prepare properly, and sell yourself and your credibility.

**CONTROL THE PRESENTATION**  During the presentation, you must control the discussion, maintain the pace of the presentation, and stay focused on the agenda — especially when answering questions. Although you might be more familiar with the subject material, you should not display a superior attitude toward your listeners. Maintain eye contact with the audience and use some humor, but do not make a joke at someone else's expense.

**ANSWER QUESTIONS APPROPRIATELY**  Let your audience know whether you would prefer to take questions as you go along or have a question-and-answer session at the end. Sometimes the questions can be quite difficult. You must listen carefully and respond with a straightforward answer. Try to anticipate the questions your audience will ask so you can prepare your responses ahead of time.

When answering a difficult or confusing question, repeat the question in your own words to make sure that you understand it. For example, you can say, "If I understand your question, you are asking ..." This will help avoid confusion and give you a moment to think on your feet. To make sure that you gave a clear answer, you can say, "Have I answered your question?" Allow follow-up questions when necessary.

**USE EFFECTIVE SPEAKING TECHNIQUES**  The delivery of your presentation is just as important as its content. You can strengthen your delivery by speaking clearly and confidently and projecting a relaxed approach. You also must control the pace of your delivery. If you speak too fast, you will lose the audience, and if the pace is too slow, people will lose their concentration and the presentation will not be effective.

Many speakers are nervous when facing an audience. If this is a problem for you, keep the following suggestions in mind:

- Control your environment. If you are most nervous when the audience is looking at you, use visual aids to direct their attention away from you. If your hands are shaking, do not hold your notes. If you are delivering a computer-based presentation, it is a good idea to use a handheld wireless device to control the slides. Concentrate on using a strong, clear voice. If your nervousness distracts you, take a deep breath and remind yourself that you really do know your subject.

- Turn your nervousness to your advantage. Many people do their best work when they are under a little stress. Think of your nervousness as normal pressure.

- Avoid meaningless filler words and phrases. Using words and phrases such as *okay, all right, you know, like, um,* and *ah* are distracting and serve no purpose.

- Practice! Practice! Practice! Some people are naturally gifted speakers, but most people need lots of practice. You must work hard at practicing your presentation and building your confidence. Many schools offer speech or public speaking courses that are an excellent way of practicing your skills. It also can be advantageous to preview your presentation with one or more people and ask for input.

## Online Presentations

In addition to face-to-face meetings, you might have to deliver an **online presentation**, possibly with two-way communication between you and the audience. You have several options. You might use PowerPoint 2010 to broadcast a live presentation, as shown in Figure A-11, and your online audience would see the slides in a Web browser. Your presentation also could include an audio narrative. If you want real-time participation, you might consider Cisco's WebEx, which is shown in Figure A-12, or a similar product. WebEx can handle live audio and video, and allows you to deliver a fully interactive Webinar. Microsoft also offers a robust Web-conferencing platform called Live Meeting, shown in Figure A-13, which supports presentations, group meetings, and collaboration.

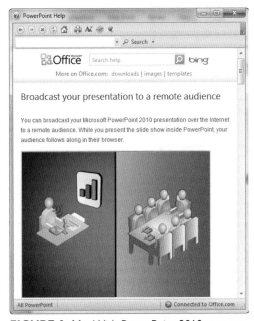

**FIGURE A-11** With PowerPoint 2010, you can broadcast a live presentation to a remote audience, who can view it in a Web browser.

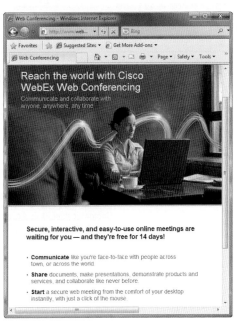

**FIGURE A-12** Cisco's WebEx can handle live audio and video, and allows you deliver an interactive Webinar.

**FIGURE A-13** Microsoft Live Meeting supports presentations, group meetings, conferences, and collaboration.

## MANAGING YOUR COMMUNICATION SKILLS

More than ever, employees must rely on their personal skills and experience. In an uncertain world and a turbulent economy, individuals should think of themselves as profit-making companies, complete with assets, liabilities, strengths, and areas for development. In Chapter 2, you learned that a company must have a strategic plan, and the same is true for an individual. Armed with a plan to improve your communication skills, you are much more likely to reach your full potential.

Communicating is like any other activity — the more you practice, the better you become. Many resources are available for students and IT professionals who want to improve their written and oral communication skills. For example, the Vocational Information Center site shown in Figure A-14 offers a wide range of free resources and links that can help you become a better writer, presenter, and public speaker. The Association for Computing Machinery (ACM) also offers many online courses and tutorials for members, including students and IT professionals.

**FIGURE A-14**   The Vocational Information Center offers many online courses and tutorials on communications skills.

Some people find it difficult to stand in front of a group and deliver a presentation or report. For many years, membership in Toastmasters, International has been a popular way to gain confidence, overcome stage fright, and develop public speaking skills. As shown in Figure A-15, Toastmasters offers a friendly environment where members critique each speech in a positive manner, note the strengths, and offer suggestions about what might be improved. With more than 200,000 members in 92 countries, this organization offers an excellent way to develop better public speaking skills.

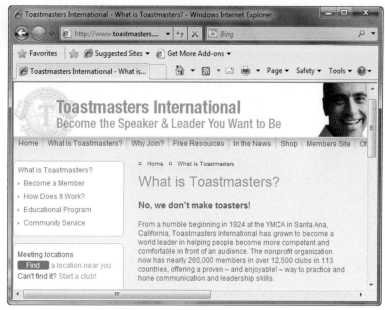

**FIGURE A-15** Toastmasters International is famous for helping people become better public speakers.

## APPENDIX SUMMARY

Your success as a systems analyst depends on your ability to communicate effectively. You must know why you are communicating, what you want to accomplish, who your targets are, what is expected of you, and when to go into detail. You must know your subject and how to use good written and oral communications techniques.

You will be judged by your written work, so it must be free of grammatical, spelling, and punctuation errors. You should write e-mail, letters, and memos clearly, and the writing style should match the situation. Many firms have standard formats for letters and memos, and you can use templates to achieve consistency.

Your writing must be clear and understandable. You can use readability measurement tools such as the Flesch Reading Ease score and the Flesch-Kincaid Grade Level score.

You will prepare various reports during systems development, and the format will vary depending on the nature of the report. Your reports should have a cover memo and might include an introduction, an executive summary, findings, recommendations, time and cost estimates, expected benefits, and a data section.

In addition to written communications, you must communicate effectively in person. You might have to deliver several presentations to different audiences at different times during the SDLC. Presentations are an important form of oral communication, and you should follow specific guidelines in preparing your presentation. You prepare by defining your audience, identifying your objectives, and organizing the presentation itself. You also need to define technical terms and prepare visual aids to help your audience understand the material. Most important, you must practice your delivery to gain confidence and strengthen your presentation skills. You may also want to deliver your presentation through an online venue.

When you develop slide presentations, you should follow the 6 by 6 rule or 7 by 7 rule and other guidelines that will make your slides easy to read and understand. You should select fonts and point sizes carefully, and strive for a consistent look and feel throughout the presentation. Special effects can be interesting, but do not overuse them.

When you give the presentation, you are selling your ideas and your credibility. You must control the discussion, build a good rapport with the audience, answer all questions clearly and directly, and try to use good speaking techniques. Again, the best way to become a better speaker is to practice.

Every IT professional should have a strategic plan to manage and improve written and oral communication skills. Many online resources offer courses, tutorials, and support to help you develop the skills you will need in the workplace.

# Key Terms and Phrases

6 by 6 rule *641*

7 by 7 rule *641*

active voice *633*

corporate culture *633*

Flesch-Kincaid Grade
  Level score *634*

Flesch Reading Ease score *634*

grammar checker *634*

groupware *636*

netiquette *635*

online presentation *643*

oral presentation *639*

passive voice *633*

presentation software *640*

readability *634*

spell checker *634*

template *635*

visual aids *640*

why, who, what, when, and
  how of communications *632*

workgroup software *636*

# Appendix Exercises

## Review Questions

1. Describe the why, who, what, when, and how of communications. Explain each term and give an example. Also, what is a corporate culture and why is it important?
2. Mention five specific techniques you can use to improve your written documents.
3. What techniques can help to improve your e-mail communications?
4. Describe the main sections of a written report to management.
5. When preparing an oral presentation, what six tasks should you perform?
6. When you organize the presentation, what three stages do you plan?
7. Why are visual aids important? Give at least three examples of different types of visual aids, and explain how you would use each type in a presentation.
8. What can you do during your presentation to improve its success?
9. Name three specific strategies you can use if you get nervous during a presentation.
10. Why is practice so important when preparing a presentation?

## Discussion Topics

1. Most people agree that business e-mail can be more conversational than formal written documents, but even e-mail has its limits. As a manager, what guidance would you give people regarding e-mail style and usage?
2. Is it possible to overcommunicate? For example, in Chapter 4 you learned to avoid leading questions, which might suggest an answer. Can you think of other examples, like newspaper headlines, where "less is more"?
3. Many articles stress the importance of body language. Think of examples where you noticed a person's body language. Did it relate to something they were trying to communicate — or something they were trying *not* to communicate?
4. Should e-mail monitoring by an employer always be permissible, never permissible, or does the answer depend on specific factors? If so, what are they?

## Projects

1. *The Elements of Style* by William Strunk, Jr. and E. B. White is a popular reference manual for proper English usage. The book identifies many words and phrases that are commonly misused, including *between* and *among, affect* and *effect, different from* and *different than, like* and *as,* and *infer and imply.* Review *The Elements of Style* or another source, and explain how these words should be used.
2. Using Microsoft PowerPoint or another program, prepare a presentation on "How to Prepare an Effective Slide Presentation." Assume that your audience is familiar with presentation software, but has no formal training.
3. As a training manual writer, choose a simple hardware or software task and write a two- or three-paragraph description of how to perform the task. Then use your word processing software to check the readability statistics. Try to keep the Flesch Reading Ease score above 60 and the Flesch-Kincaid Grade Level score to 8.0 or less.
4. View at least three examples of public speaking. You can investigate TV network news broadcasts, C-SPAN, or any other source. Describe each speaker's gestures, expressions, voice levels, inflections, timing, eye contact, and effectiveness.

# APPENDIX B

# Software Engineering

In **Appendix B**, you will learn how CASE tools can help you perform systems development and maintenance tasks.

## INTRODUCTION

## OBJECTIVES

*When you finish this part of the Appendix, you will be able to:*

- Explain CASE tools and the concept of a CASE environment

- Trace the history of CASE tools and their role in a fourth-generation environment

- Define CASE terms and concepts, including a repository, modeling tools, documentation tools, engineering tools, and construction tools

- Explain an integrated development environment

- Provide examples of CASE tool features

- Describe CASE tool trends, and how they relate to object-oriented analysis and agile methods

Computer-aided systems engineering (CASE), also called **computer-aided software engineering,** is a technique that uses powerful software, called **CASE tools,** to help system developers design and construct information systems. In this part of the Systems Analyst's Appendix, you will learn about the history, characteristics, and features of CASE tools. You will see specific examples of CASE tools and how they are used in various development tasks. In addition, you will learn about integrated software development environments.

## APPENDIX INTRODUCTION CASE:   Mountain View College Bookstore

**Background:** Wendy Lee, manager of college services at Mountain View College, wants a new information system that will improve efficiency and customer service at the three college bookstores.

In this part of the case, Tina Allen (systems analyst) and David Conroe (student intern) are talking about CASE tools and concepts.

| | |
|---|---|
| **Participants:** | Tina and David |
| **Location:** | Tina's office, early in the systems planning phase |
| **Discussion topics:** | CASE tools, integrated development environments, CASE terms and concepts |

**Tina:**   David, before we get too far into the project, let's talk about CASE tools and concepts and how we can use them in the development process.

**David:**   *Sure. I saw examples of CASE tools in my systems analysis course. CASE stands for computer-aided systems engineering, right?*

**Tina:**   Yes. Some people say CASE stands for computer-aided *software* engineering instead of computer-aided *systems* engineering. There's really no difference. Either way, CASE tools are an integral part of the systems development process, and can be used with structured, object-oriented, or agile development methods.

**David:**   *Will we use CASE tools on the bookstore project?*

**Tina:**   Yes. We'll start by identifying and modeling business functions and processes. That information will become part of a central repository, which is a database that stores all the characteristics of the information system.

**David:**   *Then what?*

**Tina:**   We'll use CASE tools to draw various diagrams, including DFDs, UML diagrams, functional decomposition diagrams, and business process diagrams. You'll learn about these as we go along. We might also use CASE tools to generate program code, screens, and reports. Also, depending on the software environment we select, we might use an integrated development environment.

**David:**   *What's that?*

**Tina:**   An integrated development environment is like a built-in CASE tool that a vendor integrates into a software product.

**David:**   *Anything else?*

**Tina:**   Well, before we decide on a CASE tool, we'll take a look at several examples. Here's a task list to get us started:

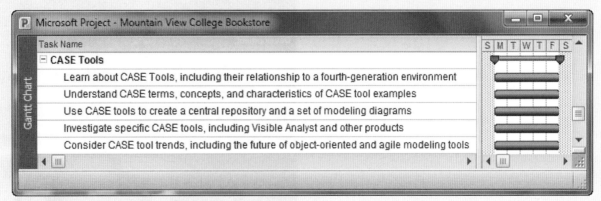

**FIGURE B-1**   Typical CASE tool tasks.

## OVERVIEW OF CASE TOOLS

If you ask a carpenter for an example of a tool, the response might be a hammer, drill, or screwdriver. Put the same question to a chef, and the answer might be a measuring cup, knife, or spatula. Every type of work requires specific tools to do the job properly, and system development is no different. CASE tools can reduce costs, speed up development, and provide comprehensive documentation for future maintenance or enhancements.

The Carnegie Mellon Software Engineering Institute (SEI) is a leader in software engineering and development. SEI helps organizations improve their software capabilities and develop or acquire high quality software. As shown in Figure B-2, SEI focuses on overall architecture, system design, software development, tools, and methods.

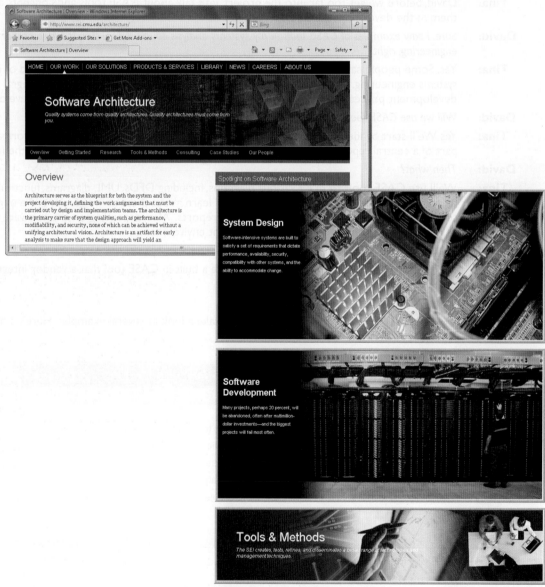

**FIGURE B-2**  As a leader in software standards and quality management, SEI focuses on overall architecture, system design, software development, tools, and methods.

## CASE Tools History

As early as the 1960s, programmers used tools such as editors and code debuggers to write mainframe computer applications. Today, in our software-driven world, CASE tools have evolved into powerful resources that systems analysts need to build and maintain complex information systems.

Traditional code was written in **procedural programming languages** such as COBOL, which required a programmer to create a command for each processing step. In contrast, modern languages such as Visual Basic or Java are called **non-procedural**, or **event-driven**, programming languages because instead of writing a series of instructions, a programmer defines the actions that the program must perform when certain events occur. Because non-procedural languages are **object-oriented programming languages (OOPL)**, they make it easier to implement an object-oriented system design, which you learned about in Chapter 6.

Another trend involves powerful programming languages called **fourth-generation languages (4GLs)** that are part of the **fourth-generation environment**, which was described in Chapter 7, Development Strategies. In a fourth-generation environment that includes modern CASE tools, system developers can develop accurate prototypes, cut development time, and reduce expense.

**ON THE WEB**

To learn more about fourth-generation languages, visit the Management Information Systems CourseMate Web site at **www.cengagebrain.com**, navigate to **On the Web Links** for Appendix B, and locate the Fourth-Generation Languages link.

## The Marketplace for CASE Tools

The CASE tool marketplace includes a wide variety of vendors and products, and no one tool dominates the market. You can use a site such as the one shown in Figure B-3 to locate CASE tool products and vendors. Depending on their features, some CASE tools can cost thousands of dollars, while others are available as shareware, or even as freeware, as shown in Figure B-4 on the next page.

You also can visit Microsoft's download center to sample various Express Editions, which are free, but limited, versions of various software development tools, as shown in Figure B-5 on the next page.

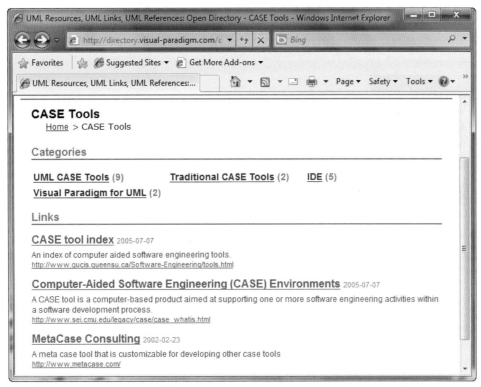

**FIGURE B-3**  Visual Paradigm's Web site offers information about many types of CASE tools.

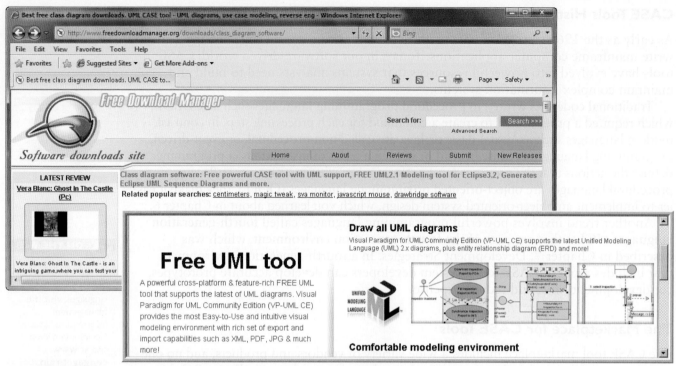

**FIGURE B-4**  This site offers many free downloads, such as the UML modeling tool shown here.

**ON THE WEB**

To learn more about the CASE tool marketplace, visit the Management Information Systems CourseMate Web site at **www. cengagebrain. com**, navigate to **On the Web Links** for Appendix B, and locate The CASE Tool Marketplace link.

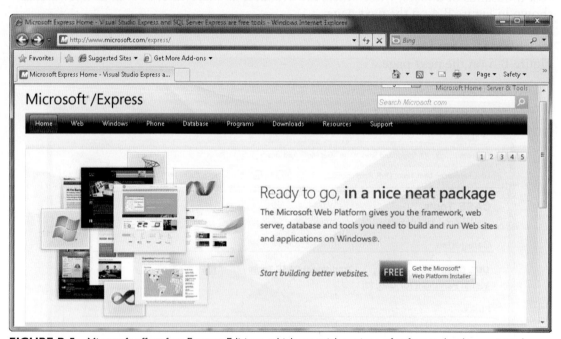

**FIGURE B-5**  Microsoft offers free Express Editions, which are trial versions of software development tools.

How do you select a CASE tool? The answer depends on the type of project, its size and scope, possible budgetary and time constraints, and the preferences and experience of the system development team. After you study the terms, concepts, and examples in this part of the Appendix, you will be able to evaluate various products and make an informed decision. The first step in learning about CASE tools is to understand basic CASE terms and concepts.

## CASE TERMS AND CONCEPTS

A typical CASE tool is actually a set of individual tools that share a repository of information. The important terms and concepts are explained in the following sections.

### Repository

A **repository** is a database that serves as a central storage location for all information about the system being developed. Once a data element has been defined in the repository, it can be accessed and used by processes and other information systems. For example, your sales processing, accounts receivable, and shipping systems all might require data about customers. After the CUSTOMER data element is entered in the repository, all three systems can share a consistent, up-to-date definition.

When you define a data element in the repository, you can assign a data type and format, a range of acceptable values, and one or more aliases. An **alias** is an alternative name for a data element. The repository can be searched, and all instances of the data element will be listed. For example, Figure B-6 shows a Visible Analyst search for the data element named CUSTOMER NUMBER. As the screens show, you can search the entire repository, or among specific types of diagrams, and the results will show all instances of the data element.

**FIGURE B-6**  A Visible Analyst repository search for the data element named CUSTOMER NUMBER. The results will show all instances of the data element.

### Individual Tools

An integrated set of CASE tools can be used to model, document, engineer, and construct the information system, as explained in the following sections.

**MODELING TOOLS**  Throughout the SDLC, system developers use modeling tools and diagrams to represent the system graphically. The textbook describes many examples, including Unified Modeling Language diagrams and functional decomposition diagrams (Chapter 4), data flow diagrams (Chapter 5), various object diagrams (Chapter 6), entity-relationship diagrams (Chapter 9), and structure charts (Chapter 10). Most popular CASE products offer these modeling tools, among others. One of the most important benefits of a **CASE environment** is that it provides an overall framework that allows a developer to create a series of graphical models based on data that has already been entered into a central repository.

**DOCUMENTATION TOOLS**  The main source of system documentation is the repository, which was explained in the previous section. In most CASE software, the repository automatically identifies the new entries and adds them to the database. In addition to the repository itself, many CASE products provide tools that check automatically for inconsistent or incomplete information in forms, reports, and diagrams. This is especially important in large, complex systems.

**ENGINEERING TOOLS** Engineering tools include forward engineering and reverse engineering tools. **Forward engineering** means translating business processes and functions into applications. Some CASE tools allow you to build the system either by editing objects and code directly, or by modifying graphical representations such as DFDs and UML diagrams. As you learned in Chapter 1, CASE tools such as System Architect and Visible Analyst allow you to develop a business model that can be translated into information system components. **Reverse engineering** allows you to examine an existing application and break it down into a series of diagrams, structure charts, and source code. Using a reverse engineering CASE tool, an analyst can transform existing application source code into a working model of the system. This can be especially important when integrating new systems with legacy systems or systems that were developed in different environments. Figure B-7 shows an example of a Visual Paradigm reverse engineering tool.

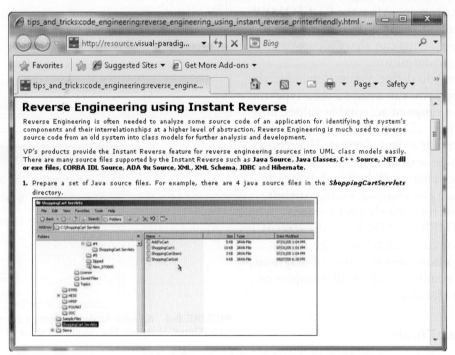

**FIGURE B-7**  An example of a CASE tool that allows reverse engineering.

**CONSTRUCTION TOOLS** A full-featured CASE tool can handle many program development tasks, such as generating application code, screens, and reports.

- An **application generator**, also called a **code generator**, allows you to develop computer programs rapidly by translating a logical model directly into code. As shown in Figure B-8, the Tangible Architect states that it easily can create .NET database applications. In this crowded marketplace, other vendors offer products that can generate applications in languages such as C, C++, Java, and AgileC.

- A **screen generator**, or **form painter**, is an interactive tool that helps you design a custom interface, create screen forms, and handle data entry format and procedures. The screen generator allows you to control how the screen will display captions, data fields, data, and other visual attributes. Modern CASE tools usually include a screen generator that interacts with the data dictionary. As shown in Figure B-9, Gillani Software's FourGen® CASE tool set includes a form painter and a screen code generator, along with many other powerful features.

**FIGURE B-8** Tangible Architect includes a code generator that can create .NET database applications.

**FIGURE B-9** Gillani's FourGen® CASE tools include a form painter and a screen code generator.

- A **report generator,** also called a **report writer,** is a tool for designing formatted reports rapidly. Using a report generator, you can modify a report easily at any stage of the design process. When you are satisfied with the report layout, the report writer creates a report definition and program code that actually produces the report. You also can input sample field values to create a **mock-up report** for users to review and approve.

## INTEGRATED DEVELOPMENT ENVIRONMENTS

**ON THE WEB**

To learn more about integrated development environments, visit the Management Information Systems CourseMate Web site at **www. cengagebrain. com**, navigate to **On the Web Links** for Appendix B, and locate the Integrated Development Environments link.

An **integrated development environment (IDE)** uses a built-in CASE tool that a software vendor includes to make it easier to plan, construct, and maintain a specific software product. For example, firms such as Microsoft, Oracle, and IBM offer IDEs that support their family of products. The following sections explain how these tools are used.

### Examples of Integrated Development Environments

Although generic CASE tools can be used to plan and design any type of information system, it usually is easier to use an integrated tool that the vendor provides. For example, as shown in Figure B-10, Oracle provides Oracle Designer, which is packaged with Oracle's application software. According to the company, Oracle Designer models business processes, data entities, and relationships — and can transform the models into applications. Other leading firms, such as SAP and Sybase, also offer powerful development tools.

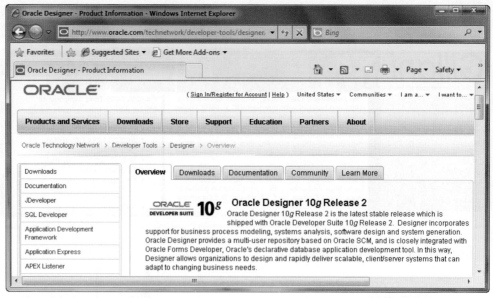

**FIGURE B-10**   Oracle Designer is a modeling and application development tool packaged with Oracle's application software.

Figure B-11 shows Microsoft's Visual Studio 2010, which is another example of an integrated development environment. Visual Studio 2010 includes various application development tools that are specifically designed to support Microsoft's .NET Web-based application development strategy. In addition to these commercial packages, programmers can use open-source software such as Java-based NetBeans IDE and Eclipse.

IBM's approach to integrated development stresses integration and teamwork. In the Redpaper® shown in Figure B-12, authors Bruce Powel Douglass and Mats Gothe

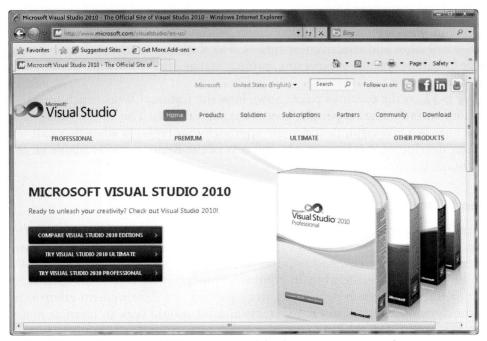

**FIGURE B-11** Visual Studio 2010 is an integrated development environment that supports Microsoft's family of .NET applications.

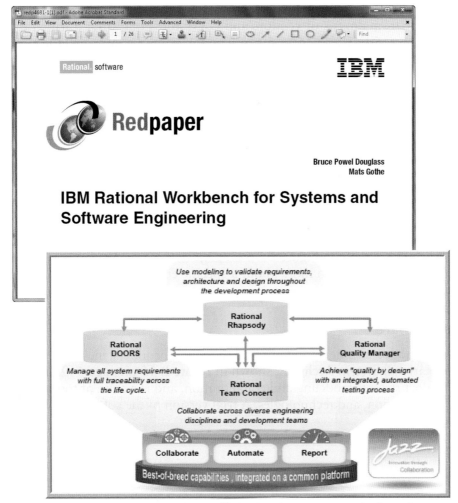

**FIGURE B-12** IBM describes its Rational® Workbench as an integrated solution for systems life cycle management.

describe IBM's Rational® Workbench as an integrated solution for systems life cycle management. Without integration, they claim, systems and software teams operate in what they call *silos*, and effectiveness suffers. The Rational Workbench spans multiple categories, such as systems engineering, project management, software development, and quality management.

Figure B-12 on the previous page shows how the Rational Workbench uses IBM's Jazz™ platform to integrate people, processes, and projects. The authors suggest that the Jazz platform is a powerful, flexible new approach that replaces what they call *one-size fits no one* development solutions. The full text of the Redpaper is available at *www.ibm.com/redbooks*.

### Pros and Cons of Integrated Development Tools

In a specific software environment, an integrated development tool is highly effective because it is built into the vendor's software package. The only possible disadvantage is that each IDE is different, and requires a learning curve and skills that might or might not be readily transferable. In contrast, non-specific CASE tools such as Visible Analyst or Rational System Architect can be used in any development environment. Given the dynamic changes in IT, a systems analyst should seek to learn as many development and CASE tools as possible.

## CASE TOOL EXAMPLES

To learn more about the Visible Analyst CASE tool, visit the Management Information Systems CourseMate Web site at **www. cengagebrain.com**, navigate to **On the Web Links** for Appendix B, and locate the Visible Analyst CASE Tool link.

You can choose from dozens of vendors and CASE tools that offer a wide range of functions, characteristics, and appearance. The following sections include examples of several popular CASE tools.

### Visible Analyst

Visible Systems Corporation is an important player in the software development market. Visible offers tools for data and application modeling, code generation, and software configuration management.

The Visible Analyst® CASE tool can generate many types of models and diagrams. Figure B-13 shows sample diagrams for a library system: an entity-relationship diagram, a data flow diagram, and a structure chart. All three examples are integrated with a central data repository.

Visible Analyst also provides a full range of Help features, including the error message analysis screen shown in Figure B-14 on page 660. When a user clicks an alphabetic letter, he or she can learn more about a specific error message that the program has displayed.

### Rational Software

To learn more about the Rational System Architect, visit the Management Information Systems CourseMate Web site at **www. cengagebrain.com**, navigate to **On the Web Links** for Appendix B, and locate the Rational System Architect link.

IBM offers many systems development and modeling products, including a powerful tool called Rational System Architect, shown in Figure B-15 on page 660. IBM claims that the product stresses modeling and collaboration, and is a suite of tools that can align processes, information, and technologies. A trial version of the software can be downloaded from IBM's site.

**FIGURE B-13** Three sample Visible Analyst diagrams are integrated with the central data repository for a library system.

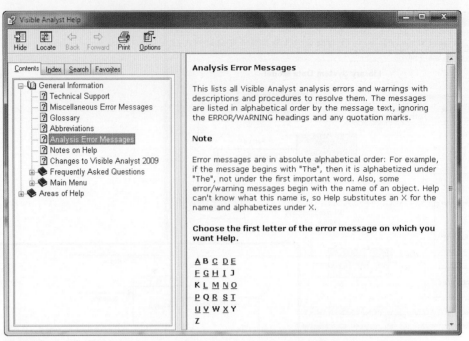

**FIGURE B-14** Visible Analyst provides error message analysis. When a user clicks an alphabetic letter, he or she can learn more about a specific error message.

**FIGURE B-15** IBM's Rational System Architect stresses modeling and collaboration.

# CASE TOOL TRENDS

Traditional CASE software evolved from simple utilities, such as code editors, to powerful multipurpose tools that can help you envision, plan, and build an entire information system. The evolution of CASE software will continue, as developers seek even more powerful tools that can model complex business processes and integrate with customer and supplier systems.

Just as modern spacecraft could not have been built without specialized, high-technology tools, future software will be planned, constructed, and maintained with a new generation of CASE tools. The following sections discuss CASE tool trends and method-specific tools.

## New Products and Features

CASE tool vendors constantly offer more features and greater flexibility. One example is a framework to help transform business processes into an information system. A **framework** organizes and documents system development tasks. For example, the **Zachman Framework** shown in Chapter 4 on page 158 arranges traditional fact-finding questions into a useful matrix.

As software becomes more powerful and complex, the lines between traditional CASE tools and other modeling tools continue to blur. For example, Microsoft Visio can model networks, business processes, and many types of special diagrams. Visio offers a variety of online tutorials and training sessions (Figure B-16). Step-by-step examples are provided for many tasks, such as creating cross-functional flowcharts, and EPC (Event-driven Process Chain) diagrams, as shown in Figure B-17 on the next page.

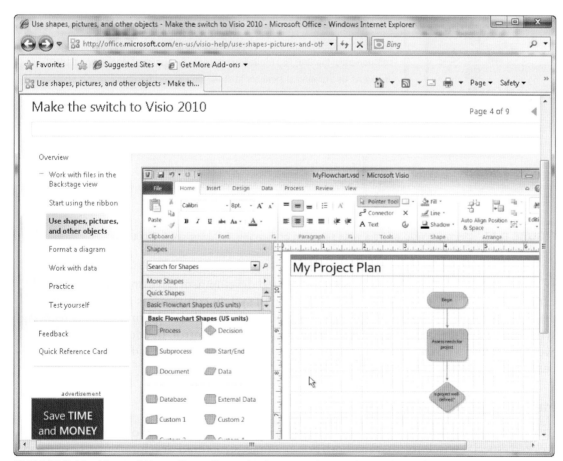

**FIGURE B-16**   Microsoft Visio offers self-paced online tutorials, complete with a self-assessment feature.

Create an EPC diagram

**FIGURE B-17**   Microsoft Visio offers a wide selection of diagrams, including cross-functional flowcharts and EPC diagrams.

Another trend is the increasing use of integrated development environments. Chapter 11 explains how an IDE can simplify the integration of system components and reduce code development time. An IDE typically includes built-in tools such as real-time error detection, syntax hints, highlighted code, class browsers, and version control. In addition to IBM's WebSphere and Microsoft's .NET, programmers can use open-source IDEs such as Java-based NetBeans IDE and Eclipse.

## Method-Specific CASE Tools

As Chapter 11 explains, each systems development approach has a set of tools that has worked especially well for that method. For example, structured development relies heavily on DFDs and structure charts. Object-oriented methods use a variety of diagrams, such as use case, class, sequence, and transition state diagrams. Agile methods tend to use spiral or other iterative models. In Chapter 1, Figure 1-25 on page 21 lists several method-specific modeling tools. System developers also use multipurpose tools to help them translate the system logic into properly functioning program modules. These generic tools include entity-relationship diagrams, flowcharts, pseudocode, decision tables, and decision trees.

**Structured analysis** is a traditional approach that is time-tested and easy to understand. Structured modeling tools are described in detail in Chapter 5, Data and Process Modeling. However, as Chapter 1 points out, **object-oriented analysis and design (OOAD)** is very popular. Widespread use of object-oriented languages has spurred interest in O-O CASE and UML-based modeling tools, which provide seamless development from planning to actual coding. Other O-O features include modular design and reusable code, which can reduce costs and speed up development. Object-oriented analysis and design tools and techniques are described in Chapter 6, Object Modeling.

The most recent trend is the popularity of agile methods. Chapter 11 includes a detailed description of an agile project, including the iterative cycles and the intense contact between developers and users. According to Scott W. Ambler, a well-known IT consultant, agile developers use a wide range of modeling tools, including CASE tools. However, many agile teams find that simple whiteboard sketching works best for them, as shown in Figure B-18.

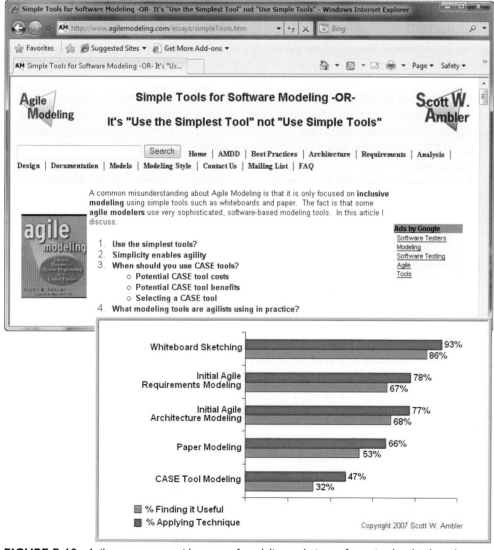

**FIGURE B-18**  Agile teams use a wide range of modeling techniques, from simple whiteboards to CASE tools.

Although it is difficult to predict the future, it seems clear that CASE tools will continue to evolve and become more powerful. At the same time, system developers will sometimes choose simpler, low-tech methods and techniques as modeling tools.

## APPENDIX SUMMARY

CASE stands for computer-aided systems engineering. CASE tools are software programs that system developers use to help them design and construct information systems. CASE tools can reduce costs, speed up development, and provide comprehensive documentation that can be used for future maintenance or enhancements.

Older systems used program code that was written in procedural languages such as COBOL, which required a programmer to create code statements for each processing step. Modern languages such as C++ and Java are non-procedural, or event-driven, languages because a programmer defines the actions that the program must perform when certain events occur.

Non-procedural languages, called 4GLs, are object-oriented programming languages (OOPL). 4GLs are important components of a fourth-generation environment that allows system developers to develop accurate prototypes, cut development time, and reduce expense.

A repository is a database that serves as a central storage location for all information about the system being developed. Once a data element has been defined in the repository, it can be accessed and used by processes and other information systems. An alias is an alternative name for a data element. The repository can be searched, and all instances of the data element will be listed.

An integrated set of CASE tools can be used to model, document, engineer, and construct the information system. Modeling tools represent the system graphically by using various types of diagrams, including data flow diagrams (DFDs), Unified Modeling Language (UML) diagrams, functional decomposition diagrams, structure charts, and network diagrams.

The main source of system documentation is the repository, which identifies new elements and adds them to the database. Additional documentation is provided by tools that check automatically for inconsistent or incomplete information in forms, reports, and diagrams.

Forward engineering means translating business processes and functions into applications. Reverse engineering allows you to examine an existing application and break it down into a series of diagrams, structure charts, and, in some cases, source code.

A CASE tool can handle many program development tasks, such as generating application code, screens, and reports.

An integrated development environment (IDE) uses a built-in CASE tool that a software vendor includes to make it easier to plan, construct, and maintain a specific software product. Examples of IDEs include Oracle Designer and Microsoft's Visual Studio 2010.

Two trends seem clear: CASE tool vendors will continue to include powerful new features, and the popularity of object-oriented tools will continue to grow.

# Key Terms and Phrases

alias 653

application generator 654

CASE environment 653

CASE tools 648

code generator 654

computer-aided software engineering (CASE) 648

computer-aided systems engineering (CASE) 648

event-driven programming language 651

form painter 654

forward engineering 654

fourth-generation environment 651

fourth-generation languages (4GLs) 651

framework 661

integrated development environment (IDE) 656

mock-up report 656

non-procedural programming language 651

object-oriented analysis and design (OOAD) 663

object-oriented programming languages (OOPL) 651

procedural programming language 651

report generator 656

report writer 656

repository 653

reverse engineering 654

screen generator 654

structured analysis 663

Zachman Framework 661

## Appendix Exercises

### Review Questions

1. Define CASE, CASE tools, and a CASE environment.
2. Explain the difference between procedural and non-procedural languages.
3. Describe 4GLs and their characteristics.
4. Define a repository, and explain its role in the systems development process.
5. What are forward and reverse engineering tools, and how are they used?
6. Provide an example of an application generator and a screen generator.
7. How is a report generator used, and what is a mock-up report?
8. Explain the concept of an integrated development environment and provide two examples of IDEs.
9. What are some features of the Visible Analyst CASE tool?
10. What is the emerging role of object-oriented analysis and design methods? Agile methods?

### Discussion Topics

1. Would a systems analyst be better off in a position where he or she works with an IDE, or where generic CASE tools are used? Explain your answer.
2. Visit the Web sites for Rational System Architect and Visible Analyst. If you could choose only one of these products, which one would you select, and why?
3. If you were a programmer, would you prefer to work with procedural or non-procedural languages? Explain your reasons.
4. Review the Dilbert© cartoon on page 141. Although the example might be far-fetched, perhaps future software will be able to identify business opportunities and requirements. Meanwhile, if the trend toward more powerful CASE tools continues, many of the tedious program development tasks might be performed automatically. Is there a limit to the capabilities of future CASE software? Could a complete information system be designed by describing a business operation and specifying certain inputs and outputs? Explain your answer.

### Projects

1. Go to the site shown in Figure TK B-3 on page 651 and choose a CASE tool. Visit the vendor's site and learn all you can about the product. Write a brief report that describes your experience.
2. Visit the *freedownloadmanager.org* Web site shown in Figure TK B-4 on page 652, and download the free UML modeling tool. Experiment with the program and write a brief report that describes your experience.
3. Search the Internet and locate an example of a screen generator. Visit the vendor's site and learn all you can about the product. Write a brief report that describes your experience.
4. Go to the site shown in Figure TK B-9 on page 655 and learn more about Gillani's FourGen CASE Tools. Write a brief report summarizing your findings.

# APPENDIX C

# Cost-Benefit Analysis

In **Appendix C**, you will learn how to use financial analysis tools during the planning, analysis, design, implementation, support, and securing of an information system.

## INTRODUCTION

### OBJECTIVES

*When you finish this part of the Appendix, you will be able to:*

- Define economic feasibility

- Classify costs and benefits into various categories, including tangible or intangible, direct or indirect, fixed or variable, and developmental or operational

- Understand chargeback methods and how they are used

- Use payback analysis to calculate the length of time that it takes for a project to pay for itself

- Use return on investment analysis to measure a project's profitability

- Use present value analysis to determine the value of a future project measured in current dollars

Appendix C of the Systems Analyst's Appendix shows you how to use various tools to calculate a project's costs and benefits. As a systems analyst, you need to know how to calculate costs and benefits when you conduct preliminary investigations, evaluate IT projects, and make recommendations to management.

Financial analysis tools are important throughout the systems development life cycle. For example, in Chapter 2 you learn that economic feasibility depends on a comparison of costs and benefits. A project is economically feasible if the future benefits outweigh the estimated costs of developing or acquiring the new system. In Chapter 7, when you analyze development strategies, you apply financial analysis tools and techniques as you examine various options. Then, as Chapter 12 explains, you use these tools again to recognize the end of a system's useful life.

## APPENDIX INTRODUCTION CASE:   Mountain View College Bookstore

**Background:** Wendy Lee, manager of college services at Mountain View College, wants a new information system that will improve efficiency and customer service at the three college bookstores.

In this part of the case, Tina Allen (systems analyst) and David Conroe (student intern) are talking about financial analysis tools and techniques.

| | |
|---|---|
| **Participants:** | Tina and David |
| **Location:** | Mountain View College Cafeteria, during the systems planning phase |
| **Discussion topics:** | Economic feasibility, chargeback methods, cost-benefit classification, payback analysis, return on investment analysis, and net present value analysis |

**Tina:** Hi, David. Before we go any further with the preliminary investigation, I wanted to meet with you to discuss financial analysis tools and techniques, and how we will apply them.

**David:** *Fine with me. Where do we start?*

**Tina:** Well, because economic feasibility depends on a project's costs and benefits, the first step is to classify those costs and benefits into specific categories. For example, costs can be tangible or intangible, direct or indirect, fixed or variable, and developmental or operational.

**David:** *Okay, I understand. What do we do after we classify everything?*

**Tina:** Then we use one or more financial analysis tools: payback analysis, return on investment analysis, and net present value analysis. We'll learn how to use them to evaluate the system and compare alternatives. We'll also talk about chargeback methods.

**David:** *What are they?*

**Tina:** A chargeback method is just a way to allocate costs for an IT system. We'll have to talk to Wendy about that. Meanwhile, here's a task list we can work on:

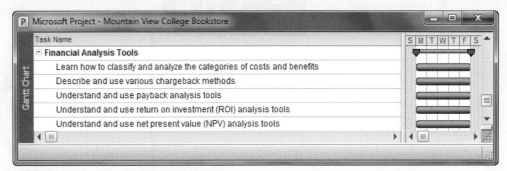

**FIGURE C-1**   Typical financial analysis tasks.

## DESCRIBING COSTS AND BENEFITS

As a systems analyst, you must review a project's costs and benefits at the end of each SDLC phase so management can decide whether or not to continue the project. Before you can use the economic analysis tools described in this section of the Appendix, you must learn how to identify and classify all costs and benefits.

As you learned in Chapter 2, **economic feasibility** means that the projected benefits of the proposed system outweigh the projected costs. When you determine economic feasibility, you must consider the project's benefits compared to the project's **total cost of ownership (TCO)**, which includes ongoing support and maintenance costs, as well as acquisition costs.

Figure C-2 shows an online TCO analysis tool provided by HP Services. HP stresses the importance of TCO analysis, and points to studies showing that the majority of total IT costs occur *after* the purchase, and that nearly half the costs lie outside the IT department's

**FIGURE C-2**    HP Services offers an online TCO analysis tool.

budget. HP also cites a study that shows a staggering TCO of $21,000 for a $2,000 PC when all costs are considered over a five-year period. HP noted that the most significant cost factor is user support, including peer-to-peer assistance that rarely is documented or measured.

Cost-benefit analysis tools also are available from various vendors and organizations, including the Info~Tech Research Group site shown in Figure C-3. Info~Tech's free TCO tool provides a three-year planning horizon and graphical output.

**FIGURE C-3**   Example of cost-benefit analysis software available on the Web.

Figure C-4 on the next page shows a cost-benefit tool that focuses on technology evaluation. The vendor, New Venture Tools, offers a demo version and a step-by-step tutorial.

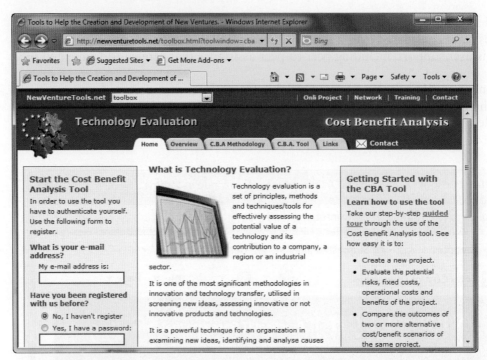

**FIGURE C-4**  New Venture Tools claims that technology evaluation requires a set of principles, methods, techniques, and tools.

## Cost Classifications

Costs can be classified as tangible or intangible, direct or indirect, fixed or variable, and developmental or operational. **Tangible costs** are costs for which you can assign a specific dollar value. Examples of tangible costs include employee salaries, hardware and software purchases, and office supplies. Tangible costs also include the interest charges that firms must pay when they need to borrow money for working capital or to finance new projects. In times of high interest rates, these costs can be significant and must be considered.

In contrast, **intangible costs** are costs whose dollar value cannot be calculated easily. The cost of customer dissatisfaction, lower employee morale, and reduced information availability are examples of intangible costs.

If the analyst examines an intangible item carefully, however, it sometimes is possible to estimate a dollar value. For example, users might dislike a system because it is difficult to learn. Their dissatisfaction is an intangible cost, but if it translates into an increase in errors that must be corrected, you probably could assign a tangible dollar cost. You should try to work with tangible costs whenever possible.

**Direct costs** are costs that can be associated with the development of a specific system. Examples of direct costs include the salaries of project team members and the purchase of hardware that is used only for the new system. In contrast, **indirect costs**, or **overhead expenses**, cannot be attributed to the development of a particular information system. The salaries of network administrators, copy machine rentals, and insurance expenses are examples of indirect costs.

**Fixed costs** are costs that are relatively constant and do not depend on a level of activity or effort. Many fixed costs recur regularly, such as salaries and hardware rental charges. **Variable costs** are costs that vary depending on the level of activity. The costs of printer paper, supplies, and telephone line charges are examples of variable costs.

**Developmental costs** are incurred only once, at the time the system is developed or acquired. Those costs might include salaries of people involved in systems development, software purchases, initial user training, and the purchase of necessary hardware or furniture. **Operational costs** are incurred after the system is implemented and continue while the system is in use. Examples of operational costs include system maintenance, ongoing training, annual software license fees, and communications expense.

Some costs apply to more than one category of expenses. For example, overtime pay for clerical staff during the systems analysis phase would be classified as developmental, variable, and direct. A monthly fee for maintaining the company's Web site would be regarded as operational, fixed, and indirect.

## Managing Information Systems Costs and Charges

Management wants to know how much an information system costs, so it is important for the systems analyst to understand direct costs, indirect costs, and methods of allocating IT charges within the company.

Direct costs usually are easier to identify and predict than indirect costs. For example, the salaries of project team members and the purchase of hardware, software, and supplies for the new system are direct costs. After a new information system goes into operation, other direct costs might include the lease of system-specific hardware or software.

Many IT department costs cannot be attributed directly to a specific information system or user group. Those indirect costs can include general hardware and software acquisition expenses; facility maintenance, air conditioning, security, rent, insurance, and general supplies; and the salaries of operations, technical support, and information center personnel.

A **chargeback method** is a technique that uses accounting entries to allocate the indirect costs of running the IT department. Most organizations adopt one of four chargeback methods: no charge, a fixed charge, a variable charge based on resource usage, or a variable charge based on volume.

1. **No charge method.** Some organizations treat information systems department indirect expenses as a necessary cost of doing business, and IT services are seen as benefiting the entire company. Thus, indirect IT department costs are treated as general organizational costs and are not charged to other departments. In this case, the information systems department is called a **cost center**, because it generates accounting charges with no offsetting credits for IT services.

2. **Fixed charge method.** With this method, the indirect IT costs are divided among all the other departments in the form of a fixed monthly charge. The monthly charge might be the same for all departments or based on a relatively constant factor such as department size or number of workstations. By using a fixed charge approach, all indirect costs are charged to other departments, and the IT group is regarded as a profit center. A **profit center** is a department that is expected to break even or show a profit. Under the profit center concept, company departments purchase services from the IT department and receive accounting charges that represent the cost of providing the services.

3. **Variable charge method based on resource usage. Resource allocation** is the charging of indirect costs based on the resources used by an information system. The allocation might be based on connect time, server processing time, network resources required, printer use, or a combination of similar factors. **Connect time** is the total time that a user is connected actively to a remote server — some Internet service providers use this as a basis for charges. In a client/server system, **server processing time** is the time that the server actually responds to client requests for processing. The amount a particular department is charged will vary from month to month, depending not only on that department's resource usage, but also on the total resource usage. The IT department is considered a profit center when an organization uses the resource allocation method.

4. **Variable charge method based on volume.** The indirect IT department costs are allocated to other departments based on user-oriented activity, such as the number of transactions or printing volume. As with the resource allocation method, a department's share of the costs varies from month to month, depending on the level of activity. In this case, the IT department is considered a profit center.

### Benefit Classifications

In addition to classifying costs, you must classify the benefits that the company expects from a project. Like costs, benefits can be classified as tangible or intangible, fixed or variable, and direct or indirect. Another useful benefit classification relates to the nature of the benefit: positive benefits versus cost-avoidance benefits. **Positive benefits** increase revenues, improve services, or otherwise contribute to the organization as a direct result of the new information system. Examples of positive benefits include improved information availability, greater flexibility, faster service to customers, higher employee morale, and better inventory management.

In contrast, **cost-avoidance benefits** refer to expenses that would be necessary if the new system were not installed. Examples of cost-avoidance benefits include handling the work with current staff instead of hiring additional people, not having to replace existing hardware or software, and avoiding problems that otherwise would be faced with the current system. Cost-avoidance benefits are just as important as positive benefits, and you must consider both types when performing cost-benefit analysis.

## COST-BENEFIT ANALYSIS

**Cost-benefit analysis** is the process of comparing the anticipated costs of an information system to the anticipated benefits. Cost-benefit analysis is performed throughout the SDLC to determine the economic feasibility of an information system project and to compare alternative solutions. Many cost-benefit analysis techniques exist. This section covers discussion of only the three most common methods: payback analysis, return on investment analysis, and present value analysis. Each of the approaches analyzes cost-benefit figures differently, but the objective is the same: to provide reliable information for making decisions.

## VIDEO LEARNING SESSION: PAYBACK ANALYSIS

Video Learning Sessions can help you understand key concepts, practice your skills, and check your work. To access the sessions, visit the Management Information Systems CourseMate Web site at **www.cengagebrain.com** and navigate to the **Video Learning Sessions** for this book. This session is about payback analysis. You'll learn how to calculate the payback period for a project and how to use a spreadsheet to determine a project's payback period.

## Payback Analysis

**Payback analysis** is the process of determining how long it takes an information system to pay for itself. The time it takes to recover the system's cost is called the **payback period**. To perform a payback analysis, you carry out the following steps:

1. Determine the initial development cost of the system.

2. Estimate annual benefits.

3. Determine annual operating costs.

4. Find the payback period by comparing total development and operating costs to the accumulated value of the benefits produced by the system.

When you plot the system costs over the potential life of the system, you typically see a curve such as the one shown in Figure C-5. After the system is operational, costs decrease rapidly and remain relatively low for a period of time. Eventually, as the system requires more maintenance, costs begin to increase. The period between the beginning of systems operation and the point when operational costs are rapidly increasing is called the **economically useful life** of the system.

**ON THE WEB**

To learn more about payback analysis, visit **scsite.com/** the Management Information Systems CourseMate Web site at **www.cengagebrain.com**, navigate to **On the Web Links** for Appendix C, and locate the Payback Analysis link.

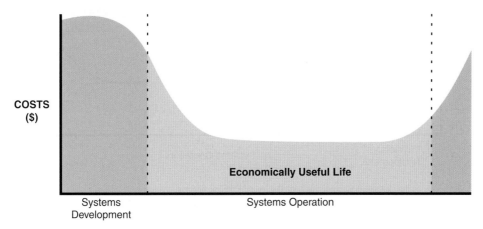

**COSTS ($)**

**Economically Useful Life**

Systems Development

Systems Operation

**TIME**

**FIGURE C-5**   The costs of a typical system vary over time. At the beginning, system costs are high due to initial development expense. Costs then drop during systems operation. Maintenance costs begin to increase until the system reaches the end of its economically useful life. The area between the two dashed lines shows the economically useful life of this system.

When you plot the benefits provided by an information system against time, the resulting curve usually resembles the one shown in the upper graph in Figure C-6. Benefits start to appear when the system becomes operational, might increase for a time, and then level off or start to decline.

When conducting a payback analysis, you calculate the time it takes for the accumulated benefits of an information system to equal the accumulated costs of developing and operating the system.

In the lower graph in Figure C-6, the cost and benefit curves are plotted together. The dashed line indicates the payback period. Notice that the payback period is not the point when current benefits equal current costs, where the two lines cross. Instead, the payback period compares accumulated costs and benefits. If you graph current costs and benefits, the payback period corresponds to the time at which the areas under the two curves are equal.

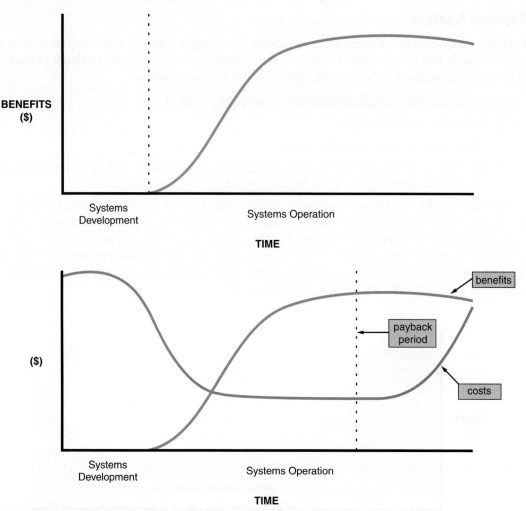

**FIGURE C-6**   Benefits of an information system change over time, as shown in the upper graph. The lower graph shows costs and benefits plotted on the same graph. The dashed line indicates the payback period, when accumulated benefits equal accumulated costs.

Figure C-7 contains two cost-benefit tables. The tables show the anticipated annual costs, cumulative costs, annual benefits, and cumulative benefits for two information systems projects. Year 0 (zero) corresponds to the year in which systems development begins. The development of Project A takes less than one year, so some benefits are realized in Year 0. Systems development for Project B requires more than one year, so the benefits do not begin until some time in Year 1.

In Project A, by the end of Year 4, the cumulative costs are $135,700, which slightly exceeds the $132,000 cumulative benefits. By the end of Year 5, however, the cumulative benefits of $171,000 far exceed the cumulative costs, which are $157,700. Therefore, at some point in time during Year 5, the accumulated costs and benefits are equal, and the payback period is established. In Project B, a similar situation exists. By the end of Year 4, Project B's cumulative costs are $191,000, which is greater than the cumulative benefits of $156,000. At some point during Year 5, cumulative benefits will exceed cumulative costs, and the system will have paid for itself.

If more specific information is available regarding the timing of costs and benefits during a year, you can calculate the payback period more precisely. Another approach is to create a chart that shows the exact point when cumulative benefits exceed cumulative costs, which is explained in the following section.

Some managers are critical of payback analysis because it places all the emphasis on early costs and benefits and ignores the benefits received after the payback period. Even if the benefits for Project B in Year 6 soared as high as $500,000, the payback period for

**PAYBACK ANALYSIS EXAMPLES**

**PROJECT A:**

| YEAR | COSTS | CUMULATIVE COSTS | BENEFITS | CUMULATIVE BENEFITS |
|------|-------|------------------|----------|---------------------|
| 0 | 60,000 | 60,000 | 3,000 | 3,000 |
| 1 | 17,000 | 77,000 | 28,000 | 31,000 |
| 2 | 18,500 | 95,500 | 31,000 | 62,000 |
| 3 | 19,200 | 114,700 | 34,000 | 96,000 |
| 4 | 21,000 | 135,700 | 36,000 | 132,000 |
| 5 | 22,000 | 157,700 | 39,000 | 171,000 |
| 6 | 23,300 | 181,000 | 42,000 | 213,000 |

**PROJECT B:**

| YEAR | COSTS | CUMULATIVE COSTS | BENEFITS | CUMULATIVE BENEFITS |
|------|-------|------------------|----------|---------------------|
| 0 | 80,000 | 80,000 | —— | —— |
| 1 | 40,000 | 120,000 | 6,000 | 6,000 |
| 2 | 25,000 | 145,000 | 26,000 | 32,000 |
| 3 | 22,000 | 167,000 | 54,000 | 86,000 |
| 4 | 24,000 | 191,000 | 70,000 | 156,000 |
| 5 | 26,500 | 217,500 | 82,000 | 238,000 |
| 6 | 30,000 | 247,500 | 92,000 | 330,000 |

**FIGURE C-7** Payback analysis data for two information systems proposals: Project A and Project B.

that project still occurs during the fifth year of operation. In defense of payback analysis, the earlier cost and benefit predictions usually are more certain. In general, the further out in time that you extend your projections, the more unsure your forecast will be. Thus, payback analysis uses the most reliable of your cost and benefit estimates.

Payback analysis rarely is used to compare or rank projects because later benefits are ignored. You would never decide that Project A is better than Project B simply because the payback period for A is less than that for B; considering all the costs and all the benefits when comparing projects makes more sense.

Even with its drawbacks, payback analysis is popular. Many business organizations establish a minimum payback period for approved projects. If company policy requires a project to begin paying for itself within three years, then neither project in Figure C-7 would be approved, though both are economically feasible because total benefits exceed total costs.

## Using a Spreadsheet to Compute Payback Analysis

You can use a spreadsheet to record and calculate accumulated costs and benefits, as shown in Figure C-8 on the next page. The first step is to design the worksheet and label the rows and columns. After entering the cost and benefit data for each year, you enter the formulas. For payback analysis, you will need a formula to display cumulative totals, year by year. For example, the first year in the cumulative costs column is the same as Year 0 costs, so the formula in cell C6 is =B6. The cumulative cost total for the second year is Year 0 cumulative total + Year 1 costs, so the formula for cell C7 is =C6+B7, and so on. The first worksheet shows the initial layout and the second worksheet shows the finished spreadsheet.

After you verify that the spreadsheet operates properly, you can create a line chart that displays the cumulative costs, benefits, and payback period, which is identified by the intersection of the cost and benefit lines, as shown in Figure C-9 on page 679.

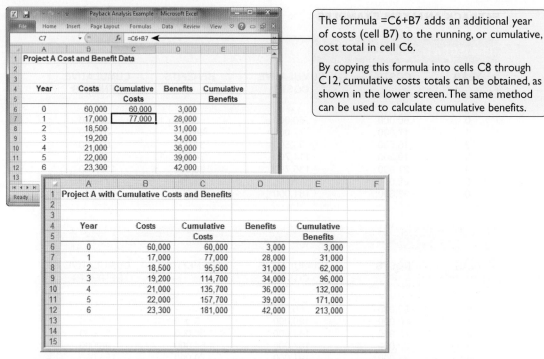

The formula =C6+B7 adds an additional year of costs (cell B7) to the running, or cumulative, cost total in cell C6.

By copying this formula into cells C8 through C12, cumulative costs totals can be obtained, as shown in the lower screen. The same method can be used to calculate cumulative benefits.

**FIGURE C-8**  A Microsoft Excel worksheet displays payback analysis data for Project A in the upper screen. When cumulative cost and benefit formulas are entered, the finished worksheet in the lower screen appears.

# VIDEO LEARNING SESSION:  RETURN ON INVESTMENT

Video Learning Sessions can help you understand key concepts, practice your skills, and check your work. To access the sessions, visit the Management Information Systems CourseMate Web site at **www.cengagebrain.com** and navigate to the **Video Learning Sessions** for this book. This session is about return on investment (ROI) analysis. You'll learn how to calculate ROI for a project and how to use a spreadsheet to determine a project's return on investment.

 **ON THE WEB**

To learn more about return on investment analysis, visit the Management Information Systems CourseMate Web site at **www. cengagebrain.com**, navigate to **On the Web Links** for Appendix C, and locate the Return on Investment Analysis link.

## Return on Investment Analysis

**Return on investment (ROI)** is a percentage rate that measures profitability by comparing the total net benefits (the return) received from a project to the total costs (the investment) of the project. ROI is calculated as follows:

ROI = (total benefits − total costs) / total costs

Return on investment analysis considers costs and benefits over a longer time span than payback analysis. ROI calculations usually are based on total costs and benefits for a period of five to seven years. For example, Figure C-10 shows the ROI calculations for Project A and Project B. The ROI for Project A is 17.7%, and the ROI for Project B is 33.3%.

In many organizations, projects must meet or exceed a minimum ROI. This minimum ROI can be an estimate of the return the organization would receive from investing its money in other investment opportunities such as treasury bonds, or it can be a higher rate that the company requires for all new projects. If a company requires a minimum ROI of 15%, for example, then both Projects A and B would meet the criterion.

You also can use ROI for ranking projects. If Projects A and B represent two different proposed solutions for a single information systems project, then the solution represented

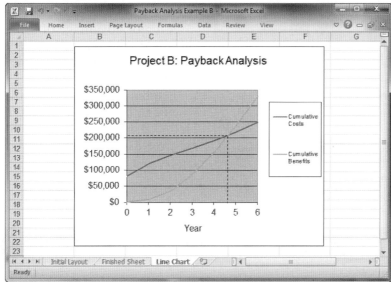

**FIGURE C-9** Microsoft Excel can be used to show the payback period by creating a chart of cumulative costs and benefits. Note that Project A has a shorter payback period than Project B.

by Project B is better than the Project A solution. If Projects A and B represent two different information systems projects, and if the organization has sufficient resources to pursue only one of the two projects, then Project B is the better choice.

Critics of return on investment analysis raise two points. First, ROI measures the overall rate of return for the total period, and annual return rates can vary considerably. Two projects with the same ROI might not be equally desirable if the benefits of one project occur significantly earlier than the benefits of the other project. The second criticism is that the ROI technique ignores the timing of the costs and benefits. This concept is called the time value of money, and is explained in the section on the present value analysis method.

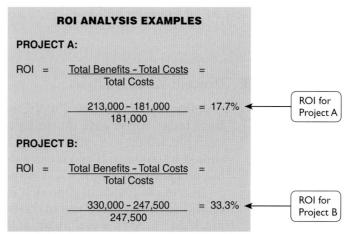

**FIGURE C-10** Return on investment analysis for Project A and Project B shown in Figure C-7 on page 677.

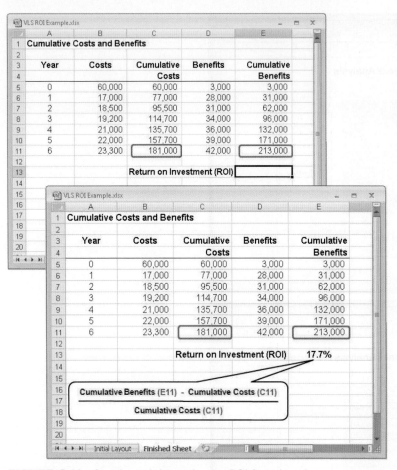

**FIGURE C-11** Sample worksheets showing ROI formula and analysis.

## Using a Spreadsheet to Compute ROI

You also can use spreadsheet programs to calculate the ROI. To do so for Project A, first set up the worksheet and enter the cost and benefit data. You can use cumulative columns (as you did in payback analysis) but you also will need two overall totals (one for costs and one for benefits), as shown in Figure C-11.

The last step is to add a formula to calculate the ROI percentage rate, which is displayed in cell E13 in Figure C-11. As stated previously, the ROI calculation is total benefits minus total costs, divided by total costs. Therefore, the formula that displays the ROI percentage in cell E13 is = (E11–C11)/C11.

A major advantage of using a spreadsheet is if your data changes, you can modify your worksheet and calculate a new result instantly.

A spreadsheet can be a powerful tool when combined with an ROI template. Hall Consulting and Research offers several free ROI templates, as shown in Figure C-12.

---

# VIDEO LEARNING SESSION: PRESENT VALUE ANALYSIS

Video Learning Sessions can help you understand key concepts, practice your skills, and check your work. To access the sessions, visit the Management Information Systems CourseMate Web site at **www.cengagebrain.com** and navigate to the **Video Learning Sessions** for this book. This session is about present value analysis. You'll learn how to calculate net present value (NPV) for a project and how to use a spreadsheet to determine a project's net present value.

To learn more about present value analysis, visit the Management Information Systems CourseMate Web site at **www. cengagebrain.com**, navigate to **On the Web Links** for Appendix C, and locate the Present Value Analysis link.

## Present Value Analysis

A dollar you have today is worth more than a dollar you do not receive until one year from today. If you have the dollar now, you can invest it and it will grow in value. For example, would you rather have $100 right now or a year from now? The answer should be obvious. If you receive the $100 now, you can invest it in a mutual fund that has an annual return of 8%. One year from now, you will have $108 instead of $100.

You might decide to approach ROI from a different direction. For example, instead of asking, "How much will my $100 be worth a year from now?" you can ask, "How much do I need to invest today, at 8%, in order to have $100 a year from now?" This concept is known as the **time value of money**, as shown in Figure C-13, and it is the basis of the technique called **present value analysis**.

The **present value** of a future dollar is the amount of money that, when invested today at a specified interest rate, grows to exactly one dollar at a certain point in the future. The specified interest rate is called the discount rate. In present value analysis, a company uses a discount rate that represents the rate of return if the money is put into relatively risk-free investments, such as bonds, instead of being invested in the project.

Most companies require a rate of return that is higher than the discount rate because of the degree of risk in any project compared with investing in a bond. Companies often reject projects that seem attractive because the risk is not worth the potential reward.

To help you perform present value analysis, adjustment factors for various interest rates and numbers of years are calculated and printed in tables called **present value tables**. Figure C-13 shows a portion of a present value table, including values for 10 years at various discount rates.

To use a present value table, you locate the value in the column with the appropriate discount rate and the row for the appropriate number of years. For example, to calculate the present value of $1 at 12% for five years, you look down the 12% column in Figure C-13 until you reach the row representing five years. The table value is 0.567. To determine what the present value of $3,000 will be in five years with a discount rate of 12%, multiply the present value factor from the table by the dollar amount; that is, PV = $3,000 × 0.567 = $1,701.

Many finance and accounting books contain comprehensive present value tables, or you can obtain this information on the Internet, as shown in Figure C-14.

To perform present value analysis, you must time-adjust the cost and benefit figures. First, you multiply each of the projected

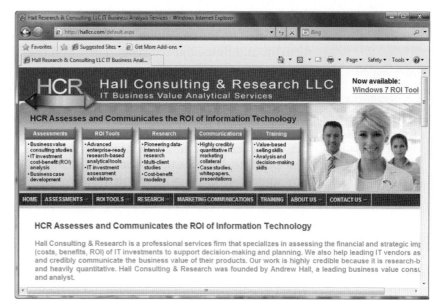

**FIGURE C-12** Hall Consulting and Research offers ROI information and templates.

| PERIODS | 6% | 8% | 10% | 12% | 14% |
|---|---|---|---|---|---|
| 1 | 0.943 | 0.926 | 0.909 | 0.893 | 0.877 |
| 2 | 0.890 | 0.857 | 0.826 | 0.797 | 0.769 |
| 3 | 0.840 | 0.794 | 0.751 | 0.712 | 0.675 |
| 4 | 0.792 | 0.735 | 0.683 | 0.636 | 0.592 |
| 5 | 0.747 | 0.681 | 0.621 | 0.567 | 0.519 |
| 6 | 0.705 | 0.630 | 0.564 | 0.507 | 0.456 |
| 7 | 0.665 | 0.583 | 0.513 | 0.452 | 0.400 |
| 8 | 0.627 | 0.540 | 0.467 | 0.404 | 0.351 |
| 9 | 0.592 | 0.500 | 0.424 | 0.361 | 0.308 |
| 10 | 0.558 | 0.463 | 0.386 | 0.322 | 0.270 |

**FIGURE C-13** Portion of a present value table showing adjustment factors for various time periods and discount rates. Values in the table are calculated using the formula shown in the text. Notice how the factors decrease as time and percentages increase.

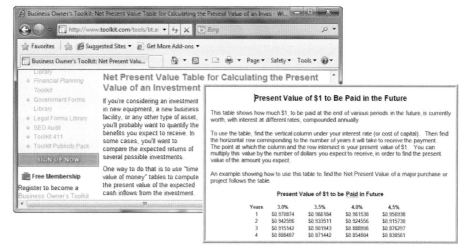

**FIGURE C-14** The Business Owner's Toolkit site provides valuable information, such as these present value tables.

benefits and costs by the proper present value factor, which depends on when the cost will
be incurred or the benefit will be received. The second step is to sum all the time-adjusted
benefits and time-adjusted costs. Then, you calculate the **net present value** (**NPV**) of the
project, which is the total present value of the benefits minus the total present value of the
costs. Figure C-15 shows the calculation of net present value for two sample projects.

In theory, any project with a positive NPV is economically feasible because the project will produce a larger return than would be achieved by investing the same amount of
money in a discount rate investment. Remember that risks are associated with any project, however, and management typically insists on a substantially higher return for high-
risk projects. For example, both projects in Figure 3-16 have positive net present values
and appear economically worthwhile.

Suppose, however, that you knew one of the projects had a 90% probability of
achieving its goals, while the other project had only a 70% chance. To be attractive, the
project with the higher risk would have to offer a corresponding higher reward. Chapter 3
explains how project managers evaluate risks. Figure 3-33 on page 122 shows a matrix
that includes various combinations of risk probability and impact.

Net present value also can be used to compare and rank projects. All things being
equal, the project with the highest net present value is the best investment. Figure C-15
shows that Project B is a better investment than Project A because it has a higher net
present value.

## NET PRESENT VALUE EXAMPLES

**PROJECT A:**

| | Year 0 | Year 1 | Year 2 | Year 3 | Year 4 | Year 5 | Year 6 | Total |
|---|---|---|---|---|---|---|---|---|
| Benefits: | 3,000 | 28,000 | 31,000 | 34,000 | 36,000 | 39,000 | 42,000 | |
| Present Value Factor (12%): | 1.000 | 0.893 | 0.797 | 0.712 | 0.636 | 0.567 | 0.507 | |
| Present Value: | 3,000 | 25,004 | 24,707 | 24,208 | 22,896 | 22,113 | 21,294 | 143,222 |
| Costs: | 60,000 | 17,000 | 18,500 | 19,200 | 21,000 | 22,000 | 23,300 | |
| Present Value Factor (12%): | 1.000 | 0.893 | 0.797 | 0.712 | 0.636 | 0.567 | 0.507 | |
| Present Value: | 60,000 | 15,181 | 14,745 | 13,670 | 13,356 | 12,474 | 11,813 | 141,239 |
| Net Present Value: | | | | | | net present value of Project A | | ➤ **1,983** |

**PROJECT B:**

| | Year 0 | Year 1 | Year 2 | Year 3 | Year 4 | Year 5 | Year 6 | Total |
|---|---|---|---|---|---|---|---|---|
| Benefits: | —— | 6,000 | 26,000 | 54,000 | 70,000 | 82,000 | 92,000 | |
| Present Value Factor (12%): | —— | 0.893 | 0.797 | 0.712 | 0.636 | 0.567 | 0.507 | |
| Present Value: | —— | 5,358 | 20,722 | 38,448 | 44,520 | 46,494 | 46,644 | 202,186 |
| Costs: | 80,000 | 40,000 | 25,000 | 22,000 | 24,000 | 26,500 | 30,000 | |
| Present Value Factor (12%): | 1.000 | 0.893 | 0.797 | 0.712 | 0.636 | 0.567 | 0.507 | |
| Present Value: | 80,000 | 35,720 | 19,925 | 15,664 | 15,264 | 15,026 | 15,210 | 196,809 |
| Net Present Value: | | | | | | net present value of Project B | | ➤ **5,377** |

**FIGURE C-15**   Net present value analysis for Project A and Project B.

Present value analysis provides solutions to the shortcomings of payback analysis and return on investment analysis. Unlike payback analysis, present value analysis considers all the costs and benefits, and not just the earlier values. In addition, present value analysis takes into account the timing of costs and benefits, so their values can be adjusted by the discount rate that provides a common yardstick and recognizes the time value of money. Even so, companies often use all three methods to get more input for making decisions. Sometimes a project will score higher on one method of analysis and lower on another.

## Using a Spreadsheet to Calculate Present Value

There are two ways to calculate present value using a spreadsheet program such as Microsoft Excel. You can enter the discount adjustment factors from an external table, and use a simple formula to apply the factors. However, many analysts find it easier to use a built-in NPV formula that handles the calculations. The two methods are described in the following sections. The example shows costs and benefits for a proposed information system with a one-year development period, a three-year useful life, and a 6% discount rate.

**USING EXTERNAL FACTORS** The first method is to create a spreadsheet similar to the one in Figure C-16. Starting with the estimated benefits, you would enter adjustment factors in cells C6, D6, and E6. Then you would create formulas in cells C7, D7, and E7 that multiply the three factors times the dollar amounts for each year, with a total shown in column F. You would do the same thing for the estimated costs. Finally, when you subtract total costs from total benefits, the net present value for the proposed system displays in cell F13.

**PV Analysis: Proposed Information System**

|            | Year 0  | Year 1 | Year 2 | Year 3 | Total  |
|------------|---------|--------|--------|--------|--------|
| Benefits   | -       | 20,000 | 30,000 | 40,000 |        |
| Factor     | -       | 0.943  | 0.890  | 0.840  |        |
| PV of Benefits | -   | 18,860 | 26,700 | 33,600 | 79,160 |
|            |         |        |        |        |        |
| Costs      | 30,000  | 10,000 | 10,000 | 10,000 |        |
| Factor     | 1.000   | 0.943  | 0.890  | 0.840  |        |
| PV of Costs | 30,000 | 9,430  | 8,900  | 8,400  | 56,730 |
|            |         |        |        | Net Present Value: | 22,430 |

**FIGURE C-16**  This sample spreadsheet shows how you can use external discount factors and formulas to calculate present value.

**USING A BUILT-IN FORMULA** The second method uses a built-in spreadsheet function to calculate present value. You enter the amounts, the discount rate, and number of time periods, and the program does the rest. Using this approach, you perform four steps, starting with the benefits.

1. First, create a spreadsheet with cost and benefit data arranged similar to Figure C-17. You will enter the NPV functions in column I.

2. Next, select cell I5, and click the Function button on the formula bar. Select the NPV function, and you will be prompted to enter a rate. You are using a 6% discount rate, so enter .06.

3. Now enter the three benefit amounts: 20,000 for Value 1, 30,000 for Value 2, and 40,000 for Value 3.

4. When you click OK, a net present value appears in cell I5. Now follow the same method to enter the cost amounts, subtract costs from benefits, and the net present value displays in cell I8. Notice there is a slight difference in the two methods because Excel uses more decimal places. The difference is not significant.

**FIGURE C-17**   This sample spreadsheet shows how you can use a built-in NPV function to calculate present value.

## APPENDIX SUMMARY

As a systems analyst, you must be concerned with economic feasibility throughout the SDLC, and especially during the systems planning and systems analysis phases. A project is economically feasible if the anticipated benefits exceed the expected costs. When you review a project, you work with various feasibility and cost analysis tools.

You must classify project costs as tangible or intangible, direct or indirect, fixed or variable, and developmental or operational. Tangible costs are those that have a specific dollar value, whereas intangible costs involve items that are difficult to measure in dollar terms, such as employee dissatisfaction. Direct costs can be associated with a particular information system, while indirect costs refer to overhead expenses that cannot be allocated to a specific project. Fixed costs remain the same regardless of activity levels, while variable costs are affected by the degree of system activity. Developmental costs are one-time systems development expenses, while operational costs continue during the systems operation and use phase.

Every company must decide how to charge or allocate information systems costs and the chargeback method. Common chargeback approaches are no charge, a fixed charge, a variable charge based on resource usage, or a variable charge based on volume.

Some companies use a no charge approach because IT services benefit the overall organization. This method treats the IT group for accounting purposes as a cost center that offers services without charge. In contrast, if management imposes charges on other departments, the IT department is regarded as a profit center that sells services that otherwise would have to be purchased from outside the company.

You also must classify system benefits. Many benefit categories are similar to costs: tangible or intangible, fixed or variable, and direct or indirect. Benefits also can be classified as positive benefits that result in direct dollar savings or cost-avoidance benefits that allow the firm to avoid costs that they would otherwise have incurred.

Cost-benefit analysis involves three common approaches: payback analysis, return on investment (ROI) analysis, and present value analysis. You can use spreadsheet programs to help you work with those tools.

Payback analysis determines the time it takes for a system to pay for itself, which is called the payback period. In payback analysis, you compare total development and operating costs to total benefits. The payback period is the point at which accumulated benefits equal accumulated costs. A disadvantage of this method is that payback analysis analyzes only costs and benefits incurred at the beginning of a system's useful life.

Return on investment (ROI) analysis measures a system by comparing total net benefits (the return) to total costs (the investment). The result is a percentage figure that represents a rate of return that the system offers as a potential investment. Many organizations set a minimum ROI that all projects must match or exceed and use ROI to rank several projects. Although ROI provides additional information compared with payback analysis, ROI expresses only an overall average rate of return that might not be accurate for a given time period. Also, ROI does not recognize the time value of money.

Present value analysis adjusts the value of future costs and benefits to account for the time value of money. By measuring all future costs and benefits in current dollars, you can compare systems more accurately and consistently. Present value analysis uses mathematical factors that you can derive or look up in published tables. You also can use a spreadsheet function to calculate present value. Many companies use present value analysis to evaluate and rank projects.

# Key Terms and Phrases

# Appendix Exercises

## Review Questions

1. What is economic feasibility? How do you know if a project is economically feasible?
2. How can you classify costs? Describe each cost classification, and provide a typical example for each category.
3. What is a chargeback method? What are four common chargeback approaches?
4. How can you classify benefits? Describe each benefit classification, and provide a typical example for each category.
5. What is payback analysis, and what does it measure? What is a payback period, and what is the formula to calculate the payback period?
6. What is return on investment (ROI) analysis, and what does it measure? What is the formula to calculate ROI?
7. What is present value analysis, and what does it measure?
8. What is the meaning of the phrase, *time value of money*?
9. Why is it difficult to assign a dollar figure to an intangible cost? When and how can it be done? Provide an example with your explanation.
10. What is a system's economically useful life, and how is it measured?

## Discussion Topics

1. Suppose your supervisor asks you to inflate the benefit figures for an IT proposal, in order to raise the priority of his or her favorite project. Would this be ethical or not? Does internal cost-benefit analysis affect company shareholders? Why or why not?
2. In this Appendix, you learned how to use payback analysis, ROI, and NPV to assess IT projects. Could these tools also be used in your personal life? Give an example of how you might use each one to help you make a financial decision.
3. Is there a role for intuition in the decision-making process, or should all judgments be made strictly on the numbers? Explain your answer.
4. The time value of money is an important factor when analyzing a project's NPV. Is the time value of money more important, less important, or of the same importance in periods of low inflation compared with periods of high inflation? Explain your answer.

## Projects

1. Suppose you are studying two hardware lease proposals. Option 1 costs $4,000, but requires that the entire amount be paid in advance. Option 2 costs $5,000, but the payments can be made $1,000 now and $1,000 per year for the next four years. If you do an NPV analysis assuming a 14% discount rate, which proposal is less expensive? What happens if you use an 8% rate?
2. Assume the following facts:
   A project will cost $45,000 to develop. When the system becomes operational, after a one-year development period, operational costs will be $9,000 during each year of the system's five-year useful life. The system will produce benefits of $30,000 in the first year of operation, and this figure will increase by a compound 10% each year. What is the payback period for this project?
3. Using the same facts as in Project 2, what is the ROI for this project?
4. Using the same facts as in Project 2, what is the NPV for this project?

# APPENDIX D Internet Resources

In **Appendix D**, you will learn about Internet resource tools that can help you perform your duties and achieve your personal and professional goals.

## INTRODUCTION

### OBJECTIVES

*When you finish this part of the Appendix, you will be able to:*

- Describe the characteristics of the Internet and the World Wide Web

- Plan an Internet search strategy, review your information requirements, use the proper search tools and techniques, evaluate the results, and consider copyright and data integrity issues

- Use search engines, subject directories, and the invisible Web to locate the information you require

- Demonstrate advanced search techniques, including Boolean logic and Venn diagrams

- Describe Internet communication channels including social networking, newsgroups, newsletters, blogs, podcasts, RSS feeds, Webinars, mailing lists, Web-based discussion groups, chat rooms, instant messaging, and text messaging

- Provide examples of IT community resources of value to a systems analyst

- Explain the benefits and disadvantages of online learning opportunities

The Internet offers a wealth of information about every conceivable subject. Without a good road map, however, it is easy to become overwhelmed by the sheer volume of material. Appendix D of the Systems Analyst's Appendix will describe various Internet resources, assist you in formulating an effective information gathering strategy, and explain Internet resource tools and techniques that you can use to access the information you need.

## APPENDIX INTRODUCTION CASE: Mountain View College Bookstore

**Background:** Wendy Lee, manager of college services at Mountain View College, wants a new information system that will improve efficiency and customer service at the three college bookstores.

In this part of the case, Tina Allen (systems analyst) and David Conroe (student intern) are talking about Internet resource tools.

| | |
|---|---|
| **Participants:** | Tina and David |
| **Location:** | Mountain View College Cafeteria, near the end of the systems analysis phase |
| **Discussion topics:** | Internet resource tools |

**Tina:** Hi, David. Did you get a chance to try that new search engine?

**David:** *I sure did. First, I formulated an Internet search strategy, as you suggested, and then I did a search using the logical operators that we talked about. I liked the way the search engine organized the results for me. I also followed your suggestions about checking out the quality of the results.*

**Tina:** Sounds good. But remember — sometimes it might be better not to start your search with a search engine.

**David:** *Why not?*

**Tina:** Well, the Internet is a huge place. In some situations, you might want to get a broad overview of a topic before plunging into a specific search. If so, you might want to use a subject directory like Yahoo! or the Librarians' Index to the Internet. Another important resource is called the invisible Web, which is a collection of searchable databases that usually are not accessed by search engines.

**David:** *Okay. What about using other communication channels like social networking sites, newsgroups, newsletters, blogs, podcasts, RSS feeds, Webinars, mailing lists, Web-based discussion groups, chat rooms, instant messaging, and text messaging?*

**Tina:** They all are important ways to get online information. Also remember that the IT community has many resources that can help you locate information, keep up with IT developments, and advance your career with knowledge and training.

**David:** *It seems like the more I know about the Internet, the more I have to learn.*

**Tina:** I feel the same way. Let's see what else we can learn about Internet resource tools. Here's a task list to get us started:

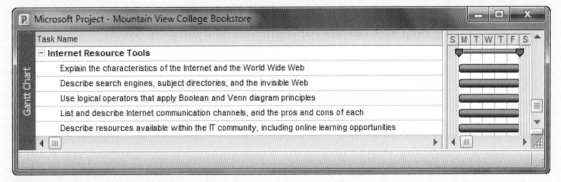

**FIGURE D-1** Typical Internet resource tasks.

## OVERVIEW

As a systems analyst, you rely on your knowledge, skills, and experience. Fortunately, you have access to the Internet, where an enormous storehouse of information is available to you at little or no cost. The **Internet** is a worldwide network that integrates many thousands of other networks, which in turn link millions of government, business, educational, and personal users around the globe. The Internet can assist you with technical problems and can help you advance your career by offering access to training, education, and communication with other IT professionals.

The Internet allows you to visit the **World Wide Web**, usually referred to as the **Web**, which contains billions of text and multimedia documents called **Web pages**. A collection of related Web pages is called a **Web site** and is stored on a computer called a **Web server**. A **Web browser**, or **browser**, is a software program that allows you to access and display Web pages that are delivered to you by a Web server. Microsoft Internet Explorer, Mozilla Firefox, and Apple Safari are popular browsers that offer powerful graphic interfaces to help you navigate the Web.

This Appendix begins with a step-by-step plan for Internet research, followed by a summary of search basics and a detailed discussion of search engines, subject directories, and the invisible Web. Internet communications tools are covered next, including social networking, newsgroups, newsletters, blogs, podcasts, RSS feeds, Webinars, mailing lists, Web-based discussion groups, chat rooms, and instant messaging. The last section presents valuable online resources available within the IT community.

**ON THE WEB**

To learn more about the World Wide Web, visit the Management Information Systems CourseMate Web site at **www. cengagebrain. com**, navigate to **On the Web Links** for Appendix D, and locate the World Wide Web link.

## PLANNING AN INTERNET RESEARCH STRATEGY

An Internet research strategy is necessary to avoid frustration and wasted time. A pilot or ship captain would not begin a journey without knowing the destination. Similarly, you can use a four-step plan to navigate efficiently and confidently toward your objectives:

Step 1.  Review your information requirements.

Step 2.  Use the proper search tools and techniques.

Step 3.  Evaluate the results.

Step 4.  Consider copyright and data integrity issues.

Over time, you will gain experience and develop your own preferences for using the Internet. You should remember that each research situation is unique, and several tools and techniques might be necessary to achieve the results you seek.

### Step I. Review Your Information Requirements

The first step to finding information online is to make sure you really understand what you are seeking. You need to think about the topic to ensure that you are casting an appropriate net. For example, a supervisor might ask you to help decide between two specific CASE products. Your initial inclination might be to find a review of various CASE applications. Upon reflection, however, you realize it would be more useful to understand CASE tools in a general sense before comparing specific products. Therefore, you decide to start with a more generalized search instead of going directly to vendor sites.

## Step 2. Use the Proper Search Tools and Techniques

Once you feel that you understand the information required, it is time to pick an initial tool. At this point, you face some choices. Should you use search engines or subject directories? Should you seek commercial sites, IT publications, professional associations, newsgroups, or other areas to explore? What about social networking?

As you gain experience, you will be able to handle a wide range of Internet tools and resources. As with most skills, the more you use them, the more expertise you acquire. In time, you probably will develop your own list of favorite tools and resources.

## Step 3. Evaluate the Results

By definition, the Internet is essentially open and unregulated. On the plus side, a huge diversity of information is available. The quality of content, however, varies greatly. Unlike published journals or textbooks, almost anyone can post **content**, or material, on the Web. This means that the searcher must review the information very carefully. Questions to ask when accessing content include the following:

**SOURCE** Is the author identifiable? Does the author have expertise on the subject? You might need to trace back through Web site addresses or URLs to find biographical information, or do a separate search on the author's name.

**ACCURACY** Does the information come from a commercial source that is offering its own solution? Is it from an association with an inherent bias? Often, it is very difficult to find completely objective information. Identifying biases and finding information from a variety of sources is a way to address this problem.

**SCOPE** Is the information specific enough? If not, you should narrow and refine your search and seek additional resources until you locate the information you need. When you use a search engine, one way to do this is to perform a **subsearch** using the results of the initial search as a starting point.

**CURRENCY** How old is the information? Is the topic static or dynamic? In the IT world, technology changes very quickly. If you locate information that appears to be out of date, you might seek more recent data to ensure that your results are valid.

**LOOK AND FEEL** Is the information easy to access and navigate? If the site is designed in a logical manner and offers value-added links to worthwhile pages and resources, do not be overly concerned with style — some excellent material is created by authors and producers who focus on content, not design.

If you find the content useful, be sure to credit the source properly when you use it. You must observe legal and ethical standards when you deal with Internet material. To learn more about proper citation and to view specific examples of how to cite electronic material, you can visit the excellent collection of resources at *www.aresearchguide.com*.

## Step 4. Consider Copyright and Data Integrity Issues

Before you copy or download your search results, you must ensure that you legally can use the material, and that the content is safe and free of threats.

The first issue involves copyright law. Many people regard the Web as a public domain, but in reality, it is more like a book or a CD. In other words, you might own a CD, but you do not own the material on that CD — you only possess a license to use the content in certain ways. On the Web, you should look for copyright notices and restrictions. If in doubt, you might have to contact the copyright holder to seek permission.

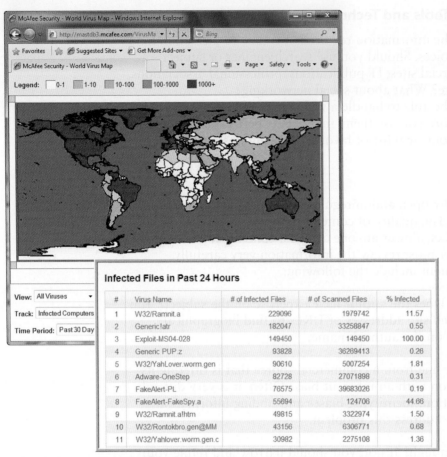

**FIGURE D-2**  McAfee's site shows how many computers and files are infected at any given time.

The second issue involves data integrity. It is important to protect your network and computer system from any unwanted viruses or **malware,** which is malicious software that might jeopardize your security or privacy. Unlike intellectual content, which is easy to evaluate, it is impossible for you to determine the integrity and validity of the internal file structure and format without a virus detection tool. As Figure D-2 shows, many thousands of viruses are identified each day. Viruses and other intrusions cost businesses many millions of dollars in lost data and additional effort. Without proper protection, you run the risk of not only corrupting your own files or hard drive, but bringing your entire company network down.

If the information is legally usable and safe, you can save it to your hard drive or network, depending on the content and purpose. The information you find may be in one of many formats, including word-processing documents, spreadsheets, and databases; Adobe PDF files; and multimedia material with file extensions such as .jpg, .mp3, .flv, and .mov.

You can download files directly to your hard drive from many Web sites. If this option is not offered explicitly, you can try right-clicking a link or embedded object to display a list of choices that includes downloading the selected information.

The following sections discuss search engines, subject directories, the invisible Web, and other Internet tools in more detail.

## SEARCH BASICS

As you journey on the Internet, you will use various navigation tools and techniques. To reach your destination, you must know how to use search engines, subject directories, and a collection of searchable databases called the invisible Web.

A **search engine** is an application that uses keywords and phrases to locate information on the Internet. **Meta-search engines** are tools that can apply multiple search engines simultaneously. For most people, search engines are the workhorses of information gathering. Search engines employ a variety of approaches to gathering information, and although they are extremely valuable, users should be aware of potential problems. For example, search results can be affected if the search engine permits commercial users to achieve higher priority based on payment of fees. Also, search engines access only a portion of the Internet.

A **subject directory** or **topic directory** is a Web site that allows you to find information by using a hierarchy, starting with a general heading and proceeding to more specific topics. A subject directory is an excellent starting point when you want an overview of a topic before proceeding to specific Web sites. Typically, a subject directory is created by an editorial staff that visits, evaluates, and organizes the sites into various categories and subcategories.

The **invisible Web**, also called the **deep Web** or **hidden Web**, refers to a vast collection of documents, databases, and Web pages that are usually not detected by search engines, but can be accessed using other tools and techniques. The invisible Web is a huge information storehouse, many times larger than the searchable Web, and includes thousands of university, scientific, and government libraries.

The following sections cover search engines, subject directories, and the invisible Web in more detail.

# SEARCH ENGINES

A search engine often is the best starting point for gathering information. A well-planned search will narrow the range of content to a manageable level and will allow you to explore the choices or execute a subsearch within the focused results. As with any tool, it is important to understand the intended use and limitations of a search engine before applying it to a task.

## Search Engine Concepts

Search engines use a specialized computer program called a **spider** or **crawler** that travels from site to site **indexing**, or cataloging, the contents of the pages based on **keywords**. The results are compiled into a database, so what you are searching is not the Web itself, but the contents of the search engine's database.

No single search engine can catalog the shifting contents of the Web, and even the most powerful engines cover a fraction of known Web content. If a particular site is not widely linked, or its author does not submit it to major search engines, then the material is invisible to them. Also, any site that requires a visitor to type in data, such as a name, cannot be accessed by search engines.

Although search engine indexes are incomplete and often dated, they are capable of delivering an overwhelming number of results, or **hits**. The real issue is quality versus quantity. When comparing search engines, it is important to know the company's policy toward allowing commercial sites to boost their ranking in a **pay for performance** arrangement. Links that are subsidized by companies are called **sponsored links**.

Not all search engines work the same way. By understanding the underlying algorithms, or specific rules, that drive these information engines, it is possible to better target your search. For example, some sites, like Google, rank their pages by analyzing the number of other sites that link to that page. Other search engines organize results differently. For example, Ask.com uses an interesting approach called ExpertRank™ technology, which ranks a site based on the number of authoritative sites that reference it, not just based on general popularity.

You usually can determine an engine's approach by clicking the *About* tab or link on the search site. The following section describes several examples of search engines, which are shown in Figure D-3 on the next page.

**ON THE WEB**

To learn more about search engines, visit the Management Information Systems CourseMate Web site at **www. cengagebrain. com**, navigate to **On the Web Links** for Appendix D, and locate the Search Engines link.

**FIGURE D-3**   Bing and Google are examples of indexed search engines, ixquick is an example of a meta-search tool, and Ask is a combination engine that includes ranked pages, suggestions to refine or narrow the search, and an expert-compiled resources section.

**INDEXED SEARCH ENGINES** Google and Bing are **indexed search engines** that organize and rank the results of a search. Although they have much in common, each tool has its own search algorithms, features, and user interface. Other examples of indexed search engines include Yahoo! and AltaVista, among others.

**META-SEARCH ENGINES** Meta-search engines can apply multiple search engines simultaneously. A meta-search engine examines the indexed results of several search engines to provide broader coverage. In addition to ixquick, other examples of meta-search engines include Metacrawler and Dogpile, which claims to use meta-search technology to remove duplicates and bring the most relevant sites to the top of the list.

## Search Techniques

Consider the following suggestions when you begin a search:

- Refine your topic. Unless you limit the scope of your search, you might be overwhelmed by the number of results. If you are looking for general information on a broad topic, consider a subject directory site.

- Translate your question into an effective search query. Searches are executed on keywords. You will improve your success if you pick the proper keywords. Try to find unique words or phrases and avoid those with multiple uses. For example, a search for the term *hard drive* might produce information about a computer hardware device or a difficult auto trip. Also consider using advanced search techniques, which are described in the following section.

- Review the search results and evaluate the quality of the results. If the search needs refinement or additional material, you can either use the site's advanced search techniques or select a different Internet resource altogether.

- It is important to organize the results of your search, so you can recognize and revisit important sites. Some search engines offer a personalized search history, which you can review and edit for this purpose. Many people find that the easiest solution is to create favorites or bookmarks in their browser for sites visited in important searches, using a set of folders and subfolders. If you do this, you can wait until you start the search, or you can create your filing system ahead of time.

To be effective, you should understand the mechanics of the search engine, use proper spelling, find unique phrases, and experiment with a variety of approaches. If you are consistently returning too many results, try using topic-specific terms and advanced search techniques. Conversely, if too few results are returned, eliminate the least important terms or concepts, broaden your subject, or use more general vocabulary when you select terms. An excellent tutorial, which includes a glossary and a comparison of several search engines, can be found at the University of California at Berkeley Library site, as shown in Figure D-4.

## Advanced Search Techniques

Many search engines offer powerful features that allow you to refine and control the type of information returned from searches. These features can include the option to search within returned results and the ability to search within specific areas, such as newsgroups. Perhaps the most powerful advanced feature is the option to use Boolean logic.

**Boolean logic** is a system named after British mathematician George Boole and refers to the relationships among search terms. You can use various combinations of the **logical operators** OR, AND, and NOT to improve your search success greatly. Figure D-5 on the next page graphically illustrates the use of the operators with search terms. The circles shown in the figure are called Venn diagrams. A **Venn diagram** uses circular symbols to illustrate Boolean logic. Venn diagrams are named after John Venn, a nineteenth-century scholar who devised a scheme for visualizing logical relationships. In the sample diagrams, the shaded area indicates the results of the search.

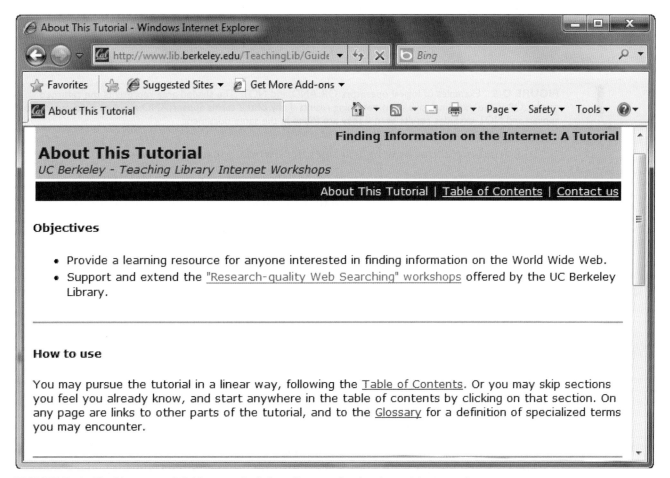

**FIGURE D-4**  The University of California at Berkeley offers search-related tutorials, tips, and resources.

| LOGICAL OPERATORS | EXAMPLE | VENN DIAGRAM (SHADED AREA INDICATES RETURNED RESULTS) |
|---|---|---|
| A or B | Baseball **or** Football | Baseball ◯◯ Football |
| A and B | Baseball **and** Football | Baseball ◯◯ Football |
| A not B | Internet **not** Web | Internet ◯◯ Web |
| A or B or C | Colorado **or** Mining **or** Gold | Colorado ◯◯◯ Mining / Gold |
| A and B and C | Colorado **and** Mining **and** Gold | Colorado ◯◯◯ Mining / Gold |
| A and B not C | Colorado **and** Mining **not** Gold | Colorado ◯◯◯ Mining / Gold |

**FIGURE D-5**   Examples of logical operators OR, AND, and NOT.  The shaded area represents the returned results.  OR is the most inclusive term, returning results if any of the terms appear; AND requires all keywords to appear; and NOT excludes results even if they are found in the same document.

To learn more about how logical operators work, consider the following diagrams:

**OR** The first diagram at the top of Figure D-5 shows that the **OR** term will retrieve all results containing either term. Notice that the shaded area includes both circles. The OR operator can be used when you need a wide search net.

**AND** The second diagram in Figure D-5 shows that the **AND** term will retrieve only those results in which all terms linked by the AND operator are present. Notice that the shaded area includes only the overlapping portion of the two circles. The more terms or concepts combined in an AND search, the fewer pages will be returned. The AND operator often is used to narrow a set of search results.

**NOT** The third diagram in Figure D-5 shows how the NOT operator can be used to exclude certain records. In this diagram, consider the closely related terms, Internet and Web. It is likely that these terms both appear in many Web pages. The **NOT** operator will strip out the results containing the unwanted term. For example the search string, Internet NOT Web, will return only those pages with the term, Internet. You should use the NOT operator carefully, because the term you want to exclude may be intertwined with the term you seek in many documents that would be useful to you.

The last three diagrams in Figure D-5 illustrate other combinations of logical operators where three search terms are involved.

Figure D-6 shows an excellent online tutorial that explains Boolean logic and provides many examples of OR, AND, and NOT operators.

**USING PHRASES** Suppose you want to find sites that sell board games that require players to use strategy, such as Monopoly®. In your search, you could specify both terms, *strategy* AND *game*, but your results probably would include many documents that describe game strategies used in various sports, which is not what you are seeking. A better approach might be to search using the phrase "strategy game" enclosed in quotes. A **phrase** is more specific than an AND operator, because it specifies an exact placement of terms. In this example, the phrase "strategy game" will not retrieve any documents unless they contain that exact phrase.

The implementation of Boolean logic varies by search engine. Some engines require the use of full Boolean searching using the complete operators (OR, AND, NOT) in the search window. Others use implied Boolean logic with keyword searching. In **implied Boolean logic**, symbols are used to represent Boolean operators, such as a plus sign (+) for AND, and a minus sign (-) for NOT. If two search terms are entered in the search window with a space between them, some search engines may assume an OR; others assume an AND. You need to consult the site's Help files to understand the underlying rules.

**FIGURE D-6**   This is an example of an online tutorial about Boolean logic, complete with various of examples of OR, AND, and NOT operators.

**USING FILL-IN FORMS** Most search engines provide an **advanced search** feature that offers a fill-in form similar to the Google example shown in Figure D-7 on the next page. Notice that the Google site also offers advanced search tips.

## Search Checklist

Many people find it helpful to prepare for an Internet search by using a checklist similar to the following.

- Does the topic have any unique words, phrases, or acronyms? If so, use these terms in the search.

- Do any of the search terms have other spellings or names? If so, include these with an OR operator in the search.

**FIGURE D-7**   For users unfamiliar with Boolean terms, many search engines offer an advanced search feature with fill-in forms. This example shows that *all these words* is like the AND operator, *this exact wording or phrase* is like putting quotes around the search terms, *one or more of these words* is like the OR operator, and *any of these unwanted words* is like the NOT operator.

- Are certain additional words or phrases likely to appear in any Web document? If so, consider adding an AND operator to narrow the search.

- Is there any unrelated material that my search terms might pick up? If so, consider using the NOT operator to exclude these documents.

- Are any organizations, publications, or institutions likely to have an interest in my topic? If so, try to locate their Web sites and then conduct a further search using the site indexes and databases available on the site.

- Is the search returning results too numerous to examine? If so, keep adding additional terms to narrow the search and reduce the number of hits until a reasonable number is achieved.

**ON THE WEB**

To learn more about subject directories, visit the Management Information Systems CourseMate Web site at **www. cengagebrain.com**, navigate to **On the Web Links** for Appendix D, and locate the Subject Directories link.

## SUBJECT DIRECTORIES

A subject directory collects and organizes Web sites in a top-down format, based on subjects and topics. An analogy might be a corporate organization chart, where you could go to the top person for an overview, then visit with lower-level employees to obtain specific information about their areas.

A subject directory is an excellent tool when you want general information about a topic before plunging into an array of specific Web sites. Yahoo! offers a popular subject directory that serves as a **portal**, or entrance to other Internet resources. Other academic and professional directories target the specific needs of researchers and users who concentrate on particular subjects. Many subject directories are reviewed by human experts, rather than computer robots, to ensure relevance and quality of links.

### A Subject Directory Example

Subject directories organize information into various categories and provide an overall framework for finding information. For example, suppose you wanted to use the Yahoo! Directory to learn more about IT security magazines. You could visit the Yahoo! site, and start with a list of main topics, one of which is called *Computers & Internet*. When you click this item, you would see a display similar to the second screen in Figure D-8, which shows various subtopics, including *Security and Encryption*. As you continue, you would click the *Magazines* link shown in the third screen, and you would see a list of publications that you could explore, some of which appear in the bottom screen.

In addition to Yahoo!, other popular subject directories include About.com and an organization called ipl2, which was the result of a merger between the Internet Public Library (IPL) and the Librarians' Internet Index (LII). The new entity, which has a Web site at ipl2.org, offers a free question-and-answer service staffed by volunteers who are professional librarians and library science graduate students.

## Advantages and Disadvantages of Subject Directories

The main advantage of a subject directory is that it provides an overview when you are not sure of the size and scope of your topic. Later, when you have a better understanding of your subject, you can use a search engine to seek additional information and examples.

Subject directories also have shortcomings. Many subject directories use human expertise to formulate the subject organization and determine the placement of links. This process involves subjective decisions that might affect the quality of search results. Some subject directories are updated continually; others might not be current. Also, unlike a search engine, a subject directory forces you to work your way through a series of levels, rather than using specific words and phrases to locate directly the material you seek.

## THE INVISIBLE WEB

Everyone is familiar with what is called the **visible Web**, which refers to Web sites that are indexed by the major search engines and are publicly accessible. As discussed earlier, much more information is available on the Internet that is not indexed. This valuable information source includes numerous text, graphics, and data files stored in collections that are unreachable by search engines.

The invisible Web includes searchable databases that contain an enormous amount of information in university and government libraries, as well as thousands of specialized databases that are maintained by institutions and organizations around the world.

Much of the invisible Web is open to the public, but some databases are password protected. Many sites allow guest access, but some areas can be accessed only by members of a specific group.

In an article in the *Journal of Electronic Publishing*, author Michael K. Bergman compared Internet searching to dragging a net across the surface of the ocean. He stated that "While a great deal may be caught in the net, there is still a wealth of information that is deep, and therefore, missed. The reason is simple: Most of the Web's information is buried far down on dynamically generated sites, and standard search engines never find it." Mr. Bergman pointed out that traditional search engines create their indices by spidering, or crawling, through many millions of Web pages. He pointed out that "To be discovered, the page must be static and linked to other pages.... Because traditional search engine crawlers cannot probe beneath the surface, the deep Web has heretofore been hidden."

**FIGURE D-8** In the example shown, the user has visited the Yahoo! Directory, clicked the *Computers & Internet* topic, then clicked the *Security and Encryption* link, and the *Magazines* link, which displays a list of IT security magazines.

**ON THE WEB**

To learn more about the invisible Web, visit the Management Information Systems CourseMate Web site at **www. cengagebrain.com**, navigate to **On the Web Links** for Appendix D, and locate the Invisible Web link.

## Invisible Web Examples

A few examples of information on the invisible Web include the following:

- Specialized topic databases: subject-specific collections of information, such as corporate financial filings and reports, genealogy records, or Ellis Island immigration data
- Hardware and software vendors: searchable technical support databases for large sites such as Microsoft's or Oracle's knowledge bases
- Publications: databases of published and archived articles
- Libraries: searchable catalogs for thousands of libraries, including the Library of Congress and numerous university and institutional libraries
- Government databases: census data, statutes, patents, copyrights, and trademarks
- Auction sites: searchable listings of items, bidders, and sellers
- Locators: telephone numbers, addresses, and e-mail addresses
- Career opportunities: job listings and résumé postings

## Navigation Tools for the Invisible Web

You can access the invisible Web in several ways. One approach is to use a search engine to locate a portal, or entrance, to a searchable database by including the word, database, as a required search term. For example, if you are searching for information about printer drivers, you could specify "printer drivers" AND database. The additional term will narrow the search results and increase the likelihood of finding searchable collections of printer drivers.

You also can access the invisible Web by using specialized portals that list and organize searchable databases. An example of an invisible Web portal is CompletePlanet.com, which is shown in Figure D-9. CompletePlanet.com claims to access over 70,000 invisible Web databases that are frequently overlooked by traditional searching, and also offers a special search tool called the Deep Query Manager™.

**FIGURE D-9**   The CompletePlanet site is organized by topics, and has links to many searchable databases whose contents cannot be indexed by traditional search engines.

If you spend a significant amount of time searching the invisible Web, you might want to use special navigation software to assist you. For example, EndNote is an application offered by Thomson Reuters, as shown in Figure D-10. EndNote uses a special information transfer method that allows a user to connect directly to hundreds of government and university databases on the invisible Web.

Figure D-11 shows a recap of the Internet tools and resources: search engines, subject directories, and the invisible Web. Notice that each has advantages and disadvantages.

**FIGURE D-10**  Many researchers use EndNote, which is an application that allows you to connect directly to hundreds of government and university databases.

## Recap of Internet Search Resources

| RESOURCE | POSSIBLE USES | ADVANTAGES | DISADVANTAGES | NOTES |
|---|---|---|---|---|
| Search Engines | Good initial starting point, especially if you have an overall understanding of the topic. Search engines can lead you to important government, professional, or commercial sites. | Flexibility. You can choose from many different engines with various features. Some allow newsgroup access as well. Meta-search engines can return and rank results from multiple sources. Advanced search techniques can be used. | Frequently produces information overload. Can return many irrelevant or out-of-date links. Without a refined search, it is impossible to examine results carefully. Some sites allow companies to improve their hits by "pay for performance." | You can improve search effectiveness significantly by using advanced search techniques based on logical operators. |
| Subject Directories | Good way to get a broad overview of a topic before accessing specific sites. | With a subject directory, you can maintain broader focus and perspective, and work from the general to the specific without getting lost in a maze of Web sites. | Material is organized by human intervention; quality, currency, and accuracy might vary. | Once you work your way through the various levels, you might be able to bookmark the resource for more direct future access. |
| Invisible Web | Information from nonindexed databases and searchable directories such as company financial reports, library holdings, industry reports, and government information. | Very diverse resource. Many more pages on the Web are non-indexed rather than indexed. | Can be difficult to access unless you know where to look. Navigating a searchable database can be more difficult than using a traditional search engine, because no common interface exists. | Portal sites are available to help you navigate the invisible Web. You can use a general search engine to locate searchable databases by searching a subject term and the word *database*. |

**FIGURE D-11**  A recap of the three main Internet search resources: search engines, subject directories, and the invisible Web. Notice that each option has advantages and disadvantages.

## INTERNET COMMUNICATION CHANNELS

Suppose that you are asked to analyze your organization's virus protection requirements. As part of your research you would want to learn about relevant news, developments, and the latest virus threats. You also might want to suggest several specific products. Assume that you performed your research using a search engine. Now you want to check your conclusions by getting feedback from other IT professionals. You can consider using social networking sites, newsgroups, newsletters, blogs, podcasts, Webcasts, RSS feeds, Webinars, mailing lists, Web-based discussion groups, chat rooms, and instant messaging.

### Social Networking

**Social networking** sites such as MySpace, Facebook, Twitter, and LinkedIn have gained enormous popularity in recent years. Many people use these communication channels along with more traditional choices, such as e-mail, blogs, chat rooms, and instant messaging. As a systems analyst, social networking allows you to connect to an extended family of personal and professional contacts, with unlimited opportunities.

### Newsgroups

Most people are familiar with bulletin boards they see at school, at work, and in their communities. Using thumb tacks or tape, people post information and read what others have posted. A **newsgroup** is the electronic equivalent of the everyday bulletin board. Newsgroups offer online discussion forums that address every conceivable subject and interest area. A newsgroup can put you in touch with the knowledge, experience, and opinions of a large online community.

Some search engines and subject directories allow you to conduct a specific search among newsgroups. Figure D-12 shows some of the many newsgroups that can be searched by the Google search engine. This portal provides a convenient entry point for a systems analyst who wants to explore and participate in a wide range of computer-related discussions.

To understand how newsgroups work, consider the following example. In your research on virus protection, which was mentioned in the previous section, assume that you have narrowed the product choices down to two. You are having trouble, however, differentiating between them and would like feedback from current users. You might want to visit individual product sites for user testimonials, but you would be unlikely to find a negative opinion on a vendor's site. You also could poll your professional colleagues, but you want to survey a variety of users that goes beyond your limited circle.

**FIGURE D-12**   Google provides easy access to numerous discussion groups.

At this point, you might decide to tap into an appropriate newsgroup and see if there have been any postings that are relevant to you. Some newsgroups are moderated, in which articles are sent to a person who approves them before they are posted for the group. Before you post, you should read the FAQ files associated with each newsgroup. The term **FAQs** stands for **frequently asked questions**. FAQs are a common method of providing guidance on questions that users are likely to ask. In many cases, FAQs describe the particular **netiquette**, or Web guidelines for protocol and courtesy, that exist on a particular newsgroup or site. You can learn more about netiquette in Appendix A of the Systems Analyst's Appendix.

As you gain experience, you might decide to subscribe to newsgroups that address topics of interest to you, including some of the ones listed in Figure D-12.

## Newsletters, Blogs, Podcasts, and Webcasts

**Newsletters** are a convenient way to keep current on topics of interest. Many online magazines and other groups offer free e-mail newsletters to subscribers interested in specific topics. For example, as shown Figure D-13, *InfoWorld* readers can access a wide range of newsletters, blogs, and podcasts.

**ON THE WEB**

To learn more about newsgroups, visit the Management Information Systems CourseMate Web site at **www. cengagebrain. com**, navigate to **On the Web Links** for Appendix D, and locate the Newsgroups link.

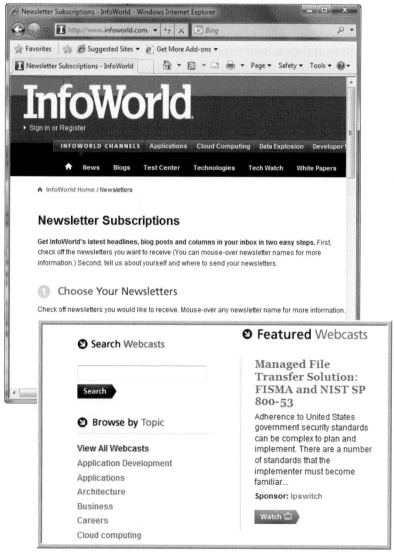

**FIGURE D-13** InfoWorld offers free newsletters, Webcasts, and other valuable online resources.

A **blog** is a Web-based log, or journal. Computer-related blogs can provide valuable information for a systems analyst. Also, many vendors offer Web-based training options, including podcasts. A **podcast**, sometimes called a **Webcast**, refers to online material that can be delivered as a streaming download to users, who can receive multimedia files and open them on a computer or download them to an iPod®, iPad®, smart phone, or other portable player. Podcasts can be pre-scheduled, made available on demand, or delivered as automatic updates, depending on a user's preference. An advantage of a podcast is that users, called subscribers, can access the material anywhere, anytime.

### RSS Feeds

**ON THE WEB**

To learn more about RSS feeds, visit the Management Information Systems CourseMate Web site at **www. cengagebrain.com**, navigate to **On the Web Links** for Appendix D, and locate the RSS Feeds link.

The term **RSS** stands for **Really Simple Syndication**. RSS is a format for publishing frequently updated content to users who subscribe to an RSS download, also called a feed, an **RSS feed**, or a **Web feed**. Web publishers such as Yahoo!, Google, CNN, MSNBC, and many other newspapers, magazines, vendors, and blogs use RSS feeds to distribute news and updates to subscribers, who can read the content with software called an **RSS reader**, a **feed reader**, or an **aggregator**.

Figure D-14 shows how Yahoo! uses RSS feeds to publish news items, and a sample of the wide variety of available topics. Many main headings, such as *Technology*, also contain a lengthy list of subtopics. In addition, Yahoo! allows you to create a custom RSS feed by typing a term or phrase into a search box, which is shown at the bottom of Figure D-14. For example, if you were especially interested in news updates about Cisco routers, you could create a Yahoo! feed that would capture and download all articles on that topic.

Yahoo! feeds make it easy for an IT professional to stay well informed on topics of interest. However, notice the important caution regarding the use of the content. Yahoo! states that the feeds are free for individuals and non-profit organizations for non-commercial use, but that proper attribution is required.

### Webinars

A **Webinar**, which combines the words *Web* and *seminar*, is an Internet-based training session that provides an interactive experience. Most Webinars are scheduled events with a group of pre-registered users and an online presenter or instructor. A prerecorded Webinar session also can be delivered as a Webcast.

### Mailing Lists

A **mailing list**, also called a **listserv**, is similar to a newsgroup in that it provides a forum for people who want to exchange information about specific topics. Like a newsgroup, users can post messages and view postings made by others. Instead of a bulletin board approach, however, a mailing list uses e-mail to communicate with users. A computer called a **list server** directs e-mail to people who subscribe to, or join, the mailing list.

**FIGURE D-14**   Yahoo! uses RSS feeds to publish news about a wide variety of topics. You also can create a custom feed by typing a term or phrase into the search box at the bottom of the Web page.

When a person subscribes to a list, he or she can receive e-mail messages as they are posted. Subscribers also can access a collection of messages called a **digest**. Many mailing lists maintain Web sites where users can search message archives.

A systems analyst would be interested in mailing lists that focus on information technology. To locate IT-related mailing lists, you can visit the Web sites of professional organizations, and you can try adding the phrase *mailing list or listserv* to your search topic. Also, as shown in Figure D-15, you can visit Web sites such as *lsoft.com* and *tile.net* that organize mailing lists by name and subject.

## Web-Based Discussion Groups

Another online communication resource is called a **Web-based discussion group**, which is an online community that combines features of mailing lists and newsgroups. Web-based discussion groups can be accessed through portals, such as Yahoo! or Google, or by visiting vendor sites, such as Cisco, IBM, or Apple. Group members can receive messages either individually or in digest form like a mailing list, and they can browse messages stored on the group's Web site. In addition to text messages, group Web sites often include membership lists and contact information, photo galleries, and links of interest to members.

Web-based discussion groups are popular because they offer a convenient and free meeting place with a graphical interface that makes it easy for users to access information and exchange messages.

## Chat Rooms

A **chat room**, also called a **channel**, is an online meeting place where users can interact and converse in real time. The chat room concept originated with **IRC**, which stands for **Internet Relay Chat**. IRC is a multichannel system supported by servers that enable conversations, group or individual, on a worldwide basis. You can learn more about IRC at the Web site *www.irc.org*, and you can follow links to see a list of available IRC channels that might be of interest to you.

Various companies also provide chat rooms that are available to IT professionals interested in specific topics. For example, Microsoft offers a wide variety of technical chat rooms, as shown in Figure D-16.

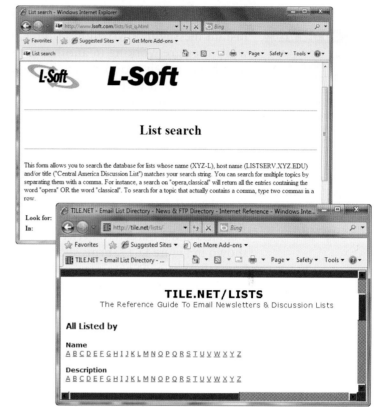

**FIGURE D-15** Lsoft.com and tile.net are examples of Web sites that organize mailing lists by name and subject.

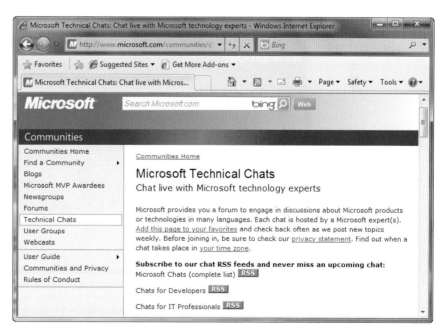

**FIGURE D-16** Microsoft offers a wide variety of technical chat rooms where users can interact and converse in real time.

## Instant Messaging and Text Messaging

**🌐 ON THE WEB**

To learn more about IM and texting abbreviations, visit the Management Information Systems CourseMate Web site at **www. cengagebrain. com**, navigate to **On the Web Links** for Appendix D, and locate the IM and Texting Abbreviations link.

**Instant messaging (IM)** allows online users to exchange messages immediately, even while they are working in another program or application. Users are alerted that other members of their group are available online, and users can send and receive messages or enter into a chat with other users.

Although instant messaging began as a popular feature in home-oriented services such as AOL and Yahoo!, it has become an important business communications tool, and many firms use enterprise-wide IM tools such as  Microsoft Office Communicator. Corporate use of IM, however, raises serious security and privacy concerns because it is relatively uncontrolled. Also, certain industries such as banking and health care must observe legal regulations that govern all their communications, including IM, which must be logged and documented. Corporate security can be compromised by unauthorized instant messaging and exchange of files. Also, applications such as Skype and other computer-based voice channels add a burden to network bandwidth and efficiency. To combat these threats, as shown in Figure D-17, firms such as Blue Coat offer software that can manage instant messaging and provide necessary security and controls.

Many people use **text messaging**, or **texting**, to send brief written messages from one mobile phone or wireless device to another. Users can also send text messages from a computer to a handheld device. The popularity of IM and texting has given rise to numerous abbreviations that reduce message size and speed up the communication process. Some well-known examples are *BTW* (*by the way*), *JMO* (*just my opinion*), and *TIA* (*thanks in advance*).

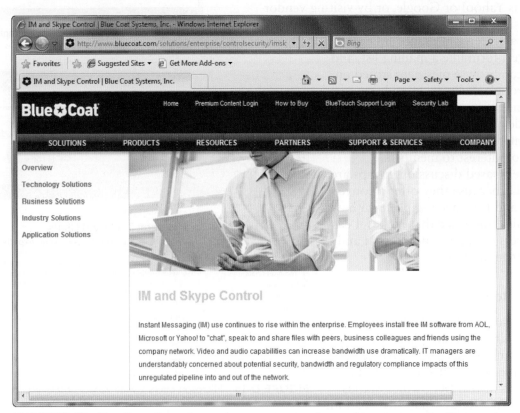

**FIGURE D-17**    Blue Coat offers software that can manage and control instant messaging, Skype, and other types of communication that use the company's network.

Figure D-18 shows a recap of online IT channels that can assist a systems analyst in online research and communication: social networking sites, newsgroups, newsletters, mailing lists, RSS feeds, Web-based discussion groups, chat rooms, and instant messaging. Notice that each resource has advantages and disadvantages.

## Recap of Internet Communication Channels

| RESOURCE | POSSIBLE USES | ADVANTAGES | DISADVANTAGES | NOTES |
|---|---|---|---|---|
| Social Networking Sites | Communicating with others who share similar interests. | Opens up new resources that can help you personally and professionally. | Your network can become too large and impersonal. Too much activity can be distracting. | Extremely convenient, popular, and no subscription fees. |
| Newsgroups | Answers to technical questions, advice, and support. | Can find information on every conceivable subject — good place to exchange views with other analysts. | Cumbersome to search through message threads. Need to assess quality of information carefully. | Some major search engines allow newsgroup access. |
| Newsletters, Blogs, and Podcasts | Good way to follow trends and developments regarding specific IT topics. | Most newsletters, blogs, and podcasts are free to users who can subscribe to specific topics. | Not interactive, and the amount of information can be overwhelming. Difficult to filter irrelevant items. | Some newsletters, blogs, and podcasts are published daily; others weekly or monthly. |
| RSS Feeds | Provide news and updates for readers of online newspapers, magazines, and blogs. | Convenient way to keep posted on virtually any topic of interest. | Unless topics are specific, the volume of information might be difficult to sift through. | Rapid growth is expected to continue, as more users discover this valuable resource. |
| Webinars | Internet-based training that can provide an interactive experience. | Users can plan, schedule, and pre-register for online sessions. | Only available when scheduled — otherwise not interactive. | Very popular technique because of convenience and cost-effectiveness. |
| Mailing Lists | Members can exchange information with others about specific topic of interest. | Messages arrive by e-mail, rather than in the form of bulletin board postings. | Amount of material might be difficult to read and analyze. | Some mailing lists, or listservs, allow members to search archived messages. |
| Web Discussion Groups | Members form a Web-based community regarding topics of common interest. | Combine many convenient features of newsgroups and mailing lists. | Although free, these groups usually must be accessed through a Web portal. | Web discussion groups offer a mix of features and convenience. |
| Chat Rooms | Online meeting places where users can interact and converse. | Many IT chat rooms attract professionals who are willing to help each other solve problems. | Discussions take place in real time, which might not be convenient. Dialog might be unfocused and irrelevant to your needs. | Many large vendors, such as Microsoft, offer technical chat rooms. |
| Instant Messaging and Text Messaging | Users can exchange messages immediately, either online or by cell phone. | Highly efficient means of real-time communication on topics of interest. Good way to collaborate on team projects. | Can be distracting to a busy user, and sheer volume of nonessential messages can be a problem. | IM and text messaging have moved beyond the personal desktop and are acceptable business communication tools. |

**FIGURE D-18** A recap of Internet communication channels that can assist a systems analyst in online research and communication. Notice that each option has advantages and disadvantages.

## INFORMATION TECHNOLOGY COMMUNITY RESOURCES

If you were asked to check a stock price or research the weather in a distant city for a business trip, you probably would not use a search engine. Instead, you would visit a favorite site you use regularly to access specific information. Similarly, when you require IT information, you can access a huge assortment of sites and resources that can be called the **information technology (IT) community**. This vast collection includes many sites that IT professionals can use to research specific questions or obtain background information. As a systems analyst, you are a member of this community. Like most communities, it offers you resources and support, including answers to technical questions, updates on new products and services, and information about training opportunities. The IT community includes numerous publications and online magazines, searchable databases, Web-based discussion groups, and mailing lists.

Four important components of the IT community are corporate resources, government resources, professional resources, and online learning resources, which are described in the following sections.

### Corporate Resources

Corporate resources can provide general IT knowledge and background, as well as help solve specific business challenges. It is very important to evaluate corporate content carefully, because some sites are developed by companies with an interest in selling you a specific solution or product. Figure D-19 shows a site that offers product reviews and helpful information.

If you are looking for help on a software application, it is a good idea to start by reviewing the software documentation. In many cases, technical support is included free of charge for a specific period of time. If you are working with an application with expired technical support, the software provider's Web site will describe support options that are available to you, including various fees and charges. Common problems often are addressed in the FAQ section.

An important corporate resource to systems analysts is their own internal company Web site or intranet. An intranet must be easy to access and provide access to valuable information. Companies increasingly are using intranets as a means of sharing information and working towards common solutions. Intranets can contain company policies and procedures, lessons-learned files, and financial information. They also enable employees to access and update their personal benefit information. In many organizations, the intranet is reducing the volume of paper memos and reports by serving as an enterprise-wide library and clearinghouse.

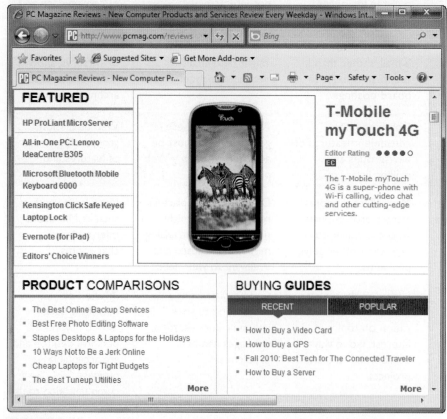

**FIGURE D-19**   PC Magazine is an example of a site that offers product guides and reviews.

## Government Resources

The IT needs of the federal government are enormous. Not surprisingly, a number of excellent federal IT resources are available on the Internet. Many sites offer comprehensive, nonbiased information and valuable advice for IT professionals. For example, recent U.S. General Accounting Office (GAO) reports on the IT industry have covered everything from an analysis of the information security practices to a framework for assessing IT investments. Additionally, government sites can provide information on federal, state, and local business policies and regulations. The General Services Administration (GSA) site depicted in Figure D-20 is a good source for federal policies and regulations, especially for firms that do business with the government.

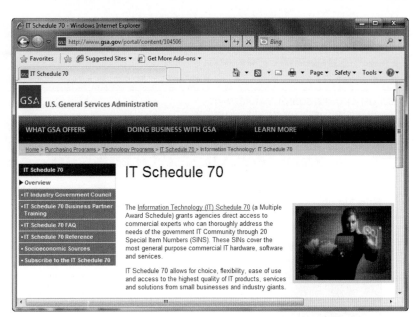

**FIGURE D-20** The GSA site contains information about federal IT policies, news, and related links. The screen shows a sample from the IT Regulations, Guidelines and Laws section.

## Personal and Professional Resources

Most individuals have friends, acquaintances, and other people that they know or would like to meet. Whether the communication channel involves e-mail, chats, newsgroups, or social networking, the goal is to expand contacts and opportunities. Some observers have compared social networks to small virtual communities or neighborhoods, where people can meet and share information. Their objectives might be personal, or might relate to technical matters, career topics, or professional growth.

In addition to social networking, a systems analyst can consider membership in one or more IT-related associations. Many organizations focus on a specific topic such as project management, software engineering, or information security. Membership in some associations is free or relatively inexpensive, and employers often subsidize professional memberships that are directly related to a person's job duties. The links provided by these sites often are quite useful. Professional organizations, such as the **Information Technology Association of America (ITAA)** or the **Association for Computing Machinery (ACM)**, which is shown in Figure D-21, also sponsor seminars and training. Many associations offer electronic newsletters that relate to your area of interest and are delivered to you by e-mail on a periodic basis.

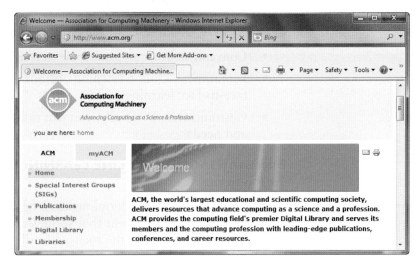

**FIGURE D-21** The ACM site is one of many resources that a systems analyst can use to keep up with current issues, trends, and opportunities.

## Online Learning Resources

It is difficult to keep up with the constantly changing IT landscape. Targeted professional development is a way for IT workers to remain focused and current in their

**FIGURE D-22**   The GoLearn.gov Learning Center offers a wide range of online training for federal employees.

chosen areas. In the past, this goal often meant attending lengthy and expensive off-site training courses. Advances in bandwidth and processing power have made online learning an increasingly attractive option for many IT professionals.

**Online learning**, also referred to as **e-learning**, is a term that refers to the delivery of educational or training content over the public Internet or an intranet. You can locate learning opportunities by searching the Web or through various professional associations. Many schools and colleges have seen a tremendous increase in demand for online learning and have increased their course offerings accordingly. The GoLearn.gov Learning Center shown in Figure D-22 is a government site with many online learning information and opportunities for federal employees.

Online learning can take many forms, ranging from individual self-paced instruction with little or no instructor involvement, to interactive, instructor-led groups with streaming audio and video capability. When choosing an online learning method, your learning goals and the quality of the content are the most important considerations. You need to think about your personal learning preferences. For example, you might learn better in a collaborative environment rather than working alone. If that is the case, consider options that include an interactive peer community. The following are some advantages and disadvantages that apply to the use of online resources:

**BENEFITS OF ONLINE LEARNING**   Benefits of online learning include the following:

- Convenient. You can participate in training when and where you want.

- Economical. Online learning options generally are less expensive than traditional face-to-face learning.

- Customizable. Generally, you can tailor the learning experience to your interests and needs.

**DISADVANTAGES OF ONLINE LEARNING**   Disadvantages of online learning include the following:

- Interaction. Although online learning can be highly collaborative, it lacks the face-to-face component that some learners find necessary. Additionally, you are less likely to receive the focused feedback that you would get when participating in traditional classroom training.

- Interface. Although bandwidth and computing power have increased greatly in recent years, the interface in an online learning experience might be a limitation. For example, you might experience slower processing performance, especially if the training uses interactive video, audio, or high-resolution graphics.

- Suitability. Online learning might not be the best option, particularly if the content is complicated and unfamiliar to you.

Figure D-23 shows a recap of online IT resources, including possible uses, advantages, and disadvantages.

## Recap of Online IT Resources

| RESOURCE | POSSIBLE USES | ADVANTAGES | DISADVANTAGES | NOTES |
|---|---|---|---|---|
| Corporate Resources | Specific technical hardware or software help, training opportunities. | First stop for troubleshooting proprietary software or hardware. | Very often an agenda is associated with the site — for example, advocating a particular product or service. | Vendor sites contain valuable specific product or solution information (check the site's FAQs). Many offer newsletters for interested visitors. |
| Government Resources | Information on IT regulations. | Wide variety of general topics, from congressional studies to industry-relevant government regulations. | Not all information can be accessed via the Web — sometimes sites refer to a document number for ordering. Information tends to be general and not always relevant. | Suggested sites: Library of Congress, General Accounting Office, Government Computer News. |
| Personal and Professional Resources | A combination of social networking, access to professional sites, and membership in IT organizations can expand personal and professional resources related to IT ethics, technical issues, and career opportunities. | Social networking is fun, because it involves person-to-person contact. IT industry-related sites often provide valuable links and inform-ation on training opportunities. | Social networking is not a precise tool for specific issues. Conversely, many IT sites are too specialized to be of general interest. | Some IT sites can serve as portals to a collection of online resources. |
| Online Learning Resources | An IT professional needs to stay current in a constantly changing technology environment. Online learning can provide job-specific skills and support for career advancement. | Convenient, economical, and customizable. You can participate in training when and where you want, and online learning options are generally less expensive than traditional face-to-face learning. | Online learning lacks the face-to-face component that some learners find necessary. Learners are less likely to receive focused feedback. Also, the interface in an online learning experience might be a limitation. Online learning might not be the best option, if the content is complicated and unfamiliar. | When considering online learning, you must know your personal learning style. You should examine the entire range of options, from individual self-paced instruction with little or no instructor involvement, to inter-active, instructor-led classes. |

**FIGURE D-23** A recap of online resources that a systems analyst can use to keep up with current issues and trends in IT. Notice that each option has advantages and disadvantages.

## Appendix Summary

The Internet is a worldwide network that integrates many thousands of other networks, which in turn link millions of government, business, educational, and personal users around the globe. The Internet can assist you in your daily work by helping you solve technical problems and in the ongoing development of your career by providing access to training and professional education.

The Internet allows access to the World Wide Web, usually called the Web, which refers to the global collection of electronic documents stored on the Internet. These documents are referred to as Web pages, which are organized and stored on individual Web sites.

An Internet research strategy should use a four-step approach: review your information requirements, use the proper search tools and techniques, evaluate the results, and consider copyright and data integrity issues. Many people find it helpful to prepare for an Internet search by using a checklist to identify key terms, phrases, and characteristics of the topic.

The primary research tools include search engines, subject directories, and a collection of searchable database resources called the invisible Web. A search engine uses keywords and phrases to locate information on the Internet and list the results of the search. Users should be aware that results can be affected if the search engine permits commercial users to achieve higher priority based on payment of fees. Also, search engines access only a portion of the Internet. Meta-search engines are tools that can apply multiple search engines simultaneously.

A subject directory is a Web site that allows you to access topics by using a hierarchy, starting with general headings and proceeding to more specific topics. A subject directory is an excellent starting point when you want an overview of a particular topic before proceeding to specific Web sites.

The invisible Web, or hidden Web, describes numerous text, graphics, and data files stored in collections that are unreachable by search engines.

Many analysts use social networking as a primary online tool to expand personal and professional contacts and communication. Other Internet tools that might be of value to a systems analyst are newsgroups, newsletters, blogs, podcasts, RSS feeds, Webinars, mailing lists, Web-based discussion groups, chat rooms, and instant messaging. Newsgroups, which are part of the Usenet, are online discussion groups that address every conceivable subject and interest area. Newsletters are published by numerous commercial and nonprofit groups that offer membership subscriptions to users who are interested in specific topics. A mailing list, or listserv, allows subscribing members to post and receive messages forwarded to them by a list server. A Web-based discussion group, usually accessed through a portal such as Yahoo!, combines features of newsgroups and mailing lists for its members. A chat room is an online meeting place where users can interact and converse in real time. Instant messaging allows online users to exchange messages immediately, even while they are working in another program or application.

When an IT professional needs to research a topic or seek background information, he or she can turn to an assortment of sites and resources called the information technology (IT) community. The IT community includes corporate, government, professional, and online learning resources.

Professional development through online learning is a way for IT workers to remain current in their chosen areas. Online learning refers to the delivery of educational or training content over the Internet or an intranet. Online learning is convenient, economical, and customizable. Some disadvantages, however, include a lack of face-to-face interaction, limitations of the interface, and the fact that not everyone works well with this type of training.

# Key Terms and Phrases

advanced search 697
aggregator 704
AND 696
Association for Computing Machinery (ACM) 709
blog 704
Boolean logic 695
browser 690
channel 705
chat room 705
content 691
crawler 693
deep Web 693
digest 705
e-learning 709
FAQs (frequently asked questions) 703
feed reader 704
hidden Web 693
hits 693
implied Boolean logic 697
indexed search engine 694
indexing 693
Information Technology Association of America (ITAA) 709
information technology (IT) community 708
instant messaging (IM) 706
Internet 690
Internet Relay Chat (IRC) 705
invisible Web 693
IRC 705
keywords 693
list server 704
listserv 704
logical operators 695
mailing list 704
malware 692

meta-search engine 692
netiquette 703
newsgroup 702
newsletters 703
NOT 696
online learning 709
OR 696
pay for performance 693
phrase 697
podcast 704
portal 698
RSS (Really Simple Syndication) 704
RSS feed 704
RSS reader 704
search engine 692
social networking 702
spider 693
sponsored links 693
subject directory 693
subsearch 691
text messaging 706
texting 706
topic directory 693
Venn diagram 695
visible Web 699
Web 690
Web-based discussion group 705
Web browser 690
Web feed 704
Web page 690
Web server 690
Web site 690
Webcast 704
Webinar 704
World Wide Web 690

## Appendix Exercises

### Review Questions

1. Describe the size and characteristics of the Internet and the World Wide Web.
2. How do search engines differ from subject directories? Compare these approaches and describe their advantages and possible disadvantages.
3. What is the invisible Web, and how can it be accessed?
4. What steps should you follow when planning an Internet research strategy?
5. What questions should you ask when evaluating the quality of Internet research results?
6. What are sponsored links, and how can they affect the quality of your search results?
7. What is Boolean logic? Provide three examples.
8. How do Venn diagrams show the effect of the three logical operators?
9. Describe social networking, newsgroups, newsletters, blogs, podcasts, RSS feeds, Webinars, mailing lists, Web-based discussion groups, chat rooms, and instant messaging. How can these tools be used in Internet research?
10. What is the information technology community, and what resources does it offer for Internet research tasks?

### Discussion Topics

1. The textbook explains that some companies pay to obtain a higher ranking when search results are displayed. Is this good, is it bad, or does it not matter to you as a user? Explain your position.
2. Some people rely heavily on social networking, instant messaging, and texting to communicate with friends and business colleagues. Others find these methods distracting. Do you use social networking, instant messaging, or texting? Why or why not?
3. Could Boolean logic and Venn diagrams be useful in everyday life? How might they be used?
4. The Internet has affected many aspects of our society. What are the most important benefits of the Internet, and what problems have been created by it?

### Projects

1. Use a search engine and enter the following words: presidential candidates in 2016. Run the search and notice how many results appear. Now place quote marks around the phrase and run the search again. Explain the difference in the results.
2. Will the search phrase "*commercial television*" return the same results as the phrase "*television commercial*"? Experiment with a search engine, and explain the results you obtain.
3. Use the Yahoo! subject directory to identify two dictionaries of technical terms. Begin with the subject *Computers and Internet*, and then follow the appropriate links until you obtain results. Describe the results of your research. What other research strategies could you use for this task?
4. Perform research on the Web to learn more about RSS feeds. Then write a practical, step-by-step guide for users who want to set up RSS feeds at their workstations.

# INDEX

organization's databases and applications. They are often used to facilitate complex business transactions. 464, 465

**application software** Software such as e-mail, word processors, spreadsheets, and graphics packages used by employees. 8

**application service provider (ASP)** A firm that delivers a software application, or access to an application, by charging a usage or subscription fee. 291, 299, 302, 469–470
  described, 291
  user references supplied by, 306

**applications programmer** A person who works on new systems development and maintenance. 579

**archived** The storage of previous version of a system when a new version is installed. 583

**ASCII** Stands for American Standard Code for Information Interchange, a data storage coding method used on most personal computers and workstations. 433, 544

**asset** Hardware, software, data, networks, people, or procedures that provide tangible or intangible benefit to an organization. 590

**Association for Computing Machinery (ACM)** A professional association for the IT industry that sponsors seminars and training and has a Web site where members can keep up with current issues, trends, and opportunities. 709

**associative entity** An entity that has its own set of attributes and characteristics. Associative entities are used to link between many-to-many (M:N) relationships. 407

**attack** A hostile act that targets an information system, or an organization itself.
  described, 592
  overview, 592–593
  profiles, 592

**attribute** A single characteristic or fact about an entity. An attribute, or field, is the smallest piece of data that has meaning within an information system. For example, a Social Security number or company name could be examples of an attribute. In object-oriented analysis, an attribute is part of a class diagram that describes the characteristics of objects in the class. Also known as a data element. 254, 402, 519
  database design and, 402
  described, 222, 250
  representing objects and, 252, 253

audiences, defining, 640

**audit fields** Special fields within data records to provide additional control or security information. Typical audit fields include the date the record was created or modified, the name of the user who performed the action, and the number of times the record has been accessed. 436

**audit log files** Audit log files record details of all accesses and changes to a file or database and can be used to recover changes made since the last backup. 436

**audit trail** An audit trail records the source of each data item and when it entered a system. In addition to recording the original source, an audit trail must show how and when data is accessed or changed, and by whom. All these actions must be logged in an audit trail file and monitored carefully. 313

**authorization zone** Part of a form that contains any required signatures. 361

**automated facsimile** A system that allows a customer to request a fax using e-mail, the company Web site, or a telephone. The response is transmitted in a matter of seconds back to the user's fax machine. 358

**automatic update service** Enables an application to contact the vendor's server and check for a needed patch. 602

**availability** One of the three main elements of system security: confidentiality, integrity, and availability (CIA). Availability ensures that authorized users have timely and reliable access to necessary information. 590

**avoidance** One of four risk control strategies. In avoidance, the risk is eliminated by adding protective safeguards. 592

**B2B (business-to-business)** A commercial exchange (e.g. products or services) between businesses, typically enabled by the internet or electronic means. 14, 400

**B2C (business-to-consumer)** A commercial exchange (e.g. products or services) between businesses and consumers conducted over the Internet. 13

back door attacks, 593

**backup** The process of saving a series of file or data copies to be retained for a specified period of time. Data can be backed up continuously, or at prescribed intervals. 436, 607, 608–609

**backup media** Data storage options, including tape, hard drives, optical storage, and online storage. 607

**backup policy** A backup policy contains detailed instructions and procedures for all backups. 607, 608

**balancing** A process used to maintain consistency among an entire series of diagrams, including input and output data flows, data definition, and process descriptions.
  described, 212
  examples, 214–216

**bandwidth** The amount of data that the system can handle in a fixed time period. Bandwidth requirements are expressed in bits per second.
  described, 586, 587
  network standards and, 482, 483
  system architecture and, 472, 482

**baseline** A formal reference point that measures system characteristics at a specific time. Systems analysts use baselines as yardsticks to document features and performance during the systems development process. 583

**Basic Service Set (BSS)** A wireless network configuration in which a central wireless device called an access point is used to serve all wireless clients; also called infrastructure mode. 483

**batch** A group of data, usually inputted into an information system at the same time. 369

**batch control** A total used to verify batch input. Batch controls might check data items such as record counts and numeric field totals. For example, before entering a batch of orders, a user might calculate the total number of orders and the sum of all the order quantities. When the batch of orders is entered, the order system also calculates the same two totals. If the system totals do not match the input totals, then a data entry error has occurred. 368

**batch input** A process where data entry is performed on a specified time schedule, such as daily, weekly, monthly, or longer. For example, batch input occurs when a payroll department collects time cards at the end of the week and enters the data as a batch. 368, 369

**batch processing** In a batch processing system, data is collected and processed in groups, or batches. Although online processing is used for interactive business systems that require immediate data input and output, batch processing can handle other situations more efficiently. 475–476

Bay Systems, 481

**benchmark** A benchmark measures the time a package takes to process a certain number of transactions.
  described, 306
  development strategies and, 296, 306–307
  prototyping and, 315

**benchmark testing** Benchmark testing is used by companies to measure system performance. 585

**best-case estimate** The most optimistic outcome is called the best-case estimate. 107

**binary digit** The smallest unit of data is one binary digit, called a bit. 433

**binary storage format** A format that offers efficient storage of numeric data. For example, when you specify numeric data types using Microsoft Access, you can choose from a variety of storage formats, including integer and long integer, among others. 434

Bing, 694

**biometric devices** Devices that identify a person by a retina scan or by mapping a facial pattern. 60

**biometric scanning systems** Mapping an individual's facial features, handprint, or eye characteristics for identification purposes. 60, 594

**BIOS-level password** A password that must be entered before the computer can be started. It prevents an unauthorized person from booting a computer by using a USB device or a CD-ROM. Also called a power-on password or a boot-level password. 595

**bit** The smallest unit of data is one binary digit, called a bit. 433

**black box** A metaphor for a process or action that produces results in a non-transparent or non-observable manner. In data flow diagrams, a process appears as a black box where the inputs, outputs, and general function of the process are known, but the underlying details are not shown.
  balancing and, 216
  described, 201, 256
  overview, 201–202
  viewing objects as, 256

**black hole** A process is said to be a "black hole" if it has no output. 203

BlackBerry (Research in Motion), 173–174

**block** A block, or physical record, is the smallest unit of data that is accessed by the operating system. 433

**block sequence** codes Block sequence codes use blocks of numbers for different classifications. 423

**blocking factor** The number of logical records in one physical record. 433

**blog** A Web-based log, or journal. 289, 703
  described, 704
  development strategies and, 305, 317

**Bluetooth** A form of wireless transmission very popular for short-distance wireless communication that does not require high power. 173, 371, 485

**body zone** The main part of the form. It usually takes up at least half of the space on the form and contains captions and areas for entering variable data. 361

**Boolean logic** A system named after British mathematician George Boole and refers to the relationships among search terms. 695, 697

**boot-level password** A password that must be entered before the computer can be started. It prevents an unauthorized person from booting a computer by using a USB device or a CD-ROM. Also called a BIOS-level password or a boot-level password. 595

**bottom-up technique** A bottom-up technique analyzes a large, complex project as a series of individual tasks, called project tasks. 105

**brainstorming** A fact-finding technique for gaining information, through the use of a small group discussion of a specific problem, opportunity, or issue. 159

**brick-and-mortar** Is used to describe traditional companies whose business model predated electronic commerce. Many brick-and-mortar companies have successfully established profitable Internet storefronts. 12

Brooks, Frederick, 124

**Brooks' Law** This interesting concept was stated by Frederick Brooks, Jr., an IBM engineer, who observed that adding manpower to a late software project only makes it later. 124

**browser** A Web browser, or browser, is a software program that allows you to access and display Web pages that are delivered to you by a Web server. 399, 690

**buffer** A segment of computer memory used for temporary storage. 433

**bug tracking software** System developers use defect tracking software, sometimes called bug tracking software, to document and track program defects, code changes, and replacement code, called patches. 529

Bugzilla, 529

**build or buy** Choice between developing in-house software and purchasing software, often called a build or buy, or make or buy, decision. 293, 294

**bus network** In a bus network, a single communication path connects the mainframe computer, server, workstations, and peripheral devices. Information is transmitted in either direction from any workstation to

another workstation, and any message can be directed to a specific device. 479

**business case** Refers to the reasons, or justification, for a proposal. 52, 58–59

business case analysis
feasibility studies and, 66–69
overview, 52–99
project management and, 64
setting priorities, 69–71

**business continuity plan (BCP)** A plan that defines how critical business functions can continue in the event of a major disruption. 608–609

business information systems, 15–18

**business logic** Business logic determines how a system handles data and produces useful information. Business logic, also called business rules, reflect the operational requirements of the business. Examples include adding the proper amount of sales tax to invoices, calculating customer balances and finance charges, and determining whether a customer is eligible for a volume-based discount. 201, 464

**business model** A business model graphically represents business functions that consist of business processes, such as sales, accounting, and purchasing. 10

**business process** A business process describes specific events, tasks, and desired results. 10, 150

**business process model (BPM)** A graphical representation of one or more business processes. 10, 150

**business process modeling notation (BPMN)** A standard set of shapes and symbols used to represent events, processes, and workflows in computer-based modeling tools. 10, 150

**business process outsourcing (BPO)** The outsourcing of a basic business process. 290

**business process reengineering (BPR)** An attempt by companies to simplify operations or reduce costs. 18

**business profile** A business profile defines a company's overall functions, processes, organization, products, services, customers, suppliers, competitors, constraints, and future direction. 10

business requirements
development strategies and, 294–295
system architecture and, 467

**business rules** Business rules determine how a system handles data and produces useful information. Business rules, also called business logic, reflects the operational requirements of the business. Examples include adding the proper amount of sales

tax to invoices, calculating customer balances and finance charges, and determining whether a customer is eligible for a volume-based discount. 201

**business support systems** Business support systems (BSS) provide job-related information support to users at all levels of a company. 16

**byte** A group of eight bits is called a byte, or a character. A set of bytes forms a field, which is an individual fact about a person, place, thing, or event. 433

C (high-level language), 318

C++ (high-level language), 25, 250, 318, 523

C# (high-level language), 523

CAIT (Center for the Application of Information Technologies), 537, 538

**calendar control** A calendar control allows the user to select a date that the system will display and store as a field value. 348

Camtasia, 543

**candidate key** Sometimes it is possible to have a choice of fields or field combinations to use as the primary key. Any field that could serve as a primary key is called a candidate key. For example, if every employee has a unique employee number, then you could use either the employee number or the Social Security number as a primary key. 402, 403

**Capability Maturity Model (CMM)** A model developed by SEI that integrates software and systems development into the process improvement framework. 508

**Capability Maturity Model Integration (CMMI)** An SEI-developed process to improve quality, reduce development time, and cut costs. A CMM tracks an organization's software development goals and practices, using five maturity levels, from Level 1 (relatively unstable, ineffective software) to Level 5 (software that is refined, efficient, and reliable). 508–509

**capacity planning** A process that monitors current activity and performance levels, anticipates future activity, and forecasts the resources needed to provide desired levels of service. 587, 588

**cardinality** A concept that describes how instances of one entity relate to instances of another entity. Described in entity-relationship diagrams by notation that indicates combinations that include zero or one-to-many, one-to-one, and many-to-many. 263, 408

**cardinality notation** Notation that shows relationships between entities. 408, 409–410

career opportunities, 32–33

**CASE environment** A CASE environment is more than a set of CASE tools; it includes any use of computer-based support in the software development process.
agile methods and, 148
described, 653
requirements modeling and, 144, 149–153, 158, 170
Zackman Framework for Enterprise Architecture and, 158

**case for action** A part of the preliminary investigation report to management that summarizes project requests and makes specific recommendations. 81

**CASE tools** Powerful software used in computer-aided systems engineering to help systems analysts develop and maintain information systems.
construction tools, 654–656
data dictionaries and, 218
described, 20, 648
DFDs and, 215
documentation and, 217–224, 653–654
engineering tools, 654–655
example, 57
history, 651
marketplace for, 651–652
method-specific, 662–663
modeling tools, 653
O-O analysis and, 266, 267
overview, 648–666
system architecture and, 481, 486
system implementation and, 511–512, 520, 525
user interface design and, 342

**category codes** Category codes identify a group of related items. For example, a local department store may use a two-character category code to identify the department in which a product is sold. 423

**certification** A credential an individual earns by demonstrating a certain level of knowledge and skill on a standardized test. 32

Certiport, 32

**change control (CC)** A process for controlling changes in system requirements during software development; also an important tool for managing system changes and costs after a system becomes operational. 582

**channel** A chat room, also called a channel, is an online meeting place where users can interact and converse in real time. 705

**character** A group of eight bits is called a character, or a byte. A set of bytes forms a field, which is an individual fact about a person, place, thing, or event. 432

**character-based report** A character-based report is created using a single mono-spaced character set. 351

**forward engineering** Forward engineering means translating business processes and functions into applications. 654

**four-model approach** Using the four-model approach means that a physical model of the current system, a logical model of the current system, a logical model of the new system, and a physical model of the new system are all developed. 231

**fourth-generation environment** Term used to describe an efficient software development environment that is created through the use of powerful CASE tools, application generators, report generators, screen generators, and fourth-generation languages (4GLs) during prototyping. 316

**fourth-generation language (4GL)** Non-procedural programming languages that are especially valuable in implementing an object-oriented system design. 316, 651

**framework** Conceptual structure that organizes and documents system development tasks. 661

frequency, of records, 222

FTP (File Transfer Protocol). *See* File Transfer Protocol (FTP)

**full backup** A complete backup of every file on the system. 607, 608

**functional baseline** The functional baseline is the configuration of the system documented at the beginning of the project. It consists of all the necessary system requirements and design constraints. 583

**functional decomposition diagram (FDD)** A top-down representation of business functions and processes. Also called a structure chart. 150, 341, 511

**functional primitive** A process that consists of a single function that is not exploded further. The logic for functional primitives is documented in a data dictionary process description. 211

**functionally dependent** Functional dependence is an important concept for understanding the second normal form (2NF). The field X is said to be functionally dependent on the field Y if the value of X depends on the value of Y. For example, an order date is dependent on an order number; for a particular order number, there is only one value for the order date. In contrast, the product description is not dependent on the order number. For a particular order number, there might be several product descriptions, one for each item ordered. 413

future needs, anticipating, 312

**fuzzy logic** An approach used in knowledge management systems

that allows logical inferences to be drawn from imprecise relationships. 17

**Gane and Sarson** A popular symbol set used in data flow diagrams. Processes, data flows, data stores, and external entities all have a unique symbol. 200–201

**Gantt chart** A horizontal bar chart that illustrates a schedule. Gantt charts were developed many years ago by Henry L. Gantt as a production control technique and still are in common use. 104–106, 109, 119

**garbage in garbage out (GIGO)** The concept that the quality of the output is only as good as the quality of the input. 360

Gartner, Inc., 292, 299

**gateway** A router or other network device used to connect to a larger, dissimilar type of network, such as the Internet. 481

**Gbps (gigabits per second)** A bandwidth or throughput measurement. 586

**global outsourcing** The practice of shifting IT development, support, and operations to other countries. 292, 293

Goal Seek feature, 587–588

Google, 12, 693–694, 697, 702, 704–705
  Apps, 472
  Desktop, 605–606
  Docs, 171, 637

government regulations, 64

**grammar checker** A software tool that can detect usage problems and offer suggestions. 634

graphic modeling software, 171

**graphical user interface (GUI)** A graphical user interface (GUI) uses graphical objects and techniques that allow users to communicate with a system. A well-designed GUI can help users learn a new system rapidly, and work with the system effectively. 338, 365, 459

**gray hole** A process is said to be a "gray hole" if an input is obviously insufficient to generate the shown output. 203

**group footer** A group footer appears after the last detail line of a group. Group footers could include items such as a subtotal, an average, or a count of the records in that group. 355, 356

**group header** A group header appears above the first detail line of a group. 355, 356

**groupware** Programs that run on a company intranet that enable users to share data, collaborate on projects, and work in teams. Also called workgroup software. 17

GroupWise (Novell), 17

growth, future, estimating, 301–302

hackers, 592

**hardening** Making a system more secure by removing unnecessary accounts, services, and features. 601

**hardware** The physical layer of the information system, to include computers, networks, communications equipment, and other technology-based infrastructure. described, 8
  development strategies and, 295, 302

Harris Corporation, 121

**hash totals** Hash totals, or batch control totals, are not meaningful numbers themselves, but are useful for comparison purposes. 368

**Hawthorne Effect** A phenomenon where employees who know they are being observed are more productive. 165

HCI (human-computer interaction). *See* human-computer interaction (HCI)

**heading zone** Area of a form that usually contains the company name or logo and the title and form number. 360

help, navigating, 345

**help desk** A centralized resource staffed by IT professionals that provides users with the support they need to do their jobs. A help desk has three main objectives: to show people how to use system resources more effectively, to provide answers to technical or operational questions, and to make users more productive by teaching them how to meet their own information needs. 29, 572–574
  described, 297, 572
  development strategies and, 297
  outsourcing, 573

Help dialog box, 345

Hewlett-Packard, 292, 300, 470–471, 481, 537, 538, 670–671

**hidden Web** The terms invisible Web, hidden Web, or deep Web, are used to describe this valuable information source, which includes numerous text, graphics, and data files stored in collections that are unreachable by search engines. 693, 699–701

**hierarchical network** In a hierarchical network, one computer (typically a mainframe) controls the entire network. Satellite computers or servers control lower levels of processing and network devices. 478

**histogram** A common tool for showing the distribution of questionnaire or sampling results. It takes the form of a vertical bar chart. 171

**history file** In a typical file processing environment, a history file is a file copy created and saved for historical or archiving purposes. New history files, unlike new

security files, do not replace the old files. 394

**hits** Although search engine indexes are incomplete and often dated, they are capable of delivering an overwhelming number of results, or hits. 693

**horizontal application** A software package that can be used by many different types of organizations. 293

horizontal system A basic system, such as an inventory or payroll package that is commonly used by a variety of companies. 8

**hot site** A separate IT location, which might be in another state or even another country, that can support critical business systems in the event of a power outage, system crash, or physical catastrophe. 609

**HTML (Hypertext Markup Language)** The language used to write Web pages for the Internet. 289, 318, 400–401
  described, 399
  system architecture and, 467
  system implementation and, 523

**hub** A hub is at the center of a star network. The hub is the central computer or device that manages the network. 480, 483

**human-computer interaction (HCI)** describes the relationship between computers and the people who use them to perform business-related tasks. HCI concepts apply to everything from a PC desktop to the main menu for a global network. 338–341

IBM (International Business Machines), 11, 124, 656–658, 662, 705
  changes in the world foreseen by, 5, 6
  DB/2, 398, 426
  history of, 4–5
  Lotus Organizer, 173
  outsourcing and, 292
  RUP and, 27
  system architecture and, 457, 466–467, 481
  training solutions, 537, 538
  user interface design and, 336, 338–340
  WebSphere, 287, 288, 289, 457, 523

**I-commerce (Internet commerce)** Transactions (e.g. buying and selling of goods and information) that occur on the internet. Includes both business-to-consumer, and business-to-business. Used interchangeably with e-commerce. 13. See also e-commerce (electronic commerce)

Ideas International, 296–297

**identity management** Controls and procedures necessary to identify legitimate users and system components. 604

**IEEE (Institute of Electrical and Electronics Engineers)** A

conversations to occur on a worldwide basis. 705

**Internet-dependent** Company that bases its primary business on a commercial Web site, rather than using traditional business channels. Dot-com (.com) is also used to describe this type of firm. 12

**interpersonal skills** "People" skills that help a systems analyst work with personnel at all organizational levels, and balance sometimes conflicting user needs. 143

Intershop, 469

**interview** A planned meeting during which information is obtained from another person.
  conducting, 76–77
  described, 159
  documenting, 162–163
  evaluating, 163
  objectives, 159–160
  preparation for, 161–162
  questionnaires versus, 169
  questions, 160–161
  requirements modeling and, 159–164
  unsuccessful, 163–164

**intranet** A private, company-owned network that provides Web-based access to internal users. 399–400

**invisible Web** The terms invisible Web, hidden Web, or deep Web, are used to describe this valuable information source, which includes numerous text, graphics, and data files stored in collections that are unreachable by search engines. 693, 699–701

IP (Internet Protocol) packets, 481

iPhone (Apple), 173–174

IRC IRC, or Internet Relay Chat, is a multi-channel system supported by servers that enable group and individual conversations to occur on a worldwide basis. 705

**Ishikawa diagram** Also called a fishbone diagram. It is an analysis tool that represents the possible causes of a problem as a graphical outline.

ISO (International Organization for Standardization). *See* International Organization for Standardization (ISO)

**ISO 90003:2004** A set of guidelines established and updated by the International Organization for Standardization (ISO) to provide a quality assurance framework for developing and maintaining software. 510

**iteration** The completion of a process step that is repeated until a specific condition changes. 225

**iteration cycle** An agile development cycle that includes planning, designing, coding, and testing one or more features based on user stories. 522

**iteration planning** meeting In agile development, a meeting held at the beginning of each iteration cycle to break down user stories into specific tasks that are assigned to team members. 522

**iterative** An adaptive method typically uses a spiral development model, which builds on a series of iterations. 25

Java, 25, 318, 651
  O-O analysis and, 250
  system architecture and, 457
  system implementation and, 523

**JDBC (Java database connectivity)** JDBC enables Java applications to exchange data with any database that uses SQL statements and is JDBC-compliant. 398

job titles, 33

Johnson, Jim, 102

**joint application development (JAD)** A popular systems development technique that uses a cross-matrixed task group of users, managers and IT professionals that work together to gather information, discuss business needs, and define the new system requirements. 26–27, 58, 143–145

**just-in-time (JIT)** The exchange or delivery of information when and where it is needed. For example, just-in-time inventory systems rely on computer-to-computer data exchange to minimize unnecessary inventory. 63

Karat, Clare-Marie, 340–341

**Kbps (kilobits per second)** A bandwidth or throughput measurement. 586

**key fields** Key fields are used during the systems design phase to organize, access, and maintain data structures. The four types of key fields are primary keys, candidate keys, foreign keys, and secondary keys. 402–404

Keynote (Apple), 171

**keystroke logger** A device that can be inserted between a keyboard and a computer to record keystrokes. 594

**keywords** Words used by a spider to catalog or index pages from Web sites. 693

**knowledge base** A large database that allows users to find information by clicking menus, typing keywords, or entering text questions in normal phrases. 17

**knowledge management systems** Systems that simulates human reasoning by combining a knowledge base and inference rules that determine how the knowledge is applied. Is sometimes used interchangeably with expert systems. 16–17

**knowledge workers** Includes professional staff members such as

systems analysts, programmers, accountants, researchers, trainers, and human resource specialists. 19

Kyocera, 173

LAN. *See* local area network (LAN)

language compilers, 525

**leading questions** Questions that suggest or favor a particular reply. 160

**legacy data** Data associated with an older, less technologically advanced legacy system. 462

**legacy systems** Term used to describe older systems that are typically less technologically advanced than currently available systems.
  database design and, 392–394
  described, 9, 457
  development strategies and, 295
  system architecture and, 457, 462, 466

**length** The maximum number of characters for an alphabetic or character data element, or the maximum number of digits and number of decimal positions for a numeric data element. 219

letters, tips for writing, 634–635

**leveling** The process of drawing a series of increasingly detailed diagrams to reach the desired level of detail. 212–217

**library module** In a structure chart, a library module is a module that is reusable and can be invoked from more than one point in the chart. 514

**lifeline** In a sequence diagram, a lifeline is used to represent the time during which the object above it is able to interact with the other objects in the use case. An x marks the end of a lifeline. 264

**limit check** A limit check occurs when a validation check involves a minimum or a maximum value, but not both. Checking that a payment amount is greater than zero, but not specifying a maximum value, is an example of a limit check. 367

**link testing** Testing two or more programs that depend on each other is called link testing, or integration testing. 526

LinkedIn, 702

Linux, 318

**list box** A list box displays a list of choices that the user can select. 348

**list server** A computer that directs e-mail to people who subscribe to, or join, a particular mailing list. 704

**listserv** A listserv, also called a mailing list, is similar to a newsgroup in that it provides a forum for people who want to exchange information about specific topics. 704

**local area network (LAN)** A local area network (LAN) allows the sharing of data and hardware, such as printers and scanners. Advances in data communication technology have made it possible to create powerful networks that use satellite links, high-speed fiber-optic lines, or the Internet to share data.
  described, 460
  file sharing architecture and, 360
  protocols and, 477
  routers and, 481
  security, 592, 600
  topology, 478, 479, 483

**log** Record typically kept by operating systems and applications that documents all events, including dates, times, and other specific information. Logs can be important in understanding past attacks and preventing future intrusions. 313, 602

**logic errors** Errors in the underlying logic that produce incorrect results. 525

**logical design** The logical design of an information system defines the functions and features of a system and the relationships among its components. 311

**logical model** A logical model shows what a system must do, regardless of how it will be implemented physically. 175, 198, 200–205, 231–232

**logical operators** The logical operators OR, AND, and NOT are used to create combinations of search terms to improve search success greatly. 695, 696

**logical record** A logical record contains field values that describe a single person, place, thing, or event. Application programs see a logical record as a set of fields, regardless of how or where the data is stored physically. 433

logical rules, 225

**logical storage** Refers to information as seen through a user's eyes, regardless of how or where that information is organized or stored. 432, 433

**logical structures** Logical structures, or control structures, serve as the building blocks for a process. Logical structures have one entry and exit point. They may be completed in sequential order, as the result of a test or condition, or repeated until a specific condition changes. 224

**logical topology** A view of a network that describes the way the components interact, rather than the actual network cabling and connections. 477

**long integer format** A type of binary storage format. The long integer format can store numbers from 2,147,483,647 to

2,147,483,647 using only four bytes of storage. 434

loop In a structure chart, a loop indicates that one or more modules are repeated. 318, 515, 517–518

looping Looping, or repetition, refers to a process step that is repeated until a specific condition changes. For example, a process that continues to print paychecks until it reaches the end of the payroll file is looping. 225

loose coupling Loose coupling means that the objects can interact, but are essentially independent. 318

loosely coupled Modules that are relatively independent. Loosely coupled modules are easier to maintain and modify, because the logic in one module does not affect other modules. 516

Lowe's, 12, 13

lower-level diagrams, 212–217

Macintosh, 341

magnetic data strip A magnetic data strip is used for automated data input. 369

mail bombing, 593

mailing list A mailing list, also called a listserv, is similar to a newsgroup in that it provides a forum for people who want to exchange information about specific topics. 704

mainframe architecture A system design where the server performs all the processing.
  client/server architecture and, comparison of, 462
  described, 458
  history of, 459
  overview, 458–459

maintenance
  management, 578–584
  requests, 580–582
  system architecture and, 464, 471
  tasks, 574–578
  tools, 588–589

maintenance activities Maintenance activities include changing programs, procedures, or documentation to ensure correct system performance; adapting the system to changing requirements; and making the system operate more efficiently. Those needs are met by corrective, adaptive, perfective, and preventive maintenance. 574

maintenance agreement A maintenance agreement specifies the conditions, charges and time frame for users to contact the vendor for assistance when they have system problems or questions. 307

maintenance expenses Maintenance expenses vary significantly during the system's operational life and include spending to support maintenance activities. 574

maintenance release A formal release of a new system version that contains a number of changes. 583

maintenance release methodology A system of numbered releases used by organizations (especially software vendors) that helps organize maintenance changes and updates. 583

maintenance team A maintenance team consists of one or more systems analysts and programmers. 578, 579–580

make or buy (build or buy) decision The choice between developing in-house software and purchasing software often is called a make or buy, or build or buy, decision. 293, 294

malware Malicious software that might jeopardize your security or privacy. 593, 601, 692

man in the middle attacks, 593

MAN (metropolitan area network) MANs (metropolitan area networks) use 802.16 standards, which are broadband wireless communications protocols. 485

managed hosting Another term for Internet business services (IBS). An operation is managed by the outside firm, or host. 291

management. See also managers
  information systems, described, 16
  presentation of systems analysis to, 309–310, 311
  system implementation and, 533, 549

managers. See also management
  interaction with, 71–72
  middle, 18–19
  preliminary investigation and, 71–72
  presenting results/recommendations to, 81
  requirements modeling and, 144
  top, 18

many-to-many relationship A type of entity relationship. A many-to-many relationship, abbreviated M:N, exists when one instance of the first entity can be related to many instances of the second entity, and one instance of the second entity can be related to many instances of the first entity. 407, 419

market basket analysis Market basket analysis can detect patterns and trends in large amounts of data. 432

master file In a typical file processing environment, a master file stores relatively permanent data about an entity. For example, a PRODUCT master file might contain one logical record for each product a company sells. 394

MAU (Multistation Access Unit), 480

Mbps (megabits per second) A bandwidth or throughput measurement. 482, 586

memory, 433

menu bar A bar of user-selectable software application options, usually located across the top of the screen. 344, 347, 348

mergers, 292

mesh network A network design in which each node connects to every other node. While this design is very reliable, it is also expensive to install and maintain. 480–481

message An object-oriented command that tells an object to perform a certain method. 255–256, 346
  described, 25, 250
  O-O design and, 25
  sequence diagrams and, 264

meta-search engine A tool that can use multiple search engines simultaneously. 692, 694

method A method defines specific tasks that an object must perform. A method describes what and how an object does something.
  described, 25, 250
  overview, 519, 254–255
  representing objects and, 253

metrics Workload measurements, also called metrics, include the number of lines printed, the number of records accessed, and the number of transactions processed in a given time period. 585

Microsoft. See also specific applications
  certifications and, 32
  development strategies and, 305, 317
  network diagrams and, 105
  outsourcing and, 292
  turnkey systems, 469
  user interface design and, 338–339, 341

Microsoft Access, 171, 298
  database design and, 405, 426, 428–430, 433
  Help screen, 345
  input masks and, 365–366
  physical storage and, 433
  referential integrity and, 405
  report design tools, 350–351
  system implementation and, 523–524
  user interface design and, 356

Microsoft Dynamics, 454–455

Microsoft Excel, 78, 171, 297, 587–588, 678

Microsoft Expression Studio, 317

Microsoft Live Meeting, 643

Microsoft Management Console (MMC) A collection tools for administering networks, computers, services, and other components. The MMC includes built-in security tools such as password and lockout policies, user rights, audit policies, and more. 590

Microsoft Office, 170–171, 293, 297, 298. See also specific applications

Microsoft Outlook, 173, 635, 637

Microsoft PowerPoint, 171, 537, 640–641, 643

Microsoft Project A powerful, full-featured program that holds the dominant share of the project management software market. 64, 109, 113
  described, 118
  network diagrams and, 119–120
  risk management and, 122

Microsoft Solutions Framework (MSF) A Microsoft approach to systems development. The objective of MSF is to define and analyze business requirements and provide IT solutions. 27

Microsoft Visio, 10, 19–20, 172, 481

Microsoft Visual Basic, 318, 523, 651

Microsoft Visual Studio, 317, 656–657

Microsoft Web Apps, 171

Microsoft Windows
  Azure, 472
  Event Viewer, 602
  Live MovieMaker, 541
  user interface design and, 347

Microsoft Word, 167, 171, 297

middleware Software that connects dissimilar applications and enables them to communicate and exchange data. For example, middleware can link a departmental database to a Web server that can be accessed by client computers via the Internet or a company intranet, 289, 400–401, 457, 465, 466

milestone A milestone, or event, is a reference point that marks a major occurrence. Milestones are used to monitor progress and manage a project. 106

military computers, 477, 480

mission statement A document or statement that describes the company for its stakeholders and briefly states the company's overall purpose, products, services, and values. 55–56

mission-critical system An information system that is vital to a company's operations. 7

mitigation One of four risk control strategies. Mitigation reduces the impact of a risk by careful planning and preparation. For example, a company can prepare a disaster recovery plan to mitigate the effects of a natural disaster should one occur. 122, 592

M:N A type of entity relationship. A many-to-many relationship, abbreviated M. 407, 419

mnemonic codes Mnemonic codes use a specific combination of letters that are easy to remember. Many three-character

products, support for new, 60

**profit center** A department expected to break even, or show a profit. 673

**program documentation** Program documentation starts in the systems analysis phase and continues during systems implementation. Systems analysts prepare overall documentation, such as process descriptions and report layouts, early in the SDLC. Programmers provide documentation by constructing modules that are well-supported by internal and external comments and descriptions that can be understood and maintained easily. 529

**Program Evaluation Review Technique (PERT)** The Program Evaluation Review Technique (PERT) was developed by the U.S. Navy to manage very complex projects, such as the construction of nuclear submarines. At approximately the same time, the Critical Path Method (CPM) was developed by private industry to meet similar project management needs. The important distinctions between the two methods have disappeared over time, and today the technique is called either PERT, CPM, or PERT/ CPM. 105–106

**programmer/analyst** A designation for positions that require a combination of systems analysis and programming skills. 579

Project (Microsoft), 64, 109, 113
  described, 118
    network diagrams and, 119–120
    risk management and, 122

**project coordinator** The project coordinator handles administrative responsibilities for the development team and negotiates with users who might have conflicting requirements or want changes that would require additional time or expense. 103

**project creep** The process by which projects with very general scope definitions expand gradually, without specific authorization. 74, 123

**project management** The process of planning, scheduling, monitoring, controlling, and reporting upon the development of an information system. 22, 28, 101–138, 514

**project manager** The project manager, or project leader, usually is a senior systems analyst or an IT department manager if the project is large. An analyst or a programmer/analyst might manage smaller projects. 103, 115–116, 144–145

**project monitoring** Project monitoring requires guiding,

supervising, and coordinating the project team's workload. 103, 114–115

**project planning** Project planning includes identifying project tasks and estimating completion time and costs. 103–104

**project reporting** Project reporting tasks include regular progress reports to management, users, and the project team itself. 103, 115–116

**project scope** A specific determination of a project's boundaries or extent. 74

**project scheduling** Project scheduling involves the creation of a specific timetable to facilitate completion of a project. Scheduling also involves selecting and staffing the project team and assigning specific tasks to team members. 103

**properties** Characteristics that objects inherit from their class or possess on their own. 24–25

**protocol** A set of standards that govern network data transmission. Also, preset conditions used by firewalls to determine whether or not to allow traffic to pass. 400, 477

**prototype** An early, rapidly constructed working version of the proposed information system. 20, 315
    agile methods and, 25
    limitations of, 317
    user interface design and, 342

**prototyping** The method by which a prototype is developed. It involves a repetitive sequence of analysis, design, modeling, and testing. It is a common technique that can be used to design anything from a new home to a computer network. 315–317

**proxy server** A networking device that provides Internet connectivity for internal LAN users. 481

**pseudocode** A technique for representing program logic. 225, 513

**public key encryption (PKE)** A common encryption technique. Each user on the network has a pair of keys: a public key and a private key. The public key encrypts data that can be decrypted with the private key. 597

punched card system, 4–5
Python, 25, 318, 523

**qualitative risk analysis** Evaluating risk by estimating the probability that it will occur and the degree of impact. 121

**quality assurance (QA)** A process or procedure for minimizing errors and ensuring quality in products. Poor quality can result from inaccurate requirements, design problems, coding errors, faulty documentation, and ineffective testing. A quality

assurance (QA) team reviews and tests all applications and systems changes to verify specifications and software quality standards. 29, 508–510

**quantitative risk analysis** Evaluating risk in terms of the actual impact in terms of dollars, time, project scope, or quality. 122
Quanttro Pro (Corel), 171

**query by example (QBE)** A query-by-example (QBE) language allows the user to provide an example of the data requested. 396, 397

**query language** A query language allows a user to specify a task without specifying how the task will be accomplished. Some query languages use natural language commands that resemble ordinary English sentences. 396

**questionnaire** A document containing a number of standard questions that can be sent to many individuals. Also called a survey. 166–167, 169, 171

**radio button** A radio button, or option button, represents a group of options. The user can select only one option at a time; a selected option contains a black dot. 348

**radio frequency identification (RFID)** Radio frequency identification (RFID) technology uses high-frequency radio waves to track physical objects. 16, 62, 454

**RAID (redundant array of independent disks)** A RAID system may be part of an organizations backup and recovery plans. A RAID system mirrors the data while processing continues. RAID systems are called fault-tolerant, because a failure of any one disk does not disable the system. 607

**random sample** A random sample is taken in a random, unplanned manner. For example, a random sample might be a sample that selects any 20 customers. 168

**range check** A type of data validation check that tests data items to verify that they fall between a specified minimum and maximum value. The daily hours worked by an employee, for example, must fall within the range of 0 to 24. 367

**range-of-response questions** Closed-ended questions that ask the person to evaluate something by providing limited answers to specific responses or on a numeric scale. 160

**rapid application development (RAD)** A team-based technique that speeds up information systems development and produces a functioning information system. RAD is similar in concept

to joint application development (JAD), but goes further by including all phases of the System Development Life Cycle (SDLC). 58, 143, 315
    described, 26–27
    objectives, 147
    overview, 145–147
Rapid Economic Justification (REJ), 156
Rational System Architect, 658–660

**Rational Unified Process (RUP)** According to IBM, RUP offers a flexible, iterative process for managing software development projects that can minimize risk, ensure predictable results. 26

**read-only properties** Elements of an application that can be configured so users can view, but not change the data. 298

**readability** Readability analyzes ease of comprehension by measuring specific characteristics of syllables, words, and sentences. 634

**reasonableness** check A type of data validation check that identifies values that are questionable, but not necessarily wrong. For example, input payment values of $0.05 and $5,000,000.00 both pass a simple limit check for a payment value greater than zero, and yet both values could be errors. 367

**record** A record, also called a tuple, is a set of related fields that describes one instance, or member of an entity, such as one customer, one order, or one product. A record might have one or dozens of fields, depending on what information is needed.
    alternate name, 223
    attributes, 223
    definition/description, 223
    documenting, 223
    name, 223
    overview, 217, 402
    security and, 372
    user interface design and, 365

**records retention policy** A records policy that is designed to meet all legal requirements and business needs for keeping records. 372

**recovery** The process of restoring data and restarting a system after an interruption. 607

**recovery procedures** Recovery procedures involve restoring data and restarting a system after an interruption. Recovery procedures can be used to restore a file or database to its current state at the time of the last backup. 607

**referential integrity** A type of validity check. Referential integrity is a set of rules that avoids data inconsistency and quality problems. 367, 404, 405

describe business processes and requirements generally. 151, 250, 663
  cardinality and, 263, 408
  overview, 259–266
  representation of objects, 251–54
  requirements modeling and, 151–152
  use case modeling overview, 259–261

**uninterruptible power supply (UPS)** Battery-powered backup power source that enables operations to continue during short-term power outages and surges. 595

**unit testing** The testing of an individual program or module. The objective is to identify and eliminate execution errors that could cause the program to terminate abnormally, and logic errors that could have been missed during desk checking. 525, 526

**Universal Security Slot (USS)** Can be fastened to a cable lock or laptop alarm. 595

**unnormalized** An unnormalized record is one that contains a repeating group, which means that a single record has multiple occurrences of a particular field, with each occurrence having different values. 411

unstructured brainstorming A group discussion where any participant can speak at any time. 159

U.S. Commerce Department, 121
U.S. Defense Department, 477
U.S. Navy, 105

**usability metrics** Data that interface designers can obtain by using software that can record and measure user interactions with the system. 342

**usage model** A service model that charges a variable fee for an application based on the volume of transactions or operations performed by the application. Also called a transaction model. 291

USB (Universal Serial Bus), 371

**use case** A use case represents the steps in a specific business function or process in UML (Unified Modeling Language). 259–261

**use case description** A description in UML (Unified Modeling Language) that documents the name of the use case, the actor, a description of the use case, a step-by-step list of the tasks required for successful completion, and other key descriptions and assumptions. 260

**use case diagram** A visual representation that represents the interaction between users and the information system in UML (Unified Modeling Language). 151–152, 261–262

**user(s)** Employees, customers, vendors, and others who interact

with an information system. Sometimes referred to as end users.
  business case analysis and, 71–72
  considerations, for systems design, 312–313
  database design and, 396–397
  described, 10
  groups, 603
  involvement, 71–72, 144, 315, 346, 353, 487
  notification, 582
  prototypes and, 315, 316
  requirements modeling and, 144
  responsible, use of the term, 220
  security and, 603–606
  surveys, 78
  "thinking like," 341–342

**user application** User applications utilize standard business software, such as Microsoft Office 2003, that has been configured in a specific manner to enhance user productivity. 297–298

**user design phase** In this phase, users interact with systems analysts and develop models and prototypes that represent all system processes, outputs, and inputs. 146

**user documentation** Instructions and information to users who will interact with the system. It includes user manuals, help screens, and tutorials. 510–533

**user ID** A method of limiting access to files and databases to protect stored data. 435

**user interface** A user interface includes screens, commands, controls, and features that enable users to interact more effectively with an application. *See also* graphical user interface (GUI)
  consistency in, 356
  control features, 347–349
  described, 297
  development strategies and, 297–298
  easy to learn, 344
  evolution of, 336–337
  guidelines, 342–249
  overview, 334–388
  security issues, 370–372
  transparent, 343

**user productivity systems** Systems that provide employees of all levels a wide array of tools to improve job performance. Examples include e-mail, word processing, graphics, and company intranets. 17

**user rights** User-specific privileges that determine the type of access a user has to a database, file, or directory. Also called permissions. 435, 601, 603

**user story** In agile development, a short, simple requirements definition provided by the customer. Programmers use user stories to

determine a project's requirements, priorities, and scope. 521

**user support** A function typically performed by individuals within an IT department. User support provides users with technical information, training, and productivity support. 29, 572–574

**user training package** The main objective of a user training package is to show users how the system can help them perform their jobs. 572

**user-centered** A term that indicates the primary focus is upon the user. In a user-centered system, the distinction blurs between input, output, and the interface itself. 337, 341–342

**user-selected** Under the control of the system or application user. For example, user-selected help displays information when the user requests it. 345

validation, 367, 404–405, 602

**validity check** A type of data validation check that is used for data items that must have certain values. For example, if an inventory system has 20 valid item classes, then any input item that does not match one of the valid classes will fail the check. 367

**validity rules** Rules that are applied to data elements when data is entered to ensure that the value entered is valid. For example, a validity rule might require that an employee's salary number be within the employer's predefined range for that position. 220

**value-added reseller (VAR)** A firm that enhances a commercial package by adding custom features and configuring it for a particular industry. 293

**variable charge method based on resource usage** Resource allocation that is based upon the connect time, the server processing time, the network resources required, printer use, or a combination of similar factors. 673

**variable charge method based on volume** In this method, the indirect information systems department costs are allocated to other departments based on user-oriented activity, such as the number of transactions or printing volume. 674

**variable costs** Costs that vary depending on the level of activity. For example, the cost of printer paper or telephone line charges are variable costs. 672

vendor. *See* software vendor

**Venn diagram** A Venn diagram uses circular symbols to illustrate Boolean logic. Venn diagrams are named after John Venn, a nineteenth-century scholar who devised a scheme for visualizing logical relationships. 695

**version control** The process of tracking system releases. 583, 584

**vertical application** A software package that has been developed to handle information requirements for a specific type of business. 294

**vertical system** A system designed to meet the unique requirements of a specific business or industry, such as a Web-based retailer or video rental chain. 8

video tutorials, 540–543

**virtual private network (VPN)** Uses a public network to connect remote users securely. Allows remote clients to use a special key exchange that must be authenticated by the VPN. 599

Visible Analyst, 10, 20, 57, 215, 218–224, 658–660
  ERDs and, 409, 410
  process models and, 22
  requirements modeling and, 151, 158

**visible Web** Refers to Web sites that are indexed by major search engines and are publicly accessible. 699

Visio (Microsoft), 10, 19–20, 172, 481

**visual aids** Tools such as whiteboards, flip charts, overhead transparencies, slides, films, and videotapes used to enhance a presentation. 640

Visual Basic (Microsoft), 318, 523, 651

Visual Studio (Microsoft), 317, 656–657

volume
  of records, described, 222
  of transactions, estimating, 301–302

**vulnerability** A security weakness or soft spot. 591

Wal-Mart, 12, 15

**waterfall model** A type of graph that depicts the result of each SDLC phase flowing down into the next phase. 22–23

**Web** The Internet allows you to visit the World Wide Web, usually referred to as the Web, which contains billions of text and multimedia documents called Web pages. 690

**Web 2.0** A second generation of the World Wide Web that enables people to collaborate, interact, and share information much more dynamically, based on continuously available user applications rather than static HTML Web pages. Interactive experience is a hallmark of Web 2.0. 289, 472–473

**Web browser** An application that enables the user to navigate, or browse the Internet and display Web pages on his or her local computer. 399, 690

**Web feed** Data format for providing users with frequently updated Web content on all kinds of topics, available by subscription. Also called a feed or RSS feed. 704

Web Host Industry Review (WHIR), 287

**Web page** Text and multimedia documents that are found on the World Wide Web. 399, 690

**Web server** A computer that is used to store and house Web sites. 400, 465, 467
  described, 399, 690
  system architecture and, 463

**Web services** Internet-based support programs that can be executed as an integral part of an information system; Web-based modular applications that can perform functions that can be quite simple or more complex. 318

**Web site** A collection of related Web pages. 399, 690

**Web support** Web support involves design and construction of Web pages, monitoring traffic, managing hardware and software, and linking Web-based applications to the company's existing information systems. 29

Web-based database design, 398–401

**Web-based discussion group** An online community that combines features of mailing lists and newsgroups. 705

**Webcast** A one-way transmission of information or training materials, such as a Webinar session, available on demand or for a specific period to online participants. 305, 537

**Web-centric** A strategy or approach that emphasizes a high degree of integration with other Web-based components. A Web-centric architecture follows Internet design protocols and enables a company to integrate the new application into its e-commerce strategy. 400

WebEx (Cisco), 643

**Webinar** A Webinar, which combines the words Web and seminar, is an Internet-based training session that provides an interactive experience. 537, 704

**WebSphere** IBM's Web-based development environment. 287, 288, 289, 457, 523

**weight** Weight is an important value that managers add to estimates so they can be analyzed. 107

**what-if** A feature of business support systems that allows analysis to define and account for a wide variety of issues (including issues not completely defined). 16–18, 31

**what-if analysis** What-if analysis allows you to vary one or more elements in a model in order to measure the effect on other elements. 587

**why, who, what, when, and how of communications** Good communications must answer these basic questions: Why is one communicating? Who is the target audience? What is expected? When is detail required? How does one communicate effectively? 157, 632

**Wi-Fi (wireless fidelity)** Family of popular IEEE local area network wireless networking standards, also known as 802.11, including 802.11a, b, g, and n. 802.11n is the most recent standard. 371, 482–484

**Wi-Fi Alliance** A nonprofit international association formed in 1999 to certify interoperability of wireless network products based on IEEE 802.11 specifications. 484, 598

**Wi-Fi Protected Access (WPA)** A common method used to secure a wireless network. This approach requires each wireless client be configured manually to use a special, pre-shared key, rather than key pairs. The most recent and more secure version is WPA2. 598

**wide area network (WAN)** A wide area network (WAN) spans long distances and can link users who are continents apart. 460, 478, 481

**wiki** A Web-based repository of information that anyone can access, contribute to, or modify. 289, 473, 531–532

Wikipedia, 432, 597

**WiMAX** IEEE 802.16 specifications, which are expected to enable wireless multimedia applications with a range of up to 30 miles. 485

Windows (Microsoft)
  Azure, 472
  Event Viewer, 602
  Live MovieMaker, 541
  user interface design and, 347

**Wired Equivalent Privacy (WEP)** One of the earliest methods used to secure a wireless network, superceded by WPA and WPA2. 598

**wireless access point (WAP)** A central wireless device that provides network services to wireless clients. Also called an access point. 483

**wireless local area network (WLAN)** A wireless network that is relatively inexpensive to install and is well-suited to workgroups and users who are not anchored to a specific desk or location. 482, 483, 484

wireless network(s)
  communication devices, 173–174
  overview, 482–485
  security, 598
  standard, 482–483
  topologies, 483–484
  user interface design and, 357–358

Word (Microsoft), 167, 171, 297

WordPerfect (Corel), 171

**work breakdown structure (WBS)** Breaking a project down into a series of smaller tasks. 104, 106, 109, 116–119

**work file** In a typical file processing environment, a work file is a temporary file created by an information system for a single task. Most often a work file is created by one process in the information system and used by another process within the same

system. Work files also are called scratch files. 394

**workgroup software** Workgroup software offers many features in addition to basic e-mail capability. These features include calendars, task lists, schedules, contact lists, and document management, among others. Also called groupware. 637

**World Wide Web** The Internet allows you to visit the World Wide Web, usually referred to as the Web, which contains billions of text and multimedia documents called Web pages. 690

**worst-case estimate** The most pessimistic outcome is called the worst-case estimate. 107

**WPA2** WPA2 is based on a new standard called 802.11i that provides a significant increase in protection over WEP and WPA. 598

written communications, 633–639. *See also* communication

XML. *See* Extensible Markup Language (XML)

XP (Extreme Programming), 26, 512, 520–523

**XY chart** Also called a scatter diagram, a tool used by system analysts to graphically show the correlation between two variables. 78–79

**Y2K issue** A problem faced by many firms in the year 2000 because their computer systems used only two digits to represent the year; most dates now use a four-digit format for the year (YYYYMMDD). 312, 434

Yahoo!, 12, 694, 698, 704–705

**Yourdon** A type of symbol set that is used in data flow diagrams. Processes, data flows, data stores, and external entities each have a unique symbol in the Yourdon symbol set. 200–201

**Zachman Framework for Enterprise Architecture** A model that asks the traditional fact-finding questions in a systems development context. 157, 158, 661

zero or many relation, 263

# PHOTO CREDITS

Phase 1 DILBERT: © Scott Adams/Dist. By United Feature Syndicate, Inc; Figure 1-7 Courtesy NASA/JPL-Caltech; Figure 1-9 © joyfull/Shutterstock; Figure 1-13 Courtesy of Intel Corporation; Figure 1-18 © Rolf Vennenbernd/dpa/Landov; 1-Ready for a Challenge © Pete Saloutos/Shutterstock; Figure 2-8 Courtesy of Ingersoll Rand Security Technologies; Figure 2-10 © iStockphoto; Figure 2-10 PRNewsFoto/Verizon Wireless; Figure 2-11 Courtesy of Intermec Technologies; Figure 2-15 PRNewsFoto/Verizon Wireless; Figure 2-15 © Dmitry Rukhlenko/Shutterstock; Figure 2-22 © Jupiterimages/Getty Images; Figure 2-23 © Tim Brown/Getty Images; 2-Ready for a Challenge Stephen © McSweeny/Shutterstock; Figure 3-2 © Peter Close/Shutterstock; Figure 3-10 © Phillip Simpson Photographer/Getty Images; Figure 3-23 © Stockbyte/Getty Images; Figure 3-35 AP Photo/Paul Sakuma; 3-Ready for a Challenge © Roca/Shutterstock; Phase 2 DILBERT: © Scott Adams/Dist. By United Feature Syndicate, Inc; Figure 4-7 © Richard Martin/Reuters/Landov; Figure 4-18 © mammamaart/iStockphoto; Figure 4-21 © Mark Richards/PhotoEdit; Figure 4-25 © Image Source/Getty Images; 4-Ready for a Challenge Herbert Kratky/Shutterstock; Figure 5-2 Courtesy of Luidia, Inc; Figure 5-4 © INSADCO Photography/Alamy; Figure 5-14 © vario images GmbH & Co.KG/Alamy; Figure 5-38 © Dennis MacDonald/Photo Edit; 5-Ready for a Challenge © sportsphotographer.eu/Shutterstock; Figure 6-3 © Mark Segal/Photolibrary; Figure 6-7 © PhotoSpin, Inc/Alamy; Figure 6-11 © Jeff Baker/Getty Images; Figure 6-26 © Sean Locke/iStockphoto; 6-Ready for a Challenge © muzsy/Shutterstock; Figure 7-11 © Hans Neleman/Getty Images; Figure 7-23 © Gary Herrington; Figure 7-27 Courtesy of Intermec Technologies; Figure 7-28 Courtesy of NASA; 7-Ready for a Challenge Jonathan Larsen/Shutterstock; Phase 3 DILBERT: © Scott Adams/Dist. By United Feature Syndicate, Inc; Figure 8-05 © Wojtek Kryczka/iStockphoto; Figure 8-38 © Tom Grill/Getty Images; Figure 8-39 © Radu Razvan/iStockphoto; Figure 8-37 Courtesy of Ingenico, N.A.; 8-Ready for a Challenge commuzsy/Shutterstock; Figure 9-2 © Eliza Snow/iStockphoto; Figure 9-27 © Michelle D. Bridwell/PhotoEdit; Figure 9-35 © Susan Van Etten/Photo Edit; Figure 9-48 © DenGuy/iStockphoto; 9-Ready for a Challenge © Herbert Kratky/Shutterstock; Figure 10-6 © Comstock; Figure 10-8 Bloomberg via Getty Images; Figure 10-30 © Karlheinz Schindler/dpa/Landov; Figure 10-38 © Patrick Seeger/dpa/Landov; 10-Ready for a Challenge © Mana Photo/Shutterstock; Phase 4 DILBERT: © Scott Adams/Dist. By United Feature Syndicate, Inc; Figure 11-5 © Bob Daemmrich/PhotoEdit; Figure 11-31 © Walter Hodges/Getty Images; Figure 11-36 © Chris Schmidt/iStockphoto; 11-Ready for a Challenge © Olga Besnard/Shutterstock; Phase 5 DILBERT: © Scott Adams/Dist. By United Feature Syndicate, Inc; Figure 12-3 © Catherine Yeulet/iStockphoto; Figure 2-9 DoD photo by Airman Charlie Whetstine, U.S. Navy; Figure 12-26 © Boris Roessler/dpa/Landov; Figure 12-38 Tony Avelar/Bloomberg via Getty Images; 12-Ready for a Challenge © Jonathan Larsen/Shutterstock.

# PHOTO CREDITS